ECONOMICS

of

AMERICAN INDUSTRY

ECONOMICS

of

AMERICAN INDUSTRY

BY

E. B. ALDERFER

AND

H. E. MICHL

Members of the Industry Department
Wharton School of Finance and Commerce
University of Pennsylvania

FIRST EDITION

McGRAW-HILL BOOK COMPANY, INC.

NEW YORK AND LONDON

1942

191941

338.40973
A361e

To

ALFRED H. WILLIAMS
Friend, Teacher, and Former Colleague

PREFACE

The purpose of this book is to present an introductory survey of the principal manufacturing industries of the United States. For a considerable number of years the subject matter, in mimeograph form, has been taught to students in the Wharton School. During this time the material was constantly revised, a task in which the authors were guided by their own classroom experience and that of their colleagues. Each industry is analyzed in accordance with the plan set forth in Part I, and an effort is made to interpret for the student the predominant economic characteristics of the industries considered. With this in view the presentation is intentionally varied from one industry to another.

At the Wharton School this book is used in a course taken by two groups of students—those who intend to specialize in industry, for whom it serves as a preparation for the study of industrial management and industrial relations, and those who take it on an elective basis to supplement their work in economic theory. Since the latter group far outnumbers the former, it is felt that the book may be found useful in other schools of business and in liberal arts colleges where it may serve as a helpful adjunct to courses in elementary economics.

To Alfred H. Williams, formerly dean of the Wharton School and now president of the Federal Reserve Bank of Philadelphia, the authors owe an inestimable debt of gratitude. Dr. Williams first suggested the writing of this book, and until he left the Wharton School in 1940, he gave much of his time, thought, and energy to the project. He helped to formulate the general plan and made available his files of notes collected over a period of more than twenty years. He read most of the manuscript and offered innumerable constructive suggestions. For practically all but the final revision the authors had the benefit of Dr. Williams's interest and wise counsel. Since he was unable to participate in the work of the final draft the authors assume full responsibility for the opinions expressed and the errors unwittingly made.

The authors also wish to express their thanks and appreciation to their present colleagues, Prof. W. R. Hockenberry, Messrs A. H. Keally, Robert Riddle, and Glen Cunningham, all of whom read the manuscript and offered many valuable suggestions. To their former colleagues, G. W. Barnwell, F. G. Connor, and others, credit is likewise due for helpful assistance when the book was in its formative stages.

The authors cannot adequately acknowledge the assistance they received from a wide variety of sources. However, they wish to thank the various publishers who have, without exception, permitted the reproduction of charts and statistical data. The authors are likewise grateful to the many trade associations, labor unions, and business organizations that have freely supplied information and photographs. A sincere effort has been made to give proper acknowledgment at various points in the book for material and ideas used, but it is obviously impossible to indicate all the specific sources because of the widespread origins from which material was garnered. Any inadvertent omissions, it is hoped, will be rectified in the bibliography at the end of the book.

E. B. ALDERFER,
H. E. MICHL.

PHILADELPHIA,
June, 1942.

CONTENTS

PART IX

THE CHANGING PATTERN OF AMERICAN INDUSTRY

PART I
THE PLAN OF THE STUDY

CHAPTER I

THE STUDY OF AMERICAN MANUFACTURING: THE INDIVIDUAL INDUSTRY APPROACH

The average length of life of a business enterprise in the United States is 66 months. This fact, perhaps as well as any other, focuses attention upon the unstable nature of our economic system. In no realm of economic activity is instability more apparent or bewildering than in the field of manufacturing. In this book we shall study this area of our national life—in many respects the most important area—in an attempt to bring to our readers a better understanding of its origins, its dynamic nature, and its socially important problems. Before discussing the plan of approach, let us look at the field as a whole and note the position it occupies in the economy of the nation.

IMPORTANCE OF MANUFACTURING IN THE UNITED STATES

Manufacturing and Employment.—As an economic activity, manufacturing may be compared with agriculture, mining, construction, trans-

TABLE I.—GENERAL DIVISION OF OCCUPATIONS IN THE UNITED STATES IN 1940

Class of occupation	Number of workers (000 omitted)	Per cent of total
Manufacturing and mechanical industries.	13,865	26.3
Agriculture.	9,272	17.5
Trade.	7,278	13.8
Clerical occupations.	5,521	10.5
Domestic and personal service.	5,413	10.3
Transportation and communication.	4,874	9.2
Professional service.	3,583	6.8
Public service.	1,518	2.9
Extraction of minerals.	1,140	2.2
Forestry and fishing.	270	0.5
All occupations.	52,734	100.0

Source: ANDERSON, H. D., and P. E. DAVIDSON, "Occupational Trends in the U. S.," pp 16–17, Stanford University Press, Stanford University, Calif., 1940.

portation, trade, finance, and other major economic activities. Among
these it ranks first, based upon the number of workers gainfully employed.
As shown in Table I, over a quarter of all gainfully employed people were
engaged in manufacturing occupations.

Manufacturing and National Wealth.—Unfortunately no recent
studies or estimates have been made of the amount of capital tied up in
manufacturing enterprises. The Federal Trade Commission estimated
the wealth of all manufacturing corporations in 1922 at 34 billion dollars.
This sum was 33 per cent of the wealth of all corporations, and it represented 10 per cent of the total estimated wealth of the United States.
The National Industrial Conference Board estimated the net capital
(total assets less investments) of manufacturing industries in 1936 as
46 billion dollars, which according to their study represented 15 per cent
of the national wealth.

Manufacturing: the Chief Source of Income.—The relative importance of manufacturing may also be shown by comparing it with the other
industrial sources of national income. The Bureau of Foreign and
Domestic Commerce estimated the national income for 1939 at 69 billion
dollars of which the largest single share, or 15.4 billion dollars, was contributed by manufacturing. Thus, on the basis of income produced,
manufacturing is the most important industrial division.

The relative contribution to our national income of our two most basic
economic activities, agriculture and manufacturing, reflects the progress of
industrialization of the United States. This is shown in Table II by

TABLE II.—PERCENTAGE OF TOTAL INCOME PRODUCED BY AGRICULTURE AND MANU-
FACTURING

Year	Agriculture	Manufacturing
1849	31.7	12.5
1859	30.8	12.1
1869	24.1	15.9
1879	20.7	14.5
1889	15.8	21.1
1899	21.2	19.6
1909	22.1	20.1
1919	22.9	25.8
1929	12.7	26.2
1939*	8.1	22.2

* Survey of Current Business, June 1940.
Source: National Industrial Conference Board, "National Income in the U. S. 1799–1938," pp.
60–61, New York, 1939.

decades. From the founding of Jamestown to the period 1879–1889
agriculture furnished our principal income. About 1885 manufacturing

passed agriculture as a source of income, and in the decades that followed the United States became a predominantly manufacturing nation.

PLAN OF THE STUDY

In organizing the material in this book we have been guided by an old German proverb which says, "The hope of mastery lies in limitation." The whole field of manufacturing will be divided into the smaller areas familiarly known as industries. An industry is a homogeneous group of enterprises or companies. Such companies may be similar to each other in several respects. They may have common raw materials as in the rubber industry, or common technology as in the chemical industry, or a common market as in the confectionery industry. Some industries are much less nearly homogeneous than others. It will be necessary further to subdivide the field in discussing the less homogeneous industries. An instance of this is the rubber industry, where there are sharp distinctions in the manufacture of tires, footwear, and industrial rubber products such as power transmission belts.

This matter of homogeneity has a direct bearing on our plan of study, and it is important to the reader to be clear at the outset about our attitude toward it. Homogeneity is to be regarded as a relative matter. At the one extreme we can have standards as to similarity so exact that no two companies can qualify as being similar. In fact, every business enterprise is unique in many important respects—its personnel differs, its capital structure differs, its products differ from those of every other enterprise. At the other extreme, we can regard all business enterprises as similar. The economist generally so regards them when he writes about all entrepreneurs using land, buildings, machinery, and labor to carry out their business projects. But we cannot solve many problems by regarding all companies as alike or by regarding each one as meriting separate treatment. We are forced by administrative necessity if by no other reason, to take a middle of the road course. This is the attitude usually taken. The companies belonging to the same industry are commonly regarded as similar. They are so grouped by businessmen, tariff officials, tax authorities, legislators, and many others. Import duties are imposed, processing taxes levied, hours of work set, minimum wages established, etc., for entire industries on the assumption that the units which compose them are essentially alike and therefore should be treated alike.

Since so much of our legislation, administration, policy making, and thinking is in terms of specific industries, the individual industry shall be the unit of analysis, and the matter of homogeneity will receive attention. It is our belief that errors of understanding and judgment arise from failure to take into account important variations between groups of companies within an industry—variations as to size, markets, capital structure, costs, etc.   Obviously, all the known facts about an industry cannot be recorded.   Such facts as seem to be significant we shall discuss under three major headings: (1) the place and structure of the industry in our economic order; (2) the development of the industry in the sense of its historical evolution; (3) the competitive aspects of the industry.

PLACE AND STRUCTURE OF THE INDUSTRY IN THE ECONOMIC ORDER

Of fundamental importance in the analysis of an industry is its position in the economic order.   How important is the industry, and what part does it play in the economic life of the nation?

The concept of "importance" is a loose one and almost useless if expressed in general terms inasmuch as all of our industries are important in our complex, interrelated present-day world.   "Importance" may or may not be related to "size."   Certain industries are very important, although large size as measured by any of the usual yardsticks is not their characteristic; for instance, the manufacture of chemical glassware, such as test tubes, beakers, etc., is quite essential to the conduct of other industries, as we learned in the First World War.   But, since we do make comparisons, it will be helpful to use the best methods.

The economic importance of the work done by an industry is measured only in part by *value of output*.   Two industries may have outputs of equal value and yet differ widely in capital investment, number of workers, and value added.   The flour milling industry has approximately the same output as the paper industry, yet it gives employment to only one-fourth as many workers and has a "value added" that is only one-third as great. Where the processes are simple, as in the milling industry, little of value is added to the raw materials and therefore the amount of employment offered is relatively small.

Number of workers is a better test of importance than value of output, although it, too, has the limitation of presenting only one view of a complex phenomenon.   In testing a group of industries for size, "number of workers" produces about the same ranking as "value added."   This is because the money paid to workers as wages and salaries is an important percentage of value added.   However, "number of workers" sometimes loses its significance as a test of relative importance because of the different degrees of mechanization reached by different industries.   Number of workers employed in the cigarette industry, for example, understates the importance of that industry because it is so highly mechanized.

If one were comparing industries as to the economic importance of their processes of manufacturing and were limited to one test, it would be the figures showing *value added*.   This is because manufacturing is a transformation of raw materials, and the industries under scrutiny should be judged, not by the quantity or the value of the products leaving the factories, but by the addition to the utility or to the money value of the materials entering the factories. From the value of the output is deducted the value of the raw materials, supplies, fuel, and power, and the result is the increase in utility that has resulted from the manufacturing operations. In 1939 the meat packing industry purchased about 2,600 million dollars' worth of raw materials, supplies, etc., and by its plant operations added some 400 million dollars to the value of these materials. In that same year the cotton industry accomplished almost precisely the same result by purchasing 600 million dollars' worth of raw materials, supplies, fuel, and power.

Demand for the Product.—Since all industries are brought into being in response to a demand for their products and continue to exist only so long as this demand continues, an analysis of the demand for the product throws much light on its place in the industrial economy.

Generally speaking, the products of manufacturing industries fall into one of two classes, *i.e.*, producer's goods or consumer's goods. Producer's goods comprise such products as machinery, blast furnaces, rails, cement, etc., in short, goods that are not manufactured primarily for use by the ultimate consumer but rather for other industries that do produce goods for his use. For example, a loom is a producer's good, or capital good, manufactured for the textile industry which uses it to weave cloth. Consumer's goods, on the other hand, include such things as food, clothing, radios, automobiles, and the hundreds of thousands of other products that are purchased directly by the ultimate consumer for his own use.

Consumer's goods may be classified according to their degree of perishability. The National Bureau of Economic Research, in a recent monograph, divided consumer's goods into three classes. Those goods lasting 3 years or more, such as automobiles, luggage, or household electrical appliances, are called durable consumer's goods. Articles which render service for 6 months to 3 years are classed as semidurable, for example, textiles, clothing, shoes, or automobile tires. Goods lasting less than 6 months are classed as perishable commodities. Typical examples of this class are foods, petroleum, and tobacco products.

An important distinction between durable and perishable goods is that the former are much less regularly produced than the latter. The reason for this is not difficult to find. Nondurable goods, as has been explained, are of an ephemeral nature and must be replaced within a short period of time. Durable goods, on the other hand, wear out slowly, and replacement can frequently be postponed indefinitely. In periods of depression, when purchasing power shrinks and the business world is gloomy, the purchase of durable goods is postponed, and the volume of production drops. Production of nondurable goods also decreases, but generally not

to the same extent.   This is illustrated in Fig. 1, which shows employment of factory workers in durable and nondurable goods industries.

Note from Fig. 1 that in the major depressions the durable goods
industries experienced a relatively greater decline in production than the
nondurable goods industries.   Note also that while durable goods industries fall to lower levels in periods of depression, the converse is true in
periods of activity—the durable goods industries stage a greater recovery.

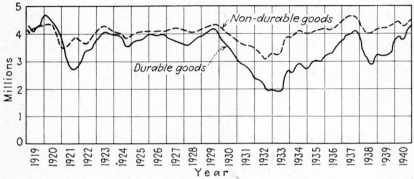

Fig. 1.—Employment of factory workers. (*The Cleveland Trust Company, Business
Bulletin, Mar.* 15, 1941.)

We may summarize this by saying that nondurable goods, as a class,
have a more immediate claim upon the national income and, from the
standpoint of physical volume of production, have a more sustained
importance in the economy of the nation.

Nondurable Goods Industries Vary in Stability.—It must not be
assumed from the foregoing that all industries in the nondurable goods field
enjoy the relative stability that is characteristic of the group.   The degree
to which an industry can maintain its production depends, as has been
said, upon the need that it satisfies and the competition from other industries that can also meet the need.   The demand for textile products,
especially in the form of clothing, is relatively stable, but the stability
of textiles as a group does not assure stability of demand for every industry within the group; for example, the demand for cotton may shift, in
part, to silk or rayon.   During the depression beginning in 1929, the per-
capita consumption of cotton cloth in the United States decreased, but the
consumption of rayon increased at a very high rate.   The food industries,
as a group, show a high degree of stability, but since the demand for food
can be met by a wide variety of products there can be, and is, considerable
shifting from one product to another.

Direct or Derived Demand.—For some products the demand is direct.
This means the goods are purchased directly for the utility they will yield
the purchaser.   The demand for clothing is an example of this type of

demand.   However, the demand for many goods arises, in part, from the demand for some other goods.   The demand for window glass, for example, arises chiefly from the demand for houses, and the demand for tires arises mainly from the demand for automobiles.   This kind of demand is said to be a "derived demand," *i.e.*, the demand for flat glass and tires may be thought of as reflecting, respectively, the demand for houses and automobiles.   Generally speaking, the demand that is derived is relatively less elastic than the demand that is direct.   The reasons for this are not difficult to ascertain.   The cost of window glass, to continue with this example, represents but a very small part of the total cost of constructing a building, and changes in its price, either upward or downward, will not cause significant changes in the demand for houses and, therefore, for glass.   Accordingly, the opportunity to expand an industry that produces this type of product depends more upon developments in the field from which the demand is derived than upon developments within the industry itself.   Reductions in cost arising from technological improvements will not cause as rapid an expansion in the market as would be the case in goods for which the demand is direct.

Having viewed an industry from a sufficiently distant vantage point to get a picture of the place it occupies in our national economy, let us draw closer and sharpen our focus in order to get a picture of its structure. This should bring within our range of vision such things as the number of units comprising the industry, the size of the individual units, and the prevailing cost structures.   Each of these three aspects is an essential part of the whole picture of an industry.

Number of Units in an Industry.—The number of units composing an industry may be measured by counting either the number of establishments or the number of companies.   An establishment is a single factory, mill, or plant—a physical entity which we think of as producing some tangible good or useful service.   A company, whether incorporated or not, is a firm, concern, or business—a financial entity which we think of as a money-making venture.   A manufacturing company must have at least one plant, but an increasing proportion of our industrial products are turned out by multiplant enterprises.   In 1939, the Census listed 184,000 establishments or plants (not including those producing less than $5,000 worth of goods annually) which turned out a stream of goods valued at approximately 57 billion dollars.   Obviously this volume of goods was not the product of 184,000 companies because some companies operated two or more plants.   A necessary part of the structural picture of an individual industry must include, therefore, both the number of companies and the number of plants, for the two are seldom if ever identical.   The point we wish to stress here is that with respect to each of the industries coming under scrutiny we ought to know whether there are few or many units in terms of companies and of plants.   The number of companies is a poor index of size of an industry, but it is significant from the standpoint of competition.

The relation of the number of companies in a given industry to the nature and amount of competition in that industry is complex; furthermore it varies according to industries.   Economic theory relates the state of competition directly to the number of the competitors.   Competition is said to exist where the sellers and buyers are so numerous that the influence of any one of these is negligible, whereas pure monopoly implies the existence of only one seller or one buyer.   In between are varying gradations of competition and monopoly.   There are, of course, influences other than number of companies which affect the amount and form of competition, but the number of companies has a direct effect.

Scale of Operation.—Another important aspect of the structure of an industry, and one in which significant differences exist between industries, is its scale of operations, *i.e.*, the size of the individual plants and companies that constitute the industry.   To understand the term "scale of operation" it is necessary to make a distinction between company and plant, because it is frequently applied to both, although the factors that determine the scale, or size, of the individual plant may be—in fact usually are—different from those that affect the scale of company operations.

The scale of individual plants, as will be shown in the chapters that follow, is usually determined by the prevailing technology and by the nature of the product.   There are definite limits to the maximum and minimum size of sewing machines, blast furnaces, lathes, cement kilns, petroleum refining stills, and all other kinds of industrial machines; and there are also limits in each industry as to the number of machines in a plant that can be effectively supervised and managed.   In some industries the scale of plant operation is determined more by the nature of the product manufactured and its market.   If the product is perishable, as in the case of bread, the plant is restricted in size; if the product is heavy or bulky in relation to value, like cement, there are definite limits to the size of the area that a given plant can serve efficiently.

The scale of company operation, on the other hand, is usually determined by commercial and financial rather than technological factors.   A company may be very large, but its individual plants may be quite small. The economies or other advantages, if any, which it enjoys arise from advertising, marketing, buying power, financing, etc.

The scale of a plant or company can be measured by several yardsticks: capital investment, number of workers, physical output, value of output, and productive capacity.   We have selected number of wage earners as less limited in usefulness than any of the others.   Those who use this unit are warned against its drawbacks.   It may understate the over-all size of plants and companies in industries that are highly mechanized or where value added is relatively low and may overstate the over-all size of the unit in industries that have a high proportion of labor costs. For example, according to the census data of 1939, flour mills employ on the aver-

TABLE III.—AVERAGE NUMBER OF WORKERS PER ESTABLISHMENT

All manufacturing.. 43

Small-scale Plants

Baking—bread..	11
Flour milling..	12
Paint, varnish, and lacquer..............................	19
Drugs and medicines.....................................	20
Liquor—distilled..	30
Clothing—women's and children's........................	34
Brick and tile..	36
Canning—fruit and vegetables...........................	49
Foundries...	50
Clothing—men's and boys'...............................	56
Liquor—malt..	60

Medium-scale Plants

Meat packing..	82
Cigars..	85
Rubber products other than tires and tubes..............	97
Leather tanning...	106
Aluminum...	106
Chemicals—miscellaneous................................	111
Beet sugar..	123
Silk and rayon weaving..................................	145
Cement..	149
Petroleum refining......................................	150
Clay products—electric and sanitary ware...............	157
Rayon—filament...	161
Shipbuilding..	164
Paper...	173
Machine tools...	183
Hosiery—full-fashioned.................................	195
Shoes...	204
Woolen and worsted manufacturing........................	208
Pig iron..	241

Large-scale Plants

Glass...	305
Cotton..	328
Pottery—table and hotel china..........................	334
Automobiles...	377
Aircraft..	390
Sugar refining—cane....................................	524
Copper smelting and refining............................	532
Cigarettes..	807
Rubber tires and tubes..................................	1,020
Steel works and rolling mills...........................	1,460

Based upon Census of Manufactures, 1939, *Preliminary Report.*

age only 12 workers each in contrast with 208 for woolen and worsted mills.   However, flour milling is a larger scale industry than wool manufacturing because the bulk of flour mill products is turned out by a very small percentage of the very largest units in the industry.

Having selected number of workers as our criterion of size of plant, we encounter the problem of standards in applying the criterion.   Scale of operation is usually referred to as "large" or "small."   We hear of "giant" corporations and "big business."   Such terms have different meanings according to the industry, the time in question, and the people who use the terms.   A recent study[1] of size uses a "dead level" standard of 1,000 employees.   If above this figure, a plant is large; if below, it is small.   We shall use a different method which we believe to be somewhat less arbitrary.   Instead of selecting a number like 1,000, as in the previous illustration, to separate the large-scale from the small-scale enterprises, we shall interpose a group or area containing 50 per cent of the plants or companies.   In Table III the two-score industries covered by our study are arranged in ranked order according to average number of workers per establishment.   Those in the top quartile we shall call large-scale plants, those in the lowest quartile will be referred to as small-scale plants, and the second and third quartile plants are to be known as medium size. Justification for this practice is strengthened by the fact that the gradations in size from industry to industry are small and fairly uniform.

Information on the scale of company structure is not published in the regular U. S. Census reports, but some data are available in special census compilations, in corporation manuals, and in special studies.

Cost Structure.—There are wide variations from industry to industry in the range of the principal items of cost.   The Census throws light on two of these items, wages and materials.   Table IV from this source shows the relation of wage cost to value of product in the industries before us. On the basis of these figures we have adopted the following standards: (1) A *low labor cost industry* is one whose wage bill ranges up to 10 per cent of the value of the output.   (2) A *high labor cost industry* is one whose wage cost exceeds 25 per cent of the value of product.   (3) Any industry with wage costs ranging between 10 and 25 per cent we shall designate a *medium labor cost industry*.   It will be noted that these figures correspond roughly to the quartile distribution of wage costs.

Similarly, Table V covers the relation of cost of raw materials (including fuel and purchased power) to value of products.   From these percentages we have adopted the following standards: (1) A *low raw material cost industry* is one in which this item is less than 40 per cent.   (2) A *high raw material cost industry* is one with raw material expenditures in

[1] Big Business: Its Growth and Its Place," Twentieth Century Fund, New York, 1939.

excess of 65 per cent of value of product. (3) *Medium raw material cost industries* have a range of from 40 to 65 per cent.

In the chapters that follow we shall examine and interpret for each industry these principal structural aspects—number of units, scale of operation, and the cost structure.

COURSE OF DEVELOPMENT OF AN INDUSTRY

Importance of Historical Information.—August Comte's adage that "no conception can be understood except through its history" can be applied with profit to the analysis of industries. Industries are the product of an evolutionary past which has shaped their present structure and practices. Prevailing practices and policies in an industry that appear in the present to be uneconomic and difficult to understand take on a new meaning when viewed in the light of the industry's development. For example, many students of the cotton textile industry express bewilderment at its complicated structure and an inability to understand the apparent lack of integration between the manufacturing and marketing branches, to which they attribute several of the industry's problems. A study of the history of the industry and the circumstances surrounding its early development explains much of its present structure and makes that structure appear more logical and economically justifiable. With respect to each industry, its technology, location, number and size of units comprising it, marketing channels—all reflect peculiarities that require some historical interpretation.

The Measurement of Growth or Decline.—One aspect of the development of an industry is concerned with its growth. The problem of measuring the growth of an industry is as difficult as those encountered in measuring size and scale. There are several yardsticks, and each has its limitations.

"Number of establishments" is rendered unsuited as a measure because in many of our most rapidly expanding industries there has been a steady decline in number of plants. As industries became mechanized, plants have decreased in number, but those that remain are of much larger size, and the output of each has greatly increased.

"Capital invested" and "horsepower installed" have similar defects as measures. An increase in capital invested may merely mean that an industry is shifting from manufacture by hand to manufacture by machines, without increasing its total output. An increase in horsepower installed may be the result of the same basic change, a shift from manual to mechanical production.

A more reliable measure of growth is "number of workers" employed, although this, too, has its limitations. If the industry has been changing its production by shifting from hand to machine labor, a decline in the number of workers might be accompanied by a large increase in physical output and value added. This measure is also affected by changes in the length of the working day or week. A reduction in the number of hours

TABLE IV.—WAGES EXPRESSED AS A PERCENTAGE OF VALUE OF PRODUCT

	Per Cent
All manufacturing	16.0

Low Labor Cost Industries

Cigarettes	2.5
Copper smelting and refining	2.7
Sugar refining—cane	4.2
Flour milling	4.3
Pig iron	5.1
Petroleum refining	5.2
Meat packing	6.1
Drugs and medicines	6.6
Paint, varnish, and lacquer	7.4
Liquor—distilled	8.9
Beet sugar	9.0

Medium Labor Cost Industries

Canning—fruit and vegetables	11.1
Chemicals—miscellaneous	11.3
Liquor—malt	11.8
Paper	15.3
Aluminum	15.3
Rubber tires and tubes	15.5
Automobiles	16.0
Leather tanning	16.5
Cement	16.6
Woolen and worsted manufacturing	19.4
Clothing—women's and children's	19.7
Rubber products other than tires and tubes	20.0
Steel works and rolling mills	20.8
Cigars	21.1
Silk and rayon weaving	21.1
Baking—bread	21.6
Clothing—men's and boys'	23.4
Rayon—filament	24.3
Glass	24.6

High Labor Cost Industries

Shoes	25.0
Cotton	25.1
Aircraft	27.5
Machine tools	28.5
Clay products—electric and sanitary ware	28.6
Brick and tile	30.0
Shipbuilding	31.8
Foundries	33.8
Hosiery—full-fashioned	36.5
Pottery—table and hotel china	48.7

Based upon Census of Manufactures, 1939, *Preliminary Report*.

per day or week that employees are permitted to work would lead to an expansion in the number of workers on the pay roll with no necessary increase in production.

TABLE V.—RAW MATERIALS EXPRESSED AS A PERCENTAGE OF VALUE OF PRODUCT

	Per Cent
All manufacturing	56.5
Low Raw Material Cost Industries	
Pottery—table and hotel china	27.1
Brick and tile	28.2
Machine tools	29.4
Liquor—malt	31.0
Drugs and medicines	31.4
Rayon filament	31.6
Clay products—electric and sanitary ware	32.5
Glass	33.8
Aircraft	34.3
Cement	35.8
Foundries	37.6
Medium Raw Material Cost Industries	
Hosiery—full-fashioned	43.3
Chemicals—miscellaneous	44.1
Rubber products other than tires and tubes	46.5
Shipbuilding	46.8
Baking—bread	46.8
Cigars	49.0
Liquor—distilled	50.0
Cotton	51.0
Shoes	52.8
Clothing—men's and boys'	55.9
Paint, varnish, and lacquer	56.5
Paper	57.0
Steel works and rolling mills	57.8
Clothing—women's and children's	58.3
Rubber tires and tubes	59.0
Canning—fruit and vegetables	60.7
Silk and rayon weaving	61.1
Woolen and worsted manufacturing	61.4
Aluminum	63.0
Beet sugar	63.4
High Raw Material Cost Industries	
Leather tanning	66.1
Automobiles	67.3
Sugar refining—cane	76.3
Flour milling	77.8
Cigarettes	78.2
Petroleum refining	78.5
Meat packing	84.0
Pig iron	84.1
Copper smelting and refining	91.2

Based upon Census of Manufactures, 1939, *Preliminary Report.*

"Value of product" loses some of its importance as a measure of growth or decline because it is expressed in dollars and has all the faults of that imperfect measure of value. Changes in the price level, either upward or downward, materially affect this figure but would reveal little concerning the amount of goods produced. During the First World War, for example, the prices of many products more than doubled or trebled. The value of products for these industries therefore increased out of all proportion to the increase in physical output. In the same way a drop in the price level, such as was experienced during the years 1930–1933, would grossly overstate the decline in physical production. Improved methods of manufacture that lead to large economies in production and lower selling prices might result in a large increase in amount of goods sold without a corresponding increase in value of product.

The best single test of growth and decline is found in the trend of physical quantity of output, *i.e.*, yards of cloth sold, suits of clothing, number of automobiles, tons of steel, pounds of copper, etc. This measure also lacks precision because, over a period of years, the quality of a product may change. For certain purposes comparisons made on this basis may lead to somewhat defective conclusions. Despite this reservation, physical output is the best single test of growth or decline of a manufacturing industry.

Law of Industrial Growth.—We shall notice when we analyze the industries included in this book that some are young and vigorous, some

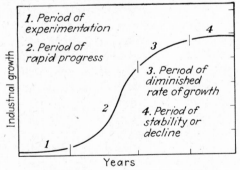

Fig. 2.—Curve of industrial growth.

are mature and stable, others are old and declining and that, although they are changing at varying rates of increase or decrease, they all show a tendency to follow a common pattern in their course of development. All of them pass through a period of experimentation, a period of rapid growth, a period of diminished rate of growth, and a period of stability or decline. This tendency, known as the "law of industrial growth," is portrayed in Fig. 2. It will be observed later that the curve does not have this exact shape for all industries because the length of the entire cycle or the duration of any component part may differ from one industry to another, depending upon developments within and without the industry and upon the nature of the product.

The factors responsible for the change in the rate of growth and decline vary from one industry to another, but the most important are the following:[1]

1. Changes in technical progress.
2. Changes in demand.
3. Competition from foreign countries.
4. Competition from new industries.
5. Developments in supplementary industries.
6. Changes in population growth.

The effects of these changes are frequently difficult to trace, for they are not independent of each other. Let us, however, examine the curve of industrial growth to see how it is influenced by these factors.

In the period of experimentation, both the product and the process of producing it are defective. Many experiments must be made, and during this period the cost of the product is high and its quality poor. The high price and the poor quality, together with the consumer's ignorance of the product, restrict the demand; the market is small. The latter part of this period, and sometimes the first part of the next period, has been referred to by Kettering, president of General Motors Research Corporation, as the "shirt-losing" period because many enterprises enter the field and many are forced to drop out via bankruptcy.

As a result of the period of experimentation, both the product and the process have been materially improved as the industry enters its second phase of growth. The growth is further accelerated by reduction in the price of the product and by improvements in the marketing of it. One improvement leads to another, and the price is further reduced. New markets are tapped, the demand swells, and the industry is in a position to manufacture on a larger scale and to reduce price still further. More new devices are brought into play, better merchandising channels are established, export sales may be pushed, and installment selling may be inaugurated. Consequently, the second period is one of rapid progress.

The industry passes next to the third stage, diminished growth. The rate of technical progress begins to slacken. Since the industry has already made great improvements in process, further improvements are more difficult to make; usually only refinements of existing processes are effected. Costs, and therefore prices, cannot be reduced to the same extent as before, and further increases in sales can be obtained only with greatly increased efforts. Demand grows, but at a lower rate than in the preceding period. All who desire the product and have the purchasing

[1] Kuznets, Simon S., *Secular Movements in Production and Prices*, pp. 1–58, Houghton Mifflin Company, Boston, 1930.

power to buy it at the prevailing price are already customers of the industry. Improvements in quality extend the life of the product, so replacements need not be made as often. Those who desire the product but cannot pay the current price cannot be reached because the existing process does not permit further reductions in price.

During the third period external forces may be at work counteracting the efforts of the industry to expand and forcing it into the fourth period, that of stability or decline. Competing industries may be established in foreign countries, and competition from them not only reduces exports but frequently results in reduced domestic sales. New industries whose products are direct substitutes for the products of the older industry may arise, and the market must be shared by both. Frequently, the products of the new industries are not direct substitutes, but the results may be the same. If the new products strike the public fancy and the old product is dispensable, purchasing power will be diverted from the old to the new industry.

The rise of new industries adds another complicating factor to the disadvantage of the older industry. The new industries must compete against all other industries for capital, labor, and raw materials, and the additional competition increases the prices of these factors, making the competitive position of the older industry more insecure by further reducing its ability to lower prices and maintain its market.

It was pointed out earlier in the chapter that some industries sell, not to the ultimate consumer, but to other industries. The expansion of such an industry is limited by developments in the consuming industry, especially if the product represents only a small part of the consuming industry's total cost of production. Reduction in the price of the supplying industry's product will not expand the market proportionately.

Expansion is sometimes retarded by the failure of the raw material producing industries to keep pace with technical progress in the consuming industry. The improvements in process of the consuming industry lead to marked reductions in cost, and since the conversion costs have been reduced the cost of raw materials represents a much higher percentage of the total cost of production than formerly. Unless the raw material industry can reduce its costs, further substantial reductions in the cost of the finished product are difficult to make, and demand will not grow at its former rate. For example, the meat packing industry has increased its efficiency by the subdivision of labor and the utilization of by-products to the point where value added represents only 15 per cent of the value of product. If this industry could reduce its conversion[1] costs 50 per cent by developing a new technique, the reduction in price would amount to only 7 per cent. On the other hand, if the cost of raising live-

[1] That is, all costs other than costs of raw materials.

stock were reduced only 25 per cent, the price of the finished product could be decreased by 20 per cent.

Expansion may also be retarded by a slowing up in the rate of population growth. This is an especially important factor in industries that produce staple goods like certain foods. The demand for flour is relatively inelastic, and growth must come chiefly from increases in population.

When an industry enters into a state of decadence, heroic efforts are often made to give it a new lease on life. These efforts take the form of intensive research to improve the product or to find new uses, or to develop a process of manufacture that will reduce costs. If the efforts are successful, especially if a revolutionary technique of manufacture is discovered, the industry may again enter a new period of growth and repeat the cycle of industrial development.

It should be added that while an industry is in its period of rapid growth (or decline) individual companies within the industry may have experiences directly opposite to the trend of the industry. Failure to keep pace with technological improvements, either in process of manufacture or in design of product, may cause some companies to pass out at a time when demand is rapidly expanding. On the other hand, an individual company, through progressive management and aggressive merchandising, may gain for itself an increasing share of the declining business of an industry.

COMPETITIVE CONDITIONS IN AN INDUSTRY

The third general phase of an industry, its competitive relations, is of more direct interest to all of us than either its structure or its historical development. Every businessman in the competitive arena is prone to regard his own industry as the most competitive. In his quest for profits he is always on the alert to find new ways to circumvent competition. The rest of us, as consumers, also have a stake in competition. This is because we live in a competitive economy. We rely upon competition to give us goods that are varied in nature, excellent in quality, and low in price. If competition does not exist, society loses. The consumers pay more for their commodities or have a limited choice as to variety and price range. Competition is most important to all of us in another respect: we rely upon it to *coordinate* the economic system as a whole. The economic system is a vast, intricate machine consisting of many parts each of which must be geared into and synchronized with all other parts. Unless the machine is synchronized it will get out of balance; it might produce too much wheat and not enough meat, too many shoes and not enough suits, too much cotton and not enough silk, too many of all these things and not enough blast furnaces, looms, and other producer's goods. In our economic system, competition is relied upon to maintain the balance between industries and to direct the flow of raw materials, labor, and capital into the various industries in proportion to the demand for their respective products.   Because we rely upon competition to produce these important results we have laws in the United States that are designed to preserve competition or, stated differently, that make it a crime to suppress competition.

The amount and the nature of competition which exists in a given industry at any time are the result of many influences: the stage of the business cycle, the secular trend in prices, the nature of the product—to mention only a few.   In the industries we shall discuss, our interest will be focused not on those competitive factors which are common to all business but rather on those which are peculiar to the industry in question.   The competitive behavior of each industry is the outcome of a composite set of factors, some general to all industry and others specific to the industry in question.   Let us look now at the latter.

Nature of the Product and Competition.—The competitive pattern of an industry is influenced greatly by the extent to which its product is standardized or, to put it conversely, is differentiated.   Where it is difficult to distinguish between the products of the several producers, as in the Portland cement industry, the article tends to be sold on a price basis. On the other hand, the manufacturer who differentiates his product from those of his competitors in a manner acceptable to consumers has what may be a semimonopolistic position; he is partially sheltered from competition.   In one industry the manufacturer achieves this by engineering, in another by beauty of design and texture, in still another by care in the selection and processing of raw materials.

Is the product made from agricultural or mineral raw materials, and are these raw materials an important item in the cost of the final article? Agricultural materials are more unstable in price than minerals owing to the vagaries of the weather and the difficulties of controlling the larger number of producers.   Gluts and shortages, "invisible" supplies, and the notorious independence of the farmer, the rancher, and plantation owner upset, as we shall see, many careful plans to control competition.

In industries where much time elapses between the purchase of raw materials and the sale of finished products the hazards of competition are great unless the risk can be shifted through hedging on a commodity exchange.   In numerous industries no such price insurance opportunities exist, and here the strategy of buying and selling becomes all the more important, especially if raw materials constitute a major item of cost.[1]

Scale of the Enterprise and Competition.—In a market of a given size the scale of the enterprise determines, of course, the number of competitors.   The number of competitors, as we have already noted, affects their

[1] See Table V, p. 13.

actions toward each other. In the cigarette industry, where the "Big Three" produce two-thirds of the total output, each company does nothing of importance without calculating the probable effect of its action on the other two. On the other hand, in the baking industry, where there are at least 18,000 producers, it is difficult, if not impossible, to obtain anything approaching unity of action. Competition is therefore much more free and independent. In some industries one company may be outstanding in size and be tacitly accepted as a leader. In others there may be a few large companies and many small ones, and the division is between the "big fellows" and the "independents."

Technology and Competition.—The technology of an industry bears directly upon its competitive aspects because of the relation of technology to the scale of enterprise, the cost structure of the industry, and the existence of "overcapacity." The technique of production may predispose companies to operate on a large scale, with heavy fixed investment in plant and a long-time supply of raw materials, as in the manufacture of newsprint paper. Here power requirements have led the companies to develop hydroelectric projects and to buy large tracts of standing timber to meet their future raw material requirements. Such ventures call for large amounts of capital, obtained in part by the issuance of bonds. The taxes on the land and the interest on the bonds demand regular and fixed payments. This ever-recurring call for money sets up pressures which cause the companies to cut the price when most of the trade feel price is already low in relation to cost. It causes them to maintain or increase production schedules even though stocks on hand are heavy and rate of consumption is low. If a textile mill's fixed costs (interest, depreciation, obsolescence, taxes, insurance, superintendence, etc.) are $100,000 and the mill can produce 400,000 pounds a month, the fixed cost per pound of finished product amounts to 25 cents. If production is decreased to 200,000, the fixed cost *per pound* is 50 cents. In other words, fixed costs per pound vary inversely with production, decreasing as production increases and increasing as production decreases. This explains why manufacturers frequently choose to operate their plants at a loss. They prefer to run at a loss rather than to shut down because that would entail greater loss. The effect on competition is obvious.

At the opposite extreme is the industry with a technology that calls for relatively little investment in plant and machinery. An example is the dress industry, where one may begin on a "shoestring" basis. The principal item of equipment is a sewing machine, which is not costly; indeed, it need not even be purchased, since leasing is a common practice. Capital investment is further minimized by the existence of loft buildings in sections of New York City where the garment industries congregate. This situation makes for ease of entrance into the industry and keen competition. It is true that the marginal firms are constantly on their way out of the industry via bankruptcy, but it is equally true that ambitious foremen and others step forward to try their skill as entrepreneurs, and this they are able to do because of the low capital requirements imposed by the industry's technology. The result is more firms than are needed and a severe struggle for survival.

The discussion thus far of the relation of technology to competition has dealt only with technology as it exists in a given industry at a given moment of time. Equally important in its influence on competition is the trend of an industry's technology over a period of time. From this point of view some industries are quite stable inasmuch as no basic changes in technique occur for a long period of time. In contrast, other industries experience important changes in rapid succession. We are not referring here to the change that comes during the "period of experimentation" when an industry is just getting under way and technical obstacles are being ironed out. Nor are we referring to the relatively minor improvements that all industries are constantly making; rather we mean the changes that materially alter the technique of production. From the standpoint of competition the important aspects are the rates and the cost of such changes.

A good illustration of a technically immature industry is rayon production. This product was produced commercially as early as 1889, and during its entire life of half a century it has been undergoing marked and ceaseless change, improvements not of a minor nature but substantial in character, so as to put at a competitive disadvantage the companies unable to put them into effect. This largely accounts for the heavy mortality of rayon producers despite a rapidly expanding market. In a technically stable industry, as we have defined the term, there exist companies with outmoded equipment and processes which struggle fiercely to avoid bankruptcy. Even when they fail the struggle is not over, for the physical plant, purchased perhaps at a few cents on the dollar, is recapitalized at the lower figure and reenters the market to compete again.

Capacity.—Technological progress is also an important cause of overcapacity, which may be defined as the ability of an industry to produce goods in excess of what the market can absorb at a price that will yield a profit. The introduction of a new and more efficient process by one company compels others in the industry to make similar installations, with the result that the industry's productive capacity expands beyond the requirements of the market and causes severe competition. Overcapacity in an industry sometimes arises not from technological developments within the industry but from technological advances in a competing industry. Thus, the rapid improvements in rayon manufacturing increased the use of rayon in all types of hosiery, displacing large amounts of combed and carded yarns formerly used for that purpose and resulting in considerable idle capacity in the cotton yarn industry. Similarly, the shift in the garment industry from the use of narrow-width fabrics to fabrics of greater widths made idle many of the narrow looms in the textile industry.

Whatever the causes of overcapacity may be—and, as will be shown in the chapters to follow, they frequently differ from one industry to another —it is one of the chief sources of competition in many of our industries. While its importance as a competitive factor is generally recognized, there is considerable difference of opinion among students as to the amount of capacity and, therefore, excess capacity that our industries have. Estimates of the annual productive capacity of the shoe industry, to cite only one case, vary from 400 million to 900 million pairs of shoes. Estimates of capacity and excess capacity of other industries show equally wide variations.

The existence of such wide differences of opinion on what would appear to be a matter of factual determination indicates that the concept of capacity and the best method of measuring it are by no means settled issues. Some students measure it by estimating the amount of goods that could be produced by an industry if the existing machinery were operated continuously throughout the year. The difference between this theoretical maximum and the amount actually produced during the year represents excess capacity. That this method is unsatisfactory should be apparent, because continuous machine operation has never been achieved, and hence actual capacity falls short of the theoretical capacity. Allowances must be made for breakdowns, repairs, maintenance as well as for spoiled materials. In addition to these factors, other variables determine the capacity of an industry. Among the most important are the following:
1. Customary hours of work.
2. Size and nature of orders.
3. The condition and balance of the mechanical plant.
4. Factory organization and managerial ability.
5. The supply and efficiency of labor.
6. The amount and quality of raw material available.

In continuous-process industries, such as steel and paper, machinery is operated 24 hours a day if it is operated at all. In other industries, however, the technique permits flexible operation, and management can choose to operate one or more shifts per day, depending upon its own wishes and the state of demand for its products. Some industries are traditionally one-shift industries, and it would be an exaggeration of their actual capacity to calculate it on the basis of two- or three-shift operation. Under certain conditions, one-shift industries may change from single-to double-shift operation, almost doubling their capacity without the installation of any additional equipment.

The productivity of a given amount of labor and equipment will vary with the size and nature of orders. For example, a worsted mill can produce more cloth in a given period of time if its production is limited to long runs of blue serge than it could produce if the orders called for short runs of various styles. In the latter case, the looms would be "down" for a considerable period of time to permit reharnessing for each different style.

The machines in a mill or industry are not of equal efficiency. In the paper industry, for example, some of the machines are quite old and some, although not old in years, are inefficient because they have not been properly maintained. Accordingly, to calculate the capacity of the industry without making allowance for these variations would lead to erroneous conclusions. In some instances the capacity of a mill is affected by the lack of balance between various departments. For example, some worsted mills operate their combing departments on a three-shift basis but can produce enough wool "top" to run their spinning and weaving plant on two shifts. Unless these mills added additional combing equipment, the spinning and weaving departments could not operate on a three-shift basis because there would be a deficiency of "tops."

Two mills of the same size and with equal amounts of labor will experience different production results if one is well managed and the other poorly managed. In one mill, for example, there may be a greater subdivision of labor and the mill's equipment will be more intensively used.

Machines do not operate themselves. They require the help of labor. Since all labor is not of the same efficiency, the productivity of machinery will vary with the type of labor employed. If the spinners in a cotton mill are highly skilled and alert and quickly repair breaks in the yarn, the productivity of the spinning department will be greater than if labor were less efficient.

An industry may be adequately equipped with machinery and labor, but unless there is an adequate supply of raw materials available the full and continuous utilization of the plant is not possible. Thus, an isolated cannery may have facilities to put up 250,000 cases of tomatoes per month, but if the local supply of tomatoes is below this amount the cannery will not be able to use all its facilities. If the raw materials are not uniform in quality but vary from one batch to another, as is so frequently the case in the silk industry, the productivity of equipment and labor will be limited by the quality of the raw material.

Thus, it can be seen that the measurement of capacity of a mill or an industry involves more than a mere counting of the machinery. It involves this and, in addition, the above factors.   Accordingly we shall define capacity as the physical output of given specifications that an industry operating on its customary schedule with its existing men, machines, and methods can manufacture.

For each industry the relation between its capacity and actual production, its own peculiar technology, the scale of plant and company operation, the personnel of its workers and executives, its historical development, the nature of its markets—all these and other factors, individually and severally, go to make up a distinctive competitive pattern.   All industries are competitive, but the form and intensity of competition vary from one industry to another.   By using, as tools of analysis, the concepts developed in this chapter it is hoped that the reader may obtain a realistic image of the competitive pattern of each of the industries discussed in the following chapters.

PART II
THE METAL INDUSTRIES

CHAPTER II

THE PLACE AND STRUCTURE OF THE IRON AND STEEL INDUSTRY

The Place of Iron and Steel in Modern Civilization.—The appropriateness of beginning our analyses of specific industries with a survey of iron and steel production rests on the vital position of these metals in modern—especially modern American—civilization. Although it is true that any one of many widely used goods could be listed as a *sine qua non* of existence, so delicately interrelated is the structure of economic life, nevertheless this term aptly fits iron and steel. This is because our present economy is (1) a machine economy, and (2) an exchange economy.

A machine economy means production of goods by mechanical rather than manual power. It is of recent origin, dating from the commercial application of the steam engine 150 years ago. Prior to that time man made practically all of his goods by the use of hand-operated tools. After Watt designed an engine that was commercially suitable, man harnessed the inanimate power of nature and since then has been performing an ever-increasing share of his work with machinery. Production of goods by machinery calls for metal. Machines can be made of wood, as are handmade wooden clocks, but they are crude, costly to construct, and short-lived; machines therefore are made of metal, and—it is significant to note—they are made of cheap metal. Of the half dozen so-called useful metals, none can come within competing distance of iron and steel if quality is considered in relationship to price. Table VI shows clearly the preference based on price that steel enjoys.

An exchange economy means a mode of life characterized by trade. This rests on subdivision of labor or specialization of task. Individuals, communities, and entire nations make only a limited variety of goods and exchange their surpluses to mutual advantage. Subdivision of labor is limited by the "extent of the market," as Adam Smith once observed. The extent of the market, in turn, is limited largely by legal barriers and the cost of transporting goods. Iron and steel reduce the costs of transportation; ships, automobiles, locomotives, and pipe lines are made principally of iron and steel. Without a cheap and efficient metal all transportation would be curtailed, standards of living would fall, and we would revert toward the pioneer days of self-sufficiency. In this country, about the time of the Civil War, trade was hampered by inefficient transportation, owing chiefly to the limitations of iron as a metal. Steel was immediately seized upon by the railroads with stimulating results to trade and economic life in general.

TABLE VI.—APPROXIMATE CONSUMPTION AND PRICES OF MAJOR METALS, 1940

Metal	Consumption, short tons (000 omitted)	Average price, cents per pound
Tin	83	50.0
Aluminum	206*	19.0
Lead	655	5.0
Zinc	663	7.0
Copper	1,005	11.0
Steel	67,000*	2.65

* Production.
Source: Metal Statistics, American Metal Market, New York, 1941.

Place of Iron and Steel in American Civilization.—If the present mode of life depends on iron and steel, this is doubly true of the American phase of it. This country, with roughly 6 per cent of the world's population, has lately been producing about one-third of the world's iron. Before the world depression the United States had a per capita iron production of 689 pounds in contrast with 500 pounds in France, 412 pounds in Germany, and 331 pounds in the United Kingdom. The production of steel in this country likewise is high, representing 35 per cent of the world's production. Per capita production of steel is shown in Fig. 3.

Our position as an exceptionally heavy producer of iron and steel is due to many interacting causes. We shall consider only a few of the principal ones.

Perhaps the most important factor is the extensive use of machinery. Our manufacturers, faced by a relative scarcity of labor, have been forced to use machines, whereas an abundant labor supply in Europe has caused businessmen there to hesitate about increasing their capital costs by using machinery. Machine production with its heavy demand for ferrous metals has been fostered in the United States by conditions so favorable that they have come to be known collectively as the "American system."

Closely linked with the use of machines is the factor of a market that is homogeneous enough to absorb the floodlike stream of standardized goods. Machines are best adapted to produce such products. The United States, populated with 130 million persons of similar tastes and containing no interior tariff barriers, offers a large market, the natural result of which is machine production.

Not only is the United States market large in terms of population but also it is large in geographical extent. The great expanse of territory means that all of us are mutually reliant on transportation. This transportation problem in the United States has been solved by the use of iron and steel in the form of railroads, trucks, automobiles, and pipe lines. A

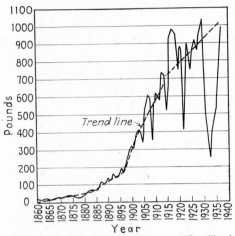

Fig. 3.—Per capita United States steel production. (*The Cleveland Trust Company, Business Bulletin, Oct.* 15, 1937.)

measure of the importance of steel in moving goods and people is the fact that 30 per cent of our steel consumption goes to the automobile industry and the railroads, and if we add to this the amount that goes into ships, oil and gas lines, and similar uses, the total amount of steel used for

TABLE VII.—STEEL MARKETS

(Percentage distribution of hot-rolled iron and steel production)

Consuming Groups	1932–1938 Average
Automotive	20.8
Construction	16.0
Railroads	10.1
Container	8.4
Agriculture	6.0
Oil, gas, and water	6.0
Exports	5.5
Machinery	4.2
Furniture and furnishings	3.6
Shipbuilding	0.9
Mining	0.5
Miscellaneous	18.0
Total	100.0

Source: United States Steel Corporation "T.N.E.C. Papers," Vol. 1, p. 380, 1940.

transportation is probably close to 50 per cent of our entire output.   The principal markets for finished steel are shown in Table VII.

Another factor of importance in influencing heavy consumption in this country is an abundance of raw materials of iron and steel—iron ore, limestone, and coking coal.   This will be discussed in a later chapter.

If we turn from the present position of the industry to its past and note its trend of development, we find that the rate of growth has been extremely rapid.   This point is established in Table VIII.   The growth of iron and steel production is compared with the growth of population, manufacturing in general, several other construction materials, two products used for clothing, and two products used for food.

TABLE VIII.—RATE OF AVERAGE ANNUAL GROWTH OF IRON AND STEEL INDUSTRY
COMPARED WITH OTHER PRODUCTS 1870–1930

	Per Cent
Steel	10.4
Population	1.9
Manufacturing, general	4.3
Lumber	1.8
Cement, Portland	18.8*
Cotton	3.5
Wool	1.7
Flour	1.3
Raw sugar	3.4

* 1880.

Source: BURNS, ARTHUR F., "Production Trends in the United States since 1870," pp. 57–59, National Bureau of Economic Research, New York, 1934.

The Structure of the Iron and Steel Industry.—The structure of this industry appears at first glance to be very intricate: there are thousands of products which have hundreds of thousands of uses.   The Federal Bureau of Internal Revenue lists 2,700 corporations in the iron and steel group. One way of simplifying this intricate structure is to think of the industry in terms of functions rather than products.   In these terms the task of the industry is to

1. Mine the raw materials (iron ore, coal, and limestone).
2. Smelt the iron from the ore.
3. Refine the iron into steel.
4. Shape the steel into
    a. Finished products such as rails, pipes, wire, nails, etc.
    b. Semifinished products such as plates, sheets, bars, etc.
5. Fabricate the semifinished products into finished products such as tanks and railway cars.

Let us turn from this simplified setup of functions and look at the companies which perform them.   The enterprises may be classified as follows: integrated companies, semiintegrated companies, nonintegrated companies, and merchant blast furnace companies.

The companies in the integrated class perform all the operations from the mining of the raw materials to the rolling of finished steel products. Here belong such concerns as United States Steel Corporation, Bethlehem Steel Corporation, Republic Steel Corporation, Youngstown Sheet & Tube Company, Jones & Laughlin Steel Corporation, and other large companies whose names are familiar. These concerns, with certain exceptions, own ore and coal mines, limestone quarries, coke ovens, blast furnaces, steel works and rolling mills, forge shops, steel foundries, and, in a number of instances, fabricating shops.

Companies in the semiintegrated class make no pig iron. They buy rather than make the basic metal and therefore begin their operations with the manufacture of steel. This class includes companies such as Allegheny Ludlum Steel Corporation, Lukens Steel, and Granite City Steel Company. The third class, the nonintegrated companies, purchase steel and begin with the rolling of steel. The fourth class, the merchant blast furnaces, produce pig iron which they sell to semiintegrated steel companies and to iron and steel foundries. The number of companies and the distribution of capacity in each class are shown in Table IX.

TABLE IX.—ORGANIZATION OF THE IRON AND STEEL INDUSTRY, 1938

Degree of integration	Number of companies	Pig iron capacity, per cent	Steel capacity, per cent	Finished hot-rolled product capacity, per cent
Fully integrated*	18	89	91	85
Semiintegrated	56	. . .	9	9
Nonintegrated	150*	. . .	. . .	6
Merchant furnace	26	11		
Total	250	100	100	100

* Approximately.
Source: Calculated from "Iron and Steel Works Directory," American Iron and Steel Institute, New York, 1938.

Much of the confusion as to what constitutes the industry disappears in the light of Table IX. Three important facts emerge from an analysis of this table: (1) The 18 fully integrated companies dominate the production and rolling of iron and steel. (2) The nonintegrated companies are important in numbers only. They make no iron or steel whatever, merely shaping purchased steel. The 150 nonintegrated companies possess only 6 per cent of the rolling capacity. (3) The merchant pig-iron industry is unimportant, relatively. When the man in the street speaks about the iron and steel industry he has in mind not the several thousand companies loosely grouped by the Bureau of Internal Revenue when it reports on iron and steel and allied products, or the several hundred companies listed by the Bureau of Census, but the dozen and a half companies that have 89 per cent of the pig-iron capacity, 91 per cent of the steelmaking capacity, and 85 per cent of the hot-rolling capacity of the entire country.

IMPORTANT CHARACTERISTICS OF THE INDUSTRY

Large-scale Operation, Both Company and Plant, Is the Rule.—The amount of capital necessary to engage in the manufacture of iron and steel

PLATE 1.—Aerial view of Irvin Works of Carnegie-Illinois Steel Corporation near Clairton, Pa. (*Courtesy of U. S. Steel Corporation.*)

products varies from one class to another, and from one company to another in each class. Total capital invested per company in the integrated group varies from about 18 million dollars for the Sharon Steel Company to 1,900 million dollars for the United States Steel Corporation. The principal companies in the semiintegrated group employ from 10 to 23 million dollars of capital. The average investment in the noninte-grated companies, according to government estimates, is around $1\frac{1}{4}$ to 2 million dollars, and the amount of capital necessary for merchant blast furnaces is indicated by the fact that a modern blast furnace plant costs approximately $4\frac{1}{2}$ million dollars.

Enough data has been presented to indicate that iron and steel manufacture cannot be conducted "on a shoestring." This is true of the operation of either an individual plant or a company. Let us consider the reasons.

The economies that come from increasing the size of an individual iron and steel plant are primarily technical in nature and will be better appreciated after we have analyzed, in the next chapter, prevailing methods of manufacture. It is sufficient to note here that technical economies are largely savings incident to heating, shaping, and moving the product in large masses. This results in low fuel and power and labor costs. Fuel and power costs for pig-iron manufacture are more than eight times the average for all industries; for steel manufacture they are more than twice the average. This item therefore becomes an important one in which to economize. This is done by heating, shaping, and moving the metal in large rather than small masses since large bodies do not dissipate their heat as readily as small ones. These great masses of metal are moved mechanically and are not allowed to cool until shaped because this would necessitate reheating in order to work them again. Approximately 90 per cent of our pig iron is "consumed" by the companies which produce it, usually in liquid form. Low costs of mechanical handling are promoted by the large size of individual lots. The apparatus for heating and shaping and moving these heavy products is costly and means heavy fixed capital investment. A measure of this is the fact that 68 per cent of all capital employed by the leading iron and steel companies is in the form of fixed property. This may be compared, for example, with 38 per cent in the automobile industry or 25 per cent in the confectionery industry. Another measure of this same condition is the ratio of dollars of sales to dollars of fixed property investment. In the iron and steel industry this runs 70 cents in annual sales for each dollar of fixed property investment. This is in contrast with $9.62 in the meat packing industry.

In contrast to the size of individual plants, the scale of operation of entire companies is determined only to a minor extent by technology. We have already noted the tendency toward vertical integration. This may proceed from mining to smelting, to refining, to shaping, to fabrication. We have seen that the amount of investment in the integrated class ranges from 18 millions to over 1,900 millions per company.

One explanation of these large investments is the real or fancied need for large reserve holdings of raw materials, principally ore lands. The United States Steel Corporation when it was formed put 700 million dollars, according to its own valuations, or approximately 50 per cent of its capital, into ore lands. Although there is a question, because of current and prospective developments in this industry, whether such reserves are now necessary, such question is beside the point. If steel companies have considered the reserves necessary and have collected the capital with which to secure them, they undoubtedly increase the scale of company operations.

Another explanation is that most companies have sought to have many plants and to spread these plants geographically. This question of the number and location of a company's plants leads into a discussion of transportation costs and methods of pricing which are presented respectively in the chapters on location and competition.

Another explanation is the desire for a "balanced line," *i.e.*, sales which are distributed over a diversified market—sheets, bars, plates, etc. Such balance, or diversity, makes for more stable and profitable operating results since important items of cost such as administrative, supervisory, and sales expenses are spread over a larger volume of output. Such balance is frequently secured by mergers. In the last period of rapid expansion, 1925–1929, when the integrated companies increased their steelmaking capacity 15 per cent, fully one-fourth of this was the result of mergers.

Still another reason for large-scale company operation is the desire to protect markets. As competition becomes keener and the risk of losing customers or the effort necessary to obtain new ones becomes greater, companies integrate forward toward the ultimate consumers. It was presumably for this reason that Bethlehem bought a company that fabricates bridges and buildings and U. S. Steel acquired an oil-well supply company.

This Business Is "a Feast or a Famine."—The iron and steel industry has wider swings in the business cycle than industry in general; that is to say, it falls to greater depths during depressions and rises to greater heights during prosperity than most other industries. This is because its primary function is to supply us with the metal from which we make so many of our durable goods. Other manufacturing industries, transportation, and construction turn to the iron and steel industry for raw materials. It will be noted from Table VII that the chief markets for steel are in the durable goods field. In 1929 the construction industry alone took 16.5 per cent of the steel output, and close to 50 per cent of the steel was used by industries producing goods for transportation. Only a small percentage of steel is produced for the nondurable consumer's goods industry, of which metal containers is the best example.

When business in general is brisk, all industries optimistically replace their existing equipment and perhaps expand their plant and equipment. These orders spell activity for the construction and equipment industries, that is, the makers of machine tools, rolling stock, storage tanks, and myriads of other durable articles. The construction and equipment

industries, in turn, translate their orders into orders for raw iron and steel.
Funneled back to the iron and steel industry, these orders cause great
activity in this area.   The flow of activity in the steel industry, like that
in a great river system, is the concentrated result of what takes place in a
wide drainage basin.

On the other hand, when a recession sets in or is in prospect, durable
goods because they are durable need not be replaced.   The railroads and

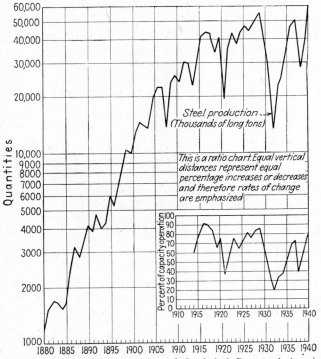

FIG. 4.—Steel production, 1880–1940. (*Annual Statistical Report of American Iron &
Steel Institute*, 1939; *Iron Age, Jan.,* 1941.)

factories and builders play safe by spending less for capital equipment.
Construction slows down, expansion is halted, and the iron and steel industry gets the full impact of the recession.   If the recession develops into a
major depression, as was the case following 1930, a cloud of gloom per-
vades the business world, replacement of equipment is almost entirely
halted, wide unemployment causes a drop in the demand for durable
goods, and orders for steel dry up almost completely.   When the depression gives way to revival and the business world becomes optimistic and
financially stronger, the pent-up demand for improved equipment is

released.   Increasing employment widens the market for automobiles and other durable goods, and iron and steel activity reaches great heights.

The unusually wide swings in activity of the steel industry are shown in Fig. 4.   Note that steel production dropped from 40 million to 20 million tons between 1920 and 1921—a 50 per cent contraction.   In the latter year the industry was operating at only 35 per cent of capacity in contrast with 75 per cent capacity operation the preceding year.   Again, production rose from a low of 13 million tons in 1932 to 51 million tons in 1937.   This represents a rise in operating capacity from 20 to 72 per cent. Thus we see that the rising and falling tides of business affect this industry with cumulative force and create violent fluctuations which result in feast or famine.

We shall return with increased appreciation, we hope, to some of the ideas presented in the foregoing discussion after we analyze the industry's technique of production.

CHAPTER III

THE TECHNOLOGY OF IRON AND STEEL MANUFACTURE

TYPES OF IRON AND STEEL

The rather intricate processes of iron- and steelmaking can be understood more readily if we examine first the nature of ferrous products. Iron rarely occurs in pure form; perhaps the nearest approach is in meteorites. Commercially, iron always contains foreign ingredients. In fact, the task of the iron and steel manufacturers is to regulate these ingredients, adding certain ones that produce desirable changes, removing others that have injurious effects. One of the most important of these foreign ingredients is *carbon*. This is because of its action; one amount weakens iron, another strengthens it. Carbon seems to be the indispensable ingredient in each of the hundreds of different kinds of iron and

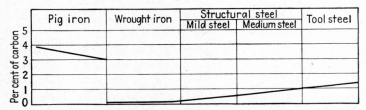

FIG. 5.—Carbon content of ferrous metals.

steel; it is present in each in varying amounts. It determines the difference between iron and steel, between pig iron and wrought iron, between mild steel and carbon steel. There are other important differences, but to the layman the statement may be made that carbon is the critical element.

Pig iron is the basic material of all iron and steel products. It is obtained by smelting iron ore which contains sand, clay, etc., that must be removed. Heat is required in the smelting process, and this is obtained by burning coke; the molten iron absorbs carbon from the coke, and the result is iron with a carbon content that is very high, ranging from 3 to 4 per cent. This high carbon content limits very severely the usefulness of pig iron, and it is necessary to perform other manufacturing operations of a refining nature.

The first, historically, of these refining processes is wrought iron manufacture. It consists of melting iron and burning out most of the carbon so that the finished product contains only about one-sixteenth to one-eightieth as much carbon as pig iron, or a range of 0.05–0.25 per cent. Although wrought iron possesses many desirable qualities, which we shall learn later, it is costly to make. Its use is therefore very limited.

Another refining operation developed at an early date was the manufacture of crucible steel. This consisted of melting the carbonless wrought iron and then adding small predetermined amounts of carbon, about 1.5 to 2 per cent. But crucible steel, like wrought iron, proved costly to make. Its use, therefore, has been limited to edged tools and other articles capable of bearing the heavy cost.

Low-carbon steelmaking was the next refining operation to develop. It consists of reducing the carbon and then putting some of it back along with other alloys. Low-carbon steel, made by the open-hearth or Bessemer process, is today the major product of the primary iron and steel industry, as Table X indicates.

TABLE X.—FERROUS METAL PRODUCTION, 1940
(In thousands of net tons)

Pig iron	47,200
Open-hearth steel	61,573
Bessemer steel	3,709
Electric steel	1,700
Crucible steel	1

Source: *Iron Age*, May 8, 1941.
Note: The production of steel is greater than that of pig iron because of the use of scrap metal.

The last refining operation to develop was electric steel manufacture. It produces steel with unusual qualities because of the high temperatures that can be attained and because it is the only process in which impurities are not absorbed by the steel during the operation. Thus far electric steel has been a high-cost steel and its production has been for special rather than general purposes.

In the foregoing sketch of the development of iron- and steelmaking, distinctions between the several major products have been made, for the sake of simplicity, on the basis of the amount of carbon which the metal contains. This is somewhat inaccurate because there are other elements in these metals which vitally affect their qualities. Two of the most injurious of these are sulphur and phosphorus; among the desirable ingredients may be mentioned chrome, nickel, tungsten, and many other alloying metals. Iron- and steelmaking is somewhat more complicated than adding and removing carbon; however, what has been said does focus attention on a major aspect of the process and may provide at the outset a perspective that will be useful as we go into further detail.

THE MANUFACTURE OF PIG IRON

As previously stated, pig iron is produced by a smelting operation. This takes place in a tall, cylindrical furnace, pictured in illustration.

Four raw materials are put into the furnace: (1) *iron ore,* which consists of iron in chemical and physical combination with sand, clay, sulphur, silicon etc.; (2) *coke;* (3) *limestone,* which acts as a flux; *i.e.,* it lowers the melting point of some of the ingredients and also absorbs some of the impurities which must be removed; (4) *hot air,* which is forced into the bottom of the furnace under pressure, the oxygen in the air combining with the carbon to produce heat. From these ingredients there is obtained (1) molten iron; (2) molten slag, which is derived largely from the limestone and the earthy materials of the ore; (3) blast furnace gas which is an inflammable product. The following table presents the above information in more detail.

TABLE XI.—RAW MATERIALS AND BY-PRODUCTS OF ONE TON OF PIG IRON
(Approximate)

Intake	Output
2 tons iron ore	1 ton pig iron
1 ton coke	$\frac{1}{2}$ to 1 ton slag
$\frac{1}{2}$ ton limestone	$5\frac{1}{2}$ to 6 tons gas
4 tons heated air	

The Equipment of a Blast Furnace Plant.—A blast furnace plant consists of one or more furnaces and a number of pieces of auxiliary apparatus. The main piece of equipment is of course the blast furnace. This is an upright steel shell, 90 to 100 ft. high and 20 ft. in diameter, lined with firebrick. The upper 70 ft. of the furnace is referred to as the stack. It is here that the coke, limestone, and ore, which are charged into the top of the furnace, are gradually heated by the ascending gases and thereby reduced in volume as moisture is driven off and coke consumed. The stack portion of the furnace is sometimes referred to as the "zone of reduction." Below the stack is a section called the "bosh," which is about 12 ft. in height. By the time the descending materials have reached this point they have heated sufficiently to reach a state of fusion. The molten iron drips down into a third section called the "hearth." Because of the difference in the specific gravity of the iron and the slag, the latter floats on top of the iron in the hearth. About every 4 hours, the molten iron and slag are tapped out of the hearth into ladles. About 80 to 120 tons of iron are removed, so the average daily capacity of a furnace would range from 500 to 700 tons. The furnace is in continuous operation for a period of months or until it becomes necessary to "bank" it, as we do a household furnace at night, owing to lack of orders, or to cease operations completely for repairs.

The metal, tapped from the furnace, flows into huge ladles and is transported either to near-by steel mills or to casting sheds where it is poured into small molds arranged as a continuous chain belt. Originally the metal was run out onto a sand floor. Here it flowed from main

PLATE 2.—Blast furnaces. Note battery of eight ovens between the blast furnaces. (*Courtesy of U. S. Steel Corporation.*)

PLATE 3.—Tapping a blast furnace. (*Courtesy of U. S. Steel Corporation.*)

channels into slight depressions similar in size and shape to the metal molds just mentioned. The appearance of the metal in the molds attached to the main runner resembled suckling pigs, hence the term "pig" iron.

Near the furnace are the storage facilities and equipment for handling the raw materials. These consist, as the illustration shows, of *bins* for limestone, coke, ores, as well as automatic hoists, immense cranes, cardumpers, etc. Other apparatus consists of *stoves* for heating the air that

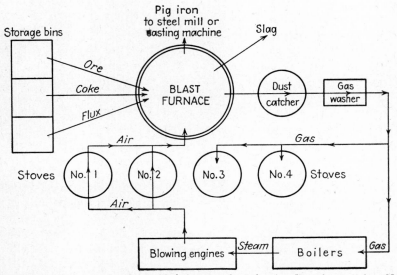

Fig. 6.—Diagramatic sketch of a blast-furnace plant showing flow of materials. Note: the piping to and from stoves is so arranged that every half hour No. 1 and 2 may exchange performance with No. 3 and 4.

the furnace consumes. In appearance these stoves are not unlike the furnace itself. Each stove contains a combustion chamber and regenerative flues consisting of bricks set in checkered pattern so as to permit the passage of air through them. After these bricks have been heated by gas flame, air is passed over them. The air absorbs the heat and then enters the furnace. By having a battery of four stoves (see Fig. 6) it is possible to have a continuous supply of hot air for the furnace since the stoves are operating in pairs, alternating with one another. Other essential pieces of equipment are the *blowing engines* which compress the air and force it into the furnace and the *boilers* to produce the steam which operates the blowing engines.

From this brief description it is readily seen that the present-day blast furnace with its surrounding equipment is a very elaborate affair.

A modern blast furnace together with the necessary auxiliary equipment costs 4 to 5 million dollars.

THE MANUFACTURE OF WROUGHT IRON

Pig iron as it comes from the blast furnace is of limited usefulness. It is very hard and brittle when cold, and when hit with a hammer it flies into many pieces. It retains this brittleness even when red hot, so it cannot be worked under a hammer. At a temperature greater than red heat, it suddenly becomes liquid without passing through a pasty stage. As a result, the only way that it can be formed into useful articles is by pouring the liquid metal into molds of the desired shape. Upon cooling, the metal retains the shape given to it by the mold. Certain articles made in this manner, a steam radiator for instance, are satisfactory, but there are many other needs which such iron cannot fulfill.

In order to escape from the limitations just outlined, men sought for an easy method to remove the impurities from pig iron. One outcome of these efforts was the puddling furnace. This consists of a hearth where pig iron and scrap metals are placed, a firebox which contains a coal fire, a sloping roof to deflect the flames down toward the hearth, and an air space for generating ample draught.

The operation of the furnace until very recently was entirely by hand. A puddler using a long metal rake "puddled" the molten mass, exposing fresh surfaces to the flame and in this manner reducing the carbon content to a very low point. As the carbon burned out the mass changed from a liquid to a paste, whereupon it was removed by means of tongs manipulated by the puddler and was processed in a rolling mill. Great skill as well as stamina were required, and the puddlers were highly paid.

The properties of wrought iron are for the most part desirable. Its softness, because of the scarcity of carbon, makes it easily worked into all manner of shapes, either hot or cold. It may be pounded or welded together so that there is no "joint." The fact that it does not rust easily, owing to the low carbon and the presence of small microscopic pieces of nonmetallic slag interspersed throughout the mass, makes it popular as a material for water and steam pipes. It is readily magnetized by a current of electricity and immediately loses its magnetism, which makes for its use in electric generating machinery.

The principal charge against wrought iron is its high cost. In the face of improvements in the rust-resisting and welding qualities of mild steels and the marked cost advantages of these metals, wrought iron has been fighting a losing battle. The time necessary for the process, coupled with the small quantity produced at a time, the intermittent operation, and the large amount of highly skilled hand labor, all combine to make the cost high.

Numerous attempts have been made to mechanize the process, and recently considerable success seems to have been achieved. One process is reported to be commercially successful. This consists of refining pig iron in the same manner as ordinary steel and then pouring the refined iron into a ladle of molten slag. The metal, chilled by the lower temperature of the slag, settles in the bottom of the ladle. As it does so it absorbs some of the slag and becomes a spongy, porous mass, similar to puddled wrought iron. If this process produces a good wrought iron at low cost, this metal may hold its own.

THE BEGINNINGS OF STEEL MANUFACTURE

At no time did either pig iron or wrought iron meet fully the demand for an efficient metal. Pig iron has been described as too brittle, although easily produced in large quantities and cheap; wrought iron, although tough and fibrous, was too expensive. Man had need for a metal somewhere in between these two, a metal that could be tempered to take a fine cutting edge, that could be worked under a hammer, that would possess strength to withstand shock. He early learned how to make such a metal, as the swords of Damascus, the armor of the Moors, and the suits of mail of the Italians prove. But the art by which these steels of fine quality were produced was lost, and we had to begin anew and by the slow process of trial and error work up to present-day methods. The first of these methods of which we have accurate historical record resulted in what is known as "cementation steel." This consisted of putting bars of wrought iron in a furnace and covering them with powdered charcoal. The product was slowly baked, which caused the carbon to penetrate the iron and produce a medium-carbon product which we loosely call steel. But cementation steel varied greatly in quality. Some bars contained a great deal of carbon; others had scarcely any. An English watchmaker was dissatisfied with this steel for he could never depend on his watch springs. He sought to remedy the defect by cutting up the cementation steel, putting it in a refractory (heat-resistant) earthen pot, and remelting it so that a product of uniform consistency was produced.

From the watchmaker's efforts, a process was evolved which is still used to a slight extent. It consists of putting pieces of wrought iron in a crucible, melting them, and then adding carbon. The product is known as "crucible steel" because of the refractory pot made of graphite or clay. It is a high-cost steel because it is made in very small quantities, usually only a few hundred pounds at a time, and its use is largely limited to fine tools, etc.

But crucible steel, as late as 1850, was far too costly to allow its extensive use, so the demand for a cheap, efficient metal was still unsatisfied. Pig iron, while cheap enough, was too brittle for many purposes.

Wrought iron was not only high in price, but was too soft for general use. It will be recalled that railroads had been in existence for 20 years in this country and were limited in supplying the growing demand for their services by the shortcomings of wrought iron. The first rails were wooden beams laid on crossties; later, strips of wrought iron were spiked on top of the wooden rails; finally, with the increase in speed and weight of trains, it became necessary to make the rails entirely of wrought iron. But the almost prohibitive cost of wrought iron limited not only railroad extension but other types of industrial development.

INDUSTRY GETS LOW-COST STEEL

After many years of waiting, low-priced steel was finally obtained by two fundamentally different processes. These were the Bessemer and the open-hearth processes. Like many fundamental inventions, these two techniques seem, in retrospect, absurdly simple. The Bessemer process consists of putting molten pig iron into a container and forcing air through the mass. The oxygen in the air, bubbling up through the iron, burns out the carbon and other impurities. The iron, now having a composition somewhat akin to wrought iron, is then changed to steel by the addition of a small but carefully measured quantity of carbon and other alloys. There is a dispute as to the inventor of this method; the courts of this country sustained the claim of a Kentucky ironmaker named William Kelly, but public acknowledgment and financial reward went to an Englishman, Henry Bessemer, who was knighted for his achievement.

The open-hearth method was the outcome of many efforts to make steel by the puddling process. All these efforts had failed because the temperature of the furnace could not be raised high enough to keep the contents liquid. It will be recalled that in the puddling furnace iron becomes pasty as the carbon burns out; this is because relatively pure iron melts at a much higher temperature than when it is combined with carbon. This problem of keeping liquid a mass of low-carbon iron was solved about 1865 when the regenerative furnace was perfected. The essential feature of this furnace is an apparatus for preheating the fuel so as to raise the furnace temperature. With these preliminary distinctions in mind, let us examine the two processes in greater detail.

THE MANUFACTURE OF BESSEMER STEEL

The principle employed in the Bessemer process is the "oxidation" of the impurities. Oxidation is the chemical uniting of oxygen, generally from the air, with other elements such as iron, silicon, and carbon. If the oxidation is slow, as in the "rusting" of iron, the resulting heat dissipates as fast as it is generated and the change is hardly noticeable. If, however, the reaction occurs rapidly and with enough vigor, we say that the material "burns." The latter sort of oxidation is what is called "combustion." In the Bessemer process, the oxygen of the air blown through the molten metal directly oxidizes or burns out the carbon, silicon, and manganese.

The pig iron in the converter, then, furnishes its own fuel. No outside combustible is needed. This is made possible by the fact that in every ton of molten pig iron there are approximately 70 lb. of carbon, 25 lb. of silicon, and 15 lb. of manganese, or a total of about one ton in the 15-ton charge of molten metal that goes into the ordinary steel plant converter.

The Converter.—A converter is a huge metal egg swung "amidships" on trunnions or pivots. This great egg of steel is lined with refractory

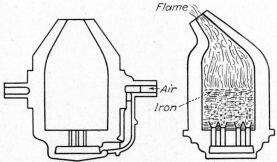

Fig. 7.—Cross section of Bessemer converter. (*U. S. Tariff Commission, Report No.* 128.

bricks and has an open top. Air from a blast pipe is admitted through one of the trunnions. To the other is geared a hydraulic ram, which turns the converter into a horizontal position for charging and discharging and into an upright position for blowing (see Fig. 7).

As the refractory bottoms are quickly burned away, they are usually detachable, being held to the vessel by hooks and links. The "tuyeres" are cylindrical clay bricks that are pierced with a number of openings. The air passes through these openings into the "bath" in large bubbles or in a fine spray depending upon their size and the pressure of the blast. The modern converter generally holds from 15 to 20 tons of molten metal, and there are three of them in the typical plant. Of these one serves as a spare, and two are used concurrently, one blowing while the other is being cleaned and recharged.

Operation of a Converter.—The vessel is charged when in a horizontal position, the pig iron being run in by means of a spout. The blast is then turned on, and the vessel is brought to a vertical position, when the pressure of the air rushing up through the tuyeres prevents the metal from running out through them. Sparks, small particles of slag, and flames issue from the vessel during the "blow," which only takes from 10 to 15 minutes.   When the blowing is finished, the vessel is turned down to a horizontal position, the blast shut off, and a recarburizer and other alloys are added.   The metal is poured into the ladles by tipping the vessel still more.

PLATE 4.—Bessemer converter.   Note that the converter is supported "amidships" so it can be tilted for charging and discharging.   (*Courtesy of U. S. Steel Corporation.*)

THE MANUFACTURE OF OPEN-HEARTH STEEL

The open-hearth process is in marked contrast to the Bessemer method.   Instead of a 15- to 20-ton converter it employs a furnace with a capacity ranging up to 300 tons.   This furnace, a low rectangular structure with walls of firebricks, is similar to the puddling furnace in that the molten metal is held in a shallow open hearth and heated by gas or oil flames beating over the surface.   The raw materials—molten pig iron, cold scrap, limestone, and iron ore—are charged into the furnace on one side; the products of the operation—raw steel and slag—are tapped from the furnace on the other side, as shown in Fig. 8.   Figure 9 shows the regenerative principle of preheating the fuel.   By reversing at regular time intervals the direction of the flow of the air and gas through the checker brickwork chambers, the hot spent gases are made to give up

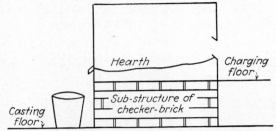

FIG. 8.—Cross section of open-hearth furnace.

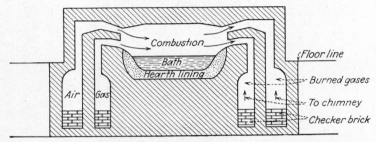

FIG. 9.—Cross section of open hearth showing regenerative preheating.

PLATE 5.—Charging liquid pig iron into the open-hearth furnace. (*Courtesy of Republic Steel Corporation.*)

their heat to the incoming cold air and gas, and this preheating maintains higher furnace temperatures. The operation takes from 8 to 10 hours.

PLATE 6.—Tapping finished steel from the open-hearth furnace. The smaller ladle is receiving the slag overflow. (*Courtesy of Republic Steel Corporation.*)

The Contrast in Development of Bessemer and Open-hearth Steel.—
Although the two processes of steelmaking just discussed came into existence at about the same time, they have followed, since 1905, widely different courses (see Fig. 10), until today Bessemer steel is far behind, its annual production being only one-twelfth that of open-hearth steel.

Why has Bessemer steel, after such an auspicious start, been outdistanced by open-hearth in the competition for the general steel market? One would have expected Bessemer to fare better; plant investment per ton of capacity is only one-fourth as great as in the open-hearth process; the process is completed in minutes instead of hours; the operation is fuelless. The explanation of the supremacy of open-hearth steel centers around two factors—*quality and cost.* The quality of steel is adversely affected by the presence of phosphorus; it makes iron and steel brittle.

It was soon discovered that the Bessemer process could not handle pig iron that contained more than 0.10 per cent of phosphorus. Then an amateur chemist, a clerk in a London police court, discovered a method of removing phosphorus—provided there was enough of it. He used a limestone rather than a sandstone lining in the Bessemer converter, and the basic qualities of the limestone neutralized the phosphorus and removed it. But it was necessary to have at least 2 per cent phos-

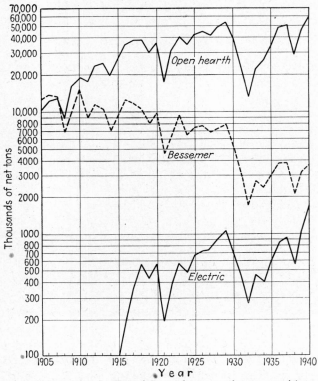

Fig. 10.—Steel production in the United States by type of process. (*Annual Statistical Report of American Iron and Steel Institute*, 1939; *Iron Age*, January, 1941.)

phorus because the converter is heated by the impurities it burns. To state it differently, low-phosphorus iron can be used in the acid Bessemer converter; high-phosphorus iron can be used in the basic Bessemer converter; medium-phosphorus iron (0.1 to 2 per cent) is not adapted for use in either. The iron ores of the United States have been largely of this intermediate type, and they may be handled successfully in the open-hearth furnace as was learned during the eighties and nineties.

In recent years another cost factor has favored the use of the open-hearth process. This is the ability to use scrap iron and steel. Whereas the Bessemer converter consumes only molten pig iron, the open-hearth furnaces take scrap metal in amounts ranging from 40 to 60 per cent of their output. A few open-hearth plants, because of their isolation from other raw materials, consume scrap metal almost exclusively. Although there are wide variations in the price differential between pig iron and scrap, the latter is usually cheaper than the former by an amount ranging from 10 to 45 per cent.

Our growing dependence upon scrap iron and scrap steel is revealed by the fact that the annual production of steel has exceeded the annual production of pig iron ever since 1910, scrap metals accounting for the difference.

The quality factor also has favored the displacement of the Bessemer process.[1] The quality of steel is determined by factors other than phosphorus; carbon content must be controlled within a very narrow range, and as steel specifications become more detailed and exacting the same is true of other ingredients. This calls for manipulation and control of the batch, and here the open-hearth process has an advantage. During the 8 or 10 hours of operation frequent tests can be made, ore and scrap added to reduce carbon content, silica to increase acidity, etc. As one commentator has put it, "it is wonderfully like an old-fashioned cook who tastes her soup and adds a pinch of this, a bit of that, and a spoonful of the other, seasoning until the product 'just suits her.'" As users of steel called for better qualities, the makers of steel turned to open hearth.

ELECTRIC STEEL

In 1880 there appeared a forecast of still another method of producing steel which was to take its place beside the crucible, Bessemer, and open-hearth processes. In that year the prolific inventor, Siemens, described to an English technical society a furnace in which he had made steel by means of heat generated from electricity. This first experimental furnace, however, was ahead of its time, for it was not until 16 years later that a commercial furnace for the steel industry was brought out by Stassano of Italy. Various models appeared rapidly about 1900 in Sweden, France, and other European countries.

It is of interest to note that all of these early furnaces were invented in Europe, where hydro-electricity was low in cost and mineral fuels high in price. The situation was somewhat different in the United States. Electric power, while lower in price than formerly, was largely generated by steam. Such hydroelectricity as we did produce was sold on the price basis of competing steam power. For this reason electric furnaces for the

---

[1] In 1939 it was reported that the photoelectric cell had been successfully adapted to controlling quality in Bessemer steel production. This may arrest the down trend in Bessemer steel as shown in Fig. 10.

United States had to be more efficient in their consumption of electricity than European furnaces, so it was not until 1908 that electric steel appeared in production statistics with one furnace and an output of 55 tons.

General Sketch.—The electric furnace as it has been developed in the steel industry is a steel shell, usually somewhat spherical in shape, lined with either acid or basic refractory bricks.   The raw materials are put in

PLATE 7.—Tapping a 6-ton arc-electric furnace.   (*Courtesy of Bethlehem Steel Company.*)

through the top or through a small door in the side, and the finished product is poured from a spout by means of tilting the entire furnace by hand or by electrically operated gears.   The electricity that furnishes the necessary heat is conducted into the furnace through electrodes projecting through the roof.

There are several uses to which the furnace may be put, and the charge varies accordingly.   It may be used to refine pig iron direct and thus resembles the open-hearth furnace or the Bessemer converter; it may be used to remelt and refine cold scrap iron and steel in somewhat the same manner as the crucible; or it may be used in the finishing stage of a duplex or triplex process in which the pig iron is partially refined in the Bessemer or open-hearth and then finished in the electric furnace.   The charge then may consist of cold or molten pig iron, iron or steel scrap, partially refined steel, ore and alloys.   In practice, the charge is usually 100 per cent scrap metal.   Mechanically and chemically the furnace acts the same as the open-hearth except that the oxidizing influence of the gas flame is absent.   It usually requires about 4 hours to complete the refining of a charge.

It should be borne in mind that the sole use made of the current of electricity is that of producing heat.   It is claimed that steel produced in the electric furnace possesses qualities thought to be given it by the electricity used in its manufacture, but these have not been proved conclusively.

Advantages of Electric Heating.—The advantages of the electric process are said to be: (1) Higher temperatures than are economical under the open-hearth method.   These higher temperatures bring about more complete separation of the slag from the metal and reduce the loss of alloys from oxidation.   (2) Greater control of heat.   (3) Cleanliness of the heating agent, since no impurities are introduced by the electric current.   (4) Better assimilation of alloys.   (5) Reduction in the loss of scrap material which, when introduced into other types of furnaces, such as open-hearth, are likely to oxidize too much, particularly if they are in the form of fine metal shavings.   (6) Equipment occupies less space.

Because of these advantages, the production of electric steel increased rapidly in this country, particularly following the outbreak of the first World War.   There is evidence at this time that electric steel is meeting direct competition from alloy steels made in open-hearth furnaces.

Alloy Steels.—A comparatively recent development deserving some attention at this point is the rapid improvement in the technology and use of alloy steels.   Alloy steels are special quality steels made by adding materials other than carbon to the bath of molten iron.   Small quantities of chromium, nickel, molybdenum, titanium, zirconium, columbium, or copper when added in certain combinations produce steels of certain desired physical properties.   Alloy steel first attracted attention some 50 years ago when Frederick W. Taylor, the father of scientific management, developed high-speed cutting tools from alloy steel.   However, it was not until comparatively recent years that alloy steels have been extended beyond the narrow field of machine-tool steel.   The exacting requirements of the rapidly growing automobile industry were largely responsible for the growth in both tonnage and variety of alloy steels. Annual production is approximately 3 million tons, and some 60 varieties are recognized by the Iron and Steel Institute.   Most of the tonnage is made by the open-hearth and electric processes.

Stainless steel, containing chromium and nickel, has attracted widespread interest because of its use in consumer's goods.   Aside from kitchen ware and cutlery, stainless steel is used in building streamlined trains, in the manufacture of radiator shells, hub caps etc., for automobiles.   It is an ideal metal for certain parts of laundry and milk-bottling machinery where sanitation demands a rust-free metal.   It is especially valuable

DIAGRAM OF STEEL MANUFACTURE

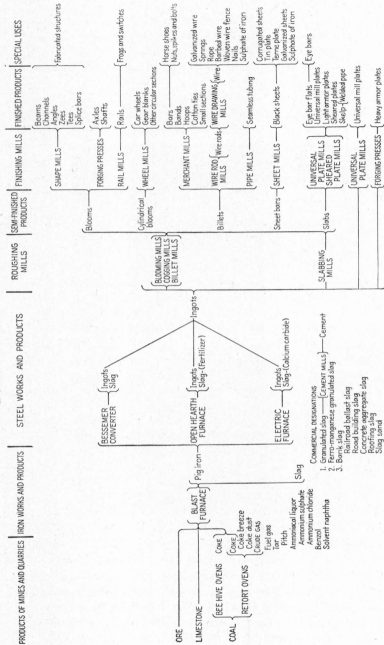

FIG. 11.—Diagram of steel manufacture. This diagram shows the principal processes and operations involved in the manufacture of finished steel products from the iron ore. It is apparent that all of the steel and iron making processes are not shown in this diagram. For example, the crucible and cementation processes for producing steel are not described, as they are being rapidly displaced by other methods. The production of finished products of iron and steel by the casting method is not considered, nor is the product of the puddling furnace—wrought iron. The student should study this diagram carefully, as it briefly summarizes much of the work covered in the previous assignments on iron and steel. (*Courtesy of United States Steel Corporation.*)

in the chemical industries. For example, it is rapidly replacing wooden vats in the dye houses of textile plants. Stainless steel is immune to the action of strong acid dyes. In changing from one color of dye to another, the stainless steel vat can be cleaned easily by flushing with warm water, whereas several hours are required to boil out the color from wooden vats.

SHAPING STEEL PRODUCTS

Finished steel products, such as car wheels, crankshafts, steel girders, or piano wire, are given form by one of several processes of shaping. It

PLATE 8.—Pouring liquid steel into ingot molds. (*Courtesy of Republic Steel Corporation.*)

should be observed at the outset that the following description of shaping processes applies, with minor exceptions, to the shaping of nonferrous metal products as well.

Shaping metal products falls into two broad classes of operations (1) preliminary, or rough, shaping and (2) final, or precision, shaping. The difference is primarily one of degree of accuracy or precision required in the final product. The sawmill cuts up timber into lumber sufficiently "finished" for such uses as joists and studs for the construction industry.

However, the cabinetmaker must further shape sawmill lumber by sawing, chiseling, planing, etc., in order to obtain the exact dimensions his products require.   Similarly, a steel rolling mill turns out rails and girders sufficiently "finished" for their intended use, but the automobile manufacturer requires hundreds of parts that must be machined down to highly precise dimensions.   The latter operations will be discussed in a later chapter.   Here we are concerned only with rough shaping.

The principal rough-shaping operations are rolling, forging, pressing, and casting.   Except for casting, the molten steel tapped from the furnace is first poured into molds and allowed to solidify into ingots.   An ingot is a solid chunk of steel, slightly tapered, with dimensions approximately 60 by 20 by 16 in.

Rolling.—Rolling is one of the earliest forms of mechanical shaping and, based on tonnage output, is still the most important shaping process.

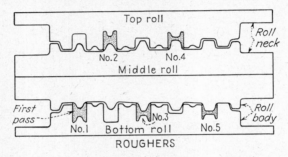

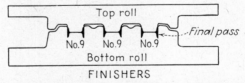

Fig. 12.—Typical passes for 6-in. beams as rolled in 28-in. structural mills.   Note: Solid black areas in this diagram show the cross-sectional changes which occur during the production of a standard beam.   The consecutive numbers show the sequence of passes through the rolls.   (*Steel Facts, December,* 1938, *No.* 30.)

It is a process of gradual reduction whereby an ingot, through successive passes between heavy power-driven steel rolls, is flattened into sheet steel or converted into such shapes as rails or girders.   Roughing mills, equipped with smooth-surfaced rolls, serve either to reduce an ingot into sheet steel or to reduce an ingot in cross section and elongate it in preparation for the finishing mills.   Finishing mills equipped with grooved rolls, as illustrated in Fig. 12, turn out such products as H-, I-, or T-shaped girders and railway rails.

The outstanding recent improvement in rolling technology is continuous rolling. Briefly, this consists of arranging, in tandem, a number of rolling-mill units so that finished steel products can be made without breaking the continuity of the operation. The first unit of a continuous rolling setup consists of a roughing mill which starts reducing the ingot, and the last unit consists of a bank of four high-finishing mills which turn out sheet steel 90 in. in width at the rate of 12 miles an hour.

PLATE 9.—Continuous sheet and strip mill. (*Courtesy of Republic Steel Corporation.*)

Continuous rolling was introduced in 1926 by the American Rolling Mill Company, and by 1940 the industry had built 28 continuous sheet mills representing an investment of 500 million dollars. Much of the installation was made during a period of business depression, and there have been rumors that the new process has not attained technical perfection. Perhaps this indicates that the installations were enforced upon the industry by competitive necessity rather than by seasoned engineering judgment. Once the new technique made its appearance, other companies could not afford to be without it.

Forging.—Forging is another widely used mechanical shaping process. There are four types of forging processes: (1) steam hammer work, (2) drop forging, (3) hydraulic pressing, and (4) drawing.

Steam hammer work, as the name implies, is nothing other than the application of power to a hammer. The device, invented by a Frenchman about 1842, consists of two upright steel columns supporting a cylinder with a hammer attached to the piston. Secured to the floor directly below the hammer is an anvil. Steam power raised the hammer, and the force of gravity of the falling hammer imparted shape to the object placed on the anvil. In 1888 the Midvale Steel Company perfected a double-acting hammer, that is, steam power was also applied to the down stroke.

PLATE 10.—Continuous sheet and strip mill. Steel emerges at a speed up to 2,120 ft. minute. (*Courtesy of Republic per Steel Corporation.*)

Drop forging is an adaptation of the steam hammer. New England manufacturers hit upon the idea of cutting an impression, or die, into the "anvil" and hammering the hot plastic metal into it. Later a detachable die was also mounted on the surface of the hammer head. Thus, unlike the products of the steam hammer where each part is "handmade" and therefore subject to slight variations, all drop forgings made from the same pair of dies are exactly alike—an ideal process for quantity-production manufacturing. In fact, the process was developed in response to huge orders from the British government for parts for the famous Enfield rifle. Today such products as automobile crankshafts and steering knuckles are made by drop forging.

Hydraulic pressing is another type of forging, but unlike hammering, which imparts a blow to the surface of the metal, it imparts slowly acting but intense pressure throughout the entire mass of the metal. The press is constructed upon the same general lines as the hammer, but the uprights support a hydraulic cylinder. By admitting water under pressure into the cylinder at the top, intense pressure is applied to the metal until it yields. Thus a kneading takes place, and the absence of a shock, characteristic of the hammer, prevents internal stresses and strains. The hydraulic press is especially well adapted for the manufacture of such products as heavy shafts, armor plate, and ordnance.

Drawing is a special type of forging confined to wiremaking. It consists of pulling a bar through a slightly tapered die which reduces the cross section of the bar and increases its length. By successive drawings through successively smaller dies extremely fine wire can be made.

Casting.—Casting consists of pouring molten metal into a specially prepared mold so that the metal upon solidification will have assumed the shape of the mold. The process requires four steps: (1) making a pattern, (2) forming a mold, (3) melting the metal, and (4) pouring the metal.

The pattern is a wooden or metal counterpart of the article to be made. Its shape must be identical with and its size slightly larger than the desired casting to allow for subsequent machining to exact size.

The mold is a cavity, made by the pattern, in moist sand mixed with a clay binder. Upon withdrawal of the pattern the depression left in the sand will obviously be that of the pattern. Molten metal is then poured into the mold. Upon solidification, a casting of the desired shape is obtained. Casting is a shaping process especially adapted for producing highly intricate shapes such as radiators or automobile cylinder blocks, products which have hollow interiors.

A somewhat recent innovation of casting is "die casting." In this process the mold consists of two metal dies clamped together tightly. Molten metal, usually one of the soft metals such as the various alloys of aluminum, zinc, tin, and lead, is forced under pressure into the mold. The castings take the exact form of the dies and cool quite quickly so that the forms may be unclamped at once and the casting released. Frequently as many as 650 castings are made in an hour. This process is used in making such things as vacuum-cleaner parts, condenser cradles for radios, etc., and extremely precise results are obtained.

Almost half of the $5\frac{1}{2}$ million tons of cast-iron products produced annually in this country are in the form of pipe, so a brief discussion of a new technique in this field of casting is of more than passing interest.

The old method of casting pipe consists of placing a cylindrical core upright in a vertical hole in the sand and pouring the metal into the opening. A new mold and core are required each time, and frequently the core goes off center, forming pipe that is thicker on one side than on the other.

In the deLavaud process, the molten metal is poured into a revolving horizontal steel cylinder. The centrifugal force formed by this revolving cylinder throws the hot metal against the outer casing which is water-jacketed so that the hot metal will not stick. The metal cools almost immediately and can be withdrawn in the form of finished pipe. The wall is much more uniform in thickness and of greater density.

The foregoing description of technology, while by no means complete, includes the major operations performed in a steel mill and should be helpful in obtaining a grasp of the economics of steel manufacture.

CHAPTER IV

LOCATION OF THE IRON AND STEEL INDUSTRY

Before an examination is made of the precise location of the iron and steel industry, it may prove helpful to consider some general factors in locating manufacturing industries. Why are industries located where they are? Why do they change their location?

The list of location factors is familiar to all of us: raw materials, market, fuels and power, labor and climate, etc. Inasmuch as these influence location because of their effect upon costs, the general observation may be made, subject to some qualification, that costs rule supreme in determining location. The problem, then, of determining where to place a plant is the problem of selecting the point which will give us the "lowest cost combination"; it is essentially a problem of equilibrium or balance.

It is not very helpful merely to list a number of factors and say these determine location. The factors vary in relative importance from industry to industry, from plant to plant, and from time to time within the same industry. The significant information deals with their relative importance; the important question is, how much weight should be attached to each of the items? Several years ago, the International Nickel Company had a committee make a thorough study of prospective sites in a wide area for a new refinery and rolling mill. Not only did this committee list the factors to be considered, it went so far as to ascribe definite values or weights to each. Thus, fuel carried a weight of 33 per cent, water supply 10 per cent, living conditions 10 per cent, etc. After determining specific costs at each point and weighting these costs according to the predetermined scale, the committee presumably selected the site that would yield the lowest cost combination.

The extent to which the International Nickel Company or any other company, in this world of rapid economic and technological change, can determine with precision and for any considerable length of time the relative importance of any one item, fuel for instance, may be questioned by skeptics. Raw materials are changing, markets are changing, modes of transportation are changing, processes are changing, prices—the common denominator of all these variables—are changing. However, the illustration points to a move in the right direction. "Knowledge insufficient for prediction may be most valuable for guidance," as John Stuart Mill observed. Companies do select locations; industries do move from place

57

to place.   The complexity of the influences back of these is all the more reason for an attempt to make a thorough analysis of the problem.

Location Factors in the Iron and Steel Industry.—In the light of the emphasis just placed upon getting a combination of costs that will give the least total, let us consider the location problem in iron and steel manufacture.   The operation of a blast furnace requires, as stated in a previous section, roughly two tons of iron ore, one ton of coke, and a half ton of limestone to make one ton of iron.   Pig iron sells for $15 to $20 a ton, or less than a cent a pound.   In other words, $3\frac{1}{2}$ lb. of raw materials are purchased, transported, and processed for less than one cent.   This focuses attention upon a key factor in the location of this industry, namely, the necessity for low costs of assembling raw materials and distributing finished product.   Reduced to its simplest terms, therefore, the location of a blast furnace resolves itself into the selection of that site which promises access to raw material, fuel, and a market at least total cost.

There was an old English saying, "ore moves to the fuel," that apparently was based upon their relative importance in the diet of a blast furnace.   However, a comparison of the ore and coke map (Fig. 13) reveals that although ore moves to the fuel in some instances, in others fuel moves to the ore, and in still others both move to a junction point. Furthermore, the modern tempo of business places ever greater emphasis upon speedy delivery of goods, which gives an advantage to those plants which have their markets near by.   The location of recent plant additions and new construction seems to confirm this observation.   Consumers of iron or steel, for the sake of economy, prefer to operate with a minimum of capital tied up in inventory, and therefore the furnace which is in a position to offer hand-to-mouth delivery enjoys a competitive advantage. Probably the most precise statement that can be made with respect to the relative importance of the ore, the coal, and the market is that they are of approximately equal importance, the latter being perhaps slightly more important than either of the others.

The market for 90 per cent of our pig-iron production, however, consists of steel companies that produce their own pig iron.   In other words, the blast furnace department is just one division of these integrated concerns.   Independently operated or "merchant" furnaces sell most of their output to isolated or nonintegrated steel mills and to foundries.   Accordingly, we might expect to find the location of steel mills coinciding approximately with that of blast furnaces.   This is less true than formerly, since steel mills are less dependent upon blast furnaces owing to the growing use of scrap.   A steel mill can operate almost entirely on scrap, provided there is enough scrap available to meet its requirements.   Proximity to a densely populated territory or to a general industrial area is therefore a good location for a steel mill because the raw material and the market are in this instance found together. Bearing in mind, therefore, that the sources of ore, coal, and the market are of approximately equal importance in determining the location of a blast furnace, and that the sources of scrap and a market are of strategic importance in the location of a steel mill, let us examine the actual location of iron and steel plants.

The Iron and Steel Districts of the United States.—At present there are 400 steel mills in more than 250 communities in 29 states of the United States. Some of these plants are in the nature of fabricating mills, that is, they may be engaged in converting steel into wire or pipe; the production of primary steel is more highly localized in a few favored territories than the above statistics suggest. Mills engaged in the production of primary steel are concentrated in 21 districts, according to a classification adopted by the American Iron and Steel Institute. To simplify the analysis, these 21 districts may be combined into five major districts: (1) the Eastern; (2) Pittsburgh; (3) the Great Lakes; (4) the Southern, and (5) the Western. This or any other classification is necessarily somewhat arbitrary, but these five major districts are, with exceptions noted later, more or less separate areas. Before turning to a detailed consideration of each district, attention is called to Table XII which presents in summary form the present and past relative importance of each, based upon their production of iron and steel respectively.

TABLE XII.—IRON AND STEEL PRODUCTION OF UNITED STATES BY MAJOR DISTRICTS
(In percentage of total)

District	Pig iron			Steel		
	1904	1929	1936	1904	1929	1936
Eastern................	13.8	12.2	18.4	25.7	17.0	17.3
Pittsburgh.............	63.8	56.4	42.8	53.5	52.5	44.7
Great Lakes...........	11.4	22.6	30.7	16.1	23.2	32.0
Southern..............	8.8	6.5	6.8	2.9	4.7	3.4
Western...............	2.2	2.3	1.3	1.8	2.6	2.6

Source: Calculation based on *Report* of American Iron and Steel Institute and *Report* of NRA on Operation of Basing-point System in the Iron and Steel Industry, November 30, 1934.

Eastern District.—This includes New England, New York, New Jersey, Maryland, Virginia, and all of Pennsylvania except the region west of Johnstown. A large part of the production of this district is in the hands of the Bethlehem Steel Corporation, whose principal plants are in Buffalo, Johnstown, Bethlehem, and Sparrows Point.

This district is the oldest in the country; its origin goes back to colonial days when population clustered along the Atlantic seaboard and smelting furnaces were built of stone and operated at low temperatures with local ores and charcoal. Later, about 1840, when the industry turned from charcoal to anthracite, the Lehigh, Susquehanna, Schuylkill, and Lebanon valleys of eastern Pennsylvania came into their own. However, this advantage of local raw materials was of short duration, for the period from 1850 to 1890 saw a transition to bituminous coking coal and Lake ores. Raw material transport costs proved an effective handicap to the growth of this district.

Since the turn of the century, the trend has been slowly downward, and would have been rapidly downward were it not for the inclusion of Buffalo and Johnstown.

The present-day ability of the district just about to hold its own in the face of aggressive developments in the Lakes district is due to the factor of transportation costs. On a cost basis, the Lake Superior ores are too remote, so the plants in this district, with the exception of those in Buffalo, import most of their iron ore from Cuba, Chile, Spain, and Africa. The general area of competitive advantage for imported ore is a strip along the Atlantic and Gulf coasts extending about 200 miles inland. The district is also favorably situated for the transport of finished products; the Sparrows Point, Md., plant, which is on tidewater, is reported to be handling an extensive export business as well as important oil field business from the Southwest. Another factor that has enabled the district to fight off precipitate decline has been the development of by-product coke. This district is much less dependent than formerly upon the use of Connellsville beehive coke. These favorable factors, however, apply largely to the big, integrated concerns. The competitive going has been rough for the small, detached furnaces which do not have modern equipment or which, not being tied in with steel companies, do not have a backlog of internal business. However, the growing importance of scrap and the trend toward "tailormade" steel is probably the reason that independent steel mills in this area have shown some recent evidence of revival.

Pittsburgh District.—This district includes (1) Pittsburgh and the adjacent steel towns such as Homestead, Braddock, McKeesport, and Donora; (2) Youngstown district which lies in the Mahoning valley to the north; (3) Sharon district in the Shenango valley to the north; (4) Wheeling which is some distance to the southwest; (5) scattered plants throughout the territory just outlined, including the south Ohio river section. The plants clustered in Pittsburgh and the immediate vicinity are the most important, having roughly one-third of the output of the entire area; the Youngstown group rank next in size with about one-fourth of the output. Youngstown and Sharon are sometimes grouped by the trade and referred to as the "valleys."

Originally, this general district used local ores and fuel. It possessed no striking advantages until the industry turned from charcoal and anthracite to coke. This was about the time of the Civil War and shortly afterwards. In the decade 1873 to 1883, while charcoal iron remained stationary and anthracite iron increased 50 per cent, the production of coke-made iron increased 175 per cent. This shift to coke brought the center of the industry to western Pennsylvania where the fuel was cheap and of excellent quality. The fame of Connellsville coal from which the finest coke was made soon spread. After the shift to coke, local ore continued to be used for some years for it was not until the early eighties

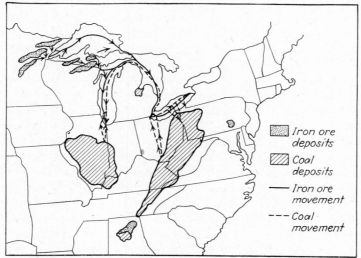

Fig. 13.—Location and transportation of iron ore and coal to blast furnaces. (*Iron and Steel, U. S. Tariff Commission Report No.* 128.)

that iron ore from Lake Superior began to arrive. Today, the region is primarily dependent on Lake ore as Fig. 13 reveals. Fortunately for the area, the importation of Lake ore has not been prohibitively costly. The haul is mostly by water with only a short overland journey. However, it costs $1.15[1] to move a ton of iron ore a little over 100 miles from Lake Erie to Pittsburgh by rail in contrast with only 83 cents to move it some 800 or 900 miles from the head of Lake Superior to Lake Erie ports.

Since we have stressed so heavily the factor of transportation in this industry, it is appropriate to point out that the general contour of the land, through its effect on transportation costs, favors Pittsburgh. The drainage basin of the upper Ohio is full of deep, sharp valleys, and the

[1] DAUGHERTY, C. R., *et al.*, "The Economics of the Iron and Steel Industry," Vol. I, p. 380, McGraw-Hill Book Company, Inc., New York, 1937.

railroads, to eliminate the expense of steep grades, all run with the streams which gather into rivers converging at Pittsburgh. These are the general location aspects of a territory that today produces about 45 per cent of the country's output of iron and steel and almost as much as the combined output of Germany and France.

Despite its splendid location, the Pittsburgh area is not progressing so rapidly as some other sections; in other words, it is losing in relative importance. During the period 1904–1929, when the plants bordering on the Great Lakes increased their share of the country's production from 16 to 23 per cent, Pittsburgh's share remained almost stationary. These, of course, are percentage figures and therefore show relative and not absolute changes. The Pittsburgh district, the first to develop large-scale production after the change from iron to steel, could not possibly retain its early position in the face of more widely dispersed production. The significance of the figures lies in their indication of continued relative change. Pittsburgh no longer has the only supply of good coking coal. With the rapid adoption, following 1915, of the by-product method, which uses almost any kind of bituminous coal, the Connellsville area declined.

In view of the failure of the Pittsburgh district to hold its own it may seem surprising that the United States Steel Corporation chose to locate its recently completed Irvin Works in this district. The explanation, according to one of the officials of the company, is that the Irvin Works, a modern continuous mill designed to produce sheets, strip, and tin plate, has no ingot steelmaking facilities. Since the company already has ample ancillary facilities, such as coke ovens, blast furnaces, and open-hearth furnaces, in the Pittsburgh district, the new plant was located there in order to obtain fuller use of its raw steel producing capacity and to serve more effectively the markets in Cleveland, Pittsburgh, and the East.

Another factor that has influenced the geographic distribution of the industry can only be briefly noted at this point. Pittsburgh's strength as a producing area was in part sustained for more than a quarter of a century by the "Pittsburgh-plus" system. This consisted in quoting and selling steel, regardless of where it was produced, at the price prevailing in Pittsburgh plus the addition of freight charges from Pittsburgh (rather than from the point of production) to the point of consumption. This system was, in essence, a device to control competitive relations. It should be noted that it favored the Pittsburgh area and that since its gradual abandonment, beginning in 1924, Pittsburgh has suffered in competition with lower cost areas. This point will be discussed more fully in Chap. V.

Great Lakes District.—As the name implies, this district centers on the Great Lakes basin. It produces about a third of the iron and steel of the United States. The plants in it are widely scattered, Duluth on the west being 900 miles distant from Erie in the east. Chicago is the center of one cluster of plants that produces more than half of the output; Cleveland is the center of another group that has about one-fourth of the output. Despite the great extent of the territory, it is essentially one economic unit.

Historically, the region has developed since the Civil War. Its growth awaited the exploitation of the ore ranges of Lake Superior which today supply 85 per cent of our domestic consumption, the development of the by-product manufacture of coke which has made available near-by coals, and the growth of a large Midwestern market owing to the general industrial and agricultural development of the region. All three trends are of significance because of their effect on transportation costs. Lake-shore plants eliminate one handling of ore. They also eliminate rail haul of ore. Rail haulage, although short, has now become a significant cost under keenly competitive conditions. In 1934, it cost only $1.74 per gross ton to deliver Lake ore at Lake-shore plants in contrast with $2.97 for delivery at Pittsburgh or $2.64 at Youngstown.[1] With pig iron selling at or under $20, this transportation differential substantially favors the plants on the Lake shores.

As early as 1900, the Lackawanna Steel Company shifted from a site at Scranton, which it had occupied for 60 years, to the immediate vicinity of Buffalo,[2] in order to get lower costs. In 1907, the United States Steel Corporation met its need for more capacity by erecting a gigantic plant on the sand dunes of Lake Michigan at Gary, Ind. In 1910, it opened a modern plant at Duluth. The growth to date has been more rapid than the general expansion of the industry.

Such cost comparisons as we have indicate that there are important differences within the territory. The strategy of location can be explained with reference not only to ore costs but to total costs of raw materials. Using the costs of assembling raw materials for pig-iron manufacture, as revealed in Table XIII, we observe that Chicago is most favorably located with respect to ore cost but least favorably located with respect to coal cost. On the other hand, Pittsburgh is most favorably located with respect to coal cost, but ore costs run relatively high for reasons already mentioned. However, total costs of assembly at Pittsburgh are very low because coking coal is obtainable at a cost well below that at any other major producing center. A development which is tending to upset normal cost relationships is the growing utilization of scrap metal.

[1] *Ibid.*

[2] Geographically and economically, Buffalo should be included in the Great Lakes district. We included it in the Eastern district only because the American Iron and Steel Institute does so and does not report statistics separately.

Scrap originates principally in large metal-consuming centers like Detroit, and this is said to be an appreciable factor in the rapidly growing steel industry of that city.

TABLE XIII.—ESTIMATED ASSEMBLY COSTS IN THE PRODUCTION OF PIG IRON,
SUMMER OF 1937
(In dollars per gross ton of pig iron)

Producing center	Iron ore	Coal	Flux	Total
Weirton-Steubenville	$5.508	$0.468	$0.337	$6.313
Pittsburgh	5.804	0.284	0.337	6.425
Cleveland	3.497	2.714	0.241	6.452
Buffalo	3.497	2.909	0.241	6.647
Detroit	3.497	3.249	0.086	6.832
Youngstown	5.193	1.979	0.170	7.342
Chicago	3.487	3.867	0.241	7.595

Source: WORTHING, MARION, Comparative Assembly Costs in the Manufacture of Pig Iron, *Pittsburgh Business Review*, VIII, No. 1, Jan. 31, 1938, pp. 21–25, Table 1.

Before leaving the Great Lakes district, there is to be noted a movement of recent origin which, though it bulks small in the total picture, has disturbed competitive relations. This is the growing importance of the Detroit area. Several companies have recently started manufacture there in order to take advantage of the large local demand of the automobile industry, the local supply of scrap metal, and the quick delivery to automobile companies who calculate their production schedules in terms of hours rather than days and who make strenuous efforts to keep inventories low. These plants are located to take advantage of water transport of raw materials and truck transport of finished goods.

Southern District.—This district, with 7 per cent of the pig iron and 3 per cent of the steel output of the United States, includes Alabama, Kentucky, Tennessee, Georgia, Virginia, and Texas. At the outset, it must be emphasized that this region is not a homogeneous unit, historically, commercially, or technically. Alabama is to be distinguished from the other centers. It did not develop in its present form until after 1870, whereas ironmaking in Virginia, Kentucky, and Tennessee had its heyday prior to the Civil War. One of the first enterprises of the Jamestown colonists was ironmaking, and since that time there has been a scattered belt of local furnaces, using local materials and supplying local markets, that runs from Virginia on the northeast to Texas on the southwest. The Alabama section has large-scale, integrated plants which produce over half the output of the South; the other states, for the most part, have small merchant blast furnaces and scattered steel plants. Furthermore, many of the analyses of iron- and steelmaking in the South fail to distinguish between the trends in production of these two areas. E. C.

Eckel, a well-known consultant on minerals, points out that during the period 1905–1929, Alabama iron-ore production increased from 3.8 to 6.6 million tons or at about the same rate as that of the United States, whereas the rest of the South declined from 1.9 to less than 0.4 million tons. When iron production statistics of the South are presented, they refer, then, largely to Alabama.

The Alabama area, as is indicated by the ore map, centers around Birmingham. It uses local ore, coke, and limestone. The ore is deposited in an elliptical area 75 miles long and 40 miles wide. It is a low grade of ore, usually about 30 to 40 per cent iron. It contains phosphorus in such quantities that its exploitation awaited the development of the basic open-hearth process about 1875. Some of the ore is self-fluxing, that is, it is high in lime content. The other raw materials, coal and limestone, are more favorably located with respect to ore than in any other section of the country. The United States Steel Corporation acquired plants in the Birmingham region in 1907, and it seems logical to infer that expansion since that time has not been hampered by lack of capital.

The failure of this region, with its favorable distribution of raw materials and low labor costs, to progress at a rate faster than that of the country as a whole is to be attributed largely to the slow industrial development of the South. Although the markets of the Southern steel industry appear to be restricted largely to the South, some products such as tin plate, produced in Alabama, are shipped to the West coast and Hawaii. It is not to be inferred, however, that the prospects are unfavorable; rather, it emphasizes the point that the future of this iron- and steel-making district is tied up with the general industrial development of the South which is reasonably sure to take place.[1]

The Western District.—The Western district, like the Southern district, embraces a large, heterogeneous territory extending from Pueblo, Colo., on the east to the Pacific Coast on the west and from Los Angeles in the south to Seattle in the north. Like the Southern district also, the outstanding center of production is confined to one region—Colorado—which specializes in rails and track accessories and also wire products for farms and ranches. The district produces only slightly more than one per cent of our total pig-iron output and only about 2.5 per cent of the country's steel. It is the smallest district because of its limited market and geographical isolation. Its future growth, like that of the Southern district, will doubtless be determined by the growth of other industries within the region.

Stability and Change in Location.—Shifts in location, like other economic phenomena, are subject to constant change. Shifting markets,

---

[1] The reader is referred to the discussion in Chap. V of the probable effect on the South of the recent change in the pricing system of the steel industry.

technical discoveries, greater use of scrap, or new pricing policies, to mention only a few, are factors constantly tending to remold the locational pattern. For example, during the decade ending with December, 1937, the United States Steel Corporation dismantled nearly 5 million tons of obsolete rolling equipment and built about 6 million tons of modern equipment. It is significant to note that much of the modern equipment was installed in areas other than those where the abandoned plants were located. In his annual report to the stockholders, Myron C. Taylor, chairman of the board of directors of the company, said that after a great deal of study it was decided that the corporation could achieve its highest efficiency by grouping its main producing units in the Pittsburgh, Chicago, and Birmingham districts.

Among the plants abandoned by the corporation for reasons of poor location were two nail mills, a sheet mill, and a tin mill in Ohio; three blast furnaces, two wire mills, a cold-rolled strip mill, and a galvanized sheet mill in Pennsylvania; a blast furnace and five open-hearth furnaces in Minnesota; and a tin mill in West Virginia. This illustrates how an industry undergoes constant change in location to the accompaniment of ceaseless change in technology.

CHAPTER V

COMPETITION IN THE STEEL INDUSTRY

Since 1850, when the steel industry as we know it today began to take form, three rather distinct competitive patterns can be traced. The first emerged in the period 1850–1900; the second came out of the years 1901–1920; the third may be pieced together from the developments since 1921.

THE PERIOD 1850–1900

The Arrival of Cheap Steel.—The industrial world of 1850 had great need for a general-purpose, low-cost metal. For centuries it had used a form of wrought iron, later some pig iron, and to a slight extent a high-carbon steel. Each of these had drawbacks that severely limited its general usefulness: pig iron was too weak for heavy duty because of its crystalline nature; wrought iron, although fibrous, tough, and noncorrosive, was costly; crucible steel was technically limited to production in small quantities and therefore was so high in price that its use was confined to toolmaking and a few other special purposes.

Meanwhile, the market was hungry for a strong, cheap, all-purpose metal. Conditions then existing in the field of transportation illustrate this. Rivers had reached their peak as carriers of commerce (the all-time high for Mississippi River commerce occurred in the middle of the fifties). The railroads, after 25 years of expansion, were only reaching Chicago in 1850. The extension of the railheads to the Pacific and the opening of the rich grain and grazing lands in Minnesota, the Dakotas, and Nebraska, as well as the further industrialization of the East, were being held in check. The railroads needed for their mature development the stimulus of cheap steel.

It seems more than a coincidence that the need just outlined should have been satisfied at the same time by two widely separated inventors, Henry Bessemer in England and William Kelly in the United States. As the epoch opened, both men were at their experiments; finally, in 1864, a commercial form of the metal now known as Bessemer steel appeared on the American market. Four years later another satisfactory structural steel, open-hearth, appeared. Conditions were now ripe for translating potential demand into effective demand.

Expansion of the Market and the Changes It Wrought.—The new steels found ready uses. Heavier and stronger rails were laid down, the

67

transcontinental railroads were completed, car capacity increased in the decade of the sixties from 18 to 40 tons, the steel tank car was devised for the newly founded petroleum industry, the refrigerator car laid the basis for Midwest meat packing, fields were enclosed with a new fencing material called barbed wire.   As if to make expansion doubly sure, the American market, which had been supplied in 1850 with 60 per cent of its requirements by British steel, was now protected by a high tariff with the result that the early seventies saw the last of the heavy importations of British iron and steel.   From approximately 6,000 tons in 1850 steel production shot up by decades to 10 million tons at the turn of the century.

This increased production immediately revealed the inadequacy of existing fuels and ores, and the industry turned from charcoal and anthracite to beehive coke made from cheap, western Pennsylvania bituminous coal, and from the small scattered supplies of local ores to the rich surface deposits of the Lake Superior region.   Altogether, this was a formative period in which each year brought new records in production, new types of furnaces, new sources of raw materials, and new outlets for the product.

These changes brought vast opportunities for profits.   None seized these with surer acumen than Andrew Carnegie, who had arrived in Pittsburgh in 1847 as an impoverished Scotch immigrant lad.   He rose rapidly to be division superintendent of the Pennsylvania Railroad Company; then, perhaps sensing the coming need for railroad steels, he entered the steel business in the early sixties.   From that time on, as if in accord with a preconceived 35-year plan, he marched into each domain of the business just as it became ripe for commercial exploitation.   His keen sense of timing enabled him to follow with great personal gain his preachment that "pioneering doesn't pay."   First it was railway car axles, then in succession railway bridges, pig iron, Bessemer steel, open-hearth steel, coke, an ore-hauling railroad, a fleet of ore boats, and ore lands.   Finally, in the nineties, he reorganized the whole of his industrial empire into a closely knit compact corporate unit.   In 1900 the value of this vast aggregation was set by the Carnegie partners at 500 million dollars.   As evidence that it was worth the price, they could point in that year to net earnings of 40 millions.

During these years the competitive going was rough.   Many entered the field to harvest the lush growth, and the "captains of industry" earned the sobriquet by following policies of blood and iron.   Ethical standards in business condoned commercial bribery, rebating, espionage, and cutthroat price cutting, although occasionally, when the competition was too keen, the market was divided under formal pooling arrangements or the more informal "gentlemen's" agreements.   But these were soon broken, and the struggle for dominance or survival was renewed. From this competition there emerged by the time of the nineties two groups of companies, the primary and the secondary producers.

The primary producers, three in number, manufactured steel which they sold to other companies for further processing. The most important of these companies was the Carnegie Steel Company, which had practically all of its capacity in the Pittsburgh area. In the Chicago territory the leading primary company was the Federal Steel Company, a 110-million-dollar consolidation arranged by the J. P. Morgan interests and headed by an Illinois attorney, Elbert H. Gary. The third primary company was National Steel Company, a 75-million-dollar enterprise in the Ohio Valley.

The secondary group was made up of hundreds of small mills which bought crude steel and rolled it into tin plate, pipe, wire, etc. These companies had been hard hit during the depression years 1893–1898, and when business revived in the latter year numerous promoters took advantage of the improved earnings and prospects to effect horizontal mergers according to products. The Moore brothers, of Diamond Match and National Biscuit fame, brought together several hundred tin plate mills; John W. Gates promoted the merger of the wire companies, and the banking house of Morgan joined the tube companies and the steel hoop companies.

But the highly capitalized secondary companies, with their increased dividend requirements, faced a black future when business fell off sharply in 1900. To improve earnings, they turned to backward integration and planned to produce the raw steel they had hitherto been buying at high prices from the primary producers. Upon receipt of this news, Carnegie announced plans to integrate forward to the market. The first step was to be the erection of a huge finishing mill at the Lake Erie end of his ore-carrying railroad. This would give the road pay traffic both ways—ore to Pittsburgh and ingot steel from Pittsburgh back to the finishing plant. It would also give the Carnegie company low-cost water transportation of finished products. A struggle of gigantic proportions seemed to be in the making. It was prevented, to the satisfaction of all concerned, including the bankers, by the consolidation of both groups in a unit called the United States Steel Corporation.

THE PERIOD 1901–1920

A Period of Friendly Competition.—"The Corporation" ushered in a new competitive era in steel manufacture. Unlike the cutthroat days prior to 1900, the first two decades of the present century were characterized by friendliness among the steel producers. The policies of the United States Steel Corporation were so well mannered and mild that they have been accurately summed up as "live and let live." The reasons behind this course of action will be more apparent if we first examine the theoretical aspects of the situation.

Inherent in steel manufacture are the elements of violent competition. In the first place, all the companies have heavy fixed investment. United States Steel Corporation, for example, has fixed costs of 180 million dollars —costs which the company must bear no matter how large or how small the tonnage produced. Seventy per cent of their total capital is tied up in blast furnaces, open-hearths, rolling mills, coke plants, interplant railroads, etc. To illustrate the point differently, they have $1 invested in fixed property for every 70 cents of annual sales. This means that overhead costs, relative to direct costs, are heavy. Specifically, it means that the industry as a whole does not earn enough to meet its full overhead costs until it is operating at 50 per cent of capacity. When operations fall below this point there is a strong urge to cut prices in order to get volume back to the "break-even" point. Any price that yields something beyond out-of-pocket costs contributes just as much toward overhead. On the other hand, when operations get beyond the 50 per cent figure the cost of the additional output falls sharply and profits climb rapidly. Costs and profits, then, are particularly sensitive in this industry to changes in the rate of operation.

The rate of steel-plant operation, as noted in Chap. II, fluctuates violently. When production falls below 50 per cent (it got down to 12 per cent in 1932), there arises an almost irresistable urge, even among companies with fat surpluses, to cut prices. On the other hand, in boom times when everyone wants steel immediately and profits skyrocket there is the urge to expand plant and to distribute easy earnings too lavishly. A prince or pauper industry tends to be a strongly competitive industry.

A third aspect of the industry that has an important bearing on competition is its zone nature. Every steel plant is the center of a territory in which it and near-by plants have a competitive advantage as regards costs of delivery. The width of this zone of advantage will vary from plant to plant; if water routes with their low rates are available the territory is larger than it otherwise would be; if the product is of low value relative to bulk and weight, the territory is smaller than it otherwise would be; if the product is made by only one or two companies the territory is larger than it would be if many widely scattered plants made it. Beyond the zone of advantage is the territory favorable to some other plant or group of plants. But, and this is important, these faraway pastures look green. When orders are low in volume it is tempting to enter the distant markets by absorbing some of the freight charges rather than passing them on to the buyer. A net mill price that yields anything beyond out-of-pocket costs will help to meet the inescapable overhead. Even when business is moderately brisk there is the temptation to invade "foreign" territory, for profits may be regarded as coming from the nearby orders and "dumping" in the distant markets may be looked upon as helping to reduce overhead costs. These three conditions—high overhead costs, wide fluctuations in production, and the zone nature of steel markets—can be expected on theoretical grounds to produce severe competition. The fact is that for almost a quarter of a century after the formation of the United States Steel Corporation in 1901 severe competition did not arise.

Why, in the face of the theory, did severe competition fail to develop during all these years? The answer is obvious enough; producers, in order to avoid its rigors, controlled and restrained competition. The way in which the restraint was achieved is not so obvious, especially because restraints were then as now banned by the Sherman Antitrust Act. The technique was a pricing system that has come to be known as "Pittsburgh plus."

"Pittsburgh Plus"—Its Operation and Results.—Under this system, all steel companies regardless of location quoted on a given order the price set by the United States Steel Corporation at Pittsburgh. Pittsburgh, rather than some other city, was the basing point because it was the most important steel center in the country and at all times, except very dull ones, consumers had to come to the Pittsburgh district to complete their requirements. Furthermore, the largest producer and the price leader, U. S. Steel, owned three-fourths of the capacity in the Pittsburgh area.

All companies, in addition to quoting Pittsburgh prices, added the cost of transporting the steel from Pittsburgh to the point of consumption, even though the product might be made at some other point. If a Chicago producer sold to a Chicago consumer, he quoted the Pittsburgh price and then added the cost of freight from Pittsburgh although no such transportation was involved. If a Chicago producer sold steel farther west, say in Omaha, he again charged freight from Pittsburgh although, obviously, shipment was made from Chicago. When a consumer asked for bids from scattered companies he got only one price inasmuch as all mills were quoting the price U. S. Steel had established at its Pittsburgh mills plus the cost of transportation from such mills to the consumer. Some of the questions which this price system stimulates in the mind of the reader may be answered if we consider separately the positions of the Corporation and the "independents."

The United States Steel Corporation, at the outset of its existence, faced the problem of what its corporate competitive policy was to be. The decision as to what attitude it would take toward other steel companies, even though not formally phrased or made all at one time, was a real one and could not be evaded. It could elect to proceed along isolationist lines and forget the others. It owned from half to two-thirds of the capacity in the several branches of the entire industry, and this gave it an initial advantage, since the cost of making steel, as distinct from the cost of marketing it, decreases as the scale of operation increases. It could cut prices to build up further volume on the assumption that distant markets helped take care of overhead and thus increased the profits on the near-by business. In other words, it could elect not only to hold but to increase its relative position in the industry. On the other hand, it was big enough to follow a policy of "live and let live." It could set prices high enough to enable the smaller producers to make profits—which of course would ensure handsome profits for itself. If under this policy the smaller producers shaved the high prices in an attempt to increase their own business, the Corporation's size could be used to coerce them back into line, pricewise.

The Corporation adopted the "live and let live" policy. Whether this was due to the belief that the demand for steel is conditioned by the operations of the business cycle and cannot be expanded much by vigorous competition or whether it was due to the trust-busting ideas of Theodore Roosevelt, then beginning to take form, cannot be said; we do know, however, that the policy was one of "friendly competition." U. S. Steel set the prices and the others followed. It set them at a level that would yield itself a profit. During periods of brisk business it sought to avoid "runaway" prices by not charging all the traffic would bear; during slack times it did not lower prices sharply in an effort to stimulate sales. Under this middle-of-the-road policy it prospered and expanded. It added a modern unit on the sand dunes of Lake Michigan around which mushroomed the city of Gary, Ind.; it bought the mines and mills of its present unit in Alabama; it erected furnaces in Duluth near the ore supplies; it rebuilt its South Chicago and Pittsburgh equipment. It is true that during this period the Corporation's share of the total business slowly declined to about 40 per cent. But it is quite probable that this decline was not objectionable to the management: while the decline was taking place some 500 to 700 millions in "water" in the original capital structure was replaced with solid assets; earnings beyond dividend requirements were plowed back until total assets had increased from 1,400 to 2,000 millions; finally, the policy came to full flower in 1920 in a Supreme Court decision. In that year the efforts of the Federal government to prove that the steel producers were acting in restraint of trade, which efforts in their various forms go back to 1905, failed. The Court decided, four to three (two judges not participating) that the Corporation had not violated the Sherman Antitrust Act and was therefore entitled to exist.

The wisdom of the man who had formulated the policy, Judge Elbert H. Gary, chairman of the board of the Corporation, was thus justified.

The advantages of "Pittsburgh plus" to the independent producers were almost wholly the result of the actions of the Corporation. When U. S. Steel set prices with a view to earning dividends on watered stock it thereby automatically enabled the high-cost producers to make a profit. If any of the independents cut prices aggressively in an attempt to "hog the business" the Corporation's competitive strength benefited all except the aggressor. Not only was the leader large and strong but, quite important, its strength was soon well distributed geographically, as we have just noted. If an independent sought to take advantage of the "Pittsburgh plus" system by quoting low prices in near-by territory where it had a natural monopoly it found that U. S. Steel was able to do likewise since it too had a plant near, if not in, the area. Furthermore, such aggressors stood revealed by "Pittsburgh plus" inasmuch as all prices were supposed to be identical, namely, the Pittsburgh price plus freight from Pittsburgh. The sensible action, of course, was to follow the leader.

Consumers of steel were in much the same position as the independent producers in the matter of price cutting. If they turned to the price cutter during times of moderate or depressed business, they paid for the disloyalty during times of brisk business when necessity forced them to ask the Corporation to sell steel to them. It is true that some "chiseling" took place, but it was secret and of minor importance. It is likewise true that under the policy Bethlehem, Youngstown, and other independents were growing at a rate faster than that of the leader; but, as already intimated, the Corporation was later to make use of this fact in court. The system, then, stabilized price changes, revealed price cutters, and enabled a leader that had little disposition to use its strength for other than policing purposes to lead everyone to the ultimate goal—profits. Lest we regard "Pittsburgh plus" as a primary cause of monopolistic competition rather than a mere technique for carrying it into effect, we should remember that throughout these years the market for steel was an expanding one. From 10 million tons production at the outset of this period in 1900, it expanded to 42 million tons in 1920. When orders are plentiful a leader can enforce policies that are ill suited to more strenuous times.

THE PERIOD 1921–1940

The Decline of Friendly Competition.—Competitive relationships do not often change overnight. This is especially true if throughout an entire industry they have run to a common pattern and have been stable enough to persist for several decades. This was the case in the steel industry. The beginnings of the new competitive era were minor in importance, slow in development, and mixed in character.   In retrospect we see what even steel men were unaware of for some years: a new competitive order was being compounded of such diverse and seemingly unimportant elements as a few changes in the technology of steelmaking, the death of Judge Gary, some consolidations among the smaller companies, the arrival of the closed-body type of automobile, the advent of hand-to-mouth industrial buying, and a few concessions to steel consumers who complained about "Pittsburgh plus."

The year 1921 is set down as the beginning of a new period because in that year steel consumers started an organized fight against "Pittsburgh plus."   Fifteen hundred consumers of rolled steel west of Chicago brought complaints to the Federal Trade Commission against the industry's practice of using Pittsburgh as the sole basing point.   Their grievance may be illustrated as follows: A Des Moines fabricator who bought his steel in Chicago found that he had to pay the Pittsburgh costs and in addition the fictitious freight charges from Pittsburgh to Chicago.   This practice handicapped the Des Moines fabricator in two ways: first, it caused the price of steel to be higher in Des Moines than it otherwise would be and thus tended to restrict the use of steel as a building material; second, it enabled outside fabricators to come into the Des Moines territory and compete.

In 1924 the Federal Trade Commission ordered the producers to abandon the system, and as a result there was a gradual increase in the number of basing points.   At present there are some 80 towns or cities which are basing points for one or more types of steel, and of these perhaps a dozen may be considered as major basing points.   The buyer now pays the price prevailing at the basing point nearest to him plus the freight from that point to his door.

After 1924, as the number of basing points slowly increased, the price policies of individual companies became more independent.   In 1928 the president of the Bethlehem Steel Corporation told the members of the Institute that "The avoidance of uneconomic price cutting was necessary to stabilization."   By 1930 "price shading" was reported to be widespread, and the business was likened to "selling rugs at a Turkish street fair."   "Base prices were no longer those announced by the Steel Corporation and price competition had demoralized the system not only through instability in base prices quoted but through concessions and allowances made in the method of calculating delivered prices."[1]   By 1932 the industry had reached a point where "trade practices that destroy profits, disorganize trade, and create bitter competition under perilous

[1] DAUGHERTY, C., *et al.*, *op cit.*, Vol. I, p. 541.

circumstances" prompted the appointment of a former member of President Hoover's cabinet as executive director of the Iron and Steel Institute.

It would be inaccurate to say that this increase in competition was caused only by the abandonment of "Pittsburgh plus," for there were several other developments that affected competition. These were consolidations among the independents, a shift in the markets for steel, and a change in the technique of rolling steel.

Consolidations.—In rapid succession, beginning in 1922, Bethlehem absorbed a large plant on the lakes at Buffalo, erected a modern mill on tidewater in Maryland, bought a big plant in Johnstown and a company on the Pacific coast. Another important consolidation was the merger in 1930 of the Republic Iron and Steel Company, the Central Alloy Steel Corporation, the Donner Steel Company, and the Bourne Fuller Company. A third important merger brought together the National Steel Company, composed of steel plants located in West Virginia and the Detroit area, and the blast furnace properties of the M. A. Hanna Company.

Shifting Markets.—While these changes in company structure were going on, competition was also being affected by changes in the markets of the industry. The most important of these changes was the rapid increase in consumption of light sheet and strip steel. These products, which in the four years 1920–1923 had accounted for about 12 per cent of the total output of hot-rolled steel, increased until in the six years 1933–1938 they totaled in excess of 30 per cent. This expanded production found an outlet in such new products as closed automobile bodies, mechanical refrigerators, radio cases, steel furniture, and household washing machines. In the automobile industry, which alone takes 20 per cent of all steel produced, cars with closed bodies increased from 10 per cent of the total in 1919 to 93 per cent of the total in 1931. On the other hand, there was both a relative and an absolute decline in the market for many heavy steel products; rail production dropped from about $2\frac{1}{2}$ million tons per year to only slightly more than a million tons. Plates and structural shapes declined from 23 per cent of the total hot-rolled products to less than 15 per cent during the period mentioned above. Another important change in markets was the expansion of the demand for alloy steels. Improvements in metallurgy, particularly in Germany, produced steels with special properties such as resistance to corrosion and heat, and these found ready markets. Most of these were made in small lots to consumer specifications and may be described as "tailor-made" steels.

Improved Technology.—The expansion of the market for light steels just discussed was both the cause and the result of a marked change in methods of rolling such products. The continuous-rolling process which has been described in the chapter on technology was introduced shortly after 1925 and immediately adopted by the industry under licenses from the American Rolling Mill Company. Within 14 years 28 mills were built at a cost of nearly 500 million dollars.

The competitive significance of these relatively rapid changes was that a number of the independents, either foreseeing the changes or recognizing their importance as they occurred, accommodated themselves to them. Business acumen was displayed by American Rolling Mill when it acquired the patents on the continuous rolling mill, by Bethlehem when it diversified its holdings, by National when it went after the automobile sheet business, and by Republic when it absorbed companies which specialized in the rapidly expanding alloy field. In contrast, United States Steel was either unprepared to shift as markets shifted or did not see the necessity for doing so. The result was that in 1934 only 9 per cent of its business was in the automobile field in comparison to 20 per cent for the steel industry as a whole. But more important as an indicator of the extent to which U. S. Steel was lagging in the competitive race was the failure of its earnings to keep pace with those of the independents. It will be noted in Table XIV that the Corporation fell behind not only during the recent depression but also during the period immediately after the depression. Almost as significant as the financial showing, and no doubt caused by it, was the recent reorganization of U. S. Steel. This took the form of concentrating production in the most efficient plants, consolidating subsidiary companies, erecting new mills in the Pittsburgh area, injecting new personnel into the financial and personnel departments,

TABLE XIV.—EARNINGS OF SOME OF THE LEADING STEEL COMPANIES
(In percentage earned on invested capital)

Year	U. S. Steel	Inland	Youngstown Sheet & Tube	Jones & Laughlin	American Rolling Mill	Bethlehem
1929	9.9	13.2	11.6	10.2	8.2	7.2
1930	4.9	7.9	4.9	4.5	1.8	4.6
1931	0.8	2.8	1.2(d)	0.9(d)	0.7(d)	1.1
1932	3.2(d)	1.3(d)	4.6(d)	3.9(d)	0.2(d)	1.9(d)
1933	1.5(d)	2.2	2.0(d)	2.2(d)	1.5	0.3(d)
1934	0.8(d)	5.9	0.9	1.4(d)	3.3	1.2
1935	0.4	10.4	3.1	0.1(d)	6.4	1.8
1936	3.2	11.9	7.1	2.6	7.6	3.3
1937	5.9	10.6	7.6	3.4	7.0	5.9
1938	0.03	4.8	1.1	1.8(d)	0.9(d)	1.9
1939	3.1	8.4	3.8	2.6	3.2	4.8
1940	7.1	10.4	6.2	5.7	5.7	8.4

(d) Deficit.
Source: Standard and Poor's Corporation.

and shifting managerial responsibility and authority from New York City to manufacturing points. The last change was made desirable by the changed buying habits of customers. Buyers of steel had installed during the period under discussion systems of inventory control and were ordering steel in smaller quantities and to more exact specifications. Such orders could be handled to advantage only by companies that had flexible organizations and policies.

Competition Intensified.—The growing intensity of competition is reflected very clearly by two major developments that occurred in the late thirties. The industry split into two opposing camps with respect to labor policies, and it instituted a new price policy which appears to have shattered much that remained of the criticized "Pittsburgh-plus" system.

In 1937 the Corporation for the first time in its history signed a general trade agreement with a labor union, much to the surprise and disappointment of the independents. The full import of this shift in policy can only be appreciated in the light of the historical background of labor relations in the industry.

Before the advent of cheap tonnage steel about 1865, the skilled puddlers and rollers of wrought iron were highly unionized. In order to retain their position of influence the union reorganized in 1876, taking in the skilled furnace men and rollers of the rapidly expanding Bessemer and open-hearth divisions. The union, which has since been known as the Amalgamated Association of Iron, Steel and Tin Workers, enjoyed a 15-year period of moderate success. In 1892 it lost a decisive battle at the Homestead plant of the Carnegie Steel Company and thereafter it never played an important part in labor relations in the industry. The Corporation, from its inception in 1901, adopted a vigorous anti-union policy in which it was supported almost unanimously by the remainder of the industry. Despite recurring efforts on the part of the workers to secure collective bargaining, the companies remained adamant in their insistence upon the open-shop principle. The Corporation carried on the fight for the industry in the great steel strike of 1919 which resulted in another of a long series of defeats for labor. Trade unionism had receded to a point where only 2 per cent of the employees in the industry claimed membership when the NRA was ushered in.

A change of the political administration in 1933 gave organized labor a fillip which led to an unexpected climax in the steel industry. The controversial 7A clause of the NRA guaranteed employees the right to bargain collectively through representatives of their own choosing. Immediately labor seized the opportunity to enter the promised land but was met with militant opposition in the early skirmishes. In 1936 the Committee for Industrial Organization appropriated a half million dollars and assigned 350 of its best organizers to the task of organizing, on an industry-wide basis, all employees in the steel industry.

Early in 1937, after preparations had been made in anticipation of the impending struggle, U. S. Steel announced that it had signed a contract with the Steel Workers Organizing Committee. This dramatic reversal of policy on the part of the Corporation precipitated much speculation as to whether political or economic considerations had prompted the action. It had all the earmarks of a strategic move, for it left the independents stranded to fight their own labor battles.

The Corporation made a second break with tradition when in the summer of 1938 one of its subsidiaries, Carnegie-Illinois, announced substantial price reductions. This aroused considerable animosity, not because the company had elected to reduce prices for, as pointed out above, price cutting was already a well-established practice, but because existing basing-point differentials were swept away. Since the abolition of "Pittsburgh plus," prices in other steel-producing centers had been $1 to $3 a ton above the Pittsburgh prices. These price differentials, established under the leadership of the Corporation, were designed to preserve the status quo. Although they were not strictly adhered to, they did serve to maintain substantial equality of delivered prices in the principal consuming markets. A mill could invade a distant market only under penalty of "absorbing" the additional freight involved in going beyond its own immediate market, but under pressure of idle capacity such invasion of distant markets was commonplace. By abolishing the price differentials the independents were put at a greater disadvantage in competing in those areas where the Corporation had plants because the invasion of such areas by distant mills entails the absorption of greater freight charges than formerly, which leaves a lower net mill realization.

The independents retaliated at once by establishing competitive basing points of their own. For example, Bethlehem Steel made Buffalo and Sparrows Point basing points, thereby forcing U. S. Steel to absorb higher freight charges on such business as it chose to accept in the Eastern market. The elimination of price differentials together with the increase in number of basing points does not necessarily confine each mill to its own immediate market, but it does impose heavier costs upon the producer who encroaches upon a competitor's market.

Although the immediate effect is more intensive competition, one can only speculate as to which of the many forms the intensified competition will assume. In areas such as Pittsburgh, where consumption of steel is only about a third of the production, the hunger for tonnage may occasionally precipitate serious price cutting. In areas such as Detroit, where steel production is only about a third of consumption, it may stimulate the expansion of additional capacity. It may take on a number of other forms such as the relocation of mills, the realignment of companies, greater utilization of water transportation, pressure upon the railroads for lower freight rates, or greater decentralization of fabricating mills. However, it is not to be expected that any of these changes will take place overnight. The zone nature of the industry, the prince and pauper aspect of its market, and the rigidity of its cost structure have in the past served to check any rapid changes in the competitive pattern. Since these same conditions are still in existence there is no reason to anticipate a revolutionary change in the competitive pattern.

The Temporary National Economic Committee held extended hearings on the subject of multiple-basing-point pricing or zone pricing and in its final report, issued in March, 1941, recommended that Congress abolish this form of pricing. The committee acknowledged but was unimpressed by the argument that legislative outlawing of basing-point systems would create serious disturbances in business. The position taken by the committee was that any disruption to business caused by such legislation would only be temporary and that it would be overshadowed by long-run gains to the public interest.[1]

[1] *Final Report and Recommendation* of the T.N.E.C., Senate Document No. 35, 77th Congress, 1st Session, p. 33.

CHAPTER VI

THE COPPER INDUSTRY

The copper industry presents a number of striking contrasts to the steel industry. In contrast to the literally hundreds of kinds of special quality steels there is only one dominant grade of copper. Accordingly, the quality of copper produced by any one refinery is identical with that from any other refinery. The homogeneity of the metal conditions many of the characteristics of the industry. It influences technology, financial organization, competitive pattern, price structure, in fact, almost every aspect of the industry.

Copper enters more freely into international trade than steel. A substantial percentage of our annual copper production enters international trade, whereas foreign trade in steel is negligible. The significance of this fact is that copper is bought and sold in a world market; therefore the American copper industry is very sensitive to the foreign copper industries as well as to general business conditions abroad.

Another peculiarity is the by-product origin of some copper. Each year a certain amount of the metal enters the market as a by-product of other mining—silver, lead, zinc, etc. In Canada, one of the world's large copper-producing countries, half of the annual copper production is a by-product of nickel mining. Although by-product copper does not assume such large proportions in the United States, this aspect of the industry, in view of the international flow of the metal, has an important influence upon supply and therefore upon price.

The price behavior of copper is very much unlike that of steel. Numerous steel products are characterized by so-called administered prices, that is, prices predisposed to minor and infrequent variations. Copper prices, on the contrary, fluctuate violently and frequently. This contrast is especially noteworthy in view of the fact that the concentration of financial control is even greater in copper than in steel.

On a tonnage basis, the consumption of copper is far below that of steel. The annual consumption of copper is less than a million tons in contrast with 30 to 40 million tons of steel consumption. The explanation is that steel is a general-purpose metal whereas copper is a special-purpose metal. However, copper is the most widely used nonferrous metal. It is used chiefly in the electrical industries because of its high electric conductivity. The principal uses of copper are summarized in

Table XV. It has been estimated that about half of the annual copper consumption is associated with the use of electricity. The miscellaneous uses of copper which together account for almost a fourth of the total consumption include such items as clocks, watches, water heaters, washing machines, wire cloth, ammunition, coinage, etc. One important use of copper Table XV does not reveal. In times of war or armament expansion, large amounts of copper are diverted into these channels. In fact, copper is one of the key metals from the standpoint of national defense.

TABLE XV.—ESTIMATED USES OF COPPER IN THE UNITED STATES, 1939

Use	Percentage of Total Consumption
Electrical manufactures	23.1
Other wire	11.9
Buildings	11.1
Automobiles	10.6
Light and power lines	8.4
Telephone and telegraph	4.9
Refrigerators	1.3
Manufactures for export	6.5
Other uses	22.2
Total	100.0

Source: *Yearbook* of American Bureau of Metal Statistics, 1939.

Copper ranks first among the nonferrous metals because of its physical characteristics and low cost. In addition to electric conductivity, it is noncorrosive. A low melting point facilitates its extraction from the ore. It is easily worked, hot or cold, by any of the metal shaping processes. Copper unites readily with other metals to form alloys such as brass, bronze, and babbit metal. Finally, copper is cheaper than aluminum, its greatest potential competitor among metals from the standpoint of similarity of physical characteristics.

Copper refining is not a large industry. The 1939 Census reported only 23 smelting and refining establishments giving employment to approximately 12,000 wage earners. The industry's total output was valued at 635 million dollars, 90 per cent of which was represented by cost of raw materials.

From Mine to Market.—The technique will be sketched by tracing the flow of material from mine to market. Manufacturing operations embrace five major steps—mining, concentration, smelting, converting, and refining.

Copper occurs in nature usually in the form of an ore such as an oxide or a sulphide, the latter being the more prevalent in the United States. The ore occurs in veins or in irregular masses, and most of it is extracted by underground mining. Where the ore exists near the surface it is extracted by open-pit mining. Some deposits are sufficiently large to permit working the mines for many years. The metal content of the ore ranges between one per cent in lean ores and 7 per cent in rich ores. American ores average about 1.5 per cent metallic copper. This is in sharp contrast with American iron ores, which yield 30 to 60 per cent ferrous metal. Consequently copper ores require extensive processing.

PLATE 11.—Froth flotation. The mineral-carrying bubbles are being skimmed off the top by paddles. (*Courtesy of Anaconda Copper Mining Company. Photo by Frank Ehrenford.*)

After the ore has been mined, part of the barren material is removed by a process known as "concentration." This consists of water concentration usually supplemented by froth flotation. In water concentration, the crushed ore is washed across oscillating trays which separate the heavier mineral-bearing particles from the refuse. Flotation is a process whereby pulverized ore is treated in a tank containing a mixture of water and oil. The combination is agitated to a froth. When this is allowed to settle, particles containing copper adhere to the oil and are carried to the surface while the gangue, or refuse, settles on the bottom of the tank whence it is drawn off. The copper concentrate is then easily recovered from the oil scum. Froth flotation, introduced about 1914, is one of the outstanding improvements in copper technology. It has added millions to our national ore reserves because it permits the utilization of low-grade ores that formerly had no commercial value.

Smelting, which follows concentration, removes additional impurities from the concentrate. It is performed in either blast furnaces or reverberatory furnaces. The copper blast furnace is smaller than the iron blast furnace but otherwise the two furnaces are similar. The reverberatory furnace resembles the steel industry's open-hearth. Prior to the introduction of flotation, smelting capacity was about equally divided between these two types of furnaces. In 1939, only three blast furnaces remained;

PLATE 12.—Copper converter. Converter in foreground is discharging blister copper. (*Courtesy of Anaconda Copper Mining Company. Photo by Frank Ehrenford.*)

94 per cent of the total smelting capacity consisted of reverberatories. Froth flotation hastened the obsolescence of the blast furnace because this type of furnace is ill adapted to smelt the finely pulverized concentrate. Furthermore, the efficiency of reverberatories has been increased through building larger furnaces more economical in fuel consumption.

The liquid product of the smelter, known as "copper matte," is conveyed by ladles to the converter. In the converter, which operates on the same principle as the Bessemer converter for iron, additional impurities are removed.

The product of the converter, called "blister copper," though 99 per cent pure metallic copper, ordinarily undergoes a final refining process.

The purpose of refining, by the principle of electrolysis, is to recover the precious metals, gold and silver, and to remove the baser metals, such as lead and zinc. The former are worth recovering as valuable by-products, and the latter must be extracted if the copper is destined for use in the electrical industries. Based on recent experience, every ton of refined copper yields as by-products an average of 0.009 fine ounces of gold and 0.414 fine ounces of silver. Electrolytic copper, the product of the

PLATE 13.—Electrolytic refining. (*Courtesy of International Smelting & Refining Company. Photo by Frank Ehrenford.*)

refinery, is now ready to be drawn into wire, rolled into sheets, or fabricated into various forms of finished products.

Location.—Over 90 per cent of our domestic copper comes from three producing areas. The Great Lakes district was opened up first (1845) and continued to be the most important producing area until 1887 when it was surpassed by Montana. In 1907, Arizona became the largest producing state. Since then, the Southwestern district has supplied most of our domestic copper.

Smelter works are usually located near the mines that supply them with the ore, thereby obviating the cost of transporting a material of small value per unit of bulk. Except for a few smelters located on the coast specializing in imported concentrates, the smelting establishments are located in the principal copper-producing states indicated in Table XVI.

TABLE XVI.—PRODUCTION OF COPPER IN UNITED STATES BY DISTRICTS, 1938
(Smelter output, fine copper, in thousands of short tons allocated to areas whence the ore originated)

Districts	Tons	Tons	Per cent
Southwestern district...........................	...	409	73
Arizona......................................	210		
Utah...	115		
Nevada.......................................	47		
New Mexico...................................	22		
Colorado.....................................	15		
Northwestern district...........................	...	78	14
Montana......................................	78		
Great Lakes district............................	...	38	7
Michigan.....................................	38		
Scattered......................................	...	37	6
Alaska.......................................	17		
Other states..................................	20		
Total......................................	...	562	100

Source: *Yearbook* of American Bureau of Metal Statistics, 1939.

Refineries, on the contrary, are located in the eastern part of the United States (see Table XVII). It is apparent that almost 70 per cent of the refining capacity is on the Atlantic seaboard conveniently located to supply the copper-fabricating industry of Connecticut and to refine the imported copper coming into the New York area.

TABLE XVII.—ELECTROLYTIC COPPER REFINING COMPANIES OF UNITED STATES, 1939

Company	Plant location	Annual capacity, short tons (000 omitted)	
		Plant	Company total
American Smelting & Refining Company..	Baltimore, Md.	360	
	Barber, N. J.	132	
	Tacoma, Wash.	120	612
Anaconda Copper Mining Company.......	Great Falls, Mont.	180	
International Smelting & Refining Co....	Perth Amboy, N. J.	240	
Inspiration Consolidated Copper Co....	Inspiration, Ariz.	36	456
Phelps Dodge Refining Corporation			
(Nichols Copper Co.)	Laurel Hill, L. I.	150	
	El Paso, Tex.	150	300
American Metals Co , Ltd...............	Cartaret, N. J.	204	204
			1,572

Source: Adapted from *Yearbook* of American Bureau of Metal Statistics, 1939.

Organization of the Industry.—The physical setup of the copper industry may be visualized as a pyramid. At the apex are nine refineries, shown in Table XVII, which refine the entire output of 16 smelters. These smelters, in turn, are supplied with ore by approximately 200 mines, which constitute the base of the pyramid. One reason why there are so few smelters is the fact that many mines operate intermittently. Ore deposits differ in formation, depth, richness of ore, etc. When the price of copper is low only the rich deposits are mined. To assure continuous operation, a smelter must therefore be in a position to draw from several sources. Furthermore, a smelter can operate more efficiently by blending various grades of ore. This assures greater uniformity of the charge. Refineries are fewer in number and larger in size than smelters because refining is a simple operation that adds very little value to the final product.

The copper industry is dominated by four large companies. American Smelting & Refining, Anaconda, and Phelps Dodge control 85 per cent of the total refining capacity, as shown in Table XVII. Kennecott has no electrolytic refineries, but it is the largest copper-mining company in the United States. During the early years of the present century most of the copper companies bent their efforts toward the acquisition of mining properties, with the result that consolidations were primarily of the horizontal type. The growing industrial demand for copper stimulated exploration, and as new rich deposits were discovered copper companies eagerly sought to add them to their holdings in order to increase their earning power. As a result of this type of growth, Kennecott is today the largest domestic producer of copper. This company has the capacity to turn out half a million tons annually, or 75 per cent of the total United States copper production.

Beginning about 1920 a very definite trend toward vertical consolidation set in. Anaconda was the first to complete its integration. The ownership of extensive copper deposits in Chile and Mexico together with its domestic mines gives Anaconda a productive capacity about equal to that of Kennecott. In order to provide a more effective outlet for its copper mines, Anaconda acquired subsidiary companies owning smelting and refining equipment. The integration was carried a step further by the acquisition of two large fabricating concerns—the American Brass Company and a wire and cable company. The other leading companies followed Anaconda's example. Phelps Dodge integrated forward toward the market by the acquisition of Nichols Copper, a refining company, and National Electric Products, a fabricating company. American Smelting & Refining pushed its integration in both directions. It integrated forward by acquiring substantial interests in General Cable and Revere Copper & Brass, both fabricating units, and it integrated backward by the acquisition of mines and the Federated Metals Division Company, the largest factor in the scrap-metal trade. Even Kennecott, which still farms out half of its smelting and all of its refining business, has gone into copper fabrication.

The stampede toward integration was a defensive measure brought on by the First World War legacy of overexpanded productive capacity. During the four years following the outbreak of the war, the world produced some 6 million tons of copper—over half as much as the entire nineteenth-century output. The American copper industry, exclusive of foreign-owned properties, supplied 60 per cent of the wartime demand.

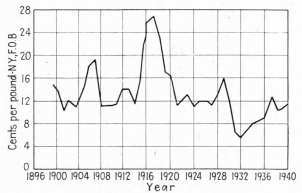

Fig. 14.—Electrolytic copper prices. (Cents per pound, f.o.b. New York.) (*Metal Statistics, American Metal Market, New York*, 1941.)

This was accomplished by large-scale operations, improved technology, and greater mechanization. Witness the fact that some deposits yielding only 17 to 20 lb. of copper per ton of ore were being operated at a profit. However, this required tremendous increases in fixed capital expenditures, and when the postwar curtailment in demand for the metal set in the industry had not only an overexpanded capacity but also a less flexible cost structure. Unit costs rose as idle capacity increased, and companies looked to integration as an avenue for sustained demand.

Competition.—Copper is purchased spasmodically because it is a highly durable capital good. The copper that is not fabricated by the producers is sold by the producers' selling agents, 10 such agents handling the bulk of the business. Much of the copper is taken by large consumers like the Western Electric, General Electric, Westinghouse, and John A. Roebling Sons. These large fabricators usually calculate their manufacturing requirements on a quarterly basis and place their orders with one or several producers, calling for periodic delivery to suit their demand. They sometimes deviate from this policy, however, and may buy more or less than their estimated short-run requirements, depending upon their inventories and anticipated price changes.

Competition is usually mild in markets consisting of few buyers and few sellers. Since the output of copper is virtually controlled by four companies, some measure of price control would seem to be both feasible and desirable. According to economic theory a perfectly competitive market is predicated upon two assumptions: (1) the existence of a large number of buyers whose separate and independent actions have but a negligible effect upon price; (2) a large number of sellers who must take what they can get because the total sales of any one seller have likewise a negligible effect upon price. In the copper industry neither of these conditions is fulfilled by reason of the small number of both buyers and sellers. Copper prices might therefore be expected to be "sticky," that is, characterized by infrequent change. The facts, however, do not conform to the theory, as an analysis of the prices of copper will show. Figure 14 portrays the average annual price of copper since 1900. The price is characterized by highly irregular fluctuations throughout the entire period, and if monthly or daily prices were plotted the irregularity would be still more pronounced. What is the explanation of this great price irregularity where, as above implied, the opposite might be expected? There are several possible reasons.

Electrolytically refined copper, as previously noted, is a perfectly homogeneous substance. A yard of cotton cloth varies from one manufacturer to another in tensile strength, fineness of the yarn, regularity of weave, etc.; a gallon of gasoline differs from another in flash point, freedom from carbonization, tendency to vapor-lock, etc.; but a pound of refined copper is like any other in every respect. This removes all traces of quasimonopoly attributable to one producer's product and transfers more of the competitive efforts to the market place where it manifests itself in the form of higgling over price. This aspect of the copper market together with the small number of buyers and sellers may explain why copper prices are so irregular.

Another possible reason is the influence of imports and exports. Partly because of its homogeneous character, copper enjoys a world market. Although the United States has been the world's largest producer of copper for many years (60 per cent during the First World War, now less than 40 per cent), the foreign producers exert a considerable influence upon the American market. A commodity having a world-wide market is subject to more severe price competition as a result of a greater range of regional differences in cost of production. Costs of producing copper in 1941 have been estimated to range from 4 to 6 cents per pound in Chile and 2.5 cents in Africa to 6 to 12 cents in the United States.

Secondary or scrap copper is exerting an increasingly important influence upon the price of copper. Copper is practically indestructible. Despite the fact that there is an annual loss of copper in the sense that some of it, once used, is never salvaged, such losses are considerably less than the annual production of virgin copper. Consequently, a net annual increment is added to the world's copper stock, and this con-

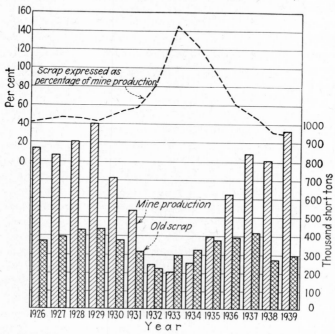

Fig. 15.—United States copper mine production and recovery from old scrap. (*From Elliott et al, "International Control in Non-Ferrous Metals," The Macmillan Company, New York, 1937; Mineral Industries, 1940.*)

stitutes an increasing potential threat to the virgin copper producers. The importance of old scrap is shown in Fig. 15. Note the proportion of scrap to virgin copper. Remelting and refining scrap is less costly than the extraction of copper from ores and alloys of copper can be fabricated anew without breaking them down into their constituent elements. Figure 15 clearly reveals that the supply of scrap entering the market is relatively constant. Consequently virgin copper production absorbs the brunt of the widely fluctuating demand for the metal.

Stabilizing the Market.—The volatility of copper prices is a constant source of despair to the copper producers. The problem has been attacked from three different angles. The industry has endeavored to expand the uses of copper, it has tried numerous valorization plans, and it has obtained tariff protection.

The integration movement, as explained above, was an effort on the part of individual companies to expand the market for copper. The formation of the Copper and Brass Research Association represented a joint effort to accomplish the same end. Its stated purpose was "to advance, through cooperative effort, the knowledge and uses of copper and copper products."

The formation of the Copper Export Association, in 1919, was the first experiment in valorization. This was a cartel for the conduct of export trade. Authorized by the Webb-Pomerene Act, which permitted American companies to combine for purposes of export trade, the specific purpose of the Copper Export Association was to liquidate the large post-war stocks of copper held by the government and the refiners. Aided by a rising demand for copper, this association had successfully accomplished its purpose by 1923, when it was dissolved.

A second valorization plan was inaugurated in 1926. This association, known as Copper Exporters, Inc., included 95 per cent of the world's copper producers. Its immediate aim was to eliminate copper brokers, to establish daily copper prices in Europe, and to ration sales among its members. For a while the association seemed to be successful. Copper prices rose from 12 cents in 1927 to 20 cents early in 1929, and when a reaction set in the cartel succeeded in pegging the price at 18 cents for several months. However, in the spring of 1930 copper prices broke and retreated in disorder to less than 6 cents a pound. Since that time no less than four world conferences of copper producers were called to restore order, but all broke up in discord.

The basic cause for the failure of the several attempts to administer price control is the advent of new low-cost copper-producing areas. Since 1925, African copper (Belgian Congo and Rhodesia) has increased from 6 to 16 per cent of the world's annual output. Ore from the Belgian Congo contains 6.5 per cent copper, as against 1.4 per cent in the United States. During the world-wide depression African copper was mined, smelted, refined, and delivered in European or American ports at 7 cents a pound. Since 1925 Canadian copper production has increased from 4 to 10 per cent of the world output. The efforts to boost the price of copper, though successful at the outset, served only to stimulate the exploitation of these richer deposits. As a result of the new low-cost areas American copper production in 1939 was less than a third of the world output in contrast with 55 per cent in 1925. Other reasons that have contributed to the failure of attempts to revive valorization are the refusal of Canadian producers to curtail their output of by-product copper, the widespread depreciation of currencies during the decade of the thirties, and the imposition of a duty on copper imports into the United States.

Domestic copper producers have been shielded from low-cost foreign copper since 1932 when a 4-cent duty was imposed on imports. The strongest proponents of the tariff were the small producers whose costs were higher than those of the large companies such as Kennecott, Anaconda, and Phelps Dodge. However, the large producers raised little objection because copper was then selling at 5 cents, stocks on hand were up to 500,000 tons—a full year's supply under normal conditions—and demand was very small.

The importance of copper as a basic war material is illustrated by recent developments. The gradual resumption of business raised the price from 5 cents in 1932 to about 9 cents in 1936. The sudden spurt in business activity in 1936–1937 sent the price up to 15 cents, stocks on hand having receded to a mere 100,000 tons. Thereupon, President Roosevelt warned business of his disapproval of speculative up-bidding of prices. The brief boom in business collapsed, and in 1938 copper was again down to 9 cents. The Second World War stimulated the demand for copper, and prices rose following the placement of French orders in the American market. Huge orders for copper were placed in 1940–1941 by domestic manufacturers after our national defense efforts got under way. It is estimated that the copper industry will produce 1,800,000 tons of copper in 1942. About 1,000,000 tons will be needed for military purposes and 400,000 tons for essential civilian use. In 1942 civilian consumption of copper was prohibited for such things as building supplies, hardware, burial equipment, and jewelry.

Future of the Industry.—Since copper is a highly durable producer's good, the industry is extremely sensitive to the pulse of business during periods of international peace. Because it is an indispensable material of war, the immediate outlook is naturally colored by the prospects of the duration of present hostilities. Demand for copper will last as long as the Second World War lasts, and the American copper industry will undoubtedly prosper as long as we are engaged in the job of strengthening our national defenses. The long-term outlook is extremely uncertain, but the prospects for the American copper industry, especially its position in the world market, are none too hopeful because of the existence of large copper mines in other parts of the world that can be mined at much lower costs and because of the ease with which copper enters into international trade.

CHAPTER VII

THE ALUMINUM INDUSTRY

Aluminum is a man-made metal, that is to say, unlike iron or copper, it has never been found in nature in metallic form. This accounts for the fact that the aluminum industry did not develop until shortly before the dawn of the twentieth century. It also accounts for the fact that for many years there was only one company manufacturing the metal in the United States.

The Development of the Industry.—For convenience the development of the industry may be divided into three periods.

1. Period of laboratory experimentation—up to 1888.
2. Formative period—1888–1904.
3. Period of rapid growth—since 1904.

The first period is characterized by a long struggle to separate the metal from the raw material. Over a century has elapsed since scientists first attempted to isolate aluminum. About 1825 a Danish chemist succeeded in obtaining a small quantity of the metal. Thirty years later a French professor, Deville, developed a chemical process which reduced the cost of aluminum to approximately $90 a pound. The most significant development in this period was the simultaneous discovery, in 1886, by Charles M. Hall in the United States and P. L. T. Heroult in France, of the electrolytic process. This discovery brought aluminum out of the price class of precious metals and opened the way for a new industry.[1]

The second period is characterized by intensive efforts to improve the technology of production and to find a market for the metal. During this period the price of aluminum was brought down from $5 a pound to 33 cents a pound. Commercial production was begun in 1888 by the Pittsburgh Reduction Company which was organized that year by Hall and several Pittsburgh capitalists. The principal use of aluminum during this period was for cooking utensils. In seeking to expand the market, efforts were made to substitute aluminum for brass castings and sheet brass. Aluminum wire for electrical purposes was made as early as 1898. Owing to a lack of fabricating equipment and a lack of knowledge as to the proper ways of shaping aluminum products, the Pittsburgh Reduction Company built foundries and sheet and wire mills to promote

[1] WARSHOW, H. T., *Representative Industries in the United States*, p. 7, Henry Holt and Company, Inc., New York, 1928.

the uses of the new metal. Progress, however, was slow. In 1904 annual production was still less than 5,000 tons despite the fact that the price had been brought down to 33 cents a pound.

Beginning in 1904, aluminum production entered the stage of rapid growth (see Fig. 16). In 1940, production was over 200,000 tons. Although production increased fortyfold in this period, the other industrial metals suffered no perceptible competition. In 1940 aluminum

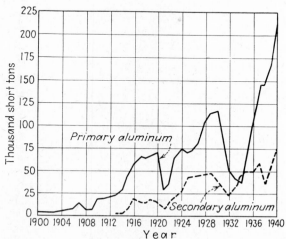

Fig. 16.—United States production of aluminum. (*U. S. Bureau of Mines.*)

production was only a fourth that of copper and less than 0.5 per cent that of steel. Comparison by weight, however, somewhat understates the relative importance of aluminum because of its lightness.

The rapid growth of the industry during this period was the result of numerous developments. The first World War opened a new market for aluminum in military aircraft because of its light weight. The rise of the automobile industry also provided a large outlet. It has been estimated that in 1920 the average automobile, excepting Fords, utilized 120 pounds of aluminum. Steel-cored aluminum cable virtually supplanted copper cable for high-tension power lines. Aluminum and aluminum alloys found increased usage in machinery of various kinds, especially in reciprocating parts, where again its lightness was advantageous. Improvements in the art of fabrication further increased the uses of aluminum. Parts for washing machines, vacuum cleaners, radios, and electrical appliances were made as a result of improved die casting of aluminum. Furniture and structural shapes for aircraft were made from aluminum following the development of extrusion. This process consists of forcing hot aluminum ingots through a die—analogous to forcing toothpaste out of a tube. Finally, the long-run price trend of aluminum throughout this period was slowly downward. Consequently, the uses of aluminum were multiplied as it became cheaper.

Present-day Methods of Manufacture.—In the present state of the arts, bauxite is the only commercially useful aluminum ore. Arkansas is the principal domestic source of bauxite suitable for aluminum manufacture. The aluminum industry normally consumes half of the tonnage

PLATE 14.—Open pit mining of bauxite. (*Courtesy of Hobbs, D. B., "Aluminum," Bruce Publishing Company. Photo by Margaret Bourke-White.*)

of bauxite mined each year. The abrasive and chemical industries utilize the remainder. The major foreign bauxite deposits are in British, Dutch, and French Guiana, southern France, and Hungary.

The manufacture of aluminum from bauxite involves two distinct steps: first, the purification of the ore; and, second, the conversion of the aluminum oxide, called alumina, into the metal—aluminum.

1. After the ore has been mined, it is crushed, washed, and baked in rotary kilns to remove moisture and other impurities as far as possible. After screening, the bauxite is ready for concentration to separate the alumina. Of several methods used, the wet Bayer process predominates.

The ore concentrate is treated with caustic soda and a solution formed from which the iron, silica, and other impurities are removed; the aluminum hydrate is then precipitated, purified, and dried—the end product being aluminum oxide (alumina). Until 1938, when a plant was built in Mobile, Ala., the East St. Louis plant was the only concentration plant in North America.

2. The manufacture of aluminum from the concentrate, alumina, is performed by electricity in a series of reduction cells, each producing about 250 pounds of aluminum per day.

PLATE 15.—Washing bauxite ore. (*Courtesy of Hobbs, D. B., "Aluminum," Bruce Publishing Company. Photo by Margaret Bourke-White.*)

To start the operation, cryolite, a sodium-aluminum-fluoride mineral, is first dissolved by the passage of an electric current through the carbon lined cell, illustrated in Fig. 17. When the cryolite has been fused, alumina is added. The electric current breaks down the alumina into its component parts—aluminum and oxygen. The oxygen, liberated in the reaction, combines with the carbon of the anodes. The resulting carbon dioxide and carbon monoxide escape through the crust at the top where the carbon monoxide burns. The molten aluminum is deposited on the bottom of the cell and about every two days is tapped into a large mixing ladle from which it is cast into pigs.[1] Since the cryolite bath material is not affected in the operation, more alumina is added to the molten cryolite, thus making the process a continuous one.

[1] This description is adapted from a pamphlet entitled "The New Industrial-Arts Metal—I," by Douglas B. Hobbs.

The production of one pound of aluminum requires approximately two pounds of alumina, one pound of caustic soda, three-quarters of a pound of carbon electrode, and 12 kilowatt-hours of electricity, an amount sufficient to keep a 40-watt lamp burning constantly for 12½ days.

PLATE 16.—Rotary kiln bakes the ore to remove moisture and impurities. (*Courtesy of Hobbs, D. B., "Aluminum," Bruce Publishing Company. Photo by Margaret Bourke-White.*)

The importance of cheap power has restricted the location of reduction plants to places where cheap hydroelectric power is available in large amounts.

The reduction plants of the Aluminum Company of America are located at (1) Niagara Falls, N. Y., where power from the Falls is used, (2) Massena, N. Y., which uses water power from the St. Lawrence river, (3) Badin, N. C., utilizing water power from the Yadkin river, (4) Alcoa, Tenn., where power is derived from the Little Tennessee river system, and (5) a plant at Vancouver, Wash., where electricity is obtained from the water of the Columbia River. The aluminum industry uses in one day enough electricity to supply a city of 17,000 homes for one year.

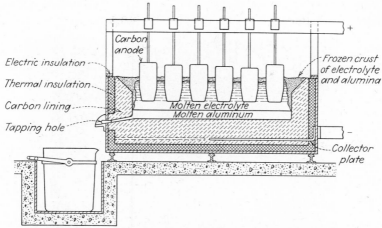

Fig. 17.—Cross section of an aluminum reduction cell. (*Courtesy of Aluminum Company of America.*)

Plate 17.—Aluminum reduction cells. (*Courtesy of Hobbs, D. B., "Aluminum," Bruce Publishing Company.*)

Many attempts have been made to lower the cost of manufacturing the metal. Efforts to utilize lower grade ores are mentioned below.

Considerable research is being directed toward the improvement of aluminum technology to make possible, among other things, the direct smelting of the ore and the production of aluminum alloys by direct smelting rather than by a mixture of the pure metals.

PLATE 18.—Pouring pig aluminum.   (*Courtesy of Hobbs, D. B.,* "*Aluminum,*" *Bruce Publishing Company.   Photo by Margaret Bourke-White.*)

Properties and Uses of Aluminum.—Aluminum, like copper, is a special-purpose metal. This fact grows out of its peculiar physical properties. Its outstanding quality is light weight. A given volume of aluminum weighs only 30 per cent as much as an equal volume of copper. Naturally aluminum is preferred in all uses where lightness is an important factor. Hence its use in the transportation field and particularly in air transportation. Aluminum is a good conductor of heat. This property together with light weight explains its usefulness for kitchen ware. Aluminum is a good conductor of electricity—only slightly inferior to copper. Allowing for differences in weight and electric conductivity, the margin of indifference is about two to one, *i.e.*, aluminum is the cheaper conductor when its price per pound is not over twice the price of copper. More than 400,000 miles of steel-cored aluminum cable are in use for transmission of high-tension electricity. The advantage of aluminum for this use lies in the fact that, because of its light weight, towers can be spaced farther apart, resulting in lower costs of power-line construction and maintenance.

TABLE XVIII.—USE OF VIRGIN ALUMINUM PRODUCED BY THE ALUMINUM COMPANY OF AMERICA

(Average over a period of years)

	Per Cent
Transportation (land, air and water)	33
Cooking utensils	16
Electrical conductor	12
Machinery (elec. appliances, etc.)	11
Building construction	6
Chemical	6
Nonferrous foundry and metal working	5
Iron and steel metallurgy	4
Food industry	4
Miscellaneous	3
Total	100

Source: Aluminum Company of America.

Aluminum is soft and therefore easily shaped by rolling, forging, casting, extrusion, or drawing, and it can also be welded. It unites easily with certain other metals to form alloys. Its affinity for oxygen led to the discovery of the Thermit process for separating other metals from their oxides. It has therefore cheapened the process of manufacturing pure chromium, manganese, vanadium, tungsten, molybdenum, and rarer metals. Table XVIII summarizes the principal uses of aluminum.

The Structure of the Industry.—The aluminum manufacturing industry embraces the mining of bauxite, the concentration of the ore, the reduction of alumina to aluminum, and, finally, the fabrication of the aluminum into finished products.

Bauxite for aluminum manufacture is mined by only one company, the Republic Mining and Manufacturing Company, a subsidiary of the Aluminum Company of America. Several other companies engage in bauxite mining in the United States, but their production is entirely for the chemical and abrasive industries.

The two concentration and five reduction plants in the United States are the property of the Aluminum Company of America—the successor to the Pittsburgh Reduction Company. Until recently, there was only one other plant in North America—located on the Saguenay River in the province of Quebec. The Canadian plant is owned by Aluminum, Ltd., with which the Aluminum Company of America has financial connections.

In the fabrication branch of the industry, which includes sand foundries, sheet rolling mills, powder and paint factories, and cooking utensil manufacturers, etc. there is more decentralization of ownership. The Census of Manufactures in 1939 lists 162 establishments employing about 17,000 workers and producing products valued at 170 million dollars, of which 63 million dollars is value added by manufacture.

The Aluminum Company of America and Its Present Position in the Industry.—The history of the domestic aluminum industry is largely the history of one company, the Aluminum Company of America, organized in 1907. Until 1941 it was the sole producer of primary aluminum. Its productive capacity in 1926 was just slightly less than the combined capacity of the four foreign producers who made up the international aluminum cartel, and in that year it produced in its North American plants about 43 per cent of the world production of aluminum. The rapid expansion of the industry in other countries and the rise of new foreign producers such as Japan and the U.S.S.R. reduced its share in 1939 to about a third of the world production.

The Control of Bauxite.—The strong position of the Aluminum Company has long been attributed to its alleged monopoly of domestic bauxite deposits. Early in its history the company followed the policy of acquiring bauxite deposits in the United States and between the years 1905 and 1909, according to a report of the Federal Trade Commission, "acquired a monopoly of the commercially available bauxite in the United States suitable for the manufacture of aluminum." It also obtained control of substantial deposits in British and Dutch Guiana and interests in bauxite mining companies in Europe. Again in 1926 the Department of Justice alleged that the company "owns practically all the bauxite lands in the United States."[1] These charges of monopoly of bauxite deposits are vigorously denied by the Aluminum Company, which claims that it owns less than one-half of the well-known deposits of the United States and only a small fraction of the available bauxite deposits of South America.

While the Aluminum Company has up to the present vigorously followed the policy of acquiring bauxite deposits, it is believed that the future will witness the abandonment of this policy for the following reasons: (1) the little likelihood that new producers entering the production of primary aluminum will offer serious competition, and (2) the possibility that the high-grade bauxite now used may not be essential to aluminum production.

For a great number of years many attempts have been made to find a substitute for bauxite, such as labradorite and kaolin, and to develop a process that would permit the utilization of lower grade bauxite. Several years ago the Republic Mining and Manufacturing Company was reported to have perfected a process capable of utilizing low-grade bauxite. A mineral called "Alunite" seems to offer the best prospect

[1] Benham Report, Department of Justice, p. 84.

as a substitute for bauxite. The Bohn Aluminum and Brass Company and Kalunite Inc. have done considerable research on this mineral, and in 1941 it was announced that the latter company was seeking 16 million dollars of capital to erect three plants in the West to make aluminum from this mineral. It is estimated that alumina made from alunite will cost \$35 a ton in contrast with \$33 for alumina made from bauxite. However, the new process yields by-products (sulphuric acid and sulphate potash) worth about \$25 a ton of alumina produced. The chief drawback to the use of Alunite seems to be the limited deposits of the mineral.

Control of Primary Aluminum.—The ownership of vast domestic bauxite deposits gives the Aluminum Company substantial control over the production of primary aluminum in the United States. Fabricators of primary aluminum cannot avoid the price control of the Aluminum Company by the importation of metal from abroad. This is due to (1) the financial connection between the company and the Canadian aluminum producer, Aluminum, Ltd.; (2) the control of world aluminum production by the international aluminum cartel of which the Canadian Company is a member; and (3) the duty imposed by the United States tariff.

Canada is our chief source of imports, but it has never been an important source for the general aluminum market as is indicated by the fact that practically all imports from it are handled by the Aluminum Company of America for its own use. The cartel agreement between foreign producers has not been made public, but there is reason to believe that it includes some regulations of aluminum exports into the world market. Whatever the contract may be, imports of aluminum, other than those for the Aluminum Company, during the period 1924–1933 amounted to less than 10 per cent of the total annual United States supplies of all aluminum.[1] Such aluminum as does come in must pay a duty imposed by the tariff, because this industry has always received the benefit of tariff protection. Under the Payne-Aldrich Act (1909) the duty was 7 cents per pound. This was decreased to 2 cents in the Underwood-Simmons Act (1913) and later raised to 5 cents by the Fordney-McCumber Act (1922). The tariff act of 1930 provided for a duty of 4 cents per pound. That these duties were used not so much to reduce imports but rather to maintain prices is indicated by the fact that the company has always changed its prices in accordance with changes in the tariff. The net results of the tariff are higher prices for the consumer and greater profits for the Aluminum Company.

Thus these three factors, the tie-up with Aluminum, Ltd., the cartel, and the tariff, give the Aluminum Company virtual control over the price of primary aluminum. Note in Fig. 18 that the price of primary alumi-

[1] "Report on Aluminum Industry," N.R.A. Research and Planning Division, p. 8.

num was slowly declining during the widespread business prosperity of the late twenties. Observe also that the price of aluminum declined very little during the great depression of 1930 when prices of most other commodities were scraping bottom.

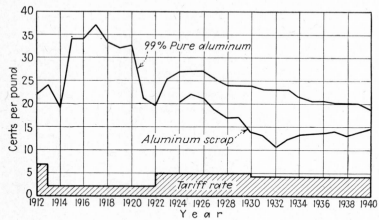

Fig. 18.—Average annual price of new aluminum and scrap aluminum. (*Metal Statistics,* *American Metal Market, New York,* 1941.)

Secondary Aluminum.—Since aluminum is an indestructible metal and has a high value per pound it is to be expected that some of it will eventually return to the market in the form of scrap to be remelted. The scrap at present arises from borings and machine-shop scrap, heavy castings scrap, fabricating scrap, drosses and skimmings, and miscellaneous scrap. For certain purposes, especially for aluminum castings, secondary or scrap aluminum is as efficient as the virgin metal.

While the supply of aluminum scrap is gradually increasing, as shown in Fig. 16, its price still appears to be controlled by the price of primary aluminum as shown in Fig. 18. The chief reasons for this are (1) that the Aluminum Company would have to cut drastically the price of primary aluminum to push secondary aluminum entirely out of the market, a policy which would greatly reduce its income; (2) producers of scrap aluminum also have nothing to gain by widening the price differential between the two metals because the total supply of scrap is limited and relatively inelastic. As long as the demand for aluminum is large and the supply of scrap limited, a small price differential is sufficient to absorb the available supply of scrap. However, the trend in the supply of scrap is upward, as Fig. 16 shows, and when it represents a larger proportion of the total supply of aluminum than it now does the price of the virgin metal will have less influence over the price of scrap, and either the differential will widen or the price of aluminum will have to decline. This may be one explanation for the downward price trend of virgin aluminum since 1926.

Aluminum Fabricators.—The comparatively recent introduction of aluminum as an industrial metal and the reluctance with which it was received made it necessary for the Aluminum Company to enter the field of fabrication. The company also undertook intensive research for the purpose of promoting the use of aluminum.

Despite the increase in the number of independent fabricating companies, the position of the Aluminum Company in this branch of the industry is very strong, as Table XIX shows. During the period 1924–

TABLE XIX.—PLACE OF THE ALUMINUM COMPANY OF AMERICA IN THE SEVERAL BRANCHES OF THE INDUSTRY

Product	Percentage produced by Aluminum Co.
Bauxite, for aluminum	100.00
Alumina	100.00
Aluminum, virgin	100.00
Fabricated aluminum	
Aluminum sheets	60.00
Extruded shapes	40.00
Aluminum forgings	40.00
Aluminum tubing, wire, bar, rod, etc	60.00
Aluminum foil	50.00
Aluminum pistons	22.00
Aluminum bronze powder	50.00
Aluminum cooking utensils	50.00

Source: Division of Research & Planning, N.R.A., and *U. S. v. Aluminum Company of America*, Petition filed April, 1937.

1933, the Aluminum Company retained for its own use from one-half to three-fourths of its primary aluminum production. Thus, the Aluminum Company not only supplies its customers with virgin aluminum but is also their chief competitor. This dual relationship, according to the company's critics, gives it an important advantage over its competitors. It is claimed that the company maintains too high a price for the primary aluminum it sells to its competitors and sells its fabricated products, in competition with them, at a price which does not fully cover their costs. The profits made on the former more than make up the losses on the latter. Thus, the public pays too high a price for aluminum products and the progress of independent fabricators is impeded.

Profits of the Aluminum Company.—Although it is difficult, if not impossible, to determine the extent to which the Aluminum Company has extracted monopoly gains from its consumers, there is no doubt that the company's activities have been extremely profitable. Since its founding, Aluminum Company of America has paid its stockholders 227 million dollars in cash and securities. This represents an annual return of 55 per cent on the paid-in capital according to the government authorities, who point out that 18 million dollars of the total paid-in capital of 21 millions was not paid until 1925. On the other hand, the company officials allege that the earnings average only 10 per cent per year on the stockholders' equity.[1] The difference between these two rates of return is due to the different bases used. The one expresses earnings as a percentage of capital paid in and the other expresses them as a percentage of capital employed which includes both paid-in capital and earnings ploughed back, *i.e.*, capital and surplus.

The Aluminum Company and the Government.—During the past 20 years the conduct of the Aluminum Company has been investigated several times by various agencies of the Federal government. Practically every charge that can be made against a monopoly has been made against this corporation. In 1912 the government investigated the company, and in what is known as the consent decree of 1912 the company agreed to abstain from certain practices. In 1924 the company's activities came under the scrutiny of the Federal Trade Commission. The company was accused by independents of canceling orders without sufficient warning or cause; of unreasonable delays in deliveries; of discouraging potential competition in certain fabricating lines by refusing to accept orders for pig aluminum from certain companies; of price discrimination; of full line forcing; and several other charges were made. After protracted hearings the Commission decided that the charges had not been proved. In 1931 the Bausch Machine Tool Company, an independent aluminum fabricator, instituted a suit against the company for 9 million dollars damages. The lower court decided in favor of the Bausch Company, but was overruled by the United States Court of Appeals which ordered a retrial. The case was finally settled out of court. In 1937 the Department of Justice again brought suit against the company under the Sherman Antitrust Act accusing the company of monopoly, conspiracy, and alleged general misconduct. In October 1941, Judge Caffey rendered a decision in favor of the company, stating that the government had failed to sustain any of its charges.

In view of the large profits earned by the company it is surprising that attempts have not been made by others to enter this industry. The newspapers have reported, from time to time, that new interests were contemplating entering into the production of primary aluminum. However, until recently, no one else has chosen to go into the business of making primary aluminum. The reasons for the hesitation, heretofore, of outsiders to enter the industry may be listed as follows:[2]

[1] *Fortune*, May, 1941.
[2] WARSHOW, H. T., "Representative Industries in the U. S.," p. 62, Henry Holt and Company, Inc., New York, 1928.

1. All the available high-grade bauxite deposits are already controlled by the Aluminum Company of America and other aluminum producers of the world.

2. No water power sites remain to be developed without the expenditure of a huge outlay of capital.

3. An enormous capital investment is necessary, not only for plant and equipment, but also for the possible conduct of trade and price wars.

4. There is fear that the Aluminum Company may restrain and intimidate new competition.

5. Few technical men familiar with aluminum technology are available.

The tremendous upsurge in demand for aluminum caused by the initiation of the national defense program has finally ushered in at least a few competitors for the Aluminum Company of America. About 90 per cent of the weight of an airplane is aluminum; consequently, the aircraft boom begun in 1940 speedily created a bottleneck in aluminum. Since the Second World War began United States aluminum capacity has been increased from 160,000 to 425,000 tons annually, but that is not enough. To relieve the shortage an RFC loan of 16 million dollars was made in 1940 to the Reynolds Metal Company, a fabricator of nonferrous metals, to build an aluminum ingot plant at Lister, Ala. Before that plant of 20,000-ton capacity was completed, the company began building another plant of 30,000-ton capacity in Washington where it can use electric power from the Bonneville Dam. The government has also subsidized the construction of a 35,000-ton plant to be operated by Bohn Aluminum and Brass Company, a 30,000-ton plant for Union Carbide and Carbon Company, and a 15,000-ton plant for the Olin Corporation.

Future of the Aluminum Industry.—Current developments in the industry seem to indicate that this field, heretofore dominated by one company, will be opened to competition. Some competitors already have a foothold, and if national defense demand for the metal continues to expand, others may be encouraged to enter, especially in view of the hydroelectric power available in the West and the not-too-friendly attitude of the government toward the leading company. However, we cannot be too optimistic about the future growth of competition because the Aluminum Company of America is likewise expanding capacity and reducing prices to meet the present emergency, and after the emergency has passed, this company may have an effective monopoly despite the existence of several comparatively small competitors.[1]

The industrial position of aluminum is not necessarily secure. Aluminum competes to a limited extent with copper and stainless steel. Where

[1] In October, 1941, the Aluminum Company of America cut the price of ingot aluminum to 15 cents a pound.

light weight, as in aircraft, is especially important, aluminum has had clear advantage but another lightweight metal, magnesium, appears to be on the threshold of commercial development. Magnesium is only two-thirds the weight of aluminum, and it can now be made almost as cheaply. Naturally an airplane made of magnesium could carry a heavier pay load than one made of aluminum.

It may be appropriate to close this section of our study of primary metals with just a word about technology. What has just been said about aluminum may be equally applicable to the other primary metals; i.e., their place in the industrial world of the future may be seriously challenged by technological developments. Already we hear of the possible use of plastics as a substitute for light sheet steel in automobile bodies and fenders. It has been predicted that within a generation the steel industry will shrink in size to a point where one large company can supply all of our needs for that metal. Except in times of war, copper is used primarily as a conductor of electricity, but copper for this purpose is not necessarily assured because experiments are already being conducted, with some success, in wireless transmission of electric power.

PART III
THE METAL FABRICATING INDUSTRIES

CHAPTER VIII

MAKING ASSEMBLED METAL PRODUCTS—
THE DEVELOPMENT OF MASS PRODUCTION

Thus far we have studied the primary metal industries: iron, steel, copper, and aluminum. The processes by which these and other metals are converted into finished products are known as metal fabrication. This appears, offhand, to be a bewildering task, for the products are countless in number and infinitely varied in size, shape, and purpose. They range from delicate wrist watches to mammoth ocean liners, and intermediate on the scale are locomotives, automobiles, printing presses, refrigerators, vacuum cleaners, etc. However, these utterly dissimilar articles are made by processes that are basically similar.

It is to be noted, first of all, that all of the products are composed principally of the four metals we have mentioned. It is true that glass, cloth, rubber, and other nonmetallic materials enter into their composition, but, primarily, they are metal products. The first step, as we saw, is to shape the raw materials as they come from the refining furnaces. This is done by rolling, casting, and hammering. But these processes give only crudely shaped castings or forgings, or rolled stock such as sheets, plates, rods, and bars. For most purposes we must have metal parts that are accurately and precisely shaped. For this, we turn to machine tools which do such work as drilling, boring, planing, and grinding.

Shaping the Parts to Be Fabricated.—A machine tool is a tool which is mechanically operated, is nonportable, and removes metal in the form of chips. Originally, most, if not all, tools were held and operated by hand. For instance, a plane is a tool for smoothing a flat surface. Every carpenter working with wood uses one. If the plane is driven by mechanical rather than hand power, you have a machine tool called a planer. Likewise, if we mechanically actuate a saw, or a chisel, or a brace and bit, or any of the other familiar hand tools, we have thereby created machine tools. The term "machine tool" is associated today entirely with the finishing of various metals to very accurate dimensions.

There are dozens of different kinds of machine tools, and it may be helpful if we consider each of these as consisting of five main parts: (1) the bed or column; (2) the table or chuck for holding the work; (3) the driving mechanism for driving the work; (4) the tool or cutter; (5) the tool feed or mechanism for moving the tool.

Bed or Column.—The bed or column serves to support all the driving and work-holding parts. It is comparable to the foundation of a house. The bed or column is usually of great strength and weight so that it can absorb all strain and vibration encountered in cutting metal.

Table or Chuck.—The work to be machined is held in place by means of either a table or chuck. A table is a flat surface to which the work is clamped with the aid of auxiliary attachments known as "jigs" or "fixtures." A chuck is a circular work-holding device equipped with jaws that operate on the principle of a vice. Jigs guide the cutting tool, and fixtures hold the work rigidly.

Driving Mechanism.—This part of the machine tool furnishes the power to the work by means of pulleys, cams, gears, etc. Various speeds are obtained by changing gears, using the same principle as is employed in an automobile engine. Usually this part of the machine tool applies to driving the work only.

Tool or Cutter.—The cutting tool is the part that removes the metal. It may be a carborundum wheel or a twist drill, a chisel, or a more intricate cutting tool such as the milling cutter. The cutting tool itself may be only a few inches in size and may appear to be dwarfed to insignificance because of the great contrast in size between it and the other parts. However, it is the heart of the mechanism, the part that actually does the work.

Tool Feed.—The tool must move in relation to the work or it would be cutting in one spot only. The mechanism for moving the tool is called the tool feed. The tool feed is usually power-driven because the metal being cut offers great resistance.

Classes of Machine Tools.—It has been stated previously that there are dozens of different types of machine tools. However, all machine tools may be divided into two broad classes—rotating and plane, depending upon whether they are designed to remove metal from cylindrical or flat surfaces. The principal rotating types are lathes, grinders, boring mills, and drill presses.

Lathes.—The lathe is the oldest of machine tools. In many respects, it is the most important machine tool because of its widespread use. Almost no general shop of any size is without one. It was developed in response to the need for a tool to turn the pistons and bore the cylinders of the early steam engines. In fact, the perfection of the steam engine awaited the development of the engine lathe, so called because of this early application. In its simplest form, the work to be machined is mounted between two spindles, one of which is mechanically driven.

PLATE 19.—Engine lathe. (*Courtesy of Pratt & Whitney Company.*)

PLATE 20.—Turret lathe. Showing turret holding six different cutting tools, which are used in sequence. (*Courtesy of The Warner and Swasey Company.*)

A cutting tool is held against the work by mounting it on a sliding mechanism, known as the "carriage." As the work is revolved, the tool is slowly moved across the work, parallel to the axis of the work. The result is a turned cylinder, round, and the same diameter from one end to the other.

Grinders.—As greater need for accuracy and precision arose in the working of metals, the modern precision grinder was designed. A com-

PLATE 21.—Grinder. Grinding an automobile crankshaft. (*Courtesy of the Norton Company.*)

mon type is the cylindrical grinder. It is similar to a lathe but many times heavier. This is necessary to absorb vibration which would interfere with the accuracy of the work. Like the lathe, it has a live center spindle or "headstock" and a dead center spindle or "tailstock." Instead of a cutting tool, it uses a large abrasive wheel turning at very high speeds. Work is usually turned to about $\frac{1}{64}$ in. of size on a lathe and then finished to exact size on the grinder. This machine will grind round or straight within limits of plus or minus 2/10,000 in.

Boring Mills.—Most boring mills are of the vertical type, which is used for turning, boring, and facing large and heavy castings such as car

PLATE 22.—Boring mill. Boring an automobile cylinder block. (*Courtesy of The Heald Machine Company.*)

PLATE 23.—Radial drill. Drilling holes in a 6,000-lb. cast-steel frame. (*Courtesy of Cincinnati Bickford Tool Company.*)

wheels, flywheels, pistons, etc. A vertical boring mill has a heavy bed upon which is mounted a rotating circular table to which the work is clamped. Behind this table and attached to the bed are two vertical columns supporting a crossrail. The crossrail supports the cutting tool

PLATE 24.—Planer. (*Courtesy of The G. A. Gray Company.*)

which feeds sidewise in either direction. In principle, the vertical boring mill is similar to a lathe set on end. This machine tool is especially designed to work on large heavy castings because, as some one has said, "It is easier to lay a heavy piece down than to hang it up."

Drill Presses.—The most widely used drill press is the upright drill. This consists of a rotating drill spindle mounted vertically in bearings supported by an upright column. The cutting tool is a spiral drill firmly secured in a socket at the lower end of the spindle. The work to be drilled is supported by a table directly below the drill. Vertical pressure or feed is applied by hand or power to push the drill through the work as the drill rotates.

The principal plane types of machine tools are the planer, the shaper, and the milling machine, all of which are designed to remove metal from flat rather than cylindrical surfaces.

Planer.—The planer has a long heavy bed with deep V-shaped slide-ways running the entire length of the bed. A heavy rectangular table, called a platen, to which the work is clamped, slides on these ways. Near one end of the bed are two upright columns which support a crossrail. The cutting tool is mounted on the crossrail. As the platen moves back

PLATE 25.—Milling machine. (*Courtesy of Kearney and Trecker.*)

and forth through the full length of the bed, the work comes in contact with the rigidly held cutting tool which planes the top surface. The cutting tool is moved horizontally by a feed mechanism so as to plane the entire surface of the work.

Shaper.—The shaper works on the same principle as the planer with one exception. Instead of the work being moved back and forth under a rigidly held cutting tool, as on the planer, the work is stationary and the planing is done by a reciprocating cutting tool. The shaper, therefore, is used to plane small sections, whereas the planer is best adapted to plane heavy castings with larger cross sections.

Milling Machines.—The first milling machine was built about 1818 by Eli Whitney and was used for the manufacture of gun parts for the United States government. Many improvements and adaptations of this original miller have since been made.   Today, the universal miller is the most commonly used type in machine shops of the kind we are discussing.   The principle of the milling machine is that of the circular saw.   The cutting tool is a small rotary cutter with numerous teeth on its circumference.   The work moves in one direction and the cutter revolves in the opposite direction.   In addition to plane work, the miller performs intricate profiling.

Other Machine Tools.—In addition to lathes, drills, milling machines, planers, and grinders, there are many other kinds of machines but these are, for the most part, specialized adaptations of the standard machines we have been discussing.   For instance, during the first World War we endeavored in this country to make 75-mm. and 155-mm. guns of French design.   The French had always produced them by hand, but we could not follow this practice and make them in quantity as was necessary. As a consequence, we developed a number of special-purpose machine tools.   One of these, called a "lapper," was for the purpose of polishing the interior surfaces of the chambers of the recoil mechanisms of the guns. Similarly, other specialized machines have been built.

In recent years, an important trend in the development of machine tools has been the creation of combination machine tools.   Manufacturers now combine several machines into one.   For instance, the Bullard Machine Tool Company of Bridgeport makes what it calls a "Mult-au-matic" machine that is designed to do "boring, turning, facing, drilling, reaming, threading, grooving and a host of kindred operations."   The saving which such a machine effects in setting up and handling costs is readily apparent.   More work is done at one spot than formerly, and fewer setups are required.   This trend may be expected to continue.   To the extent that it does, existing classifications of machine tools will disappear.

Progress in the State of the Art of Machine Tools.—While on the subject of machine tools, we may note some of the ways in which improvements have been brought about in "the state of the art."   For many years, the "neck of the bottle" was the cutting tool.   The machine as a whole was no better than its cutting tool.   This was the critical point in the removal of excess metal from castings, forgings, stampings, or bar stock.   Great heat is generated from the friction of metal cutting metal. For example, in planing a plate of steel that is to be used for armor on a battleship so much friction is generated in cutting through the very hard steel that the chips coming from the operation become very hot.   The tool itself wore down quickly and this proved to be costly, not so much because of the price of the tool but because of the expense incident to stopping the machine, changing tools, etc.   Most important, perhaps, was the fact that the wear on the part of the tools made for inaccuracy in the product that was being turned out.

All these handicaps were reduced when Frederick W. Taylor began his notable experiments in the art of cutting metal at the Midvale Works in Philadelphia. Out of these experiments not only came principles of "scientific management," but also alloy tool steel which today enables the machine to be operated at much higher speeds, to take deeper cuts of metal, and to operate with much less frequent changes in tooling.

Great improvements have also been made in machine-tool beds. They are much more rigid and more accessible for repair and adjustment. They have been so designed as to contain magazines which hold material to be worked upon and which automatically feed these parts to the work point. Machines are now designed with more rigid housing so that a number of operations are performed simultaneously or successively.

Driving mechanisms likewise have been improved. Originally, machines were driven by belts attached to overhead shafts by means of pulleys. If it were necessary to operate one machine, the entire shaft had to be actuated. This wasted power. Now, machines are individually driven by motors, and these motors are built into the machine. This permits more flexible operation. Furthermore, individual machines now have a greater variety of speeds than formerly. They are also more automatic than formerly, stopping when the work is completed and starting at a prearranged time. They complete cycles of work and then begin again without the attention of the operators.

Jigs and fixtures have also been greatly improved in accuracy. The great expense that is sometimes incurred in these is fully justified by the extent to which they make for more accurate work, for the utilization of lower grades of labor, and for the reduction in what is known as setting-up time.

Finally, it is to be noted that with the improvements in the form of machine tools has come automatic lubrication which renders it unnecessary for the operator to know much about the maintenance of the machine. This, of course, enables the management to employ semiskilled rather than skilled workers.

ASSEMBLY OF PARTS INTO FINISHED PRODUCTS

The final step in the fabrication of metal products is the assembly. The several parts or components that make up the final article are now in the form of castings, stampings, and forgings, and all of them have been reduced, by machining operations, to exact dimensions. The task that remains is to combine or join these components so that, when assembled, they will operate in unison; in other words, the parts must be so arranged that they will function as a machine.

The methods used in assembling the parts depend very largely on the number of finished machines that are to be made. This matter of the quantity to be made has a great influence on all three of the major divisions of processing that we have been discussing, namely, shaping, machining, and assembly. Indeed, it influences all aspects of the management of the individual company. Because of this influence of quantity upon method let us center our discussion around this aspect.

Fabricated articles are made in quantities ranging from a single item such as a custom-built special-purpose ship, designed for example for the West Indies banana trade, all the way up to hundreds of thousands of an identical item, such as a low-priced automobile. For our purposes let us distinguish three classes of assembled products: (1) custom built, (2) mass production, (3) job lot. We shall start with the manufacture of the custom-built item and trace the evolution of assembly production methods.

Making a Custom-built Assembled Product.—Let us assume that there is a special order for a large Fourdrinier papermaking machine. The purchaser has in mind definite specifications: he will ask the maker to guarantee the capacity of the machine. It must turn out so many feet of paper per minute, consume only so much power per unit of output, be well adapted to certain types of raw material, etc. He will specify the conditions under which the machine is to operate. He will ask the maker to draw up preliminary designs and submit them along with estimates of cost.

When the contract is awarded, the successful firm then makes the drawings of the machine. Next, patterns for the castings are made and sent to the foundry for execution. Then the castings, forgings, bar stock, etc. are sent to the machine shops for finishing. Finally, the work of assembly begins.

The principal component is placed on the factory floor, or over a construction pit, or on a platform somewhat elevated above the shop floor. The workmen then bring other components and fix them in place and do any adjusting or fitting that is necessary. Sometimes the units that are brought together have themselves been assembled elsewhere within the plant or perhaps bought from outside suppliers; these are subassemblies. As mentioned before, the parts that do not fit are adjusted by filing or cutting or remachining. After assembly, the machine will be put on a test run. If the results are satisfactory, it is taken apart and shipped to the customer. A crew of workmen goes along to reassemble the parts and finally test the complete machine in the purchaser's plant under operating conditions. Six months may have been required to do all this work.

The foregoing description applies to most products that are made to special order. If the order calls for several identical machines, essentially the same methods are used. Apparatus or equipment or machines that fall into this category are specialized machine tools, ships, certain types of locomotives, chemical apparatus, unusual power-generating machinery, etc. A special-purpose article, however, is seldom unique in all respects. Some of its parts are common to a variety of models and wherever possible these common or standard components are used. But the emphasis that has been placed in this description on the lack of standardization is essentially accurate.

The Beginnings of Mass Production of Assembled Articles.—At the beginning of the factory system the manufacture of a custom-built product was even more expensive than it is today. In the early days it was called the "cut-and-try" system. Then the methods of shaping and machining the parts were so crude that the pieces could be fitted together only after repeated efforts which involved much filing, scraping, and polishing and a high degree of mechanical ability and judgment. Furthermore, the assembled article could not be readily repaired. A broken or worn-out part had to be replaced by one that was made and fitted by hand. In the case of rifles this was a great drawback in time of war. The first effort to improve on this system of production was made in small-arms manufacture by Eli Whitney about 1820.

Solution of the difficulties lay in the direction of (1) establishing strict limits to the dimensions of all parts, (2) developing more precise methods of shaping the parts so that they would fall within the prescribed limits, (3) accurate and, at the same time, more easily applied measurements of the parts, (4) separation of the shaping operations from the assembly work.

1. Standard sizes were established for each part, and from these standards only very limited departures were allowed. A part that was oversize or undersize to an appreciable degree was not acceptable. By thus strictly limiting the deviations or "tolerances," all accepted parts were, for practical purposes, identical.

2. It was soon found that it was one thing to establish a rigid standard and another matter to live up to it while keeping costs low. Efforts to do this brought forth improvements in methods of shaping and machining. Instead of forging a part by hand on a flat anvil, the drop-forge hammer was devised; jigs and fixtures and other appliances were contrived in order to make the crude machine tools of the day more accurate. The machine tools, as we saw, steadily became more precise and embodied more and more of the operator's skill.

3. Equal in importance to narrow tolerances and improved methods of shaping and machining was the development of accurate but simplified testing. The importance of this phase of progress should not be underestimated. It was only by a process of measurement that one could tell whether a part had been precisely machined. The more precise the parts

the more efficient the final product, provided, of course, that it was a product calling for precision. The difficulty of keeping the component within the limits that had been set was an ever-present one, even with the best of production methods. For example, there was a constant "growth" of the component as the tool wore down. Unless there were frequent checkups, the part would not fit.

The old method of checking the size of a part was to adjust a caliper or micrometer (measuring devices) to the actual size of the work, read

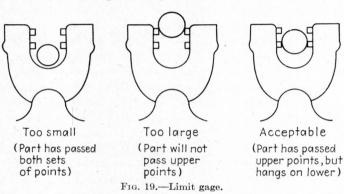

Too small	Too large	Acceptable
(Part has passed both sets of points)	(Part will not pass upper points)	(Part has passed upper points, but hangs on lower)

Fig. 19.—Limit gage.

the scale on the caliper, and then determine whether the size was acceptable. This method was slow; furthermore, it required skill and care on the part of the worker. Moreover, this method was too accurate for mass production. Under mass production it is unnecessary to determine the actual size of the part; the only criterion is whether its size falls within the upper and lower limits.

In order to supply this more simple test and do it in the most direct manner, so-called "limit gages" were devised. These were of several types, one of which is illustrated herewith (Fig. 19). These gages have this in common: they are set to the upper and lower limits of acceptable size and their use involved few motions and little skill. They require no adjustments, no reading, and no mental comparisons.

When manufacturers were able to establish standard dimensions and to achieve these dimensions within very narrow limits, they had reached their goal. This goal was interchangeability. When parts became interchangeable it was possible for the first time to have mass production of assembled products. As Charles F. Kettering, head of the research division of General Motors Corporation, expresses it, "that word 'interchangeable' is the key to mass production." The reason this is so is that it makes possible low-cost assembly. Since all the reproductions of a given component are duplicates, any one of these may be selected for assembly and will be found to fit without alterations; hence there is no delay in the assembly operation or no need for skilled mechanics to do the work. Furthermore, the work of assembly can be physically segregated from the form-giving operations, and specialized techniques and managerial skill can be developed in the field of assembly.

Assembly operations, after it became possible to carry them on separately with the type of labor just described, went through an evolution as follows:

1. At the beginning there was *stationary assembly*. All the components of a given assembly, such as a lock, were given to a worker who put them together.

2. Next came *moving assembly*. The components of an article, such as a watch movement, were distributed among a number of assemblers in a line. The first man began the work and each added to the partially completed mechanism until the task had been completed. Each man became a specialist, and the greater the number of assemblers in the line —up to a certain limit—the less the total assembling time and the better the quality of work.

Although the moving assembly was developed at an early date the idea was not adapted to the manufacture of large and heavy articles such as automobiles until 1913. To Henry Ford is attributed the first efforts along this line. A Ford car contains about 5,000 parts including small parts such as screws and washers. Some parts are bulky, others no larger than watch parts. Originally a car was put together in the same way that a house is built, at one spot on the floor to which workers brought the required parts. The first departure from that method was the policy of bringing the work to the men instead of having the men go to the work. That was in 1913 when the first experimental assembly line was set up. Prior to that time a worker required about 20 minutes to assemble, by the old method, the flywheel magneto. By subdividing the work into 29 operations and assigning one worker to each of these tasks the assembly time was reduced to 5 minutes.

Somewhat later the same technique was applied to the assembly of the chassis. Stationary assembly of the chassis had required 12½ hours. The first step in the development of a moving assembly was to draw the chassis with a rope and windlass down a line 250 ft. long. Six assemblers traveled with the chassis and picked up parts from piles placed along the line. This reduced the assembly time to slightly less than 6 hours per chassis. By elevating the assembly lines, one to 26¾ in. and another to 24½ in., the principle of "man-high" work was adapted to squads of different heights. Further subdivision of the work subsequently cut the assembly time per chassis to 1 hour and 33 minutes.

3. *Motor-driven moving assembly*. The windlass introduced by Ford soon gave way to motors which moved belt and chain conveyors.

These conveyors were geared to move at a speed that allowed each worker on the line a predetermined amount of time to perform his allotted task. With these mechanized assembly lines came overhead monorail conveyors, gravity chutes, and other mechanical means of bringing parts to those who are assembling them. (The Ford plant at River Rouge has 27 miles of conveyors.) Specialization of task has been worked out for both individuals and gangs. Crews specialize in the various subassemblies, such as motor, body, chassis, and differential subassemblies.

4. *Automatic assembly.* The assembly operations thus far described have been almost wholly manual ones and require of the operator not so much in the way of technical knowledge as they do close attention, constant activity, and considerable manual dexterity.

It has remained for the A. O. Smith Company of Milwaukee to eliminate manual labor almost completely from assembly operations. They have done this in the manufacture of automobile frames. After 5 years of effort, and at a cost of 8 million dollars, they perfected a machine, or rather a series of machines, to fabricate automobile frames at the rate of 7,200 per day. The patent application on this automatic unit, with all its intricate machinery, is contained in 245 pages of brief and 65 pages of illustrations. The ingenious processes by which this unit automatically inspects the strip steel, chemically treats it, bends the various members of the frame, rivets and welds these together, paints the final product, etc., defy description. The need for workers is largely at "supervisory, visual inspection, and control stations." There are 552 operations required on an ordinary frame, and the unit is capable of turning out over 7,000 frames a day or about 4 million operations.

We have noted that quantity production methods as applied to assembled articles originated in the small-arms industry. They were next used in the manufacture of clocks and watches, then of agricultural implements, next of typewriters and bicycles; finally, they reached the advanced state of development we have noted in the automobile industry. Lately, the technique has been adapted to the manufacture of radios, washing machines, refrigerators, and other assembled products where the output seems to warrant it.

Job-lot Production.—Somewhere between the two extremes of custom production and mass production falls the manufacture of products in job lots. Job-lot production is employed by a great number of plants manufacturing various types of machines in quantities from 10 to 100 identical units per order.

The assembly procedure is somewhat similar to that described under custom production except that parts are made interchangeable as far as possible. Usually the stationary line is used for both the subassemblies and the final product. If, for example, 10 machines are to be made, 10 subassemblies will be placed in line together with their component parts. The assembler moves from one unit to the next, performing only a portion of the assembly job. Others follow, performing different operations until the work is completed. This procedure costs less than building each unit completely before proceeding to the next.

Successful operation in job-lot manufacturing is dependent upon production control and planning procedures. Common parts are run in "batches" and held in the stockroom until needed for assembly. One of the largest cost items in job-lot production is the time required in getting ready to make the part on a machine, *i.e.*, the "setup" cost. For example, if 1 hour is required to set up a machine and 1 hour to machine the part, the total time is 2 hours. If 10 pieces are made on one setup, the setup cost is distributed over 10 pieces and the time is reduced to 1.1 hours per piece. Hence the importance of careful planning. It cuts down over-all manufacturing time, reduces inventory investments, and facilitates assembly.

IMPORTANT ASPECTS OF MASS PRODUCTION OF ASSEMBLED PRODUCTS

Increasing Investment of Capital in Machines and Equipment.— Throughout the century of development which we have been sketching, there has been an ever-present and increasing urge to decrease labor costs per unit of output. This was met largely through increased capital costs. Machines have supplanted workers as the skill of the mechanic has gradually been built into the machine. What amounts to the same thing, machines have become more and more specialized. We have noted that metal-forming and metal-cutting machines became more automatic, more specialized in the tasks they performed, and more expensively equipped with appliances and fixtures.

In this development of special-purpose machinery, the urge to improve came from both the makers and users of such capital goods. The users of machine tools, namely the fabricators, came to the machine-tool industry and requested that machines be designed to meet their special needs. Likewise, the makers of machine tools came to the users with improvements which they (the makers) had worked out on their own initiative; the forces of competition caused the users to adopt the improvements. Furthermore, it was possible to expend large sums on this design and developmental work because first costs were insignificant compared to the operating economies of such special machinery provided it was efficient. These operating economies were tremendous because any economy in turning out a single piece was multiplied by the number of pieces produced. In the automobile industry, during the period 1910–1915, when the standardization of parts was being pushed so vigorously, there was marked technological improvement of this nature.

Reaction against Special-purpose Machinery.—In recent years, especially since the depression of 1929, there has been a reaction against special-purpose machinery. The demand for the products turned out by these machines tends to fluctuate more violently than formerly and cannot be calculated closely in advance. These shifts in demand are induced by increasingly rapid and violent style changes and by products being rendered obsolete by improvements. Special-purpose machines are frequently very expensive, and have a high overhead cost for interest, depreciation, and obsolescence. In periods of depression, when the demand for durable goods sinks to very low levels, the carrying cost of a special-purpose machine as against a general-purpose machine may easily create too heavy a burden for the company to carry. The economies of the former in active periods may be more than absorbed by the overhead expense in periods of slack business. Entirely aside from fluctuations in business owing to the business cycle, the installation of too much special-purpose machinery may be dangerous because of style changes and changes in design, which may render highly specialized machines useless. This growing instability of demand has caused manufacturers to strive for plant flexibility, and they have turned to general- or multipurpose machinery. This enables them to retool their plants more cheaply when the market changes and gives them a smaller overhead to carry in periods of depression.

Misapplication of Mass Methods.—The zeal of the devotees of the mass-production idea has frequently caused them to overreach themselves in another manner. This has taken place in industries where the products were in the promotional or early commercial stage. A management engineer cites "electrical refrigerators as a horrible example of mass production entered into on a large scale before the time was right; *i.e.,* before the style and engineering features had been definitely and finally determined. It was some years before the public had enough experience with this radically new product to make up its mind as to just what it wanted in the way of an electrical refrigerator for domestic use. Likewise it took time for the engineering features to be finally determined. But the manufacturers, obsessed with the mass-production enthusiasm, proceeded to set up their plants on that basis and naturally developed a number of single-purpose machines which promptly became obsolete with the development of new types that better suited the public taste and with working out of more economical factory methods. The radio industry when young suffered from much the same mistake."[1]

Other Problems of Management.—In addition to avoiding an investment in specialized machinery and equipment that is highly inflexible

[1] DONALD, W. J., Editor, "Handbook of Business Administration," pp. 637–638, McGraw-Hill Book Company, Inc., New York, 1931.

and costly while turning out a product that is precise and yet not too costly, the management of companies in this field of quantity fabrication have been confronted with many other problems of control. Although these problems confront all manufacturers, they are intensified in this field of mass production of assembled articles. These problems include: (1) the layout of the factory, which is of especial importance here because of its influence on the flow of the work, which is divided into so many operations; (2) estimating probable sales and translating them into production requirements; (3) the timing of the work on the many diverse components so that the flow of these parts will be synchronized; (4) the execution of the timing or scheduling in such a manner that the machines are always utilized and yet at the same time do not produce parts in such quantities as to tie up too much in inventories; (5) rapid means of intercommunication to permit detailed schedules to conform with changes in sales requirements; (6) the layout of the work and the instruction of the operators as to how to perform their tasks, both of which become increasingly important as low-priced labor is employed; and (7) adequate maintenance of equipment and reserve units to prevent costly shutdowns.

CHAPTER IX

THE SHIPBUILDING INDUSTRY

A ship is the largest and most expensive movable thing man makes. The S.S. *Queen Mary*, for example, is almost a fifth of a mile long, and cost 30 million dollars to build. The same expenditure of money in an automobile factory would produce 50,000 motor cars. Ships are made by the custom building process in contrast with the mass production process employed in automobile manufacturing. The utter dissimilarity between the two processes is one reason why the United States ordinarily produces about 80 per cent of the world's automobiles and less than 10 per cent of the world's ships.

Except when we are involved, directly or indirectly, in a war, shipbuilding is not one of our leading industries. In 1939, for example, the industry produced only 327 million dollars worth of ships and gave employment to only 66,000 workers. However, the industry is invaluable from the standpoint of national defense. A nation exposed on two ocean fronts and having numerous insular possessions cannot afford to be without an adequate navy and merchant marine. Despite its comparatively small size, the shipbuilding industry must expand many times its normal size when national emergencies, such as the present (1942), arise. In a study of American manufacturing industries the shipbuilding industry also deserves special treatment because it is the best example of the custom-building type of manufacturing.

THE PROCESS OF SHIPBUILDING

A ship must be custom built. It is too big to be made on a moving assembly line, and the demand for ships of identical specifications is too small to make parts by mass-production technique. Each ship is specially designed to meet the peculiar needs of its purchaser. The United States had, in April, 1941, 1,528 merchant vessels of 2,000 gross tons and over in contrast with 31 million motor vehicles. Obviously the total demand for ships is too small to call for mass production. More important, however, is the necessity for building vessels to specifications of shippers. A ship for the coastwise trade calls for specifications entirely different from those of a lake ore boat or a trans-Atlantic passenger vessel.

The principal operations in shipbuilding are (1) designing, (2) patternmaking, (3) shaping and machining, (4) assembly, and (5) fitting out.

124

PLATE 26.—Drafting room. (*Courtesy of Newport News Shipbuilding and Dry Dock Company.*)

PLATE 27.—Mold loft where patterns are made. (*Courtesy of Newport News Shipbuilding and Dry Dock Company.*)

Designing.—Designing is the first and, in many respects, the most important step in building a ship. It is, as someone has aptly said, a cross between a girder, a hotel, a locomotive, a pendulum, and a sky-scraper. The basic requirements of all ships are watertightness, stability,

PLATE 28.—An early stage in ship building. (*Courtesy of Newport News Shipbuilding and Dry Dock Company.*)

and strength. To stay afloat a vessel must obviously be watertight. When a ship encounters rough water it pitches and rolls. To avoid upsetting it must have stability. In designing, therefore, due regard must be given to the relation between its center of gravity and its height so that, like a pendulum, it will always return to its normal position. It must have sufficient strength to prevent breaking in two when supported only in the mid-section by the crest of a wave causing a strain known as "hogging" or when supported at each end causing the mid-section to sag.

In addition to the general requirements of watertightness, stability, and strength, each ship is designed for some special purpose. Specifications vary with the nature of the cargo, the size of the vessel, the desired speed of travel, the type of power plant, the length of voyages, the type of fuel consumed, the nature of climate encountered, and many other factors.

Designing calls for engineering and architectural skill of a rare type and represents roughly 7 to 10 per cent of the ultimate cost of the vessel.

PLATE 29.—The hull begins to take form. (*Courtesy of Newport News Shipbuilding and Dry Dock Company.*)

For a large merchant vessel approximately 4,000 primary, as distinct from detail, drawings are required. Designing costs for a large battle-ship may run to a million dollars or more.

Patternmaking.—The designs are next translated into patterns. The ship must be laid out in life-sized wooden or composition templates on the floor of the mold loft. Here the curving lines of a ship's hull are made from basswood or pine scantling. The pieces are nailed together to form mock plates which must be accurate in every respect because the steel plates are ultimately made to conform to these templates.

Shaping and Machining.—When the templates are completed, they are sent to the plate and angle shop, usually located directly below the mold loft. There, the layout men place the patterns on steel plates and indicate just where the plates are to be sheared, punched, and countersunk. They likewise indicate just where and how the steel plates are to be bent, so as to conform to the shape of the hull as shown by the curvature of the templates.

PLATE 30.—Construction on the way nears completion. (*Courtesy of Newport News Shipbuilding and Dry Dock Company.*)

Materials that have to be shaped into angles or pronounced curves are placed in heating furnaces. When sufficiently heated to permit working, they are removed and bent to proper shape in accordance with the templates. This work is done largely by skilled metal workers. After being shaped, some of the pieces are joined into larger sections by riveting or welding to expedite work on the ways.

Meanwhile, parts for the ship's machinery and running gear such as propellers, turbine housings, rotors, etc., are cast in the foundry, or shaped in the forge shop and machined to proper size in the machine shop.

Assembly.—Assembly of the ship takes place on the "way." A shipway is the foundation for the timbering or scaffolding erected, at the waterfront, to support the ship during the course of construction and to facilitate its launching upon completion. Assembly begins with the laying of the keel plates. Then comes the vertical keel—a long girder extending throughout the entire length of the hull and constituting its "backbone." Other plates for the bottom shell of the hull begin to arrive from the plate and angle shop. These are laid on the vertical keel and "shored" or supported by wooden piling. Longitudinal girders are next placed in position and bolted to the hull plates. Then the transverse frames are fitted into their proper positions. As in the mold loft, work begins amidships and proceeds in all directions. Soon the hull begins to take shape. Before it is completed, the engines and other heavy machinery are installed. Whenever possible, sections such as bulkheads are sub-

PLATE 31.—Launching the vessel. (*Courtesy of Newport News Shipbuilding and Dry Dock Company.*)

assembled. After the hull is completed and the heaviest machinery is installed, the vessel is launched. To do this the keel blocks are removed, allowing the vessel to slide down the way into the water.

Fitting Out.—Immediately after the launching, tugboats escort the vessel to the fitting out basin. Here, innumerable finishing touches are applied prior to the trial run. Final touches in the fitting-out basin include such things as interior painting and decorating, installation of small hardware, plumbing and electrical fixtures, etc. There is considerable latitude in the stage of completion of a vessel at the time of launching. If a shipyard has a large backlog of business, incomplete vessels are launched as soon as possible to make room for laying the keel of the next ship. Labor plays a prominent part in shipbuilding, and it is significant to note that much of the labor is highly skilled. Labor costs represent 32 per cent of the value of product as reported by the Census of Manufactures. Labor costs are higher in shipbuilding than in most other manufacturing industries, not because the industry pays higher rates for comparable work, but because most of the work offers little opportunity for mechanization.

GROWTH OF THE AMERICAN SHIPBUILDING INDUSTRY

Throughout the three and a third centuries of American shipbuilding, the industry has gone through alternate phases of expansion and decline. The growth of the industry may be divided into five periods. These are (1) the colonial period, from 1607 to the War of the Revolution; (2) the period from the Revolution to the Civil War; (3) the period from the Civil War to the First World War; (4) the First World War period, and (5) the period since the First World War.

The Colonial Period.—Shipbuilding flourished throughout the greater part of the colonial period. This is explained largely by the abundance of domestic raw materials and the commercial policy of England, the mother country.

In this early period, ships were built of wood. The heavy stands of virgin timber furnished an almost inexhaustible supply of raw materials. Numerous shipbuilding towns sprang up in New England from Gloucester (Cape Ann) on the north to New Haven in the waters of the Sound on the south.

As early as 1651, England passed the Navigation Act which, among other things, restricted colonial trade to British and colonial vessels. The enforcement of this act raised ocean freight rates and this, in turn, stimulated colonial shipbuilding. Another stimulus was the prevailing custom of English merchant traders to send manufactured goods to the colonies where the proceeds from the sale of the cargoes were used to buy ships which were loaded with lumber or other raw material for the English or south European markets where both cargoes and ships were sold. Toward the latter part of this period, shipbuilding declined because of rising labor costs. Shipbuilding costs rose from $9 a ton in 1700 to $15 a ton at the time of the Revolution.

Shipbuilding from the Revolution to the Civil War.—At the dawn of the nineteenth century, the United States surpassed England as a shipbuilding nation, and leadership was maintained until the Civil War, as Fig. 20 shows. The peak of shipbuilding activity occurred in 1855 when American shipyards launched over 2,000 vessels. This was the heyday of American maritime activity. American "clipper" ships were the fastest sailing vessels in the world. They operated in every sea and without subsidy.

The supremacy of American shipbuilding during this period may be attributed to a number of factors. The navigation law of 1817 restricted Great Lakes and coastwise trade to American vessels. The maritime activities of New England were a constant source of demand for ships. The gold rush of 1849 reinforced the need for shipping capacity. Yankee

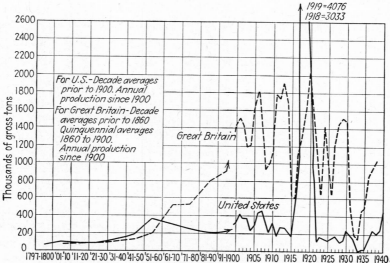

FIG. 20.—American and British shipbuilding. (Merchant vessels of 100 gross tons and over.) (*Encyclopaedia Britannica and Engineering Feb.* 10, 1939.)

clipper ships established repeated records for speedy crossing of the Atlantic. The technical superiority of Yankee clippers established the fame of American-made ships, and the domestic shipbuilding industry benefited by the receipt of numerous foreign orders. As long as wooden hulls were in use the abundance of raw materials favored American shipbuilding. The United States had an ample supply of white oak for frames, yellow pine for planking, ash and locust for fastenings, and white pine for masts.

Shipbuilding from the Civil War to the First World War.—This period is characterized by a marked decline of American shipbuilding activity and the ascendancy of Great Britain as the leading shipbuilding nation. The explanation lies partly in what happened here and partly in what occurred abroad.

Our industry was obviously interrupted by the Civil War, but this does not explain its permanent decline. The basic explanation is that the technology of shipbuilding changed. The iron and steel ship propelled by steam displaced the wooden sailing vessel. Note, on Fig. 21, the transi-

tion from wood to iron and steel construction.   The iron and steel industry in England was about a half century ahead of the development of the
iron and steel industry of the United States.   Therefore, with the change
in technology of shipbuilding, England gained the ascendancy which, as
we shall see, was never challenged save for the brief First World War
interlude.

Throughout the greater part of this period, maritime activity declined.
Industrial activity was confined almost exclusively to internal develop-

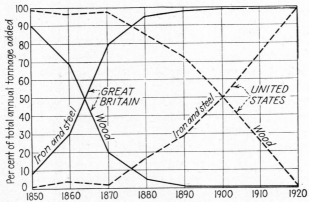

Fig. 21.—Transition from wood to iron and steel shipbuilding.   (*Smith, H. Gerrish,
Shipbuilding and Its Relation to the Iron and Steel Industry, American Iron & Steel Institute,
May 22, 1931.*)

ment.   Agriculture was expanded by pushing settlement westward to the
Pacific.   The boom in railway construction took place during the seventies and the eighties.   The post-Civil War period also witnessed the rise of
such basic industries as iron and steel, coal, copper, and petroleum.
Shipbuilding, for the time being, was neglected.

In England, on the contrary, maritime activity flourished.   English
shipbuilding profited not only by the early shift to the steel ship but also
by cheaper raw materials, low-priced labor, government aid, and the
cooperation of shipping, shipbuilding, and steel interests.   Furthermore,
England's insular position demanded both a large navy and a large merchant marine.

Shipbuilding during the First World War.—At the outbreak of war,
the shipbuilding industry throughout the world was stagnant, and the
war caused no initial stimulus.   The war was expected to be a short one
and existing tonnages of ships were considered adequate; otherwise
England would not have allowed 1,500 Belfast shipyard workers to enlist
in the army within a week after the outbreak of hostilities.   All this was
changed by Germany's campaign of submarine warfare.   In 1915, sub-

marines sank 1.7 million tons of ships; in 1916, over 3 million tons of ships were destroyed. Before the end of the war, 15 million tons, or one-third of the world's 1914 tonnage, had been sunk. The resulting shortage caused freight rates on ocean shipping to skyrocket, and shipbuilding received a stimulus such as it never had before.

In 1916, the United States Shipping Board was created to foster an American merchant marine and to control shipping. However, it was not until April, 1917, when the United States entered the war, that feverish activity began. The Shipping Board immediately created the Emergency Fleet Corporation to buy, build, and operate ships. All existing facilities were expanded, and additional shipways were constructed. Shipways were increased from 184 to 1200. The result is shown in Fig. 20. The Emergency Fleet Corporation build 2,312 ships totaling 13.6 million tons capacity. The tonnage of production during the war period was more than our total production of the two decades preceding the war plus the two decades following the war.

Wartime Shipbuilding Industry Adopts Mass Production.—The phenomenal wartime expansion was accomplished by the application of mass-production technology. The all-important need was additional shipping tonnage. Ships were turned out as rapidly as possible without regard to cost of construction. This required considerable departure from the established routine of manufacture as described at the outset of this chapter. Instead of individual designs for each ship, one design was used for numerous ships. Instead of graceful, sweeping lines and curved decks, the ships were given straight lines and virtually flat decks. They resembled power-driven cheese boxes, to use a homely analogy. Every available steel plant in the country was pressed into service to supply the shipyards with ready-made beams, plates, windlasses, castings, engines, pumps, etc. These parts arrived in a steady stream at the shipyards, where the task of "shipbuilding" was reduced to the relatively simple job of assembly. In short, the technique of mass production was used insofar as possible.

Shipbuilding since the First World War.—Following the cessation of hostilities, the shipbuilding industry receded to its prewar stagnation. Tonnage on the ways at the signing of the armistice was completed. The postwar surplus of shipping tonnage was as great as the prewar deficiency. The government retired from the industry. It eventually sold, for 337 million dollars, 1,450 ships which had cost 2,300 millions. Some yards, notably Hog Island and Cramp's in the Delaware basin at Philadelphia, were closed completely. Other yards attempted to curtail their losses through diversification. Newport News shifted to other steel products, such as railway cars and structural steel. New York Shipbuilding Company combined with Brown Boveri in order to utilize its capital equipment in the manufacture of heavy electrical machinery. Between 1922 and 1928, not a single transoceanic boat was launched in the United States.

An attempt was made to revive the industry in 1928 by the passage of the Jones-White Act. This act authorized the Postmaster General to make more liberal mail-carrying contracts and to foster shipbuilding, and a revolving fund of 250 million dollars was established to enable shipbuilders to borrow at the rate of $3\frac{1}{2}$ per cent up to 75 per cent of the value of the ships built. Shipbuilding was slightly stimulated as Fig. 20 shows. Then came the depression of 1930, whereupon the industry utterly collapsed. In 1933, only 11,000 tons were built.

Merchant Marine Act of 1936.—The low estate to which maritime activities fell led to another legislative effort to revive shipping and shipbuilding. The Merchant Marine Act created the Maritime Commission, empowered with more effective means for stimulating American shipbuilding. The government makes outright grants to shipbuilders and charges the cost to national defense. To the builders of ships that are approved by the Maritime Commission, the government pays from one-third to one-half the cost of construction and lends three-fourth of the rest, such loans to be amortized over a 20-year period.

The building program calls for the construction of a ship a week for 500 weeks or a total of 500 vessels over a 10-year period involving a gross expenditure of 1,250 million dollars. The government's stake in the program is revealed by two novel features. First, all ships are constructed so that the navy can easily convert them for its use. Second, all ships are built to four standard patterns—cargo, tanker, passenger, and combination passenger and cargo vessels. Standardizing construction has both commercial and military value. Construction costs are reduced because one set of drawings and templates can be used for several ships of the same class, thereby utilizing to a limited degree the fundamentals of mass-production technology. From the military angle, 10 ships aggregating 100,000 gross tons are more useful than 2 ships of 50,000 tons each. A small ship is more economical to operate, it possesses greater maneuverability, can enter smaller harbors, and represents less loss in case of capture or destruction.

Shipbuilding in the Crisis of the Second World War.[1]

Ships on Order.—Revival of American shipbuilding, sponsored by the Maritime Commission, had just begun when the course of the Second World War suddenly caused an inundation of orders for American ships. Great Britain requested more ships to replace her growing loss in tonnage, which by mid-1940 had attained alarming proportions. Note in Fig. 22

[1] In the following discussion the authors have drawn heavily upon articles appearing in *Fortune*, July, 1941.

the British losses of shipping as contrasted with her losses in the First
World War.

In addition to British orders, our shipbuilding industry received an
avalanche of domestic orders consisting of both merchant and fighting
craft. To begin with, the industry was working in 1941 on a backlog of
7 billion dollars' worth of naval construction consisting of 483 ships

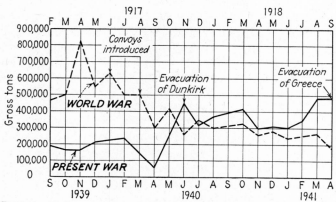

Fig. 22.—British, allied and neutral shipping losses in two wars. (*New York Trust
Company, Index, Summer,* 1941.)

ranging from submarines to 45,000-ton superdreadnaughts. In addition
to the Maritime Commission's orders of 50 ships a year, previously mentioned, the President called for 200 EC 2's, popularly known as "ugly
ducklings." They are emergency cargo ships of 7,500 gross tons each,
built to more or less standard specifications, and capable of making 10
to 11 knots an hour. On top of that order placed in January, 1941,
the President added another order in April, 1941, for 112 more EC 2's plus
100 Maritime Commission ships. The total emergency orders, including
the British order of 60 "ugly ducklings," is 472 merchant ships. Total
orders on hand in June, 1941, were 483 naval ships, 472 merchant ships,
and some private orders placed by shipping concerns.

Shipbuilding Capacity.—Shipbuilding capacity is difficult to express
accurately because of the nature of the industry. This goes back to the
point mentioned at the outset—it is an industry using custom-building
technology. How many ships we can build within a given period ordinarily depends upon three things—the facilities, the availability of the
right kind of labor, and that indefinable "know how." To these, in a
time of intense national defense efforts, must be added a fourth—availability of materials. Let us examine the situation as of mid-1941.

Our physical facilities consisted of 48 seacoast shipyards and 139 ways.
(Shipyards on the Great Lakes must be counted out because there is no

way of getting an ocean-going vessel, if built there, to the ocean.)   These 139 ways were of sufficient size to build ships of 300 feet or more in length.

Companies engaged in shipbuilding fall into two classes, according to size.   The largest companies are Bethlehem Shipbuilding Corporation, Newport News Shipbuilding and Drydock Company, and New York Shipbuilding Corporation.

The largest company is the Bethlehem Shipbuilding Corporation, Ltd., a subsidiary of the second largest steel company of the United States.   It has 23 ways in its four shipyards located at Quincy, Mass., Sparrows Point, Md., Staten Island, N. Y., and San Francisco Bay.   In its 23 years of corporate life up to 1940, it has constructed over a billion dollars' worth of ships at an estimated total profit of 100 millions.   This company not only is the leader in size, but it has the facilities and the technical staff to turn out literally almost any kind of ship.

Newport News Shipbuilding and Dry Dock Company ranks next in importance.   It has eight ways on its James River yard where it recently constructed the *America*, the largest (26,482 gross tons) liner ever built in the United States.   This company is likewise capable of building a wide variety of merchant and naval craft.   For example, it built the battleship *Indiana*, and the aircraft carrier *Hornet*.

Smallest of the big three is the New York Shipbuilding Corporation.   It has five ways on its Delaware River shipyard at Camden, N. J. Approximately one-third of its tonnage is for the United States Navy. From its yard came the battleships *Idaho, Colorado, Oklahoma*, the aircraft carrier *Saratoga*, and the merchant ships *Manhattan* and *Washington*.

The smaller companies are the Bath Iron Works on the Kennebec, Me.; Federal Shipbuilding and Drydock, a subsidiary of U. S. Steel, located at Kearney, N. J.; Sun Shipbuilding at Chester, Pa., a company specializing in tankers; Pusey and James at Wilmington, Dela.; Moore Drydock at Oakland, Calif.; Tampa Shipbuilding and Engineering at Tampa, Fla.; and Pennsylvania Shipyards at Beaumont, Tex.   Submarines are built at Groton, Conn., by Electric Boat Company; and Todd Shipyards Corporation, long in the ship repairing business at Seattle, is expanding and building new yards at San Francisco, Los Angeles, Houston, Tex., Portland, Ore., and South Portland, Me.

In addition to these privately owned facilities, there are eight continental navy shipyards located at Portsmouth, Boston, Brooklyn, Philadelphia, Norfolk, and Charleston on the Atlantic; Mare Island (Calif.) and Bremerton (Wash.) on the Pacific.   These yards, assisted by the "big three" privately owned yards, are busy expanding our one-ocean navy to a two-ocean navy.   To build the tremendous backlog of orders, the yards are being expanded as rapidly as possible, but it takes time to build more ways together with cranes, machinery, and all the appurtenances of an operating shipyard. National defense plans call for the construction of enough additional ways to step up production capacity to 500 ships or 4 million gross tons annually plus the naval building program of battleships, cruisers, etc.

The next requirement is labor. To build a ship, all kinds of labor, much of it highly skilled, is required—draftsmen, pipefitters, carpenters, welders, electricians, anglesmiths, galvanizers, calkers, riveters, shipfitters —a vast assortment of skilled and semiskilled craftsmen. It has been estimated by government officials that the two-ocean navy program alone calls for roughly 2 million man-years of labor. At least 500,000 workers will have to be trained for the special skills needed to get the desired volume of production. Labor will be conserved wherever possible. That is why we are building "ugly ducklings"—they are the nearest approach to a standardized ship that can be attained. They conserve the labor of designing and drafting, and from 2 to 5 per cent savings can be effected in the shipyards by using standard templates and standard procedures. The substitution of welding for riveting also saves labor. A welding crew of two men can accomplish as much as a riveting crew of four men. Welding also requires less inspecting, and recruits can be taught welding in less time than riveting.

The know-how of shipbuilding begins on the designing boards and does not end until the finished vessel is put into service. This aspect of the problem of shipbuilding capacity is being met by subcontracting as much business as possible to inland manufacturers who have the facilities, the operations being controlled and supervised by the shipbuilders. Another way in which the problem is being solved is by utilizing the managerial skill of Great Lakes shipbuilders, who have released some of their best talent for the duration.

The final problem of capacity is materials. Four million gross tons of ships call for a huge volume of metal in the form of sheets, plates, pipes, structural shapes, castings, forgings; plus lumber, wire, tubing, and machine-shop products of almost endless variety. If time were no factor, these materials would all be forthcoming in due course, but time is the very essence of the whole program because these materials are also being demanded in other sections of our defense program with almost equal urgency. To speed up this aspect of shipbuilding capacity, numerous concessions are made. For example, the British are taking their EC 2's powered by the old-style reciprocating engines instead of turbines, and they are made to burn coal instead of oil.

The Outlook.—The future of the American shipbuilding industry must be considered in two phases—the immediate future and the distant future. The immediate future can be foreseen with considerable clarity. The industry has enough business on its books to keep it going at top speed for

4 or 5 years at least.   The distant future is extremely vague.   It depends upon too many unknowns.   How long will the Second World War continue?   How much more existing tonnage will be sunk before the conflict closes? etc?   The emergency expansion very closely parallels the First World War expansion.   Therefore it might be supposed, to continue the parallel, that the industry is heading for another postwar collapse. Obviously, the industry will not continue indefinitely at its present accelerating pace, but the post-war decline may be less drastic unless it is likewise accompanied by a world-wide disarmament program such as we had in the early twenties.

CHAPTER X

THE DEVELOPMENT OF THE AUTOMOBILE INDUSTRY

The automobile industry is often and quite properly cited as the classic example of mass production. It converts a vast stream of diversified raw materials into highly standardized products for sale at prices which yield comparatively high wages to its employees, big dividends to its stockholders, and large values to its customers. These results are obtained, in part, through the technique of mass production, characterized by large-scale operation, tapered integration, special-purpose equipment, subdivision of labor, and power-driven assembly. Annual redesign of product, shrewd buying, and able merchandising also play a prominent part, as we shall see.

The motor vehicle industry, in its broadest aspect, embraces the manufacture of pleasure cars, motor trucks, automobile bodies, and parts. As such, the industry represents a capital investment of 1,300 millions; it employs about a half million workers and it produced 5 billion dollars' worth of products according to the 1939 Census of Manufactures. The industry ranks first in raw materials consumed, value of products, and value added by manufacturing. However, our analysis, in this and the following chapter, is confined to the automobile industry, *i.e.*, the manufacture of pleasure cars.

The automobile industry, in the restricted sense just defined, is nevertheless an industry of first magnitude. In 1940 it produced 4 billion dollars' worth of cars. Compared with other manufacturing industries, it ranked first in the consumption of materials, second in value of products, fourth in total pay roll—it employs approximately 400,000 workers. The industry ranks first as a consumer of steel, rubber, plate glass, nickel, lead, and mohair. It is also one of the best customers of the aluminum, copper, zinc, cotton, machine tool, and chemical industries. Despite its large size, the industry consists of only 11 companies— these companies turn out from 1 to 5 million cars annually.

The huge size of the motor industry is especially noteworthy in view of its comparative youth. Automobile manufacturing is a twentieth-century industry. In 1895, there were only four registered automobiles in the United States. In 1940, there were 27 million passenger vehicles— enough to carry simultaneously the entire population. Before analyzing the industry, let us note how it attained its present position of importance in our economic structure.

The development of the automobile industry may be divided into three periods. The first, extending to 1908, was an experimental period. The second, ending approximately 1921, was a period of rapid growth, as Fig. 23 shows. The third period, from 1921 to the present, is characterized by a diminishing rate of growth.

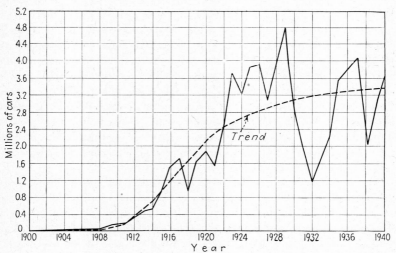

FIG. 23.—United States automobile production. (*Automobile Facts and Figures* 1941.)

THE EXPERIMENTAL PERIOD—PRIOR TO 1908

Although the automobile is a twentieth-century product, the idea of a self-propelled vehicle operating without trackage goes back much earlier. As early as 1770, Cugnot, a French artillery captain, built a horseless carriage propelled by steam. During the nineteenth century, little progress was made because of, first, technical difficulties and, second, the development of railroads. By 1880, approximately 100,000 miles of railway trackage had been built which met our basic transportation needs.

The immediate stimulus to the development of the automobile was the appearance, about 1880, of the internal-combustion gasoline engine. It was invented simultaneously by Otto, a German, and Selden, an American. George Selden, a patent attorney, filed application for a patent in 1879 although he had not yet completed a working model. He apparently realized that the market was not "ripe" for his device because he deliberately delayed, by means best known to a patent attorney, the granting of the patent until 1895. By that time, a number of pioneers were working on experimental models. Among these were Ford, Haynes, and Duryea, each of whom made sufficient contributions to share the distinction of having built America's first motor car. In their footsteps quickly followed machinery makers, such as Cadillac and Marmon, bicycle makers, such as Pope and Jeffery, carriage makers, such as Studebaker and Mitchell, and parts makers, such as Chandler and Dodge.

Slow Early Development.—During the experimental period, the youthful automobile industry was beset with technical, legal, and economic difficulties. The early automobiles were large, heavy, noisy, and unreliable. Almost every make had some notorious mechanical defect. Alloy steels were unknown, manufacturing methods were crude, and the products were highly unstandardized. The lack of standardization may be illustrated by the fact that cars were powered by gasoline, steam, or electricity. In some cars, the motor was found under the hood, in others, under the rear seat or under the front seat. Cars equipped with gas engines were either two-cycle or a four-cycle, single-cylinder or multiple-cylinder, air-cooled or water-cooled, etc. Over 800 different sizes of lock washers and 1,600 different sizes of steel tubing were used. The great diversification of mechanical construction made for high costs of production and unreliability of performance.

Another barrier to the early development was a protracted litigation over the basic Selden patent. In 1899, Selden sold his patent to The Electric Vehicle Company. This company sought to collect royalties from all manufacturers using the gas engine. Some of these, notably Ford, objected and refused to pay. The suit against Ford was not settled until 1911, when the United States Court of Appeals rendered a verdict in favor of Ford. The decision turned upon a technicality in which the court held that Ford had not infringed upon the patent. Thereafter, the industry operated under a cross-licensing agreement which provided for the pooling of all but major inventions.

Economic barriers, too, exerted a retarding influence on the early development of the industry. Railways offered more reliable transportation between the principal population centers. Highways suitable for automobile travel were few. Automobile manufacturers had great difficulty obtaining capital. No banker and few private capitalists could be found who were willing to risk capital in the industry. Consequently, motor car manufacturers generally resorted to the practice of buying materials and supplies on time and selling cars for cash. Since manufacturing costs were high and sales were made on a cash-on-delivery basis, the industry catered only to a limited clientele in the upper income group.

PERIOD OF RAPID GROWTH—1908–1921

Although commercial production of automobiles had begun about 1900, it was not until 1908 that the motor car received widespread acceptance. Note in Fig. 23 the rapid rate of increase after 1908. Physical volume of production rose from 40,000 cars in 1907 to almost 2 million cars in 1920.   This increase was largely accounted for by the phenomenal growth of one concern—the Ford Motor Company.

Ford Dominates the Market.—Henry Ford, in partnership with others, made motor cars for sale as early as 1898.   His partners were too conservative to suit him, so in 1903, Ford organized his own concern—the present Ford Motor Company.   During the 35 years ending with 1937, the company produced 27 million motor cars which yielded a total revenue of 14 billions and a total profit of 1 billion.

During the early years of the company's history, Ford, like his competitors, offered a variety of models at a variety of prices.   However,

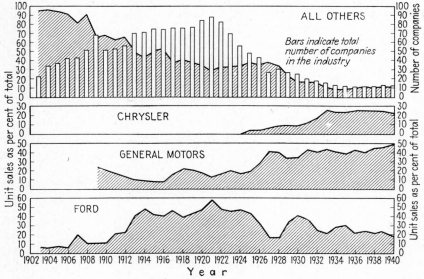

Fig. 24.—Division of the automobile market.

after only moderate success, Ford decided, in 1908, to embark upon quantity production of a relatively low-priced car.   He designed the model "T"—which remained substantially unchanged until 1927, when competition finally forced him to design a new car.   The model "T" was noted for its simplicity of construction, ruggedness, and ease of operation. Within 6 years after the introduction of this car, Ford was producing as many cars as all the rest of the industry together.   His production rose, with few interruptions, from 10,000 cars in 1909 to a peak of over 2 million cars in 1923.   Throughout the lifetime of this model, Ford made approximately one-half of all American passenger cars as shown in Fig. 24. Ford ploughed most of the profits back into the company for further plant expansion.   From an initial cash investment of $27,000, the company grew to its present huge size.

Standardization the Key to Ford's Success.—Ford's phenomenal success was largely due to his production and marketing policies. His production policies were characterized by product standardization, based upon the use of highly specialized machine tools, power-driven conveyor assembly, minute subdivision of labor, intensive supervision, and high wage rates. This combination of factors, working in harmony, made for low manufacturing costs. Furthermore, Ford built a highly integrated business unit. When he discovered a parts supplier making a big profit, Ford designed a machine and made the part himself. For example, a

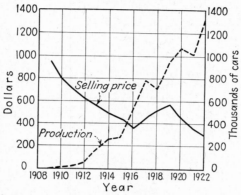

Fig. 25.—Annual Ford production and average annual price of Ford touring car. (*Seltzer, Lawrence H., "Financial History of the Automobile Industry," Houghton Mifflin Company, New York, 1928.*)

certain part which he had been buying at $50 a thousand, he later made for himself at a cost of $8.50 a thousand. He constructed his own blast furnaces, steel mills, glass factories, etc., bought coal mines, ore deposits, timber land, and water-power sites in order to make himself more independent of suppliers.

Ford's marketing policies were characterized for many years by an almost total absence of paid advertising and by a progressive series of price reductions. Advertising was superfluous because Ford cars so greatly outnumbered all other cars that the Ford was its own best advertisement. As volume of production increased, manufacturing costs per unit declined. Ford passed on to his customers some of the savings in the form of lower prices. Between 1909 and 1922, the price of the Ford was progressively reduced from $950 to $295. Note in Fig. 25 the relation between price and volume of production. Lower prices increased sales, and this, in turn, brought added savings in production costs. Until 1925, Ford's market continued to respond favorably to the magic charm of price reduction. Thereafter, sales fell off rather sharply. Before going into that, let us note what was taking place in the other half of the industry during this period dominated by Ford.

The Other Half of the Industry.—While Ford was reaping the harvest, numerous other companies were struggling to secure a foothold in the industry. One student[1] of the automobile industry points out that, of the 181 companies engaged in passenger car production between 1903 and 1926, only 44 survived as of the latter date. The median length of life of the 137 companies retiring from the field was five years, and most of the "exits" occurred prior to 1921. Two major causes for this high mortality are offered. First, the hazards incident to rapid changes in design and construction are especially severe in a young industry making a complex fabricated product. Companies erred by being either too radical or too conservative in both the degree and frequency of restyling. Second was the difficulty of adjusting production schedules to the market. Companies erred by making either too many models which entailed high manufacturing costs or too few models which attracted only a limited clientele.

The large company turnover during this period is sufficient evidence of the competitive struggle. Nevertheless, until 1921, companies entered at a faster rate than they withdrew, as Fig. 24 reveals. There are several explanations for this. The motor car had come to be an accepted form of transportation. An endless succession of technical improvements had made it a reliable and comfortable vehicle for travel. Thousands of miles of hard-surfaced roads were constructed. Prospective manufacturers found less difficulty in obtaining capital. The First World War and postwar prosperity increased buying power. By 1920, the industry had attained sufficient size to be regarded as an important factor in our national economy. Although the industry suffered a severe setback in the depression of 1920–1921, many economists credit the immediately ensuing period of prosperity to the rapid recovery of the automobile industry.

PERIOD OF RETARDED GROWTH—1921–1940

After 1921, the automobile industry entered a new phase of growth. Its market became more and more a replacement market. Used cars became an increasing obstacle to the disposal of new cars. Buyers became more discriminating in their demands. Cars were bought for their appearance rather than for their economy. Closed cars replaced touring cars. Installment sales outnumbered cash sales. Manufacturers became fewer. Small companies fell by the wayside or were absorbed by larger companies. Large companies became larger. General Motors and, later, Chrysler rose to challenge the undisputed leadership hitherto held by Ford.

---

[1] Epstein, Ralph C., "The Automobile Industry," McGraw-Hill Book Company, Inc., New York, 1928.

Early History of General Motors.—General Motors went through a long period of trial and error before it became the leading company in the industry. As a matter of fact, it was organized in 1908, the year Ford embarked upon quantity production of his low-priced car. General Motors never was a small company. During the first year of its operation it produced over 20 per cent of the industry's cars. It sprang into existence as the largest company of the industry, and that precisely was its biggest weakness. Within a few years it was surpassed by Ford, and 16 years elapsed before General Motors again outsold Ford, as Fig. 24 shows. General Motors was founded by a promoter who divided his attention between Wall Street and Detroit.

General Motors was a consolidation of approximately two dozen existing companies, half of which had been motor companies and the others, accessory manufacturing companies. It embraced some of the then leading motor companies, such as Buick, Oldsmobile, and Cadillac. Unfortunately it also embraced numerous other concerns long since unheard of. Durant, the promoter, failed to include the Ford Motor Company only because he was unable to raise the cash stipulation of Ford's 8-million-dollar asking price. Durant had consolidated more than he could profitably manage. Two years later, in 1910, the company fell into the hands of the bankers, who administered it for a period of 5 years. They kept the most profitable units and got rid of the others. Meanwhile Durant acquired control of the Chevrolet Motor Company. He used this company as a springboard to jump back into control of General Motors in 1915. Once more in command, he resumed his policy of vigorous expansion. However, the business depression of 1920–1921 caught him totally unprepared, and he was forced to retire permanently. Control of the company thereupon fell into the hands of duPont and Morgan interests.

The new management instituted more conservative administration and laid the foundations for the company's subsequent rise to its present position. Numerous subsidiary units were consolidated, a centralized budget was installed, and a system of centralized-decentralized administration was set up. The major divisions, such as Cadillac, Buick, Oldsmobile, Pontiac, Chevrolet, and Fisher Body, operate with decentralized control and authority but with centralized assistance from General Motors. The manager in charge of each division is responsible for making his unit a profitable adjunct of General Motors and is therefore given complete control over all operating functions. Thus, the operating divisions are virtually autonomous units, but they receive aid from General Motors in matters like finance, engineering, and research.

General Motors Assumes Leadership.—Based on volume of production, General Motors became the leading company in 1927 and has

retained that position.   The company turned some of its corporate lega-
cies to good account.   Its geographically scattered plants were very
profitably converted into either specialized parts-manufacturing plants or
district assembly plants.   The latter resulted in considerable savings in
freight charges.   The acquisition of Fisher Body proved profitable as a
result of the growing popularity of the closed car.   General Motors was in
a strategic position to reap the harvest of the public's increased buying
power.   Producing cars that ranged from the low-priced Chevrolet to
the luxurious Cadillac, General Motors offered, to quote from its own
advertisements, "a car for every purse and purpose."   With Morgan-
duPont financial backing, the company was well prepared to take over the
business of consumer financing.   As early as 1919, the General Motors
Acceptance Corporation was created for this purpose.

General Motors likewise profited by the basic change that occurred in
the nature of the market during the twenties.   It was a decade of intensive business activity characterized by widespread prosperity, rising
prices, and rising standards of living.   Buoyed by the growing prosperity,
the public became more style-conscious.   Consumers showed a marked
preference for cars that were smartly styled, beautifully upholstered, and
equipped with the very latest mechanical improvements and accessories.
Motorists bought new cars more frequently, and manufacturers hastened
the process of obsolescence by making sufficiently noticeable style changes
each year.   New styles were widely publicized by the annual automobile
shows.   General Motors was quick to perceive that the market had
become more discriminating.

Rise of Chrysler Motors.—The unusual success of the Chrysler Motor
Corporation, despite its comparatively late entry into the industry, is
largely attributable to Walter Chrysler, the founder.   Chrysler, like
Ford, had unusual mechanical ingenuity.   Furthermore he had a keen
sense of market psychology.   Chrysler received his early training with
General Motors.   He had served as general manager of the Buick division and as vice-president of General Motors.   He resigned from General
Motors with intent to retire when a group of bankers sought his aid in
rehabilitating the semidefunct Willys-Overland Company.   This company, like most motor companies that did not actually fail during the
1920–1921 business depression, emerged with a weakened financial structure.   Having salvaged one automobile company, Chrysler was next
prevailed upon to resurrect the Maxwell, which had also barely survived
the depression.   After rehabilitating two run-down motor companies,
Chrysler decided to go into business for himself.

Chrysler had a keen appreciation of the public's desire for sweeping
lines, delicate shades, and luxurious appointments.   He designed and
exhibited at a private showing in 1924 the first Chrysler car.   It had a

streamlined, low-slung body, hydraulic brakes, and a high-speed, high-compression motor. The car at once attracted a large and enthusiastic following. In fact, it "stole" the annual automobile show.

The next year the Company introduced the Chrysler "50," "60," "70," and the "80"—model numbers indicative of their respective speeds. Stockholders received a 10-million-dollar dividend at the end of the year.

Chrysler Expands.—In 1928, when the Dodge properties were put up for sale, Chrysler bought them and thereby acquired a foundry and a ready-made nation-wide dealer organization. The DeSoto was added to bridge the price gap between the Chrysler and the Dodge. The same year the Plymouth was added for the purpose of invading the low-priced market. This gave the company a price line almost as broad and complete as that of General Motors. Two years later, Chrysler, DeSoto, and Dodge dealers were required to add the Plymouth to their franchises. That marks the beginning, as Fig. 24 shows, of the company's rise to large-volume production.

Ford Temporarily Eclipsed.—In the middle twenties, Ford was temporarily eclipsed by the vigorous growth of General Motors. In the late twenties, when Ford emerged, Chrysler loomed on the horizon as another formidable competitor. After 1921, Ford sales had begun to decline, relative to the total industry production. Two years later, Ford sales decreased in both relative and absolute numbers. The model "T," of 1908 vintage, had outlived its usefulness. Finally, in 1927, after continuous shrinkage in sales, Ford closed down his plant and designed a new car. About 70 per cent of the machinery had to be altered or replaced. Fully 18 months elapsed before the plant was again operating at full capacity.

During the Ford shutdown, General Motors obtained 40 per cent of the automobile business, a proportion which it persistently holds. Since 1930, Chrysler has been producing 25 per cent of the total volume. In recent years, Ford's share of the total industry output has declined, and his annual production has been more irregular than that of his two big competitors. Since Ford abandoned the model "T," the company has just about broken even. It is not to be inferred that Ford is on the way out. The company has no dividends to pay other than those required by the family; furthermore, it has a tremendous surplus upon which to draw. Like General Motors and Chrysler, Ford has broadened his price line by introducing the Lincoln-Zephyr and the Mercury. That Ford is a mechanical genius and a rugged individualist needs no argument. There is no end of rumors as to what he will do next. For example, he has taken out patents on a car with the motor in the rear. In 1939, the company broadened its line by the addition of an inexpensive lightweight farm tractor.

The "Big Three" against the Field.—Since 1921, when the growth of the automobile industry began to slacken, there occurred a pronounced decline in the number of competing manufacturers. The initial exodus began with the business depression of 1920–1921, but it has continued despite the ensuing period of prosperity, and, in 1940, only eight companies remained to compete with the "big three." The eight companies[1] share only 10 per cent of the business. Their total annual volume fluctuates between 100,000 cars when business is poor and 400,000 cars when business is good. Their production is highly irregular because, for the most part, they manufacture either medium- or high-priced cars, sales of which are very sensitive to general business conditions. Because of the reciprocal relationship between volume and cost, it is almost impossible for a small manufacturer to attain that critical volume which brings unit costs down to the point where he can enter the low-priced field. Ford's success in the low-priced field attracted many followers; however, only Chevrolet and Plymouth succeeded.

The small manufacturer encounters other handicaps. Retooling the plant, incident to annual style change, is expensive. This is a large item of cost which requires large volume to absorb the capital outlay. The small manufacturer cannot offer as great a variety of models as his large competitor without incurring heavy costs. That is to say, he lacks the advantages of mass production. Advertising costs are large. Building a nation-wide dealer organization is a slow and expensive task. Most people prefer to buy a car from a well-established company rather than run the risk of buying a car which may shortly become an "orphan."

With this background we shall examine, in the next chapter, the competitive pattern of the automobile industry.

[1] Crosley, Graham-Paige, Hudson, Hupp, Nash, Packard, Studebaker, Willys-Whippet.

CHAPTER XI

TECHNOLOGY AND COMPETITION IN THE AUTOMOBILE INDUSTRY

Automobiles at 25 Cents a Pound.—Mass production is a distinctly American contribution to the manufacturing arts, and in the automobile industry it is seen in its highest form. This is basically the reason why automobiles can be made to sell for as little as 25 cents a pound. By contrast, this price is well below that of other consumer goods of comparable durability. The price of mechanical refrigerators, sewing machines, washing machines, and radios ranges from 40 cents to $1 per pound. Our earlier automobiles were just as costly as these products, but by continuous improvement of the product and the technology of production, the automobile has been made available to people of modest means.

HOW MOTOR CARS ARE MADE

The three major steps in the manufacturing process are (1) designing and engineering, (2) machining, and (3) assembly. The relative importance of these three steps depends very largely upon the degree of integration. For example, very little machining is done by the small automobile manufacturer. The small nonintegrated company merely designs a car, buys the subassemblies, such as the motor, wheels, body, etc., assembles the car, and markets it under its own name. However, this procedure has become the exception since the "Big Three" do 90 per cent of the business. Let us see how the large company operates.

Designing and Engineering.—The designing and engineering department of a motor company has the task of creating a car that dealers can sell. This calls for a delicate balance between creative imagination and economy of production. Approximately 30,000 man-hours of work are required to design a car. Designing is begun about a year before the car ultimately appears on the market. Miniature models, executed in either clay or wood, are made and submitted to the proper company officials for criticism. After the general style has been tentatively selected, larger models are made, to exact scale, from metal, glass, rubber, etc., to permit execution of detail. Upon final decision as to style and variety of models, engineers write specifications for all component parts.

Machining.—Mass production as applied to the foundry and machine shops requires equipment which may be operated with unerring accuracy

PLATE 32.—Pressing body sections.   (*Courtesy of General Motors Corporation.*)

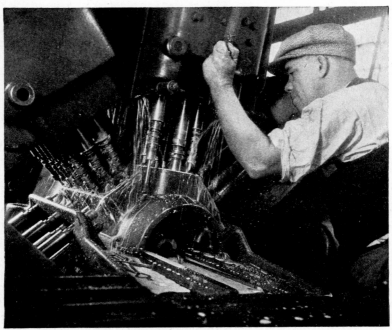

PLATE 33.—A machining operation showing the simultaneous tapping of 79 holes in the Ford V-8 engine block.   (*Courtesy of Ford Motor Company.*)

by semiskilled labor. Special-purpose machine tools, of the types described in Chap. VIII, are used almost exclusively. In the foundry, for example, sand molds are made by automatic molding machines. In the Ford foundry, the V-8 cylinder-block core assembly takes place on a moving chain conveyor. Individual core pieces, of which more than 50 are required for each motor, are fed to monorail conveyors. The finished castings are turned out in endless succession by continuous pouring from a large reservoir, containing the molten metal, into a traveling car ladle, synchronized with the pouring conveyor, filling the molds while in motion. In the Buick foundry, to cite another example, an automatic shot-blast cleaning device cleans the motor block castings at the rate of three per minute.

The highest forms of mechanized production are found in the machine shops. In the Plymouth plant at Detroit, cylinder blocks are rough bored, two at a time, by a six-spindle boring machine. A multiple-spindle drill press drills 110 holes simultaneously into the top and sides of the block. A special automatic six-spindle grinder faces the hard valve seats at the rate of 90 motor blocks per hour. Pistons are machined to identical dimensions by a specially designed milling machine which also weighs each piston accurately. These are examples of hundreds of similar mechanical operations.

The labor cost of machining operations has been reduced drastically by the use of special-purpose machine tools. The skill which formerly depended upon the dexterity and judgment with which the worker plied his hand tools has been "built into" the machine tools. Furthermore, many of these machine tools are so automatic that the function of the operator is reduced to the simple task of feeding raw stock and removing the finished product. Inexperienced workers can therefore be employed after a very brief training period. Consequently the manufacturer can obtain most of his workers in the general labor market and need pay no more than the prevailing rate of wages for semiskilled labor.

An outstanding exception is found in certain key occupations, especially tool and die making. Numerically a small proportion of the total labor force, the tool and die makers are the aristocrats in contrast with the rank and file workers. They are the highly skilled mechanics who make the cutting tools, dies, jigs, and auxiliary fixtures with which the specialized machine tools must be equipped every time the manufacturer changes models.

Assembly.—The automobile industry has probably made its greatest contribution to mass-production technology in the art of assembly. A first glance at the interior of an automobile assembly plant leaves an impression of utter confusion. Overhead wires feed electric power to portable motorized tools, such as screwdrivers and welding irons. Bodies,

PLATE 34.—Bar-welding the body in a jig.   (*Courtesy of Ford Motor Company.*)

PLATE 35.—Lowering motor onto chassis.   (*Courtesy of General Motors Corporation.*)

PLATE 36.—Lowering the body onto the chassis.   (*Courtesy of Ford Motor Company.*)

PLATE 37.—Finished automobile coming off the assembly line.   (*Courtesy of General Motors Corporation.*)

hoods, and fenders float through the air; skeleton cars, in various stages of completion, creep along the floor in single files.   However, upon closer inspection it will be observed that the apparent chaos is order of the highest type.

The layout is such as to accommodate two or more parallel final-assembly lines extending throughout the length of the building.   Tributary to the final-assembly lines are subassembly and unit-assembly lines, supplying, at appropriate intervals, such subassemblies as the body, the motor, and the wheels to be installed on the chassis frame, the initial member of the final-assembly line.   From the finishing end of the assembly line, the completed motor cars are driven away, under their own power, at the rate of two or three a minute during the height of the busy season.

Economy of production in the assembly department is attained through emphasis upon extreme subdivision of labor and motorized transportation of materials.   Enough workers are assigned to the assembly lines so that each man has a very simple task to perform, such as inserting and spreading a cotter pin or drawing up several bolts.   Material handling is reduced through the use of elaborate conveyor devices, such as motorized chain conveyors, overhead monorail conveyors, and tiering trucks.

THE ECONOMIES OF BIG BUSINESS

The " Big Three " reap additional economies of operation as a result of their integration, standardization, multiple line of cars, and regional assembly plants.

Tapered Integration.—Ford, the most highly integrated of the three leading motor companies, is in the best position to obtain the economies of integrated operation.   Through the ownership of coal and ore mines, steel plants, glass factories, tire factories, etc., the company is in a position to obtain most of its materials at cost.   However, this is a competitive advantage only when independent producers of steel, glass, tires, etc., are asking higher prices than the costs incurred by the integrated manufacturer—a condition generally obtaining during periods of brisk business activity.   When the demand for cars is, let us say, only 50 per cent of the manufacturer's capacity, the fully integrated organization incurs the costs of idle capacity in every manufacturing division.   Ford, however, turns integration to good account by taking a position known as tapered integration; *i.e.*, his capacity for producing steel, tires, and other raw materials is geared to only a fraction, let us say 50 per cent, of his normal demand for these materials._ Consequently, these anterior manufacturing facilities can always be utilized and when the demand for cars calls for raw materials in excess of his production capacity, he can obtain them from independent manufacturers. Much of the burden of idle capacity is, therefore, shifted to the independents. General Motors and Chrysler are also partially integrated, but Ford has extended his farther back to basic raw materials than his competitors.

Volume Production of Standardized Parts.—Each of the "Big Three" motor companies derives its principal revenue from its low-priced car division. In each instance, large volume, low price, and low costs are obtained by simplicity of design and standardized production. Machines and dies are very costly, but the cost per car is small because of the large volume of production absorbing these costs. For example, a set of dies for stamping out the body of a car costs approximately $750,000, but annual production of Fords, Chevrolets, and Plymouths averages between 400,000 and 700,000 cars each, so that the die cost per car is only $1 or $2. The huge press equipped with these dies costs $367,000, but only a part of its cost need be charged to depreciation each year because the machine is serviceable for a number of years. Annual change of body design requires new dies but not new presses.

Multiple Price-line Economies.—Through their wide range of cars, General Motors and Chrysler have made the most of economies peculiar to multiple car production. One advantage arises from the possibility of utilizing numerous parts in common for the different priced cars. As a result of this practice, die costs per car are still further reduced. Although it is not generally appreciated, some Pontiac parts are made from Chevrolet dies without sacrificing quality in the higher priced car. Similarly, Dodge and Plymouth have numerous parts in common made from the same set of dies. The savings effected are obvious.

Mechanically, there is very little difference between a manufacturer's low-priced car and his car in the price class immediately above it. The standard Dodge, for example, has numerous refinements to justify the small price differential between it and the standard Plymouth, but careful scrutiny reveals that they are almost identical, structurally. However, there are vast differences between a company's lowest priced car and its highest priced car. Parts for the former are usually made in the companies' own shops, whereas parts for the latter are frequently purchased from specialty suppliers. For example, one of the companies bought patented piston rings at $1.10 per set for its highest priced car, and made the rings in its own machine shop at a cost of only 7 cents a set for its lowest priced car.

Regional Assembly Plants Save Freight.—Detroit is the center of the automobile industry, but the leading companies have geographically scattered assembly plants located in their principal markets. In their Detroit plants they manufacture parts and unit assemblies such as wheels, fenders, frames, and motors, for shipment to their several regional plants where the cars are finally assembled. Only four completely assembled motor cars can be loaded in a freight car, but unassembled, the equivalent of more than 40 automobiles can be shipped in one car. The ultimate buyer pays freight f.o.b. Detroit on the fully assembled basis, but the manufacturer incurs shipping costs on the unassembled basis. The differential recently amounted to a saving of $46 per car on a model assembled in New Jersey.

PROFITS OF MANUFACTURERS

Concrete evidence of the advantages of large-scale automobile manufacturing is found in the profits made by the leading companies. General Motors is particularly outstanding in this respect. In the 11 years, 1927–1937, General Motors earned 36 per cent on its invested capital. Its total earnings represented 80 per cent of all profits made by the entire industry. This company made more profits than any other manufacturing corporation in the country despite the fact that it was not the largest company as measured by total assets. General Motors makes a great variety of products, practically everything requiring a motor, ranging from electric fans run by 0.01-hp. motor to locomotives powered by 6,000-hp. Diesels. Nevertheless, auto manufacturing is the principal source of profits. It is estimated that 60 per cent of its profits come from automobiles directly and 20 per cent from automobile parts and accessories, the remainder from other products.

It is not to be inferred that General Motors is the only profitable company. The industry as a whole surpasses all major manufacturing industries in profitability. During the 20 years ending with 1937 the automobile industry averaged 17 per cent on its net worth. This is in contrast with 8 per cent earned by a representative group of companies consisting of 200 leading concerns in various lines of manufacturing and trade. Taking the good and bad years together, auto manufacturing has been more than twice as profitable as industry generally.

Profits of Automobile Dealers.—The distribution of automobiles requires about as much capital and as many people as auto manufacturing, but there is a marked contrast between the profitability of automobile manufacturing and automobile merchandising.

Thus far it has been impossible to obtain a comprehensive survey of dealer profits because of the large number of dealers, some operating as corporations, others as partnerships, and the vast majority as private enterprisers. However, such studies as have been made suggest that dealer profits, on the basis of volume of business, are substantially less than manufacturers' profits. One survey of 250 dealers revealed that in 1935 2.4 million dollars' profit was made on 59 million dollars' worth of business, but that profit was offset by 2.3 million dollars' losses sustained on used cars traded in. The net profit for the year was $400 per dealer. According to a Federal Trade Commission survey covering the sale of 120,000 cars of all makes in 1937, net operating profits per new cars sold by retail dealers were derived entirely from the sale of parts, accessories, supplies, and services, which represented only 15 per cent of the total business done by the dealers covered in the survey. Excessive used-car allowances wiped out virtually all profits on new-car sales. "For distributor-dealers, whose business combined both wholesaling and retailing, the showing was that nearly 97 per cent of their profit of $13.10 per new car sold was derived from sales of parts, accessories, supplies and service representing less than 12 per cent of their total business."[1] Another indication of the small profits in automobile retailing is found in the high mortality among dealers. Approximately 25 per cent of the automobile dealers retire from business each year. Though the evidence is fragmentary, it is apparent that dealer profits are considerably less than manufacturers' profits.

The bountiful returns on automobile manufacturing, in contrast with the small returns in distribution, cannot be attributed entirely to the internal economies of large-scale production. The concentration of production has given rise to a competitive pattern which redounds with especial favor upon the large manufacturing concerns.

THE COMPETITIVE PATTERN

Automobile manufacturing is concentrated, as we have already noted, within the hands of 11 companies, and three of these produce 90 per cent of the annual output. The competitive practices of the "Big Three" thus virtually determine the competitive pattern for the industry.

The manufacturers consume an enormous stream of raw materials, parts, and accessories. They buy these materials from several thousand independent manufacturing concerns which are very eager for the business because of its sustaining volume.

On the other hand, the auto manufacturers produce an enormous stream of motor cars which calls for a gigantic task of merchandising. This function is performed by more than 40,000 dealers scattered throughout almost every hamlet in the country.

The structure of the industry, in its broadest sense, is analogous to an hourglass. Centrally located, between a large number of suppliers on the one hand and a large number of distributors on the other hand, are three concerns practically constituting the auto manufacturing industry, in the narrowest sense of the term. Let us see what advantages this structure has to offer the manufacturers.

[1] Federal Trade Commission, *Report* on Motor Vehicle Industry, House Document No. 468, Seventy-fifth Congress, First Session, p. 1064.

Buying Policies.—Raw material costs run high in automobile manufacturing because of the great variety of raw materials required and because many of the purchases, such as generators, batteries, etc., are the finished products of antecedent manufacturers. As such, they embody not only materials but also labor. In the auto manufacturers' cost structure the total money outlay for these purchases appears as cost of raw materials. Based upon census reports, raw materials in auto manufacturing constitute 67 per cent of the value of products in contrast with 57 per cent for manufacturing generally. Thus it is apparent why auto manufacturers exert every effort to secure the lowest prices.

When the big automobile companies enter the market for basic raw materials, such as steel, glass, and paint, they place orders for large quantities. Most of the producers of these materials are large companies, and as such they are all too frequently in need of large orders for sustaining volume. The automobile companies, realizing this, will naturally place their orders where the hunger for tonnage is the greatest, for there is where they can get the biggest price concessions.

The leading companies in the industry have a reputation for shrewdness in buying. On several occasions the industry is reputed to have "broken" the price of steel, a product long noted for its price rigidity. The president of one of the major steel companies stated in 1939 that the automobile manufacturers had "chiseled away" the $6 to $8 a ton savings effected by the new process of continuous rolling.

The bargaining power of the automobile companies is most pronounced in the market for parts, subassemblies, and accessories. This is a highly competitive market by virtue of the great number of suppliers. Chrysler, for example, does business with 1,400 suppliers. The auto manufacturers with large orders to award can get preferential prices; moreover, they can also use low bids as a wedge for still lower bids from competing suppliers. The integrated companies produce their own parts when they regard prices of suppliers too high. By these and similar measures, pressure is brought to bear upon the suppliers so that the automobile manufacturers often buy at prices very close to cost. Unable to do business at substantial margins with the auto companies, some suppliers have been known to take orders at figures slightly above prime costs for purposes of sustaining volume and strive to recoup, in the replacement market, what competitive conditions prevent them from earning in the original equipment market.

Selling Policies.—The distribution of automobiles is organized so that the burden of competition falls upon the dealers rather than upon the manufacturers. The manufacturers get the advertised prices of their cars less the stipulated commissions paid their distributors. However, for the dealer, the advertised price is only the beginning of a "horse trade" between him and the customer because most buyers already have old cars to trade in. In these transactions the prospective buyer frequently has the upper hand because of the vast number of dealer outlets. The buyer simply shops around until he gets the maximum allowance on his used car, which is often in excess of its resale value. Nor is this the end. The disposal of the used car frequently demands the acceptance of another trade-in. It has been estimated that every new-car sale gives rise to three second-hand sales. Fortunate is the dealer who has retained his commission by the time all the used cars have been disposed of. Thus the burden of competition in merchandising automobiles falls upon the dealers through no malicious design of the manufacturers except insofar as they "encourage competition" through excessive dealer outlets.

However, the distributors who sell the popularly priced cars are subject to a great deal of supervision by the manufacturers. The nature of this manufacturer control is revealed in the following provisions in the manufacturer-dealer agreements.[1]

1. That the dealer shall make a capital investment that is satisfactory to the manufacturer; that no capital withdrawals may be made without the consent of the manufacturer and that, if the manufacturer so indicates, the dealer must leave in the business such part of the profits thereof as may be necessary to increase the investment to a point satisfactory to the manufacturer.

2. That the dealer shall at all times maintain salesrooms, service facilities, and signs satisfactory to the manufacturer.

3. That the dealer shall develop his sales territory to the satisfaction of the manufacturer, including the maintenance of sales and service personnel approved by the manufacturer.

4. That the dealer shall comply with all the manufacturer's policies, whether set out in the agreement, or in addenda thereto, or communicated by letters, or even by oral statements of his field agents who make most of the contacts with the dealers.

5. That in carrying out these policies, the dealer places orders that are binding upon him, but are not binding upon the manufacturer until accepted.

6. That the manufacturer disclaims all financial responsibility for the dealer's commitments, even though they may have been made at the instance of the manufacturer's field men who, by terms of the agreement, can not bind the manufacturer in any way by statements, promises or understandings that are not reduced to writing, signed by the designated officials of the manufacturing company and made a part of the dealer's written agreement.

7. That the dealer must either sell exclusively the line of the manufacturer signing the agreement, or that another, or competing, line may not be handled by the dealer without the consent of the said manufacturer.

[1] "Motor Vehicles Industry, Summary and Conclusions," *Report* of the Federal Trade Commission Prepared and Submitted Pursuant to H. J. Res. 594, p. 13, Seventy-fifth Congress, Third Session (Public Resolution No. 87).

8. That an agreement may be canceled by the manufacturer upon short notice, compared with the dealer's ability to readjust his investment and financial obligations.

Although dealer agreements have been revised since the above complaints were made, not all of the causes for dealer dissatisfaction have been removed. Contracts vary with the times. In lean years, manufacturers are prone to exert greater pressure upon their dealers. In prosperous years, pressure is relaxed and dealers earn reasonable returns on their investments.

THE FUTURE OF THE AUTOMOBILE INDUSTRY

Frequently the question is asked, has the automobile industry entered the last stage of its life cycle—the period characterized by lack of growth or perhaps by decline? There is no debate as to the firm hold it now has on the American consumer. We spend annually about one-sixth of the national income for automobiles and their operation. The automobile challenges clothing for third place in the family budget, and during the depression of the thirties individuals on relief traded food tickets for gasoline. There are many reasons why motor cars appear to be indispensable to Americans: our large continental area, the increase in suburbanization, our restless energy—all these call for flexible and personalized transportation which thus far has been supplied best by the automobile.

The demand for automotive transportation is now taking a significant form. New-car demand averages each year about 3 million units. Most of these are purchased by the upper three-tenths of the population whose income is in excess of $1,700 per family. Since most of these families already own motor cars, the market is primarily a replacement market. New-car buyers "trade in" their used cars which are resold to customers in a lower income group. At this lower level, similar exchanges are made. Thus used cars filter down through successively lower income groups until the resale value approaches scrap value. The long-run expansion of the volume of new-car business depends, then, on the increase in the number of multicar owners, on the extent to which present owners can be induced to buy higher priced cars, and on the increase in exports of automobiles to other countries. There is also, of course, the factor of the rapidity with which the cars now in use are consumed. This calls attention to the increased instability in recent years of the demand for automobiles. This instability is brought out clearly in Fig. 26 and calls for an explanation.

In years of widespread business prosperity more new cars are absorbed at the top level and more used cars are discarded. In years of adversity, fewer new cars are bought because new-car owners at all income levels feel the urge to economize, which they do by postponing the purchase of a new car. The replacement is easily delayed because of the durability of the product. Note in Fig. 26 the disparity between the demand for transportation and the demand for new cars. The gasoline consumption of automobiles during the depression years of the last decade was almost as uniform as the consumption of bread. This was not true of new-car sales. An economic statistician of the Chrysler Corporation has pointed out[1] that from the end of 1923 to the end of 1929 the public increased its inventory of unused passenger-car mileage (by buying more new cars) from 500 billion to 1,090 billion miles. Then the public proceeded to draw on this inventory (by reducing its new-car purchases) until at the end of 1934 the cars on the road contained only 750 billion miles. The decline was equivalent to the mileage built into 5 million new cars. Then,

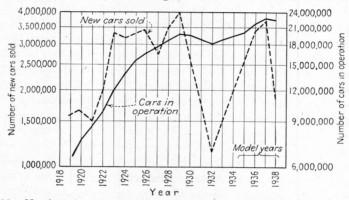

FIG. 26.—Number of cars in operation and new cars sold in United States. (*Dynamics of Automobile Demand, based on papers presented at a joint meeting of the American Statistical Association and the Econometric Society in Detroit, Mich., Dec. 27, 1938. Published by General Motors Corporation, 1939.*)

during the next 3 years, 1935–1937, the unused mileage was again built up some 200 billion miles. Throughout these several periods the amount of automobile driving did not vary greatly. The great cyclical swings that have been noted are, then, variations in production and sales and not in use.

This instability is of especial significance in the automobile industry because, owing to the nature of the production process, costs rise very sharply as production decreases and fall just as sharply when production increases. The net result of this increasing instability which Fig. 26 shows, will be even greater swings in the profits and losses of the producing companies. When general business is brisk and purchasing power high and automobile sales are responding vigorously, gross profit will be disproportionately high. When business activity slumps and consumers

[1] *Proceedings* of the 1938 Ohio Conference of Statisticians, Ohio State University Publications, College of Commerce Conference Series, No. 5, Columbus, Ohio, 1938.

postpone new-car purchases and draw on the potential mileage they have accumulated in their garages, auto sales will fall off sharply.   They did this in 1937 without any warning and caught General Motors, according to their own testimony, totally unaware.   And, in the future, it is not likely that the companies will be able to bring costs into line with these sudden and irregular declines in sales.   Auto workers are now unionized and already have written into their collective bargaining agreements provisions that cushion them against the adverse effects of slack work. Moreover, costs are not as flexible as formerly because of the increased relative importance of overhead.   In the automobile industry, as in most other industries, investment in machinery is constantly becoming heavier. Huge presses and dies are now used for stamping out metal body tops; whereas, in the old days, the hickory and fabric tops were built up by hand.   Investment in a $200,000 press creates overhead costs that cannot be reduced when sales volume declines.   In periods of prosperity earnings will have to be shared to an increasing extent with the tax collector and the workers.   Accordingly, it is unlikely that the future of this industry will be as profitable as its past.   Indeed, the days of adversity have already come to one major producer, the Ford Motor Company. During the 11-year period 1927–1937 inclusive, the Ford company on that portion of its investment which was devoted to the motor vehicle business (534 millions) showed an annual average loss of almost one per cent.

The industry, of course, has virile management, and its product is by no means a mature one.   Automobiles with engines in the rear, with engines of much higher compression and therefore smaller size, automobiles with plastic bodies and with gear shifting entirely eliminated are already a reality or a near prospect.   In other words, technical and style obsolescence can continue for some time to create "dissatisfied" customers.   None of the three leading companies makes any major change of competitive policy without fully taking into account the likely effect of the change on the other two.   In other words, we have in this industry the conditions which make for "monopolistic competition" and therefore we are not likely to witness another case of the Kilkenny cats who consumed each other.   Furthermore, the automobile companies have been steadily increasing the diversity of their products and stand ready to enter aircraft manufacture on a large scale when, as, and if this latter industry attains the stage of mass production.   These and other factors make the above prediction concerning the long-run profit trend in automobile manufacturing no more than a considered guess—which is all it is intended to be.

CHAPTER XII

THE AIRCRAFT MANUFACTURING INDUSTRY

Ships are made individually, tailored to specifications; automobiles are produced *en masse* according to standard specifications. The former exemplifies custom building, the latter mass production. Which technique is used to make airplanes? The answer is—neither, precisely, and both, in part—a hybrid process which may be called job-lot production. Ships, autos, and airplanes are utterly dissimilar except that they have a common use—transportation. An airplane is larger than an auto, smaller than a ship, faster than either, and it travels through a medium unstable at best. Air varies greatly as to density, temperature, and velocity. To operate safely in its unstable medium, aircraft must be made, therefore, to withstand a wide variety of natural conditions.

Instability characterizes the aircraft industry as well as the medium through which its products operate. The industry is young and therefore has attained no clearly defined position in our industrial economy. Its products undergo rapid change—new designs are constantly replacing their predecessors. Its technology of manufacture is ever changing to meet new demands. Its location is shifting. Production is sporadic, earnings irregular, and the future uncertain. Before the national defense emergency arose in 1941, the industry was small sized, in contrast with other industries. The latest census data report 125 plants, 49,000 workers, and 280 million dollars' worth of planes and parts produced. But that was in 1939. Since that time the industry has grown so fast that the above figures are of interest only to the historian.

Milestones in the Development of Aviation.—Mankind's desire to fly probably antedates the dawn of civilization. Actual experiments were made as early as the thirteenth century by Roger Bacon and in the fifteenth century by the versatile Leonardo da Vinci. In the nineteenth century, numerous individuals, both here and abroad, experimented with gliders. The first power-driven airplane capable of sustained flight was perfected by the Wright Brothers. They made their historic flight at Kitty Hawk, N. C., in December, 1903, with a biplane equipped with a 16-hp. motor, both of their own design. Success crowned their efforts very largely because their motor was just below the critical weight of 16-lb. per horsepower. Curiously, the achievement of the Wright brothers failed to stimulate an immediate interest in aviation. This interest first developed abroad, following Orville Wright's demonstration flying, in 1908, in France.

After that time, a series of record flights was made which foreshadowed the military and commercial possibilities of the airplane. In 1909, Bleriot flew across the English Channel. In 1910, Curtiss flew from Albany to New York. In 1919, Alcock and Brown spanned the Atlantic by flying from Newfoundland to Ireland. These flights, however noteworthy as milestones in the development of aviation, were completely overshadowed by Lindbergh's flight, in 1927, from New York to Paris. Lindbergh's flight started a stampede of dare-devil flights by others. Although many of these flights ended in disaster, numerous long-distance records were established. For example, in 1931, Post and Gatty flew around the world in $8\frac{2}{3}$ days. In 1938, the time for encircling the globe was cut to 3 days and 19 hours.

GROWTH OF THE AIRCRAFT MANUFACTURING INDUSTRY

Commercial production of aircraft began about 1909 when the United States Army bought a plane from the Wright brothers. Ever since that time, with few exceptions, the army and the navy have been the largest customers. There was very little production prior to the First World War. Approximately 15,000 planes were made during that war, which served as a proving ground for the airplane. Immediately after the war, production collapsed and civilian flying was confined chiefly to barnstorming by aviators who bought some of the army's surplus stock of planes. Flying was hazardous because technically the airplane had scarcely emerged from the "haywire and tomato crate" stage and flying facilities, such as landing fields and beacons, were nonexistent.

Between the First and Second World Wars American aircraft manufacturing expanded but not phenomenally. Although orders for military craft continued to be the chief source of demand, the expansion in civil aviation produced a growing demand for nonmilitary planes. Underlying favorable factors were, first, the rapid strides in improved design, proof of which was the numerous epochal flights; second, the ease with which the industry obtained capital—speculative mania was rampant during the twenties so that almost any kind of a security was marketable; and, third, the government assumed a growing interest in promoting flying—both civil and military.

Before describing the recent developments growing out of the sudden intensification of national defense efforts, let us pause to examine the aircraft industry in a period that may be regarded as normal. This will help us to appreciate the gigantic task of expansion that President Roosevelt imposed on the industry.

ORGANIZATION OF THE AIRCRAFT INDUSTRY

The aircraft industry consists of approximately 30 major companies in the sense that each one of these produces one or more types of planes marketed under its own name. These companies fall into two groups based upon the degree of integration—the integrated and the nonintegrated. An integrated company is one having the facilities for making a complete plane, including the major units such as airframes, motors, and propellers, within its own organization. The nonintegrated companies make planes of their own design by assembling ready-made units, such as motors and propellers, produced by either the integrated companies or aircraft supply manufacturers. There are approximately 200 companies producing aircraft supplies and accessories such as instruments, tires, parachutes, etc.

There are three integrated companies, as defined above—United Aircraft Corporation, Curtiss-Wright Corporation, and The Aviation Corporation. The largest of these is Curtiss-Wright. It embraces the St. Louis Airplane division, producer of large land transports; the Curtiss Aeroplane division, the oldest airplane manufacturer which in recent years has specialized in military craft (bombers, pursuit, and scout-observation planes); the Wright Aeronautical division, producer of airplane motors, and the Curtiss Propeller division.

United Aircraft Corporation makes the Pratt and Whitney engines, Hamilton Standard propellers, and Vought-Sikorsky planes.

Aviation Corporation, the smallest of the integrated companies, produces Stinson and Vultee planes, Lycoming motors, and hollow steel propellers.

TABLE XX.—SOME LEADING AIRCRAFT MANUFACTURERS
(In millions of dollars)

Company	Net Sales, 1939
United Aircraft	$52
Curtiss-Wright	49
Lockheed	35
Douglas	28
North American	28
Glenn L. Martin	24
Boeing	12
Consolidated	4
Aviation Corporation	3
Piper	2

Source: *Standard Statistics* and *Moody's*.

The nonintegrated companies may be classified roughly as producers of commercial transports, military and small private planes depending upon which of the three types predominates. Douglas, Boeing, and Lockheed are the leading producers of commercial transport planes. Brewster,

Consolidated Aircraft, Grumman, Glenn L. Martin, and North American are among the leading producers of military craft. Outstanding producers of small private planes are Piper, Taylorcraft, and Aeronautical Corporation of America. The relative size of the leading companies based on volume of business for 1939 is shown in Table XX.

To the above roster of outstanding names in aircraft manufacturing should be added Allison, the liquid-cooled motor manufacturing subsidiary of General Motors, and two outstanding aircraft supplies manufacturers—Sperry Corporation and Bendix.

TECHNOLOGY OF MANUFACTURE

Aircraft is manufactured by the job-lot type of production. Until recently mass production was inapplicable because, first, the total volume was too small; second, planes were made in a great variety of models; and third, obsolescence occurred with startling rapidity.

The aircraft industry had a relatively busy year in 1938, yet the total volume of production was only 3,675 planes. This is in contrast with the 2 to 4 million motor cars produced annually. The great variety of airplane types also prevented mass production. The 1938 production consisted of 1,800 military planes, 1,425 light commercial, 300 private and business, and 150 airline transport planes. Each of these groups is composed of numerous subclasses. Military planes, for example, include bombers, transports, trainers, pursuit, attack, scout, and numerous other classes of planes. Mass production of planes will be difficult as long as designs change so rapidly. A manufacturer frequently spends several hundred thousand dollars designing a plane that is outmoded by a new and improved design when only a few have been produced.

Designing.—Designing an airplane is somewhat like designing a ship. There are many kinds of planes, each for its own special purpose. Some are designed for overland service and others for oversea service; some are designed to fly at normal altitudes, others for stratosphere flight; some are designed for exceptionally high-speed operation, others for heavy loads at normal speed, etc. These and other considerations determine whether it shall be a single or multimotor, monoplane or biplane, low or high wing, fixed or retractable landing gear, etc. The recent Douglas 42-passenger transport, the DC 4, required 500,000 hours of engineering time and 100,-000 hours of laboratory testing time.

Machining.—Machining operations in an aircraft factory differ from machining in a mass-production factory in that most of the equipment consists of multipurpose machine tools, such as the jig borer. Fewer but more versatile machine tools are used so that maximum utilization can be obtained from this costly equipment. This naturally calls for more highly skilled labor than is required in mass-production industries. Wages in the aircraft industry are 27.5 per cent of the value of product in contrast with 16 per cent in the automobile industry.

Assembly.—In the larger aircraft factories, semiassembly-line production methods are employed. With respect to both the unit assemblies and the final assembly, overhead conveyors are used to move, at periodic intervals, the incomplete assembly from one work station to the next. One of the chief differences between the semiassembly line and the mass-production assembly line is that, in the latter, the conveyor moves continuously, whereas, in the former, it does not. In the assembly of the

PLATE 38.—Assembly of the fuselage. (*Courtesy of Vultee Aircraft, Division Aviation Manufacturing Corporation.*)

fuselage, for example, a series of approximately 20 work stations is set up along the assembly line. For several hours at a time the line remains stationary as the workers at each station install unit assemblies and subassemblies on each fuselage in various stages of completion. At periodic intervals, the conveyor moves all planes forward to their next work stations. From one to six completed planes come down the semiassembly line per day, depending upon the size of orders.

Costs of Production and Profits.—The cost of building an 11-passenger transport plane, convertible into a bomber, is approximately $75,000, exclusive of designing and engineering costs. The selling price (in quantities) may be $100,000 depending upon what equipment is included, but it must not be concluded that the manufacturer has made a $25,000 profit.   The development costs must be reckoned with.   They amount to approximately $300,000 for a plane of this type.   Net profits per plane depend, therefore, upon how many planes are sold before the design becomes obsolete.   Some measure of the relation between volume and cost is shown by the bids submitted, in 1939, to the government for single-engine interceptor pursuit planes.   Seversky, the low bidder, submitted figures ranging from $34,080 to $23,507 in lots from 1 to 300 planes—*i.e.*, the contract price per plane depended upon the size of the order.

TABLE XXI.—EARNINGS OF AIRCRAFT MANUFACTURERS
(In percentage earned on invested capital)

Year	Avi-ation Corp.	Boeing	Con-soli-dated Air-craft	Curtiss-Wright	Douglas	Lock-heed	Martin	North Amer.	United Air-craft
1929	4.0(d)	....	30.7	2.8(d)	12.9	....	1.2		
1930	19.2(d)	....	4.2	15.3(d)	20.3	....	6.0		
1931	17.4(d)	....	7.2(d)	11.6(d)	15.3	....	4.4	2.0(d)	
1932	50.6(d)	....	14.8(d)	2.1(d)	2.8	....	4.8	1.5(d)	
1933	3.9	....	....	0.5	1.2	9.7	1.4	14.8(d)	
1934	16.4(d)	7.1(d)	....	1.3	0.9	52.8(d)	1.6(d)	18.0(d)	0.2(d)
1935	3.9(d)	12.7(d)	13.6	0.1	22.5	31.0	12.2(d)	0.3(d)	2.8
1936	0.9	5.0	5.2	3.6	9.3	4.1	12.6	0.1	8.8
1937	4.2(d)	4.3	12.0	6.7	10.0	5.5	13.6	8.3	16.2
1938	2.0	7.7(d)	32.2	11.4	19.9	10.5	16.8	24.4	22.8
1939	19.9(d)	86.3(d)	19.0	15.1	20.7	36.3	22.9	72.4	28.8
1940	0.6	3.2	23.4	34.0	48.7	12.3	25.7	56.2	36.0

(d) Denotes deficit.
Source: Standard and Poor's Corporation.

   Profits in aircraft manufacturing have been rather small and exceedingly irregular.   Earnings of the leading companies, expressed as a percentage return on capital invested, are shown in Table XXI.   Note the frequency of deficits and the small return on capital invested not only during but also since the depression of the thirties.   However, earnings after 1935 show marked improvement—a reflection of large military orders of both domestic and foreign origin.   Douglas and Martin are the only companies that have demonstrated a rather consistent earning power.   For the industry as a whole, the record of profits looks, as someone has aptly said, like a fever chart.   Profits are fitful because of the adverse combination of small volume of business, irregular orders, and rapid obsolescence.   The data of Table XXI are summarized and presented in somewhat different form in Fig. 27 which reflects more clearly the irregularity of earnings of the leading companies.

The constant change in aircraft design fostered by manufacturers, in their quest for profits, is a boon and at the same time a source of despair to the commercial transport companies.   Barring accidents and obsolescence, a transport plane is serviceable for 8 to 10 years.   Actually obsolescence reduces the serviceable life to only 2 to 3 years.   Plane manufacturers solicit new business by constant redesigning of new and improved planes, and the airlines, likewise, solicit business by constantly striving to be equipped with the latest transports.   For example, in 1933, United Airlines spent $2,500,000 for 55 new Boeings.   Within 6 months there-

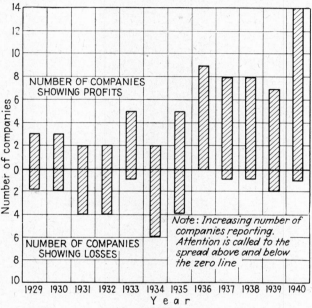

Fig. 27.—Profits and losses of leading aircraft companies. (*Standard and Poor's Corporation.*)

after, Douglas brought out a new plane that outloaded and outsped the Boeings.   T.W.A. promptly bought a fleet of the new Douglases, and immediately United had to spend another $1,500,000 to revamp its Boeings.   Shortly thereafter both Douglas and Boeing again brought out new models which were better than their predecessors.   Before a new plane is rolled out of the shops, engineers are already at work on their drafting boards, designing a better model.   The impact of such rapid obsolescence upon manufacturers' costs and profits is obvious.

THE AIRCRAFT INDUSTRY IN NATIONAL DEFENSE

In the spring of 1940 when France was on the verge of collapsing under the German invasion she frantically called for "clouds of planes."

England was busy defending herself, so the American aircraft industry was the best potential source of aid. Emphasis, however, must be placed upon the word "potential" because the United States was just awakening to the need for national defense. Our aircraft industry was woefully unprepared to render assistance to anyone. That same spring, in a message to Congress, President Roosevelt expressed a need for 50,000 planes a year. For an industry geared up to an annual production of about 5,000 planes, that was indeed a formidable task. Almost immediately, however, the industry accepted the challenge and by August, 1941, it was on schedule with production running at the rate of 18,000 planes a year.

The enormity of the task is difficult to appreciate. Witness the fact that one prominent automobile manufacturer replied to the President that within 6 months he could produce 1,000 planes a day if they were of one type and the design were completely frozen. The foregoing "ifs" plus several others are the major obstacles to mass production of airplanes.

Military planes, whatever the total number required, are not and cannot be of one type. The army and navy each need 12 to 14 distinct types of planes. Actually the industry produces about 50 types, including several British types. It is estimated that variety cannot be cut below 35 to 40 kinds of planes without sacrifice of military efficiency.

Rapidity of obsolescence is even more true of military than commercial planes. For reasons of military necessity, especially during war, plane designs literally push each other off the drawing boards. Under such conditions it is easy to imagine the difficulties of getting started on mass production. The essence of mass production is interchangeability of parts, but with rapidly changing design of product, standardization of parts is almost impossible.

Other difficulties, though somewhat less serious, standing in the way of mass production of airplanes are: first, the huge size of planes in contrast with automobiles; second, the high degree of precision and perfection of workmanship required; and third, the reluctance to embark upon mass production in view of the uncertainty as to when the market will collapse. The first difficulty is met by "breaking up" a plane into integral units or subassemblies which can then be put together in semifinal and final assemblies. For example, a medium-sized bomber consists of some 30,000 single parts which are made into 650 minor subassemblies. The latter, in turn, are made into 32 major subassemblies before the final assembly takes place. The manufacturer is guided by the precept—"Keep the parts (subassemblies) from becoming too big."

Precision and perfection of workmanship are attained by high standards and minute tolerances plus frequent inspection. For example, the motor for a plane of the type just mentioned contains about 5,000 parts, each of which must be inspected from one to ten times. Thus approximately 25,000 inspections are required.

Reluctance to set up mass production is overcome by financial aid rendered by the government. The solution is government-built (British and American) plants privately operated.

The Backlog.—In the middle of the year 1941, the aircraft industry had 7,500 million dollars' worth of unfilled orders. Using the 1939 output as a base, the 1941 backlog represented 30 years' business. In other words, there were enough orders to keep the industry busy for 30 years at the 1939 rate of output. This comparison indicates the huge task that confronts the industry.

The Plan.—How soon can the industry produce 50,000 planes a year as called for by the President? That goal will be reached by 1944 according to the estimate of one authority on aircraft. The past and estimated future production is shown in Fig. 28.

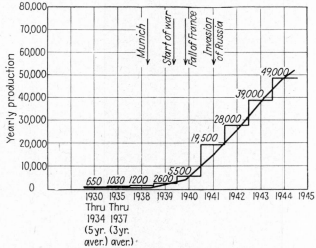

Fig. 28.—Estimated production of military aircraft 1941 to 1944. (Combined program of United States Army and Navy and British Purchasing Commission.) (*T. P. Wright, The Truth about Our National Defense Program, Aviation,* Jan. 1941.)

The Execution.—In order to produce 50,000 planes a year, the industry must expand its manufacturing facilities in all directions. Factory floor space must be increased from 14 to 40 million sq. ft. to produce the airframes. Approximately two and one-half engines are required per plane. Floor space for making the engines must be expanded in roughly similar proportions. Within a year after plans were laid, Wright Aeronautical Corporation started making 1,700-hp. engines in its new plant in Cincinnati. The plant covers 2,120,000 sq. ft. Prior to the national defense expansion, aircraft plants were heavily concentrated in Los

Angeles, Baltimore, and Buffalo.   For military reasons, the new plants are being located at strategic points between the Appalachian and Rocky Mountain ranges.

Labor requirements will have to be expanded from 120,000 to 400,000 workers.

In addition to this great expansion, the aircraft manufacturers are using all possible facilities of the automobile industry.   An automobile manufacturer cannot shift to airplane manufacture immediately, but, under proper guidance of an aircraft manufacturer, a large part of the productive facilities of an auto plant can be used to make parts and subassemblies for aircraft.   Ford's new airplane plant at Ypsilanti, Mich., will make subassemblies for both Consolidated, which is operating a huge government-built plant at Fort Worth, and Douglas, which is operating another government-built plant at Tulsa.   General Motors will make subassemblies for North American, which is operating a large government-built plant at Kansas City.   Another large plant built by the government at Omaha will be operated by Glenn L. Martin, with subassemblies supplied by Chrysler, Goodyear, and Hudson.   Studebaker is cooperating with Wright Aeronautical to build engines.   Packard, Nash, and Continental Motors are likewise producing aircraft motors, parts, and accessories.

Plane production is being accelerated by still another method—mass-production technique—not as we know it in the automobile industry, but in a modified form.   The greatest stumbling block to quantity production of airplanes is the need for optimum design excellence.   Despite this outstanding difficulty, the industry uses mass-production technique insofar as possible.   This may be illustrated with reference to designing, machining, and assembly.   As already indicated, numerous types of planes are called for and designs change rapidly.   However, wherever possible individual parts and subassemblies are standardized for use in two or more types of planes.

In machining, the industry is increasing productivity by using more automatic machine tools, intricate jig borers, 5,000-ton presses, high-capacity air drop hammers.   For example, Wright has developed the famous Greenlee machine to drill, countersink, ream, and tap aluminum cylinder heads.   This machine automatically performs 71 separate machining operations with 134 cutting tools.   Production is stepped up from 2 to 35 cylinder heads per hour.   Although it is an expensive machine, it requires a smaller amount of skilled labor to operate.   Machining costs have also been reduced by the greater use of specially designed jigs and fixtures.

Productivity has likewise been increased by improved assembly methods, semiassembly production lines, as already described, still predominate, but they have been lengthened and more plants are using this method. Lockheed makes interceptor pursuit planes in its Burbank, Calif., plant whose final assembly line is 820 ft. long. Throughout its length there are 30 work stations where 30 planes, in various stages of completion, are being assembled. Trainer planes come off the final assembly line at Vultee in Los Angeles at the rate of one every 2½ hours. This line is fed with subassemblies, such as fuselage sections, wings, tail units, by overhead conveyor spur lines. Engine production has attained continuous moving assembly.

THE FUTURE

To predict the future of the aircraft industry is to predict the duration of the Second World War. Prior to the Japanese attack upon Pearl Harbor, the American aircraft industry had already expanded from one of our smallest to one of our largest industries. Until the war ends, the aircraft industry will continue to expand production as rapidly as existing supplies of materials, tools, and labor will permit.

As for the postwar period, one can only speculate. It is extremely unlikely that the peacetime demand will take up where the military demand leaves off. However, the war will very likely stimulate postwar private flying. In 1941, there were over 100,000 certified pilots; after the war there will be a great many more, and they will constitute a large potential demand for aircraft.

PART IV
THE NONMETALLIC MINERAL INDUSTRIES

CHAPTER XIII

THE CEMENT INDUSTRY

The cement industry produces a product used almost wholly by the building and construction industry. This dependence of cement upon building determines, as we shall see, many of the characteristics peculiar to the cement industry. Its early struggle for recognition as a durable building material, its subsequent manufacture to standard specifications, its carefully controlled technique of manufacture, the rapid rate of growth of the industry, its pronounced irregularity of production—both seasonal and cyclical—its price rigidity—all stem from this interrelationship.

Definition of Cement.—Portland cement may be defined as an intimate mixture of pulverized lime, alumina, and silica burned to the point where fusion begins and the resulting clinker ground to a very fine powder. When cement is mixed with gravel, slag, sand, and water and the whole mass allowed to set, the resulting artificial stone is known as concrete.

Prior to the development of Portland cement, so called because of its resemblance to a rock found on the English Isle of Portland, the principal cements were natural cement and puzzolan. Natural cement is made from cement rock, a naturally occurring raw material that needed only to be burned and pulverized. As early as 1820 it was used in the building of the Erie Canal, and until 1900 it represented over 60 per cent of the total cement produced in the United States. Puzzolan cement is a mixture of slaked lime and granulated blast furnace slag. Since these two cements constitute today less than one per cent of the total output, our chief concern is with Portland cement.

Historical Development of the Industry.—Portland cement was first made in 1824 by Joseph Aspdin, a bricklayer of Leeds, England. His method of manufacture differed from earlier methods in that he mixed several ingredients not already combined by nature and burned them at a very high temperature until they formed a clinker. Prior to that time all methods were deliberately designed to avoid the latter result by burning the materials at lower temperatures.

The new cement did not receive a ready acceptance because of the great importance of the natural cement industry in England and the high reputation of the natural product. It was not until the fifties that Portland cement proved its superiority over natural cement, and after that the industry expanded rapidly in England and spread to other European countries, notably Belgium, Germany, and France.

Despite the great increase in general industrial construction in the United States after the Civil War and the consequent heavy demand for cement, the manufacture of Portland cement in this country lagged behind developments abroad. The first Portland cement mill was not established until 1872, approximately 50 years after the experiments of Aspdin and 25 years after the development of commercial production abroad. The reasons for this delay are twofold. First, we had a large supply of natural cement. Second, after information of the new cement spread to this country and its qualities were appreciated, there was a marked preference for European cements. The popularity of the foreign cements over the domestic product was so great that many of the early manufacturers were compelled by dealers to market their cement under foreign brand names. Between 1878 and 1893 imports of Portland cement increased greatly, and it was not until 1896 that domestic production exceeded imports and not until 1900 that it exceeded natural cement.

The real development of the industry began after 1900 with the coming in of the rotary kiln, which was developed just prior thereto, and the standardization of the product immediately following. Prior to the development of the rotary kiln cement was burned in upright stationary kilns, which had to be charged and unloaded after every burning. While these kilns were economical in the consumption of coal they required large amounts of labor. The rotary kiln, on the other hand, operated continuously and while it consumed more coal it was much more economical in its labor requirements. Since the United States had large supplies of cheap coal the new development by conserving labor lowered the cost of production.

In the early years of the industry the quality of cement varied greatly from mill to mill and from one batch to another. The lack of uniformity retarded the use of the product because engineers and architects could not accurately determine its strength and durability. In 1904 the American Society for Testing Materials adopted rigid specifications of specific gravity, fineness, tensile strength, setting time, and chemical composition. These specifications have been improved upon from time to time, and finally cement became a highly standardized product, the output of one manufacturer being identical with that of another. The uniformity of cement greatly increased public confidence and widened the market for its uses. Whereas during the period 1880 to 1899, production of Portland cement expanded slowly, after 1900, as Fig. 29 shows, Portland cement grew at a very rapid rate and natural cement entered into a decline.

The growth of the industry after 1900 was stimulated by a number of other factors. On the supply side, the important factor was the steady decline in the price of cement. In 1880 it sold for $3 a barrel, but with the introduction of the rotary kiln and larger and more efficient grinding equipment the price declined rapidly. Since 1920 the price declined from $2 to $1, but since the low point in 1932 it has again increased to about $1.50. The decline put cement on a competitive level with other

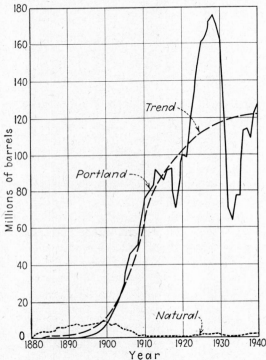

Fig. 29.—United States cement production 1880 to 1940. (*Mineral Resources*, 1940; *Survey of Current Business.*)

building materials. On the demand side, the market was responsive to the decreasing price. Construction was increasing rapidly, and the greater heights of buildings required stronger and more durable materials. The rapid rise of the automobile industry created a greater demand for more and better roads. For both of these uses, and for many others, cement was superior to competitive materials. It was not only cheap in price, it was easily handled and in several ways, was much superior. In the case of roads, for example, while the original cost of concrete is higher than most competing materials, the maintenance cost, as shown in Table XXII, is lower than any other type. The Federal Aid Road

Act, 1916, made available large sums of money for the development of roads, and by 1934 about 35 per cent of the Federal Aid roads in the country were constructed of concrete.

Location.—Cement manufacturing in the early years was heavily concentrated in the Lehigh Valley because of the excellent limestone deposits and the concentration of the population in the eastern section of the country. This district produced about 70 per cent of our cement in 1900. Although it has since grown in production, it has declined relative to the total industry production, and today it produces less than 20 per cent of the aggregate output. The relative decline of the Lehigh district may be explained largely by technical developments permitting the utilization of lower grade raw materials, the growth in the application of fuels other than coal, and the rise of distant markets in the West and South, too far removed from the Lehigh district to be economically served by it. Cement is now being manufactured in almost every state in the union. The heaviest concentration of productive capacity is in Pennsylvania, New York, Ohio, Indiana, and Illinois. In other words, the distribution of cement mills is roughly proportionate to the distribution of population.

TABLE XXII.—ANNUAL ROAD MAINTENANCE COSTS PER MILE
(Various types of roads)

Concrete	$ 97.18
Brick—concrete base	221.58
Bituminous concrete	248.93
Bituminous macadam	342.87
Macadam	541.42
Gravel	276.79
Rock asphalt	154.78

Source: "Cement and Concrete Reference Book," Portland Cement Association, Chicago, Ill., 1941.

The factors having the greatest influence on the location of cement mills are the relative positions of raw materials and the market. Though the fuel consumption is quite large and represents a large portion of the cost of manufacturing, there are few, if any, areas in the United States where at least one of the fuels, coal, oil, or gas, cannot be obtained. Cement, like pig iron, has a low value per unit of weight, and nearness to market is of paramount importance. When we consider the raw materials, however, we find that a cement mill must be located at the source. The widespread distribution of limestone together with the widespread supply of fuel has permitted the location of cement mills with primary consideration being given to the market.

Technique of Manufacture.—The first step in the manufacture of cement is the quarrying, mining, or dredging of the raw materials. The method employed depends upon the material; cement rock, limestone, and shale are quarried; clay is dug from pits; marl is dredged; and mining is resorted to only when the topsoil is too thick to permit economical stripping.   Of the three methods, quarrying is the most important.

After the raw material has been obtained it is crushed in immense gyratory crushers that reduce the large blocks of rock to small pieces about one inch in diameter.   The material is then passed through rotary dryers, which measure 5 to 8 ft. in diameter and 50 to 80 ft. long and are fired by powdered coal or oil.   This is known as the "dry process" and is used with dry materials such as cement rock and limestone.   If the raw materials have a high moisture content, the wet process is employed.[1] In this process the material is crushed and mixed with water and reduced

PLATE 39.—Quarrying limestone rock.   (*Courtesy of Universal Atlas Cement Company.*)

to the consistency of thin mud.   While both methods find about equal use in this country, the wet process is considered the better.   It makes grinding easier, eliminates the drying, the material is easier to handle, and there is less dust.   The disadvantage of the wet process is that more fuel is required and greater kiln capacity must be provided.

The next step, common to both the wet and dry process, is grinding. This is done in steel tubes, 7 to 10 ft. in diameter and 22 to 40 ft. long, half filled with steel balls from $1\frac{1}{2}$ to 5 in. in diameter.   As the tube revolves the balls pulverize the materials into particles finer than flour. When the materials leave the tube they are stored to permit chemical testing and the mixing of any necessary ingredients to assure uniformity of quality.

[1] In 1938 about 53 per cent of the industry's capacity employed the dry process.

Once the materials have been tested and properly apportioned, they pass into the giant rotary kilns. Kilns vary greatly in size, ranging from 110 to 400 ft. in length and 6 to 12 ft. in diameter. They are mounted horizontally on ball bearings and are inclined at a pitch of about ¾ in. per foot to facilitate the passage of the materials through the kiln. The pulverized mixture or "slurry" is fed into the upper end. As the kiln rotates the slurry works its way toward the discharge end. Coming in from the other end is a powerful flame, caused by blowing in pulverized coal, oil, or gas. The temperature at the hottest point is about 2800°F., and the material is fused into a clinker. The kiln is operated continu-

PLATE 40.—Rotary kilns. (*Courtesy of Universal Atlas Cement Company.*)

ously 24 hours per day and 7 days per week, and a moderate-sized kiln can burn over 800 barrels per day.

After the clinker is cooled it goes into the storage yards, where it can be kept indefinitely without deterioration, or it is mixed with gypsum and ground into a finer powder. It is then ready for shipment either in bags or in bulk.

Technological progress in the industry has permitted the increased use of lower grade raw materials and the use of less fuel per barrel of cement. The latter development is of major importance because fuel is a large item in the cost of manufacturing cement. The decrease in fuel requirements has been brought about chiefly by increasing the size of kilns and by utilizing waste heat from the kilns for the production of power. Another development along the lines of waste-heat utilization is the development of a clinker cooler designed to cool the clinker and to recover the dissipated hot secondary air for combustion in the kiln.   In 1934 the Valley Forge Cement Company announced the installation of a flotation process.   It is a method of removing calcite, an impurity, by first treating the slurry with an acid which has an affinity for calcite. After adding a frothing agent, the mixture is whipped up by introducing air into the flotation cells.   When the mixture is allowed to settle a froth of fine bubbles appears on top, carrying with it the calcite particles which are then skimmed off.   The process, it is claimed, will increase reserves through utilization of lower grade stone, reduce quarrying costs through elimination of selective quarrying, decrease grinding costs of both raw stock and clinker, eliminate the purchase of high-grade limestone, and make possible the economical production of special cements through control of kiln feeds.

TABLE XXIII.—CAPITAL REQUIREMENTS PER BARREL OF ANNUAL CAPACITY FOR A MODERN PLANT

Land and deposits*	$0.25
Cement plant equipment	1.65
Waste-heat equipment	0.40
Total fixed capital	$2.30
Working capital	0.37
Total capital required	$2.67

* Variable.
Source: NRA *Hearings* on The Cement Industry, July 11, 1934.

Cement manufacturing is conducted on a large scale.   It is estimated that a new plant, equipped with the most modern machinery, cannot operate efficiently with a clinker capacity of less than 1.5 million barrels. This represents a capital investment of about 3.5 million dollars.   Add to this a minimum working capital requirement of $500,000 and the total minimum capital becomes 4 millions.   In Table XXIII the principal items of capital are broken down to a per-barrel basis.

TABLE XXIV.—AVERAGE NUMBER OF MAN-HOURS REQUIRED TO PRODUCE 100 BARRELS OF CEMENT IN 88 MILLS, 1934, BY ANNUAL PLANT CAPACITY

Annual capacity (million barrels)	Number of plants	Man-hours per 100 barrels
All plants	88	47.6
Over 3	4	40.0
2.5 to 2.9	6	47.5
2.0 to 2.49	10	49.3
1.5 to 1.99	29	48.5
1.0 to 1.49	29	56.0
Under 1	10	64.5

Source: *Monthly Labor Review*, March, 1936, p. 575.

Cement plants are operated on a large scale because of resulting economies of labor, fuel, and overhead. The effect of plant size on labor costs is shown in Table XXIV.

Fuel costs in cement manufacturing run very high. For the industry as a whole, fuel cost 30 cents per barrel of cement in 1935, in contrast with a cost of approximately 27 cents per barrel for labor. Stated in another way, fuel and power costs represent about 35 per cent of the total value of cement produced. Large-scale operation cuts down fuel consumption, as shown in Fig. 30. The same temperature must be attained regardless of the size of the kiln, and more effective use of that heat is obtained in larger kilns because doubling the kiln capacity does not require twice as much fuel. Cement producers have made strenuous efforts to economize

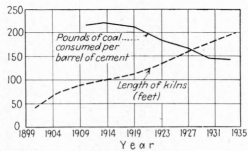

Fig. 30.—Trend in length of kilns and consumption of coal. (*Technology and the Mineral Industries, National Research Project, Philadelphia, April,* 1937.)

on fuel—note, in Table XXIII, that the capital expenditure for waste-heat reclamation is 60 per cent more than the investment in land and deposits.

Structure of the Industry.—In 1939 the cement industry comprised about 78 companies, with 160 mills employing approximately 24,000 workers. The five leading companies (Universal-Atlas, Lone Star, Lehigh Portland, Alpha Portland, and Penn Dixie) control about 40 per cent of the total industry capacity. The six mills next in size control about 15 per cent of the capacity. Thus, 11 of the 78 companies have 55 per cent of the total capacity. All of the large companies, and some of the smaller, own two or more plants. The five largest producers, for example, had between them a total of 59 mills, and the six next in size had 27 mills. In such companies the mills are not concentrated at one point but are located near several markets. This is due to the limited demand in any one market and the difficulty of shipping to distant markets because of the high transportation costs. Expansion of existing companies, therefore, took the form of construction or purchase of mills in new areas rather than expansion of the original plant. The five largest companies achieved expansion by the acquisition of mills through consolidation and merger.

Wide Fluctuations in Demand.—The nature of the market for cement subjects the cement industry to wide fluctuations in demand. As Table XXV shows, the construction industry is the largest single market and together with road construction represents over 50 per cent of the total market for cement. Since almost all cement is used out of doors, the nature of construction work and road building favors activity in the spring, summer, and fall months. In large part this is due to the effects

TABLE XXV.—DISTRIBUTION OF USES OF PORTLAND CEMENT, 1938

Use	Per Cent
Paving: Roads, streets and airports	24
Structural: Buildings, bridges and railroads	29
Conservation: Reclamation, water supply and sewerage	17
Housing and miscellaneous uses	20
Farm	10
Total	100

Source: "Cement and Concrete Reference Book," Portland Cement Association, Chicago, Ill., 1939.

of inclement weather upon construction materials, but in part it is due to custom. Despite the progress that has been made in laying concrete in cold weather, the milder months are still favored for construction.

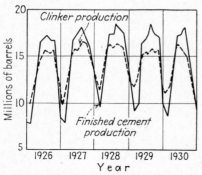

FIG. 31.—Seasonality in Portland cement production. (*America's Capacity to Produce, The Brooking's Institution, Washington, D. C.*, 1934.)

The importance of construction and road building in the market for cement, therefore, causes wide seasonal swings in the demand. (See Fig. 31.) Shipments of cement of the entire industry are from two to four times as large in May, June, July, August, and September as in the other months of the year. The seasonality in the North is even more pronounced than that of the industry as a whole.

Of even greater importance to the instability of the industry are the wide cyclical fluctuations in demand. These fluctuations, like the seasonal ones, are due to the importance of construction in the market for cement. Construction activity, as is true of most durable goods industries, is determined largely by general business conditions, rising to great heights in periods of prosperity and sinking to very low levels in periods of depression. The fluctuations in construction activity and its relation to cement shipments are shown in Fig. 32.

The wide fluctuations in the demand for cement impose a heavy burden upon the industry. To serve the market it is necessary to have sufficient capacity to meet the peak seasonal and cyclical demands. These peaks, as has been stated, are considerably above the valleys, and since the cement plants must always operate 24 hours a day if they operate at all, the peak demand cannot be met, as in many other industries, by increasing the hours of operation per day. Since operations must be conducted on a continuous basis, the rate of operation in a cement mill is determined by the number of kilns in operation. Consequently, in a five-kiln mill only five different levels of operation are possible: 20, 40, 60, 80, and 100 per cent. Therefore, sufficient equipment must be installed to meet the peak loads. This gives rise to excess capacity, and since the average fixed investment per barrel of capacity is approximately

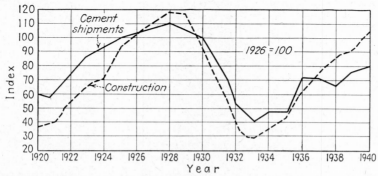

Fig. 32.—Cement shipments and volume of construction. (*Cement and Concrete Reference Book*, 1937. *Standard and Poor's Corporation.*)

$2.30, the financial burden that must be carried in periods of low activity is apparent.

To minimize the excess capacity, the industry irons out some of the seasonality by manufacturing clinker for storage in the slack months. Cement in the clinker stage does not deteriorate and can be stored for grinding in the busy season. This practice reduces the kiln capacity, which represents the major part of plant investment, and increases the need for grinding capacity. There is, of course, a limit to the amount of clinker that can be stored, because storage facilities and carrying charges require the investment of capital. The ratio of kiln capacity to grinding capacity varies from one plant to another, but for the industry as a whole kiln capacity is about 10 per cent less than grinding capacity. The results of this practice upon plant utilization are indicated in Fig. 31; clinker production fluctuates less than finished cement production. The distinction between clinker capacity and grinding capacity must always be kept in mind in measuring the capacity of the cement industry. Grinding capacity figures overstate and clinker capacity figures understate actual production capacity.

The idle capacity arising from seasonality of the industry is aggravated by the business cycle. While the long-run trend of production has been upward, annual production has varied considerably. In periods of general prosperity production has been very high; in periods of depression very low. Each succeeding cyclical rise was accommodated by the installation of additional capacity which was partially idle during the intervening periods of depression. The utilization of capacity, as shown in Fig. 33, varies greatly from one stage of the cycle to another.

The wide variations in production give rise to wide fluctuations in costs and earnings. Since the capital investment in a cement plant is high, the ratio of constant costs to total costs is also high. Interest on investment and depreciation represent a substantial part of the constant

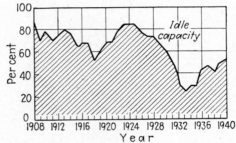

Fig. 33.—Utilization of Portland cement capacity. (*Minerals Yearbook, Washington D. C.*, 1940.)

costs and cannot be reduced. Administrative and selling costs also tend to be constant, and, since even partial operation requires a minimum crew, some of the operating labor tends to be a constant cost. (A five-kiln plant, operating at 20 per cent capacity—*i.e.*, four kilns being idle—requires 140 per cent more labor per barrel of cement produced than when operating at full capacity.) The variable costs are fuel, supplies, power, and some of the labor. It has been estimated that 60 per cent of the total costs of making cement are constant costs and the remainder variable. Operating under such a cost structure the industry is very sensitive to changes in production and prices. A small change in either may mean the difference between profits and deficits.

Competition.—Our analysis of the industry has revealed conditions that, theoretically, should make for very severe competition. Five such conditions are outstanding.

First, cement is a homogeneous product. It is manufactured to rigid specifications and standards laid down by the American Society for

Testing Materials. Since the product is standardized[1] no manufacturer can secure a premium for his product because of quality.

Second, the demand for cement is relatively inelastic because it is a derived demand arising chiefly from the demand for the products of the construction industry. The cost of cement represents only a small part of the total cost of construction, as is very clearly revealed in Table XXVI. Since cement constitutes so small a fraction of total construction costs,

TABLE XXVI.—COSTS OF CEMENT USED IN TYPICAL CONSTRUCTION PROJECTS

Project	Total cost	Cost of cement at $1.67 per barrel	Per cent cement cost is of total cost
Reinforced-concrete girder bridge— 60-ft. span 44 ft. wide..........	$129,494	$10,550	8.1
Apartment building, structural-steel frame, encased in concrete.......	170,206	8,465	5.0
Factory building, reinforced-concrete frame and floors...........	201,600	5,677	2.8
Paving, reinforced concrete, 68,000 sq. yd........................	238,921	39,500	16.5

Source: Portland Cement Association, private communication.

its demand is relatively inelastic, *i.e.*, a decrease in the price will not bring forth any appreciable increase in consumption. Therefore, when the construction industry is at low ebb one might expect cement producers to cut prices severely to obtain the few available orders.

Third, no company has sufficient capacity or a sufficient proportion of the business to constitute a monopoly or to offer continuous price leadership. Universal-Atlas, the largest company, has only 14 per cent of the industry capacity.

Fourth, idle capacity induced by seasonal and cyclical declines, together with high capital costs, should create strong pressure for continued operation by price cutting on the part of individual mills. Theoretically, it should pay the manufacturer, burdened with a heavy overhead, to cut his price to any point higher than his prime costs if by so doing he can maintain his operations at a high level of activity. Any income in excess of his prime costs could be applied to his overhead costs. Since other producers in the same area could not maintain their prices in the face of his cuts, the product being standardized, they would be obliged to meet his prices, cut by cut.

[1] Except for "high-early-strength" cement which sets quickly and waterproof and colored cements. High-early-strength cement is a small percentage (less than 5 per cent) of all cement produced, and the others are largely in the experimental stage.

Fifth, the difference in operating costs between old and modern plants is another possible cause of price cutting. Although no revolutionary developments in technology have occurred since the introduction of the rotary kiln, there has been a steady increase in plant efficiency. The size of kilns has been increased, grinding equipment has been improved, waste-heat utilizing units have been installed, etc. Therefore, modern mills should have a higher technical efficiency and a cost advantage over older mills. This advantage, one might suppose, would force out the inefficient mills in the scramble for orders during periods of shrinking business.

In the light of these conditions, let us see what has been the recent price behavior of cement. During the 21 years portrayed in Fig. 34, three distinct patterns of price behavior stand out. During the first period,

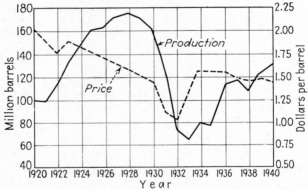

Fig. 34.—Portland cement production and price. (*Mineral Yearbook, Washington, D. C.,* 1940.)

1920–1928, prices and production showed an inverse relationship. Production rose from 100 million to 175 million barrels. This was the period of our secondary postwar business expansion during which industrial construction shared in the general prosperity of the times. The expanding market for cement was eagerly accommodated by newly installed cement-producing capacity, and this was instrumental in forcing the price of cement down from $2 to $1.60 per barrel. Net profits during this period averaged 14 per cent on the capital invested.

During the second period, 1928–1932, building virtually ceased and road construction was severely curtailed, thereby drying up the principal markets for cement. Production declined from its peak of 176 million barrels to 70 million. It was accompanied by a substantial, though somewhat less precipitate, price decline. The shrinkage of the market caused a contraction in mill operations to only 30 per cent of capacity as is shown in Fig. 33. Faced with such a large amount of idle capacity and a heavy burden of fixed costs, mills underbid each other until prices declined to $1 a barrel, the lowest level during the period.

The declining price trend was reversed in 1932 despite the fact that production continued to decrease. By 1934 prices had increased approximately 50 per cent over 1932, although production was only slightly higher. If the industry was unable to check the price decline in the early years of the depression, how was it able to increase prices after the industry's statistical position became worse? The answer appears to be that while idle capacity and heavy overhead costs initiate a downward spiral in prices, such as occurred between 1928 and 1932, there finally comes a time when many companies have exhausted their financial resources and realize that any further price cutting is futile. Price cuts by one company will give it only a temporary advantage, since they will be met by their competitors. Under such conditions there comes a point when individual mills, like a drowning man grasping at a straw, accept any price leadership offered. An announcement of an increase in price by one company is followed by similar increases in another. The fear of provoking another price war is sufficient argument to persuade mills to "cooperate." If the announcement of higher prices is later followed by an increase in business, the higher prices can be maintained and, perhaps, further increased. This happened after the summer of 1933 with the entrance of the government as a heavy purchaser of cement. During the 30 depression months ending in December, 1935, purchases of cement by both the Federal and state governments for public works and highways absorbed two-thirds of the industry's output.

The assumption that the technically superior company will force out the less efficient is not always supported by the facts. All the available evidence indicates that in the short run the former cannot push their technical superiority to the limit. Let us see why this is so. The cost of any manufactured product is the total of the direct costs and the overhead costs, or, to put it another way, the sum of the prime and capital costs. In an industry where capital costs are low and direct costs high, the manufacturer does not hesitate to scrap old equipment because new equipment will bring about a substantial reduction in labor or material costs. In an industry with high capital costs there is a greater reluctance to scrap old equipment, because, first, the new equipment is costly and increases the capital investment, and second, the reduction in direct costs will be small. Accordingly, while a modern plant has a higher technical efficiency, *i.e.*, uses less fuel or less labor per barrel of cement produced, the efficiency is obtained only by the investment of more capital. The older mills consume more coal and require more labor, but since their plants have been depreciated their overhead costs are low. If the latter are very low their total costs may not be very much out of line with the technically more efficient.   In such cases the modern mills, in order to obtain a larger share of the available business, would be obliged to drive prices to a point that would render them unable to meet the commitments imposed by their heavy capital investment.   Furthermore, plants are not subject to complete obsolescence because improvements in technology do not occur simultaneously in all departments.   Improvements occur gradually and affect only certain processes.   Therefore, a well-managed company that has not permitted itself to fall too far behind may be economically efficient despite its old equipment.   It is not to be inferred from this that a modern plant has no operating advantages over an old plant.   It does mean, however, that, in an industry with high capital costs such as this, a mill utilizing 40 man-hours per 100 barrels as against another requiring 50 may have a total cost that is only slightly lower than the latter.

The ability of the cement industry to check price declines and to increase prices as it did after 1932, an occurrence that is not unfamiliar in the history of this industry, is attributed by its critics to collusion among the producers.   To sustain their charge they point to the identical bids submitted by mills on government contracts.   On several occasions in recent years governmental agencies have received from several companies bids that were identical to the fourth decimal point.   When the bids were rejected and new bids called for the results were the same. Federal agencies have threatened from time to time to undertake the manufacture of cement for their own projects, and several states are already operating cement plants.   The identical bids it is charged are the results of collusion and the utilization of the multiple-basing-point system of pricing.   The operation of this system in the cement industry is similar to that of the steel industry described in an earlier chapter.

The industry explains away the identical bids by pious reference to the law of one price, namely, that in a given market a given commodity (in this case a highly standardized one) can have only one price, and to the fact that the prevailing price in any given market is known to all producers.   Accordingly, they insist all bids must necessarily be identical. This explanation is not satisfactory to the critics, who very properly point out that if the prevailing price is known, some producer, anxious to obtain a contract, would shade his price slightly below it.

While the industry has been investigated several times by government agencies no conclusive evidence has been found of collusion or monopolistic practices, other than the utilization of the basing-point system of pricing.

Summary and Conclusion.—At the turn of the century Portland cement, a comparatively new building material, "arrived" when the Federal government approved its use in fortifications.   Its subsequent manufacture to standard formula and its approval by scientific societies gave it unquestionable acceptance as a reliable building material and furnished the impetus for a rapid development of the industry. Its average annual rate of growth during the half century ending with 1929 was 18.8 per cent—a rate surpassed by no major industry except aluminum. Although Portland cement is a comparatively new industry, the secular trend of its growth, shown in Fig. 29, suggests its entrance into the fourth or final stage of the growth cycle. In other words, the industry gives every sign of an early old age. If we are entering an era of sharply retarded industrial growth, as is believed though not conclusively established by many economists, the cement industry may have to rely more and more on government business. In this event the industry may come in for more vigorous attack on its pricing policies, if not for more governmental regulation. The problem of idle capacity is likely to become more acute in the future because additional capital will flow into the industry to meet the peak cyclical demands for cement.

CHAPTER XIV

THE CLAY-WORKING INDUSTRIES

"An industry is really nothing more than a group of men behaving in a certain manner, part under the immediate pressure of earning a living, associated in structural relationships in a situation where tradition and convention, inertia and sheer accident all play their parts."[1] This definition aptly characterizes the clay-working industries. Their products are highly diversified, their markets are influenced by different competitive factors, and their manufacturing processes are not identical. Indeed, even the characteristic which is the basis of their census classification, the use of clay as their common raw material, is a doubtful one for purposes of comparison, since they must use different types of clay.

In 1939, this group of industries comprised 1,400 establishments, employed 90,000 workers, and had a value of product of 265 million dollars. The products manufactured range from the common building brick, drain tile, and refractory brick to toilet and bathroom fixtures, porcelain electrical supplies, garden pottery, and high-grade tableware. The first group, designated by the Census as "clay products other than pottery," is the more important, having 1,200 establishments, 70,000 workers, and a value of product of 165 million dollars. The second group, known as the "pottery industry," has only 200 establishments, employs only about one-fourth as many workers, and has a value of product of 100 million dollars. Since the range of products is so wide and since they have so little in common, we shall not discuss these industries as a group; instead, we shall select the brick and tile industry as typical of the first group and the manufacture of general and sanitary ware as illustrative of the second group.

THE BRICK AND TILE INDUSTRY[2]

The origin of brick as a building material is lost in antiquity, but archeological excavations indicate that it was first used in Babylonia, thousands of years before the earliest recorded history. The art of brickmaking in this ancient civilization and in Egypt was developed to a high state, the bricks being of high quality and excellent in appearance. From

[1] MEIKLEJOHN, H. E., "Prices and Price Policies," edited by W. H. Hamilton, p. 300, McGraw-Hill Publishing Company, Inc., New York, 1938.

[2] In writing this section, the authors have drawn heavily on M. E. West, "The Brick and Tile Industry," National Research Project, Philadelphia, Pa., 1939.

these centers, knowledge of brickmaking gradually spread to other parts of the world and was finally introduced by the Romans into Europe, where it soon found wide use.

Development of Brickmaking in the United States.—The first brick houses in colonial America were built of materials imported from Holland and England, but brickmaking made its appearance in Virginia as early as 1611 and in Massachusetts in 1629. By 1849 about 17,000 workers were employed at brickmaking, and the value of product in that year was in excess of 6 million dollars. The industry grew rapidly as the population of the country increased. In addition to the stimulus that came from the demand for brick as a building material, new uses were found for the products of this industry: in the rural areas tile found increasing

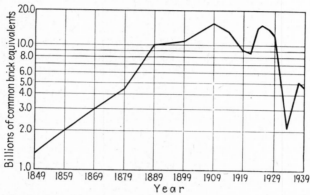

FIG. 35.—Production of brick and tile. (*Adopted from A. J. Van Tassel, and D. W. Blueston, Mechanization in the Brick Industry, National Research Project, Report No. M-2 Philadelphia, 1939.*)

use in the draining of lands, and in the cities, in the sixties and seventies, bricks began to find use as street-paving material. The increase in the height of buildings, which called for stronger walls to support the structure, gave a further impetus to the industry. The combination of these factors permitted the industry to grow rapidly, and up to 1909 it expanded at a rate of 40 to 50 per cent per decade.

The year 1909 marked the turning point in the production trend of the industry. Thereafter, as Fig. 35 shows, production declined until 1921 when the great expansion in building returned brick and tile to temporary favor.

The decline that occurred between 1909 and 1921 was only in part due to a recession in building activity. More important were the changes that took place in other industries, namely, in the art and science of building construction and the rapid development of Portland cement manufacturing. The introduction in the nineties, and the rapid extension during the present century, of the use of structural steel frames in construction made unnecessary the use of brick walls for structural support and made possible the application of substitute building materials. At about the same time, it will be recalled from the preceding chapter, important technological changes in cement manufacture resulted in rapid reductions in cement costs which greatly stimulated the consumption of this new material. Whereas in 1900 cement production amounted to only 10 million barrels, by 1910 it was almost 80 million barrels, and during the next decade cement production reached 100 million barrels.[1] Much of the expansion of the cement industry was at the expense of the brick industry, especially in roads and pavements, for which cement was regarded as superior to the older material. Thus, the growth of this old industry was checked by the vigorous growth of a young industry and by the introduction of cheap steel which made revolutionary changes in construction methods.

Process of Manufacture.—The manufacture of brick and tile involves the mining of the raw material, the forming of the brick or tile, and burning to give the products rigidity and strength.

Clay and shale, the principal raw materials, are usually mined by mechanical devices similar to those used in mining raw materials for the cement industry. From the clay and shale pits the materials are transported, usually by mechanical means, to the near-by machine house. There the materials are placed in a granulator equipped with steel knives, which cuts them into smaller pieces. After granulation the material passes through a set of conical rolls which remove the stones.

The actual forming of the brick and tile may be accomplished by one of three methods: the stiff-mud process, the soft-mud process, and the dry-press method. If the stiff-mud or soft-mud processes are employed, the ground clay must go to the pug mill where it is mixed with water to give it the proper consistency.

In the stiff-mud process the most common type of brick machine is the auger type in which an encased revolving screw forces the clay through a hard steel die from which it emerges as a ribbon of clay onto a belt conveyor which carries it to the cutting machine. This is synchronized with the brick machine and cuts the ribbon of clay into brick and tile of the desired size. Different dies are used for each type of product manufactured. After cutting the bricks are carried away on . . . a belt from which they are removed . . . and are set on cars. In the stiff-mud process the machine operations form one continuous operation.

The forming of soft-mud bricks usually requires more hand labor. The brick machine forces the clay into molds which have been sanded to prevent the sticking of clay and which have been placed in the machine by hand. The top surface of the brick is then smoothed by a hand operator, and the molds are ejected by the

---

[1] See Fig. 29, Chap. XIII.

machine onto a table where they are bumped by hand to loosen the bricks. These are dumped by another man onto metal pallets. The more modern equipment includes automatic sanding, dumping, and ejecting devices which are built into or are attached to the standard type of brick machine. . . . Because of the quantity of water added in mixing the clay, the bricks made by this process are too soft to handle by hand and must be carried off on the pallets on which they are dumped.

In the dry-press method the clay, after it has been tempered, is conveyed to a rotary mixer from which it drops into a mold box containing 5 to 10 molds. The dry clay is then formed into bricks by a press exerting high pressure. The lifting of the press automatically ejects the bricks from the molds onto a table from which they are taken by hand and placed on trays which are wheeled directly to the kiln for burning.[1]

Bricks made by the stiff-mud and soft-mud processes contain much moisture and are, therefore, so fragile that they must be dried before being placed in the kiln for burning. Formerly the green bricks were dried by open-air methods, which required from 5 to 12 days, but in recent years drier kilns, heated by steam heat or by waste heat from the burning kilns, have supplanted the earlier methods and have reduced the drying time to 1 to 3 days.

After drying, the bricks are moved to the burning kilns, of which there are several kinds. In the early years of the industry the most popular kiln was the beehive type, a circular brick structure similar to the beehive coke oven. While the beehive kiln had a high fuel efficiency, it was displaced by the rectangular kiln which had a capacity of from 400,000 to a million bricks as compared with only 50,000 for the beehive. The high fuel costs of both of these kilns stimulated the search for more efficient methods of burning, and the next development was the continuous system of rectangular kilns. In this method a large rectangular kiln is divided into a number of chambers in which the bricks are piled. A fire is lighted in one of the chambers, and the flue gases from that chamber are used to preheat the bricks in other chambers. Later, a fire is lighted in another chamber, and the flue gas used to preheat the bricks in other chambers. Thus, at a given moment only one chamber has a fire, and the bricks in the various chambers are in different stages of the firing process.

While the continuous kiln was more efficient in the use of fuel than the intermittently operated rectangular or beehive kilns, the amount of labor necessary was about the same. To reduce the high labor costs arising from the loading and unloading of the kilns, the tunnel kiln was introduced. In this method, bricks are piled on kiln cars which are slowly pushed on rails through a tunnel-shaped kiln. The fire is located at one central point so there is no heat loss through the alternate heating

[1] WEST, *op. cit.*, p. 8.

and cooling of individual kilns. Despite the fuel and labor economies of the tunnel kiln, it has not been generally adopted by the industry. Only about 30 such kilns are in use. The chief factors responsible for the slow installation of this kiln is the high capital cost, about twice that of other types, and the fact that its economies are realized only when it is operated at peak capacity.

Structure of the Industry.—The foregoing description indicates that the manufacture of brick and tile is a relatively simple process, but one that requires the use of considerable labor despite the development of machinery. Even in the case of the highly automatic brick machine much labor is involved in the transferring of bricks from one stage of the process to another. During the period 1925–1929, one of high production, wages represented 30 per cent of the value of product, and as Table IV, Chap. I, shows, among the 40 industries listed only four have higher labor costs. Under such circumstances, with labor representing so large a percentage of costs, there are no appreciable economies in large-scale production.

Another factor that limits the tendency towards large-scale operation is that, because brick and tile are bulky, transportation costs are high. This restricts the marketing area of a plant and forces it to rely primarily on a local market. The combination of these forces, therefore, tends to make brick and tile plants small in scale. This is shown in Table XXVII. It will be noted that the average number of workers per establishment was

TABLE XXVII.—AVERAGE SIZE OF BRICK AND TILE PLANTS

Major product	Average number per establishment	
	Wage earners	Common brick equivalents (000 omitted)
Vitrified brick......................	83	22,400
Face brick.........................	59	16,000
Hollow building tile...............	50	15,000
Drain tile.........................	11	2,600
Average........................	38	10,000

Source: WEST, *op. cit.*, p. 15.

only 38, and in plants making drain tile an average of only 11 workers was employed. Table III, Chap. I, shows that only six manufacturing industries had fewer employees per establishment than the brick and tile industry.

Despite the prevalence of small-scale operations and the presence of a large number of companies, there are a few large companies in the industry, such as the **Illinois Brick Company, National Fireproofing Company,**

Hydraulic Press Brick Company, Metropolitan Paving Brick Company, and the United Brick and Tile Company. Most of these companies are the result of mergers and consolidations, and their manufacturing operations are spread over a wide geographical area. The exception to this is the Illinois Brick Company whose operations are concentrated in the Chicago area. The absence of concentration is indicated by the fact that in 1934 the largest firm in the common brick branch shipped only 3.8 per cent of the total; in face brick the largest firm shipped 6 per cent; and in structural clay tile 24 per cent.

Location.—The factors that determine the location of brick and tile plants are similar to those in the cement industry. The market for brick and tile is wide, and since these products cannot be shipped long distances because of their bulk and low unit value, proximity to market is the most important location determinant. The raw material, clay, and the fuel, which may be coal, oil, or wood, are widely scattered and generally available close to the market. Accordingly, the plants in the industry are widely scattered and located primarily near large urban centers. The leading centers are the Hudson River valley and Cook County, Ill.—adjacent to our two largest cities, New York and Chicago. As in the cement industry, the distribution of brick and tile plants is roughly proportional to the distribution of population. The heaviest concentration of capacity is in New York, Pennsylvania, Illinois, Ohio, New Jersey, Indiana, Massachusetts, Missouri, and California.

The location of the plant has considerable influence upon its size and mechanization. In the large market areas, such as Chicago and New York, where there is a heavy concentration of capacity, keen competition, and high wage rates, plants tend to be more highly mechanized and larger in size.

Fluctuating Market.—Enough has been said to indicate that the principal use for the products of this industry is in the construction industry. This is not true, of course, of drain tile, which is used in agriculture. Since the demand for brick and tile arises from the demand of the construction industry, the demand for these products, like the demand for cement, is subject to seasonal and broad cyclical fluctuations.

This industry, however, has less difficulty in adjusting itself to these fluctuations than do most of the industries considered so far. Unlike the steel and the cement industries, for example, this industry, operating on a small scale and with a comparatively low investment, has rather low fixed costs. This is indicated in Table XXVIII. It will be noted that the major part of the cost of common brick is represented by direct costs, the total amount of which varies with the volume of production. With such a cost structure the plants are not confronted with the task of carrying a heavy burden of overhead costs in periods of low activity. Consequently, they do not have the urge to continue production at a high level when the market is shrinking. If they continued to produce at a high level, the price of the product would decline and they would have difficulty in recovering their "out-of-pocket" expenses, namely, labor, raw mate-

TABLE XXVIII.—COST OF PRODUCTION OF COMMON BRICK

	Per Cent of Total Cost
Labor, operating and indirect	33.4
Power	15.4
Fuel	10.4
Raw material	3.8
Overhead	13.9
Other manufacturing costs	1.7
Administration	10.4
Selling	4.1
Other	6.9
Total	100.0

Source: Adapted from WEST, *op. cit.,* p. 145.

rials, and fuel, which as we have seen represent a large percentage of their total costs. Since it is not costly to shut down, they prefer to do so until the market recovers. Thus, it is apparent that the supply of brick and tile is very flexible.

The flexibility of supply makes it possible to maintain more stable prices than one would expect from an industry whose market depends on

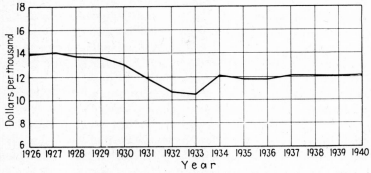

FIG. 36.—Average annual price of common brick. (F.O.B. plant.) (*United States Department of Labor, Bureau of Labor Statistics.*)

the fluctuating demand of the construction industry. (See Fig. 36.) In addition to this factor there is also evidence to indicate that in some of the large markets, where a few large companies dominate, "gentlemen's agreements" are not unknown. Early in 1940 the Department of Justice obtained indictments against many tile manufacturers, contractors, and building union leaders for allegedly "cooperating" to such an extent that competition among tile manufacturers was restrained in violation of the Sherman Antitrust Act.

Summary.—It has been shown that the brick and tile industry experienced a vigorous growth from 1849 to 1909 and that this growth was checked by the rise in competitive materials. Thus, the future growth of this industry will be determined not only by the trend in construction activity but also by the ability of the industry to compete with other building materials. This competition involves both price and style factors. With respect to price competition this industry appears to be under a handicap, especially in competition with cement, since the process involves the use of considerable labor, an item that will probably become more rather than less costly. While it is possible that the process may become more mechanized, transportation costs will always stand in the way of large-scale production. Concerning the influence of style upon the demand for this industry's products little can be said with certainty. In the field of industrial construction, where cost rather than appearance is the main consideration, there is at present no reason to believe that the trend will be reversed. In the field of residential construction the style element will play a more important role.

THE POTTERY INDUSTRY

This branch of the clay-working industries, as has been previously indicated, is smaller than the group just discussed. Like the other group, this branch manufactures a wide range of products—bathroom and toilet fixtures, hotel china, white tableware, red earthenware, stoneware, porcelain electrical supplies, and garden and art pottery. Measured by value of product, the most important in this list are general ware (household tableware and hotel china) and sanitary ware (bathroom and toilet fixtures), which together account for about one-half the total. It is with these two groups that we are concerned here.

While the pottery industry has been long established here, its introduction followed that of brickmaking. Before 1800 such table and kitchen pottery ware as was to be found here was of European manufacture and was high in price. The colonists used primarily wood and pewter utensils. The industry in this country was begun by English potters who found here crude clays capable of being made into rough products such as common stoneware, red earthenware, and drain-pipes. The manufacture of better grades of white ware did not get under way until about 1850.

In the early years the industry was heavily concentrated in Trenton, N. J. However, since the more recent expansion of the sanitary ware branch, which got under way in the seventies, and the rapid growth of the East Liverpool, Ohio, district, which includes potteries in West Virginia, Trenton has become the center of the sanitary branch, and East Liverpool the principal producer of general ware.

Raw Materials.—The principal clays used in the pottery industry are kaolin and ball clay. While both of these clays are widely available in the

United States (chiefly in the Appalachian district), the American pottery industry has long depended upon foreign sources, primarily England, for a large part of its supplies, especially for the manufacture of high-grade table and sanitary ware. Recent developments have made possible the greater use of domestic clays, but manufacturers of sanitary ware and hotel china have been slow to accept domestic clays.

Other raw materials are quartz, which gives rigidity to the body; feldspar, which acts as a flux to bind the materials as they fuse; and glazes of numerous kinds, which impart to the outer surface of the pottery a finish like a coating of glass.

Process.—The production of pottery consists of three principal operations:

1. The preparation of the raw materials.
2. Forming the ware.
3. Firing or burning.

Preparation of the raw material.—One of the most important steps in the preparation of materials is the correct proportioning of the various constituents that are to make up the finished ware. Particularly is this true of companies making high-grade ware or of companies producing branded ware. Early in the history of pottery manufacture it required extreme skill to make successive batches of pottery exactly the same, but in recent years a high degree of scientific control has entered this phase of the process, and now large quantities of identical goods can be produced. In addition to proper proportioning, the raw materials must be finely ground and intimately mixed. After the addition of water, the mixture is put through a filter press and the mass allowed to season.

Forming the ware.—There are three methods by which the clay may be given shape: (1) pressing, (2) jiggering, and (3) casting.

Pressing, used in making irregular, nonsymmetrical objects, is accomplished by pressing the prepared clay into plaster-of-paris molds.

Jiggering is used in making symmetrical objects like bowls, cups, saucers, and plates. The jigger, which is an adaptation of the potter's wheel, is an upright spindle carrying a mold to form the outside of the article and a sweep, which is a piece of wood, steel, or fired clay, fixed to an arm in such a way that when the spindle revolves the sweep cuts away the excess of material from the inside of the article to be made, and presses the clay at the same time to the shape of the mold on the spindle. In flat work, such as plates and saucers, the mold forms the inside of the article and the sweep the back or exterior.

Casting is the most recent development for the forming of pottery products. The process is entirely dependent upon the absorbent nature of the plaster mold, which may be of endless varieties as regards shape. The operation consists of pouring the liquid clay, known as "slip," into a plaster-of-paris mold. When the mold is filled with the clay suspension, the solid particles, by virtue of the water-absorbing quality of the plaster, at once adhere to the surface of the mold. A coating of clay is thus formed, the thickness of which depends upon the porosity of the mold and the length of time of contact. As soon as the desired thickness is reached, the excess mixture is poured off.

Firing or Burning.—This operation consists in subjecting the "green" clay form to heat sufficiently intense to fuse the clay. It is carried on in either stationary or tunnel kilns. The former are brick structures conical in shape, into which the clay forms are carried and stacked by hand. The tunnel kiln, a recent development, is a brick tunnel 300 to 500 ft. long, through which cars carrying the clay forms are moved. The mid-section of the tunnel kiln is heated to a temperature high enough to fuse the clay, and the temperature graduates downward toward either end. The kiln is continuous in operation, is more efficient in the use of fuel, and requires less labor. However, its economies are realized only when the kiln is operated at a high level of capacity.

Except for very common ware having no gloss there are two firings, one to fix the form of the ware, known as "biscuit" firing, and a second to vitrify the product after the glaze solution has been applied, known as the "glost" firing.

Importance of Labor.—Like the clay-working industries in general, the pottery industry requires the use of a considerable amount of labor. The process involves much handling of materials as they pass from one stage to another. Much of the labor is also highly skilled, it being estimated that 40 per cent of the operatives in the general ware branch are in the skilled classification. Furthermore, it is this branch of the industry that produces our highest grade china, such as Lenox china, where individual pieces cost hundreds of dollars because of the large amount of artistic skill lavished upon forming and decorating each object. Extraordinary accuracy and artistic ability are required of the craftsmen producing these products. This entails great expense and adds heavily

TABLE XXIX.—COSTS OF 12 COMPANIES ENGAGED IN THE MANUFACTURE OF EARTHENWARE

	Per Cent of Total Costs
Labor	54.5
Materials	23.5
Fuel	4.0
Factory overhead	10.0
Selling expenses	3.5
Administrative	4.5
Total	100.0

Source: U. S. Tariff Commission, "Pottery," *Report* No. 102, Washington, D. C., 1936.

to the cost of production.   For the table and hotel china division of the pottery industry, as Table IV, Chap. I, shows, the ratio of wages to value of product is 48 per cent, the highest ratio for the 40 industries listed.

The high labor costs have stimulated the potteries to adopt various methods to lower the importance of this item in their cost structure.   Two methods have already been mentioned, the introduction of the tunnel kiln and the more general use of the casting process. . Further economies were made by the installation of auxiliary devices such as belt conveyors and other automatic devices for transferring the green ware from one stage of the process to another.

Foreign Competition.—In contrast with brick and tile, which have a low unit value, the products of the general ware branch can absorb higher transportation costs and, therefore, can be marketed over a wide area. This fact, coupled with high labor costs, makes the industry especially vulnerable to foreign competition and very sensitive to tariff changes, which affect both the competitive and labor situations.   This is not true of sanitary ware products, which have been developed to a much higher state in this country than abroad.   In 1894 duties on general ware were lowered, and the following year the volume of imports increased by 40 per cent and the industry entered into a depression, accompanied by a decline in production and a cut in wage rates.   In 1897, when import duties were raised, imports declined and wages were raised.   In 1913 duties were again decreased, but the outbreak of the war in 1914 made it difficult to import ware into this country, and both the industry and the workers were able to avoid the adjustments that would have been necessary by the downward revision.

The importance of the tariff to the potteries and the workers resulted in the early organization of a strong employers' association and a labor union which jointly exerted their influence to obtain tariff protection.   As a result of their common interest in tariff matters, the two associations established amicable relations and for many years wages in the industry were established by national agreements, a situation then rare in American industry.   The national agreements established uniform wage scales throughout the country and tended to stabilize competition between eastern and western producers.

This relation continued until 1922 when strikes were called in both the general and sanitary ware branches.   In both instances the unions demanded higher wages and the potteries insisted upon wage cuts.   In the general ware branch the manufacturers felt that the restoration of peace in Europe would enable the foreign countries to reenter the American market despite the tariff of 1922.   In the sanitary branch the companies insisted on a downward revision of wage rates because of changes in the process of manufacture.

The union in the general ware branch was granted the wage increase, the strike was called off, and the manufacturers and the union reverted to the practice of negotiating national agreements. The strike in the sanitary branch lasted about a year and was finally lost by the union. The union has never recovered from the effects of this strike. The manufacturers abandoned national agreements and the union has been able to obtain recognition in only a few plants. The weakness of the union in this branch of the industry and the change in the attitude of the sanitary manufacturers toward national agreements were due to economic and technical developments that were occurring in this branch of the industry. In the first place, the sanitary branch had experienced marked expansion in various parts of the country and the union had failed to organize most of the new plants. In the second place, the sanitary branch was shifting from the pressing to the casting process, and the unions insisted on receiving approximately the same rates for casting as for pressing. Thus, the union potteries operated under an adverse cost handicap in competition with the nonunion mills which had lower wage rates generally and especially lower casting rates. Since the tariff was of little significance to the sanitary ware manufacturers, there was no bond of common interest to hold the employers and the union together.

Except for the periods when tariff duties were lowered, the duties were generally high enough to protect the general ware industry. Ware that was brought in over the tariff wall was relatively high in price and competed with domestic manufatures on a quality rather than a price basis. In the thirties, however, the situation changed when Japan became a more important source of supply, especially in the low price classifications. The low wage rates in Japan, the then-demoralized condition of the Japanese industry, and the depreciation of the yen, resulted in a rapid increase in imports from that source.

Changes in the domestic market have also adversely affected the demand for general ware. The most important development has been the rapidly increasing sale of articles for the same use made of pressed glass, especially pressed glass cups, saucers, and plates. These are produced on highly automatic machines at a much lower unit cost than corresponding pottery products. Another development has been the reduction in the size of dinner sets purchased. In part this was due to the business depression and in part to the smaller family living quarters.

The chief unstabilizing force in the sanitary branch is the fluctuating activity of the building industry, to which the industry must look for its principal market. Since both plants and companies are conducted on a larger scale than in general ware, and since the demand for its products is much less stable, earnings are subject to much wider fluctuations.

CHAPTER XV

THE GLASS INDUSTRY

If sand is mixed with lime and soda ash (sodium carbonate) and heated to a temperature of 2500°–3000°F., it melts to a molasseslike consistency. The mass is homogeneous and noncrystalline; furthermore, it cools slowly and may be worked while plastic into permanent shape with great ease. This product we call glass. It is difficult to define glass concisely because it has a wide range of characteristics. Most of it is transparent; on the other hand, it may be opaque or merely translucent. Most of it is brittle but it may be toughened by heat treatment until it becomes bulletproof. It is impervious to air, water, gases, and most chemicals; it is easy to clean; it does not warp or soften; it takes a high polish; it can be compounded so as to filter out the infrared or ultraviolet rays of the sun. These and other qualities have opened for it many markets.

Its major markets are three in number: (1) the container field where it is used to bottle foods, beverages, medicines, and toilet preparations; (2) the construction field where it is used for windows in buildings, automobiles, etc.; (3) the household where it serves as table and kitchen ware. The relative importance of these and other fields is shown in Table XXX.

TABLE XXX.—GLASS PRODUCTS

	Millions	Per cent
Glass containers:		
Food containers	$60	
Beverage containers	51	
Miscellaneous	47	
Total	$158	44
Flat glass:		
Plate glass	$43	
Window glass	24	
Other flat glass	4	
Total	$71	20
Tableware	40	11
Lighting ware	21	6
Technical and scientific ware	10	3
Miscellaneous	58	16
Total	$358	100.0

Source: 1939 Census of Manufactures.

Manufacture of Glass.—Before examining the various divisions shown in Table XXX we shall discuss the raw materials and principal steps in the process of glass manufacture which, regardless of type of product, consist of mixing, melting, feeding, shaping, and cooling.

Raw Materials.—As previously mentioned, sand, soda ash, and lime are mixed to make glass. Other principal ingredients are broken or scrap glass and salt cake (sodium sulphate).

The most important of the raw materials is sand (silicon dioxide). Not all sand is suitable for glassmaking. "Glass sand" must be low in iron oxide and alumina and high in silica. Iron, the most undesirable impurity, is always present to some degree and, when more than a trace (0.05 per cent) is present, cannot be tolerated except where clarity is not important. When the sand particles are small, uniform, and angular, better fusion results. But these specifications are not difficult to meet, for the industry is readily supplied with its annual requirement of some 2 million tons of sand from deposits in widely scattered states. Inasmuch as glass sand has low value in relation to its weight (in 1938 its average cost was $1.71 per ton), freight charges often represent a major cost of sand and restrict the source of supply. From 60 to 70 per cent of the entire domestic supply comes from three states—Illinois, West Virginia, and Pennsylvania; this is because of their proximity to fuels and markets for the finished goods.

Soda ash (sodium carbonate) is used to the amount of 500,000 to 700,000 tons annually as a flux to facilitate the mixing and melting of other ingredients in the batch. It costs five to six times as much per ton as sand and is made from salt, ammonia, and carbon dioxide by several large chemical companies.

Lime (calcium oxide) and limestone (calcium carbonate) together are used to the extent of about 200,000 tons annually for the purpose of giving hardness, permanency, and ease of melting and refining.

Salt cake (sodium sulphate) is used to lower the melting point and the viscosity of the glass. The industry uses about 40,000 tons although the amount has been declining in recent years as automatic temperature control has been improved.

Broken glass, or cullet, is extensively used—sometimes to the extent of 50 per cent of the batch. It shortens the melting time and reduces raw material and fuel costs.

Relatively small quantities of many other raw materials are used; the most important are metallic oxides used as colorants.

The raw materials collectively constitute only 10 to 15 per cent of the total costs of manufacture and therefore do not play a determining role in the location of the industry.

Melting.—This takes place in a regenerative furnace which has been described previously in the chapter on the technology of the steel industry. Both industries obtained the furnace from Siemens in the 1860's. Prior to that time glass was melted in small clay crucibles fired directly with wood or coal as fuels. The resultant temperatures were low and variable. By utilizing the waste gases of combustion to preheat the incoming gas and air, Siemens obtained a much more intense and uniform heat and reduced fuel costs 50 per cent. Equally important, the new

PLATE 41.—Removing pot of molten glass from furnace. (*Courtesy of Pittsburgh Plate Glass Company.*)

furnace enables the size of the batch to be increased until now furnace capacities range up to 1,400 tons. The new furnace made it desirable to locate near cheap natural gas, which proved to be an ideal fuel.

Two types of regenerative furnace are used for melting glass, the pot type and the tank type. Both are rectangular in shape. In the pot furnace are placed 12 to 20 open crucibles, each containing up to 1½ tons of glass. The tank furnace has an open-hearth or combustion chamber lined with a refractory material and divided into a melting compartment where fusion of the raw materials takes place, a refining compartment where the impurities are burned out, and a working compartment where a uniform working temperature keeps the product molten. Tank furnaces may be operated continuously with raw materials being charged and glass being withdrawn continuously. In the so-called "day furnace" the charging and melting takes place at night, and the tapping during the day.

Feeding.—This operation consists of getting the molasseslike molten glass from the furnace into the mold where it is formed. There are many methods of doing this—most of them patented. In some the glass is poured out, in others it flows out, in still others it is sucked out. The step is a crucial one because it directly affects the quality as well as the volume of production.

Shaping.—Again a resemblance to steel manufacture is observed, for the molten glass may be shaped into final form by rolling, drawing, pressing, or casting. Another and very important method is blowing the viscous material into form by means of compressed air. Each of these methods will be referred to later.

Cooling or Annealing.—It is necessary to control the rate at which the hot glass cools in order that the cooling may proceed at a uniform rate throughout the thickness of the glass. This prevents the stresses that occur when the surface cools more rapidly than the interior, which make the glass quite fragile. The tempering ovens or "lehrs" are so heated as to reduce the temperature gradually throughout their length, which ranges up to 700 ft.

FLAT GLASS DIVISION OF THE INDUSTRY

Ordinary Window Glass.—All glass of this type is today made on a continuous basis. The process, which was introduced during the First World War, is comparatively simple in its main essentials. An iron bar, 7 to 9 ft. long, is inserted horizontally in the shallow bath of molten glass. The sticky glass adheres to the bar so tenaciously that when it is withdrawn a thin sheet, 7 to 9 ft. wide, flows after it at the rate of 4 or 5 ft. per minute. It continues to flow out in an endless flat ribbon since the amount of glass being melted is equal to the amount being withdrawn.

Prior to the continuous process, window glass was made by blowing huge cylinders, first by hand and later by machine. The cylinders of hot glass were then split and flattened in sheet form. The introduction of the present method in 1917 was followed by its rapid adoption as Table XXXI indicates.

In this branch automatic production has reduced the number of plants and companies. In 1917 there were 82 plants, in 1935 there were only 21, and 8 of these were idle. More than 75 per cent of the total output was produced in 1939 by three companies: the Libbey-Owens-Ford Glass Company, the Pittsburgh Plate Glass Company, and the American Window Glass Company. Each of the companies operates several plants, most of which are located in the western Pennsylvania-West Virginia-

Ohio area. Window glass is bulky in relation to value; transportation therefore is an important cost, ranging from 20 to 35 per cent of factory cost. Insofar as fuel costs make it possible, plants are located near markets, which are closely related to population distribution.

TABLE XXXI.—PERCENTAGE OF WINDOW GLASS MADE BY CONTINUOUS PROCESS

Year	Per Cent
1919	10
1923	38
1926	39
1929	80
1932	95
1935	100

Source: United States Tariff Commission, *Report* No. 123, Flat Glass and Related Glass Products, 1937.

The complete mechanization of this branch of the industry has brought about a marked reduction in labor costs but this gain is largely offset by increased costs of raw materials, fuel, and overhead. The principal items of cost before and after mechanization are shown in Table XXXII.

TABLE XXXII.—COST OF SHEET GLASS PRODUCTION

	Cents per pound	
	1890	1929
Materials	0.457	1.04
Labor	2.198	1.264
Fuel, power, and heat	0.316	0.473
Overhead	0.336	0.695
Total f.o.b. plant	3.307	3.472

Source: U. S. Tariff Commission, *Report* No. 123, Flat Glass and Related Glass Products, 1937.

Two million dollars is now required to set up an establishment in contrast with $118,000 before mechanization. Modern plants are burdened with higher depreciation and interest charges and a more inflexible cost structure. Consequently profits vanish rapidly when prices or production decline and respond as quickly on the upturn.

All the companies in this branch have excess capacity estimated for the branch as a whole at 50 per cent in 1936. This is due in considerable part to the speed at which the transition to the continuous process took place and to the fact that this transition occurred during the building boom of the 1920's when the excessive demand, pent up by the First World War, was released. In addition to the three companies just mentioned, four of the remaining companies have organized a joint sales company to effect economies in distribution and strengthen their competitive position. An indicator of competitive conditions in this division is the wholesale price index of window glass. In 1934 when the wholesale price index (1926 = 100) of all commodities was 74.9 and building materials 86.2, window glass was 63.1. The future of this branch seems closely related to the construction industry. Capacity, which is now rated at 1,100 million sq. ft. annually, should be related to consumption, which at the peak never exceeded 700 million sq. ft. On this point there should not be overlooked the possibility of making existing window glass obsolete by low-cost

PLATE 42.—Sheets of plate glass emerging from annealing lehr are being picked up by vacuum cups for transfer to grinding and polishing room. (*Courtesy of Pittsburgh Plate Glass Company.*)

manufacture of glass with special insulating and health-giving properties. It also seems likely that glass, in relation to other building materials, will be used more extensively in the future.

Plate Glass.—Plate glass differs from window glass in that it is ground and polished. In 1922 and 1923 the Ford Motor Company and the Pittsburgh Plate Glass Company produced simultaneously a new method of making plate glass. For about a century the only process was one of pouring molten glass on a table and rolling it into flat sheets preparatory to grinding and polishing. The new method consists of continuous drawing, rolling, grinding, and polishing. The principle of continuous drawing is substantially similar to that used in plain window glass, already described.

The new method of manufacture coincided and no doubt was induced by the quick shift to the closed automobile which occurred at this time. Production of plate glass, which had fluctuated between 50 and 65 million sq. ft. in the decade 1910–1920, soon climbed to 100 to 150 million sq. ft. Production in 1923 was 17 per cent greater than in 1922 and 66 per cent

PLATE 43.—Emery grinding of plate glass.   (*Courtesy of Pittsburgh Plate Glass Company.*)

greater than in 1921.   Prices increased from 42 cents per square foot in 1922 to 85 cents in 1923.   To assure themselves of adequate and low-cost supplies, the auto companies entered the field.   Fisher Body Division of General Motors obtained control of a company with two plants.   Durant purchased a company; Ford developed the process just referred to and purchased another company.   All the automobile manufacturers, except Ford, later sold their plants to glass companies, effecting at the same time satisfactory arrangements for their requirements which today equal about 75 per cent of the plate glass production.   Since 1930, the plate glass industry has received another boon in the introduction, and later the compulsory use, of laminated or "safety" glass in automobiles. It requires the use of two sheets of glass and therefore doubles the area of glass per car.

Production which has always been limited to a few companies has now come into the hands of two companies, Libbey-Owens-Ford and Pittsburgh. Together they make in their six plants 95 per cent of all the plate glass. The Ford Motor Company, for many years well equipped to make a large part of its requirements, has produced little glass since 1931 although it has recently installed additional capacity and can produce 45 million sq. ft. annually. This is to be compared to United States annual production of 200 million sq. ft.

In this discussion of companies, it is interesting to note again a trend toward diversification. The Pittsburgh Plate Glass Company now derives less than 50 per cent of its revenue from sales of glass, the remainder coming from paints, cement, and chemicals which go chiefly to the building trade. It has recently joined with the Union Carbide & Carbon Corporation in the development of a new type of glass which will stretch and bend, and with the Corning Glass Works in the manufacture of structural glass blocks and tile. Libby-Owens-Ford likewise is extensively developing new products such as heat-absorbing glass for show windows, double glazing for insulating purposes, etc. All of these large companies, singly or cooperatively, have integrated backward to get an assured supply of high-grade sand and fuel.

THE TABLEWARE DIVISION OF THE INDUSTRY

This branch produces glass products that are used for the most part in household dining rooms and kitchens and in restaurants. Except in the manufacture of tumblers, the processes are less automatic and the plants are smaller in size than in the other divisions. The raw material is usually melted in pot furnaces, gathered by hand, and formed by hand or semiautomatic processes in which the glassmaker operates an individual mold. Some 35 plants operate in this division, the bulk of them in the three principal glass-producing states already mentioned. Competitive conditions are characterized by style piracy, *i.e.*, the copying of hand-wrought designs; the producing by automatic and semiautomatic methods of articles formerly made by hand and sold at high prices; the trend toward frequent changes in style, color, and design.

THE GLASS BOTTLE INDUSTRY

We come now to the most important and in many respects the most interesting division of the industry—the manufacture of glass bottles or containers. This branch of the industry has grown very rapidly, as indicated by Fig. 37, and it accounts for over 40 per cent of the total output of the entire glass industry. Because this output is in the form of

7 billion standardized units (bottles), highly automatic machines can be used.

Prior to the turn of the present century, bottles were made throughout the ages by skilled hand workmen who used a blowpipe and a few simple tools. The expert reached into the furnace with his pipe, got a gob of the sticky molten glass, pulled it out, dropped it into a mold, and then shaped the bottle by using his lung power and the manipulative skill of his fingers to twirl the pipe. One of the worker's biggest problems was to dip out of the tank the exact quantity of glass needed. This age-old difficulty was

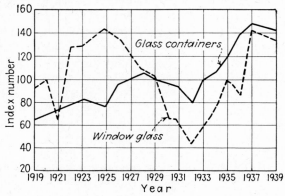

Fig. 37.—Glass production. (*Survey of Current Business*, 1940 *Supplement, U. S. Dept. of Commerce.*)

overcome in 1903 when an Ohio glass maker, Michael Owens, patented a method of getting the glass from the furnace to the mold by mechanical means.

The Owens machine employs the principle of suction to get the molten glass from the tank into the forming molds. In its main essentials it consists of arms, from 6 to 15 in number, which radiate from a central post like spokes from the hub of a horizontal wheel. It is placed at the discharge end of a continuous furnace. The wheel rotates and an arm moves into place above the furnace opening; a plunger descends and compressed air suction pulls up a fixed amount of molten glass. Then begins a series of forming operations in which the gob is successively expanded by compressing air in the molds until the bottle is completely formed and ejected onto a moving belt that transports it to the lehr or tempering oven. All these movements have been timed so that they conclude just before the arm moves again over the molten glass to begin anew the cycle. Each of the other arms does precisely the same work, with the result that bottles flow onto the belt in a swiftly moving, ceaseless stream. The Owens machine is almost completely automatic and continuous. It is almost too much so, in fact, inasmuch as its huge output—

as much as 75,000 bottles per day—and its high cost, $150,000, has limited its use to large-volume, long-run work. It now turns out only about 30 per cent of the industry's output.

In 1912 another method appeared. The new machine, controlled by the Hartford-Empire Company, instead of sucking the glass from the tank, extrudes or pushes it out in separate gobs or drops by means of a plunger. By 1917 the newer method got a foothold throughout the industry because it was less intricate, did not require as fine adjustments, was less expensive, and was adaptable to smaller orders.

The rapid mechanization of the industry has greatly increased the productivity of labor. Whereas at the turn of the century the average production per man per year was 40,000 containers, in 1935, average production per man was 245,000 containers.[1] The reduced cost of production made possible a substantial increase in output through the expansion of existing markets and the adaptation of glass containers to new uses. In 1899, 1 billion containers were produced; in 1939 production amounted to 7 billion containers. The number of employees during the same period decreased from 28,000 to about 26,000.[2] However, the labor employed now is of an entirely different type.

The Leasing System.—The most interesting aspect of the technological advance of the glass container industry is not the great increase in the productivity of the workers or the expansion in production. In these respects the industry has repeated the experiences of many other industries. Much more interesting, because of their effects on the structure of and competition within the industry, are the methods by which technical advances and their utilization are controlled through the ownership and leasing of patents.

As was previously stated, the principal processes used in the manufacture of containers are controlled by two companies, Owens-Illinois and Hartford-Empire. From 1917 to 1924 there was sharp conflict between the two companies and some patent litigation. The peace terms took the form of a cross-licensing agreement, and since 1924 the two companies have worked together with close understanding. Neither of these companies sells its equipment outright to container manufacturers. Owens-Illinois restricts the use of its machinery to its own plants, and Hartford Empire merely licenses the use of its machinery.

According to testimony presented before the Temporary National Economic Committee, the company has been very conservative in the number of licenses it has granted. Its policy is clearly indicated in the following memorandum which was presented to the Committee:[3]

[1] T.N.E.C. *Hearings*, Part 2, Washington, D. C., 1939, p. 755.
[2] *Ibid.*, p. 824.
[3] T.N.E.C. *Hearings*, Part 2, Washington, D. C., 1939, p. 769.

1. The glass industry (excluding sheet and plate glass with which we have nothing to do) was in 1912 in a backward state mechanically and just about right for change to automatic machine processes in order to meet the change of American industry toward mass production. Our development, therefore, came at the moment when it was needed and the result has been that the glass industry has absorbed from us a very large amount of expensive machinery.

2. Our process had one important rival, the Owens Bottle Company, the most powerful glass concern in the world. Its process was entirely different from ours. It came into commercial use about 1905 and dominated the industry until about 1917 when our process began to get a foothold. Up to 1924 there was sharp conflict between us and Owens, with some patent litigation. In 1924, after long negotiation, the two companies got together in a cross-licensing arrangement and have since then worked in exceptionally close understanding. There is, however, no combination between the two.

3. We began our commercial expansion in 1917 when our first feeders were put into production. It was at once apparent that if we put out these machines broadcast, without restriction, we would disorganize the whole industry, which was then divided into a large number of small units, and most of these manufacturers would not be able to refrain from using practically all the savings produced by these machines in fighting with each other. In fact, our first group of licensees said so expressly and urged us to take measures to prevent such a result.

4. Consequently we adopted the policy which we have followed ever since of restricting licensing. That is to say,

   a. We licensed the machines only to selected manufacturers of the better type, refusing many licensees whom we thought would be price-cutters, and

   b. We restricted their fields of manufacture, in each case, to certain specific articles, with the idea of preventing too much competition.

   c. In order to retain more complete control of the situation, we retained title to the machines and simply leased them for a definite period of years, usually 8 or 10 years, with the privilege of renewal of a smaller additional term.

5. In specifying the various fields of ware for a given licensee, we have, with a few exceptions, based the classification upon the use of the article rather than shape or other physical characteristics. Glass containers have so many shapes that it is practically impossible to classify them by shape and very often numerous different shapes will be used for the same purpose, so that use of the container is the basis for our classification except in a few cases.

6. Quite early in our history we foresaw that the glass industry, like others, would doubtless go through a process of combination, which as a matter of fact has occurred. We felt it to be to our best interest, as well as for the best interest of the whole industry, that we should use our influence to steady the industry as much as possible, with a long-distance view toward its general prosperity. The men at the head of our concern took this long-distance view deliberately and

have ever since maintained it. For example, although the Hartford-Fairmont Company was organized in 1912, it paid its first dividend on its common stock in 1924. Up to that time it had put back into development all of its profits and considerable amount of cash received from sale of patents abroad.

7. We have thus gradually evolved the theory of what may be called a "glass equipment concern." In this change of the industry to mechanical equipment, two courses were theoretically possible for the manufacturer—

   a. He might at his own expense develop automatic machinery and protect the same by patents for his own benefit. Such development and patent protection is an extremely expensive process, and if the manufacturers generally had followed this course, there would have been a very large duplication of effort and expense.
   b. On the other hand, the manufacturer might select some outside concern, like the Hartford-Empire Company; entrust to it the work of developing and protecting machinery of the glass industry generally; and support that concern in its development by paying a proportionate contribution which in this case was best measured by royalties on production.

8. The latter course was the one which the manufacturers very wisely chose. The result has been that the Hartford-Empire Company has now become the most important glass equipment concern in this country and probably in the world. This means that H-E has a duty toward the whole industry not only of developing and supplying machines immediately needed, but of keeping in advance of that need by inventing further improvements. It also must act as a source of service and information for its licensees in all technical matters relating to their business and must help to steady, as far as possible, the general glass industry. H-E has done this to the best of its ability; has spent enormous sums in machine development and patent litigation, as well as in research along mechanical, physical, and chemical lines.

9. As to the foreign situation, we have pursued a somewhat different policy. In most cases we have sold our foreign patents outright, it being too difficult to establish a workable licensing system abroad where we could not be in touch with our licensees and could not give them service. We have sold foreign patents in some 15 or 20 countries and have especially close working arrangements with British Hartford-Fairmont Syndicate, a London concern, and St. Gobain Glass Company in Paris. We have still a number of foreign patents unsold, especially in Central Europe.

The rapid technological advances in container manufacturing, the domination of the glass container equipment industry by two companies, and the practice of leasing equipment to "selected manufacturers of the better type" has resulted in a high degree of concentration of control. In 1904 there were 155 companies engaged in the manufacture of glass containers. In 1937 there were 40, and of this number five produced more than two-thirds of the total. Owens-Illinois, with its 17 plants, produces about 31 per cent of all containers, and the companies licensed by Hartford-Empire, some 30-odd in number, produce about 65 per cent. The so-called independent companies, only four in number, produce 4 per cent.[1]

The high degree of control in the industry is not adequately indicated by the small number of companies. From the evidence it appears that machines are licensed for the manufacture of bottles for a specified use and licensees are not at liberty to shift their machines to the manufacture of bottles for other uses. Thus, the equipment manufacturers, through their control of patents, not only control the flow of equipment into the industry; they also control the uses to which it can be applied. Accordingly, the payments the licensees make to the equipment manufacturers represent not only payments for the use of their machinery, but also insurance against too much competition.

To maintain its dominating position as a manufacturer of equipment, Hartford-Empire is not content to satisfy itself within its present patents. Recognizing that technological changes may render its patents valueless, the company has engaged in research in order to maintain its position. How the patent system facilitates this can again be shown best from the following statement of the company's policy:[2]

The Management at Hartford feels that if we are to have the same success in the future that we have had in the past, and if we are to provide for a long future of satisfactory income, we must keep in the forefront of development.

We believe that a certain proportion of our development budget must go to pure research and experimental work.

Three years is the normal period from invention to commercial success of a machine or process. Hartford must be ready to supply improvements when needed, or others, more prepared, will get the business. Hartford must therefore look ahead and be ready. . . .

In taking out patents we have three main purposes—

  a. To cover the actual machines which we are putting out, and prevent duplication of them.

  The great bulk of our income results from patents. Between a feeder protected by patents, and one not so protected, there is the cash difference between one ordinary manufacturing profit of, say, $1,500, and a royalty return of at least $30,000 over 8 years. This theory also applies to other equipment.

  b. To block the development of machines which might be constructed by others for the same purpose as our machines, using alternative means.

  We have in mind such machines as the Hillman machine; the Roirant type of machine; the Knox-O'Neill machines; improved stream feeders;

[1] *Ibid.*, pp. 762–63.
[2] T.N.E.C. *Hearings*, Part 2, pp. 775–76.

vacuum and pressure feeders; ribbon feeders; forced feeding or down suction feeding; and autoblow methods of feeding, as well as various types of pure forming machines.

To ignore this form of protection may result in a competitor's having an estoppel or hold on our own developments.

c. To secure patents on possible improvements of competing machines, so as to "fence in" those and prevent their reaching an improved stage.

There is also another, rather minor, purpose in securing patents. It corresponds with research in machine developments. Occasionally patentable ideas will appear which deal more with general principles. They may have no immediate and apparent application. But they may so relate to the possible future as to merit some time and expense.

The domination of an industry by an equipment manufacturer has some pragmatic sanction. It affords a simple and effective method of securing industry-wide support of technical research; it facilitates the withdrawal of obsolete and high-cost equipment; it discourages the entrance of weak and financially incompetent producers; it prevents excess capacity and thereby helps to stabilize production, employment, prices, and profits.

However, monopoly also has its undesirable aspects. It removes the control of the industry from the market and places it in the hands of one company, whose judgment may or may not be consistent with sound social policy. The policy of "blocking" and "fencing-in" patents of competitors may not only retard technological progress, but "freeze" it in one channel of development. It gives the controlling company dictatorial power: to favor one producer as against another; to restrict productive capacity to an uneconomic level, which is socially as harmful as excessive capacity; and to levy tribute upon the ultimate consumers of the products of its equipment.

Future.—Since the turn of the century the two principal divisions of the glass industry have experienced great growth. While their growth in the future will not be as great as in the past, neither of them has yet reached a plateau. Of the two branches, the container division seems to face the better prospect. The market for packaging materials is constantly widening and the many qualities of glass make it highly desirable material for such purposes. But this market will not come to the container industry as a matter of course. Developments in the paper and metal container industries are making inroads in the present market of the glass industry, and both of them are constantly adopting their products to new packaging uses. The extent to which the three industries will share the packaging field will be left to the arbitrament of the market, and the decision will rest upon the prices and the qualities of the materials.

PART V
THE CHEMICAL PROCESS INDUSTRIES

CHAPTER XVI

THE CHEMICAL INDUSTRIES

Scope of the Field.—What is a chemical industry? One authority answers this difficult question by defining a chemical industry as "one which produces commodities which differ chemically from the raw materials out of which they are made." According to this definition, the rayon industry, which produces synthetic fibers from cotton, or wood, or skimmed milk, is readily recognized as a chemical industry. But, according to this definition, is steel manufacture a chemical industry? The answer is not so apparent despite the fact that finished steel differs from the iron ore, limestone, manganese, silica, chrome, and numerous other ingredients from which it is usually made. Another writer has defined a chemical industry as "one which uses chemical processes to an extent that requires the employment of trained chemical technicians to control the manufacturing operations and makes highly advisable an understanding of chemistry by the general executives." Here again difficulties are encountered when the definition is applied. The paper, rubber, and glass industries meet the requirements of the definition but are not commonly regarded as chemical industries.

Perhaps it will be helpful to line up all industries according to the amount of chemical processing they do. At one end of the line will be industries that do little or no chemical processing, such as the clothing industry or machine tool manufacturers. At the other end will be those industries which do little in addition to chemical processing, such as the manufacturers of sulphuric acid or explosives. Between these extremes are industries that combine both chemical and mechanical processes in varying degree. Using this approach, chemical manufactures can be classified into three groups: (1) The strictly chemical industries which cover (a) heavy chemicals (such as soda or sulphuric acid), so called because they are heavy and bulky in relation to value; (b) fine chemicals (such as drugs and dyes) that have a high value per pound; (c) a host of organic and inorganic products such as alcohols, plastics, tanning materials, etc. The distinguishing character of these industries is that they sell strictly chemical products as such. (2) The allied chemical industries. These are closely related to the first group because they likewise do considerable processing, but differ in that their products are either blended with other materials or are manipulated mechanically. Examples are the manufactured paint, varnishes, perfumes, cosmetics, soap, etc. (3) The chemical process industries. This group includes those industries in which natural raw materials are processed chemically to change their form to one which is commercially useful; for example, cottonseed oil is converted into an edible fat by the process of hydrogenation. This group embraces such industries as rayon, fuels, ceramics, foods, rubber, paper, and many textiles.

Any classification, no matter how arbitrary, should be useful. Our object in this instance is to determine whether the industries on the chemical end of the line have common characteristics that help to explain their size, organization, capital structure, operating policies, etc. If an industry has enough chemical processing in its technology to bring into existence these characteristics, we shall be warranted, for purely pragmatic reasons, in considering it to be in the chemical group. But before attempting to generalize about the industries in this broad field let us learn more about them.

DYESTUFFS INDUSTRY

The modern dyestuffs industry came into existence in 1856 when a London college student, W. H. Perkin, in the course of an attempt to produce quinine from a coal-tar product, accidentally discovered a purplish or mauve dye. He sensed its commercial possibilities and built a plant to manufacture it. Thus the synthetic dyestuffs industry was born and the natural dyestuffs industry received a sentence to die as soon as the newcomer should reach maturity. According to one authority,[1] the industry has since passed through four phases. The first period, 1856–1871, was one of dominance by English producers. These producers were aided by a German professor and several German chemists then resident in England. Kreps describes the period as an epoch of "empirical individual experimentation" and "single-commodity production." Mauve was the first color; then came magenta; this was followed in the early seventies by alazirin or Turkey red.

The second phase extended from 1871 to 1900. This period is characterized by rapidly declining prices which came from mass production of raw materials and improved processes for making intermediates. It was also during this period that production shifted to Germany. Several reasons account for this: the return of the previously mentioned nationals to their homeland; the liberal financial support of university research;

[1] KREPS, T. J., The Dye Industry, "Encyclopaedia of the Social Sciences," Vol. 5, pp. 301–305.

the suitability of the Rhine River as a plentiful source of pure water and low-cost transportation; also the absence, until 1877, of a German patent law to protect the prior British discoveries. Another development took the form of systematic experimentation instead of the previous individual effort. Since the operation of a dyestuffs plant results in joint products, Germanic genius for systematic research led to the development of derivative products such as pharmaceuticals, flavoring extracts, perfume materials, and photographic chemicals.

The third era extended from 1900 to 1915. It witnessed the demise of the few remaining natural dyestuffs; also marked improvement in fastness to light, washing, and perspiration, of the coal tar dyes. German production was concentrated in a half-dozen large plants. Communities of interest between these were formed and agreements were made to exchange technical information and establish common price and sales policies. Furthermore, there were numerous consolidations, which culminated in 1926 in the formation of one gigantic enterprise, the I. G. Farbenindustrie A. G., which monopolizes dyestuffs production in Germany. German foreign trade in dyestuffs was pushed by a policy of "full-line forcing" whereby the consumer had to buy all the items in the line in order to obtain the few obtainable nowhere else. Throughout these years the German government seems to have been sympathetically aware of the value of the coal tar industry as a potential source of munitions, and other countries grew uneasy about German dominance in this field.

The latest period is from 1916 to date. It is marked by the establishment of dyestuffs production in the United States, as well as in England, France, Italy, and Japan. The immediate occasion for this was the First World War. It not only cut off supplies of dyes but demonstrated the value of the industry for munitions manufacture. England also used this opportunity to reestablish herself in the field.

United States Manufacture of Dyestuffs.—In the United States the industry developed in the following manner: During the war the Federal government appointed an alien property custodian to seize and keep in custody the property of enemy countries. Among the properties so seized were 4,500 German patents covering chiefly the manufacture of organic dyestuffs. Producers and consumers of dyestuffs organized a corporation, Chemical Foundation, Inc., to buy the patents and to license American manufacturers to use them. Some companies found it necessary to bring chemical engineers from Germany to lend assistance in the commercial exploitation of these patents. Although these engineers were seldom placed in responsible positions, they had the invaluable "know-how" which American companies then lacked. The income from license fees accruing to the Chemical Foundation has been used to develop and encourage the domestic chemical industries.

The American industry, off to a flying start, was protected at the outset by an embargo and later by a very high tariff. It specialized at first, and still does to a considerable extent, in large-volume, low-price products. Because of technical difficulties of production, the trade has come largely into the hands of four companies; Allied Chemical and Dye and duPont share equally 60 per cent of the total business; American Cyanamid and General Aniline Works share equally 20 per cent. The latter company, formerly known as Grasselli Dyestuffs Corporation, is owned 100 per cent by American I. G. Chemical Corporation which has a contract with I. G. Farbenindustrie A. G., for permanent rights to exploit in the United States all dyestuff patents and inventions developed by that dominant German company.

The process of dyestuffs manufacture is highly complex, calling for complicated reactions involving minute chemical control; it can be summarized for the layman in only the broadest terms. From one ton of coal there is distilled 140 pounds of tar. The tar is next processed into five "crudes" weighing only 12½ lb. The crudes after elaborate further processing yield 300 intermediate products. These are converted into 1,000 dyestuffs which finally yield some 5,000 brands of dyes. The intermediates are made on a mass-production basis and are carried in stock; this is the stage where chemical engineering plays a prominent part, giving rise to the production of ancillary products, such as germicides, insecticides, medicinals, perfumes, flavors, tanning and photographic materials. It is a comparatively simple matter to extract the dyes from the intermediates; about the only equipment required is a tub and a filter press. Since most dyes are made in very small quantities, they are usually produced on order. Kreps is authority for the statement that four dyestuffs—indigo, sulphur black, direct black, and Turkey red— account for one-half of the total quantity of dyes manufactured; that "less than 5 per cent of the modern dyes are produced in quantities exceeding 100 tons, and less than 10 per cent in amounts greater than 10 tons."

The domestic dyestuffs industry now supplies more than 90 per cent of our needs and is apparently able to fend for itself, especially because of agreements calling for international exchange of patents on both processes and products.

THE HEAVY CHEMICAL INDUSTRIES

Heavy chemicals, namely those which sell at low prices relative to weight and bulk, constitute the major portion of our chemical products. A dozen or more industries operate in this field. Although these are quite diverse they have certain common characteristics in addition to the one just mentioned. They turn out their products in thousands of tons instead of pounds. The raw materials—salt, air, sulphur, lime, etc.—are plentiful and cheap, and value added by manufacture is not high since the process is relatively simple. Soda, for instance, sells for 1 cent per pound although it requires 2 cents' worth of ammonia to make a pound of it by the Solvay process. This is commercially possible only because of highly efficient recovery of the ammonia. As transportation charges have an important place in the cost structure of these industries, plants are located near the sources of raw materials, particularly if manufacturing operations bring about a loss in weight. Many of these products do not pass through the open market because they are consumed within the chemical industries.

Sulphuric Acid Industry.—This is one of the oldest of the chemical industries. In this country, the first plant was erected in 1793. The product is widely used in industrial processes and is produced in large quantities. In 1939 the United States production amounted to 8 million tons, two-thirds of which was made for sale. The remainder was consumed in the plants of origin. The fertilizer industry usually consumes about 25 per cent, petroleum refining 20 per cent, chemicals 20 per cent, and the remaining 35 per cent is distributed throughout a wide range of industries to such an extent that the consumption of sulphuric acid is regarded as one of the best single indices of industrial activity. There are very few industries that do not use sulphuric acid.

It is estimated that more than 25 per cent of the world supply of this basic chemical comes as a by-product of other industrial processes. Tennessee Copper Company, now the Tennessee Corporation, was virtually forced into the field as a result of a Federal injunction against it to restrain it from producing noxious waste gases containing sulphur. This company is now one of the largest producers of sulphuric acid.

The Heavy Alkali Industries.—The most important alkalies are soda ash, caustic soda, and chlorine, all of which are related. Soda ash is used in this country in amounts ranging up to 3 million tons annually. The chemical industry itself is a large consumer, and soda ash is also used in the making of glass, soap, and paper and in the refining of petroleum. The most important of the numerous processes by which it is made is the Solvay method, named after the Belgian who invented it. This process utilizes as raw materials salt, limestone, coke, and ammonia. The inventor and his brother followed the practice of establishing branch plants in countries with good markets. The method was introduced in the United States in 1884 at Syracuse, N. Y. Since the First World War natural soda from California, by-product soda ash from the paper industry, and the output of numerous electrolytic processes furnish some competition. Allied Chemical and Dye Corporation alone produces about 40 per cent of the total output.

Caustic soda is produced in amounts of 600,000 to a million tons annually for the rayon, chemical, and soap industries (which together take

50 per cent of the output) and for numerous other process industries. The allied product chlorine is used as a bleach for textiles and in water purification and sewage disposal. It is also used as a raw material for the dye and explosives industries.

The plants producing these alkalies are located near great underground deposits of salt which are pumped to the surface as brine and then converted. The alkalies constitute a more or less stabilized industry as regards volume of trade, but competition is rather keen. It thus becomes important to have plants near sources of raw materials. The producers have recently built new plants on the Gulf coast. Although Mathieson Alkali Works, Inc., which specializes in this field, has deposits of salt and limestone near its main plant in Virginia that are estimated to be sufficient for over 100 years' requirements, in 1935 the company erected a 7.5-million-dollar plant in Louisiana designed to cut delivery costs through the possibilities of cheap water transportation through the Panama Canal to Pacific coast ports and through the Mississippi waterways system to interior points.[1]

OTHER CHEMICAL INDUSTRIES

In the strictly chemical field, which we have distinguished from the allied chemical and the chemical process industries, there are some 30 industries separately reported by the Census. In our discussion of the manufacture of dyestuffs and heavy chemicals we have touched upon only a few of these. The more important of the remaining ones will be discussed very briefly because of limitations of space.

The field of the industrial solvents covers the manufacture of the numerous alcohols, esters, ketones, aldehydes, and acetates for use in making paints, varnishes, resins, perfumes, drugs, and cellulose products. With the exception of water, ethyl alcohol is the most widely used solvent. It is used in the manufacture of paints, plastics, varnishes, lacquers, antifreezes, etc. It is usually fermented from molasses although it may be synthesized electrically from a derivative of natural gas or petroleum. The ethyl alcohol field is fairly well dominated by the U. S. Industrial Alcohol Company and Commercial Solvents Corporation, each of which produces about 25 per cent of the United States output.

Gases.—The field of the industrial gases is occupied largely by oxygen and acetylene which may be combined to produce a very intense flame for use in the cutting, welding, and finishing of metals. Eighty-five per cent of the output of this division is produced by Union Carbide & Carbon Corporation and Air Reduction Company, Inc. This field is closely related to the production of carbon and carbon products and electric

[1] In the foregoing discussion of dyestuffs and heavy chemicals, the authors have with permission drawn heavily upon the articles on these subjects which appear in the "Encyclopaedia of the Social Sciences," published by the The Macmillan Company, New York.

furnace ferro-alloys, and much of the work is done near the source of cheap power.   Hydrogen is another important industrial gas; it is used in the hydrogenation of vegetable oils for food purposes.

Explosives.—Explosives constitute another group of chemical products.   These may be classified into commercial and military explosives. The field is dominated by three companies; duPont, Hercules Powder, and Atlas Powder produce about 80 per cent of the total.   The remainder of the market is shared by about 25 small companies.   Explosives constitute only 7 to 8 per cent of the total dollar sales volume of duPont's business; military explosives normally account for only 1.5 to 2 per cent, sales of which are confined almost exclusively to the United States government.

Plastics.—Another group of chemical products about which much has been heard lately compose the field of the plastics.   Developments began some 70 years ago when the Celluloid Corporation brought out the nitrocellulose product from which the company took its name.   Progress was not marked, however, until the decade of the 1920's when the radio industry gave the field a fillip.   The most important class of plastics are the phenol compounds made from carbolic acid and formaldehyde. Other competing resins are (a) urea formaldehyde, made from ammonia and carbon dioxide; and (b) the vinyls, the basic substances of which are lime and coal.   There are many other plastics such as those made from the cellulose materials and the protein materials.   The latter group include plastics from milk, dried blood, and soy beans.   Another classification of the plastics is according to the way they are used.   They may be either molded, cast, or laminated.   In the first instance plastic powder (mixed with wood or some other filler) is formed under heat and pressure in molds.   Casting involves pouring the plastic sirup into molds where it hardens upon cooling or baking.   Lamination involves saturating fabric or paper with plastic and subjecting the piled sheets to pressure under heat; the resulting product shows great strength and may be used for gears and bearings.

An indication of the growing importance of the new field was the formation in 1935 of an organic plastics section of the United States Bureau of Standards.   Many companies are in the field, among them duPont, Union Carbide & Carbon, Tennessee Eastman, American Cyanamid, and Bakelite.   The market for these products is not yet clearly defined; some predict the chief sales will be to the building industry where, it is contended, it will be used for doors, walls, ceilings, floors, store fronts, table and counter tops.   One writer states: "these products have the advantages of permanent lustrous finishes.   They may be transparent, opaque, or come in a variety of colors."   They can be cut to order, eliminating wastage on the job, they do not warp, are free from expansion and contraction, have a high electrical insulating value, and are practically fire- and acidproof. Prices of the coal-tar resins have declined from about 70 cents per pound to 20 cents per pound during the period 1920–1936. The last development in the field consists of making plastics from the lignins (the soluble substance of wood) which are produced as waste products from the production of paper and which are also present in corncobs, oat hulls and sawdust.

Nitrogen Fixation.—In many respects the most important single chemical development during the past 25 years has been nitrogen fixation. Nitrogen is an indispensable element in the life cycle of plants and when combined with hydrogen and oxygen it forms nitric acid—a raw material for explosives manufacture. For many years the natural deposits of sodium nitrate in Chile supplied the leading nations of the world with their fertilizer and explosives requirements. In order to escape their dependence upon so distant a source of raw materials for military explosives, German chemists developed a process for manufacturing synthetic ammonia which can easily be oxidized to form nitric acid, the basic raw material for explosives, fertilizers, and urea-formaldehyde plastics. In the United States the process has been adapted primarily to the production of ammonia which found a rapidly growing market in mechanical refrigeration.

We have already alluded in our discussion of the dyestuffs industry to the manufacture of medicinals. If space permitted, this field could be analyzed to reveal its unusual phases, especially the development of ethical standards which play such an important part in the conduct of the industry.

CHARACTERISTICS COMMON TO MOST CHEMICAL INDUSTRIES

It is hazardous to generalize about the economic aspects of the industries comprising a field so broad and diverse as this one; nevertheless, the following attributes may be accepted with some reservation as characteristic of the group.

Changing Products and Processes.—In no group of industries is change more prevalent or more necessary than in the chemical field. New methods, new equipment, and new products prevail in all branches of it. It is easier to be positive about the existence of this constant element of change than it is to be dogmatic concerning the reasons for it. Two factors seem to account for the changing technology and structure. It is probably due in the first instance to the fact that these industries rest upon scientific knowledge rather than upon empirical or "practical" knowledge. Prior to 1880 most of the then-existing chemical industries were extractive industries with techniques that were simple, traditional, and of the rule-of-thumb variety. With the extension of knowledge of physics and chemistry and the acceptance of the scientific method as a fruitful approach to new knowledge, the chemical industries changed from reliance upon practice to reliance upon science.   This was especially true in Germany, to which country the world is greatly indebted for pioneering in this field.

Here technical education was widespread enough to provide the chemical industries with even minor executives and salesmen formally trained in chemistry.   It was therefore relatively easy to build up a close liaison between the universities and the chemical companies and to imbue the latter with the spirit of science.   Some observers go so far as to contend that Germans are peculiarly research-minded.   At any rate, continued and systematic research on a mass basis brought forth cumulative knowledge and continuous change.   This has persisted to the present day, and it is not a hazardous prediction to forecast its continuance.

Another explanation arises from the fact that most chemical industries are joint product industries.   When they produce a new commodity they are likely to get, in addition to the one they seek, a number of other products whether they want them or not.   Furthermore, these additional products are not of the same nature as would be the case in many fields such as in lumber manufacture.   For example: If methanol (wood alcohol) is manufactured by subjecting wood to pressure and heat, the producer finds himself with a supply of acetic acid (vinegar) as well as the major product.   He may be forced by competitive conditions in the acetic field to do research for more profitable outlets.   Conditions in any one chemical field may, and constantly are, being upset by the incidental results of experiments in other chemical fields.   To summarize: cumulative scientific knowledge, plus knowledge of and faith in the scientific method, plus the criss-crossing of the lines of chemical research, plus the profit motive, make change the order of the day in these industries.

Liberal Budgets for Research.—It is apparent that under the conditions just described individual companies should make ample provision for research.   It is estimated that, in 1937, the chemical industries employed 300 research workers for every 10,000 wage earners it employed. The ratios for petroleum refining and rubber manufacturing, chemical process industries, were 210 and 170 respectively.   This is in marked contrast with iron and steel, 20, leather tanning, 4, and textiles, 3 research workers per 10,000 wage earners.   The duPont company states that after it began in 1917 to pioneer in the development of an American coal-tar dyestuffs industry, it alone invested more than 40 millions and spent more than five years of research before a cent of profit was returned from the venture.   This company spends at the present time about 6 million dollars annually for research.   The large companies not only maintain research departments at each plant but also support large laboratories which are set apart from manufacturing operations and which frequently work on "pure" research problems. However, it cannot be emphasized too strongly that the research departments are held strictly accountable for results, *i.e.*, they engage in research not merely for the sake of scientific exploration but for a specific purpose such as finding a new use for a low-priced raw material or developing a cheaper process. Although companies are liberal in making appropriations for research, the research divisions must first show cause why such appropriations will prove profitable.

High Rate of Obsolescence and Depreciation.—A concomitant of the frequent changes in product and process is the rapid outmoding of plant and equipment. This makes it necessary to provide in the cost accounting of the industry for a high rate of obsolescence. Provision must be made also for a high rate of depreciation, not only because the tanks, pipes, stills, autoclaves, etc., wear out quickly as a result of the high pressures and temperatures at which they are operated, but also because the probability of obsolescence makes it advisable to exceed what would otherwise be the optimum conditions of operations. In some branches of the chemical industry it is customary to allow only 2 to 3 years for the expected life of the equipment.

Flexible Capital Structure and Conservative Dividend Policies.—The characteristics thus far noted have an influence on the financial policies of chemical corporations. Adequate provision must be made for the time when sales of a product or class of products may disappear altogether or must be made at reduced prices; when research programs must be entered into without prospect of immediate financial returns; when rates may be high in the money market and at the same time vigorous plant expansion seems advisable. These contingencies dictate a policy of borrowing only a small portion of the necessary capital by means of bond issues. They also call for a conservative policy with regard to dividends and for ample provision of working capital.

A recent survey of 15 leading chemical companies shows that eight had no bonded indebtedness and four of the remaining ones had no preferred stock outstanding. In other words, these companies were trying to avoid either fixed charges from bond issues or prior claims of preference stock. Another survey showed a funded debt in the period 1928–1932 equal to less than 2 per cent of total capital investment in contrast to approximately 13 per cent in the petroleum industry, 4 per cent in copper production, and 2.5 per cent in the electrical equipment industry. Only the automobile industry, which is well known for its freedom from bonded indebtedness, had a comparable showing, and even it had a slightly higher percentage.

Rational Procedure for Converting Research Findings into Commercial Results.—After research has brought forth a new product or process, it is necessary, of course, to adapt the findings of the research department to the requirements of commercial manufacture. Success at the laboratory stage does not ensure success when the process is carried out on a commercial scale. When the apparatus is enlarged to factory size the results may be quite different from those obtained in the small laboratory apparatus. When large masses of material are handled there may be a change in the rate at which heat is absorbed or dissipated, or in the way in which a catalytic agent or a retarder works; more frequent adjustments may have to be made which will make the cost of supervision too great; yields may be lower than under laboratory conditions. These are some of the reasons why there has developed in the chemical industries a somewhat standardized procedure for getting commercial results from research experiments with a minimum amount of risk. This procedure takes the form of steps or stages:[1]

1. *Laboratory stage.* This is the period after the question has been raised or the hypothesis formulated when the technical literature is scanned to avoid work done or difficulties encountered previously. Laboratory experiments may be performed with either standard apparatus or small-size models. Apparatus may be altered to throw light on commercial equipment needed.

2. *Pilot-plant stage.* During this period only one model may be built. It may be actual factory size. Performance is checked for the influence of change in size upon results. There is constant adjustment and close supervision.

If costs involved in full production are heavy or results are not definite enough, the plant may go through what may be called a semicommercial stage before full production is attempted. This will give a better clue to normal production yields and costs. It has the further advantage of developing the "know-how" without tying up a large investment.

3. *Commercial stage.* Full productive capacity is now secured, the experimental engineers, laboratory technicians, and other high-grade personnel may be reduced in number or replaced by straight operating personnel who follow standard policies and techniques laid down for them. The variables in the commercial operations are now well known and provided for.

Decreasing Costs Usually Prevail.—Competition in the chemical industries enforces upon each company the necessity to secure lower costs, just as in mechanical industries, but it takes a somewhat different form. In the chemical industries great emphasis is placed upon increasing yields and reducing fuel consumption. For example, one manufacturer of aniline reduced his costs from 17 to 11 cents a pound by an improved

---

[1] Adapted from Tyler, Chaplin: "Chemical Engineering Economics," McGraw-Hill Book Co., Inc., New York, 1926.

process that gave a greater yield from the same raw material. Manufacturing costs are also reduced by increasing the size of stills, evaporators, filter presses, and other equipment. This makes for increased output without proportionate increases in labor costs. Finally, growth in size of plants also produces lower costs because it permits continuity of operation.

Chemical Industries Run to Large-scale, Diversified Enterprises.—A marked characteristic of the chemical industries which has been discussed is the presence in each of them of large corporations. If we turn our attention from the industries to the corporations themselves, we will note that the largest and most successful of them occupy a number of fields. The duPont company, founded in 1802 to manufacture black powder, confined its operations to explosives and paints until the period of the First World War. Afterwards it expanded rapidly into dyestuffs, plastics, solvents, heavy chemicals, germicides, rayon, and numerous specialties. In the words of the company, it "uses a variety of closely related chemical processes which provide a large number of chemical products. Many of these in appearance show little family relationship; yet, almost without exception, they have a definite kinship with each other. These chemical products are closely related either because they have certain basic raw materials in common or because the technique involved in their manufacture is similar."

The same diversification exists in the other companies: Allied Chemical & Dye Corporation is the result of a consolidation in 1920 of five companies, each from a different chemical field. Since that time growth has been by internal expansion, and its interests now ramify throughout most of the field. The same story of diversification can be told of Union Carbide & Carbon Corporation, the American Cyanamid, the Dow Chemical Company, Monsanto Chemical Company, and many others.

A special phase of this growth of large-scale, diversified enterprise is the tendency to form alliances with foreign producers calling for interchange of process and product patents and the right to act as sales representatives of each other in their respective territories. Mention has already been made in this connection of General Aniline Works. Another arrangement, which is quoted from a prospectus filed by Morgan, Stanley & Company with the SEC in 1937, illustrates in detail the type of foreign relationship frequently effected in these industries:

In the foreign field, the (duPont) company has arrangements relating to patents and processes with various foreign chemical manufacturers, the most important of which is with Imperial Chemical Industries, Ltd. The company entered into these arrangements primarily for the purpose of securing American rights to foreign inventions and of securing a maximum return from foreign exploitation of its own developments. The arrangement . . . provides that each will afford to the other the opportunity to acquire rights under their respective patents and processes, except as to rayon, "Cellophane," military explosives and certain other products.   The payment for licenses is determined by negotiations.   Rights so granted within the licensee's exclusive territory are subject to the right reserved by the licensor to sell within the same territory, and rights granted in other territories are non-exclusive. . . . A further relationship between (the two) is represented by the ownership by each, directly or through subsidiaries, of substantially equal investments in several foreign companies, the principal ones of which are Canadian Industries, Ltd., a Canadian company, and Industrias Quimacas Argentinas "Duperial" S.A. Industrial y Commercial, an Argentine company.

Price Wars Normally Absent.—The citation of this point as a characteristic may occasion some surprise in view of the emphasis that has been placed upon shifting sources of raw materials, improvements in processes, and changing markets for finished products.   Perhaps the presence of these incitements to competition accounts for the failure of the industry, except infrequently, to engage in "cutthroat" price wars.   In the chemical industries the competitors who have a stake in stabilizing prices are relatively few in number and strong financially.   Furthermore, they have, albeit to a slight extent, the means of control at hand.   This control is in the form of an ability to alter processes and to decide which shall be major and which shall be minor products.   The flow of products onto a particular market can thus be influenced to some degree in the interests of price stability.   This is not to be understood as meaning that price declines do not take place.   Violent declines occurred in the price of wood alcohol in the period 1922–1927 when the synthetic product was displacing the natural one.   But it is accurate to state that these declines take place largely during periods of technical upheaval; once the new process is installed and costs are determined, the new price is a fairly stable one.   Another reason why prices tend toward stability is that companies in this industry sell many products to each other.

Other Characteristics.—Out of the factors already discussed grow other characteristics which will be merely mentioned.   The day labor employed in the industry is semiskilled, unorganized, and, although it is paid somewhat higher than market rates for common labor, constitutes a relatively low charge against costs of production.   Supervisory workers, on the other hand, are becoming to an increasing extent technically trained.   This extends up through the supervisory and sales forces to the top executives.   Finally, profits in the chemical group of industries run above the average for manufacturing in general.   This was especially true in the depression years following 1929.

The Future of the Chemical Industries.—The late Dr. Edward Slosson, a prolific and inspiring writer on chemical subjects, has summarized man's progress in battle against a "niggardly nature" in the following manner: We have passed through three stages in our technological development: The first we may call the "appropriative stage." Here man accepted what nature gave him: for food he ate berries; for clothing he pieced together the skins of animals with sinews; for shelter he lived in caves. In the second period, the "adaptive stage," man assumed greater control over nature by altering natural products. He improved his food supply by selecting better plants and upgrading these by cultivation; he domesticated certain wild animals to his own advantage. Nevertheless, the goods he consumed were essentially natural products. In the third epoch, the "creative stage," into which man is now beginning to enter more fully, he is remaking the natural world so that it will more adequately meet his needs. He is taking natural products, such as wood, coal, air, salt, and cotton, and, by a process of tearing down and rebuilding, is getting synthetic products which have a form utility highly superior to nature's products. As a result, we have rayon made from cotton and wood; Bakelite produced from phenol; dyes, medicines, and perfumes from coal tar; rubber from lime and coal, etc.

In the face of this development, proceeding at a swift pace, it requires no great amount of imaginative insight to predict that the role of chemistry will become increasingly important. Some go so far as to predict that our foods will be synthetic; also our building materials, our clothing and our weather. In such a stage the chemical industries may expand to embrace almost all manufacturing. Whether or not one agrees with this point of view, there need not be much doubt concerning the increasing role of chemistry in manufacturing.

CHAPTER XVII

THE PETROLEUM INDUSTRY

The petroleum industry is closely allied to the automobile industry. The connection that immediately comes to mind, of course, is that the demand for gasoline and lubricants is largely derived from the use of automobiles. But there are other relationships also. In a very real sense, the birth of the automobile industry had to await the birth of the petroleum industry in 1859. The automobile in its modern form could not operate without a lubricant that would stand up under the high temperatures generated by the internal combustion gas engine and without a liquid fuel capable of being easily distributed, easily dispensed, and of very light weight in proportion to the energy it contains.

Another important relationship between the two industries is: technical developments in each one limit or condition technical developments in the other. Before the automobile arrived the principal objective of petroleum refining was to produce kerosene; afterwards, it was to produce gasoline. The shift in emphasis greatly altered refining methods. More recently, during the period 1915–1920, changes in refining techniques produced gasolines with high antiknock qualities. This change opened up a new field for the automotive designer, and the first to enter it was Walter Chrysler with his high-speed, high-compression motor, brought out in 1924. During the years 1925–1930 all the other automobile companies followed Chrysler's lead and produced cars with higher and higher compression engines which in turn demanded fuels with higher antiknock qualities. Some engineers predict that automobiles will eventually be powered by engines the size of a cigar box and that this development awaits the coming of a fuel capable of being compressed in the tiny cylinders of such engines without knocking. Thus we see that there has been from the outset an intimate and reciprocal relationship between the two industries, as is indicated in Fig. 38.

The Structure of the Industry.—The principal branches of the petroleum industry are three in number, and it will be helpful to take a brief glance at these before discussing each in detail.

Production.—This branch of the industry includes all the activities incident to the exploration and location of petroleum lands, the drilling of wells, the extraction of crude petroleum from the earth, and its storage in the fields.

Closely related to the production of petroleum but, from our point of view, a separate and auxiliary branch is the transportation of the crude oil from the fields to the refineries. Transportation facilities take the form of pipe lines, through which the crude oil is pumped, or tank steamers if the route is overseas.

Refining.—This branch includes all the activities involved in converting the crude petroleum into the 300 or more useful products which the

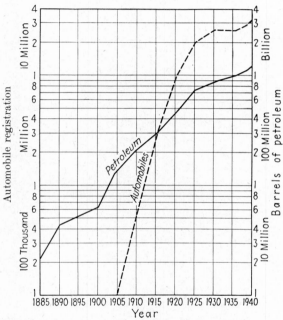

Fig. 38.—Petroleum production and number of automobiles registered in the United States. (*Automobile Facts and Figures, Automobile Manufacturers Association*, 1941; *Petroleum Facts and Figures, American Petroleum Institute*, 1941.)

industry produces. The liquid raw material, petroleum, consists of a large number of molecular combinations of hydrocarbons, and the refining process consists of separating these into marketable products ranging from solids to highly volatile liquids and gases. The refining processes are numerous and varied, but all of them employ heat, pressure, chemicals, and catalysts.

Marketing.—This branch includes, as the term implies, the distribution of the products through wholesale, intermediate, and retail channels to the ultimate consumer. Its physical facilities include storage tanks, motor trucks, tank cars, gasoline pipe lines, and the ubiquitous service stations.

Before examining each of these three divisions more closely we shall consider the nature and occurrence of petroleum or "crude oil," as it is called in the industry.

The Raw Material—Its Nature and Occurrence.—It has just been noted that petroleum is a liquid or gas composed of hydrogen and carbon. There are many theories as to its origin; the one that is usually accepted is that it is an organic creation arising from the deposit, during certain geologic eras, of countless marine organisms. These organisms have decomposed, as a result of heat and pressure, into liquid or gaseous form.

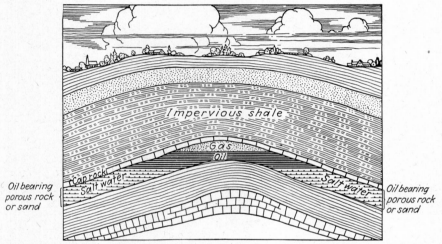

FIG. 39A.—Oil trapped in natures reservoir. (*Courtesy of The American Petroleum Institute.*)

It is invariably found in porous rock. At one time it was thought that oil was found in underground lakes and streams. We now know that crude oil is found diffused, like water in a sponge, through certain porous sand or rock strata. Gas and water are usually found with the oil, and wherever possible the gas and water pressure is utilized to drive the oil to the surface.

Crude petroleum has been found throughout a wide expanse of territory in this country. It has been estimated that it is geologically possible for half of the acreage of the country to yield petroleum. The oil found in various sections varies widely in density, viscosity, and color. In some sections it is a tar or pitchlike substance and dark in color. Elsewhere it may be yellow, brown, or green and much more volatile in substance. Originally, much importance was attached to external appearance and crudes were divided roughly into three classes according to their bases or heavy constituents. Thus, the crude from Pennsylvania was known as a paraffine-base oil and was reputed to yield superior lubricants; the California crudes were known as asphalt-base oils; and the Mid-Continent crudes were known as mixed-base oils because they were combinations of these two. But improvements in refining techniques have minimized the effects of these differences on the qualities of the finished products, so the above classification no longer means much and is falling into disuse.

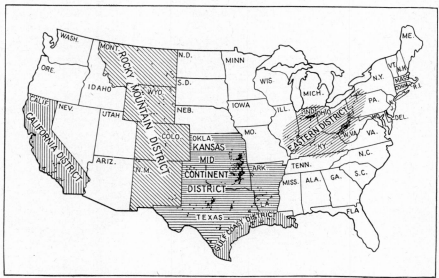

Fig. 39B.—The principal oil-producing areas in the United States. (*Courtesy of The American Petroleum Institute*, 1935.)

The principal areas of production are shown in Fig. 39B. Their importance, in terms of production and estimated reserves, is shown in Table XXXIIA.

TABLE XXXIIA.—PETROLEUM FIELDS OF THE UNITED STATES
(In millions of barrels)

Field	Production, 1939	Estimated reserve, Jan. 1, 1940
Mid-Continent and Gulf..........	821	13,049
California.......................	224	3,532
Eastern.........................	153	787
Rocky Mountain..................	65	1,106
Total........................	1,263	18,474

Source of Estimates: American Petroleum Institute.

It is evident from Table XXXIIA that the petroleum industry of this country, insofar as it relates to the occurrence and production of the crude product, is almost wholly confined to two fields—Mid-Continent and California. To state this thought differently, in 1939 three states— Texas, California, and Oklahoma—produced almost 70 per cent of our petroleum and contained about the same relative amount of our estimated future supply.

THE PRODUCING BRANCH OF THE INDUSTRY

As previously indicated, this division covers the purchase and exploration of oil lands, the drilling of wells, and the extraction of the crude. In seeking to understand the organization and operation of this branch of the industry it is helpful to remember at all times four facts about petroleum.

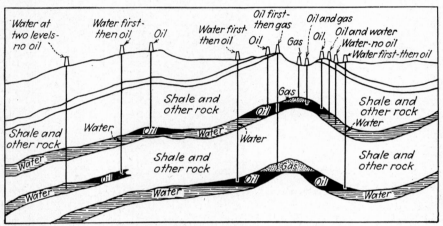

Fig. 39C.—How oil is found and missed in typical fields. (*Courtesy of The American Petroleum Institute, 1935.*)

1. The supply is finite. By this is meant that nature is no longer producing petroleum; the supply is limited; every barrel brought to the surface results in that much less for those who come after us.

2. The supply, though definitely limited in amount, is unknown. This is true not only for the country as a whole but for each of the fields, each of the hundreds of pools, and each of the 350,000 producing oil wells of the country. Experts make estimates of our supply, but their calculations are to be regarded only as estimates. Table XXXIIA gave our probable future supply as roughly 18 billion barrels and our annual production as roughly 1 billion barrels. If production and supply do not change, we shall exhaust our supply before 1960—according to the *estimate*.

3. Petroleum is fugitive. This means that it moves from place to place—the direction and extent of the movement depending on the nature of the rock, the pressure to which it is subjected by surrounding deposits of water and gas, and other circumstances. (Note Fig. 39C.) This also means that petroleum production, after everything possible has been done to make it scientific, remains a gamble.

4. Petroleum is subject in the United States to the "law of capture." This doctrine holds that petroleum is part of the land, and therefore the landowner possesses a right to all of his own and other people's oil he can obtain from the mouth of a well on that land. Some of the ways in which these four facts combine to influence developments in this branch will become apparent as we proceed with the discussion.

The Art of Discovery.—The first step in the production of crude petroleum is prospecting. This may take the form of random, hit-or-

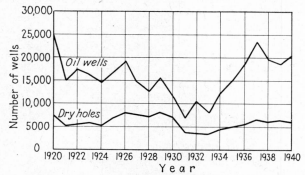

Fig. 40.—Number of producing and dry wells completed annually. (*Minerals Yearbook,* 1940.)

miss efforts known in the industry as "wild-catting" or more rational scientific efforts. There is an old saying in the industry—oil is where you find it—and the only sure test is to drill a well. During the first half century of the oil industry, prospecting was almost wholly a matter of random drilling. It was guided only by surface indications, such as oil or gas seepages, or by hunch, "doodle bugs," or divining rods.

Today, prospecting proceeds along more rational lines. Geological and geophysical analyses reveal the existence of traps—underground structural conditions suitable for the accumulation of oil as shown in the preceding illustration. Clues leading to the discovery of oil are found by such devices as the seismograph, which times the echoes of sound waves sent into the earth, the torsion balance, which measures gravity anomalies, the electrical log, which reveals the permeability of subterranean beds, and the aerial camera, which exposes surface formations otherwise invisible. These and allied scientific aids offer no sure formula for finding oil, but it has been demonstrated that exploration based upon technical data is more productive than wild-catting. Note in Fig. 40 the recent trend in the ratio between productive and unproductive drilling. The search for oil yielded only 114,000 barrels per dry hole in the wild-catting period prior to 1900, in contrast with 266,000 barrels per dry hole in the period 1931–1938 when prospecting was based almost entirely upon scientific procedure. Another proof of the superiority of scientific exploration is that throughout the history of the petroleum industry, 225 oil fields have been discovered through the aid of geological and geophysical technology in contrast with only 65 discoveries by the "wrinkle chasers."

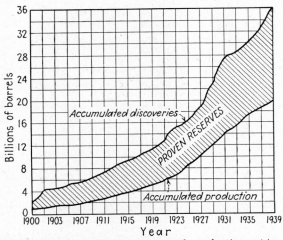

Fig. 41.—United States petroleum reserves and production. (*American Petroleum Institute and Energy Resources and National Policy, National Resources Committee, Jan., 1939.*)

As a result of constant prospecting and of improved prospecting technique, the industry has been able since its beginning to maintain proved reserves in sufficient amount to ward off exhaustion of supply. This is revealed by Fig. 41. But it must be remembered that the numerous estimates by government and other petroleum geologists, all of which have proved to be erroneous, were made so chiefly by constant and better prospecting. It is not inaccurate to describe the prospecting activities of the industry as a race between discovery and disaster. This constant, unrelenting necessity to keep on hunting for oil raises problems that affect the nation, the oil-producing states, and the individual companies. It is to the crude-oil policies of the companies that we turn at this point.

Crude-oil Policies of Petroleum Companies.—For many years the large petroleum companies were not particularly interested in acquiring oil lands. In fact, Rockefeller did not enter the raw material end of the industry until 25 years after he began to refine and market petroleum products. There were several reasons for this: prospecting was very hazardous for it was carried on wholly by "wild-catting" methods; the supply of crude above ground was usually very plentiful, was sold under highly competitive conditions, and could therefore be purchased very profitably by the companies which refined and sold it; the future supply seemed inexhaustible and no one worried much about the conservation of our natural resources. (The conservation of natural resources of all kinds did not begin on a national scale until the movement was popularized by Theodore Roosevelt about 1907.)

More recently, particularly following the First World War, all the major companies adopted the policy of assuring themselves a future supply of raw material by acquiring, through discovery or purchase, crude reserves in large quantities. It is currently estimated that between 80 and 85 per cent of the total crude reserves of the United States are held by 22 companies. The policies of individual companies vary widely; Table XXXIII shows the reserves of some of the more important companies.

TABLE XXXIII.—ESTIMATED RESERVES OF SOME MAJOR COMPANIES

Company	Millions of Barrels	
Standard Oil Company of N. J.	2,500	
4 companies	1,000	each
3 companies	500 to	750 each
9 companies	250 to	500 each
6 companies	100 to	200 each
12 companies	50 to	100 each

Source: T.N.E.C. *Hearings*, Public Resolution No. 113 (75th Congress), Part 14, Petroleum Industry, Sec. 1, p. 7392.

Care should be taken in comparing the policies of one company with those of another on the basis of the above figures. The table does not show the relative amount of each company's capital that is tied up in oil reserves, or the amount of oil each company consumes each year, or the amount of oil each company is in a position to buy on favorable terms from outside sources. Atlantic Refining, for example, which has relatively small reserves, buys 70 per cent of the oil it consumes—possibly on very favorable terms. If the latter is true it is thereby conserving much of its relatively small supply for future use.

The trend in the industry is definitely toward the passing of oil lands into "strong hands," namely, into the possession of the big companies. There are probably two major reasons for this. (1) Prospecting and production require greater and greater capital investment as they become more rational and as deeper wells must be drilled. (2) Only companies with large capital resources can afford to pursue a long-run policy with respect to the acquisition and development of reserves. For example, Standard Oil of New Jersey is shown by the above table to possess 2,500 million barrels as a reserve. This amounts, on the basis of the extent to which it drew on its own reserves for oil in 1935, to a 33-year supply. In other words, the company will not realize on some of its investment until one-third of a century shall have elapsed. An impecunious owner cannot afford to wait that long.

Production of Petroleum.—The main activity covered by this division is the drilling of wells. Drilling methods fall roughly into two classes. (1) In percussion methods a heavy cylindrical steel bar, attached to a cable, is alternately raised and allowed to drop into the hole being drilled. Inasmuch as the bar is sharpened at the free end and is of great weight, it forces its way in a succession of blows (hence the term "percussion") through the strata of rock to the point where the oil is presumed to be

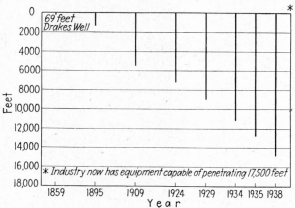

Fig. 42.—Progress in depth of drilling. (*Adapted from J. E. Pogue, Economics of the Petroleum Industry.*" *The Chase National Bank, New York, March,* 1939.)

located.   (2) Rotary drill methods employ the principle of grinding away the rock instead of hammering it to pieces as in the percussion methods. The bit, or cutting device, is screwed to the end of a shaft. As the shaft is rotated, the bit turns and the rock is ground or pulverized. Water flows down through the hollow drill pipe, washes away the pulverized rock, and wells up on the outside of the casing. As the hole becomes deeper, additional sections of drill pipe are screwed onto the upper end of the shaft to allow contact between the bit and the bottom of the hole.

It will be noted in the accompanying sketches that oil, gas, and water are all confined under great pressure. When the well penetrates the oil-bearing rock, the pressure tends to drive the oil out of the stratum to the surface. It has been increasingly realized over the years that this pressure or energy is of great importance as an agency for oil recovery. Whenever possible, gas that would formerly have been wasted is now held in the reservoir to drive oil to the bottom of the well.   Water, thought to be the greatest menace a decade ago, is now regarded as a powerful agent for the expulsion of oil.

Recent improvements in production methods have added millions of barrels to our available supply of crude. Rotary drilling is replacing percussion drilling. New drilling tools penetrate hard rock formations more rapidly. Derricks, pumps, boilers, etc., are now made to permit drilling to depths of 17,500 ft. Progress in deeper drilling, as shown in Fig. 42, has "brought in" oil pools hitherto unknown. Modern cementing procedure permits sealing off the gas overlying the oil sand so as to preserve the gas pressure. Water is similarly shut off and its pressure used to drive up the oil. Oil sands are exhausted more thoroughly by improved methods of secondary recovery. Gas, air, or water is injected under pressure in several well-heads to flush oil from the sands and force it up a centrally located well, thereby recovering more oil than can be obtained by conventional pumping. The long-declining Pennsylvania field has been rejuvenated by these repressuring methods and is now producing as much oil as it did in its heyday in the nineties.

The Problem of Overproduction.—Periodic overproduction has plagued the producing branch of the industry throughout its entire history. High crude prices immediately stimulate production, but, oddly enough, low crude prices do not immediately retard production. The explanation is to be found in the fourfold characteristics of production mentioned at the outset. The keynote of the anomaly is the law of capture.

The rule of capture, the fugitive nature of oil, and the divided oil pool serve to stimulate feverish extraction not alone in response to economic considerations of high price but out of fear of expropriation by competitors operating in the same pool. Since the subterranean area of a pool is seldom confined within the limits of a surface tract of single ownership and since the law of capture gives every landowner the right to as much oil as he can bring to the surface on his own property, the discovery of oil naturally leads to competitive drilling and extraction. Low prices will induce no one producer to curtail production because every barrel of oil left in the pool is subject to extraction by competitors. Additional pressure toward rapid exploitation arises from the multitude of interests in the pool. Oil pools are usually divided among many interests not only because the land was so divided before the discovery of oil but also because the property is subdivided among numerous operators after the discovery for the purpose of spreading the financial risk. Operators have long followed the practice of spreading their risks geographically because it costs an average of $25,000 to drill a well and not all wells are "strikes."

About 1926 Oklahoma introduced a plan, called "proration," for the purpose of keeping production within the reasonable bounds of market demand.   Originally proration merely allocated demand on a pro-rata basis among competing producers within a restricted territory.   Since that time proration has been expanded to embrace broader objectives and wider territory.   It is now practiced in every major oil-producing state (on a voluntary basis in California) with the threefold purpose of conserving petroleum, allocating production, and adjusting production to market demand.   Proration is administered by state regulatory bodies and has the sanction of the Federal government which forbids, under the Connally Act, the interstate shipment of oil in excess of quotas established by state commissions.

Although proration has gone a long way toward correcting the evil of excessive production, there still remains the problem of uneconomical drilling.   As long as the well is used as the unit for allocating demand in proration, there remains an artificial incentive for drilling.   Too many wells defeat the goal of conservation on two counts—unnecessarily increasing the costs of extraction and reducing the amount of recoverable oil through dissipation of reservoir energy.

REFINING AND MARKETING BRANCH OF THE INDUSTRY

Refining, in its elementary form, consists of heating crude petroleum in a still until it vaporizes, collecting the vapors, and condensing them into liquids.   Petroleum is a complex hydrocarbon compound, but the several products are easily extracted because each has a different heat of vaporization.   The application of heat first drives off the lightest fractions—the naphthas and gasoline.   As the heat is increased the successively heavier fractions are obtained, such as kerosene, fuel oil, lubricating oils, and finally waxes, asphalt, and coke.   Gasoline, fuel oil, and lubricating oil are the most important commercial products; together they constitute almost 90 per cent of the revenue of refineries, as Table XXXIV shows.

TABLE XXXIV.—PETROLEUM REFINERY PRODUCTS

Products	Value of products, 1939 (000,000 omitted)	Per cent of total
Gasoline	$1,424	58
Fuel oils	472	19
Lubricating oils	237	10
Kerosene	112	5
Grease, wax, asphalt, coke, etc	216	8
	$2,461	100

Source: "Petroleum Facts and Figures," 1941.

Types of Refineries.—Refineries are divided into seven major types according to their products.   Almost half (46 per cent) of the crude-oil

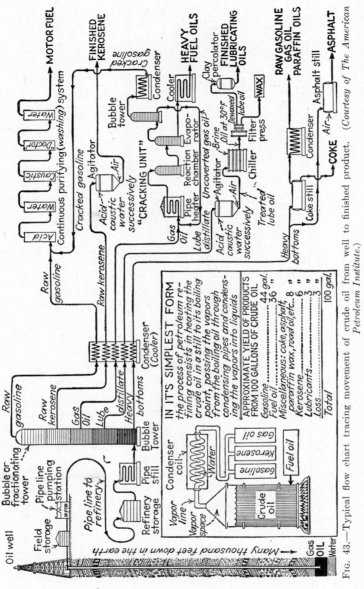

MOTOR FUEL

FINISHED KEROSENE

Continuous purifying (washing) system

Cracked gasoline

Cracked gasoline

Agitator

Bubble tower

Condenser

Cooler

HEAVY FUEL OILS

Clay percolator

FINISHED LUBRICATING OILS

Raw gasoline

Raw kerosene

Acid — caustic water successively

"CRACKING UNIT"

Reaction chamber

Evaporator rotor

Uncovered gas oil

tube oil — WAX

dewaxed

lube oil

Filter press

Pipe heater

Gas oil

Lube distillate

Brine

Agitator — Air

Acid — caustic water successively

Chiller

Treated lube oil

RAW GASOLINE

GAS OIL

PARAFFIN OILS

Heavy bottoms

Condenser

Asphalt still

Air — **ASPHALT**

Coke still

COKE

Acid · Caustic · Doctor · Water · Water

Water

Raw gasoline
Raw kerosene
Gas Oil
Lube
distillate
Heavy
bottoms

Bubble or fractionating tower

Condenser (Cooler)

Bubble Tower

Oil well

Field storage

Pipe line pumping station

Pipe line to refinery

Refinery storage

Pipe still

Condenser coil

IN IT'S SIMPLEST FORM the process of petroleum refining consists in heating the crude oil in a still to its boiling point, passing the vapors from the boiling oil through condensing pipes and condensing the vapors into liquids

APPROXIMATE YIELD OF PRODUCTS FROM 100 GALLONS OF CRUDE OIL

Gasoline	44 gal.
Fuel oil	36 "
Miscellaneous: coke, asphalt, paraffin wax, road oil, etc.	8 "
Kerosene	6 "
Lubricants	3 "
Loss	3 "
Total	100 gal.

Vapor line

Vapor space

Gas oil

Kerosene

Gasoline

Water

Crude oil

Fuel oil

Many thousand feet down in the earth

Gas
OIL
Water

FIG. 43.—Typical flow chart tracing movement of crude oil from well to finished product. (*Courtesy of The American Petroleum Institute.*)

refining capacity consists of "complete" plants, *i.e.*, refineries that produce all the major products shown in the accompanying flow chart.   The other refineries are "incomplete" plants in the sense that they extract from the crude oil only those products which are in greatest demand.   In 1938 about 35 per cent of the crude-oil refining capacity consisted of skimming plants which extract only gasoline and kerosene and sell the residue as fuel oil or gas oil for further refining.   It is apparent that these two classes of refineries have 80 per cent of the total refining capacity; the remainder consists of such plants as skimming and lubricating plants that take off gasoline, kerosene, and lubricating oil; skimming and asphalt plants that produce, as the name indicates, gasoline, kerosene, and asphalt.

Refineries vary in size, ranging from small units processing less than 10,000 barrels daily to plants with a capacity in excess of 100,000 barrels per day.   The large refineries are for the most part the complete plants.   In 1938 almost 80 per cent of the total refining capacity was represented by 104 of the 431 plants then operating.   Physically, small plants are about as efficient as large plants, but the commercial advantages of large-scale production favor mass-production operations in areas adjacent to large markets.

Location of Refineries.—The location of refineries clearly shows the importance of bulk movement of crude oil by water.   Although refineries are found in 32 states, five states—Texas, California, Pennsylvania, Oklahoma, and New Jersey—have 70 per cent of the total   refining capacity.   It is estimated that half of the gasoline supply comes from refineries located on deep water.   Crude oil is transported from the producing fields to the seaboard refineries either by tanker or by pipe line.   Oil can be transported by either of these means at less than half the cost of shipment by rail.[1]   Seaboard refineries are on the average six times as large as refineries in the interior because they have access to large markets in addition to low crude transportation costs.

Technological Developments.—Petroleum refining has become a highly automatic process characterized by low labor costs, huge investments, and rapid obsolescence.   About the only labor required is that of repair and maintenance crews and the supervisory work of reading gauges and manipulating valves.   Labor costs in this branch of the industry are only 5.2 per cent of the value of the product.   However, capital costs are quite high.   Petroleum refining employs $38,700 of capital per worker in contrast with $3,700 per worker for all manufacturing industry.   Capital costs are high not only because of the huge original investment but also because the equipment is short-lived.   Depreciation charges are heavy because the equipment is continuously subjected to high-tempera-

[1] Approximate costs per ton mile are: 1 mill by tanker, 3 mills by pipe line, 7 mills by railway or truck.

ture and high-pressure operation. Furthermore, existing equipment is rapidly outmoded by changes in the technology of refining. For example, it is estimated that most of the 120 refineries that were idle in 1938 will never be used again because of their obsolescence, despite the fact that much of this equipment has been in use only 5 to 10 years.

Since technical developments in refining are too numerous and too complex to be covered completely, only the most important changes will be indicated. The outstanding development has been the introduction of "cracking," which permits the extraction of more gasoline from a given quantity of crude than can be obtained by straight-run refining Cracking utilizes the gas-oil distillate which formerly was a drug on the market.

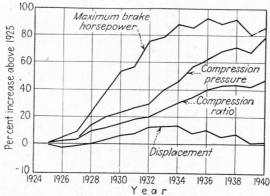

Fig. 44.—Increased efficiency of automobile motors. (*New York Times, Feb.* 11, 1940.)

By the application of higher temperatures and greater than atmospheric pressure in stills especially built for the purpose, the gas-oil is broken down into gasolines of high antiknock quality. Cracked gasoline burns more efficiently in modern automobiles equipped with high-compression motors. Note, in Fig. 44, how antiknock gasoline has accompanied the increased efficiency of motors. Cracking both improves the quality and increases the quantity of gasoline obtained from crude. Prior to the introduction of cracking only 17 per cent of the crude was convertible into motor fuel. Today, 45 per cent of our crude is converted into gasoline.

The rapidity of technological change in petroleum refining is illustrated by the recent development of catalytic cracking which threatens to displace thermal cracking. Instead of using terrific heat and pressure, catalytic cracking produces gasoline by heating either crude or gas oil distillate and passing the vapor through a catalyst at relatively low pressure and heat. One of these new catalytic processes—the Houdry process —jointly owned by Sun Oil, Socony-Vacuum, and the Houdry Process Corp., is reputed to yield 82 per cent gasoline per barrel of crude. Catalytic cracking offers the advantages of lower processing costs, higher quality of product, greater gasoline yield, and less by-product fuel oil.

Another recent development of considerable commercial importance is polymerization. This is a new gasoline-producing process essentially the reverse of cracking. Instead of breaking down the heavier hydrocarbons, polymerization produces gasoline by building up the lighter refinery gases

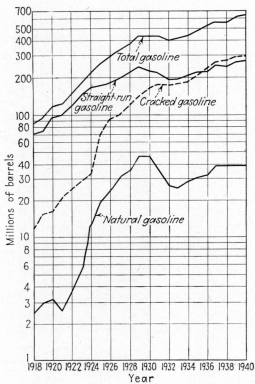

FIG. 45.—Production of gasoline by type of process. (*Minerals Yearbook*, 1940.)

as well as propane and butane obtained from natural gas. The process uses the principles of both thermal and catalytic processing and brings to the motor fuel user another source of high-quality gasoline.

A process which has been technically perfected but not commercially developed by reason of our abundant supply of crude oil is hydrogenation. This, a German invention, adds hydrogen under great pressure and heat in the presence of a catalyst and produces new hydrocarbon combinations of special qualities. Hydrogenation, though too costly in the face of our present low prices of gasoline, stands ready to supply practically any petroleum product in any proportions from any grade of crude oil. It can also utilize coal as a raw material.

The basic economic problem in petroleum refining, a multiple-product industry, is to maintain equilibrium between supply and demand of the several products. The demand for each of the joint products is conditioned by a separate set of factors, and in order to supply the demand for one product without creating large surpluses of joint products, refining must have considerable flexibility. The variability in yields offered by the new refining processes furnishes the necessary stabilizing influence.

PLATE 44.—General view of a refinery. (*Courtesy of Esso Marketers.*)

Integration of Refining and Production.—The petroleum industry is dominated by large corporate enterprises engaged in every phase of the business from oil derrick to retail gas stations. However, the integrated setup of the industry is a development of comparatively recent origin. Prior to 1911, when the Standard Oil Company was dissolved by court decree, most oil companies confined their activities to one or a few closely related phases of the business. This is very well illustrated by the rise of the Standard Oil Company.

The parent company, Standard Oil of Ohio, organized in 1870, set out in the refining division in Cleveland. After monopolizing the home market, the company, under the capable direction of Rockefeller, proceeded to acquire the refineries in Pittsburgh, Philadelphia, and New

York.   By 1879 the company controlled 95 per cent of the refining capacity of the country.   This was accomplished by vigorous price cutting, rebating, and bribery.   The refining monopoly was strengthened by the acquisition of tank cars, pipe lines, and bulk distributing stations.   The only venture into production occurred during the eighties when the Standard Oil Trust bought oil lands in the Ohio-Indiana field at bargain prices because the oil was high in sulphur content and produced foul-smelling kerosene.   Until he retired from active business at the turn of the century, Rockefeller confined the activities of Standard Oil to refining and marketing.   The wisdom of this policy is shown in the earnings.   Standard Oil earned 15 per cent on its capital invested from 1882 to 1892; 21 per cent from 1892 to 1900; and 25 per cent from 1900 to 1906.   At the time of its dissolution in 1911, Standard Oil controlled 90 per cent of the pipe-line transportation facilities, 85 per cent of the refining capacity, and 85 per cent of the marketing.

By the decree of the Supreme Court, some 33 subsidiary companies were split off from the parent holding company—the Standard Oil Company of New Jersey.   There was no immediate change in competition since each stockholder of the original company received a pro-rata interest in each of the separated companies.   For a while the several companies of the Standard group respected each other's special spheres of interest, but with the advent of new producing areas, new refining methods, new markets, and new companies in the industry, the unity of action gradually broke down.   The growth of rivalry within the family is illustrated by the invasion by Standard of New Jersey of the New England market, which Standard of New York had long regarded as its own.   Alternate periods of shortage and surplus of crude, inadequacy of refining capacity, and changes in the relative importance of marketing areas compelled each of the former members of the Standard group to integrate either forward or backward to strengthen its competitive position.

At present there are five large integrated companies of the former Standard group.   They are Standard of New Jersey, Socony-Vacuum, Standard of Indiana, Standard of California, and Atlantic Refining.   Each of these companies controls assets in excess of 100 million dollars, and Standard of New Jersey, the largest, has a capitalization of approximately 2 billions.   Adding the Ohio Oil Company, which is primarily a producer of crude, and the Standard of Ohio, which refines and markets only, there are seven Standard companies with a combined capitalization of 4,300 millions.

The demand for motor fuel has grown so rapidly that in addition to the "majors" there have come into the field a number of large integrated "independent majors."   There are 11 companies in this group with assets in excess of 100 million dollars each.   They are: Texas, (Sinclair)

Consolidated, Gulf, Tide Water, Union, Pure, Phillips, Sun, Cities Service, Continental, and Mid-Continent. This group together with Shell, a domestic subsidiary of a foreign company (Royal Dutch Shell), has an aggregate capitalization of almost 3 billions. It is estimated that the 19 "majors" have a total capitalization of 7.5 billions, which represents approximately 75 per cent of the total capital invested in the industry.

The Marketing of Petroleum Products.—Petroleum products are marketed by a physically efficient but economically inefficient distributive mechanism. From the refineries gasoline moves by tanker, barge, pipe line, or railway tank car to terminals or bulk stations of which there are some 20,000 throughout the country. It reaches the ultimate consumer by one of four principal channels: the company-owned service station, the independent dealer, the jobber, or the large consumer, such as a trucking or bus company. There are about 400,000 retail outlets almost equally divided between service stations and other mercantile establishments carrying gasoline and oil as a sideline. We now have as many retail outlets as producing oil wells.

The marketing structure with its excessive number of retail outlets arises from numerous causes, some of which go back to the First World War period. At that time large refineries entered the field of marketing by establishing their own retail service stations. Refining technology was improving rapidly. With the consequent improvement in products, the companies wished to sell their own branded products directly to the public. Another inducement was the high profit margins then prevailing in distribution. The rapid expansion in the use of automobiles and the pressure exerted by the increasing supplies of crude oil during the twenties attracted more and more distributors. Lacking the capital to build service stations rapidly enough, oil companies offered inducements in the way of free equipment and substantial margins to independent dealers. The expansion of retail outlets continued throughout the depression of the thirties because the total demand for gasoline continued to grow and many unemployed workers sought a livelihood by turning to this field of retail distribution.

More recently the major companies began to withdraw from retailing, a policy which was hastened by widespread chain store taxation. Independent dealers now handle over 50 per cent of the retail gasoline sales. With thousands of independent dealers competing with each other, each one exercising the right to sell at his own price, the inevitable results are weakness in the price structure, periodic price wars, rapid turnover among dealers, and vanishing profits. The distribution of petroleum in its present form is too unstable to continue, and we shall doubtless see considerable change before this phase of the industry attains any semblance of a permanent pattern.

A problem of much concern to the entire petroleum industry is that of increasing gasoline taxes.   Since 1920 the petroleum industry has reduced prices of gasoline by more than 50 per cent, but consumers have not realized the full benefits because of the ever-mounting gasoline taxes as

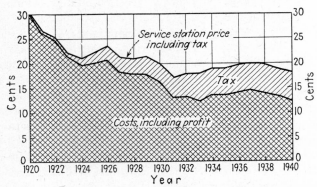

Fig. 46.—State and Federal gasoline sales.   Taxes shown in cents per gallon.   (*Petroleum Facts and Figures, American Petroleum Institute*, 1941.)

shown in Fig. 46.   Federal taxes have been quite moderate, but the states have levied upon this commodity with growing avidity.   Consumers of gasoline paid over a billion dollars in taxes in 1940, of which the states collected 75 per cent.   Originally the states taxed gasoline to construct and maintain their motor highways, but in recent years more and more of these funds are used for other purposes.

CHAPTER XVIII

THE PAPER INDUSTRY

Paper, in the modern sense of the term, is a fabric produced by the felting of individual cellulose fibers into a thin compact sheet. Paper, as such, was invented by the Chinese about A.D. 105. In developing the art of papermaking, the Chinese originally used old linen and discarded fish nets as raw materials, and they preserved the secret for several centuries. Knowledge of the art gradually spread to other Asiatic countries and then to Europe. Paper was first made in America, in 1690, by William Rittenhouse, a skilled papermaker who with the aid of William Bradford built a paper mill on a small tributary of the Wissahickon near Philadelphia.

Paper had always been made by hand, one small sheet at a time, until 1798, when Louis Robert, a Frenchman, invented a method of felting fibers mechanically in sheets of 15 to 20 yd. long. Five years later, two stationers in England, Henry and Sealy Fourdrinier, perfected Robert's idea by constructing a machine that made paper in a continuous sheet. This invention completely revolutionized the art of papermaking since it permitted the manufacture of paper in large quantities and at low cost. Despite innumerable improvements in the process, papermaking today utilizes the basic Fourdrinier principle. In the United States the transition from manual papermaking, which was an art requiring great skill, to machine production occurred about 1827.

Consumption.—Paper, in various forms, is consumed to the extent of 250 lb. per capita. Newspapers and magazines account for a third of our paper consumption. Paper is used also in the manufacture of books and for wrapping parcels; paper cartons serve as containers for shipping merchandise; paper is used for insulation and decoration. Paper is used in lieu of cotton for towels and napkins, in place of glass for drinking cups, instead of leather for book covers and binders. A summary of the principal kinds of paper consumed is shown in Table XXXV.

Although paper is now abundant and cheap, it has not always been plentiful. During the colonial period paper was very scarce and used most sparingly. In fact the shortage of paper was so great that papermakers were exempt from military service during the American Revolution. Since then, numerous improvements in the art have wrought the change from a deficit to a surplus paper economy. These improvements took place in the technique of manufacture and in the raw materials

249

consumed.   The two are so closely interrelated that neither can be discussed without reference to the other.

TABLE XXXV.—ESTIMATED PAPER CONSUMPTION, 1940

Kind	Total, Tons (000 omitted)
Paper board	6,550
Newsprint	3,600
Wrapping paper	2,350
Book paper	1,624
Tissue paper	720
Other paper	2,100
Total	16,944

Source: United States Dept. of Commerce.

Cotton and linen rags were the principal raw materials in the days when paper was handmade.   With the invention of the Fourdrinier machine, paper could be made so much more rapidly and cheaply that the supply of raw materials soon became inadequate.   In 1840, Keller, a German, invented the wood grinder.   This, however, was only a partial solution of the raw material problem because paper made from wood is inferior in quality to paper made from rag stock.   Wood did not replace rags but was used in conjunction with rags for making paper that did not have to be of the highest quality.

The next major advance came in 1867 in the discovery of a means to extract the cellulose from wood by a chemical process.   This, the sulphite process, consisted of treating wood with sulphurous acid which dissolved the woody or ligneous portion, leaving a residue of cellulose.   Sulphite pulp was first made in America in Providence, R. I. in 1884.[1]   Its general adoption was delayed owing to patent rights, a royalty of $10 per ton being exacted for many years.   After the chemical processes of extracting cellulose from wood had come into general use, the days of raw material shortage were over.   The change is reflected in the price situation.   Book paper, which sold at 12 to 25 cents per pound in the Civil War era, fell to 7.5 cents during the decade of the eighties.   Print paper dropped from 24 to 3 cents a pound in the early nineties.   These lower prices naturally multiplied the use of paper tremendously.   Today, there are literally thousands of different kinds of paper varying in strength, thickness, durability, color, weight, texture, transparency, luster, and moisture absorption, to mention only the major physical characteristics.   The quality of any particular paper depends upon two things—what it is made of and how it is made.   Accordingly, these two aspects of the paper industry will be considered briefly.

[1] Soda pulp was produced in Pennsylvania nearly 20 years earlier.   The sulphite process was discovered in 1884.

Raw Materials.—It is impossible to set up criteria of quality applicable to all kinds of paper because of the great diversity of use to which different papers are put. For some purposes, as in bags, a paper that is very strong and flexible is desirable; paper for boxes and cartons must be strong and inflexible; writing paper must be smooth and nonabsorbent. In general, however, it may be said that those raw materials which yield long, strong, and straight cellulose fibers are preferable. In addition to these physical characteristics, certain economic considerations are to be reckoned with because of their influence upon the cost of producing the pulp. They are: (1) the abundance or scarcity of the raw material; (2) the location of the raw materials, which, if materials are far removed from centers of consumption, is an important cost item; and (3) the ease or difficulty of extracting the cellulose fibers.

Wood is the most important raw material; it constitutes between 50 and 60 per cent of all paper raw materials consumed. Although the fibers are short, wood is compact, can be stored easily, and yields a fairly high degree of cellulose which can be easily extracted, chemically. Spruce, yellow pine, and hemlock, in the order named, are the most important sources of pulpwood and together account for over 70 per cent of all pulpwood used in paper manufacture.

Paper, like steel and wool, can be reprocessed. Approximately one-third of the industry's annual output is made of waste paper. Beating the waste paper back to pulp shortens and weakens the fibers, but the cellulose yield is naturally quite high—about 90 per cent. Paper made of waste is used primarily for the manufacture of paper board.

Cotton and linen rags are still the best raw materials for high-grade durable writing or book paper. Rags yield fibers that are about 1 in. in length and the cellulose yield is relatively high.

Straw, jute, esparto, and manila waste make up the remainder of raw materials consumed. Straw makes very stiff board. Very little esparto is used in the United States. Jute and manila waste, derived from old rope and burlap, make very strong paper bags.

Process.—Papermaking consists of two major operations—first, the raw materials must be reduced to pulp, and, second, the pulp is made into paper.

The Manufacture of Pulp.—The trees are felled, trimmed, and cut into logs 6 to 8 ft. long, which are hauled to the stream and floated down to the mill. There they are washed, sent through a tumbler to remove the bark and through a splitter, which removes the knots, and finally put into a machine whose high-speed rotating knives slice the logs into small chips. The chips are reduced to pulp in large kiers or digestors.[1] The

[1] About 25 per cent of the pulp produced in the United States is made mechanically. The logs instead of being cut into chips are ground into mush on huge power grind-

chemicals dissolve the wood and together with the woody structure are washed away, leaving the pure cellulose fibers, which are then sent through the beater engines.   The beaters reduce the irregular lumps of pulp into fairly uniform length and consistency.   The pulp is then run through the Jordan engine which reduces the pulp to a homogeneous slurry consisting of fibers of uniform length ready for the felting machines, which actually make the paper.

PLATE 45.—Beater reducing pulp to fine consistency.   (*Courtesy of Robert Gair Company.*)

The Manufacture of Paper.—The Fourdrinier is a large $350,000 mechanism about the length of a city block consisting of two parts, a wet end and a dry end.   The slurry spills onto an endless belt of bronze wire cloth on which the fibers are formed into a thin continuous sheet, the water being drawn off through the meshes.   The loosely felted web passes on between heavy rollers that press out additional water, and finally through a series of 40 or 50 steam-heated, smooth-surfaced drying cylinders, the paper emerging from the dry end, on some of the largest machines, at the rate of 10 to 15 miles an hour in sheets up to 300 in. wide.

For certain types of paper, such as building and board paper, the cylinder machine is used instead of the Fourdrinier.   The cylinder

stones—hence the term, "groundwood pulp."   Mechanical pulp is of inferior quality because the ligneous material is not removed and the fibers are cut too short.

machine differs from the Fourdrinier only in the wet end.   Instead of a wire cloth sheet-forming device, it has a large cylinder, covered with wire

PLATE 46.—Fourdrinier paper-making machine.   (*Reproduced by permission of the Philadelphia Commercial Museum.*)

cloth, partially submerged in a vat containing the slurry.   As the cylinder revolves, the water is drained off the wire cloth to which the fibers cling to

TABLE XXXVI.—CAPACITY OF PAPERMAKING MACHINES

	Fourdrinier		Cylinder	
	Number of machines	Capacity per 24-hr. day, short tons	Number of machines	Capacity per 24-hr. day, short tons
Newsprint.....................	42	3,098		
Groundwood specialties*.........	54	1,926		
Book paper...................	216	6,374	1	5
Cover paper..................	11	205	2	5
Writing paper................	132	2,181		
Wrapping paper...............	200	7,596	40	480
Tissue paper..................	114	1,732	70	426
Absorbent paper..............	48	541	24	66
Building paper................	7	351	71	2,520
Boards.......................	47	5,322	469	18,987
Other paper..................	14	290	13	125
Total....................	885	29,616	690	22,614

* Catalogue, hanging, poster, news-tablet, etc.
Source: *Paper Trade Journal*, Dec. 7, 1939.

form a continuous sheet. Some cylinder machines have more than one paper-forming cylinder whereby multiple layers of stock are picked up by felts and laminated. These machines can produce, for example, fancy coated cardboard consisting of two outside layers of a glossy white surface and a center section of low-grade stiff board made from waste paper stock, the whole constructed on the sandwich principle. The number of machines in use and the type of paper they make are shown in Table XXXVI. Note that the Fourdrinier is used to make a greater variety of papers than the cylinder machine.

The Role of the Paper Industry in Our National Economy.—In order to get a picture of the size of the paper industry it is necessary to define just what the paper industry includes. The Census of Manufactures reported, for 1939, the production of 2,000 million dollars' worth of "Paper and Allied Products." Breaking this down, we find it includes 220 million dollars of pulp, 930 millions of paper, and 850 millions of converted paper products. We shall not concern ourselves with the latter group, which has to do with the making of finished paper products: our interest is focused upon the manufacture of paper itself. This includes the paper mills and most of the pulp mills because the majority of them are owned and operated by integrated paper companies.

The paper industry, as defined above, employs over 100,000 workers and produces a wide variety of products. These products may be divided into two groups—mechanical papers and "cultural" papers. As representative of the first group we shall select the paperboard industry. Newsprint paper is presented as representative of the second group.

THE PAPERBOARD INDUSTRY

By tonnage or value of output the paperboard industry is the largest division not only of mechanical papers but of all branches of the industry. In 1940, the industry produced 6.5 million tons of paperboard, which was about 45 per cent of the total of all types of paper produced that year.

The Product.—Paperboard consists of primarily two products—container boards and boxboards. Boxboards, in turn, are made up of two principal kinds—folding box (bending) and set up box (rigid). The former are made into boxes to package suits, toothpaste, shaving cream, breakfast cereals, etc., and the latter are converted into articles like candy boxes, shoe boxes, etc. Container boards are heavier in weight than boxboards since they are a compound built up of several layers as, for example, corrugated shipping containers.

Growth.—The consumption of paperboard, as shown in Fig. 47, has doubled every decade since 1899, which represents the highest rate of growth for all divisions of the paper industry. This abundantly healthy growth may be attributed to the increasing cost of wooden boxes arising from the growing scarcity of lumber and to the savings in freight resulting from the use of lighter weight containers. It is not surprising to find, therefore, that capital was readily attracted to this industry, which eagerly accommodated the rapidly swelling demand.

Raw Materials.—Excluding Southern kraft manufacturers, who have only recently invaded the paperboard industry (to be discussed later), practically all paperboard is made from waste paper. Waste paper is collected by thousands of junk dealers and social welfare organizations all over the country and ultimately finds its way to the paperboard mills.

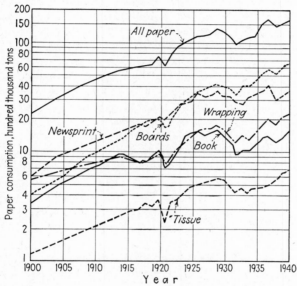

Fig. 47.—United States paper consumption. (*United States Bureau of Census.*)

The volume of waste paper collected depends very largely upon the price it commands at the board mills. Such waste paper as is not destroyed is ultimately consumed by a paperboard mill.

Capital Required.—Most paperboard is made on the cylinder machine. A modern 150-ton (per day) single-machine paper plant costs about 1.2 million dollars. Capital costs are therefore fairly large, and labor costs are relatively low. In 1939, labor costs for the industry averaged close to $7 per ton, or about 15 per cent of the value of the product, which is low in comparison with labor costs for all manufacturing. The mills are customarily operated on a 24-hour schedule, 6 days a week, until a particular bank of orders is filled.

Companies.—The industry consists of approximately 130 companies, 200 plants. Most of the companies have but one mill each. Ownership is widely scattered and no one company occupies a predominant position. The five largest companies together produce about a third of the total output, and the 15 companies next in size account for an additional 28 per cent. The leading companies are International Paper, Container Corporation, Kieckhefer, Robert Gair, and Fibreboard Products. The absence of large multiplant consolidations, except for International, which is also the leader in newsprint manufacturing, may be but a reflection of the comparative youth of this division of the paper industry.

Scale of Operation.—Paperboard plants are smaller than newsprint mills. Most board mills have a capacity of 25 to 75 tons per day. The paperboard industry presents, therefore, a picture of a relatively large number of fairly small enterprises with only a few large concerns, whose size is not sufficiently formidable to threaten the existence of the smaller producers. The manufacture of paperboard has certain inherent characteristics that seem to inhibit the expansion of plant size. Waste paper, the raw material, presents some difficulty of collection. Huge supplies are available in heavily populated areas, but in sparsely populated districts less waste paper accumulates and the cost of collection mounts as trucks are forced to go farther away from the mill. The shipping of the finished product involves costs which limit the area of profitable marketing to a maximum radius of about 300 miles. Another reason is the rather well-established practice on the part of paperboard mills of rendering extra services to their customers. These benefits consist of such things as providing convenient terms of payment, installment shipping, storage facilities, and manufacturing to particular specification. These and similar services can be rendered by the small mills just as well as the large ones. Finally, there is no great technical efficiency in size. For convenience in handling the product a machine cannot go beyond a definite limit in width, and machines cannot be speeded up indefinitely without sacrifice in quality of paper produced.

Integration.—Those mills which convert their paperboard into boxes are known as combined mills, in contrast with the independent mills that make paperboard for sale. There is only a slight predominance of integration, in this sense of the term, except for those plants specializing in solid fiber chip. In the latter class of mills, almost all are combined mills, as compared with 50 to 60 per cent integration for the rest of the industry. Prior to 1928, the integrated and large-scale firms (which two groups overlap to a certain extent) grew in size at about the same rate as the smaller companies. Since then, however, as a result of expansion and mergers, the large and integrated concerns have grown more rapidly. There is considerable product specialization in the paperboard industry. Some mills produce only glossy lining paper; others produce set-up boxboard, etc. The multimill companies, of course, can supply a wider range of products through the practice of mill specialization.

Location.—The industry is located in two major zones designated the East and the West. The line of demarcation is the western boundary of Pennsylvania extended due south. The East has 36 per cent of the plants, with the heaviest concentration in New England, New York, New Jersey, Pennsylvania, and Maryland. Most of the "Western" mills are in Ohio, Michigan, Indiana, Illinois, and Wisconsin.

Stability of Production.—Production in the paperboard industry is subject to some seasonal irregularity. The seasonal pattern shows two high points, in February and October, and two low points, in July and December. Employment in this industry is therefore somewhat unsteady, but the industry pays good wages relative to most manufacturing industries.

The paperboard industry is remarkably free from cyclical disturbances judged by the experience of the last decade. Total production decreased only from a maximum of 4.2 million tons in 1929 to 3.3 million tons in 1932. An industry that contracts only 20 per cent in physical volume during the country's worst depression is indeed almost depressionproof. The reason does not seem particularly obscure. Cardboard boxes and containers are used very extensively for the shipment of foods, drinks, drugs, and clothing, items of commerce the per-capita consumption of which is relatively stable.

Prices and Competition.—The recent price history of paperboard products presents what appears to be a peculiar combination of competitive and administrative influences. Paperboard prices exhibit both stability and instability—stability in the sense of infrequency of price change; instability in the sense of large amplitude of change. Prices of paperboard products, published by the National Paperboard Association, show for certain items an unchanging price for as long as 26 months. "Test liners," for example, remained at $65 per ton from January, 1927, until March, 1928, when they dropped to $60 per ton. During 1931, the price was $32.50 for 10 consecutive months. During 1935 and part of 1936, the price remained at $43.50 for nine consecutive months. "Single manila lined chip" prices were $55 a ton from January, 1927, until March, 1928, and at other periods the price remained the same for three to eight consecutive months. These are some of the more extreme examples of price stability. It is highly improbable that forces of supply and demand with respect to any commodity maintain such delicate balance as to bring about such extended periods of price stability. If the reported prices are accurate, it is difficult to escape the conclusion that some mysterious obstruction occasionally interferes with the forces of competition. However, with respect to many commodities, concessions are frequently made from the published prices. Actual prices may deviate considerably from the published prices and, in a service industry like paperboard, price is not the only criterion of competition.

The amplitude of variation of paperboard prices is sufficiently large to dispel all doubts as to the existence of any artificial restrictions on competition. During the decade ending in 1935, prices of test liners fluctuated between $65 and $26 a ton, corrugating material between $55 and $27, and single manila lined chip between $57.50 and $35 per ton. While there have been fluctuations of equal or greater severity in other manufactured goods during the same period, by no stretch of the imagination can it be claimed that paperboard prices are noncompetitive. Furthermore, those goods that are subject to administrative price control have, as an almost invariable concomitant, a marked amplitude of variation in physical volume of production. This is not the case with respect to paperboard products, as was previously pointed out. Indeed, in an industry where there are several hundred competitors, anything other than free and unrestrained competition would be difficult to attain. This reinforces our conclusions with respect to the "stickiness" of paperboard prices—it is apparently a case of inaccuracy which prevails in numerous commodity price reports where because of rebates and allowances actual prices differ greatly from prices published in trade journals, which are usually the asked prices. Such practices naturally give the appearance of greater stability than in fact exists.

Kraft.—A comparatively recent development in the paperboard industry is the appearance of Southern kraft production which has attained an annual output of 2 million tons. Brown kraft paper, made from Southern pine, has long been used in paper-bag manufacture for which it is admirably suited by reason of its great strength. Beginning about 1926, the kraft industry started to invade paperboard, a product where the strong kraft can be used to equal advantage. The paperboard industry is seriously concerned with this development because not only does it add additional capacity to the industry but containers made from the stronger kraft board are lighter, a real competitive advantage. Perhaps the entrance into kraft production by Container Corporation and International Paper points the way in which this new competition will be met by the paperboard industry. Northern paperboard companies, instead of resisting, are accepting the inevitable.

Profits.—The paperboard industry has been highly profitable in recent years. Even at the depth of the depression in 1932, many paperboard manufacturers succeeded in avoiding deficits or when they did have deficits were able to prevent them from attaining alarming proportions by means of vigorous internal economies. It is impossible to present anything approaching a complete survey of profits because there are so many relatively small family-owned enterprises that do not publish financial statements. According to published statements, which include primarily the larger companies, the earnings of the majority showed an eminently satisfactory trend relative to all manufacturing. The profitableness of the industry is due in part to the stability of demand for its products and the rapid rate of growth of the industry. This industry, to repeat, has doubled its production every decade during the present century. With such a rapidly growing demand, it is not strange to find that profits came easily and somewhat affluently. This condition cannot be expected to continue indefinitely, and already there are heard complaints of excess capacity in this industry.

NEWSPRINT PAPER INDUSTRY

This industry is the largest unit in the cultural group of paper producers. The industry had its beginning with the advent of journalism represented by the publication of the *Boston News-Letter* in 1704. In 1712, the *Pennsylvania Packet and General Advertiser* appeared in Philadelphia, and it is accorded the distinction of being the first daily paper published in this country. The high cost of paper limited the circulation of early colonial newspapers to coffeehouses and wealthy subscribers. The rise, during the thirties, of sensational journalism, together with the growth of advertising, public schools, and the advent of cheaper paper made from wood, assured the success of the penny daily paper thereby providing a rapidly growing demand for newsprint. The more recent advent of newspaper chains, such as Hearst, Patterson-McCormick, and Scripps-Howard, has been a material aid in pushing the circulation of daily papers to 35 million copies, equivalent to one and one-sixth per American family. Sunday papers are bought by all but 6 million of the 30 million American families. Add to this 5,000 weeklies, with a total circulation of 50 million copies, and about 2,000 monthly and quarterly magazines, with a total circulation of about 125 million copies, it is apparent whence arises the demand for the newsprint industry's annual output of 3 to 4 million tons of paper.

Inadequacy of Domestic Raw Materials.—The scarcity and high cost of paper in our early history has already been mentioned. The processing aspect of high-cost paper was solved by the invention of the Fourdrinier machine, and the quest for a cheap raw material, in turn, was solved by the mechanical and chemical wood-pulping processes. Beginning about 1870, the consumption of soft wood, particularly spruce, increased steadily. It reached such large proportions that shortly after the turn of the century great concern was expressed over the rapidity with which this industry was devouring our forests. The industry was first established in New England; after virtually stripping that region of its virgin

forests, it moved down into New York State.   After practically exhaust-
ing that region of its best timber supply, the industry moved into the
Great Lakes states of Michigan and Wisconsin, and more recently into
the Pacific Northwest.   In the meantime pulpwood and woodpulp were
being imported from Canada.   As early as 1913, the industry was
importing from Canada a fifth of its raw material.   Canada, alarmed
in the interest of her own national economy, took steps to conserve her
own forest resources.   In 1910, Quebec, following the example set by
Ontario in 1902, placed an embargo on the exportation of pulpwood.
The following year, 1911, New Brunswick did the same.   This political
action stimulated the development of a Canadian newsprint industry
(which was the purpose of the embargo), financed very largely with
American capital.   It is estimated that at present half of the 800 million
dollars tied up in the Canadian industry is American capital.   This
action, plus an act by Congress placing newsprint paper on the free list in
1913, has stimulated a steadily mounting importation of newsprint from
Canada.   We are now getting 80 per cent of the newsprint consumed
here from that source.   In addition to the great American demand and
American capital as stimuli to the rapid growth of the Canadian newsprint industry is the equally fundamental fact that Canada has large
tracts of timber and good water-power sites.

Organization of the Newsprint Industry.—In contrast with the many
companies constituting the paperboard industry, only 25 companies, with
plants located principally in Maine, New York, Wisconsin, Minnesota,
Washington, and Oregon, constitute the American newsprint paper
industry.   The aggregate capital employed is about 300 million dollars.
A self-contained mill, it has been estimated, requires an initial capital
investment of about $50,000 per ton of daily output.   A 100-ton-per-day
mill would therefore require a capital of approximately 5 millions exclusive of forest land.   Since most newsprint mills are self-contained, *i.e.*,
produce their own pulp, they require an enormous amount of power to
reduce the wood into pulp.   This applies particularly to the mechanical
pulp process, and 75 to 80 per cent of newsprint pulp is so made, the
remainder being unbleached sulphite, which is added to give the paper
greater strength.   An index of the importance of power in this industry
is the fact that a paper mill worker has at his command 23 hp., compared
with 14 in the steel industry, which is also regarded as a heavy consumer
of power.   As a result of the huge power requirements most paper mills
produce their own power, and not infrequently they sell electricity as a
by-product to neighboring industries, deriving considerable revenue
from this source.

The Leader.—The International Paper Company is the largest unit
in the industry.   Organized in 1899 by combining 34 of the largest mills,

it controlled 70 per cent of the country's output at that time. It manufactures paper in the United States and Canada. Today its paper
kingdom consists of 35 mills extending from Newfoundland to Wisconsin
and from Ontario to Florida. It produces one-fifth of the total newsprint demand of the North American continent. Its annual 700,000 tons
of newsprint output supply almost 500 daily newspapers. Twenty-six
per cent of its capacity is given over to the production of kraft and board
paper, 13 per cent to special ground wood paper, 9 per cent to bags and
bag paper, 6 per cent to book and bond paper, and it also produces
one-half of the world's bleached pulp for the rayon industry. Diversification was brought about by competitive conditions which also explain, in
part, the company's relative decline to its present 20 per cent of the newsprint capacity of North America.[1]

Large-scale Production.—The outstanding characteristic of the
newsprint industry is the large capital required to engage in this industry.
It has been stated that a normal-sized mill requires about 5 million dollars
exclusive of forest land. Interest at 6 per cent on this amount is $300,000
a year, which makes an annual fixed charge of $10 per ton of paper,
assuming the mill operates at 100 per cent of capacity. In actual practice, however, 100 per cent capacity is rare except for very short periods,
nor can forest land be excluded from the calculation. It would be rather
short-sighted business policy to erect a 5-million-dollar enterprise without
assuring an adequate raw material supply. The land, though rarely
purchased, involves nevertheless additional money outlay if leased.
International Paper Company, for example, owns stumpage rights of
over 35,000 sq. miles of forest land which, at an approximate cost of $8 per
square mile, amounts to well over a quarter million dollars. Then, too,
taxes must be paid on land so acquired, which adds to the burden of
fixed cost.

Large-scale production is economical because it permits greater
specialization in task and equipment, the substitution of mechanical for
human labor, and the subdivision of labor. In newsprint manufacturing,
labor costs per ton in large plants of over 200 tons per day are only $6.90
as compared with $12.74 in mills of 26 to 50 tons capacity. The effects
of large-scale production, however, are not all advantageous. Large-
scale production inevitably carries with it the burden of heavy fixed
costs. The heavy overhead in the newsprint industry influences directly
and indirectly price policies, competition, profits—in fact it permeates
the entire fabric of the newsprint industry.

Prices.—Prices of newsprint paper, like paperboard prices, remain
fixed for a long period of time, but the range within which they fluctuate

[1] The Crown-Zellerback Corporation controls about 80 per cent of the newsprint
capacity on the Pacific coast.

is much greater. According to the United States Bureau of Labor Statistics, newsprint prices remained unchanged for 4 years—from January, 1927, to January, 1931. Newsprint is ordinarily sold under long-term contract—a factor making for price stability. There is also the alleged price leadership of the International Paper Company whose announced price sometimes remains unchanged for many months. However, actual prices are frequently known to deviate considerably from the announced or published prices. Consequently the latter should not be taken too seriously.

When changes in the price of newsprint do occur they are likely to be quite pronounced. Over short periods the supply of newsprint is rather inflexible; it takes about 2 years to organize and construct a mill. Since it is difficult to accommodate a sudden increase in demand, the price is very likely to soar. On the other hand, the existence of idle capacity plus the pressure of heavy overhead costs is likely to precipitate a price war. If overhead costs are a large proportion of total costs, a producer who has idle capacity is tempted to take business away from his rivals so long as the price yields just a little more than his bare out-of-pocket expenses, principally for labor and raw materials. The more orders he gets the nearer he reaches capacity operation, and down go his total average costs per unit. Fear of reprisal on the part of his competitors, which may lead to a price war, is his only inhibition.[1] Of course, if he accepts orders at a price that does not cover total costs, he is in reality donating part of his capital with every ton of paper sold. Such a depletion of resources cannot go on indefinitely, but the process of adjustment is so slow that the producers may merely attempt to curtail their losses by discouraging price cutting.

The existence of excess capacity has also contributed toward a weak price situation in the newsprint industry. Brookings Institution in its "America's Capacity to Produce" alleges that "over a 30-year period (1899–1930) as a whole, the paper industry has come closer to operating at practical capacity than any other important manufacturing industry . . . "[2] but goes on to say "that the newsprint division of the industry shows a somewhat different situation from the industry as a whole. . . . "[3] The high postwar price of newsprint caused a rapid expansion of plant in the United States and Canada, most of which was justifiable. However, the industry, perhaps unaware of the decline in the rate of increase of cultural paper consumption and aided by adequate funds easily obtained by investment bankers, became overbuilt in the years following 1926. Furthermore, it takes a long time to erect a

---

[1] Hence the advantage of making secret concessions below the announced prices.
[2] NOURSE, E. G., and associates, "America's Capacity to Produce," p. 239, Brookings Institution, Washington, 1936.
[3] *Ibid.*

newsprint paper plant. Operation in newsprint is therefore estimated to have dropped from 95 per cent in 1926 to 84 per cent in 1929. The subsequent business depression obviously greatly aggravated the situation. How any idle capacity makes for a weak price situation is perfectly obvious. Idle capacity rose from 200,000 tons in 1926 to 700,000 tons in 1934, causing prices to drop from \$72 to \$40 per ton.

The capital structure of most of the newsprint paper companies has also hindered them in putting up a bold front in asking prices. The newsprint industry has drifted into a bog of costly financial management. A number of the largest companies have obtained a grossly disproportionate share of their funds for expansion in the bond market rather than in the stock market. One analysis of the capital structure of 13 of the leading companies revealed a distribution of equities as follows: bonds 31 per cent; preferred stock 14 per cent; common stock 49 per cent; and current liabilities 6 per cent. An industry that obtains one-third of its capital in the bond market must take what it can get if it deals with shrewd buyers.

Finally, the buyers of newsprint are few in number, large in size, and shrewd in purchasing. Publishers of small dailies and weeklies do not buy enough paper to influence its price materially, and they have less urgent reason to dicker over price since paper constitutes only about 14 per cent of their total costs of doing business. The large chain publishers, on the other hand, consume about two-thirds of the newsprint. They have not only more power in the price-making process, but also more interest in getting the lowest prices possible because their paper costs average about 37 per cent of their total costs of doing business.

Profits.—Profits in the newsprint industry, in contrast with the paperboard industry, have been very modest. This should be no revelation in the light of the foregoing analysis of competition and prices. In the 8 years between 1926 and 1933, the newsprint industry, as a whole, showed a profit of only 3 per cent of sales. Companies that made no profit whatever increased from 31 to 37 per cent during the same period. In this division of the paper industry, as in the paperboard division, the earnings of the leading company have not been particularly impressive. In fact, the International Paper Company has a distinctly poor record. In no year between 1934 and 1940 did the company earn as much as 6 per cent on its invested capital. Whether this is because of or in spite of its huge size we do not know, but this company does have a heavily funded capital setup. Its 1939 balance sheet showed a funded debt of 59 millions, preferred stocks outstanding 98 millions, and common stock of 15 millions.

Newsprint from Southern Pine.—White paper suitable for newsprint is now being made from Southern pine. Heretofore, inability to remove the resin from this wood has precluded its use as newsprint. This difficulty has now been overcome. By using the younger trees with low resin content and growing them on the orchard principle, it is alleged that the South, with its longer growing season, could easily displace Canada as our source of newsprint paper. It is further alleged that there is an ample supply of pulpwood and that a Southern mill could produce newsprint at $3 to $4 per ton less than the lowest cost Canadian newsprint mills. All these allegations have sufficient corroboration from sources that appear to be unbiased, and it is generally believed that the time is almost at hand for the development of a Southern newsprint industry. How this will affect the present newsprint industry is largely a matter of conjecture. However, Southern kraft has already upset the market for wrapping, bag, and sulphate pulp and is giving concern to the paperboard industry. Newsprint may be next.

Recapitulation.—The paperboard industry is the largest division of the pulp and paper industry. Newsprint is second in size. The former has grown more rapidly than the latter, indicative of a slowing up in growth of cultural paper consumption in contrast with mechanical paper. Paperboard manufacturing, while hardly a small-scale industry, is nevertheless a smaller scale industry than newsprint. There are many kinds of paperboard; it is made from waste paper, on cylinder machines, by numerous, widely scattered, closely owned, single-mill enterprises. Newsprint is made from spruce wood on Fourdrinier machines by relatively few, multimill, widely owned companies. Both newsprint and paperboard mills make their own power. Prices in both break infrequently, but when they break they drop precipitously. Profits in paperboard are adequate; in newsprint meager. Paperboard has already been invaded by Southern kraft; newsprint seems vulnerable.

THE PAPER INDUSTRY IN GENERAL

In recent years, especially during the decade of the thirties, it was frequently alleged that the paper industry was suffering from much excess capacity. It is doubtful whether the paper industry as a whole had more idle capacity than other industries, but the pressure of idle capacity was probably greater in newsprint than in the other divisions of the paper industry. High newsprint prices from 1916 to 1920 attracted additional capital into the industry, but the downward trend in prices from 1920 to 1935 cannot be attributed entirely to the overexpansion caused by the wartime prices. Of equal, if not greater, importance was the inflated capital structure of newsprint companies.

Papermaking capacity is easily overestimated because of the nature of the industry. To multiply the tonnage per hour by the customary number of hours per week operated is an oversimplified approach. It assumes ideal conditions, which practically never exist. Proper allowances must be made for idleness, for repairs, adjustments, trial runs, etc. For example, when a new order is begun, the paper turned out during the first few hours may be scorched or may have other imperfections. Such unavoidable delays are not properly chargeable to idle capacity.

The paper industry is somewhat unique in the way in which any excess capacity, whatever it be, exerts itself upon the different divisions of the industry. If there is more idle capacity in one division than in another, it appears that the less fortunate groups go foraging in their neighbor's preserves. The similarity in equipment and in manufacturing processes within the several divisions of the paper industry affords an avenue for some cross competition. A newsprint mill, for example, may reach a point where it has idle capacity on hand because it has used up all its economically available pulpwood supply or has suffered the loss of some of its market through the exigencies of competition. Rather than stand by idly, it will go into the manufacturing of wrapping paper or possibly book paper, even if some additional capital outlay is required to make mechanical adaptations. In many instances, shifts of this sort are of an evolutionary character. A newsprint mill constructed, say, in 1880, may be obsolete for newsprint purposes in 1900. A shift into a grade of paper with a high ground-wood pulp content, such as hanging or poster papers, would be a natural development. Later this same mill, when pressed too hard by the competition of larger newsprint mills seeking refuge in this grade of paper, will probably shift again into ground-wood specialties. Mounting costs of pulpwood may force it ultimately to discontinue the operation of its pulp mill, after which it may purchase pulp and shift again, this time probably into wrapping or sulphate bond paper. It is noteworthy that all of these shifts tend toward higher grade papers in an attempt to get larger returns for their raw material.[1] Definite evidence of the extent to which shifts of the type just described take place is found in a study of the capacity and production of 56 newsprint mills, between 1910 and 1934, made by the American Paper and Pulp Association. In 1910 these mills produced 733,022 tons of newsprint and 159,783 tons of other grades. In 1934 these same mills made only 684,140 tons of newsprint, but their production of other grades increased to 714,205 tons. Such shifts cause greater competition in the area within which they take place and usually leave the shifters with greater flexibility of operating capacity, facilitating further change when deemed necessary.

It has been alleged that the existence of excess capacity in the paper industry in conjunction with the flexibility of operations has been the principal cause of the failure of all past efforts to create monopolies in

[1] Private communication from Charles W. Boyce, executive secretary of the American Paper and Pulp Association.

the paper industry.   Such efforts were made in the strawboard division by the formation of the American Straw Board Company, in 1889; in the newsprint division by the International Paper Company, in 1899; in the paperboard division by the formation of the United Box Board and Paper Company, in 1902; and the United Paper Board Company in 1917. These and other attempts at monopoly failed.   They did not make the profits their sponsors anticipated nor did they succeed in obtaining the high prices their customers feared.   That the failure of all these efforts to eliminate competition can be laid on the doorstep of excess capacity and flexibility of operations seems incredible, though these doubtless contributed.   Industrial history is replete with similar failures without the same causes.   In any rapidly growing industry, it is exceedingly difficult for the leader to maintain his relative position.

CHAPTER XIX

THE RUBBER INDUSTRY

One hundred years ago Charles Goodyear discovered how to vulcanize rubber. That discovery marked the beginning of a new manufacturing industry which employs over 100,000 workers and produces between a half billion and a billion dollars worth of products. The story of its development is largely one of chemical processing.

Importance of Chemistry.—Although rubber had some utility prior to Goodyear's discovery, its use was extremely limited because of the unstable nature of the material. For example, as early as 1823, Mackintosh, a Scotchman, developed a way of waterproofing cloth by spreading over the fabric a thin layer of rubber dissolved in coal naphtha. However, these early raincoats became soft and sticky in hot weather, in cold weather they became hard and cracked. Accordingly rubber was subjected to a great deal of experimentation with a view to "fixing" its good properties. This led to Goodyear's discovery. By adding sulphur and white lead to rubber and heating the compound, he obtained rubber as we know it—a weather-resistant, coherent solid of great strength and elasticity.

Although Goodyear had little appreciation of the chemistry involved, it was the beginning of chemical pioneering in rubber, the frontiers of which are only beginning to be realized. Shortly after Goodyear's discovery, his brother Nelson found that, by increasing the sulphur content, rubber could be made exceedingly hard. Later it was discovered that rubber could be made tough without making it hard by the admixture of such chemicals as zinc oxide, clay, lithopone, carbon black—the soot obtained from burning natural gas—and other reinforcing agents. For certain uses, very soft rubber is desired. This is obtained by adding softeners, such as stearic acid, rosin, and vegetable oils. By adding pigments, rubber of any color can be made.

In more recent years the vulcanizing process has been speeded up by adding accelerators in the compounding room. Lime, litharge, magnesium oxide, etc., in proper proportions have cut down the time required to vulcanize a tire from 3 hours to less than 1 hour. Certain other chemicals are added as antioxidants, *i.e.*, materials which retard atmospheric oxidation of the finished product. This prolongs the life of rubber products exposed to the weather.

267

The use of reclaimed rubber is also a contribution of rubber chemistry. A Goodyear chemist discovered the use of dilute caustic soda as an agent to reduce finished rubber to a soft plastic for reprocessing.

Synthetic rubber promises to be one of the greatest contributions of chemistry to the rubber industry and may completely alter the future course of the industry. However, before discussing that, let us consider the industry in its present setting and its past growth.

Size of the Rubber Industry.—In 1939 the rubber industry consisted of 572 manufacturing establishments. It converted over a half million long tons of crude rubber into approximately 900 million dollars' worth of finished rubber products.

The Census of Manufactures divides the rubber industry into three major classes or subindustries consisting of, first, the rubber tire and inner tube industry; second, rubber boots and shoes; and third, other rubber goods. This last embraces a wide variety of products, such as rubber heels, soles, raincoats, hospital sheeting, transmission belts, hose, battery boxes, druggists' and surgeons' supplies, toys, flooring, bathing apparel, cable insulation, etc. This group is distinguished by its comparatively large number of small plants—over 400 in contrast with 53 in the tire and tube division. The tire and tube division is the largest; it accounts for two-thirds of the value of output of the entire industry. Unless otherwise indicated, the rubber industry will be treated in terms of the tire division. The boot and shoe division is the smallest; it accounts for only a tenth of the total value.

The Raw Material.—Rubber is a coherent elastic solid. Its physical properties are softness, toughness, elasticity, impermeability, adhesion, and electrical resistance. Chemically, it is a hydrocarbon compound, and it is extremely resistant to all but a few chemical elements.

Rubber is obtained from a milky liquid known as "latex" which is tapped from the bark of a wide variety of tropical trees. Most commercial rubber is the product of the *Hevea brasiliensis*,[1] a tree that grows wild in the Amazon valley. Until 1914, wild rubber or Para rubber, named after the Brazilian port at the mouth of the Amazon, was our principal source of supply. Today wild rubber production is negligible because it has been superseded by plantation rubber which is superior in quality.

Rubber agriculture had its beginning in 1876 when Sir Henry Wickham, an Englishman, brought *Hevea* seeds to Kew Gardens in London where he succeeded in germinating trees which he sent to Ceylon. Following this experiment numerous plantations were begun in the British and Dutch Malay Archipelago, which region long supplied most of our crude rubber. Rubber trees are set out about 100 to the acre and begin

[1] Minor vegetable gums are guayule, balata, and gutta-percha.

to yield latex in 5 to 7 years after planting. The latex exudes from an incision in the bark and flows into an attached receptacle. Daily collections are made, and the latex is brought to the estate factory where the crude rubber is extracted. This consists of coagulating the latex, mechanically milling the doughy coagulum to remove most of the moisture, curing the sheets by smoking, and drying. The resulting product, known as ribbed smoked sheets, is then packed for export. Plantation rubber thus prepared constituted most of the new rubber consumed by the American rubber manufacturing industry until the Second World War.

About 1922, the rubber industry began importing the liquid latex. To reduce the cost of transportation, the water is evaporated. By treating the product with an alkaline preservative to prevent coagulation, the liquid rubber can be shipped in tanks. In 1939 approximately 25,000 long tons of latex were imported.

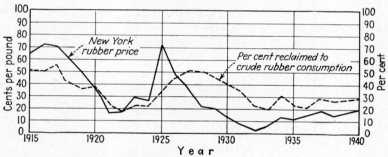

Fig. 48.—Influence of price upon use of reclaimed rubber. (*Bureau of Foreign and Domestic Commerce, Rubber Division.*)

Reclaimed Rubber.—Another source of raw material is reclaimed rubber obtained from discarded rubber products. It is used to supplement natural rubber in the manufacture of numerous rubber products. Scrap rubber is ground, washed, and chemically treated to remove fabric and other foreign matter. As Fig. 48 shows, the price of crude rubber, which is quite variable, has a definite influence upon the amount of reclaimed rubber consumption. For example, between 1922 when crude rubber averaged 17 cents a pound and 1927 when the price was 38 cents, the ratio of reclaimed to crude rubber consumption in the United States rose from 19 to 51 per cent. In 1932, when the price of rubber fell to 3.5 cents a pound, reclaimed rubber consumption was only 23 per cent of crude rubber consumption.

Process of Manufacture.—The great variety of rubber products differing in size, shape, and hardness of the rubber calls for a variety of manufacturing methods, but generally four major steps are performed.

They are (1) plasticizing, (2) compounding, (3) shaping, and (4) curing. These will be explained with reference to the manufacture of an automobile tire casing.

1. *Plasticizing.*—This is a mechanical breaking down of the crude rubber (which is very tough) in order to soften the material and make it more amenable to further processing. This operation is usually performed in two separate stages. First the crude rubber is cut into conveniently sized chunks and fed into the "cracking" mills, consisting of two corrugated rolls, rotating together at different speeds. The crackers

PLATE 47.—Cracking mill. (*Courtesy of U. S. Rubber Company.*)

tear the rubber into shreds and a stream of water washes off any impurities. Upon drying the rubber goes back to the mill room for further breaking down in mills equipped with smooth-surfaced rolls. This operation requires from 15 to 45 minutes, depending upon the product being made.

2. *Compounding.*—This consists of mixing the crude rubber with various chemical ingredients, such as sulphur, gas black, etc., in accordance with the formula of the manufacturer. This operation is performed in machines called "Banbury mixers," which operate on the principle of a dough mixer.

3. *Shaping.*—As the name implies, this is the form-giving operation and, in case of a tire, consists of building up the alternate layers of cord fabric. The tire is built over a collapsible drum about 14 in. in width

The invention of the pneumatic tire and the development of the automobile industry opened up a tremendous market for rubber which ushered the rubber industry into its second phase of the growth cycle—the period of rapid growth. Since 1900 the imports and consumption of rubber have increased more than twenty-fold. This period also witnessed the shift from wild to plantation rubber, the attempts to control prices by restricting production, the search for rubber substitutes, the mechanization of the industry, the transition from small-scale to large-scale production, the rise of Akron as a manufacturing center, the

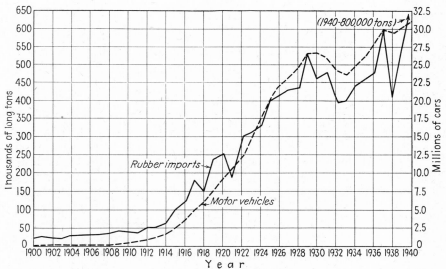

Fig. 49.—United States imports of crude rubber and motor-vehicle registration. (*Automobile Facts and Figures*, 1941; *Bureau of Foreign and Domestic Commerce, Rubber Division.*)

advent of unionism, the rise of the "big four" rubber companies, and an ever-growing intensity of competition.

Structure of the Industry.—The tire industry ranks above all major manufacturing industries in scale of operations. The industry employs about 54,000 workers in its 53 plants which average about 1,000 workers per plant. In 1921 about the same number of workers were employed, but there were more than four times as many plants. The marked decrease in number of establishments clearly indicates the shift to larger scale production.

A similar change has taken place within the corporate structure of the industry. In 1927 there were 109 tire companies, but in 1936 only 28 remained. Furthermore about 75 per cent of the business has fallen into the hands of the "big four"—Goodyear, U. S., Firestone, and Good-

rich.   Table XXXVII summarizes some of the leading characteristics
of these companies.

TABLE XXXVII.—COMPARATIVE ANALYSIS OF THE "BIG FOUR" RUBBER COMPANIES,
1940

	Goodyear	U. S.	Firestone	Goodrich
Total assets, millions of dollars......	$201	$193	$193	$140
Average ratio of inventory to total assets—1930–1939..............	26	17	24	25
Plantation acreage.................	100,000	132,000	70,000	
Per cent of requirement supplied by company acreage...............	10	25	5	
Per cent of total sales in tires.......	75	50	70	60
Daily tire-producing capacity.......	100,000	50,000	53,500	45,000

Source: Standard and Poor's Corporation.

Goodyear is the largest producer of rubber products in the world.
The company concentrates its activity upon the production of comparatively few lines of products to secure the maximum economies from mass
production.   In addition to rubber plantations, the company operates
a 37,000-acre cotton plantation in Arizona and markets its tires through
some 300 company-owned retail stores.

United States Rubber Company has the largest rubber plantation
acreage.   This company gets most of its original equipment business from
General Motors.   Both companies have substantial duPont financial
backing.

For some years Firestone has been supplying about half of Ford's
original equipment requirements and a smaller share of the General
Motors' business.   Firestone also makes miscellaneous motor accessories, such as batteries, rims, wheels, and ignition equipment which it
markets together with its tires through some 500 company-owned
service and supply stores.

Goodrich is the only one of the "big four" that does not own rubber
plantations.   This company is also distinguished by the fact that it
practices diversification to a greater extent than any of its competitors.
The company produces 30,000 rubber products.   This highly diversified
line of products may prove to be an asset of growing importance in view
of the declining profits in tire manufacturing.

The Tire Market.—During the last two decades the tire market has
undergone numerous changes, all of which have reacted unfavorably
upon the tire industry.   The market consists of the original-equipment
demand of the automobile manufacturers and the replacement demand
arising from registered vehicles in use.   The rapid growth of the auto-

mobile industry provided a rapidly swelling volume of original-equipment orders, but with the increased concentration of control of automobile manufacturing into the hands of the "big three," the downward pressure on tire prices left very meager profits for the rubber companies.   Furthermore, this source of demand is subject to large cyclical irregularity. In the decade ending with 1939 the volume of original-equipment sales ranged from 7 to 26 million tires.   Fortunately the replacement demand bulks larger than new-equipment sales, but this market has not been growing as fast as the rate of increase in new cars registered because tires have improved in quality to such an extent that the longer wear makes for less frequent replacement.   Another factor responsible for less frequent replacement is the improvement in the art of retreading used tires.   The companies foster the retreading business by manufacturing unvulcanized retread stock known as "camelback."   Note in Table XXXVIII tire sales per car in use and total replacement sales.

TABLE XXXVIII.—REGISTERED CAR TIRE CONSUMPTION

Year	Tire sales per car in use	Replacement sales (000,000 omitted)
1928	2.24	52
1929	1.91	47
1930	1.47	39
1931	1.46	39
1932	1.29	33
1933	1.36	33
1934	1.34	32
1935	1.18	29
1936	1.15	31
1937	1.02	30
1938	1.05	31
1939	1.22	38
1940	1.11	35

Sources: "India Rubber World"; Bureau of Foreign and Domestic Commerce, Rubber Division.

In their effort to obtain adequate profits, the tire companies sought new channels of distribution.   In 1926 Goodyear entered into a contract with Sears Roebuck whereby the tire company supplied the mail-order house with 60 per cent of its requirements at a price which yielded 6.5 per cent profit to Goodyear.   Subsequently the other large tire companies made similar contracts with either mail-order houses or chain retail outlets like Western Auto Supply and Standard Oil (of New Jersey) gas stations.   Firestone, Dunlap, and several others opened up a large number of retail outlets of their own.   The stampede for mass distribution completely altered the tire marketing structure.   Between 1926 and

1936, the number of independent tire dealers declined from 120,000 to 60,000. Their sales declined from 91 to 59 per cent of the total replacement sales. On the other hand, sales by mail-order houses rose from 7 to 13 per cent of the total replacement sales, and sales by oil companies and tire company stores increased from 2 to 24 per cent of the total replacement sales. However, mass distribution did not bring the tire companies the anticipated profits. On the contrary, it induced severe price cutting and losses for the tire companies. Between 1926 and 1936 there were 17 price cuts. The public and the large distributors profited more than the manufacturers by this venture in mass distribution.

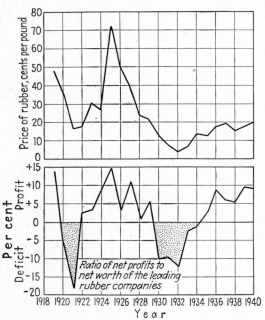

Fig. 50.—Average annual price of crude rubber and earnings of rubber companies. (*India Rubber World; Standard and Poor's Corporation.*)

The Struggle for Profits.—Rubber manufacturing, as reflected in the earnings of the tire companies, has not been very profitable in recent years. The composite net earnings, expressed as a percentage of net worth, of the leading rubber companies are shown in Fig. 50. Throughout the 20-year period these companies earned an average of only 2 per cent on their net worth. This is in contrast with 8 per cent earned during the same period by 200 large companies engaged in all kinds of industry and trade.

The comparatively poor profit showing of the rubber industry presents a marked contrast with that of the automobile industry with which it is closely allied. The rubber industry, as we have observed, experienced its most vigorous growth as a result of the rapid rise of the automobile industry, and tires still constitute its principal market. Furthermore, the rubber industry, like the automobile industry, is dominated by a few outstanding companies which, on theoretical grounds, should favor the repression of competition in its most ruinous forms. Automobile profits, as pointed out in Chap. XI, are above average. Why are rubber profits below average? One reason is the unfortunate venture into mass distribution already mentioned. Another reason is the erratic nature of the price of its raw materials.

Inventory Troubles.—As Fig. 50 reveals, there has been a very close relationship between the trend of profits and prices of crude rubber. Raw materials constitute about 60 per cent of the value of the product in this industry, and rubber, the chief item, came from the other side of the world. Five to eight months elapsed between the time a rubber company bought its rubber in the East Indies and the time it realized cash from sales of finished products. At any given instant, large sums of working capital were tied up in rubber—some afloat, some in warehouses, some in process, and some in finished goods.

The price of rubber has been very erratic in the past. This is due partly to natural causes and partly to valorization. The supply of crude rubber is rather inelastic. A sudden increase in demand of sizeable proportions cannot be accommodated instantly because of the long time required for newly planted acreage to bear rubber.

Valorization is the maintenance of an artificial price of a product by governmental interference. Though the purpose is to stabilize the price, it sometimes does the opposite, as was the case in the early efforts to stabilize the price of rubber. Following the collapse of crude rubber prices as a result of the world-wide depression of 1920–1921, the British undertook to raise prices by restricting exports from their East Indian plantations by means of a sliding-scale export duty. At the inauguration of the scheme, known as the "Stevenson plan," the British controlled 75 per cent of the plantation rubber acreage. Rubber advanced steadily until it attained a price of $1.21 a pound in 1925. However, this served to stimulate the planting of increased acreage by the Dutch, and as more rubber came into the market from this source, prices declined, and in 1928 the Stevenson plan was abandoned. The experiment caused the American rubber companies serious inventory losses whereupon they set out to acquire their own plantations.

In 1934, a second valorization plan went into effect under the auspices of the International Rubber Regulation Committee, embracing 98 per cent of the world's crude rubber suppliers. This effort, like the first, stimulated higher prices for several years. On the whole, it was more successful in stabilizing prices.   The plan was renewed in 1938, but the future of rubber prices is very uncertain as a result of the outbreak of the Second World War.

Throughout the decade 1926–1936, vast changes occurred in the rubber industry.   The price of the raw material declined from its lofty and erratic peaks of 50 cents to $1.25 a pound to 15 to 20 cents.   Processing was subjected to greater chemical control and greater mechanization.   Manufacturing fell into the hands of fewer and larger companies.   Distribution changed to mass merchandising. Finally, the efforts to find a substitute for natural rubber were beginning to bear fruit.

Synthetic Rubber.—Approximately 30 varieties of synthetic rubber have been studied.   They fall into roughly three classes.   The one which has attained the greatest commercial development is Neoprene—an elastometer pioneered by the late Reverend Nieuwland of Notre Dame University and perfected by duPont.   It is made from acetylene gas and it accounted for the greatest part of the 4,000 tons of synthetic rubber made in 1940 in this country.

Another type of synthetic rubber is Buna—a word compounded from the two essential chemicals used in its manufacture, namely, *bu* for butadiene and *na* for sodium, its polymerizing agent.   The basic raw materials used in its manufacture are coal or petroleum.   Standard Oil of New Jersey acquired the American patent rights on this process from Germany's I. G. Farbenindustrie.   In addition to operating a plant in Louisiana, Standard Oil has granted manufacturing licenses to Firestone and United States Rubber companies.   Closely related to Buna is Goodrich's Ameripol.

Representative of a third type of synthetic are Koroseal, made by Goodrich, Vinyon, made by Union Carbide, and Thiokol, made by Dow Chemical.   These products are more in the nature of synthetic resins.

Synthetic rubber, in the present state of development, is superior to natural rubber in some respects and inferior in others.   Synthetics offer greater resistance to cracking in sunlight, they withstand greater heat, and are less soluble in oil.   On the other hand, natural rubber has greater elasticity and more wearing quality.   Furthermore, synthetic rubber costs two to three times as much as natural rubber.

Rubber for War Economy.—The outbreak of war between Japan and the United States shut off our supply of rubber from the East Indies. This created an immediate problem of looking elsewhere for our supply of rubber.

Synthetic rubber promises to be the best solution for the problem of our long-run supply, but the industry is too small to be of much aid in the immediate future.   The industry can supply only about 2 per cent of our normal consumption, and to expand productive capacity to a point approaching our normal requirements would take a capital investment of about 400 million dollars. However, the principal obstacles to such an expansion program are, not the capital requirements, but rather the building materials, labor, and time required to build the synthetic rubber factories.

Other sources of natural rubber likewise offer little hope for a quick solution to our difficulty. Although certain parts of Latin America have a climate suited to rubber growing, it takes 5 to 7 years to bring *Hevea* trees into bearing. Henry Ford spent approximately 20 million dollars in an attempt to grow rubber in the Amazon basin, but his venture encountered numerous difficulties of a political and economic nature.

Rubber from the guayule shrub which can be grown in the semiarid region of California is likewise no quick solution because it would take several years to make this shrub an important commercial factor.

The most practical solutions to the problem at hand are enforced curtailment of civilian use of rubber, retreading, and reclamation. Realizing the gravity of the situation, the government placed a ban on the sale of automobile tires within a week after the Japanese attack upon Pearl Harbor. Subsequently, a plan was devised for rationing the sale of rubber products for civilian use.

The art of retreading automobile tires offers one of the best means of conserving our limited supplies. To retread the average-size tire of the kind used on most automobiles requires only 8.5 lb. of camelback (5 lb. of which is rubber) in contrast with 14 lb. of rubber required to make a new tire. A retread will give about 80 per cent of the mileage of a new tire. It is estimated that 115,000 long tons of crude rubber can be saved annually by retreading.

Finally, the use of reclaimed rubber can be relied upon as the most important solution for the immediate problem. In 1940, about 210,000 long tons were reclaimed and, under the circumstances now prevailing, it is estimated that 340,000 tons can be obtained from this source. However, it should be noted that rubber cannot be reclaimed indefinitely. Reclaimed rubber is not as good as natural rubber. In contrast with natural rubber, it is softer and loses its "nerve." To obtain best results, it should be mixed with a certain amount of new crude rubber.

Rubber is the first of the chemical process industries to feel the pinch of war, and it is highly probable that the war will accelerate the search for substitutes. However, rubber manufacturers estimate that approximately 30 million dollars will have to be spent on research in order to find substitutes that are entirely satisfactory.

PART VI
THE TEXTILE INDUSTRIES

CHAPTER XX

THE TEXTILE AND ALLIED INDUSTRIES

The textile and allied industries serve to introduce us to a new group of industries—the consumer's nondurable goods industries. The chief characteristic of this group of industries is that they produce goods primarily for direct consumption of the ultimate consumer and, generally speaking, are goods that are consumed in a relatively short period of time and must quickly be replaced. The industries discussed earlier, it will be recalled, direct their production chiefly to other industries. Their products, including that portion which finds its way to the ultimate consumer, are of a durable nature and are used up or worn out slowly. The obvious exceptions are the petroleum and chemical industries. The nature of their market and the short time required to consume their products give the consumer's goods industries behavior patterns quite different from those of the producer's and durable goods industries,[1] and make them sensitive to market forces that are of little significance to the latter.

The Scope of the Field.—The textile industries include all those mills which perform one or more of the processes involved in the manufacture of yarns and fabrics, such as spinning cotton, wool, silk, or rayon fibers into yarn; weaving or knitting yarn into cloth; finishing the fabric by dyeing, bleaching, or printing; and other preparatory or finishing operations. Some of the products of this group may be in finished form and ready for immediate use, like blankets, knitted underwear, sweaters, hosiery, and so-called square-sewn goods, like bed sheets, pillow cases, and towels. Other products may be in the form of cloth which must be processed into wearing apparel and other textile products.

The allied industries that convert the fabrics into apparel are known as the "garment" or "needle trades," such as the men's, women's and children's clothing industries. Another group comprises establishments that purchase fabrics for conversion into nonapparel articles like draperies, awnings, tents, bags, etc. The scope of the field is shown in Fig. 51.

[1] See Fig. 1, p. 6.

The wide scope of the field, the variety of raw materials used, the wide range of goods manufactured, and the many uses to which they are put, have brought about the development of a high degree of specialization. In the textile industries proper, *i.e.*, the enterprises engaged in the process-

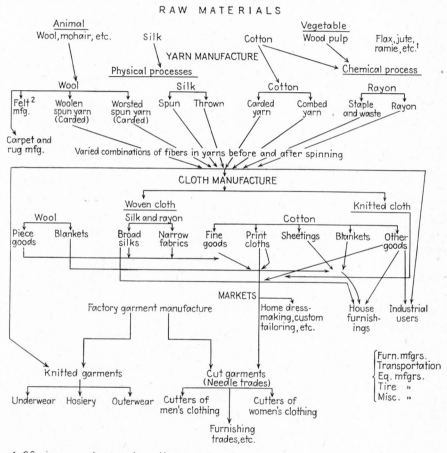

1. Of minor importance in domestic manufacture.
2. Some woven felt goods; others "felted" by special machines; major market-industrial users

FIG. 51.—The principal textile industries, relation of raw materials, processes, and markets. (*H. E. Michl, The Textile Industries, Textile Foundation, Washington, D. C.*, 1938.)

ing of yarn and cloth, mills tend to specialize on one fiber—cotton, wool, silk, or rayon—and within each of these fields mills tend to specialize still further upon a few types of yarns or fabrics. Very few of the mills are completely integrated; only a small number carry their operations through to the cutting stage. Among the allied industries, the needle trades firms, for example, tend to specialize on one type of garment. This aspect of the industry will be considered in greater detail in the chapters to follow.

The Place of Clothing in the Family Budget.—The fact that clothing is an indispensable want places the textile industries in an enviable position among the manufacturing industries of the United States. The primary physical need it satisfies makes every person in the country a customer, regardless of age, creed, color, or wealth. The importance of clothing in the budget of the American people is shown in Table XXXIX. It will be noted that the amount spent for clothing varies from 7.6 per cent for the lowest income group to 14.3 per cent for the highest, with an average of 10.5 per cent for all groups; and that it is exceeded by only three items—food, housing, and household operation.

It would be easy to explain the importance of clothing in the budget by pointing to the fundamental need it satisfies, but, as Table XXXIX shows, the demand of individuals for clothing is elastic, increasing as income increases, although not quite as rapidly. This indicates that the demand does not arise entirely or even in large part from a physical need. Important though that factor is, other considerations compel us to spend as much as we do on clothing, and among these the most important is fashion, which we shall define as a characteristic mode of expression.[1]

Importance of Fashion.—No article of consumption is more personal, intimate, or expressive of the ego than one's clothing. A person may emphasize his individuality not only by his selection of clothing but also by the manner in which he wears it, because identical garments may be worn by different people in ways which express individuality.

The possible choices of clothing available to a person are almost infinite in number because of the many possible variations in color, texture, materials, weight, and cut. The factors that govern the choice of a particular individual are many, some personal and others social in character. Certainly one of the most important is the desire for the beautiful, which is almost entirely subjective. To satisfy their desire for the beautiful, people do not necessarily look to works of art. They may also look to goods. Accordingly, even in this day of machinery and mass production, it is impossible for the textile manufacturer to separate the idea of cloth from the conception of color and design. Another factor, the will of the individual to differentiate himself from the mass, may be explained on a number of grounds. As fundamental as any, perhaps, is the desire for variety for its own sake. Certainly another is the sexual factor, the hope of obtaining recognition from the opposite sex.

---

[1] There are students who differentiate between a style and a fashion on the basis of the number of people who adopt it. We shall, however, use the terms interchangeably.

TABLE XXXIX.—PERCENTAGE OF TOTAL EXPENDITURES OF AMERICAN FAMILIES AND SINGLE INDIVIDUALS FOR MAIN CATEGORIES OF CONSUMPTION, BY INCOME LEVEL, 1935–1936

Income level	All items	Percentage of expenditures for										
		Food	Housing	Household operations	Clothing	Automobile	Medical care	Recreation	Furnishings	Personal care	Tobacco	All other
Under $500	100	44.5	22.3	9.5	7.6	2.2	3.6	1.0	1.4	2.2	1.7	3.8
$500 to 750	100	42.3	20.1	9.8	9.2	3.0	3.6	1.9	1.6	2.2	1.9	4.5
750 to 1,000	100	40.3	19.2	10.0	9.5	4.2	3.7	2.2	2.2	2.2	2.2	4.3
1,000 to 1,250	100	37.8	19.0	10.4	9.6	5.7	3.9	2.6	2.7	2.1	2.2	4.0
1,250 to 1,500	100	36.3	18.4	10.2	10.0	6.5	4.1	3.0	2.9	2.1	2.3	4.2
1,500 to 1,750	100	34.5	18.4	10.1	10.1	7.6	4.5	3.3	3.2	2.1	2.1	4.1
1,750 to 2,000	100	32.9	18.5	10.3	10.2	8.8	4.5	3.3	3.5	2.1	2.1	4.0
2,000 to 2,500	100	31.2	18.3	10.1	10.8	9.7	4.6	3.6	3.3	2.1	2.0	4.3
2,500 to 3,000	100	29.9	17.9	10.9	11.2	10.2	4.7	3.8	3.3	2.1	1.9	4.1
3,000 to 4,000	100	28.1	18.3	11.0	11.7	10.3	4.9	4.2	3.4	2.0	1.8	4.3
4,000 to 5,000	100	25.9	18.2	11.4	12.6	11.3	4.9	4.4	3.0	2.0	1.6	4.7
5,000 to 10,000	100	23.2	18.5	12.2	12.6	11.5	5.7	4.9	3.2	1.9	1.4	4.9
10,000 to 15,000	100	19.7	20.7	11.5	13.6	11.1	4.2	5.8	3.3	1.8	1.3	7.0
15,000 to 20,000	100	19.2	17.7	11.9	13.6	10.4	5.0	5.6	2.8	1.6	1.1	11.1
20,000 and over	100	15.2	20.0	13.2	14.3	12.1	6.1	6.4	2.7	1.6	0.8	7.6
All levels	100	33.6	18.9	10.6	10.5	7.6	4.4	3.3	2.8	2.0	1.9	4.4

Source: National Resources Committee, "Consumers Expenditures in the United States, Washington, D. C., 1939," p. 85.

Struggling against the personal desires of the individual is the powerful force of social pressure. Man is a gregarious animal and group life exerts certain pressures upon the individual to do or refrain from doing certain things. The pressure may take the form of laws but more often it is nothing more tangible than public opinion. The conduct of most of us is influenced by what people will say about us if we do or fail to do certain things. Fear of disapproval makes us conform to what those around us consider "right," and the "right" thing is the customary thing. With respect to clothing this means that while physical needs compel us to cover our bodies, social custom demands that we cover them in a certain way—the prevailing way. To be adequately clothed is not enough; to be correctly clothed is just as important. There is no article of apparel less useful than a necktie, yet most men in polite society would feel undressed without one.

Another aspect of the influence of social forces upon the consumption of clothing is pecuniary in nature. In a pecuniary society, such as ours, great stress is placed upon material wealth, and clothing helps to give an appearance of wealth and reputability. As Veblen in his "Theory of the Leisure Class" states it, "the greater part of the expenditure incurred by all classes for apparel is incurred for the sake of a respectable appearance rather than for the protection of the person. And probably at no other point is the sense of shabbiness so keenly felt as it is if we fall short of the standard set by social usage in the matter of dress." Again, "the commercial value of the goods used for clothing is made up to a much larger extent of the fashionableness, the reputability of the goods than of the mechanical service which they render in clothing to the person of the wearer." The service clothing performs as a symbol of social standing and wealth is one of the factors that explains the purchase of an expensive garment when one at one-half or one-fourth the price would give the same protection.

Fashion has always been important in textiles, but since the First World War it has become increasingly important. Prior to the war about 80 per cent of the cotton textile industry's output was staple in character; today it is estimated that over 50 per cent of its production is subject to the dictates of fashion. In the worsted branch of the wool industry, which once could rely upon a large market for blue serge, fashion has almost completely driven this staple from men's wardrobes.

The chief factor responsible for the increased importance of fashion was the rise of the ready-to-wear garment industry. Before the development of this industry garments were made either in the home or by the local seamstress or in the corner tailor shop from piece goods purchased from small local retail stores. Choice of materials was limited to such fabrics as the store had available, and mills could afford to minimize the problem of design. The growth of the garment industries, especially in women's clothes, has changed this. Sewing in the home is now almost a lost art, and the local seamstress has gone the way of the village blacksmith. The demands of the great garment industries for new patterns, and the tremendous buying market they represent cannot be ignored.

Coincident with the increased breadth of the area affected by fashion is the increase in frequency of fashion changes and the speed with which they are adopted, developed, and discarded. Several factors are responsible for the widened scope of fashion and the rate of change, but three stand out as most important. One is the increase in the standard of living of the masses since the turn of the century which has permitted more people to satisfy their desire for the latest style. Another factor is the great improvement in communication and transportation as evidenced by the development of faster train and ship schedules, the airplane, the automobile, the radio, the moving picture, and a large increase in magazine and newspaper advertising. No longer is it possible for a clothing manufacturer to dump old or unsuccessful styles in isolated towns and villages; today the little store on Main Street displays the same fashions as the large department store in New York and about as quickly. The third factor was the early recognition by manufacturers and distributors of the excellence of new styles as a competitive weapon to draw trade away from one another and to increase the total demand by inducing consumers to replace commodities more frequently.

The influence of fashion has not been confined to clothing fabrics. Color is playing an increasing role in such household fabrics as draperies, upholstery, curtains, and even towels, sheets, and pillow cases.

Although the demand for clothing and household fabrics increases with income and can be stimulated by fashion changes, it does not follow that an increase in consumer expenditures for these purposes will follow as a matter of course. The ever-widening variety of goods and services made available to consumers increases the intensity of the battle for the consumer's dollar, and in this battle the clothing industries so far have failed to hold their own. Figure 52 shows the trend of consumer spending for the period 1919–1937. Note that it was not the depression of 1930 which initiated the decline in the proportion spent for clothing. On the contrary, the decline set in during one of the most prosperous periods in American history, a period that brought forth many new products and made available others at lower prices. Among the most important are automobiles, radios, electric refrigerators, etc.

Nowadays when the family has had a prosperous year it is quite as likely to think of the automobile as a symbol of success as to turn to new clothes or new furniture for the parlor. At the end of the war period, motor cars were owned so seldom by wage earners and clerical workers that the schedule used in the

Bureau of Labor Statistics classified automobiles with motorcycles and bicycles. Fifteen per cent of the families covered reported some expenditures for either one of these three types of vehicles. Among families of similar composition studied in 1934–1936, approximately 50 per cent owned automobiles. . . . Apparently, American moderate-income families are wearing less than at the end of the postwar period.[1]

Studies by the Bureau of Labor Statistics of low-income groups show a similar trend. The conclusion is that as income advances consumption becomes more capricious and that staple items in the family budget do not have an impregnable position.

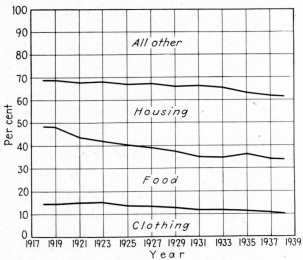

Fig. 52.—Distribution of consumers expenditures. (*National Industrial Conference Board, Enterprise and Social Progress, New York, 1939.*)

Stability of Demand.—Despite the increase in capricious consumption, a fundamental characteristic of textiles and allied industries is the fact that they possess an unusual degree of stability of demand. This is because textiles wear out rapidly and must be replaced frequently by reason of style changes. This is indicated in Table XL, which shows the percentage decline in production between 1929 and 1932 and the percentage increase in production during the recovery from 1932 to 1937. It will be noted that during the depression, production of textiles declined only 28 per cent and that only three industry groups, leather, petroleum, and food, maintained production at a higher level. An analysis of physical sales of department stores[2] shows that in 1932, the poorest

[1] *Monthly Labor Review*, November, 1938, p. 977.

[2] TEBBUT, A. R., "Behavior of Consumption in a Business Depression," Harvard University Bureau of Business Research, 1933.

year since 1928, only two departments in women's wear—cotton wash goods and high-priced dresses—had a decline of over 25 per cent from 1928, and sales of 12 items were actually greater than in that year. Sales of women's hosiery, for example, were 37 per cent higher. Apparently most people have only a minimum of clothing which must be replaced when it is worn out or has become unfashionable.

TABLE XL.—PRICE AND PRODUCTION CHANGES DURING DEPRESSION AND RECOVERY FOR NINE MAJOR INDUSTRIES

Industry Group	Per cent drop 1929–1932		Per cent recovery 1932–1937	
	Prices	Production	Prices	Production
Motor vehicles.........................	12	74	2	64
Agricultural equipment.................	14	84	9	84
Cement..............................	16	55	20	24
Iron and steel........................	16	76	20	67
Auto tires............................	25	42	27	24
Leather and products..................	33	18	29	27
Petroleum products...................	36	17	21	37
Textile products......................	39	28	24	24
Food products........................	39	10	24	−1

Source: National Resources Committee, "The Structure of the American Economy," Washington, D. C., p. 386, 1939.

The discussion of textile markets so far has been centered chiefly on the demand for clothing and household fabrics, but these account for only 60 per cent of the total market, 40 per cent for apparel and 20 per cent for household use. About 40 per cent of the total textile production goes into industrial uses, in the form of cordage, twine, tires, bags, felts, etc. The demand for textiles for industrial uses is, of course, less stable than the demand for clothing and household fabrics.

Individual Textile Industries Are Unstable.—The large aggregate demand for textile products and the relative stability of consumption would lead one to expect a high degree of stability in mill operations, prices, employment, and profits. However, instability is the rule rather than the exception in most of the textile industries. Price declines, for example, as shown in Table XL, were greater in textiles than in all the industry groups listed with the exception of foods with which it shared first place. The forces responsible for the instability vary from one textile industry to another, and attention will be directed to these in the chapters to follow, but common to most of them are the following:

1. *Fluctuating Raw Material Prices.*—All the principal textile fibers are agricultural in origin, and the nature of agricultural production makes

the supply of the fibers, rayon excepted, more dependent upon weather conditions than upon the demand for them. All the fibers are also important in world commerce. Cotton, wool, and, to a lesser extent, silk are produced in many parts of the world and are consumed as a raw material in an even greater number of countries. The international movement of textile fibers makes them, therefore, extremely sensitive to world influences. These two factors cause wide fluctuations in prices in the long run and frequent changes in the short run. Figure 53 shows

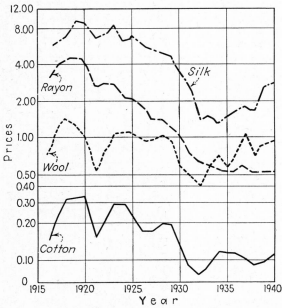

Fig. 53.—Prices of raw silk, rayon, cotton, and wool, 1916–1940. (*Rayon Organon, February,* 1941.)

the annual price changes for the principal fibers. Rayon prices fluctuate less than the prices of the other fibers. Unlike cotton, wool, and silk, rayon is a manufactured product whose supply can be more easily regulated. Prices in the short run, therefore, are very stable, and the declining long-run trend can be explained by technological developments.

The fluctuations in the prices of raw materials are a constant hazard to the industry because of the relatively high ratio of raw material costs to value of product and the importance of inventories to the mills. In the cotton textile industry, 50.3 per cent of current assets is represented by inventory; in woolen goods, 53.2 per cent; and in silk goods, 36.3 per cent.[1]

[1] BALDERSTON, C., and V. KARABASZ, "Management of a Textile Enterprise," p. 108, Textile Foundation, Washington, D. C., 1938.

The relation between raw material price movements and profits is indicated in Fig. 54.

2. *Idle Capacity.*—Since the First World War almost all the textile industries have carried a heavy burden of idle capacity and have had to undergo a process of liquidation. Although the factors that gave rise to this condition differ somewhat in each industry, the result has been the same in all—vigorous competition and resulting instabilities.

3. *Intricate Marketing Structure.*—As has been previously stated, there is a high degree of specialization in the textile and allied industries. This has resulted, in most of the industries, in a notable lack of integration and in the development of a highly complicated marketing system. This is especially true of the cotton, silk, and rayon industries, for

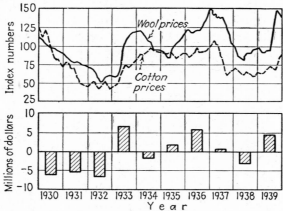

Fig. 54.—Raw material prices and profits in the textile industries. (*Adapted from Standard and Poor's Corporation.*)

reasons that will be explained in the following chapters. In these industries goods move from the mills to the distributors, converters, finishers, cutters, and finally into retail channels. The decentralization of control and the separation of manufacturing from marketing deprives the mill executive of much necessary knowledge of the movement of his goods into consumption and has injected in almost every stage of the marketing process a considerable amount of speculation. During periods of rising prices, distributors, converters, and cutters rush to place orders with mills far in advance of their needs, and mill operations, which are very flexible because of an abundance of productive capacity, expand rapidly. Total inventories at each stage reach a high figure, and purchases dry up until the inventories are liquidated.

4. *Fashion Changes.*—Reference has already been made to the importance of fashion in the textile industries. Although fashion changes have been an important factor in stimulating the demand for

textile products, it has made the operation of textile mills more difficult than would otherwise be the case. The difficulties are numerous, but they arise from one cause: uncertainty—uncertainty as to what styles the consumers will accept and how long they will continue to accept them.

Some of the style changes that take place are broad, long-run changes that occur over a period of years and cause a shift from one fiber to another. An example of this type of change is the postwar shift in women's dress goods fabrics from wool to lighter weight fabrics, such as silk, rayon, and cotton. Another example is the shift from cotton to silk and rayon hosiery. Important as these changes frequently prove to be, they generally extend over several seasons, and the mills affected have greater opportunity to adjust themselves to the change.

It is not changes of this type, however, that cause the most difficult management problems in these industries. Much more important are the short-run changes that occur each season within a specific industry, such as changes in the construction of the cloth, the weave, the texture, the weight, color, design, and finish. These changes occur quickly and are not easily predicted. If a mill makes a "strike" with a style, large profits may be made; if it guesses wrong, the season's operations may result in a loss.

The management problems that have developed as a result of the increased importance of style arise from irregular operations, short runs, and the difficulty in "timing" styles.

Not knowing what styles will "take," mills hesitate to manufacture to inventory and wait until the last possible moment before the season opens. If the mill does not do its own finishing but sells to converters (individuals who buy goods in the "grey" and have them finished according to their own specifications), it must either anticipate the type of cloth that will be called for or wait for orders from the converters. The converters also hesitate to place orders because they, too, are not certain of the style and they also do not want to assume the risk of any changes in price. Another factor that makes them hesitate is the fear that competitors may copy their design. When orders are finally placed, pressure is put upon the mills for quick delivery, frequently making it necessary to resort to overtime work, which is generally more costly.

The rapid changes in style and the short life of many styles make wholesalers, cutters, and retail stores hesitate to buy beyond their immediate needs. Unless the mill is willing to assume the risks of manufacturing to inventory, it must manufacture short runs of a particular style on a hand-to-mouth basis. This, of course, is a more expensive method of manufacture and requires great flexibility in mill management.

It is necessary to know not only what styles will strike the public fancy but also at what stage of the life of the style to enter production.

The trend of fashion may be apparent, but if the mill produces the style before the market is ready for it, sales will be too restricted. If production is held up until the style is evident beyond any doubt, the style will have reached the mass-production stage and will soon pass out. When the style reaches the mass-production stage it loses its distinctive quality and is on a competitive basis, with the profit margin small or nonexistent.

Although fashion makes itself felt in all the textile industries, the incidence of style changes is not the same for all. In the cotton, silk, and rayon industries a large portion of the output is styled after it leaves the weaving mill; in wool, on the other hand, the style is woven into the fabric.

Variations in the Textile Industries.—This chapter has been devoted to some of the general aspects of the textile industries. Since there is a high degree of specialization in the industries and in the mills within each industry, both as to fiber and product, some of the problems will vary in scope and intensity. We shall return to these problems as they appear in the various industries after considering, in the next chapter, the technology of textile manufacturing.

CHAPTER XXI

THE TECHNOLOGY OF TEXTILE MANUFACTURING—THE PRODUCTION OF YARN AND CLOTH

Since the need for clothing has long been one of the most fundamental of man's material wants, the making of cloth is one of the oldest arts. While it is impossible to say definitely when the first cloth was woven, historians believe that the art of weaving was known in Egypt five or six thousand years before Christ.

Cloth can be made by several processes, but the most important method employed today is weaving. This involves two fundamental processes—spinning and weaving. The purpose of spinning is to bind together the loose individual fibers into a continuous strand, or yarn, which will have sufficient strength to resist the strain incident to weaving. Weaving may be defined as the interlacing of yarn at right angles in such a manner as to form a fabric.

Cloth can also be made by knitting or felting. Knitting may be defined as the interlacing of a single strand of yarn into a series of interlocking loops. This is the method employed in the manufacture of sweaters, hosiery, and certain types of underwear. Felting may be defined as the manufacture of a fabric by the matting of loose fibers under pressure and moisture. This process is used in the making of hats, rugs, and certain types of shoe linings.

Early Spinning and Weaving.—The simplest and earliest method of spinning was a hand process without the use of any device. It consisted of pulling out the cleaned fibers into a strand which was twisted by rolling it between the palm of the hand and the thigh. The first implement used in spinning was simply a slender shaft of wood known as a "spindle." The operator squatted on the ground, placed the spindle at right angles across his thigh, and attached the beginnings of his strand of yarn to it. One hand drew out the loose fibers from a supply on the ground, and the other hand twirled the spindle against the thigh. By regulating the angle between the revolving spindle and the strand, the yarn could either be twisted or wound on the spindle (see Fig. 55). Another method of using the hand spindle was to supplement it with a pole or distaff on which the loose raw material was fastened.

About the sixth century there was introduced into Europe from India the first form of mechanically driven spindle, known as the "spinning wheel." A foot treadle actuated a large wheel, which in turn, by means of a belt, drove a spindle. The invention marked a big step forward, for the driving wheel and belt assured a spindle rotation that was constant instead of intermittent. Furthermore, both hands were

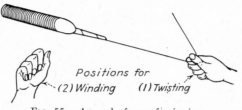

Positions for
(2) Winding   (1) Twisting

FIG. 55.—An early form of spinning.

free to draw out the fibers. The spinning wheel in its various forms was the implement used in the households of this country in colonial times.

After the yarn is made, the next process is weaving, which, as was stated above, is the interlacing of strands of yarn at right angles in such a manner as to form a fabric. The parallel threads which run the length of the cloth are called the "warp"; the crosswise yarns which intersect the warp constitute the "filler" or "weft." Figure 56 illustrates in simplest detail the structure of woven cloth. It will be noted that each filler thread alternately passes under one and over the next warp yarn. The work of laying the warp yarns parallel and inserting the filler constitutes the weaving process in its simplest form.

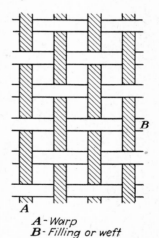

A - Warp
B - Filling or weft
FIG. 56.—Detail of a plain weave.

The weaving process involves three steps: (1) "shedding," or the raising of alternate threads of the warp; (2) "picking," or placing the filler yarn between the warp yarns separated by the first operation; (3) "beating up" or pushing the filler yarns firmly in place against the finished cloth.

The Primitive Loom.—It is impossible to interlace the strands unless the warp strands are held in a parallel position. Because of this, one of the first developments was a method of stretching the warp to keep it in position, so that the threads could easily be raised. A pole was placed parallel to the ground between two trees or forked poles, and the warp threads were tied to it and made taut by a bottom pole. This principle of keeping the warp threads taut and parallel is still employed today in the modern loom. By winding the warp threads in their proper position around the top beam and rolling up the woven cloth on the bottom beam, a great length of fabric may be made in one piece. Also the weaving can be kept at a convenient height for the weaver. These operations, likewise, are still performed—the winding of the finished cloth upon the cloth beam being known as "taking up" and the releasing of the yarn from the warp beam "letting off."

The task of separately raising every other warp thread to form a path for the filling was very laborious, and there was soon used the simple device of inserting a pointed stick all the way across the warp to form the "shed" or path for the filler. In place of using fingers to insert the filler, the yarn was first wound on a small stick and then thrown through the shed across the width of the cloth. This was the forerunner of the shuttle. Thus, during the course of the centuries, came improvements, finally culminating in the European handloom.

The European Handloom.—The handloom, used throughout Europe wherever the household system of manufacture was in vogue, represents, as there developed, the highest type of weaving device using hand power. This was the type of loom employed during the colonial period in this country. A thorough knowledge of the handloom is necessary to understand modern weaving methods since the power loom is essentially the same machine except that most of the action is automatic.

It has been stated that there are three fundamental steps in loom operation. These three steps as applied to the handloom are:

1. *Shedding.*—This operation has already been described as the raising of alternate warp threads in order to form a shed or path for the insertion of the filler yarn. It will be recalled that the original method of performing this operation was by hand, in which each thread was laboriously lifted by the fingers of the operator, and that later a stick was inserted. The European handloom did this by means of "heddle" frames. A heddle consists of a number of parallel wires supported by a rectangular frame, each wire having a small eyelet in the center. One warp thread is run through each of these eyelets. In simple weaving, where all the alternate warp threads are to be lifted at one time, two heddle frames must be used. In more intricate weaving there are sometimes as many as 12. This part of the loom is called the "harness." In a two-heddle loom all the even threads are passed through the eyelets of one frame and all the odd threads through the eyelets of the second frame. The two-heddle frames are attached to two-foot treadles, which alternately raise and lower the frames. First one frame, then the other, is raised by the foot treadle, thus furnishing an opening for the filler yarn to be carried across the shed.

2. *Picking.*—Picking or inserting the filler yarn is accomplished by throwing a shuttle from one side of the loom to the other. A shuttle is a

wooden shell shaped like a boat in which is placed a bobbin of filler yarn. As it passes back and forth the bobbin of yarn revolves and the yarn leaves the shuttle through a small hole in the side. For many years the weaver passed the filler thread back and forth by throwing the shuttle from one hand to another. Although this was a very slow process and limited the width of the cloth to the reach of a man, it continued until 1733 when Kay invented the flying shuttle, a mechanical device so arranged that, by pulling a cord, a spring was released which propelled the shuttle from one side to the other.

3. *Beating Up.*—The process of "beating up," or forcing each strand of filler yarn close up against the preceding one after it had been inserted by the shuttle, was performed by means of a comblike arrangement known as the "reed." It consisted of short strips of reed (later replaced by wire) fastened in a frame the width of the cloth. Between each two wires passed a warp thread. The frame was suspended from the top of the loom and, after every pick, the operator pulled it toward himself, thereby pressing the last thread solidly and evenly against the finished cloth. As the weaving proceeded the operator wound up finished cloth on the beam at the front of the loom and at the same time released ("letting off") more yarn from the warp beam at the rear.

The spinning and weaving methods just described prevailed until almost the fourth decade of the eighteenth century. In many parts of the world the handicraft artisan of textile fabrics still persists. It has been estimated that there are in operation in India 50 million spinning wheels and almost 2 million handlooms, which account for about 40 per cent of the total cotton cloth produced in India. In China handloom weaving still predominates over power-loom weaving, the ratio of hand weaving to power weaving, in terms of yarn consumption, being four to one.[1]

The Industrial Revolution.—Beginning in 1733 with the invention by Kay of the flying shuttle, there occurred in England a series of inventions that were of epoch-making importance. The inventions not only speeded up the making of yarn and cloth, but also introduced an era which has since become known as the industrial revolution, a revolution that caused profound changes in the prevailing social organization and stimulated the shift from home to factory production. Prior to these great inventions, textile making was largely confined to the home. This was especially true of spinning. Weaving had already become something of an independent industry. Weavers bought yarns from home artisans and wove them into cloth. Spinning was a much simpler operation than weaving, and the spinners produced more yarn than the weavers

[1] "The World Textile Industry, Economic and Social Problems," pp. 41–43, International Labor Office. Geneva, 1937.

could use. This unbalance between spinning and weaving, together with the great demand for fabrics, put the weavers under heavy pressure to improve their methods.

The invention of the flying shuttle saved much of the weavers' time and also permitted the weaving of wider cloths, with the result that output per loom increased fourfold. In 1760 Kay's son invented the "drop box" which permitted the use of several shuttles with different-colored yarns. Boxes at the end of the shuttle path were arranged so that they could be raised or lowered so as to bring the desired compartment with its colored yarn on a level with the opening in the shed. That particular yarn was then propelled through the shed. In place of the former surplus of yarn there was now a great shortage, and it was up to the spinners to improve their methods.

Within about 10 years the deficiency in yarn was met by the invention of three spinning devices. In 1770 Hargreave patented the spinning jenny, which contained eight spindles and greatly increased the output of yarn. At about the same time Arkwright developed the water frame which produced a strong warp yarn, and in 1779 Crompton patented the mule which produced a fine yarn. These three machines put the spinners far ahead of the weavers, and the market was again glutted with yarn. The demand for a more productive loom was met in 1785 by the invention of the power loom by Cartwright. The power loom substituted mechanical power for manual power in such operations as raising the heddles to make the shed, throwing the shuttle back and forth, beating up the yarn after it has been thrown across the shed, and winding up the cloth and releasing more warp yarn.

Thus, within about 50 years, the spinning of yarn and weaving of cloth were put on a mechanical basis, and factories replaced the home as the scene of their manufacture.

Present Methods of Spinning and Weaving.—The manufacture of textiles, speaking broadly, follows five successive phases, of which the first four are primarily mechanical and the last largely chemical:

1. Preparatory spinning operations. The fiber must be cleaned, softened, and drawn.

2. The fiber must be twisted into yarn.

3. The yarn must then be prepared for the loom, by slashing (starching) and beaming (spooling).

4. The yarn must then be woven into a fabric.

5. The fabric must finally be bleached, dyed, printed, starched, ironed, or otherwise finished.

Preparatory Operations.—Before the fibers can be spun and woven it is first necessary to put them through certain preliminary and intermediate operations. The first step in the operation is to remove all foreign material. Cotton comes to the mill containing small stones, leaves, twigs, etc., which adhere to the fibers as they are picked, baled, ginned, and transported. Wool contains a large amount of grease supplied by nature to protect the body of the sheep from the weather, and also burrs and vegetable matter picked up by the animal. The same condition, in varying degrees, is true of the other fibers; silk, for example, is covered by a protective gummy substance which has to be softened and removed.

The opening, cleaning, and disentangling of fibers is done by machinery, and when the fibers leave the picking room they are in the form of a lap about 40 in. wide, in the case of cotton, and about 40 to 50 yd. long. The lap is then run over a machine known as a "card" which removes much of the remaining waste, part of the very short fibers, and partially straightens the remaining fibers. The fibers emerge from the card in the form of a soft rope about an inch in diameter called "sliver."

The sliver, in turn, is made into a more uniform and thinner strand on drawing frames, and this, in turn, is drawn out and twisted on a "slubber" into smaller rope called "roving." After the roving is further drawn out and twisted, the material is ready for the final spinning. The method of accomplishing this gradual reduction may be illustrated as follows: a strand one inch in diameter is drawn out until it is one-half inch in diameter; next, two of these one-half-inch strands are combined and drawn out until the combined strand is one-half inch in diameter. Two of these strands are combined and reduced, and this process is repeated many times until there is a very uniform distribution of the individual fibers throughout the length of the strand, whereupon the half-inch strands are reduced to quarter-inch size, and thus successively down to the final size. Throughout all these drawing operations the strand is kept in as loose and fluffy a condition as possible with just enough twist in it to cause the individual fibers to cohere and not break apart under the tension or pull which is being exerted. Finally, during the last drawing operation when the yarn is coming to its final size, the strand is twisted to make the fibers cling to each other closely and thus add strength. The twisting, which has hitherto been minimized in order to make drawing easier, is now greatly increased since there will be no further drawing and since the operation ensures that the fibers will not readily pull apart in the next operation—spinning.

Spinning.—Two main types of spinning, frame and mule, embrace most of the many variations that have been worked out to fit the peculiarities of individual fibers such as wool, cotton, flax, etc. Frame spinning is the more important; measured in terms of spindles there is roughly seven times as much equipment in the combined cotton and wool industries devoted to frame spinning as there is to mule spinning. In the following descriptions of these two methods, it is to be remembered that we are discussing the last in a long series of operations, namely, the step that follows the drawing operations. The purpose of this last step is to complete the drawing out of the fibers and also to add a relatively large amount of twist.

Frame Spinning.—Frame spinning gets its name from a spinning machine consisting of a stationary frame which supports on each side a row of approximately 75 to 100 spindles. There are three subtypes of frame spinning—ring, cap, and flyer—but we shall observe only ring spinning, invented in 1829 and today the most important process.

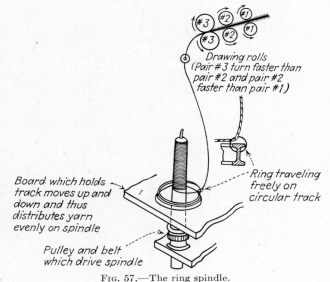

Drawing rolls
(Pair #3 turn faster than
pair #2 and pair #2
faster than pair #1)

Ring traveling
freely on
circular track

Board which holds
track moves up and
down and thus
distributes yarn
evenly on spindle

Pulley and belt
which drive spindle

Fig. 57.—The ring spindle.

The ring-spinning mechanism as outlined in Fig. 57 can be understood more readily if we think of it as performing three functions: (1) drawing out the fibers, (2) twisting them together, and (3) winding the finished yarn.

The drawing is performed by the three pairs of rollers mounted on top of the frame. By driving each pair faster than the preceding pair, a pronounced pull is set up which elongates the strand.

The twist is imparted by the unique feature of the machine, the ring. This is a tiny C-shaped steel ring called the "traveler." It snaps on to a flanged circular track on which it moves freely. As shown in Fig. 57, the yarn passes from the roller through the ring and onto the spindle. The spindle, which is mechanically driven, is made to revolve at a speed so fast that there is a very, very slight pull or tension on the yarn. Furthermore, the ring, through which the yarn passes, is dragged around the circular track by the whirling strand of yarn. The whirling action of the yarn plus the slight drag imposed by the weight of the ring imparts the twist to the fibers and completes the process. The amount of twist is controlled very accurately by regulating the speed at which the rollers release the roving and the speed at which the spindle winds the yarn. If the spindle winds the yarn faster than the rolls release it, there is a tension. This drags the ring about the track and imparts the twist.

PLATE 52.—A spinning frame.   (*Courtesy of the Farm Security Administration.*)

A very significant feature of the process is that it is continuous and not intermittent; *i.e.*, the drawing, twisting, and winding are simultaneous operations. Prior to the perfection of the ring spindle in 1829 these three operations could not be carried on at the same time. The continuous feature greatly increased the output.

Mule Spinning.—The mule, although much less important than the ring, is an older machine, invented in 1779 as a hybrid of two earlier machines, hence the term mule.

As shown in Fig. 58, the mule contains the roller feature of drawing, but its unique feature consists of a movable carriage which moves outward a distance of 8 to 10 ft. and as it does so it draws and twists the yarn. The drawing and twisting take place over a distance of about 8 to 10 ft., instead of within a space of a few inches as in frame spinning. Consequently, mule spinning is slower and more gentle, producing a softer and fluffier yarn.

Frame and Mule Spinning Compared.—Frame spinning since the introduction of the ring in 1829 has steadily forged ahead of mule spinning. One reason for this is that frame spinning is continuous whereas mule spinning is intermittent and therefore much slower. Drawing, twisting, and winding are simultaneous on a ring whereas on the mule, when the winding takes place as the carriage returns, there can be no

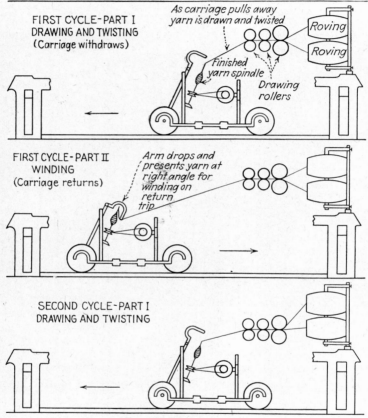

FIRST CYCLE-PART I
DRAWING AND TWISTING
(Carriage withdraws)

As carriage pulls away
yarn is drawn and twisted

Roving

Roving

Finished
yarn spindle

Drawing
rollers

FIRST CYCLE-PART II
WINDING
(Carriage returns)

Arm drops and
presents yarn at
right angle for
winding on
return
trip

SECOND CYCLE-PART I
DRAWING AND TWISTING

FIG. 58.—Mule spinning.

drawing or twisting. Furthermore, a frame is more compact and therefore requires less floor space in a mill. It also requires less skilled labor. It is not to be thought, however, that mule spinning is doomed to quick extinction. A mule produces a very soft and elastic yarn which for certain uses is very desirable; furthermore, if the fibers are extremely short, they can be spun more readily on the mule. However, frame spinning is constantly improving, whereas mule spinning seems to have reached a plateau of technical progress; so we may expect the latter to diminish in importance.   In the spinning of wool fibers the mule is still predominant in the production of woolen yarns, although most new installations are of the ring type.

Other Spinning Methods.—Up to this point the discussion has been confined to the spinning of short fibers such as cotton and wool.   When we turn to silk it is apparent that the drawing operations are not neces-

PLATE 53.—Mule spinning.   (*Courtesy of the Philadelphia Commercial Museum.*)

sary because the silk filament comes in lengths of 300 to 700 yd.   All that is necessary here is to twist two or more of these strands together to get a yarn of required size and strength.   The factories where this takes place are known as "throwing"[1] plants rather than spinning plants.

In the production of rayon yarn, cotton or wood cellulose is dissolved into a viscous, gelatinous mass forced through a fine nozzle into a chemical bath which solidifies the filament.   Since this produces a continuous yarn, spinning, in the sense we have defined it, is unnecessary.   However,

[1] Derived from the Anglo-Saxon word "thrawan," meaning to twist.

to obtain different effects, the continuous filament may be cut into short lengths known as rayon staple, and in such cases the spinning operation is necessary.[1]

Weaving.

Preliminary Weaving Operations.—The yarn which is to be used as the warp is wound on spools or cones and from them is wound on to a beam. The yarn on the beam, in turn, is run through the "slasher," where it receives a starch coating, called "size," which smooths and strengthens the yarn for weaving.

PLATE 54.—A loom. (*Courtesy of the Farm Security Administration.*)

Weaving.—When the yarn has been sized the beam is placed on the loom, and after it has been "harnessed," (warp yarns drawn through the proper heddle wires) the actual weaving begins.

For a period of a century, or until the decade of the nineties, there were no fundamental changes in the power loom of 1785. There were, of course, many improvements, but these were in the nature of refinements. The speed of the loom, which is measured in "number of picks per minute" (the number of times per minute the shuttle is thrown across), was increased. The action of the loom as a whole became smoother as a result of more accurately synchronizing its numerous moving parts. But there were still many difficulties: warp threads broke frequently and weavers had to be alert to this in order to stop the loom immediately

[1] The technique of rayon manufacture is discussed in greater detail in Chap. XXIV.

and thus minimize the output of defective cloth; furthermore, when the yarn in the shuttle became exhausted it was necessary for the weaver to remove the empty bobbin and insert a full one. Both of these necessities severely limited the number of looms a weaver could operate.

In 1895 the Northrup battery loom representing fundamental changes was introduced. It automatically ejected the empty bobbin from the shuttle and inserted a fresh bobbin during the brief interval of time (one-twentieth of a second) in which the shuttle is at rest between trips across the loom. The term "battery loom" originated from the fact that each loom had a supply or battery of filled bobbins arranged in a circular magazine, which rotated in such a manner as to move a filled bobbin into place when an empty one was thrown out. Later Northrup made applicable to looms in general what is known as the "automatic stop motion" whereby the loom is automatically stopped when a warp breaks. With these improvements weavers could tend many more looms; in fact, today on plain cotton goods a weaver sometimes operates over 100 looms.

Developments since 1900 have been along the line of greater speed and more nearly automatic operation, and the application of these automatic devices to the production of quality goods. At one stage only plain cloth could be woven; where the pattern called for several different-colored yarns, the automatic loom could not be used. Now, several shuttles are used, and these shift automatically to provide the color of yarn called for by the pattern.

Finishing.—When the cloth leaves the loom it is seldom in a condition fit for immediate use. Additional operations, known as "finishing," must be performed. Much cotton, for example, is woven in the gray, and must be bleached, dyed, or printed before final use. Silk is also frequently woven in the greige and must be dyed or printed. Woolens usually have the design woven into the fabric rather than printed on the surface of the fabric, but require shrinking and napping; and the fabric must also be dyed if it is to have a solid color.

In some cases weaving mills in the cotton, silk, and rayon industries perform the finishing operations, but usually this is restricted to the larger mills. The smaller mills either sell their goods in the gray or have it finished by an independent finisher on a commission basis. Wool manufacturers, on the other hand, generally do their own finishing.

In this chapter we have covered the main steps in textile technique. Variations, of course, occur from one textile industry to another, and when important they will be touched upon when we consider the principal industries within the textile group.

Influence of Technology on the Textile Industries.—The nature of textile technology has had important effects upon the structure of the textile industries. Among the most important are the following.

1. *A Tendency toward Small-scale Plant Operations.*—Large-scale operations are less-prevalent in the textile industries than in the industries previously discussed. Except in the manufacture of rayon filament, no branch of the textile industries is dominated by one or a few companies as in iron and steel, aluminum, copper, etc. To be sure there are large companies and mills engaged in the processing of textile fibers, but in no instance do they control more than a small percentage of the industry's capacity. In the cotton textile industry, where operations are conducted on a larger scale than in wool and silk, of the approximately 1,000 mills, 688 have less than 30,000 spindles each, or per mill less than 0.10 per cent of the total spindles in the industry.

The absence of concentration and the presence of many small mills can be explained almost entirely by the technique of manufacture and the nature of the product. Unlike the steel, aluminum, and chemical industries, no process in textile spinning or weaving requires large-scale operations to be conducted economically. Increases in the size of mills do not result in any appreciable manufacturing economies. Textile mills increase in size by adding additional machines rather than by installing larger machines, as do iron, steel, cement, and chemical manufacturers. A large mill differs from small mills only in the number of spindles, looms, and auxiliary equipment, and the labor force is larger in about the same ratio. From a strictly technical standpoint small cotton mills can operate about as efficiently as large mills.[1] The same is true of silk- and rayon-weaving mills. While there are no manufacturing operations that make large-scale production necessary, there are some, such as the blending of raw materials, that can best be carried on in a small mill. There are many grades of raw cotton and wool, and to obtain certain qualities in the fabric and to reduce costs careful attention must be given to the blending of the raw stock. The blending is not subject to scientific control, but depends upon the experience and skill of the mill superintendent. Blending is especially important in the wool industry, and efficiency or lack of it in blending can "make or break" a company.

2. *A Tendency to Move toward Low-wage Areas.*—Although practically all the textile processes are highly mechanized, the operations are of such a nature as to require considerable supervision by labor. Labor costs, therefore, are high. As Table IV, Chap. I, shows, wages represent 25.1 per cent of the value of product in cotton manufacturing; 21.1 per cent in silk; and 19.4 per cent in woven woolen goods. In some instances, depending upon the nature of the product, labor costs represent as much as 67 per cent of the value of product. The importance of labor costs and the severe competition in recent years has placed the textile industries

[1] KENNEDY, S. J., "Profits and Losses in Textiles," p. 185, Harper and Brothers, New York, 1936.

under the pressure of searching for low-cost labor. The search has been facilitated by the highly mechanized process which makes highly skilled labor less important than before and simplifies the training of workers, and by the light nature of the work, which makes possible the employment of women and young workers. According to a recent study, it is estimated that over 50 per cent of all the workers in the world textile industry are women. In the United States they represent 42 per cent of the total, in Great Britain 60 per cent, in Japan 64 per cent, and in Italy 78 per cent. These industries also employ a larger proportion of young workers than do other industries.[1]

In the United States the search for lower labor costs, in addition to stimulating the mechanization of plants, has brought about a relocation of several branches of the industry, and internationally there have occurred during the last two decades important shifts in exports from high-wage to low-wage countries. The shifts in location and the composition of the labor force raise certain social problems to a higher level of importance here than in most industries. Such questions as hours of labor per day and week, night work, and minimum wages, until recently have been the subject of legislation only insofar as they affect women and youths, and variations in legislation between textile manufacturing areas take on added significance in these industries.

The composition of the labor force, together with the fact that such a large proportion of the workers are unskilled or only semiskilled, has a depressing effect upon wage rates and earnings and has made textile manufacturing a low-wage industry. "In general, despite some exceptions, average hourly wage rates are lower for the textile industry than the corresponding national averages for all industries. Both women and men receive less per hour as textile workers than as workers taken as a whole."[2]

3. *Flexibility of Capacity.*—Most of the industries discussed earlier in the book are continuous-process industries; *i.e.*, all processes or at least the key operations must be operated continuously or not at all. A blast furnace, an open-hearth furnace, an aluminum reduction cell, a cement kiln, must operate 24 hours a day and 7 days a week. This is not the case in the textile industries. If the various departments in a textile mill are balanced, all departments in the mill can run 6, 8, 12, or 24 hours per day, depending upon management policies, state legislation, and market conditions. Until the First World War, American textile industries were day industries, but to meet the rush of war orders, most mills increased the number of shifts and operated from 16 to 24 hours per day. When the war ended many mills continued to operate on a multi-

---

[1] World Textile Industry," *op. cit.*, p. 223.
[2] *Ibid.*, p. 351.

ple-shift basis, and today most textile mills in this country operate with two shifts of 40 hours each. Many of the problems that have confronted these industries during the last 15 years are traceable to this practice. The ease with which production can be increased by the addition of another shift of workers makes available, with triggerlike action, productive capacity in excess of the needs of the market, and gives the three-shift mills a competitive advantage over those mills which cannot run night shifts because of legislation that prohibits the employment of women on night work.

Summary.—As was pointed out earlier in the chapter the making of textiles was the first manufacturing process affected by the epoch-making inventions of the industrial revolution. The spinning and weaving processes were mechanized within a period of 50 years and attained a level of technical stability long before many of our present industries were established. It is to be expected, therefore, that the technical progress of the textile industries during the present century could not *parallel* the rapid strides that were taken by the younger industries. Since the invention of the Northrup loom in 1895, the most important development since the introduction of the power loom, more than 100 years earlier, no fundamental changes have taken place. This is not to say that no improvements were made, but to emphasize that they were only refinements of existing processes rather than basic changes. During the last 10 years there has been some speeding up of technical changes in the cotton industry. In the preparatory picking operations a machine has been developed which eliminates several machines and reduces the amount of labor required. Important improvements have also been made in spinning by the development of long-draft spinning, which reduces the number of drawing operations and makes the process shorter and more continuous. Considerable progress has been made in the spooling and warping operations, and the new high-speed looms operate 25 per cent faster than the older automatic looms.

The retardation in technical developments has aggravated the difficulties of the industries. Such improvements as were made were not of sufficient importance to warrant the complete displacement of existing equipment. That is to say, the operating economies of the new machines were not large enough, in the opinion of mill managements, to justify the original cost of new equipment and the cost of discarding the old. The slow rate of obsolescence has permitted the continued use of old machinery, making possible the existence of a dangerous fringe of mills operating old machines assembled at costs of one-tenth or one-twentieth of original values. These mills can almost completely disregard those essential elements of costs (such as depreciation and obsolescence) which must enter into the calculations of a more highly capitalized modern mill.

The technical superiority of the new machinery, relative to total costs, was not great enough to enable modern mills to purge the industry of excess capacity by eliminating their technically less efficient competitors.

Mention has already been made of the tendency of the industry to shift to low-wage areas. This shifting was made easier by the technical maturity of the industry. Textile processes and machinery are so highly standardized and so well known that it is no difficult matter, from a technical standpoint, to enter the industry. Textile manufacturing on an industrial basis began in Great Britain; it soon spread to Europe and North America; more recently it was established in the Far East and Latin America. Indeed, even at this time the world-wide dispersion of textile manufacturing shows no evidence of having reached completion. Today, as before, most industrially undeveloped countries take their first step towards industrialization by entering into the manufacture of textiles. The rise of these new textile-producing countries which formerly were textile importers has seriously disturbed the balance of the world industry. The development of the industry in our own South has similarly upset New England.

Another effect of the slackening up of technological developments, although difficult to measure, is the spirit of conservatism toward technical change it bred in both management and labor. The ease with which profits were made during the period of rapid expansion insulated manufacturers from the rigors of competition and made them reluctant to accept such technical developments as did occur. For example, when the Northrup loom was introduced manufacturers in New England did not give it a warm welcome, and the machinery manufacturers were forced to turn elsewhere for a market. The market they found in the South was not influenced by the conservatism of New England. The combination of cheap labor and a new loom ushered in an era of speculative mill building in the South. The same conservatism was manifested by the industry toward other labor-saving devices and scientific management. It is significant that, despite the age of the industry, the first steps in scientific management and cost accounting were taken not in the textile industries but in the metal and automobile industries.

The early rise of trade unions in the industry also inculcated the same spirit of conservatism and enmeshed them in traditions that were not in harmony with the technical advances. In England, where the unions were much stronger than here, they refused at first to operate the North-rup loom. Later they accepted it, but arbitrarily and unnecessarily limited the number of looms the individual weaver might run. They did this in an effort to maintain a preconceived ratio of employment to production. The attitude of labor unions in certain branches of the American textile industry was not unlike that of the English unions.

The result in both cases was the same.   English mills found it increasingly difficult to compete in the world market against mills of other countries where not only the loom but also the principle of organization it implied were adopted; in the United States the established industry of the North was rapidly forced to give way to the South.

Our discussion of the textile industries so far has been in general terms and may have created an impression of considerable unity among them.   While the basic technology is essentially the same and the fibers interchangeable for some purposes, the unity is more apparent than real. Each fiber has its own qualities and uses and is sensitive to different influences, and each branch of the industry shows structural differences that distinguish it from the others.   To these we shall now turn our attention.

CHAPTER XXII

THE COTTON TEXTILE INDUSTRY

The cotton textile industry is a "sick" industry. The illness is not a phenomenon of the business cycle, for it manifested itself during the generally prosperous decade that preceded the depression of 1930. During that period when industrial profits were large and industrial shares generally reached new highs on the stock market the trend in this industry was against the generally rising tide. Profits were low and for many mills nonexistent; cotton textile shares, especially those of New England mills, sank to very low levels and bankruptcies eliminated many old names from the industry. Hourly wage rates and weekly earnings were lower than in most of our important manufacturing industries, and in a period of relative industrial peace this industry was racked with labor strife. While unemployment for the country as a whole was small, large numbers of cotton textile workers were irregularly employed and in some sections of the ·country were completely stranded. The profit record of the industry since 1926 is shown in Table XLI.

TABLE XLI.—INCOME AND DEFICITS OF COTTON MILLS, 1926–1937
(000 omitted)

Year	Corporations reporting net income			Corporations reporting no net income		
	Number of returns	Gross income	Net income	Number of returns	Gross income	Net deficit
1926	520	$ 826,578	$ 42,778	541	$635,907	$ 73,621
1927	672	1,204,845	102,108	308	196,392	26,266
1928	483	912,355	49,248	501	455,005	38,666
1929	487	914,007	54,567	420	490,356	32,550
1930	200	230,620	9,593	686	782,781	101,100
1931	208	229,858	12,544	637	580,775	76,114
1932	187	182,741	8,273	628	419,307	61,936
1933	488	660,747	49,850	288	193,528	18,022
1934	425	543,538	34,103	481	438,063	25,689
1935	373	435,437	17,743	548	477,067	28,004
1936	541	772,359	46,843	316	211,257	9,340
1937	503	816,076	52,658	358	208,202	12,195

Source: Statistics of Income, Bureau of Internal Revenue.

Unprofitable operations and the accompanying evils were not peculiar to the American industry. In Great Britain the situation was even worse and in other textile manufacturing centers only slightly better.

The difficulties of the industry in this country have not been caused by a shrinkage in the market for cotton textiles or by competition from substitutes. This is not to say that the advent of rayon, for example, has not affected the market for cotton fine goods or that paper has not replaced cotton for certain uses. To be sure in particular markets and for certain purposes cotton has been forced to give way to substitute materials, but the markets lost have been offset by the development of new uses. Bales of raw cotton consumed, as shown in Table XLII, have

TABLE XLII.—COTTON CONSUMPTION IN THE UNITED STATES
(In running bales of 500 pounds)

Year	Bales	Year	Bales
1900	3,873,165	1930	6,105,840
1905	4,621,742	1931	5,262,974
1910	4,621,742	1932	4,866,016
1915	5,597,362	1933	6,137,395
1920	6,419,734	1934	5,700,253
1925	6,193,417	1935	5,360,867
1926	6,455,852	1936	6,351,160
1927	7,189,585	1937	7,950,079
1928	6,834,063	1938	5,747,978
1929	7,091,065	1939	7,253,400
		1940	8,057,648

Source: Bureau of the Census.

substantially increased since the turn of the century and in 1940 reached the all-time high. The chief effect of substitutes on the cotton industry has been on its rate of growth, which has diminished, and on its relative position among the five principal fibers. This is shown for the period 1920–1940 in Table XLIII. It will be noted that while cotton consumption in 1939 was 417 million lb. greater than in 1920 its share of total fiber consumption declined from 88.9 to 79.6 per cent. Rayon, on the other hand, which accounted for only 0.3 per cent in 1920, increased to 10.2 per cent in 1939. Clearly the causes of the chronic difficulties of the industry can not be found in a shrinkage in the size of the market, but must be sought for elsewhere—in the territorial shifts of the industry, its structure, its raw materials, and its fluctuating market.

Territorial Shift.—The first cotton mill in the United States was built in 1790 in Pawtucket, R. I. For the next 20 years progress was very

TABLE XLIII.—ANNUAL FIBER CONSUMPTION IN THE UNITED STATES
(In millions of pounds)

Year	Total, pounds	Cotton, per cent	Wool, per cent	Rayon, per cent	Silk, per cent	Linen, per cent
1920	3,180.3	88.9	9.9	0.3	0.9	
1921	3,001.0	86.5	11.4	0.7	1.4	
1922	3,389.3	85.9	12.0	0.7	1.4	
1923	3,622.7	86.1	11.7	0.9	1.3	No data
1924	3,069.0	85.8	11.2	1.4	1.6	available
1925	3,548.9	86.6	9.9	1.6	1.9	
1926	3,684.0	87.3	9.3	1.6	1.8	
1927	4,113.8	87.2	8.6	2.4	1.8	
1928	3,692.8	86.3	9.0	2.7	2.0	
1929	4,005.5	85.5	9.2	3.3	2.0	
1930	3,103.6	84.1	8.5	3.8	2.5	1.1
1931	3,232.6	82.2	9.6	4.9	2.4	0.9
1932	2,946.9	83.6	7.8	5.3	2.4	0.9
1933	3,678.1	83.0	8.6	5.9	1.6	0.9
1934	3,169.6	83.8	7.3	6.2	1.8	0.9
1935	3,524.7	78.2	11.8	7.3	1.8	0.9
1936	4,292.6	80.8	9.5	7.5	1.4	0.8
1937	4,434.9	82.5	8.6	6.9	1.2	0.8
1938	3,587.9	80.9	7.9	9.1	1.5	0.6
1939	4,558.3	79.6	8.7	10.2	1.0	0.5
1940	3,964.4	80.6	8.4	9.9	0.7	0.4

Source: *Rayon Organon*, February, 1940, p. 31, and February, 1941, p. 35.

slow because of competition from Great Britain, but the stimulus given the industry during the War of 1812 led to a rapid expansion. Protected by the tariff after the war, the industry was able to exploit the growing domestic market and maintain its high rate of expansion. Mills were established in Lowell and Lawrence, Mass., and when they outgrew the water-power facilities there, more were built in Maine, New Hampshire, Connecticut, Rhode Island, New Jersey, and Pennsylvania. The shift to the use of steam power freed the mills from the necessity of locating at sources of water power and gave them greater choice in selecting locations. This was an important factor in the development of Fall River and New Bedford, Mass., which were ideal mill locations because of their damp climate, which facilitated spinning, and their proximity to tidewater for the receipt of coal and raw cotton. By 1870 the number of active spindles in the United States had increased to over 7 million, or more than three times as many as in 1840.

This phenomenal development, as Fig. 59 shows, was confined almost entirely to the North, principally New England. The South's chief interest up to this time was in agriculture. The invention of the cotton gin and the subsequent rapid expansion in the use of cotton made cotton growing so profitable that the South turned her back on almost all other activities and crowned cotton as king. The economic prostration of the South during and after the Civil War and the plight of her poor-white population convinced her leaders that the Southern economy was too unbalanced. After the International Cotton Exposition in Atlanta, Ga., in 1881, planned by Northern manufacturers to interest Southerners in new methods of growing and ginning cotton, the South was convinced that her salvation lay in bringing the cotton mills to the cotton fields.

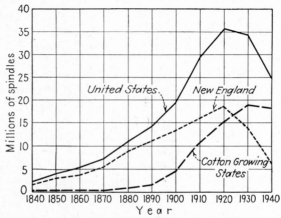

FIG. 59.—Growth of the cotton textile industry, 1840–1940. 1840 to 1900 active spindles. 1910 to 1940 spindles in place. (*Census of Manufacturers.*)

New England was not alarmed at the Southern development. Indeed Northern manufacturers laughed at the idea of the South as a cotton manufacturing center. Where would it obtain the necessary capital, the skilled labor, and the knowledge of spinning and weaving methods? Expansion in the South, however, continued. During the decade 1880–1890, as Fig. 59 shows, active spindles trebled. Capital was raised locally, frequently by popular subscription, and Northern textile machinery manufacturers helped by selling machinery on a long-term credit basis and accepting common stock in part payment. Labor was drawn from the surrounding rural areas and was quickly trained to spin the coarse yarns that were characteristic of early Southern cotton manufacture. The training of workers was facilitated by the perfection of ring spinning, which required less skill than mule spinning.

The rapid expansion of the South finally disturbed the complacency of the New England mills, but they comforted themselves with the thought that the South would not be able to manufacture anything but coarse materials. The introduction of the automatic loom, and the increase in the market, stimulated the further expansion of the industry in both areas. Competition after 1910 became more vigorous, and the future was not too bright. The consequences of the rapid expansion, however, were postponed by the outbreak of the war in 1914. Both sections expanded under the stimulus of war prices and postwar prosperity, and by 1923 New England reached its peak development with about 19 million spindles as compared with 16 million spindles in the cotton-growing states. That year marked the turning point for New England, and by 1926 the South had more spindles.

Consequences of the Southern Expansion.—The increase in spindles that took place during this period was important enough in itself to cause vigorous competition, but the fact that such a rapid expansion occurred in the South aggravated conditions. As was indicated in Chap. XXI,[1] the capacity of most textile industries is very flexible and can be increased by increasing the running time of the machinery. Prior to the first World War the cotton textile industry was primarily a one-shift industry, especially in New England where the bulk of the capacity was concentrated. During the war both areas operated on multiple shifts, and at its conclusion New England returned to single-shift operation, but the South continued with multiple-shift operations. Accordingly, the productive capacity was greater than the number of spindles in place would indicate. The extension of running time per spindle is shown in Table XLIV.

TABLE XLIV.—AVERAGE HOURS OPERATION PER YEAR PER ACTIVE SPINDLE

Year Ending July 31	United States
1923	2,945
1927	3,153
1929	3,286
1933	3,538
1937	4,183
1939	4,149

Source: Bureau of the Census.

Another aggravating factor was the cost advantage enjoyed by the South. Its favorable cost position was due to (1) a large supply of cheap labor, (2) the almost complete absence of restrictive social legislation, (3) more efficient machinery, and (4) lower taxes.

As was pointed out earlier in the chapter, the economy of the South is built on agriculture. As recently as 1930, about 45 per cent of its population lived on farms as compared with 25 per cent in the remainder of the country, and in the same year over 50 per cent of the gainfully

[1] Chap. XXI, p. 307.

employed were engaged in farming, whereas only 20 per cent are so employed in the country as a whole. The heavy concentration on cotton growing, the presence of a decadent tenant system of farming, and the heavy pressure of population on resources make the South a low-income area. It is estimated that the value of farm products per male worker in the South is only about 50 per cent of the value for other agricultural areas. It is from this low-income agricultural labor, drawn from the poor hill country, that the South has recruited its textile labor force. The large supply of labor seeking better employment than the farms could afford and the lack of other industries resulted in the establishment of wage rates substantially below those of the heavily industrialized North. Hourly earnings in New England cotton mills, during the period 1912–1920, were from 28 to 60 per cent in excess of those of Southern cotton mills. After 1920 differences in average hourly earnings between the two areas began to widen, and by 1926, hourly earnings in New England mills were 51.7 per cent in excess of Southern hourly earnings.[1] The trend since 1928 is shown in Table XLV. The differences in average hourly

TABLE XLV.—AVERAGE HOURLY EARNINGS IN NORTHERN AND SOUTHERN COTTON MILLS, 1928 TO JUNE, 1940

Period	Unweighted average			
	North, cents	South, cents	Excess of North over South, cents	Percentage South of North
1928	39.4	27.3	12.1	69.3
1930	39.7	28.1	11.6	70.8
1932	32.3	23.9	8.4	74.0
July, 1933	27.6	20.5	7.1	74.3
August, 1933*	41.1	33.7	7.4	82.0
August, 1934*	42.2	35.6	6.6	84.4
August, 1935	42.2	34.8	7.4	82.5
July, 1936	41.8	34.6	7.2	82.8
July, 1937	50.0	39.7	10.3	79.4
August, 1938	44.6	36.6	8.0	82.0
June, 1940†	47.6	39.3	8.3	82.5

* NRA.
† Wages and Hours Act.
Source: Wages in Cotton Goods Manufacturing, Bureau of Labor Statistics, *Bulletin* 663, 1938, p. 72; and *Monthly Labor Review*.

earnings, it should be pointed out, do not accurately indicate differences in labor costs, because other factors beside the wage rate influence labor costs. For example, it is the practice of many Southern mills, especially those in isolated communities, to provide company houses, schools, water,

[1] *Monthly Labor Review*, May, 1935.

and light at prices lower than could be obtained in the open market, and
to the extent that these costs are borne by the mills they must be regarded
as part of the labor costs. Another factor that must be considered, but
one which is difficult to ascertain, is the efficiency of labor in the two
areas. There can be no doubt that until recently Northern textile
workers were more efficient than those of the South. On the other hand,
the almost complete absence of labor unions in the Southern mills
freed them from any restrictions on machine loads per worker.

Closely connected with the problems of wages is the question of
legislation governing working conditions. For example, no important
Southern textile state has an 8-hour-day, 48-hour-week law for women.

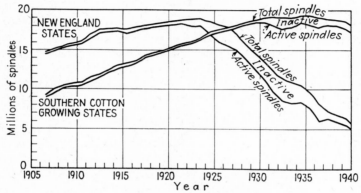

Fig. 60.—Total active and inactive spindle, 1906–1940. New England and cotton
growing states. (*Wages in Cotton Goods Manufacturing, Bureau of Labor Statistics
Bulletin* 633.)

Massachusetts, on the other hand, until 1933 limited women's work to
48 daytime hours per week. This law was recently relaxed, under
pressure of competition, to permit women in the textile industry to work
until 10 P.M. The restrictions upon night work for women put Northern
mills under a competitive disadvantage because night work in all departments was impossible since male wage rates were too high. Restrictions
on the use of young workers are also higher in New England as are other
standards of social legislation, such as workmen's compensation laws.

Since the bulk of Southern spindles came into the industry at a later
date than those of New England they are more efficient. Mention has
already been made of the reluctance with which New England accepted
the automatic loom. As recently as 1929, only 59 per cent of New
England's active plain looms were automatic as against 80 per cent of
the South; in fancy looms only 33 per cent were automatic as against 67
per cent in the South. The greater automaticity of Southern looms
permits the assignment of more looms per worker and thus reduces labor
costs per unit of output.

To encourage the establishment of mills practically all Southern states granted free lands for the construction of mills and relieved them of taxes for a period of years. While taxes represent only a small portion of the cost of manufacture, this nevertheless was an additional advantage.

The existence of excess capacity owing to machinery installations and extension of running time, and the disparity in costs between the two regions, resulted in severe competition and the liquidation, between 1925 and 1939, of almost 13 million spindles, through bankruptcy, scrapping of spindles, and plant abandonment. As Fig. 60 shows, the burden of idle spindles and the contraction in capacity rested more heavily on New England than on the South,[1] and today 73 per cent of the spindles are in the cotton growing states.

International Migrations.—The rise of a new cotton textile producing area was not peculiar to the United States. Similar shifts have occurred on an international basis. For many years the world cotton textile industry was dominated by Great Britain and the United States; in 1913 their combined capacities represented 61 per cent of the world's 144 million spindles. During the next 13 years another 21 million spindles were added to the world total, and while both the United States and Great Britain shared in the expansion, the most rapid rates of growth occurred in other areas of the world. After 1933 total world spindleage declined, but the decline was limited to the older textile-producing countries. The number of spindles in Japan, India, China, and Continental Europe continued to expand at a rapid rate.

The rapid expansion of the industry in new areas had a depressing effect on the older textile countries. On Great Britain the development was especially severe because her industry depends on an international market. The foreign developments were less severe on the United States industry because of the relative unimportance of foreign markets. Beginning in 1930, however, Japanese cotton textile exports to this country began to make themselves felt, and during the next several years increased rapidly. In 1936 imports from Japan reached such a high figure for certain types of cotton cloth that the United States industry sent a mission to Japan to persuade Japanese mills to limit their exports to this country to the average of 1935 and 1936. Under the agreement finally negotiated the Japanese agreed to limit their 1937 exports to 155 million sq. yd. and 1938 exports to 100 million sq. yd.

With these developments as a background, let us turn our attention to the structure of the industry and to other aspects of its operations.

---

[1] In the period 1923–1933 the number of mills in Massachusetts declined from 245 to 137; in Rhode Island from 153 to 93; in Connecticut from 69 to 35; and for all New England from 506 to 301. (Census of Manufactures.)

Structure of the Industry.—As was shown in Table XLIII, cotton is the most important fiber used in textile manufacturing, accounting for approximately 80 per cent of the combined consumption of cotton, wool, silk, and rayon. If jute consumption is included, cotton's share of the total represents about 70 per cent. Cotton textile manufacturing is not only the largest industry in the textile group, it is one of the largest American manufacturing industries. It has more than 1,000 mills, exclusive of finishing plants, employs in excess of 400,000 workers, and has a capitalization of about 1,500 million dollars. The cotton textile industry is not a homogeneous industry, but a group of related industries.

The processing of raw cotton involves spinning, weaving, and finishing. These processes have been discussed in Chap. XXI. Not all mills in the industry perform all three processes. Of the more than 1,000 mills, 300 are specialized spinning mills that spin yarn for the use of others, such as knitters, small weaving mills, and thread, twine, and mop manufacturers. About 85 per cent of these mills are located in the South and are quite small, over 200 of them having less than 20,000 spindles each, and all but a few of the remainder are in New England. There are about 140 mills with about 12,500 looms that are exclusively specialized weaving mills, which buy their yarn from others. These mills, too, are quite small, averaging less than 100 looms per mill. It is in this branch of the industry that areas other than New England and the cotton-growing states play an important part; for example, Pennsylvania has more mills of this type than New England and the South combined. These mills manufacture tapestry, towel, damask, drapery, upholstery, and specialty fabrics. The most important mills in the industry, measured either by the number of mills or by spindles, are the combined spinning and weaving mills, which number about 600 and have about 24 million spindles and almost 500,000 looms. These mills are much larger than either of the above types, and are concentrated almost entirely in two areas of the country—the cotton-growing states and New England. Some of these mills, about 125 in number, have finishing plants, but the majority of them sell their output in an unfinished state, known as "gray" goods, or have it finished for their account by independent finishers on a contract basis.

These mills, as a group, manufacture a wide variety of woven fabrics such as print cloth, sheetings, fine carded and combed fabrics, colored yarn fabrics, towels, ducks, napped fabrics, etc. Individual mills do not manufacture all these products but specialize on one or a few.

Marketing.—Some cloth, especially that intended for industrial uses, is sold directly by the mills to the industrial consumer. The major part of the output, however, is sold through selling houses or cloth brokers. The selling house may be either a mill-owned selling house, a mill-owning selling house, or an old-line commission house. The mill-owned selling house is a subsidiary of the mill and really acts as the sales department of the mill. It may, and frequently does, operate under a different corporate name, and may act as the sales representative of other mills. The mill-owning selling house owns, in whole or in part, one or more cloth mills. The old-line commission house is an independent house that acts as exclusive agent for a number of mills, ranging from 5 to 75, and receives for its services a commission of from 2 to 5 per cent, depending upon the type of cloth sold and the services rendered. While there may be no direct financial relations between the mill and the selling house, the business relations are frequently as close as they would be under common ownership. They render financial assistance to the mills by making advances on shipments, on goods in process, or on accounts receivable, and frequently guarantee sales accounts. Some also advise mills on market trends in cloth construction and in some instances supervise the allocation of a mill's looms for specific orders.

The cloth broker acts as an intermediary between the sellers on the one hand, either mills or selling agents, and, on the other hand, the converters and sometimes industrial purchasers. The broker is very important in the marketing of fancy weaves and fine gray goods, and is relied upon by converters to place them in contact with mills that produce the particular type of cloth desired.

The Converter.—As was previously indicated, a very substantial percentage of the cloth output is sold by the mills as "gray" goods, it being estimated that only 13 per cent of the total, consisting of colored yarn fabrics, is styled by the mills. An additional 9 per cent, consisting of sheet and pillow-case fabrics, towel fabrics, and surgical gauze, is finished by the mills or for their account. About 30 per cent goes directly into industrial use as gray goods without any finishing. The remainder, 48 per cent, must be styled or finished by other interests. The principal factor to perform this function is the converter. He buys the gray goods either directly from the mills or through a selling house or broker and has them styled or finished, either in his own or an independent finishing plant, in accordance with his own designs. The converter generally specializes on one line of goods to the exclusion of all others, because he is in a hazardous position owing to rapid changes in demand and must be quick to sense changes in consumer tastes. The finished cloth is sold by the converter to cutters-up, wholesalers, department stores, mail-order houses, etc.

Problems Arising from the Industry's Structure, Raw Materials and Products.—The difficulties that arise from the excess capacity are aggravated by other aspects of the industry—its structure, raw materials, and products.

As has been indicated earlier in the chapter, the industry is very complex and highly decentralized in control. Of the more than 1,000 mills, 688 have less than 30,000 spindles, or per mill less than 0.10 per cent of the total spindles in the industry. The 11 largest mills in the industry, each with 200,000 spindles or over, control less than 14 per cent of the total spindles.

Although the majority of the mills are combined spinning and weaving mills, for most of these mills there is a sharp separation between these functions and the finishing and marketing functions.

The small degree of forward integration makes the mills primarily sellers of gray goods with little, and frequently no, control over the styling of their product. As sellers of more or less standardized and unbranded gray goods, competition between the mills resolves itself almost entirely into price competition. A given construction of gray cloth at any moment sells at a standardized price, and the shading of the price by as little as a fraction of a cent per yard will divert an order from one mill to another. This intensity of competition prevails in practically all branches of the industry, because the equipment of the mill can readily be shifted from the production of one type of cloth to another. Accordingly, in the long run one line of production cannot be more profitable than other lines because capacity will be shifted from the low-profit to the high-profit lines.

The natural price competition that arises from the sale of a standardized, unbranded product, it is claimed, is further aggravated by the fact that so much of the industry's output is sold through selling houses. Most of the selling agents in the industry, especially the independent houses, have little or no investment in the industry, and their incomes depend on the commissions they receive for the goods sold. If the relations between the mills and the selling house are not close, as is sometimes the case, the selling house has little appreciation of the mills' costs. To obtain a quick turnover in its volume of sales, it is charged, the house induces the mill to make price concessions to buyers. A concession of one-fourth cent per yard might reduce the agent's commission by about 3 per cent, but it might entirely wipe out the normal mill profit.

The increasing importance of style in the cotton industry is also an unstabilizing factor. As has been previously stated, cotton cloth can be styled either by the mill or after it leaves the mill. In the former case, the mill must assume all the hazards incident to marketing a styled fabric,[1] but it also has an opportunity to make a profit on its styling. The gray-goods mill makes no profits as a result of style changes, but it cannot avoid the incidence of style changes. The converter hesitates

[1] See Chap. XX, p. 292.

to place orders for gray goods far ahead of his immediate needs because of his uncertainty concerning style and his unwillingness to assume the inventory risks arising from changes in the price of raw cotton. Accordingly, he delays his purchases until the last possible moment and then insists on quick deliveries, and is in a position to impose his wishes upon the mills because of the intensity of competition arising from the idle capacity.

The absence of integration and the intricate marketing structure through which cotton goods must pass as they go from the mills to the consumers have deprived the mills of much information necessary for formulating production policies. It is difficult for them to ascertain whether their goods are moving into consumption or are piling up at the several stages of the marketing process. This is especially true during a period of improving business. Converters, cutters-up, and retailers in an effort to cash in on the anticipated rise in prices increase their commitments and take a speculative position, and the mills increase production quickly and manufacture to inventory. When large inventories are accumulated buying dries up until they are liquidated.

Another unstabilizing factor in this industry was referred to in Chap. XX[1]—the fluctuations in the price of raw cotton. Raw material costs represent a large percentage of the total manufacturing cost, ranging from 33 to 70 per cent, depending upon the type of product, and changes in raw cotton prices are immediately reflected in finished goods prices. Since most manufacturers make their commitments for raw cotton early in the market season to assure themselves of a supply of the particular quality they require, and since all of them must carry some inventories of finished goods and goods in process, they are always confronted with the risks of changing inventory values.

Theoretically, the cotton mills can protect themselves from losses arising from fluctuations in the price of raw cotton by hedging their commitments on the futures market. For example, a manufacturer purchases raw cotton at 15 cents a pound, which, when manufactured into cloth, he hopes to sell at 40 cents a pound—making a profit of 2 cents a pound. However, when he does obtain an order for cloth, the price of raw cotton may have declined to 13 cents a pound. This decline would be reflected in a corresponding drop in the price of cloth. In order to ensure a profit, when the manufacturer buys raw cotton at 15 cents a pound, he immediately sells a future for an equal amount of cotton at, let us say, 17 cents a pound. Hence, if the price of raw cotton declines to 13 cents, he will not make his anticipated profit of 2 cents on the manufactured cloth, but he will be compensated by the purchase of a future. For, when the price of raw cotton declines

[1] See p. 289.

2 cents a pound, the price of futures declines in the same amount. Therefore, the manufacturer can now buy a future at 15 cents a pound, which is 2 cents less than the price for which he sold it.

Hedging, however, does not offer as complete insurance as is frequently assumed. Several factors operate to limit its effectiveness, among the most important of which are the following.

1. The hedging contract offers protection against fluctuations in the price of the standard basis grade of cotton, but the mill may require a different grade and staple. The grade and staple of cotton depend upon weather conditions, with the result that supply of each grade and staple varies each season. Changes in consumer demand, on the other hand, determine the demand for each grade and staple. In short, instead of having one price for cotton there are as many prices as there are grades and staples. Since the prices of the various grades and staples are influenced by different supply and demand factors, they do not necessarily move in the same direction or in the same ratio.

2. The differential between spot and futures prices is not constant, which is necessary for complete insurance, and losses on the one will not necessarily be offset by equal gains on the other.

3. The spread between spot cotton prices and cloth prices is also not constant, but is often subject to wide variations.

The Future of the Industry.—The future of the cotton textile industry is at best uncertain. Several of the factors that have made for instability and unprofitable operations in the past have lost much of their force. The liquidation of more than 14 million spindles, through bankruptcy and scrapping, has eliminated much of the burden of idle machinery that has harassed the industry during the last 15 years, and the recent quickening of obsolescence will undoubtedly cause a further contraction in spindles. Both of these developments are constructive because they will tend to reestablish equilibrium in the industry. How effective they will prove to be in stabilizing the industry is difficult to say, because the industry can easily change from a two-shift to a three-shift basis of operation.

The interregional competition, based primarily on differences in wage rates, will also be less important in the future now that wage rates are being stabilized through the operation of the Fair Labor Standards Act,[1] and by the gradual unionization of Southern labor.

The chief threats to the future of the industry arise from governmental control of raw cotton prices and the increasing competition from substitute materials. The great versatility of cotton, the many and

---

[1] Beginning in October, 1939, minimum wage rates for the cotton textile industry were fixed at 32.5 cents per hour. In 1941, the rate was increased to 37.5 cents per hour, and on April 20, 1942 to 40 cents per hour.

varied uses to which it is put, make it extremely vulnerable to competition from substitutes. The substitutes are not limited to textile fibers such as rayon, wool, silk, or jute. In addition to these fibers, cotton products, for certain purposes, must meet competitively such nontextile materials as paper, rubber, and leather. So far the loss of markets to these materials has been offset by gains elsewhere, but the effect of all has been to retard the growth of the industry. The most dangerous competition to the industry arises not from alternative textile materials, such as rayon, because the cotton mills with some adjustments to their equipment can process them. Indeed, many cotton mills have already shifted to the processing of rayon, both in New England and in the cotton-growing states. More dangerous is the competition from nontextile materials such as paper, which has made serious inroads in the cotton textile markets for bagging, twine, towels, window shades, napkins, etc.

Efforts on the part of the government to raise the income of cotton growers by raising the price of cotton will weaken the competitive position of cotton textiles, especially for industrial uses where competition from substitute materials is strongest.

CHAPTER XXIII

THE WOOL MANUFACTURING INDUSTRY

The wool manufacturing industry occupies a much more restricted area in the field of textiles than cotton manufacturing. The relative importance of these two industries is determined in general by fiber qualities. Cotton is a general-purpose fiber, is relatively cheap, and has many uses. Wool, on the other hand, is a special-purpose fiber and is more costly. It possesses certain properties in an unusual degree, and these properties give wool unusual utility for certain purposes. It is elastic, is a poor conductor of heat, and felts easily, qualities which make it desirable for certain types of apparel, rugs, upholstery, and household goods. The combined market for these products, however, is smaller than the market for cotton products.

However different its raw materials and products are from those of the cotton textile industry, from an economic standpoint the wool manufacturing industry has one thing in common with the former: it is a sick industry. During the 11-year period beginning in 1927, in only four

TABLE XLVI.—INCOME AND DEFICITS OF WOOLEN AND WORSTED MILLS, 1927–1937
(000 omitted)

	Corporations reporting net income			Corporations reporting no net income		
Year	Number of returns	Gross income	Net income	Number of returns	Gross income	Net deficit
1927	305	$502,062	$24,788	266	$185,148	$ 16,058
1928	291	395,375	18,719	295	297,876	19,799
1929	246	367,143	14,628	317	307,190	24,922
1930	168	113,953	5,148	380	346,952	40,475
1931	172	139,877	6,542	368	291,405	37,785
1932	78	43,409	2,069	453	250,360	39,260
1933	286	317,811	26,315	242	73,239	6,891
1934	193	158,807	7,987	370	218,690	20,156
1935	312	454,422	25,009	240	98,010	5,512
1936	326	527,749	46,843	220	80,038	3,148
1937	211	326,682	9,147	337	273,911	9,329
	Total net income $187,195			Total net deficit $223,335		

Source: "Statistics of Income," Bureau of Internal Revenue.

325

years did more than one-half the mills make a profit, and for the entire period the industry sustained a loss of about 36 million dollars. The causes of this poor record are several in number and will be better understood after an analysis of the industry's structure, history, and problems. To these we shall now direct our attention.

Definition.—Wool manufacturing can be defined to include all those industries for which wool is the chief raw material. This includes the woolen and worsted industry, the felt goods, carpet and rugs, and felt hat industries, as well as the allied service industries such as job dyeing and finishing, wool scouring, wool pulling,[1] and the manufacture of reworked wool. We shall not use this broad definition, but shall confine our discussion to what is termed the "woolen and worsted industry" by the Census of Manufactures. This consists of those mills which comb tops, spin weaving and knitting yarns for sale, and weave apparel fabrics, blankets, and automobile upholstery cloth. This restricted definition is justified because the other industries, such as rugs and carpets, require a different raw material and equipment and are not considered a part of the industry by the trade.

Development of the Industry.—The wool manufacturing industry both here and abroad is an older industry than the cotton manufacturing industry, which was a product of the industrial revolution. The manufacture and consumption of cotton on a large scale depended upon the development of cotton ginning machinery, and until a cheap method of separating the fiber from the seed was invented, cotton was in the luxury class with silk. Since sheep raising had been for centuries a part of general farming in many parts of the world, the use of wool as a textile fiber antedates cotton.

The history of wool manufacturing in this country can be divided into the following periods.

1. *Household Stage, up to* 1790.—During this period wool was converted into yarn and cloth by means of spinning wheels and handlooms operated within the household. The first process to be centralized in separate establishments was fulling[2] which required considerable skill as well as mechanical power.

2. *Establishment of Factories,* 1790–1830.—The first factory in which wool was spun by power machinery was established in 1788. From that time until the close of the period the industry grew irregularly with intervals of acceleration and retardation coming as a result of wars that

---

[1] Wool pulling is the removal of wool from the skin of a slaughtered sheep's pelt by sweating or use of a depilatory.

[2] Fulling is a finishing operation consisting of soaking the cloth in a specially prepared soap and water solution and then running it through rollers. It shrinks the cloth and gives it more body.

were then in progress. During this period the industry was hampered by the absence of good raw materials, since the sheep raised in America yielded a short, coarse fiber fit only for coarser wool products.

3. *Spread of the Industry*, 1830–1870.—In 1828 substantial tariff protection was afforded the industry, and it grew behind this wall until the outbreak of the Civil War when there were almost 1,300 plants in the country. During the Civil War and the years immediately following there was a further increase and by 1870 the number reached the record high of almost 2,000. The mills were scattered through 42

PLATE 55.—Combing machine which separates the tops (long fibers) from the noils (short fibers). (*Reproduced by permission of the Philadelphia Commercial Museum.*)

states, but about 80 per cent of them were in Massachusetts, Connecticut, Vermont, New York, and Pennsylvania. During this period there occurred a development that was later to prove of the utmost significance to the plants that were then expanding with little competition. This was the mechanization of the combing operation which hitherto had been performed by hand and therefore had been so costly as to make prohibitive the consumption of worsteds. In fact, only three worsted mills were reported in the Census of 1860.

4. *The Rise of the Worsted Industry*, 1870–1890.—In addition to the mechanical comb, the worsted industry was stimulated by the upbreeding of sheep which yielded long-fiber wool of the combing variety and by tariff legislation which encouraged the importation of wools suitable for combing. During this period foreign capital entered the industry and

established mills such as Botany, Forstmann, New Jersey Worsted, and the Rhode Island group of mills spinning on the French system.[1] The effect on the woolen branch of the growth of worsteds is shown in Fig. 61. Hundreds of small mills closed down, and many more were consolidated. From the standpoint of yards produced the trend was not as disastrous, for the total market was expanding and woolens haltingly held their own, with worsteds absorbing the increase.

5. *Period of General Prosperity, 1900–1919.*—This period was characterized by great activity and prosperity for practically the entire industry.

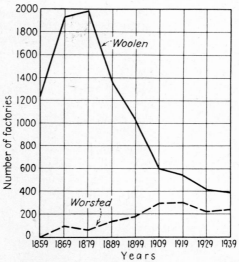

Fig. 61.—The number of spinning and weaving factories in the woolen and worsted divisions.
(*Census of Manufacturers.*)

Production of worsteds increased without interruption until 1909; woolen production expanded until 1904, receded until 1914, and then continued to expand. In addition to the stimulus given by the First World War the industry made great profits as a result of the great increase in the price of raw and finished wool.

6. *Period of Readjustment, 1920 to Date.*—The trends in production, markets, and prices that make for general prosperity in the preceding period reversed themselves in this period. Wool goods lost their popularity, raw material and finished wool prices fell steadily, and great inventory losses were sustained. Productive capacity, as a result of the previous expansion and the introduction of the automatic loom, was far in excess of the needs of the shrinking market, and painful readjustments had to be made.

[1] The French system is the application of the mule type of spinning to worsteds.

Structure of the Industry.—The woolen and worsted industry comprises 620 spinning and weaving plants of which, as Table XLVII shows, 373 are woolen plants and the remainder, 247, worsted mills. Measured by number of workers, value added and value of product, the woolen branch is outranked by the worsted division.

TABLE XLVII.—THE WOOLEN AND WORSTED INDUSTRY, 1937

	Woolen	Worsted	Total
Number of plants...............	373	247	620
Number of workers.............	64,680	87,530	152,210
Value added....................	$120,658,470	$155,375,000	$276,033,470
Value of product................	$292,336,200	$498,582,629	$790,918,829

Source: Census of Manufactures, 1937.

While wool and worsteds are generally spoken of together, they represent two distinct branches. They use different raw materials, employ different processes, and produce distinctive yarns and fabrics.

The worsted industry uses long fibers combed from virgin wools, wools that have not been previously processed. In the combing process, in which the short fibers or "noils" are eliminated, the long fibers are made to lie parallel to each other, so they may be tightly spun. The fabrics, as a result, are closely woven and have a smooth appearance, and the pattern of the weave is easily discernible.

Woolens, on the other hand, are made from short-fiber wools, or from noils, and also, from reworked wools, frequently referred to as "shoddy." Unlike the straightened fibers in worsteds, the fibers are more or less crossed and intermixed, are less tightly spun, and the fabrics, for the most part, are loosely woven and rough surfaced.

The processing of woolens involves fewer operations than worsteds. Intermediate drawing operations[1] that are important in worsteds are eliminated in woolens. Until recently, the spinning of woolens was done on the mule[2] which was better adapted to the short fibers, but in recent years in an effort to reduce costs there has been a gradual shift to frame spinning.

The difference in the number of operations makes it possible to operate woolen mills on a smaller scale than worsteds. Based on the 1937 Census, the woolen mills employed, on an average, 186 workers per mill and had a value of product of about $783,000; the worsted mills, on the other hand, averaged 400 workers per mill and produced an average of 2 million dollars' worth of products per plant.

[1] See Chap. XXI, p. 299.
[2] *Ibid.*, p. 301.

Another factor that makes for smaller scale operation in woolens is the importance of blending, *i.e.*, the mixing of various grades of virgin and reworked wools, a process which must be closely supervised. Because there is less opportunity in worsteds to manipulate fibers, since only top can be used, blending is of less importance. A third factor, less true today than formerly, is the fact that woolen mills produced more novelty fabrics while worsted mills tend to longer runs of particular constructions.

The difference in scale between the two branches can also be indicated by the number of looms in the mills. Forty-three per cent of the integrated woolen mills have less than 50 looms, and 52 per cent have between 50 and 100 looms. In the worsted division 56 per cent have from 50 to 200 looms and about 40 per cent have from 200 to 1,000 looms.

Most of the mills in both branches are completely integrated. However, there are a few small specialized weaving mills that manufacture high-style fabrics and some specialized worsted yarn mills that produce yarn for sale chiefly to knitting mills and small weaving mills. It is especially important for woolen mills to be integrated, despite the variety of yarns required for the manufacture of many patterns, because woolen fabrics are really styled on the mixing floor prior to carding, for it is the fibers used and their blending which are most important in determining both the character and the price of the finished fabric.[1]

The completely integrated character of the worsted branch has, in recent years, begun to change. An increasing number of mills are eliminating the process of top making and are looking to independent top makers as their sources of supply. Few of the top makers have combing mills of their own; the majority have the wool combed at a fixed price by worsted mills known as "commission combers," that formerly combed their own top. There are approximately 25 top makers[2] in the United States, located chiefly around Boston, and in 1937 they combed 47 per cent of all tops made in the United States. The reasons for the rise of the independent top makers will be discussed in a later section.

Finishing.—Not only are most mills in the wool industry completely integrated with respect to the preparatory processes and the spinning and weaving operations, but practically all of them also do their own finishing. There are only four job printers of wool fabrics and 53 plants engaged exclusively in finishing wool fabrics. Unlike cotton, wool fabrics are styled in the weaving mill rather than after they leave the mill.

[1] Industrial Research Department, Wharton School of Finance and Commerce, "Vertical Integration in the Textile Industries," p. 82.

[2] Garside, A., "Wool and the Wool Trade," p. 73, Frederick A. Stokes Company, Inc., New York, 1939.

Marketing.—The high degree of integration in the woolen and worsted industry makes the marketing structure much less complex than that of the cotton industry. The fact that woolens and worsteds are styled in the weaving mill or in the manufacturer's own finishing department eliminates the need of a converter. This facilitates direct selling by the mills, and the major part of all woven goods is sold directly to the cutters-up. Few, if any, of the old-time commission selling houses are now left in the wool fabric market, especially in men's wear where style is of less importance.

Wool and Cotton Manufacturing Contrasted.—The above description of the wool industry reveals several significant contrasts with the cotton textile industry.

1. *Woolen and Worsted Manufacturing on a Smaller Scale.*—The reasons for this have been previously indicated, but may be summarized here. First, blending and manipulation of fibers is much more important in the wool industry and must be closely supervised. Second, since woolen and worsted fabrics are styled earlier in the process than in cotton manufacturing, the incidence of style is greater in the wool industry and it therefore requires greater flexibility. Third, the wool industry does not have as large a volume of staples as cotton, and cannot have as long runs as the latter.

This does not imply that there are no large mills in the wool industry, for such is not the case. However, large companies such as the American Woolen Company, with its many mills in New England, Arlington Mills, in Lawrence, Mass., and Botany Worsted Mills, in Passaic, N. J., are not typical of the industry.

2. *Less Intricate Marketing Structure in Wool.*—Since woolens and worsteds are styled by the mill, there is no gray-goods market. The absence of such a market makes unnecessary the converter, reduces the number of intermediaries between the mills and their customers, and has simplified the marketing structure.

3. *Greater Geographical Concentration in Wool.*—Since its establishment the wool industry has been heavily concentrated in New England, New York, Pennsylvania, and New Jersey. While there is some wool manufacturing in other states it is relatively insignificant. Of the 620 mills in the industry, less than one-sixth are located in states other than those listed above, and of this number only a few are located in the South. The wool industry, especially the worsted branch, has not, however, been immune to migration. Since 1919 the number of worsted spindles has declined in Pennsylvania, New Jersey, and Massachusetts and increased in Rhode Island and other New England states.[1]

[1] VON BERGEN, W., and H. MAUERSBERGER, "The American Wool Handbook, 1938," The American Wool Handbook Company, New York, p. 44.

Unstable Character of the Wool Industry.—Wool manufacturing is traditionally a speculative industry. The basis of its speculative nature has been its raw material, which varies greatly in quality and in price. In recent years developments in styling, in markets, and in utilization of productive capacity have further increased the speculative nature of the industry.

The Raw Material.—Wool is produced in every state of this country, but the most important sources are Texas, California, the so-called "territory states" (Wyoming, Montana, Utah, Idaho, Oregon, New Mexico, and Colorado), and the so-called "fleece states" (Ohio, Iowa, South Dakota, Michigan, Missouri, and Minnesota). In the territory states growers maintain large flocks of sheep and make sheep growing their chief occupation. In the fleece states growers maintain only small flocks, of the so-called mutton type, and raise sheep incidentally to general farming. Territory wool represents about 42 per cent of total United States production, fleece wool about 30 per cent, Texas 21 per cent, and California 7 per cent.[1]

Formerly the United States was obliged to import a substantial part of its wool supply, but in recent years, as a result of tariff protection, the domestic growers have met about 85 per cent of our requirements for apparel wools. For carpet wools we depend entirely on foreign sources.

TABLE XLVIII.—APPROXIMATE SHRINKAGE AND YIELD OF DOMESTIC WOOL

Grade	Shrinkage, per cent	Yield, per cent
Fine	64	36
½ blood	60	40
⅜ blood	54	46
¼ blood	49	51
Low ¼ blood	44	56
Common	40	60

Source: Adapted from GARSIDE, *op. cit.*, p. 26.

The properties of wool that determine its value for manufacturing are fineness, length of staple, strength, elasticity, color, luster, and softness. These properties vary considerably depending upon the breed of sheep, the area in which the sheep are raised, and weather conditions during the growing season. Even the individual fleeces when sorted (pulled apart) yield fibers of varying qualities. Accordingly, while there has been some grading of the fleeces, by the time the wool dealers in Boston and Philadelphia offer them for sale, the mill buyer must exercise great caution in judging qualities of the wool.

[1] GARSIDE, *op. cit.*, p. 14.

The most important property he must judge is its shrinkage. Wool is a very absorbent fiber and, in addition to the natural grease which is always present, it contains dirt, sand, burrs, and other foreign matter. Table XLVIII shows the shrinkage for several grades of wool. If the buyer underestimates the shrinkage his purchase will yield him less scoured wool than he expected and his costs per pound will be correspondingly higher. Since wool is a high-cost fiber, such mistakes can be very costly.

Another hazard associated with the raw material arises from the wide fluctuation in prices. This is shown in Fig. 62.

Fig. 62.—Average yearly price of selected domestic wools in Boston, 1919–1939. (*National Association of Wool Manufacturers, Bulletin, Vol.* LXIX.)

The possibility of inventory losses, therefore, is always great,[1] especially for large mills such as American Woolen, Botany, and Arlington. Such mills find it difficult to operate on a hand-to-mouth basis, because their raw material requirements are large and it may be difficult for them to acquire particular grades of wool in the necessary amounts on short notice.

The losses arising from fluctuation in raw-wool prices are not confined to inventories of raw wool and unsold goods in process, but extend frequently to unfilled orders, because wide movements in wool prices tend to demoralize the market. During periods of rising prices, clothing manufacturers place heavy orders for fabrics, and when prices weaken or break, as for example in 1937, cutters frequently cancel their orders, leaving the mills with heavy inventories of raw wool and finished fabrics.[2]

Until recently the mills had no protection against price fluctuations, because there was no organized futures market on which they could

[1] See Chap. XX, p. 290.
[2] Botany Worsted Mills, *Annual Report,* 1937.

hedge their commitments. In 1931 trading in wool-top futures was inaugurated by the wool associates of the New York Cotton Exchange. Opinion in the industry concerning the extent of protection offered by hedging is divided. Critics of the practice point out that wool tops represent an advanced stage of processing and, therefore, cannot accurately reflect changes in raw-wool prices.[1] Others object that trading is too narrow and, therefore, that futures prices fluctuate more widely than in the spot market.[2]

Another reason for the objection of the mills to hedging is the tradition of speculation in the industry. Throughout their history the mills have always been confronted with the hazard of raw material price changes, and in recent years, when competition was so keen that manufacturing profits, if any, were very small, appreciation in inventory values was often the only source of profits. Despite the criticism mill membership in the exchange has steadily increased, and from 1931 to 1938 trading in wool-top futures increased from 5 million to 75 million pounds. The latter amount, on a raw-wool equivalent basis, was equal to about 68 per cent of the 1938 domestic wool clip.

The rise of the independent top maker, previously mentioned, has a tendency to lower the price risks that must be assumed by the mills. Since the raw material is purchased in a semiprocessed rather than in a raw state, the mills' manufacturing cycle is shortened and their inventory risks are decreased. This is not the only reason for the increasing importance of the top maker. Others may be summarized as follows:

1. The large volume of business done by the top maker and his practice of hedging permits him to do business on a very narrow margin of profit.

2. The large volume of wool handled by the top maker enables him to do a better job of blending and to produce a highly uniform quality of top.

3. The worsted mill can buy tops to rigid specifications.

4. The mills are relieved of the task of disposing of noils, the short-staple fibers produced as a by-product of top manufacturing.

Another problem that arises from the raw material, one which complicates the competitive situation, is the practice of blending reworked wool and other cheap fibers with virgin wools and selling the fabric as an all-virgin-wool product. This practice, it is claimed, is the result of pressure from the clothing manufacturers who desire cheaper fabrics. Wool growers for a long time demanded legislation that would compel manufacturers to disclose the raw material content of their fabrics. Wool

---

[1] In 1941 futures trading in raw wool was inaugurated.

[2] SHOOK, R. C., Futures Could Be More Useful, *Daily News Record*, Wool Survey, Apr. 4, 1940, p. 12.

manufacturers indicated a willingness to state the rayon content, but opposed all legislation that would force them to disclose the amount of reworked wool. Their chief argument against such legislation was that it would create the false impression that virgin wool as such is superior to all types of reworked wool regardless of the use to which it is put, and that it would be impossible to enforce such legislation, since present laboratory tests cannot easily distinguish between virgin and reworked wools. Despite the objections of the manufacturers, the Wool Labeling Act was passed in 1941. This act requires all wool products to be labeled indicating the percentages of wool, reprocessed wool, reused wool, and other fibers if they constitute 5 per cent or more of the weight of the fabric.

Problems Arising from the Market.—From 1889 to 1909 the production of wool piece goods almost doubled, and per capita adult consumption increased from 5.7 sq. yd. to 7 sq. yd. Excluding the war period, the subsequent trend was downward, and by 1929 per capita adult consumption was less than 4 sq. yd. The decline was especially marked in women's wear.

The decline, especially in women's wear, was not due to a shrinkage in the demand for clothing. The decrease can be explained only by a shift from wool to other fabrics. The shift is due to a number of factors but chiefly to general changes in living habits occasioned by the advent of the closed automobile, shifts to apartment dwelling, central heating, greater participation of women in athletics, and changed ideas as to bodily hygiene. All these factors contributed to shift the demand from wool goods to lighter weight fabrics. The wool industry either did not recognize the shift or failed to appreciate its significance. It took the women's wear mills as a whole about 10 years to learn to make sheer wool dress fabrics. In the meantime, other textile fabrics, especially rayon, became increasingly popular, and at the same time some of them, such as silk and rayon, became much cheaper. After considerable experimentation the wool industry succeeded in manufacturing lighter and more highly styled fabrics. Improvements in the processing of wool and the increased use of rayon staple hold out hopes of further progress along these lines.

The short-run style changes have also increased the problems of the industry. As Table XLIX shows, of the total yardage produced by the industry, more than 80 per cent is for apparel purposes and subject to style changes. The increasing importance of style in such a large part of the industry's production makes the risk of mill operation quite high, especially because the design is usually woven into the fabric. This requires changes in the color and construction of the yarn and cloth and frequently in the grade of wool used. These changes require adjust-

TABLE XLIX.—PRODUCTION OF WOOLEN AND WORSTED FABRICS, 1939

Type	Quantity, square yards (000,000 omitted)	Value (000,000 omitted)
Woven goods, total....................	568	$476
Apparel fabrics, total.................	482	386
Men's suitings, pantings, and coatings..	225	196
Women's coatings, suitings, and dress...	160	122
Other apparel.......................	97	68
Nonapparel fabrics...................	46	50
Auto cloths.......................	34	37
Other upholstery and drapery fabric....	8	9
Other nonapparel...................	4	4
Blankets, etc.......................	39	25
All other...........................	...	15

Source: Census of Manufactures.

ments in equipment and are particularly difficult for the large mills which were built when style was less important and when the bulk of the production, especially in men's wear, was in staples such as serge.

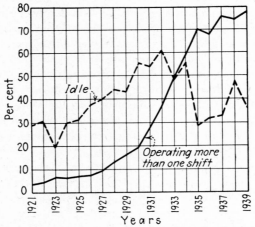

FIG. 63.—Percentage of broad looms idle and percentage of active broad looms operating on more than one shift. (*Adapted from National Association of Wool Manufacturers, Bulletin, Vol. LXIX; and United States Bureau of the Census.*)

Idle Capacity.—During the First World War activity in the industry was maintained at a high level. Mill activity was continued for some years after the war when the millions of demobilized soldiers had to be outfitted in civilian clothes. The optimism that prevailed in the industry during this period resulted in the installation of a considerable amount of additional capacity. When the decline in activity occurred, competition became very severe and some mills, in an effort to reduce costs, resorted to a familiar practice in the textile industry—the introduction of multiple shifts. As demand and prices continued to decline, more and more mills felt it necessary to calculate costs on the basis of multiple shift operation. The extent to which the practice was adopted is shown in Fig. 63.

While the resulting severe competition eliminated 17,000 looms from the industry between 1926 and 1931 alone, the equivalent of more than 5,000 looms were added through double-shift operation during the same period. Another development that reduced the effects of the liquidation of looms was the increase in the number of automatic looms, which added greatly to the productivity of the mills.

Future.—It appears that the future of the wool industry, like that of the cotton industry, depends primarily on the liquidation of more idle capacity. Until that is accomplished the industry will continue to produce for a buyers' market, and chaotic market conditions will continue to plague the industry.

So far the industry has not experienced a substantial migration of mills to the South; to date, such migration as has occurred has been confined primarily to movements within the North. Whether this will continue to be the case in the future is an open question. If the industry becomes more important in the South, it is unlikely that its growth there will be as rapid as that of cotton. The cheap labor is no longer available in abundance, and Federal regulation of wages and hours should serve as a restraining factor.

The future of the industry does have some encouraging aspects. The most encouraging, is the growing use of rayon staple fiber. The use of this fiber offers a twofold advantage to the wool industry. First, it will act as a stabilizer of wool prices, thus enabling it to offer its products at a lower price than would otherwise be the case. Of equal, if not of greater importance, is that it will give the industry greater opportunity to develop new fabrics and to style them more effectively.

CHAPTER XXIV

THE RAYON INDUSTRY

Rayon is the result of man's effort to imitate silk. For thousands of years silk was the raiment of royalty and nobility because of its rarity, brilliance, fineness, and costliness. Rayon is the first man-made fiber. As such, it is the outstanding technological development in the textile field since the mechanical inventions that ushered in the industrial revolution.

In 1664 a young English physician wrote about the possibility of a chemical substitute for natural silk. In the next 200 years, dozens of others made similar comments, but the project never got beyond the speculative stage. Finally, about 1850, active experimentation began, and by 1900 four distinct methods of imitating silk had emerged. The first, the nitrocellulose process, was patented by Count de Chardonnet. He was a student of Pasteur when the great French scientist was evolving a cure for a silkworm disease which threatened to wipe out the silk industry of France. The young student set to work to eliminate the silkworm instead of the silkworm disease. Within five years he was able to exhibit at the Paris Exposition a synthetic silk that created widespread public interest. Two years later the English investigators, Cross and Bevan, announced what is today called the "viscose process." In 1893, Cross also patented the recently popularized "acetate process." Finally, in 1899, the present-day cuprammonium method was successfully commercialized in Germany.

It is worthy of note that again we have come upon a situation where an idea remained dormant for a long period of time and then suddenly entered a phase of active experimentation in which the goal is reached by basically different routes.

Before discussing the processes that are in current use, let us look at the principal raw materials of this industry.

Raw Materials.—Rayon, like silk, is made of cellulose. Cellulose is found in all vegetable matter—in cotton, grass, sugar cane, trees, etc. But not all these sources can be utilized to provide the rayon industry with its raw material. This is because some plant material has a low cellulose content and a high content of undesirable matter such as fats, oils, resins, etc. The rayon industry has found that the best sources thus far for cellulose are cotton linters and spruce wood.

Cotton, because of its high cellulose content (80 to 90 per cent), was the first raw material to be used. At the outset, the staple itself was used, but soon it was found that equally pure cellulose could be obtained from cotton linters—the short, dark, fuzzy fibers which remain on the seed after the cotton has been ginned. The linters are cooked to remove the natural oils and waxes and to bleach the product. This "chemical cotton" when dried in sheet form is ready for the rayon manufacturing process.

Spruce wood (52 per cent cellulose) is likewise cooked to remove the natural gums, lignin, and resin and to bleach it. The resultant pulp is dried in sheet form like cardboard in appearance. It now contains 90 per cent cellulose and is ready for shipment to the rayon plant. Spruce wood constitutes 75 per cent of the raw material used by the rayon industry; cotton linters make up the remainder.

The Technique of Rayon Manufacture.—Today there are three principal methods of making rayon. (Originally there were four, but the use of the Chardonnet nitrocellulose process was discontinued in this country in 1934 because of its high cost.) These three processes, in their conversion of the commercially pure cellulose into rayon, are similar to the extent that they (1) bring the cellulose into solution; (2) force the liquid cellulose through needle-fine nozzles from which it emerges as a continuous filament; (3) convert these fine streams of liquid cellulose into coagulated or solid threads; (4) chemically wash the yarns and prepare them for shipment. There follows a brief sketch of the principal methods.

The Viscose Process.—The viscose method, which accounts for almost 65 per cent of our production, uses wood pulp principally. The relative amounts of wood and cotton linters depend on the price of the two raw materials.

1. The wood pulp is soaked in caustic soda and then milled until it assumes the consistency of bread crumbs. After these are aged for several days, they are churned in carbon bisulphide and then dissolved in caustic soda. The mass is now a thick viscous liquid and in this form is ripened for four days.

2. The spinning process consists of forcing, by means of small mechanical pumps, the thick liquid through the fine holes of a metal "spinnerette"—analogous to the sprinkler head of a bathroom shower. The size of the filaments that are being formed depends on the size of the opening in the nozzle (0.001 to 0.005 in.) and upon the amount of the solution delivered by the pump. The rayon industry is commonly thought of as solely a chemically controlled industry, but it is also one in which there is a high premium on mechanical accuracy. The pump must deliver an exact amount of the solution to the spinnerette in order to

secure uniformity of filament size. The industry is especially noted for high standards of performance in every phase of the process.

3. As the thick liquid comes from the spinnerette which is immersed in a coagulating bath (chiefly sulphuric acid, ammonium sulphate, and glucose), it is instantly hardened in the form of a filament and in that solid form comes out continuously from the machine to be coiled or wound on bobbins.

4. The final operations consist of purifying the yarn by washing, bleaching, drying, conditioning, inspecting, sorting, etc.

The Acetate Process.—The basic raw material for acetate rayon is cotton linters. These are scoured and bleached, then treated with

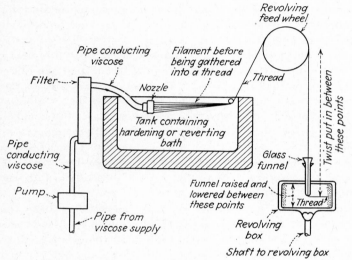

Fig. 64.—The spinning of viscose rayon. (*Courtesy of the Viscose Company.*)

acetic anhydride, glacial acetic acid, and a catalyst which produces cellulose acetate. After further processing, the mix is dissolved in acetone to form the spinning liquor. The spinning of the liquid into filaments is somewhat similar to the viscose process except that the spinnerette, instead of being immersed in a bath of coagulating fluid, is set in a tube through which a current of warm air travels. As the liquid oozes from the spinnerette, the warm air evaporates the acetone. The filaments solidify and are gathered together at the bottom of the tube and wound on a bobbin. The finishing operations are similar in purpose to those described in the viscose process.

The acetate process is now second in importance. In 1940 it contributed about 30 per cent of the total United States production. Its rate of growth has been very rapid. As late as 1924 only one company used the process, whereas in 1940 five companies employed it. The rapid growth of acetate rayon is due to the fact that acetate yarn is basically different from viscose yarn. The difference between the two is especially marked when it comes to dyeing. Acetate yarn takes dyes in a manner entirely different from viscose, cotton, or wool yarns. Acetate dyes cling to acetate rayon only. Consequently mixed fabrics, containing acetate and other yarns, produce attractive cross-dye effects. For example, when a fabric consisting of acetate and viscose yarns is dipped into a vat containing a mixture of acetate and other dyes, the acetate yarn absorbs only the acetate dye.

An all-acetate fabric has a distinctive "feel" and it is said to have especially good draping qualities. Acetate fabrics compete with the best grades of viscose fabrics in the high-quality dress goods market formerly restricted to fine silk.

The Cuprammonium Process.—This method of rayon manufacture is relatively unimportant. It now accounts for approximately 5 per cent of total rayon production. Cotton linters are used as raw material and these are dissolved in an ammoniacal-copper solution. After spinning and solidification, the resulting yarn is washed in sulphuric acid and then goes through the preparations for the market that were previously described.

Technical Progress.—We have seen that the four processes of rayon manufacture were invented in the period 1884–1899. The technical development since then has been rapid and continuous. Most of the progress has been in the nature of endless refinements, but they appeared in such rapid succession that only the financially strong companies were able to survive. Filaments have been made constantly finer. The diameter has been reduced to the point that one pound of the filament is 1,000 miles in length. With increased fineness, it is possible to multiply the number of filaments to the strand of yarn without increasing the diameter of the strand. The advantage of this is twofold; it adds to the strength and pliability of the yarn and fabric and it improves the luster. Instead of the old metallic sheen caused by the reflection of light from the unbroken, glasslike surface of the coarser yarn, the modern multifilament yarns have a soft, subdued luster, similar to silk, arising from the broken surface. Other improvements have come gradually, such as greater tensile strength, elasticity, regularity of cross section, improved insulative quality, and affinity for dyestuffs. The research chemists took natural silk as the goal of their synthesis, and although they failed, they achieved a product that is different from all natural products and superior in some respects to all of them. One expert states that "uniformity is the respect in which rayon excels most."

The outstanding single development of recent years is the perfection of continuous spinning, *i.e.*, the forming, twisting, and finishing operations are all performed in one continuous process. Industrial Rayon Corporation recently completed a new plant specially adapted to this new process. Long rows of three-tier machines, 19 ft. in height, produce the viscose yarns in continuous streams. The filaments are formed in the hooded spin baths at the top of the machines, pass through all the

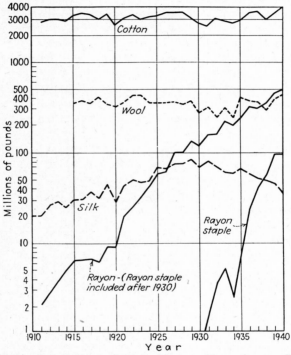

Fig. 65.—Textile fiber consumption in the United States. (*Rayon Organon, February*, 1941.)

processing stages at the intermediate level, and come out on the lower level, wound on bobbins, ready for packaging. Manufacturing time is reduced from 90 hours to 6 minutes.

Growth of the Industry.—In 1911, the year United States commercial production was begun, less than a half million pounds of rayon were produced. In 1940, the industry produced 390 million pounds. Rayon consumption is now ten times our silk consumption and the equivalent of our wool consumption. A graphic picture of the rapidity of growth is portrayed in Fig. 65. The sharp inclination of the rayon curve presents a marked contrast with that of cotton, wool, and silk. Let us consider briefly the reasons for this disproportionately rapid growth of rayon.

Although the rayon first produced was of very inferior quality, judged by present standards, it had some appeal because of its novelty. It was something new, it vaguely resembled silk, and unlike the other fibers it was a synthetic product. Extravagant claims were made with respect to its physical qualities, and pioneer weavers and knitters of cloth gave it a fair trial. However the results were somewhat disappointing. Compared with silk, rayon was harsh, inflexible, coarse, and weak. Innumerable difficulties were encountered in dyeing, twisting, reeling, and bleaching. Furthermore, it had a very high gloss which made it easily distinguishable from silk and, above all, it was unfortunately marketed under the prejudicial name of "artificial silk."

In the first decade (1911–1920), rayon went through a period of experimentation. The industry was spending great effort and considerable capital in perfecting its product. Particular attention was directed toward simulating silk. Technical advancement in the product largely centered around increasing the tensile strength and decreasing the diameter of the filament. Although total production in 1921 was still relatively small, nevertheless it was 100 per cent greater than the preceding year. This marks the transition to the second stage in the industry's development, namely, the period of rapid growth.

In 1924, the industry adopted and popularized the word "rayon" as a substitute for "artificial silk." Meanwhile additional improvements in the quality were being made. For example, the advent of crepe twist in 1925 indicates the attainment of much stronger rayon filament. Another factor contributing to the rising tide of rayon acceptance during the decade of the twenties was that rayon attained a high degree of technical perfection at a time when the textile industry was in the doldrums. While cotton, wool, and silk were going through a period of so-called profitless prosperity, the rayon producers were offering the market a progressively better product at continuously lower prices. Under these circumstances production of rayon continued to rise.

Rayon producers are now able to imitate practically all the physical qualities characteristic of silk so that the most discriminating buyer cannot tell the difference between silk and rayon fabrics unless they are properly identified. In fact, rayon has surpassed silk with respect to some qualities, and since the silkworm cannot be taught new tricks, rayon may eclipse other qualities of the aristocrat of fibers. Certainly there is no evidence as yet that rayon has approached the third period in the evolution of industrial growth, namely, the period of retarded expansion.

The Market for Rayon.—When commercial rayon first appeared, it found its most enthusiastic buyers in the hosiery industry and, until 1920, that industry consumed the largest share of the rayon output.

Since 1920, the hosiery industry has consumed a progressively smaller percentage of the annual rayon production and today only 5 per cent of the rayon output is absorbed by hosiery manufacturers. This does not imply that the hose manufacturer's demand for rayon has dried up. Approximately 17 million lb. of rayon are converted annually into hosiery in contrast with only 2 million lb. in 1920. What has really occurred is a proportionately larger consumption of rayon in other uses. These will be mentioned presently. Although the percentage of rayon produced that is used for hosiery is comparatively small, it is worth noting that about half of men's hose is made wholly or principally from rayon. Women's hosiery is made almost entirely of silk[1] which has greater elasticity than rayon. Ever since the fashion for shorter skirts

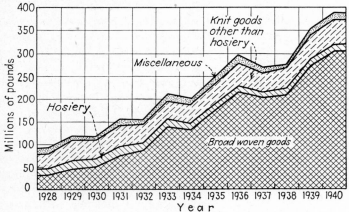

Fig. 66.—Recent trends in use of rayon. (*Rayon Organon, Special Supplement, January,* 1941.)

has emphasized the importance of hosiery, form-fitting hose has become a canon of good taste, and silk serves this purpose better than rayon.

The largest market for rayon is in the manufacture of woven and knitted cloth. The accompanying Fig. 66 shows that approximately 80 per cent of rayon is now being converted into broad woven cloth. Most of this cloth is converted into dress goods and novelty fabrics for women's apparel and into linings for men's suitings and overcoats. Rayon is less costly than silk and since the two cannot be readily distinguished, inexpensive women's dresses can be made to simulate silk dresses. Rayon dresses offer stylish appearance at low prices and as the style cycle becomes shorter the demand for rayon dress goods is likely to increase because it costs the consumer less to keep in style.

Rayon is displacing silk in other lines of apparel. It is used in underwear and negligee fabrics, outerwear fabrics such as jackets, knit jersey,

[1] This is no longer true since the silk embargo and the outbreak of war with Japan.

and sportswear. Approximately 50 million lb. of rayon are used annually by knitters other than hosiery manufacturers and much of this is made into knitted underwear. Furthermore, the sharp rise in the price of silk in 1939 stimulated the use of rayon in seamless hosiery and in the making of heels, tops, and toes of full-fashioned hosiery.

Rayon Staple.—An interesting development that is now attracting considerable attention is rayon staple. Rayon staple is made by cutting rayon filaments into short fibers of uniform length which are then spun into yarn by any of the textile spinning processes. It was introduced in Germany during the First World War but did not achieve much commercial importance until the late twenties. Spun rayon yarn has a wide range of usefulness. It has had its greatest development abroad in Germany, Italy, and Japan—countries which lay great stress upon economic nationalism. These three countries produced almost 90 per cent of the world's spun rayon yarn in 1939. By substituting this for natural fibers these countries reduce their dependence upon imported textile raw materials.

Rayon staple production was begun in the United States in 1928. In that year we produced about 165,000 lb. In 1940 we consumed 100 million lb. of rayon staple, 80 per cent of which was domestically produced, the balance imported. Rayon staple is made from the same raw materials as rayon filament. It can be produced by any of the three processes previously described, but the viscose process predominates. However, in the production of rayon staple much larger spinnerettes are used. Spinnerettes containing several thousand holes turn out the rayon in large volume—almost like a rope. This explains why it can be produced more cheaply than rayon filament. The staple is cut into 1.5-in. lengths for the cotton spinning system or into 3-in. lengths for silk spinning machines or into longer lengths for the woolen and worsted industry.

The rapid growth in consumption of spun rayon yarn in the United States cannot be explained on the ground of economic nationalism. Its widespread acceptance is due rather to its contribution to style and serviceability in fabrics. Blended with the natural fibers rayon staple produces substantially new fabrics hitherto unknown. Until about 1938 spun rayon was used chiefly in the woolen and worsted industry as an adulterant in the sense that it served as a lower cost raw material. More recently, the wool industry has come to regard rayon staple as a styling medium. Novel and attractive effects can be obtained by mixing rayon staple with wool to produce fabrics of the challis type; unusual cross-dye effects can be obtained from such mixtures.

Fabrics made entirely from spun rayon yarn can be finished to simulate linen, worsted, and silk fabrics. These fabrics are used in making women's dresses, men's summer suits, robes, neckwear, mufflers, and other forms of apparel. The fabrics are especially adaptable to the manufacture of washable shantungs for women's wear and gabardines, homespuns, twills, and tweeds for men's wear. Some textile experts predict that the use of spun rayon yarn will eclipse filament rayon yarn in the very near future. This prediction is not based upon irrational enthusiasm. Figure 65 shows very clearly that the rate of growth of rayon staple has thus far surpassed all other fibers, including rayon filament.

Rayon Companies.—The Viscose Company was the first successful American company and is still the leading producer. In 1909, the Viscose Company was organized by Courtaulds, Ltd., which was already manufacturing artificial silk in England, and the history of the industry from that date to 1920 is largely the history of the Viscose Company. This company built its first plant at Marcus Hook, Pa. In 1917 it built another plant in Roanoke, Va. Late in this period several other companies were organized, but the output of the Viscose Company represented well over 90 per cent of the total American output.

The rapid increase in consumption, shown in Fig. 65, and the high price of rayon ($5 per pound in 1920) attracted additional capital into the industry. In 1921 Viscose built another plant in Lewistown, Pa.; in 1925 a 10-million-lb. plant in Parkersburg, W. Va., and in 1927 completed the construction of another plant in Roanoke. The latter plant had a capacity of 17 million lb. per year, then the largest in the world. Among the new companies that entered into production after 1920 were duPont, Belamose, Celanese, American Bemberg, Skenandoa, and American Chatillon. The rapid technological advances and the resulting lower prices together with the increasing popularity of the new fiber required the installation of additional capacity to meet the demand. It was provided by expansion of existing companies and the organization of new companies. DuPont increased the capacity of their Buffalo plant and built additional plants at Old Hickory, Tenn.; Richmond, Va., and Covington, Va. Newcomers were American Glanzstoff (now North American Rayon Company), New Bedford Rayon, and American Enka. Approximately 15 new companies were organized between 1925 and 1929, bringing to a total of about 40 the number of companies that entered the industry since 1910. Of these 40 companies only 18 remain and, as Table L shows, Viscose controls almost half of the productive capacity. The nine largest control over 90 per cent.

In view of the rapid expansion in the consumption of rayon and the high profits that were made, it is interesting to speculate on the reasons for the failure of so many companies during this period. Some of the companies were, of course, only security promotion schemes that never got beyond the organization stage, but this is by no means the entire explanation. The chief reasons appear to be the following:

1. The manufacture of rayon requires a large capital investment for construction and installations, and cannot be conducted on a small scale. It will be noted in Table L that the smallest company has an

TABLE L.—UNITED STATES PRODUCERS OF RAYON, 1941

Company	Approximate annual capacity, pounds (000,000 omitted)	Per cent of total
Large companies:		
American Viscose Corp	191	46
DuPont	40	10
Industrial Rayon	32	8
Medium companies:		
American Enka	30	7
North American	24	6
Tennessee Eastman	24	6
Celanese Corp	22	5
Tubize Chatillon	20	5
American Bemberg	10	4
Small companies:		
Skenandoa Rayon	7	Less than 2 % each
New Bedford Rayon	5	Less than 2 % each
Hartford Rayon	4	Less than 2 % each
Delaware Rayon	3	Less than 2 % each
Woonsocket Rayon	3	Less than 2 % each
Hampton Co.*	2	Less than 2 % each
Imperial Rayon	1	Less than 2 % each
Acme Rayon Corp.*	1	Less than 2 % each
Sylvania Industrial Corp.*	1	
Total	419	100

* Plants idle in April, 1941.

annual capacity of 1 million lb. Companies with smaller plants were unable to produce at a competitive price.

2. The process must be delicately controlled and requires a long time, frequently several years, before quality yarn is produced. This period of experimentation has often drained companies of their working capital and thrown them into bankruptcy before they could produce a merchantable yarn.

3. Technological changes affecting both the method of manufacture and the quality of the product occurred with such rapidity and were of such a fundamental nature that the small companies were unable to keep

abreast of changes. Prices were determined by the efficient manufacturers rather than the marginal producers, who passed out of the industry. This usually occurs in young industries, as we saw in the case of the automobile industry. There also the number of companies was greatly decreased during the industry's period of most rapid expansion.

Location.—The 30 plants comprising the industry are located within a crescent-shaped area along the Atlantic seaboard from Massachusetts to Georgia, extending westward to Ohio. Over half of the plants are in Pennsylvania, the Virginias, Tennessee, and Ohio. The chief reasons for the wide geographical spread appear to be the limitations of water supply and the desire to avoid creating too large a demand for labor at

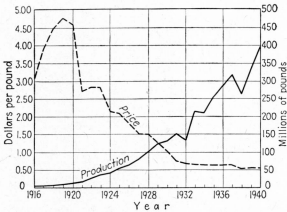

FIG. 67.—Average annual prices and production of rayon. (*Rayon Organon, Special Supplement, January,* 1941.)

any one point which would tend to increase wage rates. Rayon manufacture requires large quantities of clean soft water. For example, the Viscose plant near Chester, Pa., consumes more water than the entire city of Chester (population 60,000). For technical reasons, water supply must be given first consideration in the location of a plant. Labor is also an important factor; it constitutes about a third of the manufacturing costs and for this reason companies have chosen areas affording a large supply of cheap labor which can find alternative employment only in low-paid agricultural or industrial industries.

Competitive Relations.—One of the best measures of competitive relations in an industry is to be found in the price behavior of its product. A price that is subject to either frequent or broad changes, or both, is generally indicative of a very competitive industry. On the other hand, a price that is relatively stable is usually a sign of a well-controlled, if not a monopolistic industry. The price of rayon reveals two striking characteristics—first, the long-run trend is downward as shown in Fig. 67, and second, the short-run trend is stable, as Fig. 68 indicates.

The first characteristic occasions no surprise. The industry is still young, and technological advances occur frequently, permitting the industry to reduce prices without sacrificing profits.

The second characteristic, however, the relative stability of prices in the short run, indicates what has become known as an "administered price"; *i.e.*, a price that is determined by administered coordination

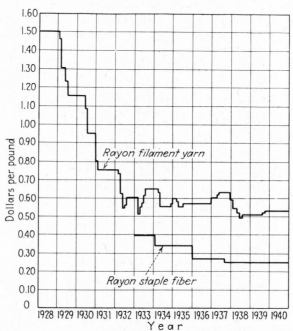

FIG. 68.—Monthly prices of rayon filament yarn and rayon staple fiber. (*Rayon Organon, January*, 1941.)

rather than by the operation of the forces of supply and demand in a free and open market. It should be borne in mind that an administered price does not necessarily mean a monopoly price. It does mean, however, a price determined in an "imperfect" market. As has been pointed out elsewhere, a competitive market requires, among other things, a large number of buyers and a large number of sellers. The presence of both in large numbers diminishes the influence of any one seller or buyer in the market. The market for rayon meets only one of these two conditions, namely, a large number of buyers. The other requirement, a large number of sellers, is absent because as we have seen there are only 18 companies in the industry and two of these control about 50 per cent

of the industry's capacity.   Accordingly, the producers are able to give
concrete expression to their common desire to avoid "spoiling the
market" by price cutting.   In short, directly or indirectly, either by
agreement or in recognition of the consequences of individual action,
prices are not permitted to reflect the full effect of short-run changes
in the supply of and demand for rayon.

Available evidence indicates that in this industry, as in the steel
industry in former years, prices are determined by the leaders.   A change
in their price lists, either upward or downward, is generally recognized
as a signal for the revision of prices throughout the industry.   Evidence
also warrants the belief that in a crisis the important producers manifest
an attitude of cooperation.   For example, in 1932 when production and
stocks were far in excess of orders, there was a simultaneous shutting
down of the plants of almost all of the large producers.   There is evidence
also that the principal producers permitted their books to be audited
by a firm of accountants to determine how closely each adhered to his
announced price list.

A few years ago a number of knitters filed a complaint against the
principal producers, charging them specifically with:

1. Fixing and maintaining uniform prices.

2. Curtailing the production of rayon by agreement.

3. Attempting to secure an agreement among rayon knitters not to
sell rayon cloth below an agreed-upon price.

4. Refusing to sell rayon yarn to those knitters who refused to abide
with the agreed price.

5. Entering into the manufacture and sale of knitted cloth so that
they might punish price cutters of knitted rayon cloth by underselling
them.

In 1937, after extended hearings, the rayon companies were ordered
by the Federal Trade Commission to refrain from engaging in these
practices.

While the published price of rayon is relatively stable, there has been
some indirect price competition through secret discounts, secret freight
allowances, and the sale of quality yarns as seconds.   The large producers also attempted to keep their customers by discouraging the practice of shopping around for lower priced rayon.   The yarn producers
protected their customers against price declines and allowed them cumulative discounts.   However, most of these practices have been discontinued since the passage of the Robinson-Patman Act in 1936 which
prohibits various forms of price discrimination.

Comparisons and Contrasts.—Strictly speaking, rayon manufacture
is not a textile industry.   Technically it is a chemical process industry.
However, it is included among the textile industry because its business

is confined almost wholly within the textile field. It may be helpful, therefore, to indicate here some major contrasts between the rayon and the other textile industries. Among the more important are the following.

1. The few companies in the rayon industry and the large size of each.

2. The great importance of large-scale manufacture, and the emphasis placed upon scientific control.

3. The close relation of the American rayon companies to foreign producers. Practically every American rayon company is controlled either in whole or in part by a European company or receives technical help from it.[1]

4. The absence of large fluctuations in the price of its raw materials and its finished product.

5. The fact that the rayon industry is primarily a yarn-producing industry, except for three companies that produce some cloth.

6. The narrow limits within which quality can be controlled. Silk, wool, and, to a lesser extent, cotton lack uniformity in quality. The quality varies from season to season and from one batch to another. This lack of uniformity limits the speed and the automaticity of the loom, and requires the use of more hand labor. Rayon, on the other hand, can be manufactured to specific standards and uniformity can be guaranteed. This makes possible greater speed in weaving and the use of more automatic machinery and less hand labor.

7. The relative youth of the rayon industry with respect to methods of manufacture, product, and market, as compared with the other textile industries, which are in a state of senescence.

The Outlook.—In Chap. XX considerable emphasis was placed upon the importance of style as a source of either profits or losses in the textile industries. Profits accrue to those manufacturers who display shrewdness in "calling the turns" in style changes. Rayon manufacturers as a class should benefit by the increasing capriciousness of the market because they are in the best position not only to adapt their products to the demand in vogue, but also to create new styles in fabrics. Rayon is a product of the chemical laboratory, and rayon companies are lavish in their expenditures for research. Many of the popular fabrics that have appeared on the market in recent years are made in whole or in part of rayon. With rayon and particularly rayon staple, fabrics can be made to simulate most of the fabrics made from the natural fibers.

It has been intimated that the rayon industry has not as yet run its full course of stage two (rapid growth) of the industrial life cycle. The rapid growth of rayon manufacture in Germany, Italy, and Japan has

---

[1] In 1941, Courtaulds, Ltd., British thread and textile makers, sold American Viscose to American bankers.

led many to believe that a similar growth will take place in the United States. However, in our opinion this is not likely to occur. In the dictator countries the tremendous expansion of rayon manufacture did not take place in response to natural competitive developments. It was rather a development which was part of a national plan to avoid the importation of natural fibers which could have been obtained at less cost than rayon, had those countries tolerated freedom of international trade.

CHAPTER XXV

THE SILK AND RAYON WEAVING INDUSTRY

The phenomenal rise of the rayon yarn industry, described in the preceding chapter, has almost completely altered the character of the silk weaving industry. Whereas in 1929 approximately 59 million lb. of silk were used for weaving, in 1939 only 9 million lb. were so consumed. During the same period the consumption of rayon yarn for weaving increased from 48 million to almost 286 million lb. So great has been the transformation caused by the introduction of the new fiber that the silk industry no longer exists as a separate industry—in its place we now have a silk and rayon weaving industry.

The silk mills, especially those of Paterson, N. J., once the center of the industry, were very slow in adjusting themselves to the new fiber, and many of their troubles during the past decade arose from their reluctant acceptance of rayon. Not all the troubles of the industry, however, can be attributed to the new raw material. War and postwar expansion, fluctuating silk prices, and changes in the industry's structure were also important causes of instability.

Development of the Industry.—Despite the long history of silk as a textile fiber and the early development of silk weaving in Europe, the industry in the United States is of relatively recent origin when compared with cotton and wool. The first silk mill in the United States was established in 1793, but as late as 1850 the Census reported only two weaving mills with a combined capital of $5,000 and a total labor force of eight people.[1] The chief limitations to the development of the industry were the lack of skilled labor and of an adequate supply of raw material.

The turning point in the development of the industry came in 1860 when certain national and international events combined to give it a great stimulus. In that year Great Britain entered into a reciprocal trade agreement with France which, among other things, eliminated all duties on manufactured silks entering Great Britain. The elimination of tariff protection virtually destroyed the British industry, and the resulting unemployment caused the migration of silk workers to the United States. At about the same time the government of the United

[1] KEIR, M., "Manufacturing Industries in America," p. 416, Ronald Press Company, New York, 1923.

States, in need of revenue, imposed a tariff on all imported silk goods. Many attempts had been made to establish a domestic sericulture industry but in 1863 the government recognized their futility and abandoned all duties on raw silk. This action made available to the domestic industry the silk of the Orient. The response of the industry to these stimuli and the concomitant development of the silk power loom was immediate. Whereas in 1860 domestic silk manufactures of all types were only 18 per cent of manufactured silk imports, in 1870 they amounted to 50 per cent, in 1890 to 235 per cent, and at the beginning of the present century the United States was the second largest silk manufacturing country in the world.[1]

During the early part of this period the industry was localized in New Jersey, chiefly in Paterson, which became known as the "silk city" of the United States. The concentration in Paterson can be explained on a number of grounds: in the first place, it is located within 17 miles of New York, the principal market and style center; second, the chief industries prior to the development of the silk industry were the metal-working industries which employed only men and left available, without any competition, their wives and children for employment in the silk mills; and third, there was available a large supply of water power to run the machinery and sufficient clean water to process the silk.[2] In the eighties improvements were made in throwing[3] equipment which made possible the employment of less skilled labor, and manufacturers looked for a cheaper source of labor. This they found in the small towns of the anthracite and cement regions of Pennsylvania where an adequate supply of female labor was available. Within 20 years the number of throwing spindles in Pennsylvania increased from 32,000 to 940,000. The shift from Paterson to other locations was not confined to throwing but extended to the manufacture of other products. The early decline in the relative importance of Paterson in other than throwing operations, it should be noted, was due less to actual migration than to the higher rate of growth of other areas. After 1910 actual migration, due to labor disturbances, played a more important role in the decline of Paterson.

During the early years of the present century the production of silk cloth expanded steadily, increasing from 88 million sq. yd. in 1899 to 310 million in 1919. "That period was the prologue for a fabulous period of prosperity and demand that followed the First World War. Silk became the everyday dress of the average woman. The ready-to-wear manufacturing industry began to take hold with its consumption of

---

[1] MATSUI, S., "History of the Silk Industry in the United States," p. 420, Howes Publishing Company, New York, 1930.

[2] KEIR, *op. cit.*

[3] See Chap. XXI, p. 303.

thousands of pieces of 60 yd. each instead of a few hundred yards that the average retail store could handle. More and more machinery was the cry. Every effort was made to speed up the loom action; new plants were built rapidly. Prices for the finished fabrics were whatever the manufacturer wanted to ask."[1]

Behind this facade of prosperity important economic and technological changes were taking place which revolutionized the industry: rayon became important as a weaving material; more automatic looms were introduced; new mills in new areas entered into the processing of rayon; and silk prices began to decline. These developments made competition very severe and, as Table LI shows, an increasing number of mills found it difficult to operate at a profit. It will be noted that in only two years did the number of profit-making mills exceed the loss-reporting mills.

TABLE LI.—INCOME AND DEFICITS OF SILK AND RAYON WEAVING MILLS, 1927–1937

Year	Corporations reporting net income			Corporations reporting no net income			Per cent of total having no net income
	Number of returns	Gross income (000 omitted)	Net income (000 omitted)	Number of returns	Gross income (000 omitted)	Net deficit (000 omitted)	
1927	403	$ 558,082	$ 60,990	408	$ 268,660	$ 15,223	50
1928	460	627,580	74,200	360	264,441	14,742	44
1929	451	615,116	57,013	374	288,961	19,849	45
1930	308	272,464	21,264	472	488,949	50,865	61
1931	267	243,666	9,504	493	319,226	42,932	65
1932	145	167,600	4,344	588	240,972	31,471	80
1933	258	297,526	32,987	528	182,994	14,728	67
1934	245	255,054	19,606	624	223,070	18,689	72
1935	243	321,500	21,127	611	196,411	15,329	72
1936	249	368,939	32,838	547	166,856	11,338	70
1937	184	320,698	34,554	530	196,405	10,927	75
Total		$4,048,225	$368,427		$2,836,945	$246,093	

Source: Bureau of Internal Revenue.

The Technique of Silk and Rayon Weaving.—As is the case in other textile industries, the three principal divisions of the industry from the standpoint of process are: (1) the preparation of the yarn, (2) the weaving of the fabric, and (3) finishing.

The nature of raw silk is such that the yarn can be made by merely twisting together several of the filaments furnished by the silkworm.

[1] CONZE, G. H., Fabric Weaving and Technological Progress, statement before T.N.E.C., T.N.E.C. Hearings, Part 30, p. 16, 881.

The worm exudes two streams of thick viscous fluid which immediately harden into gelatinlike strands, which range in length from 300 to 700 yd. and taper in size at the ends.   In unwinding the silk from the cocoon, from five to seven of these strands are brought together, slightly twisted, and put into skein form.   It is in this condition that raw silk reaches the United States.   In this country the first step is to soften and remove the wax content of the silk by the use of soap and water and then to bring together two or more of the strands, twisting them to provide the necessary strength and size.   The latter process, that of twisting, is known as throwing.

Silk from broken or crushed cocoons lacks continuity of strand, and this waste silk is cut into short staple lengths and spun by ordinary spinning methods such as those that prevail in cotton and wool.   The product is known in the trade as "spun silk," in contradistinction to thrown silk.   Spun silk amounts to only a small fraction of American silk manufacture.

Silk weaving resembles in most essential respects other types of weaving except that looms are operated more slowly than for other fibers because of the fragile nature of the yarn.   Prior to the post-war boom silk fabrics were woven from dyed yarn, but in an effort to increase production during the boom period the industry began to weave an increasing amount of greige goods.

The amount of processing required to weave rayon depends upon whether rayon filament or rayon staple fiber is used.   If the continuous filament is used, the process is not unlike that of silk, except that the yarn need not be washed and thrown.   If rayon staple is used, the fibers must first be spun into a continuous strand like cotton or wool.[1]   Both rayon filament and staple yarns can be woven on either cotton or silk looms, and many looms in the cotton and silk industry have been transferred to the weaving of rayon.   The major proportion of rayon fabrics is produced as greige goods.

The processes of dyeing and printing rayon and silk fabrics are similar to those employed in the cotton industry.

Structure of the Industry.—In 1939, according to the Census of Manufactures, the silk and rayon division of the United States textile industry, exclusive of the rayon yarn producers considered in the last chapter, comprised 829 establishments, employed 119,000 wage earners, and had a value of product of 442 million dollars.   Of the 829 establishments 275 were engaged in the weaving of rayon broad goods (18 in. wide and over); 119 in the weaving of silk broad goods; 131 in the commission throwing and spinning of silk; and 84 in the commission throwing and spinning of rayon.   The remainder were engaged in the manufacture

[1] See Chap. XXI, p. 299.

TABLE LIII.—CHANGES IN BROAD GOODS MANUFACTURING FIRMS, 1921–1929

States	Going out of business		Entering business		Discontinued branches or moved to other cities or states	
	Firms	Looms	Firms	Looms	Firms	Looms
New Jersey..............	921	30,175	964	24,856	90	8,514
Pennsylvania..............	107	22,801	155	23,083	41	4,446
Rhode Island..............	18	3,110	28	4,643	2	1,255
New York..............	36	3,403	41	3,916	2	713
Massachusetts..............	9	1,423	22	3,281	2	367
Connecticut..............	2	451	8	2,208	1	
Total..............	1,093	61,363	1,218	61,987	145	15,295

Source: COPELAND, M., and W. TURNER, "Production and Distribution of Silk and Rayon Broad Goods," The National Federation of Textiles, Inc., New York, 1935.

of the outgoing mills at bankruptcy prices. During the depression, looms that cost $400 when new were available in the second-hand market at $10.[1] With the lower overhead costs competition was intensified.

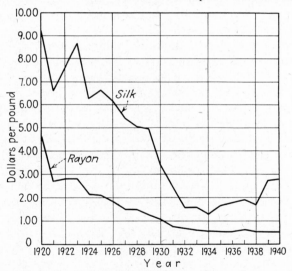

FIG. 69.—Average annual prices of silk and rayon. (*Rayon Organon, Jan.* 21, 1941.)

Raw Materials.—A concomitant, and in part a cause, of the disintegration of the industry was the declining trend of silk prices between 1923 and 1934. As Fig. 69 shows, the average annual price of silk declined from $8.65 to $1.29 a pound. The declining trend in prices

[1] SWAN, H. S., "The Plain Goods Silk Industry," p. 20, The Industrial Commission, Paterson, N. J., 1937.

put the large stock-carrying mills in an unfavorable competitive position. The commission weaver wove the raw silk of the converter who purchased it in small amounts and, in the case of the very small converters, with very little forward buying. The large mills, however, were under the necessity of carrying inventories. Accordingly, the stock-carrying mills were unable to meet the prices of the converter. The low prices of silk cloth and the narrow profit per yard made it necessary for the large mills to increase the turnover of their goods. To shorten their manufacturing cycle they sold their output in the greige to the converter. This shortened the time the goods were in their possession, decreased their carrying charges, and at the same time gave them more protection from inventory losses. Thus, the converter became both a competitor and a customer of the stock-carrying mills.

Weighting.—During the period of rapid expansion when strenuous efforts were made to increase production the industry introduced new processes that made possible the "weighting" of silk fabrics so that a given amount of raw silk would go farther in producing a yard of fabric. The weighting of silk involves the soaking of the raw silk yarn in a solution of metallic salts which are absorbed by the yarn and increase its size. As raw material costs represent a substantial part of total manufacturing costs[1] this was an effective way of cutting costs. While this practice within limits is not to be condemned, it did, and continues to, create competitive difficulties because some mills and converters overweighted the fiber and, consequently, enjoyed a price advantage over their competitors who tried to maintain quality. The practice increased as rayon, with its lower price, became more competitive in the broad goods field and created much criticism among buyers.

Variations in Quality.—The nature of raw-silk production, its dependence upon natural processes, makes for great variation in its quality. Manufacturers of high-quality silk goods buy only silk that meets rigid tests for uniformity, strength, and elasticity and often reject one-half of the silk inspected, which is sold at lower prices to other mills who purchase it to lower their costs.[2] The variations in the quality of silk have frequently been the cause of labor trouble in the industry. Agreements as to piece rates are usually posited on particular grades of yarn. Variations from these grades are likely to cause disputes between the management and the workers. If the yarn is constantly breaking, the worker must spend a great deal of his time repairing it, and since his earnings are reduced, he insists on a revision of the piece rate. If the quality of the next batch is higher, his earnings increase and management is tempted to cut the rate.

[1] See Chap. I, p. 13.
[2] Swan, *op. cit.*, p. 12.

The Advent of Rayon.—In the early years of the rayon industry, as was pointed out in the preceding chapter, the principal market for its product was in the hosiery and knit goods industries. However, as rayon improved in quality and obtained greater consumer acceptance, the rayon industry looked to the market served by the broad silk industry as an outlet for its expanding production.

The established silk manufacturers gave little consideration to the new fiber and were convinced that for outerwear silk, the "queen of the fibers," could not be displaced as the luxury fiber. The reluctance to accept rayon was especially marked in Paterson.

While the silk industry debated the merits of the new fiber and some reluctantly shifted to its use, another competitive group appeared, the cotton fine goods mills. These mills, which were seeking to avoid the increasing competition in the cotton industry, shifted to the weaving of rayon, which they could do with some minor adjustments to their equipment. The fine goods mills of Massachusetts were the first to shift, but later Southern cotton mills also shifted to rayon. In addition to the shift of cotton capacity, new mills, especially designed for rayon processing, entered the industry. Few of the new mills were located in the old silk area, and as of 1937 rayon was woven in 12 states, from Maine to South Carolina. The dispersion of the industry is shown in Table LIV.

TABLE LIV.—LOCATION OF RAYON BROAD GOODS MILLS, 1937

State	Number of establishments	Value of product
Connecticut	10	$ 9,000,000
Massachusetts	19	33,000,000
New Jersey	54	10,000,000
New York	15	13,000,000
North Carolina	26	45,000,000
Pennsylvania	73	47,000,000
Rhode Island	18	24,000,000
South Carolina	6	25,000,000
Virginia	8	9,000,000
Other states	8	14,000,000

Source: Census of Manufactures.

With this competition the silk mills were unable to cope. The rayon mills not only had the advantage of lower cost raw materials, but they also enjoyed lower processing costs. Since rayon is a man-made fiber, manufactured with scientific precision, it is uniform in quality. Therefore looms can operate at a higher speed and the fiber can be adapted more easily to the automatic loom that can silk. Thus, the loom load per worker in rayon was more than double that in the silk division.   In addition to these advantages, the rayon weaver was never confronted with any inventory hazards arising from fluctuating raw material prices.   As a result, as Fig. 70 shows, the rayon mills took an increasing share of the silk market, and the silk mills were forced to retreat.

The belated efforts made by some silk mills to shift to rayon failed to save them.   While their silk looms could match rayon looms in producing quality rayon fabrics, they could not cope with them on a cost basis.   Few of them were automatic and most of them were relatively old and inefficient.   According to a 1937 survey, 86 per cent of the nonautomatic silk and rayon looms (the latter owned almost entirely by

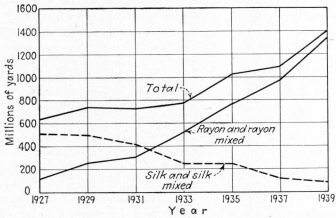

Fig. 70.—Production of silk and rayon woven goods.   (*Census of Manufactures.*)

former silk mills) were obsolete.[1]   Inefficient equipment was not, however, the only disadvantage suffered by the converted silk mills.   The converted cotton mills and the new rayon mills, as was stated before, were located outside of the former silk manufacturing area and enjoyed lower wage rates.   This was especially true in the South.   The Southern mills not only had lower wage rates and lower labor costs, but also had the economies that came from multiple-shift operation.   In a survey made by the United States Bureau of Labor Statistics in 1940, it was found that over 50 per cent of the workers in the South were employed on second and third shifts, whereas only 33 per cent of the Northern workers were employed on extra shifts.

The competitive situation between rayon and silk in the broad goods industry may be summarized with the statement that the victory of rayon is virtually complete.   Silk has been almost completely driven out of the dress goods field, and the principal market for broad silk is

[1] CONZE, *op. cit.*, p. 16,888.

in the underwear trade. Until recently, rayon fabrics did not find much favor for underwear, because it is said that they "ride." However, improvements in rayon are eliminating this objection and the amount of rayon cloth, both knitted and woven, used for underwear is rapidly increasing.

The last stronghold of silk was in hosiery, particularly women's hosiery. Full-fashioned silk hosiery, introduced about the time of the First World War, became so popular that, by 1940, all but a negligible proportion of women's hose was so made. Now this market for silk is being invaded by a new synthetic yarn—Nylon.

Nylon, a duPont product, is made from coal. In 1940, the manufacturers of women's full-fashioned hosiery began using this raw material instead of silk. Nylon hose was received so enthusiastically that the duPont company could not produce it fast enough. During the last half of the year, Nylon hose constituted 10 per cent of the total output of women's full-fashioned hosiery. The cessation of Japanese silk shipments, late in 1941, hastened the shift from silk to Nylon hose. There is no doubt that silk has met a formidable adversary in its last big market, and it is safe to predict that the longer American-Japanese hostilities exist, the more strongly will Nylon be intrenched at the expense of silk.

The Future of Textile Industries.—The textile industries were the first to feel the impact of the industrial revolution and for many years led all other industries in technological developments and in growth. As was to be expected, however, this position could not be maintained, and leadership passed to other industries. For many years the industry, in practically all divisions, languished in a state of senescence. Interregional migrations, multiple-shift operations, and changing markets required major adjustments in operation and the withdrawal of many companies in all divisions.

However, as frequently happens in the lives of industries, new developments injected new vigor. A recent rapid acceleration in technological improvements in practically all stages of the textile process is creating new possibilities and new opportunities for the industry.

Of even greater importance is the rise of new man-made fibers. The synthetic fibers, in various stages of technical and commercial development, fall into about six or seven well-defined classes. Those which are already in commercial use are, first, rayon, a regenerated cellulose fiber; second, acetate, a cellulose derivative fiber, and third, Nylon, a proteinlike fiber of mineral origin. Others that are on the eve of commercial development are the protein fibers, such as Lanital, made from milk casein, the synthetic resin fibers, such as Vinyon, and finally the fibers made from a combination of the above materials, for example,

Fibramine, a mixture of regenerated cellulose (viscose) and proteins (casein).

Just how these man-made fibers will be used we can only guess, but we know that the advent of rayon and its processing by the cotton, wool, and silk mills has already done much to obliterate the former boundary lines in the textile industries. The increasing tendency to mix fibers and the rise of new fibers will break down even more the boundaries which heretofore have separated one division of the industry from the others. In place of several distinct textile industries, each specializing in a distinct fiber, we may have a general weaving industry equipped with very flexible machinery capable of processing any fiber or any combination of fibers.

PART VII
THE APPAREL INDUSTRIES

CHAPTER XXVI

THE CLOTHING INDUSTRIES

The broad stream of goods that flows from the textile mills of the country splits, according to destination, into three lesser streams. One flows into industrial uses, another goes into housefurnishings, and the remaining one supplies us with most of our wearing apparel. This apparel—suits, overcoats, dresses, skirts, caps, shirts, millinery, etc.— is manufactured by industries known collectively as the garment trades, the clothing industries, or the needle trades. These are the subject of the present chapter.

The Technology of Clothing Manufacture.—The term "needle trades" indicates that all the members of the group employ a common technology. This consists of designing the garment, cutting the cloth, sewing the pieces together, and pressing the assembled garment. These operations in their simplest form call for a pair of scissors, a hand needle or a foot-power sewing machine, and a pressing iron. Present-day factory production of clothing, in its most mechanized form, uses high-speed electrically driven cutting devices, such as rotary disks or recipro-cating knives which cut layers of cloth up to 9 in. in thickness. More than 200 specialized forms of the power-driven sewing machine are in use. These operate at speeds ranging up to 4,600 stitches per minute and perform specialized tasks such as the sewing of buttons, buttonholes, basting, hemstitching, spiral braiding, etc. A pressing machine also has been invented. It consists of a bed plate made to fit a particular garment or part of a garment. This bed is piped for steam, as is also the head which the operator brings down after the garment has been placed on the bed.

The manual workers also perform specialized tasks such as tailoring a coat collar or inserting the sleeve in a garment. In some factories as many as 50 or 60 separate operations are involved in the manufacture of a coat.

It should be pointed out that, despite these advances in technology, clothing establishments have relatively low investments in plant and machinery. None of the equipment is heavy or bulky or expensive

367

nor is there need for specially designed buildings. On the contrary, the machine units are small and light and can be housed, if need be, in a few hundred square feet of rented space in a loft building. It has been estimated that all shops manufacturing women's clothing in New York City, probably 3,000 in number, could be housed in 64 buildings, 12 stories in height, placed in eight city blocks.[1] The low investment in plant and equipment is brought out in Table LV.

TABLE LV.—RELATION OF FIXED ASSETS TO TANGIBLE NET WORTH, AVERAGES FOR
PERIOD 1932–1936, SELECTED FIRMS

Industry	Per Cent
Women's cloaks and suits	6.91
Dresses	9.40
Men's and boy's clothing	10.06
Industrial chemicals	50.45
Confectionery	50.03
Leather tanning	37.28
Industrial machinery	46.35
Paper	78.57
Women's and children's shoes	29.21

Source: Dun & Bradstreet, Inc.

There is another important aspect of the technology of clothing manufacture. In many industries the ultra-modern machine has brought an almost complete transfer of skill and pace-setting from the worker to the machine. This is not true in the needle trades. Here the quality and the quantity of the output still depend largely on the operator, on how he guides and manipulates the materials.

It takes but a few seconds to make a seam, so far as the actual stitching is concerned; but it takes a great deal more time to pick up the parts, put them together properly, place them under the needle, bring down the attachment which holds the work in place, start the machine, and then to repeat the process for the next seam. It is estimated by engineers, on the basis of years of time studies, that the actual sewing takes only from 15 to 33 per cent of the time taken by the workers to make the garment, depending on the length of the seam and the complexity of the operation. From 67 to 85 per cent of the time is spent in handling and manipulating the garment. It becomes clear, therefore, that the effect of improvement in machinery upon the time required for an operation is sharply limited because of the comparatively low ratio of operating time to handling time.[2]

The Background of the Present-day Garment Industries, 1825–1910.
The transfer of garment making from home to shop and factory began in

[1] SELEKMAN, B., et al, "The Clothing and Textile Industries in New York and Its Environs," Regional Plan of New York, New York, 1925.

[2] United States Bureau of Labor Statistics, *Bulletin* No. 662, "Productivity of Labor in the Cotton Garment Industry," Washington, D. C., 1939, p. 36.

this country about 1825. At that time there appeared, in addition to garments that were homemade or custom tailored, clothing that was ready to wear. It was made to meet the demands of sailors who wished to replenish their apparel cheaply and quickly during brief stays in port. New York, Boston, and New Bedford were the principal cities for such trade, which was soon expanded by orders for cheap clothing for plantation slaves, and later by orders from the gold miners of California. During these early decades the designing and cutting were done in shops

PLATE 56.—Cutting clothing. Numerous layers of cloth are cut in one operation. (*Courtesy of the Philadelphia Commercial Museum.*)

and the bulk of the sewing was performed by city housewives and by women on farms, especially by the latter during the winter seasons. The industry, therefore, was largely on a "putting out" basis.

An epoch-making development came in 1846 when Elias Howe invented the modern sewing machine. It produced a stitch which, unlike the chain stitch of the other experimenters, could not be ripped apart easily.[1] Improvements on the Howe machine by Singer and others during the 1850's placed the men's cloth-industry on a sound

---

[1] Howe's machine may be described as a power-driven needle. He placed the eye at the pointed, not the blunt, end of the needle. His machine operated in a cycle of synchronized movements as follows. (1) The needle was driven down through the cloth, carrying a strand of thread with it. (2) On the other side of the cloth, a hook moved up to catch the thread and pull it into a loop. (3) Through this loop a bobbin carried a second strand of thread. (4) Finally, the needle was pulled back through

mechanical basis to take care of the boom which occurred during the Civil War. During this war, as in previous wars, there was a great increase in the consumption of men's clothing. For the first time, however, the stimulus was permanent. Army authorities had collected detailed physical measurements of millions of soldiers. This increased knowledge of the dimensions of the male form furnished the statistics for standardized clothing sizes. These, in turn, improved the fitting qualities of ready-made clothing and permanently expanded the market for such apparel.

During the remaining three decades of the century, changes continued in rapid succession. Early in the seventies the mechanized cutting tools, already referred to, appeared. Several years later there began in Austria-Hungary, Poland, and Russia, a series of pogroms and other persecutions which drove to this country large numbers of Hebrews. Most of these found their way into the garment industries. Between 1880 and 1910 1.5 million Jews migrated to this country and, although not all of them were tailors, the statistics show that the great majority of the immigrant tailors at this time were Jewish. Moreover, the group as a whole was accustomed to urban occupations and hence readily fitted into the expanding needle trades. During the nineties a heavy flow of Italian immigrants began, and large numbers of these became clothing workers. A measure of the extent of the shift to these new sources for the general labor supply of the country is found in Table LVI.

TABLE LVI.—PERCENTAGE OF TOTAL UNITED STATES IMMIGRATION FURNISHED BY ITALY, RUSSIA, AND POLAND

Decade	Per Cent
1871–1880	4
1881–1890	11
1891–1900	34
1901–1910	44

Source: United States Bureau of Census.

During these postwar decades the market for clothing was expanded by other causes than an improved technology and a plentiful supply of labor. The spread of free education, the growth in newspaper circulation, and the increase in railroad mileage all combined to "democratize" style in women's clothing and hasten the transfer of its production from the home to the factory. Another force which made for expansion in the needle trades was the general rise in the standard of living growing out of the development of the corn and wheat belts of the Midwest, the iron ores of the Lake Superior district, Pennsylvania petroleum, Western copper, and Southern textiles.

---

the cloth but its thread, because it had looped the bobbin thread, was caught on the under surface of the cloth and locked in place; hence the term "lock stitch."

But this expansion in their industry did not benefit the needle workers. The oncoming immigrants kept the supply of labor ahead of the demand for labor and the results were low wages and failure to share in the benefits which came to the general populace. The newcomers arrived at the main port of entry without funds or knowledge of our language. Most of them passed into New York City's foreign colonies. There, crowded in tenements with their kind, they remained to speak their mother tongue, observe their Old World customs as to food and religion and recreation, and retain all the other habits that constitute the fixed pattern of living.

For employment they turned to a clothing contractor. The contractor, then as now, occupied an important position in the industry. On one side of him was the clothing jobber who bought the cloth, selected the style, and cut the garment. The jobber gave the bundles of pieces to the contractor to be sewn and finished into the final garment at a set price. On the other side of the contractor stood the individual workers who during the years under discussion carried on their labors in the tenement houses where they lived. These tenement workshops were described by the New York State Factory Inspector in his report for 1887 as "foul in the extreme." The contractors or "sweaters" used a system of production known as "team and task." A team consisted of a number of workers, each of whom performed one specific part of a group task, such as the manufacture of a vest. Instead of assigning individual piece rates, a group rate was set on the total task and the workers divided the money on a basis mutually satisfactory to themselves. The group piece rate was set to yield the going or market wages for the fastest worker in the team. The fastest man served as a pacesetter and "stretched out" his slower team mates. If the earnings were good, the rate was cut and the workers forced to increase their pace or put in more hours at work. The lack of sanitary facilities, the overcrowding, the poor lighting, and the long hours of work in these "sweatshops" finally compelled public interference and by means of the Tenement House Act of 1892 the contractor was gradually forced out of dwelling buildings into loft buildings, although many of these were not much better than the premises that had been vacated.

The efforts of the workers to improve their earnings took the form of attempts to unionize themselves and to conduct strikes. These efforts began in the early eighties and for a period of approximately 30 years were unsuccessful. The consistent failures of these early years call for an explanation in view of the low wages which prevailed. What were probably the two basic causes have already been touched upon: (1) the constant downward pressure exerted on wages by the large supply of necessitous unemployed immigrants; (2) an industry set-up which interposed between the owners of the goods and the workers a group of contractors who were overly ambitious, financially irresponsible, constantly coming into and out of the industry, and at all times being played off against one another by the owners. These main causes were supplemented by minor ones. Numerous cleavages of language, customs, and temperament prevented the several racial elements among the workers from presenting a united front. Furthermore, the garment trades are highly seasonal and the resultant gluts and shortages of work made it difficult for the new unions to effect a collective bargain and make it stick.

However, the tide turned in favor of the garment workers about the year 1910. In New York City successful strikes were conducted by the shirtwaist workers in 1909 and by the cloakmakers in 1910. The latter resulted in the famous "Protocol of Peace" which may be said to have ushered in the present period of collective bargaining in the women's garment industry. This agreement, in which Louis D. Brandeis played an important part, called for a preferential shop, a joint board for the control of sanitary conditions, joint price committees to set piece rates, and provision for the arbitration of disputes.

In the other major branch, the men's clothing industry, the turn came in Chicago. A small strike in the Hart, Schaffner and Marx plant soon spread to other shops and soon 35,000 workers were out on strike. At the Hart, Schaffner and Marx Company the settlement of the dispute called for an arbitration board which agreed upon better working conditions, equitable division of work in slack seasons, machinery for orderly adjustment of grievances, a minimum wage, and a 54-hour week. The company brought in from the outside a labor economist and placed him in charge of a labor department empowered to investigate complaints, negotiate with the union, and handle cases before the arbitrators. The union likewise appointed a full-time man with similar functions.

It may be said that these developments, which placed collective bargaining on a firm basis in the field of clothing manufacture, coincided in point of time. There have been many setbacks since but the contrast between the pre-1910 and the post-1910 years is sufficiently marked to establish the year as a pivotal one. Several explanations for the change may be given: immigration tapered off soon afterward; the 30 years of failures no doubt taught the pro-unionists the necessity for reconciling their differences and presenting a united front; more able leadership appeared about that time; as did also interested outsiders. Finally, the development may have been due to the "spirit of the time," for in both New York City and Chicago help came from the feminist movement and from public-spirited citizens who had hitherto not been interested, or at least active, in the labor movement. The relative merit of each of these explanations may be debated but there can be no doubt that combined they brought a new era to labor relations in clothing manufacture.

THE MEN'S CLOTHING INDUSTRY

The men's clothing industry, like the other needle trades, is an urban industry. The relative importance of the leading metropolitan areas in the industry is shown in Table LVII.

These centers, which are known in the trade as "markets," differ from each other in important characteristics. The New York market produces 40 per cent of the output of the 10 leading cities. It specializes in cheap and high-style suits. It is also regarded as a "spot" market where goods can be produced quickly to meet unexpected turns in demand. It is aided in performing this service by the presence of the "Fourth Avenue market" where practically all of the men's wear fabrics woven in this country are marketed.

TABLE LVII.—THE LEADING METROPOLITAN CLOTHING MANUFACTURING CENTERS
(In millions of dollars)

	Value of output, 1939		
	Men's, youths' and boys'	Women's, misses' and children's*	Total
New York-Newark-Jersey City.........	$221	$380	$601
Philadelphia-Camden.................	72	18	90
Chicago............................	50	27	77
Baltimore..........................	35	3	38
Rochester..........................	32	....	32
Cleveland..........................	28	4	32
Boston.............................	21	1	22
St. Louis..........................	20	10	20
Cincinnati.........................	19	2	19
Total for 9 cities..................	486	445	931

* Dresses included.
Source: Census of Manufactures, 1939.

Following New York in size come Philadelphia and Chicago. However, the characteristics of these two markets are quite different. Philadelphia, for many years an open-shop town but now unionized, has shops that are intermediate in size and in quality of output, whereas the establishments in Chicago are for the most part large and produce higher grade clothing. One student of the industry explains the large size of Chicago plants on the grounds that when the city first developed as a clothing center in the early days of mechanization, it supplied the Western rural trade that demanded 4 to 6 months credit, which only large enterprises could supply. Chicago is the home of the original "tailor to the trade" company which came into existence shortly after 1900. This type of company uses merchants, postmasters, and others who are in a position to act as sales agents on the side. It provides them with sample "swatches," order books, and detailed instructions on how to measure the customer.

Next in size come five cities—Baltimore, Rochester, Cleveland, Boston, and St. Louis. Of these, Rochester is noted as a center for the production of high-grade clothing and Cleveland as the home of the largest of the recently developed factory-owned chain clothing stores. The latter establishments manufacture at a central point and distribute through branch stores. The product is sold at popular single prices and success is dependent on volume sales, volume cloth purchases (frequently to the clothing company's specifications), and highly mechanized and controlled production. Such plants have highly subdivided tasks and use specialized tools and women workers trained within the plant. One company which illustrates this development in its most advanced form employs 2,500 workers and operates 60 stores.

The Amalgamated Clothing Workers.—The men's clothing industry has been for 25 years one of the most strongly unionized industries in the country. The union, known as the Amalgamated Clothing Workers, was formed in 1914, shortly after the Chicago strike already referred to. From the outset it has been of the industrial rather than the craft type. In fact, the clothing workers who formed the Amalgamated did so because of their dissatisfaction with their old craft union, the United Garment Workers. They contended that the United Garment Workers and the other unions in the parent organization, the American Federation of Labor, were serving the interests of skilled workers only. Sidney Hillman, a brilliant young clothing cutter who had come to the fore as a leader in the Hart, Schaffner, and Marx strike, was elected to leadership, and policies were adopted which embraced the needs of the rank and file as well as the elite.

It is interesting to note, in the light of the current struggle between craft and industrial unionism (C.I.O. vs. A. F. of L.) that has been going on in this country since 1935 that the Amalgamated at its first convention in 1914 declared:

If in any given locality the workingmen engaged in any one of the tailoring trades will be organized in one big local union instead of in many small ones as they are now, but subdivided into branches as the convenience of the members may require, and these big trade locals will, in turn, unite in a very close alliance, there will be a solidified and powerful organization of the entire industry. . . . Our organization, in order to succeed, must be organized in the Form and Spirit of Industrial Unionism.

The new union got off to a flying start, because the clothing workers, who were of southern and eastern European origin with Jewish and Italian stock predominant, had long been out of sympathy with the old-line leadership of the United Garment Workers. Sidney Hillman, who has been the head of the union for 25 years, has furnished aggressive, dynamic leadership. In the Chicago, Rochester, and New York markets the union established a system of unemployment insurance; between 1927 and 1930 two housing projects accommodating 870 workers were completed; the union organized labor banks in Chicago and New York and engaged in small loan service; it furnished financial assistance to 10 clothing firms during the period 1924–1930; for a time it took over and operated, unsuccessfully, a bankrupt firm. In its dealings with clothing manufacturers it has encouraged the employment of full-time arbitrators, the use of time and motion studies and other techniques of "scientific management," and it has demanded "dismissal wages" for those employees who are permanently put out of employment by the progress of technology.

During the period under discussion the trend has been sharply downward in the hours of work per week and upward in the average hourly earnings in this industry. The details are to be found in Table LVIII.

TABLE LVIII.—TREND OF HOURS AND WAGES IN MEN'S CLOTHING INDUSTRY

Year	Full-time work week	Average hourly earnings
1911	54	$0.23
1914 (ACWA founded)	51	0.27
1919	48	0.45
1922	44	0.73
1924	44	0.76
1926	44	0.75
1928	44	0.73
1930	44	0.70
1932	44	0.51
1934	36	0.66
1938	36	0.77

Source: HARDMAN, J. B. S., The Amalgamated—Today and Tomorrow, Amalgamated Clothing Workers of America, New York, 1939.

Lately the union has been active in organizing related industries, on the theory that further advances in the earnings of its members are to be gained only by improvement in the purchasing power of the general populace. It has brought into affiliation with it the shirt workers, the neckwear workers, the journeyman tailors, the glove workers, the cleaners

and dyers, and the laundry workers.   During NRA days Hillman worked
with John L. Lewis of the United Mine Workers and out of their common
belief in the necessity to organize the rank and file of industrial workers
came the C.I.O.   The Amalgamated has since contributed heavily to an
organizing fund for the Steel Workers Organizing Committee and an
initial fund of $500,000 for the TWOC which seeks to organize the
1.3 million workers in the textile industries.

The fortunes of the Amalgamated have varied from time to time and
place to place.   Its hold on the New York market was intermittently
weak and strong for some years but recently it has become strongly
entrenched.   The Chicago market resisted its efforts until 1919; the
Philadelphia market proved to be unusually difficult to organize and did
not capitulate until late in the twenties.   Baltimore has also been in and
out of the union fold.   Over 90 per cent of the manufacturers of men's
clothing employing over 90 per cent of all the workers are unionized.

THE WOMEN'S CLOTHING INDUSTRY

This branch of the needle industries differs in several important
respects from the one just analyzed.   Most of these differences arise from
the increased importance of style.   Because of the dominant influence
of style the industry is even more highly concentrated in New York City
than is the men's wear branch.   Fully 80 per cent of the total output
of the 10 leading cities comes from metropolitan New York (see Table
LVII).   In the silk-dress branch this proportion climbs to 90 per cent.
The reason for this heavy localization of production in New York is the
fact that the city is the style center of the country and dresses are high-
style items.   Manufacturers must keep up with rapidly changing styles
because outmoded garments must be sold at any price.   Furthermore,
style changes cannot be forecast accurately and the producer must be
at the style center to note changes as they occur and accommodate his
production plans to such changes.

The style factor also influences the size of the manufacturing establishment.   The jobber who selects the style, buys the cloth, and cuts it, as
well as the contractor who sews the garment, attempts to master the
problems arising out of style change by limiting the scope and size of his
enterprise.   In New York City the employees average less than 25 per
shop.   The shops are also quite limited in the range of the garments they
produce.   Not only do they specialize in silk dresses, cotton dresses,
blouses, suits, separate skirts, coats, etc. but they restrict themselves
within these fields to one particular type of garment, such as evening
dresses, or sports dresses.   Furthermore, within this class they limit
their efforts to one price class, such as lines to sell wholesale at $2.95,
$3.75, or $16.50, etc.

Within New York City the heaviest concentration is in the 150 acres bounded by the Pennsylvania Railroad station on the south, Times Square on the north, Seventh Avenue on the east, and Ninth Avenue on the west. Here in loft buildings are the several thousand small enterprises that comprise the industry; two-thirds of them are of the contractor type. In the neighboring streets are also the buyers and sellers of high-style fabrics, feathers, furs, and whatnot. One author has graphically described the scene as follows:

Because it is built upon fashion and behaves accordingly, the district looks to the casual visitor more like a madhouse than anything else. To pass through its streets at lunch time is an unforgettable experience. Its sidewalks are so jammed with throngs of garment workers who have poured out of its buildings for a breathing spell that through traffic is virtually stopped. The buildings house a jumble of showrooms, workrooms, storerooms, and offices. Through them passes a stream of buyers looking for goods they can sell to the customers of the retail stores they represent. Boys push little carts around through the streets, carrying a dozen or two dresses or coats at a time from one workshop or showroom to another. In offices scattered throughout the section, employers and workers argue out their recurring disputes over wages. Throughout all these operations runs a high nervous tension.

Madhouse though it may seem, the garment center and its ways of doing business are a logical answer to the fundamental force which brought them into existence—fashion. It provides two fundamental needs: First, it enables everybody to keep in touch with what everybody else is making and with what the consumers of the country and the storekeepers who represent them in this market are buying. Second, it makes possible great speed in setting up facilities to produce a particular style while the demand for it is good, closing them down when demand falls off, dropping styles quickly before stocks have been accumulated if they fail to win demand, and copying immediately anything any competitor devises which consumers like.[1]

Jobber-contractor System.—The jobber-contractor system, already referred to as having served in the early days to recruit and utilize immigrant labor, is still most heavily concentrated in the women's wear branch of the clothing industries. It has been estimated that 80 per cent of the dresses produced in the New York area are made by contractors. One student of the industry, H. E. Meiklejohn, says[2] that the jobber-contractor system performs three principal functions at the present time: (1) Contractors relieve the jobbers of dress production and thus enable them to concentrate on the increasingly important function of styling and marketing. (2) Contractors assume almost the full burden of idle

---

[1] Cox, Reavis, "The Marketing of Textiles," p. 312, The Textile Foundation, 1938.

[2] Hamilton, W., and associates, "Price and Price Policies," McGraw-Hill Book Company, Inc., New York, 1938.

capacity during slack seasons. (3) Because of the ease with which sewing machines and manufacturing space can be rented, ambitious would-be contractors come into the industry in such numbers and compete so vigorously as to furnish dresses at the lowest possible cost of production. It also results in a high turnover among contractors. Meiklejohn quotes the report of a union investigation of 927 contract shops during the period 1926–1933: More than two-thirds of all the shops went out of business within 3 years and within the 7 years almost 82 per cent discontinued. The union contends that the system is the principal factor in keeping wages down and during the last decade has made vigorous attempts to bring it under control. Before discussing these attempts, a survey will be made of the principal union developments since the "Protocol of Peace" of 1910.

International Ladies Garment Workers Union.—The "Protocol of Peace" of 1910 imposed upon the industry conditions of industrial government that were too elaborate and far-reaching. It will be recalled that the agreement called for joint control of working conditions and the wage-setting process. The latter provision was the principal cause of the difficulty. Each time dress styles changed—and this was almost daily—new types of work were created on which new piece rates had to be established. This called for negotiation toward which both sides took a trading or bargaining approach. The union asked for twice as much as it hoped eventually to get; the contractors offered half as much as they expected eventually to yield. The result was endless negotiation. Finally, when trade became quite dull in 1915, the system bogged down and the protocol ended. Shortly afterward wartime prosperity set in; the union gained in strength and imposed a 44-hour week with a weekly minimum wage after winning a major strike in 1919. During the same year 25 agreements were made with employers in nine cities. In 1920 membership exceeded 100,000, a figure that was not to be passed until 1933 when the National Industrial Recovery Act with its famous Clause 7A, gave all union membership a fillip.

The postwar business recession brought cuts in wages, lapses in collective bargaining agreements, abandonment of weekly wage rates, reestablishment of piece rates, and unsuccessful results from the strikes which accompanied these developments. The decline in union membership continued almost uninterruptedly throughout the twenties. (It will be noted in Fig. 71 that this period was also one of declining membership for the Amalgamated.) To make a bad situation worse there broke out within the union a struggle between the right- and the left-wing elements. The latter established in New York City many so-called "family shops" alleged to be communistic in organization and objectives. Crushing defeats were suffered in the New York market in 1926 and 1932, and according to the report of the general executive board, 1932 "was a year of forced economy, of breakdown or retrenchment, and retreat on every line."

In the spring of 1933 came a great revival in organizing activity. Contracts were won in Philadelphia and New York and when the NRA came in the Code of Fair Competition which was adopted contained the terms of these new contracts almost verbatim. These included a 35-hour week, the use of the NRA label on all garments, and a classified wage scale. Membership, according to union sources, skyrocketed from 40,000 to 140,000 to 200,000 to 220,000 and finally in 1938 reached 250,000.

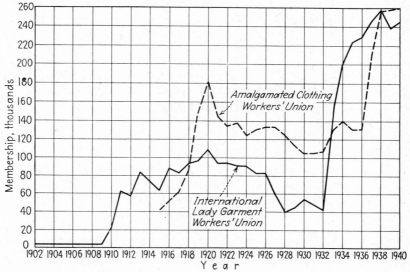

FIG. 71.—Growth of membership in clothing unions. (*L. Wolman, The Ebb and Flow of Trade Unionism, National Bureau of Economic Research, New York, 1936; I.L.G.-W.U., Trends and Profits in Women's Garment Industry, New York, 1940.*)

With these advances in membership came an increase in activities designed to create group solidarity. These include a Union Health Center which provides medical care at low rates to workers and their families, a national death benefit fund, and Unity House, which is a "country home" with 850 acres of land and recreational facilities.

On three occasions during this current period of revival the leaders of the unions that compose the International have tackled the problem of how to make the jobber-contractor system serve their purposes. They regard this system as the chief obstacle to increased wages. They contend it has this effect because it operates in the following manner. The jobbers upon the receipt of an order or upon decision to make a certain style dress send a sample dress to several contractors for estimates of production cost.   Each contractor goes into a "huddle" with a "price committee" of his workers to determine the labor price.   To this price the contractor adds a percentage for his overhead and profit and gives the estimate to the jobber.   The jobber then tells each contractor that he has received lower estimates from the other contractors and thus plays one against the other to drive down the contract price.   The workers claim that under the system they are limited in the demands they can make because they know that the workers in other shops are bidding against them.   They contend that to obtain the work at all they have to keep their wages low.   They assert, moreover, that the jobbers do not do a good job of selling, especially to the big purchasers—namely the buyers for the apparel chain stores, the group buyers, and the resident buyers.   In short, they claim that the competitive pressure which originates with the ultimate consumer is passed on successively to the stores, the jobbers, the contractors, and finally the workers who must bear it because there is no one else to whom it can be handed.   This argument is exaggerated of course, because it has been noted that there is a high turnover among contractors and it may be stated that the jobber also is in a hazardous calling.

The solutions proposed for the problem are of several kinds.   In the agreements of 1933 it was provided that the jobbers should pay the contractors a "reasonable amount" for overhead.   In the NRA code this called for a minimum of 35 per cent of his actual labor costs; in the 1936 agreement in the dress trade this figure was increased to 40 per cent on certain classes of work.

Another step designed to remedy the evils of the system was the establishment in 1933 of the principle that jobbers should deal only with contractors who agree to abide by union standards; furthermore, that the jobbers should be responsible to the union for the maintenance of wage rates by contractors.

In 1936 an even more drastic control was established.   Thereafter contractors could work for only one jobber and jobbers in turn had to show cause in order to discharge a contractor or take on additional ones.   The enforcement of these provisions was vested in a board on which the union, the jobbers, and the contractors were represented.[1]

At the time the latter control was established, a plan for setting piece rates was adopted.   In essence this calls for a joint-employer committee.   The price set for a dress must prevail in all contract shops making that particular garment and must be agreed to by the jobber for whom the contractor is working.   Furthermore, the price set for the dress must be

---

[1] In September, 1941, the Federal Trade Commission instituted proceedings against both the union and the manufacturers, charging that most of the terms of the agreements constitute unlawful restraints in trade.

based on the total of the so-called unit prices. The unit system of prices had its origin in the desire of the union to simplify the task of pricing the thousands of new styles that are produced each season. This is done by breaking down the garment into its constituent parts and determining the time necessary to make each part. As data on the task of making these parts are gradually accumulated, the work of pricing the new style resolves itself into determining its elements, most of which already have been time-studied.

Early in 1941, the union, through its Dress Joint Board, established another milestone in collective bargaining. A 3-year contract was signed by the Board which represented the 85,000 union dressmakers, and five employer associations which represented 2,100 employers. In this contract the unions demanded: first, that the employers operate their plants more efficiently, and second, that the employers make more profit. In order to achieve the first of these demands, the union specifically recommends such things as standardization of lighting and ventilation, modernization of equipment, and production planning. The union also thinks the employers could make more profits if a more effective job of merchandising were attempted. More specifically, the union offered to contribute $100,000 toward the establishment of a 3-million-dollar promotion fund: first, to promote New York as the fashion center of the world, and, second, to increase the sale of dresses by advertising New York's outstanding position in the field of style, fine workmanship, and excellent values. This industry has never been cited for efficiency of production, and there is much room for improvement in merchandizing, since the average woman spends less for dresses than she spends for hosiery and underwear. However, it is interesting to note that the pressure for reform came from the union.

The clothing industries are unique in a number of respects. In contrast with other industries, they are noted for their high degree of unionization, heavy concentration in New York City, predominance of Italians and Jews, both as workers and employers, small-scale operation, coexistence of inside and outside shops, and the curse of style. Before the rise of unions, these industries exemplified competition at its worst. For employers, survival was perilous; for workers, life was misery. The very factors which made for these unwholesome conditions gave rise later to full-fledged unionism.

CHAPTER XXVII

THE LEATHER INDUSTRY

The leather industry, by a process known as tanning, converts hides and skins, highly perishable by-products of the meat packing industry, into leather, a semidurable product of many uses.   About 80 per cent of its output is used in the manufacture of shoes.   The remainder is used in the manufacture of gloves, belting, bags, harness, upholstery, book-binding, etc.   The raw materials are the hides and skins of a wide variety of animal life: cattle, sheep, pigs, goats, horses, deer, kangaroos, seals, snakes, lizards, sharks, ostriches, etc.   The industry is closely related on the one side with the meat packing industry, and on the other with the manufacture of shoes, and this intermediate position influences to a great extent the economic aspects of the industry.

The Development of the Industry.—Leather manufacture is of primitive origin, because of the widespread occurrence of the raw materials, the simplicity of the process, and the extensive demand for its products.   At the outset in this country many colonists produced their own leather supply, since hides and skins were easily obtainable and the process of preserving them from decay was easily mastered.   But as one observer stated: "Although almost anyone could manufacture leather, it took a skilled tanner to produce good leather."   It was natural, therefore, that skilled artisans should soon develop and that tanneries should be among the first manufacturing establishments to appear in this country.   In time almost every community had its local tannery.

The equipment and process of these colonial tanneries was simple. The equipment consisted of tubs or vats sunk in the ground near streams of running water.   After soaking the hides to make them soft and pliable, the layer of fat and blood vessels was removed from the under side of the hide and the hair was scraped from the grain side.   The middle portion was tanned or converted into leather by soaking it in a solution of water and bark obtained from oak or chestnut trees.   In this operation the fibers which compose the skin are prevented from putrefying or turning into glue by the preservative action of the tannic acid contained in the bark.   The leather was then finished by making it either dense and firm or soft and pliable according to the needs of the consumer.

The operation, although a simple one, was extremely slow, requiring from nine months to a year to accomplish.   The labor was unskilled, except that of the boss tanner who, by means of his senses of sight, touch, and taste, had to determine the rate at which the tanning was proceeding and when to move the skins from time to time to vats of varying strength of tanning liquor.   Most of these early tanneries were located in New England where a localized shoe manufacturing industry had already been established.

Aside from an increase in the number of tanning materials which appeared about 1800 as a result of the experiments of Sir Humphrey Davy, the industry made little technical progress during the first three-quarters of the nineteenth century.   The most noteworthy development

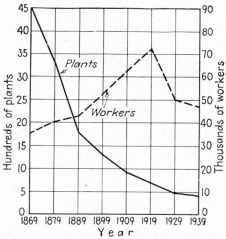

Fig. 72.—Number of establishments and workers in the tanning industry.   (*Census of Manufacturers.*)

during this period was the mushroom growth of tanneries.   In 1870 about 4,500 tanneries were in operation.   They were by this time located not only in New England, but throughout New York, Pennsylvania, south along the Blue Ridge mountains in the hardwood areas of Virginia, North Carolina, and Tennessee, and in eastern Ohio and Indiana.   Prior to the Civil War, seaboard tanneries gradually came into existence which specialized in light leather made from imported sheep and goat skins.

Since 1875 the industry has changed materially in technique, scale, and organization.   The first change to be noted was the disappearance of the local tannery.   The extent of the decrease in number of establishments is portrayed in Fig. 72.

Several developments account for this change in scale of operations. First was the substitution of tanning concentrate for tan bark.   Tanning concentrate is a distilled tannic acid made by cooking the bark at its point of origin. It is shipped in concentrated form to the tannery where it is diluted to about 10 per cent of the shipping strength.

Second was the invention in the late eighties of a tanning material from the mineral chrome. Hitherto all tannins had been of vegetable origin. Since the chrome process was best adapted to light leathers and these were manufactured predominantly from imported sheep and goat skins, such tanning establishments developed on a large scale in the Middle Atlantic states where they were in direct contact with raw-material supplies and consuming markets.

Third was the appearance of interstate meat packing establishments with centralized slaughtering and packing plants, the corn belt feeding area as the principal source of supply, and refrigerator car distribution. As a result, large-scale tanneries sprang up in Illinois, Wisconsin, and Michigan to utilize these centralized sources of leather raw materials.

Fourth was the formation of large leather companies as a result of the general consolidation movement culminating around the turn of the century. The United States Leather Company, organized in 1893, was a consolidation of 6 companies controlling about 150 establishments. It was the first corporation in the United States with a capitalization in excess of 100 million dollars and it controlled, at the outset, about 60 per cent of the sole leather production of the country. Similarly, the American Hide and Leather Company, organized in 1899, combined 23 companies and at one time controlled about 75 per cent of the United States upper leather output. In both instances, the consolidations resulted in the dismantling of inefficient plants and the transfer of their production to better located and better equipped units. Today more than half of the output of the industry is the product of establishments producing in excess of a million dollars' worth of leather each.

In 1939 the leather industry produced 346 million dollars' worth of products, according to the Census of Manufactures. About 60 per cent of this output consisted of light leather products, such as upper leather for shoes, garment and glove leather, and fancy leather products. The remaining 40 per cent consisted of heavy leather products such as sole leather for shoes, harness leather, leather for bags and luggage, and upholstery leather. Although at one time most tanning establishments produced a wide range of products, plants today specialize on a basis of raw materials and finished product to such an extent that the industry divides itself into two distinct fields—the heavy leather and the light leather division.

HEAVY LEATHER DIVISION

The first of these is the heavy leather industry. This branch produces leather from hides rather than from skins. Hides come from large animals such as cattle, horses, buffalo, and oxen. These animals yield a thick heavy hide weighing from 25 to 75 lb. About 10 to 15 per cent of our hides are imported, two-thirds of this supply coming from the Argentine. The leather that is produced from such hides is used for shoe soles, harness, belting, etc., and is sold by the pound rather than by the square foot.

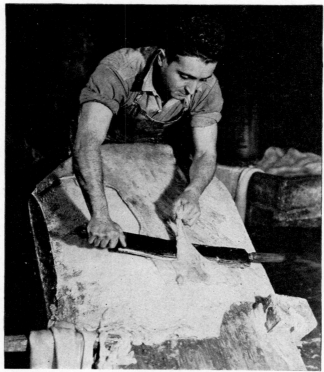

PLATE 57.—Hand fleshing and trimming. (*Courtesy of U. S. Leather Company.*)

Hides from the large meat packing establishments of the United States constitute well over half of our domestic supply. They are known as "packer" hides, in contrast with "country" hides which are secured from small packers, local butchers, and farmers who do their own slaughtering. Packer hides invariably command better prices because of their superior quality. They have fewer imperfections resulting from careless take-off, improper curing, grubs, or ticks. A 50-lb. packer hide will yield about 35 lb. of leather, but it is difficult to estimate the yield of country hides.

Process.—Hides arrive at the tannery in bundles, heavily salted to arrest decomposition while in transit. First, they are soaked for several

PLATE 58.—Interior of a tannery.   (*Courtesy of Charles S. Walton & Company Inc.*)

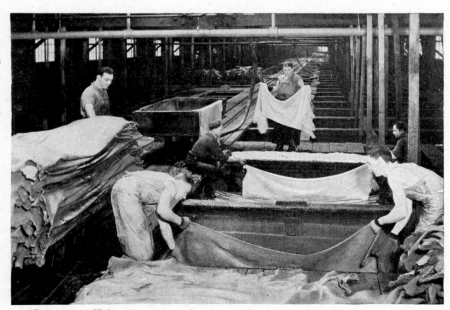

PLATE 59.—Hides going into rocker vats.   (*Courtesy of U. S. Leather Company.*)

days to remove the salt, blood, and dirt and to render them soft and pliable throughout.

The next operation is the removal of the hair. This is facilitated by soaking the hides from four to six days in a lime solution which loosens the hair. The hides are then washed and fed through a machine which removes the hair. The hair is sold as a valuable by-product. It is used as a binder in making plaster, stuffing for mattresses and more

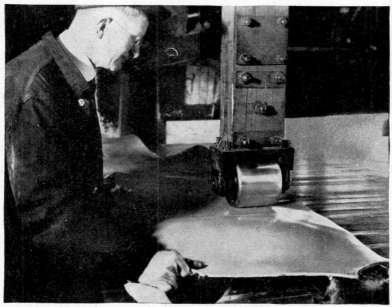

PLATE 60.—Rolling, a finishing operation to make the leather firm and flat. (*Courtesy of U. S. Leather Company.*)

recently to make Ozite, a felted fabric used as a floor covering to protect rugs.

The flesh side of the hide contains fat and blood vessels which must be removed before actual tanning begins. This operation takes place in the beam house. It is done partly by machine and finished by hand. Most of the fat and tissue is removed by a machine consisting of sharp-bladed knives mounted in spiral fashion on a cylinder revolving at high speed. Subsequently the hides are placed upon a barrel-shaped block and with the aid of a knife the flesh side is scraped as clean as the grain side. The fleshings are likewise disposed of as a by-product used in the manufacture of furniture glue and grease for soapmaking.

The actual tanning takes place in two stages of soaking in tannic acid vats. The hides are first tanned in the "rocker vats," arranged in a series so that the strongest liquor from the head or top vat flows into the top of the next vat. The hides are moved into progressively stronger solutions and during suspension they are slowly moved up and down on rockers so as to agitate the tannic acid thus assuring thorough and uniform tanning. This operation requires from 2 to 3 weeks. The hides are next piled, one on top of the other in club-sandwich fashion, in the "lay away" vats, where they are soaked in tannic acid from two to six months. Finally the hides are washed, swabbed in oil, and hung up in the drying loft. Numerous finishing operations, such as dyeing, splitting, shaving, brushing, rolling, etc., impart the desired finishes according to the needs of the customers.

Length of the Manufacturing Cycle.—Heavy leather tanning has always been and still is a time-consuming process. In contrast with 9 months to a year which was formerly required, the manufacturing cycle has been reduced to approximately 3 to 6 months. This is due not so much to improved machinery as to improved chemical control. Although tanning is essentially a chemical process, it is only within recent years that tanneries have sought the aid of chemists. Through improved chemical procedures companies now feed tannage to the hides more rapidly than hitherto. In former days, because of a lack of chemical knowledge and control, tanners always erred on the safe side and used a mild rather than a concentrated tanning liquor.

Heavy leather is made for the most part by vegetable tanning processes and although the manufacturing cycle has been shortened considerably, it is still much longer than in chrome tanning. The result is that capital tied up in work in process represents a larger proportion of the total investment than is the case in the light leather branch of the industry where chrome processes prevail. A medium-sized leather plant has a daily output of 300 to 400 hides, and the manufacturing cycle is approximately 100 days. Estimating conservatively that each hide is worth $3, it can be calculated that a minimum of $100,000 is invested in work in process. If to this total is added the value of the hides held in storage for processing, the value of finished leather held for sale, and the value of the tanning materials, it may readily be seen that although the capital invested in machinery and equipment is not as great as in the light leather division, where operations are apt to be more numerous and elaborate, nevertheless the operation of the medium-sized tannery in the sole leather branch is not a small financial venture.[1]

The Leading Producers.—The principal producers of heavy leather are few in number. The United States Leather Company is still the largest producer, but it occupies a less important position than it did

[1] WARSHAW, H. T. "Representative Industries of the United States," p. 426, Henry Holt and Company, New York, 1928.

at the outset. In contrast with 150 plants and 60 per cent of the sole-leather-producing capacity of the industry, which this company had at the time of its incorporation, it now operates about 16 plants whose combined capacity is about 20 per cent of the total for this branch of the industry. Some of the company's plants were sold with the understanding that the purchasers would not enter the leather business as competitors; they were sold therefore at little more than scrap value. Other plants were permanently closed. United States Leather's largest competitors are the National Leather Company, a Swift and Company subsidiary, and the J. K. Mosser Leather Corporation, a subsidiary of Armour and Company. The effects of the entrance of the meat packers into the leather industry will be discussed later in connection with the subject of competitive conditions in the leather industry. Other large companies in this division of the leather industry are Howes Brothers and Proctor Ellison, both Boston concerns, the American Oak Leather Company of Cincinnati, and Leas and McVitty of Philadelphia.

LIGHT LEATHER DIVISION

The second major branch of the industry engages in the production of light leather. Light leather is manufactured from skins and kips. A kip comes from immature cattle, horses, etc., and a skin comes from light animals such as calves, sheep, lambs, goats, kids, colts, pigs, etc. Whereas hides weigh 25 to 75 lb., skins weigh less than 25 lb. In dollar volume of output this division of the industry is larger than the heavy leather division.

The light leather industry differs from the heavy leather industry in a number of respects. The manufacturing cycle is much shorter, the process is more elaborate, the equipment is more extensive, and the labor is more skilled.

Process.—Skins are tanned for the most part by a mineral rather than a vegetable process. The chrome or mineral process of tanning employs chrome salts, usually bichromate of potash or bichromate of soda. These mineral ores are imported from British and Portuguese Africa, Greece, Brazil, and French Oceanica. Mineral tanning requires only a few weeks instead of months. Very few hide tanners use this process because vegetable tanning produces thicker hides which are desired by the heavy leather producers.

Chrome tanning consists of three major steps—preparation of the skins, tanning, and finishing operations. Of the three, the actual tanning is really quite simple but elaborate preparatory and finishing operations are required.

The preliminary operations are essentially the same as those used in the heavy leather division except that after the fleshing operation the skins are bated. Bating consists of soaking the skins in a reel or vat containing pancreatic enzymes to wash off the alkalies of the depilatory process. It also causes a "falling" of the skins—a disappearance of swelling.

Skins, like hides, are tanned in two stages. The first tanning is accomplished by soaking the skins in a reel containing a solution of chrome and muriatic acid. This is an overnight process. Upon removal the excess liquor is drained off by running the skins through the striking-out machine which operates upon the principle of a wringer. As soon as the skins are wrung out they are placed into another reel for a second tanning. This bath arrests the chemical transformation, that is, it permanently "fixes" the leather.

Finishing consists of a dozen or more operations, depending upon the type of leather to be made. In the case of kid leather the sequence of operations is as follows: dyeing, oiling to restore the fat previously washed off, drying, staking—a mechanical operation to soften the leather, buffing—to make it more uniform, seasoning, glazing, measuring, and inspecting. It is because of the numerous finishing operations that the light leather tanneries employ more equipment and proportionately more highly skilled labor than the heavy leather tanneries.

The Leader.—The American Hide and Leather Company is still the leader in this division of the industry. This company, like United States Leather in the sole leather branch, has also suffered a relative decline in capacity. It produces 15 to 17 per cent, of the calf leather output and 5 to 9 per cent of the "dress side upper leather"—the term applied by the trade to light leather made from "split" hides. Three-fourths of the company's output goes to manufacturers of men's shoes and 15 per cent to manufacturers of women's shoes. This company has recently introduced a number of medium-priced colored leathers for women's popularly priced shoes. Skins are processed to the coloring point and there held in stock awaiting the orders of shoe manufacturers.

ECONOMIC CHARACTERISTICS OF THE LEATHER TANNING INDUSTRY

Importance of Foreign Raw Materials.—As noted before, the advent of the chrome process in the eighties led to the establishment of a number of specialized plants in the Middle Atlantic area. These plants consume imported sheep, calf, and goat skins and turn out specially processed leathers, such as French kid, Rosebay Willow, morocco leather, etc. The light leather branch of the industry is heavily dependent upon foreign sources of raw material. Practically all of the goat skins and about half of the sheep, calf, and kip skins consumed in this country are imported.

There are a number of reasons for our great dependence upon other countries for leather raw materials. With the growth of population and

facture of a trial shoe or model; (2) the manufacture of lasts; and (3) the manufacture of patterns.

Designing.—In plants making women's shoes and men's dress shoes the designer is as important as in the clothing industry. Upon his skill and judgment depend in large measure the volume and permanency of trade secured by his company. He must have artistic skill, a knowledge of shoemaking, and a familiarity with about 2,500 different designs. From the traveling salesman he receives suggestions as to the current likes and dislikes of the public. Following a study of style trends, the designer, sales manager, and factory manager confer and decide upon their line for the coming season. Samples or trial shoes are then made for the salesman to take out and show to the trade. If sufficient orders are obtained, patterns are made and quantity production begins. This preliminary work must be done twice a year—for the spring and fall seasons.

Last Making.—A last is a wooden or metal form having the shape of a foot which serves as the model over which each shoe is built. It resembles a shoe tree used to preserve the shape of a shoe when not in use. Lasts are generally made of maple wood which cuts easily and presents a hard, smooth surface. They may or may not have a steel plate on the bottom, depending upon the type of shoe to be made. A shoe factory needs as many lasts, lefts and rights, as its weekly production schedule, including a great variety of styles and sizes, calls for. The "last" item represents no small cost of shoe manufacturing.

Patternmaking.—Patterns are the forms or shapes used in cutting the various parts of the upper portion of the shoe. A sole pattern is sometimes used, but generally it is blocked or cut out in the rough and subsequently trimmed to proper size. Master patterns are first cut by hand out of sheet iron. From these, production patterns are reproduced in cardboard by pattern machines. The cardboard patterns are then bound with metal strips which are smoothed at the corners and soldered at the joints. Finally, the patterns are stamped with size numbers, widths, and styles.

Shoemaking.—The sequence of operations depends upon the kind of shoe being made. We shall consider the Goodyear welt which is made in larger volume than any other type. The manufacturing operations fall into three major categories—namely, the making of the shoe upper, the sole assembly, and the final assembly, including lasting, bottoming, and finishing.

The upper assembly embraces the sorting, cutting, and stitching of the light leather, linings, and trimmings that go to make up the upper part of the shoe. After the materials have been sorted they are cut by hand or with a die-cutting machine. This requires skillful placing of the

PLATE 61.—The pulling-over machine.   (*Courtesy of Endicott-Johnson Corporation.*)

PLATE 62.—Outside stitching.   (*Courtesy of Endicott-Johnson Corporation.*)

patterns so as to secure the most economical use of the leather. The cut parts are then assembled and properly pieced together by stitching into the complete upper assembly ready to go on the last.

The sole assembly consists of the outer sole, welting, insoles, counters, toe boxes, and heels. These parts are first cut in the rough to approximate shape by means of dies and then cut down to precise shape in conformity with the patterns in a rounding machine. The outsole is passed through a heavy rolling machine to compress the fibers and through a splitting machine to reduce it to an even thickness.

The third series of operations begins with lasting, in which the assembled units just described are fitted over a last for the final construction of the shoe. The toe box and counter are inserted between the lining and the outer leather. The toe box and counter consist of pieces of inflexible leather or fiber which serve to give rigidity to the toe and heel respectively. The completely assembled upper is then drawn tightly over the last and temporarily tacked to it. This is done by the pulling-over machine which has replaced hand lasting. A series of "wipers" remove from the toe and heel all wrinkles, leaving a perfectly smooth surface. The trimming machine removes all surplus leather and the shoe then passes to a machine which beats the leather and counter into final shape in conformity with the last. Upon completion of the lasting operations the upper is stitched to the insole by means of the welt. The welt is a narrow strip of flexible leather extending along the edge of the shoe from the fore part of the heel around the toe and back to the heel on the other side. The heavy outsole is then stitched on to the welt, and the shoe is complete except for tacking on the heel and a series of trimming and finishing operations.

Kinds of Construction.—For many years shoes were made by either the Goodyear welt process just described, the McKay, or the pegged process. The chief distinction between types of construction lies in the method of attaching the outer sole to the upper. The Goodyear welt process attaches the insole to the upper by means of a welt in such a manner that the stitches do not penetrate the inside surface of the insole. This is accomplished by a specially designed machine equipped with a curved needle. A second sewing operation attaches the outer sole to the welt as explained above. This produces a shoe that is comfortable, durable, flexible, and one that can be readily styled and resoled.

In the McKay shoe, which antedates the Goodyear welt, the outer sole is united to the upper by a stitching which penetrates clear through the insole. The wearer's foot thus rests upon a line of stitching and clinched lasting tacks unlike the Goodyear welt. However, the McKay is a simpler construction and therefore less costly to manufacture.

Heavy work shoes are of the pegged or standard screw type. The sole is attached to the upper with metal or wooden pegs or threaded wire. This type of construction produces a heavy, inflexible, but very durable shoe suitable for all-weather purposes. These three basic types illustrated in Fig. 75 account for over half of our total output.

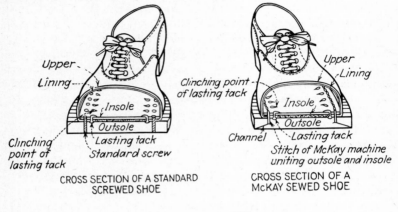

CROSS SECTION OF A STANDARD SCREWED SHOE

CROSS SECTION OF A McKAY SEWED SHOE

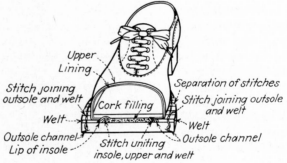

CROSS SECTION OF A GOODYEAR WELT SHOE

Fig. 75.—Types of shoe construction. (*Shoe Constructions; Circular of the National Bureau of Standards, C419, U. S. Department of Commerce, 1938.*)

The stitch-down is one of the oldest types; it is used largely in the manufacture of children's and juvenile shoes. The upper is attached to the sole by a single stitching, but the edge of the upper is turned out instead of under the insole, thus resembling the welt shoe in appearance.

The distinguishing feature of the Compo shoe is that the sole is cemented to the upper. Although it is not a recent innovation, the cemented shoe has gained rapidly since the formation of the Compo Shoe Machinery Corporation about 10 years ago. At that time it was used for women's shoes, but now men's shoes are also made by the Compo process. In 1939 this type accounted for 12 to 15 per cent of the total output. It is alleged to be as good in quality as a stitched shoe if not superior. The process is quite simple and lends itself to the production of a shoe that is light, trim, flexible, and easily styled.

Most lightweight shoes for women were formerly made by the turned process. The shoe is lasted wrong side out and finished after turning. The process of turning the shoe inside out weakens the leather and since light-weight shoes can now be made by other processes, such as the Compo, the turned shoe is almost obsolete.

The Leasing System.—The practice of leasing machinery in this industry began about the middle of the last century. With the adaptation of Elias Howe's sewing machine to shoe manufacture in 1852 there began a period of rapid mechanization. In 1858 Lyman Blake invented a machine to stitch soles to uppers. He sold this machine to Gordon McKay for $150,000 the following year. McKay made some improvements but found difficulty in selling it to shoe manufacturers, who had small businesses and were unaccustomed to heavy capital investment. Accordingly, he equipped the machines with stitch counters and began leasing them to shoemakers who paid a royalty on the basis of the number of pairs of shoes made. In 1875 Charles Goodyear brought out the welt process bearing his name. Numerous other machines appeared in quick succession. Among the more important were machines for heeling, lasting, channeling, rough rounding, eyeleting, and buttonholing. By the decade of the nineties the custom of leasing shoe machinery had become the established method of introducing any new equipment and there had arisen many shoe machinery companies among which intense rivalry existed. In 1890, for example, there were 100 machine companies in Lynn. All this was changed by a series of consolidations culminating in 1899 with the formation of the United Shoe Machinery Corporation, which acquired and still holds control of about 90 per cent of the business.

The United Shoe Machinery Corporation distributes its products by either sale or lease, but the most important machines are leased. For the use of a machine the lessee pays a royalty on each pair of shoes made. The royalty per pair ranges from $\frac{1}{2500}$ cent for the welt indenting and burnishing machine to $\frac{1}{2}$ cent for the sole-laying machine. Total royalty payments are about 5 cents per pair of shoes. The lessee is also required to pay an installation fee and a termination charge, each of which is about 10 per cent of the cost of the machine, and a minimum monthly rental charge in case the machine is idle for a long period. Including interest on investment the lease of a machine costs the lessee slightly more than would outright purchase. Nevertheless, most shoe manufacturers elect to rent the machines, thus obviating the necessity of a large initial cash outlay. Only 13 per cent of total assets in the shoe industry are tied up in fixed form, in contrast with 41 per cent for automobile and 56 per cent for full-fashioned hosiery manufacturing.

Leasing offers the shoe manufacturer several other advantages in addition to reduced capital investment. The company maintains scattered repair depots which carry spare parts. They are manned by a staff of specially trained mechanics who serve the local users of their machinery. The company also has a corps of management experts upon whom shoe manufacturers may call for advice in such matters as plant administration and factory layout. Furthermore, the company replaces obsolete equipment.

It is difficult to appraise the social effects of the leasing system upon the shoe industry because of its manifold influence. For example, there is a diversity of opinion as to whether it has retarded or stimulated mechanization of the industry. It is alleged that the United Shoe Machinery Corporation stunted technical progress by buying and suppressing new machines to protect its investment of installed machinery. Its policy of full-line forcing prior to 1922 lends support to this argument. Before the government intervention the company refused to supply a manufacturer with any of its machines unless he contracted to use its full line of machines. On the other hand, it must be acknowledged that the company has fostered mechanization as a result of, first, its large technical staff, second, its policy of leasing which facilitates easy acquisition by shoe manufacturers, and, third, its policy of modernizing old machinery by installing new attachments or by complete factory reequipment.

The leasing system is alleged to be one of the major causes of excess capacity in the shoe industry. Since an able enterpriser can get started without the financial burden of buying machinery, the argument sounds logical. However, there appears to be considerable disparity in the estimates of capacity. Some put it at 900 million pairs annually, which would be more than twice the consumption. The Brookings Institution's study of "America's Capacity to Produce" concludes that the shoe industry normally operates at an average of about 80 per cent of capacity. This study points out three reasons for the overestimates of capacity. First, the leasing system leads to the practice of stating capacity on the basis of floor space available rather than on the basis of machinery actually installed. Second, much of the installed machinery is necessarily idle owing to the great variety of types, styles, and sizes of shoes. Third, the increased rate of style change since 1921 has increased the difficulty of keeping all machinery active and has increased the element of seasonal slack[1]. The problem of excess capacity is probably no worse

[1] Nourse, E. G. and Associates, America's Capacity to Produce, p. 224, The Brookings Institution, Washington, D. C., 1934.

in the shoe industry than in other industries. If leasing does facilitate entry into the industry, it must also be recognized that it facilitates withdrawal.

The leasing system has strengthened the survival of small plants because of the absence of a sliding scale of royalties. All manufacturers, regardless of size, pay the same royalty for the use of machinery rented from the United Shoe Machinery Corporation.

The leasing system has increased the intensity of competition, both domestic and foreign. The ease of entry and withdrawal has opened the competitive arena to the small enterpriser, as a result of which we find a tendency toward a large company turnover. Furthermore, the policy of leasing machinery abroad tends to stimulate imports and discourage exports. Foreign producers, equipped with the latest American machinery, can turn their lower labor costs to better advantage, permitting them to undersell domestic producers in the home market. The effect of the leasing system on labor is closely tied up with the general question of location.

Shift in Location.—The leasing system has also been one of the factors responsible for the shift in location of shoe plants. Prior to the formation of the United Shoe Machinery Corporation, shoemaking was distinctly a Yankee industry. New England produced over half of our output. Haverhill, Lynn, Brockton, and Boston, all in eastern Massachusetts, were the principal producing cities. As long as shoemaking required skilled labor, this region, by virtue of its early start, remained the historic center of the industry. The increased subdivision of labor and mechanization stimulated by the United Shoe Machinery Corporation policies reduced the attractiveness of Massachusetts as a shoe center because skilled labor, though not eliminated, was greatly reduced in importance. The relative decline of Massachusetts is shown in Table LIX.

TABLE LIX.—PERCENTAGE DISTRIBUTION OF SHOE PRODUCTION BY LEADING STATES ACCORDING TO PHYSICAL VOLUME OF OUTPUT

State	Per cent		
	1904	1919	1939
Massachusetts	44	35	19
New York	10	19	17
Missouri	7	8	12
Illinois	5	3	7.5
New Hampshire	9	7	9
Total United States production (million pairs)	242	331	424

Source: Census of Manufactures.

Several other factors contributed toward the geographical decentralization. Not only was it increasingly possible to utilize labor outside of Massachusetts, but numerous manufacturers were eager to move out in search of other labor markets because of the unions. The industry had become highly unionized, and as the workers made increasing demands, many plants moved out of the state into areas offering a more tractable labor market. In 1939–1940, approximately only 40 per cent of the workers were organized, largely as a result of this shift.

Another development that aided the decentralization of the industry is the westward shift of the market. It is more expensive to transport shoes than the raw materials and, with the growing importance of style, proximity to the market, facilitating quick delivery, is more important than ever.

Organization of the Industry.—The shoe industry is characterized by a high degree of plant specialization and a marked disparity in scale of operations.

The industry consists of about 1,100 establishments, most of which confine their manufacturing operations to a fairly narrow range of products. Plants specialize according to process, such as Compo, welt, or McKay. Within each of these processes they specialize according to use, i.e., men's, women's, or children's shoes. Some plants make only staple or work shoes; others, novelty or dress shoes, and we find small plants producing only custom-made shoes. Furthermore, plants specialize in the different price classes of low-, medium-, and high-priced footwear.

Specialization of another type has developed in the form of materials and parts suppliers. In addition to the shoe plants described, there is a group of about 500 plants specializing in the production of cut stock, consisting of soles, shanks, heels, insoles, etc., and findings, that is, pegs, metal tips, heel plates, bows, laces, etc. Lastmaking, which was formerly the function of a separate department of every shoe plant, is now a separate industry.

This high degree of specialization is not a haphazard development but rather the practical solution to a difficulty inherent in the nature of the product. Consider the almost bewildering variety of product turned out by this industry. There are variations as to type of construction which require different combinations of machines; variations as between men's and women's shoes which call for different tools and materials; variations in sizes both as to length and width of the shoe which call for a large supply of lasts. For example, if a manufacturer restricted his output to one type of men's shoe, he would need approximately 1,000 different sized lasts. Finally, the problem of style brings infinitely more complications. In the face of this heterogeneous array of types, sizes, and styles, plant specialization is practically inevitable.

Among the thousand shoe plants proper, we find a great diversity in size of plants. They range in size from very small establishments employing 5 workers or less to large factories employing as many as 2,500 workers. Perhaps the picture as to scale of operations can best be summarized by citing the fact that 60 per cent of the plants employ no more than 100 workers each, whereas 85 per cent of all workers employed in the industry are in plants of over 100 workers each. In other words, shoe manufacturing is an industry of many small plants, but the bulk of the output is the product of the larger plants. There are several explanations for this disparity in size.

Let us consider, first, the small manufacturer. Many of these small shops are custom shoe manufacturers located in Brooklyn, Philadelphia, and Chicago, where they cater to the high price metropolitan trade. Very little capital is required to enter the industry, by virtue of the machinery, leasing system. Furthermore, cut stock, lasts, and miscellaneous supplies can be purchased from independent suppliers. The growing importance of styled and novelty footwear likewise favors the small manufacturer, who has a more flexible change of pace than his larger competitors. This is corroborated by evidence of the difference in size of plants manufacturing men's shoes as compared with women's shoes which are naturally more subject to the influence of style. Between 1920 and 1928 the average number of wage earners per plant in Haverhill, a women's shoe center, was 56.1, as compared with 209.8 in Brockton, a men's shoe center.[1]

Large plants usually manufacture the popularly priced shoes. Accordingly, they cater to the economical buyer who is interested in mechanical serviceability as well as style, and as a result of the economies of larger volume of production they compete on a price basis.

The leading producers are the International Shoe Company, Endicott-Johnson, and the Brown Shoe Company. Together these companies produce about one-fourth of the total output. The International Shoe Company is the largest. It employs 30,000 workers and produces 50 million pairs a year. Second in size is the Endicott-Johnson Company. It employs 20,000 workers and produces about 40 million pairs annually. Third in size is the Brown Shoe Company, which employs about 9,000 workers and turns out about 12 million pairs annually.

These large companies are multiplant, integrated enterprisers manufacturing a variety of shoes, but they concentrate their volume on popularly priced lines. International, for example, has 38 shoe factories, 9 tanneries, and numerous shoe findings and supply plants. Each shoe plant is given over to one particular type of shoe and is in charge of a

[1] NORTON, T. L., "Trade Union Policies in the Massachusetts Shoe Industry 1919–1929," p. 99, Columbia University Press, New York, 1932.

manager who receives special rewards contingent upon the efficiency of his unit.   These companies engage in centralized buying of leather and other supplies and distribute them among their several units in accordance with their special needs.   They tan from 50 to 75 per cent of their leather requirements so as not to be at the complete mercy of the highly volatile leather market.   They have a wide coverage of the shoe market but produce a substantial volume of conservative lines which can be manufactured for stock in off seasons to guarantee quick delivery in brisk seasons.

Technical Maturity of the Industry.—Few, if any, other industries have attained the high level of mechanical proficiency found in the shoe industry.   This has its origin in the rapid succession of inventions after 1850 and the practice of leasing which permits every plant to obtain the latest equipment on easy terms.

The early and basic inventions have already been pointed out, but, in addition to these, an almost endless flow of auxiliary machines and attachments has appeared.   As early as 1914 over 7,000 patents on shoe machinery had been issued by the Patent Office.   Today comparatively few hand operations remain in shoemaking.   In some of our larger plants the shoemaking process has been broken down to some 200 separate operations, 170 of which are done by machine.

By virtue of the leasing system, the machinery is easily available to all manufacturers on equal terms.   The United Shoe Machinery Corporation's policy of servicing machinery and replacing obsolete equipment assures high operating efficiency of machinery in place.   Furthermore, the machinery is light and therefore easy to transport and install; it is highly automatic and therefore easy to operate.

The technical maturity of the industry has brought with it lower labor costs for the manufacturer and a marked change in status for the workers. The labor cost per pair of shoes in 1863 when shoes were handmade was $4.58, in contrast with an average cost of only 45 cents in 1937.   Excepting a few special occupations, such as cutting, vamping, bottoming, lasting, and pulling over, the skilled labor formerly required has been displaced by ingenious machinery.   Shoemaking offers a striking example of the elimination of craftsmanship by machines.

Stability of Demand.—Since the shoe industry manufactures a consumer's good, it has a remarkably steady demand.   Shoes are an indispensable item of apparel, only semidurable and thus requiring frequent replacement.   The per-capita consumption of shoes varies from 2.5 pairs annually in depression years to slightly over 3 pairs in prosperous years.   The stability of demand is reflected in the total annual production shown in Fig. 76.   It is apparent that shoe manufacturing is virtually a depression-proof industry.   For the period covered in Fig. 76

the net change between any two consecutive years was never greater than 16 per cent.

Another factor which has helped to sustain demand is the element of style. Style plays a minor role in men's shoes for the most part, but since the world war, women have become ever more style conscious in their purchases of footwear. The trend toward shorter shirts gave more prominence to the shoes in a woman's ensemble, with the result that more attention was paid to the appearance of shoes. In the early twenties novelty and sport footwear appeared and today a lady's wardrobe usually includes a variety of shoes, as of dresses, for every occasion. In other words, women's shoes serve to adorn the feet as well as to protect

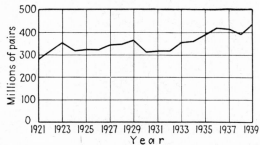

Fig. 76.—United States production of leather shoes. (*Census of Manufacturers.*)

the feet, and therefore mechanical serviceability has given way to style. Women's shoes are not worn from one season to the next. They become outmoded and are replaced by others of more recent design. Manufacturers have eagerly catered to this increasing tempo of style change by making shoes of lighter construction, which makes for lower costs. A woman can therefore afford several pairs of low-cost shoes in place of fewer high-priced shoes as formerly. This is reflected in the volume of production. Whereas the population is about equally divided between males and females, since 1914 the production of women's shoes has consistently gained over men's shoes as shown in Table LX.

TABLE LX.—RATIO OF WOMEN'S SHOE TO MEN'S SHOE PRODUCTION

1914	83	1932	154
1919	110	1933	147
1923	110	1934	146
1925	120	1935	145
1927	122	1936	156
1928	136	1937	145
1929	138	1938	153
1930	147	1939	161
1931	147	1940	146

Source: United States Department of Commerce, Bureau of Census.

Men's shoes are more conservatively styled. They are made of more durable material. Heavier leather and composition soles give longer wear. This calls for less frequent replacement.

Profitability of Shoe Manufacturing.—The depression-proof character of the shoe industry is clearly revealed in Fig. 77. Tanneries, by way of contrast, sustained deficits in 6 of the 11 years shown. Shoe companies earned no less than 4 per cent upon their capital investment during any one year of this period, which was one of the most trying of our business history. Comparative stability of earning power in the shoe industry is a reflection of the nature of the market and the nature of the industry's cost structure. Shoe manufacturers do not have to contend with violent fluctuations in demand, and such variations as do occur can easily be met because of the absence of heavy overhead costs.

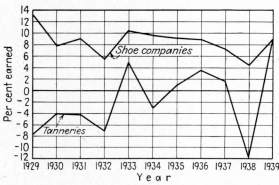

FIG. 77.—Earnings of shoe manufacturers and tanners. Based upon 5 leading shoe companies and 3 leading tanneries. (*Standard and Poor's Corporation.*)

On the other hand, profits are never fabulous in shoe manufacturing. Competition is free and open to anyone who chooses to enter. We have already noted the absence of monopoly. The leading companies must share the market with a large number of small competitors. It is an easy industry to enter and easy to leave. There is a wide range of products in which the enterpriser may elect to specialize—work shoes, dress shoes, children's shoes, etc. A shoe is a product that may or may not contain hidden values, *i.e.*, a wide range of quality exists. A cheap shoe made of inferior leather, wet-lasted, can be made attractive by concealing poor workmanship with a generous burnishing of the outside and the insertion of a nicely embossed cushion sole on the inside. However, the foot is not easy to fit well and only high-grade raw materials and careful workmanship can produce a durable, comfortable, and serviceable shoe.

In the years before the outbreak of the Second World War, manufacturers were disturbed by the rise of imports of cheap foreign-made shoes. The industry had tariff protection of varying rates for over a century until 1913 when shoes were put on the free list. A 20 per cent tariff was reimposed in 1930 as a compensatory duty for the tariff on leather provided by the same Act. In spite of the tariff, imports of cheap women's cemented shoes retailing around $1.20 increased during the thirties. Most of them formerly came from Czecho-Slovakia, the product of the Bata Company. To escape the restrictions of rising trade barriers this company has erected numerous plants in other countries. In the late thirties it acquired a site on the shores of the Chesapeake near Baltimore. The first manufacturing unit was completed in 1939, but the ambitious expansion program encountered numerous obstacles.

The Future of the Industry.—The shoe industry has apparently attained technological and economic maturity. Shoemaking is an old industry. The processes are mechanized, the equipment is efficient, and the plants are specialized. Demand is stable, capacity is more than adequate, and profits are modest. Shoes, and especially men's shoes, are firmly anchored in custom. There is little reason to expect any revolutionary change in the state of the art of either shoes or shoemaking. However, such change is not impossible. Some enterprising manufacturer may upset the apple cart by introducing a shoe embodying a wide departure from conventional material, technique, or design. The apparent security of leather as a raw material does not preclude the introduction of a substitute. The shoe of the future may be made of a plastic material, molded to the foot at a small fraction of the present cost of footwear. In the absence of any revolutionary change, manufacturers of footwear will doubtless continue to cultivate the market as intensively as possible through the medium of style changes.

PART VIII

THE FOOD, LIQUOR, AND TOBACCO INDUSTRIES

CHAPTER XXIX

FOODS: A GENERAL ANALYSIS

The food processing industries were the last of our major manufacturing industries to be established on a commercial basis. Prior to the twentieth century, the population was predominantly rural, and the family kitchen was the most convenient and economical place to prepare food for human consumption. However, the rapid urbanization of population hastened the shift from home to factory preparation, so that now the food processing industries assume a prominent position in American manufacturing.

Economic Importance.—Census data reveal foods, textiles, steel, and motor vehicles as the four largest industry groups. Of these, the food industries rank first with respect to number of establishments, dollar value of raw materials, value added, and value of product. The food industries are surpassed by others only in number of workers employed as Table LXI shows.

TABLE LXI.—COMPARATIVE SIZE OF THE FOUR LARGEST INDUSTRIAL GROUPS

	Number of establishments	Number of workers	Value of raw materials (000,000 omitted)	Value added (000,000 omitted)	Value of product (000,000 omitted)
Food industries.........	51,454	824,009	$7,021	$3,583	$10,604
Textile industries.......	6,293	1,075,702	2,088	1,809	3,897
Iron and steel..........	8,993	966,371	3,636	2,956	6,592
Motor vehicles and automobile equipment.....	1,133	398,963	2,725	1,322	4,048

Source: Census of Manufactures, 1939 (preliminary).

In value of products, the food industries rank above all others. In 1939, the food industries produced over 10 billion dollars' worth of products which represented 19 per cent of the total product value of all manufacturing industries. However, this somewhat overstates the

410

relative importance of the food industries because raw materials constitute a large part (66 per cent) of the total value. In other words, the raw materials, for the most part, undergo very little change of form and require neither complicated machinery nor highly trained labor for processing.

Scale of Manufacture.—From the previous discussion it is apparent that while the food industries are large in size, the industry is conducted on a relatively small scale. The 51,000 establishments in the industry, which account for 28 per cent of all manufacturing establishments, employ only 10 per cent of all workers engaged in manufacturing. Aside from the relative simplicity in the processes, which facilitates ease of entrance, other factors that explain the small-scale nature of the industry are the widespread sources of supply, the perishability of most of the raw materials and of many of the finished products. When these factors are absent, as in cane-sugar refining, scale of operation tends to be larger.

Far-flung Marketing System.—The large number of companies in the industry, the great variety of foods processed, and the large and geographically widespread market over which they must be distributed require the services of a far-flung marketing organization. The industry's products reach the consumers through the services of more than 20,000 wholesalers and 602,500 retail stores.[1]

Growth Factors.—It would appear that the most important factor influencing the rate of growth of the food industries is the size of the population. While the number of people to be fed is of obvious importance, growth in population does not explain the growth of the food industries, because most of them, and the group as a whole, have grown at a faster rate than population. Of much greater significance than the size of the population are the activities in which it is engaged and the extent to which it is concentrated in a few areas.

Beginning in 1860 the United States experienced a phenomenal industrial growth, and agriculture, which was once the most important occupation, has been replaced by manufacturing and other activities. The trend in occupations since 1870 is shown in Fig. 78. The industrial development of the country not only changed our methods of making a living but also our ways of living. An increasing proportion of the total population found employment in factories in the crowded industrial areas. The concentration of population gave an impetus to the food processing industries, which came into being in response to the needs of the ever-growing numbers of people divorced from agriculture. In the early years the food industries performed the more strictly primary processes, such as, for example, the milling of grain and the refining of

[1] "Facts in Food and Grocery Distribution," published by *The Progressive Grocer*, January, 1940.

sugar.   The baking of bread and canning of food and similarly more
advanced processing were still done chiefly in the home.   Gradually,
however, the food industries assumed more and more of the task of preparing food.   The decline in the contribution of the garden to the family
table, the employment of women outside of the home, the growth in

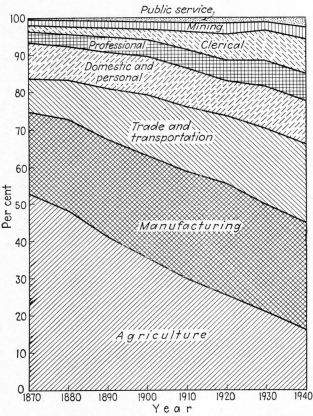

Fig. 78.—Proportion of gainfully employed over 16 years of age by major occupational
groups, 1870–1940.   ("*Recent Social Trends in the United States*," *McGraw-Hill Book Company, Inc., New York*, 1933; H. D. Anderson and P. E. Davidson, "*Occupational Trends
in the United States*," *Stanford University Press*, 1940.)

apartment living—all the result of industrialization and geographical
concentration—gave added stimulus to the growth of the food processing
industries.   The improvement in the standard of living created a desire
for greater variety of foods, a desire that could best be met by the food
industries, and the demand on the part of women for more leisure also
increased the demand for factory processed foods.   Between 1909 and
1939 the value of product of the food industries increased from less than

4 billion dollars to over 10 billion dollars. In part, the higher figure can be explained by an increase in the general level of prices, but to a much greater extent it represents the transfer of food preparation from the kitchen to the factory.

TRENDS IN FOOD CONSUMPTION

It is impossible to indicate with a high degree of precision the trend in total food consumption in the United States because statistical data, especially for the years prior to 1920, are far from complete. However, on the basis of such data as are available, it appears that per-capita food consumption has steadily declined.[1]

The decline in per-capita food consumption is the result of developments in conditions of work and living that have decreased the physiological needs of individuals.

The changing proportion of labor in exposed and sheltered occupations, which has been under way for generations, continues now with the movement out of agriculture into clerical and professional occupations. The progressive mechanization of industry and agriculture has in this latest period revolutionized those occupations requiring the greatest physical exertion. Since 1914 the reduction in hours of work has been made at a more rapid rate than ever before. The widespread use of the automobile, with the rising popularity of the closed car, has hardly been offset by the growing disposition of Americans to indulge in outdoor sports. Finally, there has been a decided improvement in the equipment of both industrial and domestic heating that has tended to effect a material conservation of body heat in colder regions and in colder weather.[2]

At the same time that per-capita food consumption was declining, significant changes occurred in the content of the reduced diet. The consumption of foods high in energy value decreased while the intake of so-called protective foods, those high in mineral salts, vitamins, and proteins, increased. Trends in the consumption of some of these foods are shown in Table LXII. It will be noted that the consumption of grain products has declined substantially among families at all levels of expenditures, especially among the families having a low level of expenditures. Meat consumption also experienced a decrease, although not as marked as that of grain products. Consumption of milk, eggs, vegetables (except potatoes), and citrus fruits has greatly increased.

The shifts in food consumption are not, of course, entirely due to the reduction in energy and heat requirements. "Man uses food as a means of satisfying many emotional needs which are so closely related to his

---

[1] "Recent Economic Changes in the United States," Vol. I, p. 27, McGraw-Hill Book Company, Inc., New York, 1929.

[2] *Ibid.*, p. 28.

physiological needs that unless they are met he fails to get the most from his food. He enjoys and even demands variety not only in foods themselves, but in methods of preparing them; he wants foods that appeal to his eyes and his senses of taste and smell; he wants to eat in pleasant surroundings."[1] The ability to satisfy this desire has been greatly increased by the great improvements in the transportation, processing, and storing of foods. The rise of the canning industry has made available fruits, vegetables, and many other foods for consumption throughout the entire year. The speeding up of transportation makes possible the shipping of fresh and perishable foods over thousands of miles, thereby reducing the seasonal aspects of food consumption. Seasonality in the consumption of fruits and vegetables has been still further reduced by the development of quick freezing methods.

TABLE LXII.—TRENDS IN AVERAGE ANNUAL PER CAPITA CONSUMPTION OF SPECIFIED FOODS BY LEVEL OF FOOD EXPENDITURES, 1885–1937

Level of food expenditures per person and period	Grain products, pounds	Meats, fish, and poultry, pounds	Milk or its equiva-lent, quarts	Eggs, dozens	Leafy, green, and yellow vege-tables, pounds	Toma-toes, citrus fruits, pounds
$1.25 to $1.87 per week						
1885–1904	294	123	41	12	24	10
1905–1914	240	124	90	12	31	15
1915–1924	174	84	101	15	35	38
1925–1934	152	85	112	12	43	37
1935–1937	155	85	118	16	53	45
$1.88 to $2.49 a week						
1885–1904	222	169	90	24	29	22
1905–1914	239	157	90	14	39	46
1915–1924	178	87	186	18	62	57
1925–1934	172	104	135	15	70	39
1935–1937	160	106	150	23	76	75
$2.50 to $3.12 a week						
1885–1914	218	204	84	20	48	59
1915–1924	204	115	180	26	67	73
1925–1934	163	129	144	24	83	68
1935–1937	174	139	191	27	95	98

Source: "Food and Life," *Yearbook of Agriculture*, p. 313, U. S. Department of Agriculture, 1939.

Place of Food in the Family Budget.—The decrease in per capita food consumption has not been accompanied by a decline in the expenditure

[1] "Food and Life," *Yearbook of Agriculture*, p. 131, United States Department of Agriculture, 1939.

for food.   Indeed, a recent study[1] made by the Bureau of Labor Statistics
of family expenditures in 27 cities indicates that the proportion of total
expenditures devoted to food has been greater in recent years than in
1917–1919, when the level of food prices was considerably higher.   The
increase in expenditures for food in the face of the decline in per capita
consumption is explained by the increasing variety in the diet, the shift
from low-price high-calorie to high-price low-calorie foods, and the
increasing dependence upon purchased and factory processed foods.

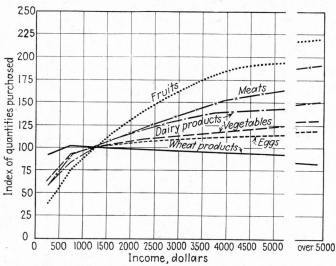

Fig. 79.—Relation of income to consumer expenditures for various food, 1935–1936.
(Nonfarm, nonrelief families.)   (*M. Perkins, "The Challenge of Underconsumption," United
States Department of Agriculture, mimeographed.*)

The importance of expenditures for food in the American budget is
shown in Table XXXIX, Chap. XX.   It will be noted that expenditures
for food are 33.6 per cent of all expenditures for all levels of income and
are the largest category of expense at every income level below $10,000.
It is also clear that the relative importance of food declines rapidly with
advances in income, although money expenditures, of course, increase.
The fact that the relative importance of food declines with advances in
income has generally been regarded as evidence that the demand for food
is inelastic.   Since the primary purpose of food is to satisfy physiological
needs and since these do not vary significantly, it was believed that the
principal difference between the food consumption patterns of low and
high income groups was chiefly in the content of the diet rather than
in the amount of food consumed.   Recent and more refined studies

[1] WILLIAMS, F. M., Changes in Family Expenditures in the Post-war Period,
Monthly Labor Review, pp. 974–976, November, 1938.

warrant the belief that the demand for food is more elastic than was formerly believed. Higher income groups not only consume higher priced foods and a greater variety of foods, but they also consume a larger total amount of food. The relationship between income and food consumption is shown in Fig. 79. It should be emphasized that the changes shown in the chart are in terms of physical quantities of the various foods rather than in terms of dollar expenditures. It will be noted that consumption of all foods, with the exception of wheat products, increases with income. The degree of elasticity is not of course the same for all foods. In the case of wheat products, potatoes, and similar staples,

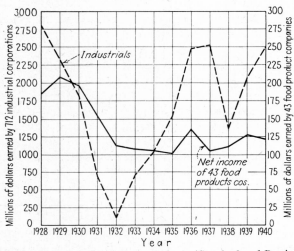

Fig. 80.—Earnings of food processing companies. (*Standard and Poor's Corporation.*)

the demand tends to be rather inelastic; the demand for poultry, green and leafy vegetables, and fruits is very elastic.[1]

While the demand for food is more elastic than was formerly believed, it is nevertheless more inelastic than the demand for all other major groups of consumer items. Although lower food prices or greater income will bring forth a greater demand for most foods, the capacity of the human stomach imposes strict limits upon the amount that can be consumed.

Instability in the Food Industries.—The indispensability of food gives the food industries a more stable demand than is enjoyed by any other major manufacturing industry. This is reflected in the earnings of food processing companies, as shown in Fig. 80. However, while the total demand for food fluctuates little from one year to another, individual food industries are not immune to fluctuations arising from the business

[1] PERKINS, M., *op. cit.*, pp. 13–14.

cycle. The instability of the individual industries arises chiefly from two sources: shifts in demand for the several foods and the nature of the raw materials.

As has previously been shown, consumers can choose from a wide variety of foods to satisfy their physiological requirements. In periods of declining purchasing power when consumers must retrench their expenditures, they do so in the case of foods not so much by eating less as by purchasing less expensive and less palatable foods. A smaller variety is placed on the table, cheap cuts of meat replace more expensive ones, fresh or high-quality canned foods are replaced by lower priced canned goods or are entirely eliminated. Highly processed, well-advertised packaged foods give place to bulk and unadvertised brands. The reduction in the sales volume of the high-priced well-advertised products more than balances the lower costs of raw materials, because expenditures for advertising them represent such a large part of operating costs and cannot safely be reduced.

The raw materials of these industries are agricultural in origin and, like most commodities, are subject to wide year-to-year and cyclical changes in price. Since they represent in most instances a large proportion of total costs,[1] particularly in the staple lines, changes in raw material prices have an almost immediate effect on prices. Consequently, in most of these industries, companies find it necessary to make frequent adjustments in inventory values. In a few industries management can minimize the risks by hedging on an organized futures market, but in the majority of industries there is no such price insurance available.

Structure of Enterprise.—Food industries have come in for their share of consolidations into large multiplant financial organizations. In meat packing, the three largest companies together control 43 per cent of the business. In flour milling, the three top-ranking companies control 38 per cent of the industry; in canned fruits, 30 per cent of the business is done by the three largest companies. The relative importance of the three largest companies in other divisions of the food industries is 13 per cent in vegetable canning, 17 per cent in baking, and 50 per cent in sugar refining. Although the concentration of control is not so great in food industries as it is in some other industries—notably, automobiles, steel, rubber, and cigarettes—nevertheless it is noteworthy, especially in view of the small-scale physical setup of the food industries.[2]

One of the principal reasons for the growth of large multiplant companies is the savings that can be made in the physical distribution of food products. Companies handling highly perishable foods like meat,

---

[1] See Table V, p. 13.

[2] The average number of workers per plant in the food industries was 16 in 1939 in contrast with 43 for all manufacturing.

milk, and bread must invest large amounts of capital in distributing equipment such as refrigeration cars, motor trucks, and delivery wagons. In order to reduce the overhead on such equipment they take on allied lines of perishable foods. For this reason, the meat packing and dairy industries have found it especially desirable to broaden their lines of products.

Furthermore, multiplant companies grow larger because they have the necessary capital to develop new food products and processes. General Foods Corporation, for example, has attained huge size not only through consolidation of existing companies but also through vigorous promotion of products it has developed and advertised nationally. This company makes 80 food specialities which are manufactured in its 45 plants and distributed through 10,000 authorized dealers. Some companies attained large size through patent protection on their products or processes. For example, the Shredded Wheat Company prior to its acquisition by the National Biscuit Company in 1930, owed much of its growth to its patent on the shredded cereal biscuit.

Another factor which has been favorable to the growth of large food processing companies has been the development of large food retailing organizations. Grocery chains, such as the Great Atlantic and Pacific Tea Company, Kroger, American, and Safeway stores, through their thousands of retail stores provide thousands of retail outlets for the manufacturers of packaged foods.

CHAPTER XXX

THE FLOUR MILLING INDUSTRY

The importance of cereals in the diet was indicated in Chap. XXIX. In the American diet, wheat is the leading cereal; it is estimated that wheat accounts for no less than 20 per cent of all the food we eat. The conversion of wheat into bread and other edible products is performed by two separate industries—the flour milling and baking industries. In this chapter we shall focus our attention upon the industry which converts wheat into flour. The term flour originally meant "the flower," *i.e.*, the best part of the grain.

The position wheat occupies in our diet may give an erroneous impression of the importance of flour milling among the food industries. The conversion of wheat into flour is one of the simplest of all manufacturing operations. It is almost wholly mechanical in nature and consists of pulverizing the grain and screening out for human use the portions most edible and palatable. The simplicity of the task results in a low "value added" and in a high degree of mechanization. A rough approximation of the role of flour milling in our economy is shown by the following contrast between milling and baking. In 1939 some 750 million bushels of wheat were ultimately converted into bread and related bakery products worth about 1,400 million dollars. In the course of conversion, the milling process added only 144 millions in contrast with 763 millions added by the baking process. The flour milling industry employs only 25,000 workers in contrast with 230,000 workers employed in baking.

NATURE OF THE PRINCIPAL RAW MATERIAL

Both the present organization and the historical evolution of flour milling in the United States are more readily understood if one possesses some knowledge of the function and structure of wheat. The wheat kernel or grain consists of four parts as shown in Fig. 81: (1) On the outside are five layers of tough, fibrous covering or husk called "bran." (2) Immediately beneath the outer coat is a hard, almost flint-like shell of yellow protein matter called "gluten." (3) In the interior of the kernel and merging with the gluten is the starch. (4) At one end of the kernel and easily distinguishable is the germ—small, dark, and both oily and sweet to the taste. Nature has thus constructed the kernel for the purpose of reproducing the wheat plant. The germ is the true seed and from it ultimately develops the plant. In order to increase the likelihood that the germ or embryo will accomplish its destined task, nature surrounds it with starch and gluten which serve as a food supply in the first stages of germination. The tough coat of bran acts as a protection in the struggle of the kernel to survive until the next season.

If we shift from biology to dietetics and economics we get a somewhat different view of these several parts of the wheat kernel. Man found through the centuries that the germ causes the pulverized grain to deteriorate and, furthermore, that it discolors the flour. Although for centuries efforts were made to remove the germ, the task was an exceedingly difficult one. Constituting less than 10 per cent of the weight of the whole kernel, it was crushed with the remainder of the kernel and could not be entirely screened out. Similarly the fibrous cover or bran (5 per cent of the kernel) was removed when possible because it discolored the flour, absorbed moisture readily, and was tough. It is likely that man sought to eliminate the bran not because of its low food value but because it was "roughage," which incidentally is now the chief reason for its limited usage. The least of the worries of our forebears was obtaining bulk or roughage in their food. When it came to the gluten in wheat (5 per cent), the miller was confronted with a dilemma. Gluten in considerable quantity was desirable in wheat because it improved the breadmaking qualities of the resultant flour. This is because, as is connoted by the word itself, which comes from the same root stem as "glue," it makes a resilient and elastic dough and one that will retain a great deal of water; the gases generated during the process of fermentation do not readily escape. Gluten accordingly increases the amount of bread that can be made from a given quantity of flour. But gluten in considerable quantity made the grinding of the grain more difficult. There were several reasons for this. The high content of flintlike gluten made it necessary to run the grinding machinery more slowly; furthermore, the increased friction generated more heat and this discolored the flour. In the choice between a high-gluten, hard wheat that was difficult to grind, and a low-gluten, soft wheat that made a somewhat inferior flour

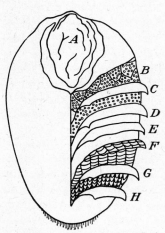

Fig. 81.—Dissected kernel of wheat. ("*Wheat and Flour Primer*," *Washburn-Crosby Company, Minneapolis, Minn.*)

(*A*) germ
(*B*) gluten cells predominate
(*C*) starch cells predominate
(*D*) interior coat of bran
(*E*) testa, coloring matter of bran
(*F*) endocarp
(*G*) epicarp
(*H*) epidermis

as the milling center was the growth of large-scale milling, the concentration of ownership, and the development of an extensive system of grain marketing.

Beginning about 1900 several new developments were set in motion which gave rise to new milling centers that ultimately eclipsed Minneapolis and the Northwest. These developments had to do with, first, the rise of new wheat-growing areas; second, changes in distribution; third, revision of freight rates; and fourth, new habits of consumption.[1]

For many years Minneapolis flour, made from high-gluten, hard spring wheat, was considered the best breadbaking flour. However, the constant repetition of sowing wheat year after year ultimately "tired" the soil with the inevitable result of decreasing yields. For a time, new strains of hardy disease-resistant wheat were tried with considerable success, but eventually they, too, yielded less wheat per acre. One type in particular (Velvet Chaff) was especially hardy and produced a high yield, but it was not a good milling wheat; consequently it sold at a discount. Because it got mixed with other types of seed wheat some millers believe it was responsible for lowering the quality of Northwestern flour with more serious adverse effects upon the reputation of Minneapolis flour. The decline of this region was retarded somewhat by Durum wheat which was introduced by a colony of Russian Mennonites. Durum is not satisfactory for bread flour; it is used by the manufacturers of macaroni.

The perfection of the gradual-reduction process, the growth in the reputation of hard-wheat flour, and the introduction of a strain of wheat peculiarly adapted to its soil and climate brought Kansas City and the Southwestern milling district into prominence. In the early seventies, there was introduced from Russia wheat which could stand Kansas's extremes of heat and cold and low rainfall. Kansas City is the milling center of this hard winter wheat region which embraces Nebraska, Kansas, Oklahoma, and part of Texas. The growth of the Southwestern wheat-producing area in contrast with the decline of the Northwest is shown in Fig. 83.

The most recent center to develop large-scale milling is Buffalo. Prior to the First World War, Buffalo mills produced annually about 600,000 barrels of flour. In 1930 Buffalo surpassed Minneapolis as a flour-milling center. Buffalo mills produce over three-fourths of the flour milled in the state of New York. The growth of this and the other milling areas is shown in Fig. 84.

In addition to the rise of new wheat-growing areas, changes in the methods of flour distribution also contributed to the shift in milling

[1] Pickett, V. G., and R. S. Vaile, "The Decline of Northwestern Flour Milling," pp. 33–55, University of Minnesota Press, Minneapolis, 1933.

centers.   Prior to 1900 most flour sales were made direct from mills to retail grocers in carload lots.   In 1902 the minimum carload weight of flour for interstate shipment was raised.   Since the higher minimum was more than many grocers wished to buy, it gave rise to an extensive flour-jobbing business.   This broke down the direct contact that had

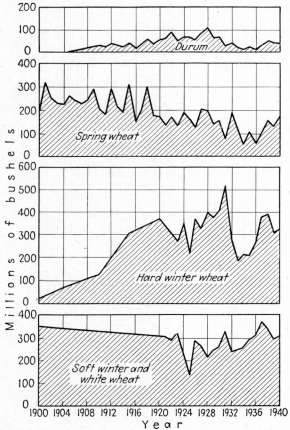

Fig. 83.—Wheat production according to classes. (*Data from* 1900–1920, *V. G. Pickett and R. S. Vaile, "The Decline of Northwestern Flour Milling," University of Minnesota Press, Minneapolis,, 1933; for period 1921–1939, The Northwestern Miller Almanac, April 30, 1941.*)

helped the Northwestern millers to hold their customers on the basis of quality flour.   The close relationship was weakened further by the growing emphasis upon price.   The rise of chain-store flour distribution likewise affected Northwestern millers adversely.   Since chain stores buy flour in large quantities and sell under their own brand names, they buy with even greater emphasis upon price and they shop around over a larger territory. In self defense the large Minneapolis millers built or bought mills in the new centers to recoup the loss of business suffered in the northwest.

Another factor which contributed to the decline of the Northwest was a change in freight rates. In 1918, freight rates were advanced on packaged goods without corresponding advances on bulk shipments on the Great Lakes. This was especially beneficial to Buffalo. Buffalo mills gained additional business at the expense of the Northwest following the 1920 changes in freight rates, which temporarily denied Minneapolis milling-in-transit privileges. Under the milling-in-transit privilege, mills buy wheat by paying the freight rate that applies from the shipping

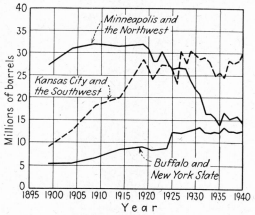

Fig. 84.—Flour production of the leading areas. (*V. G. Pickett and R. S. Vaile, "The Decline of Northwestern Flour Milling,"* p. 19, *University of Minnesota Press, Minneapolis, 1933; and The Northwestern Miller Almanac, April 30, 1941.*)

point, mill the wheat, ship the flour to its destination, and pay an additional item of freight equal only to the difference between the freight already paid and the rate applicable from the point of origin of the wheat to the destination of the flour. Proximity to large Eastern markets enables Buffalo mills to make quick delivery of flour in good condition, and the dairy region of western New York also affords an excellent market for the by-product mill feed.

Closely allied to the subject of freight rates is milling in bond— a practice which has also served to stimulate flour milling in Buffalo. Under the milling-in-bond privilege, American millers can import Canadian wheat without paying the tariff if they keep this wheat segregated during the milling process and export the flour obtained from the grind.

Finally, changes in consumer habits also reacted unfavorably upon Northwestern millers. The shift from home baking to commercial baking and the growing competition among commercial bakeries placed ever greater emphasis upon low-priced flour.   This diverted purchasing away from Northwestern quality flour.[1]

ECONOMIC CHARACTERISTICS OF FLOUR MILLING

Flour milling is characterized by large-scale production, both physically and financially, by stability of operations and earnings, and by a large amount of idle capacity.

Large-scale Production.—Most of the flour output is the product of large mills, but many small mills remain in the industry.   It is difficult

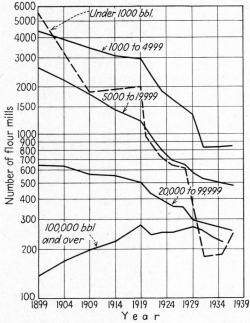

FIG. 85.—Number of mills classified according to annual output.   Mills under 1,000 barrels estimated for 1904.   (*Wheat Studies of Food Research Institute, Vol. 12, No. 8, pp. 282–84; and Northwestern Miller Almanac, Apr. 24, 1940.*)

to determine accurately the number of mills in operation or capable of operation.   This is because there are so many mills which operate intermittently, coming into production during periods of brisk business and rising prices only to retire when local supplies fail or business falls off. The last time the United States Census made a complete canvass—1919— there were some 21,000 establishments listed.   More than half of these were custom mills, *i.e.*, mills which do not buy grain but merely process

[1] *Ibid.*

the customer's grain for a fee—cash or kind. It is probable that most
of these mills were small neighborhood enterprises. *The Northwestern
Miller*, the industry's leading trade publication, estimates 3,400 mills in
1940 having a total daily capacity of 730,000 barrels of flour. The
average daily capacity of each mill is therefore approximately 215
barrels. However, most of the actual flour output is the product of the
larger mills. The trend toward large-scale milling is shown in Fig. 85.
During the present century there has been a declining trend in all classes
of flour mills except the large mills—those with an output in excess of
100,000 barrels of flour annually. This class of mill produces 80 per cent
of the total annual output.

The large mills have a number of advantages over their smaller competitors. The principal advantage enjoyed by the large miller is his
ability to produce standard grades of flour year after year. A mill
cannot produce a uniform grade of flour unless it is able to draw wheat
of the required quality from a large territory, which permits blending
varieties in such a way as to get flour that approaches uniformity. The
growth of large-scale commercial baking, as we shall see in the next
chapter, puts an ever-increasing premium upon standardized flour.
The concentration of wheat growing in a few favored areas has also
stimulated large-scale processing, especially because with a low "value
added" (22 per cent), there is an incentive toward volume operation.

Flour milling has likewise become a large-scale business from the
standpoint of financial operations. Approximately half of the annual
flour output is the product of 13 multiplant companies. The three leading companies, which together produce about 30 per cent of the total, are
General Mills, Pillsbury, and Archer-Daniels-Midland. These companies have daily capacities of roughly 70,000, 37,000 and 25,000 barrels
respectively. General Mills operates numerous flour mills in all of the
leading milling centers, plus cattle-feed mills, cereal mills, elevators, and
farm service stores. By operating widely scattered plants, General
Mills can make quick delivery of quality flour in every large market.

Stable Operations and Stable Earnings.—The term "stability"
expresses better than any other the outstanding economic characteristic
of the flour milling industry. Stability of operation is not literally applicable to all mills. The small mills, as already stated, are active in some
periods and idle in other periods but these mills, though numerous,
process no more than 20 per cent of the total grind. The large mills
responsible for most of the output are virtually immune from the cyclical
disturbances of business. Despite marked changes in the American diet,
pointed out in the preceding chapter, bread is still the staple. Consequently, flour has an assured demand the stability of which is equalled by
few if any major items of food. Observe in Fig. 86, which portrays the

annual consumption of flour since 1921, that changes in demand from year to year are very small.

Stability of earnings, like stability of mill activity, stems from the nature of the demand for flour but it is not the sole cause. Although the consumption of flour shows little change, the supply of wheat is highly irregular. The annual wheat crop fluctuates between 500 and 900 million bushels as a result of natural and economic forces. Among the principal factors influencing the size of the annual crop are: the acreage planted, rainfall, plant disease and pests, the annual carry-over, exports, etc. Wheat plays a prominent role in international trade. Countries like Great Britain, Germany, Belgium, and Brazil import

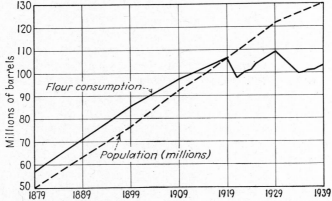

Fig. 86.—United States flour consumption. Flour consumption shown by decades prior to 1919 and yearly after 1919. (*Bureau of the Census and Census of Manufacturers.*)

large quantities from countries like Canada, Argentina, and Australia, which have large exportable surpluses. The United States is also a wheat-exporting country, though our surplus is gradually diminishing. However, our exportable surplus is very irregular. Since the First World War it has fluctuated between 300 thousand bushels and 250 million bushels annually. All these factors combined make for a highly complex combination of forces influencing the price of wheat. The price of wheat is notoriously volatile. In 1917–1918 the American farmer received an average price of $2.05 a bushel for his crop. In 1932–1933 he got only 38 cents; in 1936–1937 he received $1.03 a bushel. In the face of these erratic and unpredictable price changes and despite the fact that the raw materials and supplies constitute 78 per cent of the value of the product, flour milling is one of the most consistently profitable industries. Deficits are almost unknown. Note for example in Table LXIII how the leading companies fared during the severe business depression of the thirties.

The principal reason why earnings in the flour milling industry are apparently so little influenced by the volatile price situation in wheat is the widespread practice of hedging.[1] Data obtained from a reliable private source indicate that among commercial flour mills about 80 per cent of their combined position is either hedged or offset, *i.e.*, protected, by opposite trade transactions in the futures market for wheat. In brief, hedging affords millers substantial protection against speculative losses in inventories and thereby assures them as much manufacturing

TABLE LXIII.—RATE OF RETURN ON REPORTED CAPITAL INVESTMENT OF 11 FLOUR MILLING COMPANIES

Year	Per Cent
1929	11.36
1930	8.38
1931	6.71
1932	5.19
1933	6.65
1934	7.96
1935	8.15

Source: Federal Trade Commission, Agricultural Inquiry, Part 1, p. 818, 1937.

profit as the competitive situation permits.[2] However, hedging is characteristically a large-mill practice. Most of the small mills, in number perhaps 75 per cent of all mills, do not hedge and in fact have little or no knowledge of the futures market.

Idle Capacity.—In contrast with other manufacturing industries the flour industry has a capacity far in excess of the demand. In 1939 the industry produced less than half of the flour it was capable of grinding and that is typical of the relation between production and capacity since the turn of the century. Some allowance must be made for the fact that data on capacity are based upon rated rather than practical capacity. However, it is no exaggeration to say that the industry customarily operates near 50 per cent of capacity—using the term as defined in Chap. I.

The huge excess capacity is the result of the geographical shifts in flour milling already mentioned. The migration of the industry from Minneapolis to Kansas City and Buffalo was accomplished by the construction of new mills in these areas. The inevitable result was that numerous mills in the older centers were forced to operate less regularly and some had to shut down completely. Since 1925, mills in Kansas City and Buffalo have operated at a consistently higher capacity than those in Minneapolis.

The large excess capacity does not appear to have a particularly adverse effect upon profits. It is indeed somewhat anomalous to find an

[1] Refer to Chap. XXII for an illustration of hedging.

[2] Compare this with hedging in wool top futures, Chap. XXIII, and hedging in hide futures, Chap. XXVII.

industry that has a comparatively satisfactory earning capacity and at the same time has so much excessive productive capacity. The explanation is to be found in the nature of the milling industry. All flour mills operate on a narrow margin. Small mills find the competitive going very difficult because of the inventory hazards. Large mills have overcome the inventory difficulty by hedging and they obtain fuller utilization of their capital investment through the practice of operating 24 hours a day, but why do the large periodically idle mills in the Northwest fail to offer more competition to the large mills elsewhere? The answer is they cannot produce the types of flour now demanded at prices which leave a sufficient margin above the cost of wheat. In short, they are economically isolated because they are geographically isolated.

Idle capacity, however, is not entirely a matter of geographical location. It is also closely associated with size of enterprise. Most of the idle mills are small mills or, to state it more accurately, percentage of full time operation varies almost directly with size. For example, in Kansas City and the Southwest during the 1939–1940 crop year it was primarily the mills with a daily output of 500 barrels and over that operated in excess of 50 per cent of capacity, as Table XLIV reveals.

TABLE XLIV.—PERCENTAGE OF CAPACITY OPERATION BY MILLS OF VARIOUS SIZE IN THE SOUTHWEST, 1939–1940 CROP YEAR

State	Daily capacity				
	Over 1,000 bbl.	500 to 1,000 bbl.	200 to 500 bbl.	100 to 200 bbl.	Less than 100 bbl.
Kansas.................	74.3	54.2	46.9	11.2	10.6
Texas.................	58.7	56.3	33.7	38.6	16.0
Oklahoma.............	67.8	78.1	52.0	12.7	21.5
Nebraska.............	85.1	70.9	38.4	28.2	9.9

Source: *Northwestern Miller Almanac*, Apr. 30, 1941.

This table throws some additional light upon the relation between profits and excess capacity. Our knowledge of profits is based chiefly upon the published statements of the leading companies. These companies operate large mills which, on the whole, operate closer to their full capacity than the smaller mills. It is improbable that the smaller mills, operating at 10 to 30 per cent of capacity, have a relative earning power as great as the large companies shown in Table XLIII.

It is not to be inferred that the small millers are doomed to extinction. Many of them are sheltered by special circumstances. Some small mills produce flour of a distinctive character. An example of this is the "germ flour" produced by a small company in Chicago. By supplementing the regular grinding equipment with an auxiliary aerating process, this company produces a nonrancidifying flour containing the germ and the endosperm. In years to come we shall doubtless see a continued decline in the number of flour mills, but we do not expect a total extinction of small mills. Heretofore the decrease in the number of small mills has been the result of the rise of new milling centers and the decline in flour consumption. (Per capita consumption of flour decreased from 230 lb. in 1900 to 154 lb. in 1939.) Both of these developments appear to have run their course.

CHAPTER XXXI

THE BAKING INDUSTRY

Despite the increased variety of foods now available, bread is still the staple in our diet. Not many years ago most bread was baked in the homes where it was consumed. Today it is estimated that bakers' bread accounts for 80 per cent of the total consumption. The dietary importance of bread, together with the rise of commercial baking, explains why baking occupies a prominent position within the food industries. Baking is the largest industry of the food group, as shown by the several measures of size presented in Table LXV. Although the total dollar volume of meat packing exceeds that of baking, the value increment of baking is greater because baking requires considerably more processing than meat packing. The ratio of value added to value of product is only 16 per cent in the meat packing industry in contrast with 54 per cent for baking.

TABLE LXV.—COMPARATIVE SIZE OF THE PRINCIPAL FOOD INDUSTRIES, 1939

	Number of establishments	Value of product (000,000 omitted)	Value added (000,000 omitted)	Number of workers (000 omitted)
Baking................	18,405	$1,412	$762	231
Flour milling.............	2,143	650	144	25
Meat packing............	1,478	2,648	422	120
Sugar refining (cane).......	27	384	91	14
Canning................	2,221	653	256	114

Source: Census of Manufactures, 1939.

THE RISE OF COMMERCIAL BAKING

Since flour is the most important raw material[1] consumed in the baking process, the rise of commercial baking may be portrayed by comparing the growth of baking with flour milling. During the first two decades of the present century the two industries grew at substantially identical rates, as shown on Fig. 87. Since 1919, however, commercial baking

[1] Flour constitutes 48 per cent of the total raw material costs in baking. Sugar is 13 per cent, shortening 7 per cent, dry milk solids, 4 to 6 per cent. No other ingredient is in excess of 5 per cent.

434

has grown much more rapidly. While the milling industry has suffered a substantial decline in dollar volume of output, the baking industry has continued to expand. This represents primarily a shift from household to commercial baking.

The reasons for the transition from home to commercial baking are both economic and social. The principal economic cause is the growing urbanization of the population. The concentration of well over half of the population in towns and cities affords an excellent market for the highly perishable products of the baking industry. The shift in population has been accompanied by numerous changes in the pattern of family life. Families are smaller, and this fact, together with the decline in

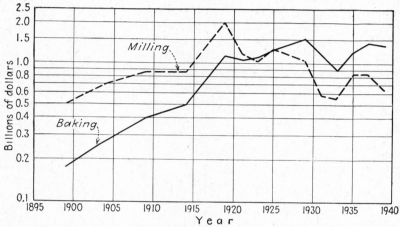

Fig. 87.—Growth of flour milling and commercial baking. (*Census of Manufacturers.*)

per-capita consumption of bread, has brought about a marked contraction in total consumption. However, commercial baking continued to expand because bread baking in the home declined almost to the vanishing point. Women have found increased opportunity for employment in industry and social activities. Housewives take less interest in bread baking, which for even the skilled home cook is a difficult art to master, particularly in view of the inadequate facilities of modern kitchens, especially the kitchenettes of our apartment dwellings. Since many families consume only two or three loaves of bread a week, the savings, if any, would scarcely repay the inconvenience of home baking.

Twofold Division of the Industry.—The baking industry produces a great variety of products. For our purposes it is sufficient to consider only the two most important products. Bread is the principal item of the division making almost exclusively soft dough products. The other division of the industry, smaller in size, makes chiefly biscuits and crackers.   The relative size of the two divisions and the principal products of each are shown in Table LXVI.

TABLE LXVI.—PRODUCTION OF BAKERY PRODUCTS, 1939
(In millions of dollars)

	Value of Product
Bread and related products	
Bread...	$ 657
Cake...	186
Rolls and coffee cake.............................	140
Pies and pastry..................................	100
Doughnuts and crullers..........................	55
Cookies...	20
Miscellaneous...................................	40
Total...	$1,198
Biscuits and crackers.............................	214
All bakery products, total.......................	$1,412

Source: Census of Manufactures, 1939.

The baking industry consists, as shown in Table LXV, of two virtually noncompeting divisions—the bread bakers and the cracker bakers.   The basic distinction lies in the degree of perishability of their products. Bread, pies, cakes, etc., grow stale very rapidly.   Unless they are marketed within about 12 hours after production the baker suffers a loss. Biscuits and crackers are less perishable and to this fundamental distinction in the nature of their products may be ascribed the differences in economic characteristics between the two divisions of the industry. Since bread and allied soft goods account for 85 per cent of all bakery products, this branch of the industry will be taken up first.

THE BREAD BAKING INDUSTRY

Process.—Except for differences owing to variations in mechanization, the principal processes of baking consist of: (1) blending, (2) sifting, (3) mixing, (4) proofing, (5) baking, and (6) wrapping.

Blending is confined to the larger establishments using two or more kinds of flour.   The operation is done by a machine which leaves each kind of flour evenly distributed throughout the whole mixture.   It assures greater uniformity, gives the baker that flour which meets his own peculiar requirements, and enables him to keep flour costs at a minimum.

From the blending machine the flour is conveyed to the sifting machine where all foreign substances are removed.   The flour is next conveyed to the storage bins, usually located on an upper floor, from which it can be dropped by gravity to the mixing room below.

The various ingredients are automatically weighed or measured and dumped into the mixer which has a capacity ranging from 1 to 5 barrels of dough.   After approximately 12 minutes of kneading in the power mixer, the dough is dumped into elongated troughs shaped like bathtubs. These are wheeled into a separate room for proofing.

Proofing is the raising or fermenting of the dough by the bacterial action of the yeast. Proofing requires careful temperature and humidity control, the process takes from 3 to 4 hours depending upon the character of the flour and other ingredients. During the process the dough is punched or worked down several times to obtain the proper texture.

The dough is then dropped into the scaling or dividing machine which cuts and delivers 2, 4, 6, or 8 pieces at a time, according to the size of the machine, each piece being the weight of the loaf desired. The pieces of dough are then rounded or rolled into balls in a rounding machine, lightly dusted with flour, dropped on a moving belt (proofer) for a 10- to 15-minute rest or proofing period. Following this the dough pieces are molded into loaf shape and are placed into baking pans for a second proofing (pan proofing) which takes approximately 1 hour.

Upon completion of pan proofing the pans are placed on the oven-hearth—either on the slowly moving conveyors of the straight traveling oven, or on moving shelves in other types of ovens, or on the tile hearth of stationary ovens. The traveling-hearth type of oven is rapidly replacing all other types. The temperature of the oven is maintained at a constant heat of 450°F., and after approximately 45 minutes the baked bread emerges from the farther end of the traveling oven. After cooling, the bread is mechanically sliced and wrapped ready for delivery.

It is apparent that the process as carried out in large baking establishments is well mechanized and scientifically controlled. Uniform standards of operation founded upon scientific determination explain why baker's bread is always uniform in quality. Blending flour assures the elimination of all but the imperceptible variations in the predominant raw material. Mechanical mixers ensure a more intimate mixture of flour and water than is attainable by hand kneading. Specially designed fermenting rooms equipped with automatic temperature and humidity control devices take the guesswork out of the most critical stage of the manufacturing process. Perhaps it is not too much exaggeration to say that in the transition from the household to the commercial bakery, baking changed from an art to a science.

Widespread Geographical Distribution.—Since bakers must deliver their bread almost immediately after it is produced, baking is a local industry. The geographical distribution of bakeries is practically identical with the distribution of urban population. Two-thirds of our bakeries are located in the 10 states leading in population density which have two-thirds of the urban population. The only exception to the correlation between urban population and number of bakeries is in the South where because of the popularity of hot breads, the development of commercial baking has been somewhat retarded. For example, annual per-capita bread consumption in Rhode Island is 150 lb., in contrast with only 17 lb. in Mississippi. The preference for home-baked hot bread in the latter state largely accounts for the difference.[1]

Predominance of Small Shops.—Since bakeries are widely scattered, it follows that they are numerous and, for the most part, are small shops. According to the 1939 Census of Manufactures, there were 18,000 establishments. This does not include the smallest bakers—those whose annual output is less than $5,000 worth of products. Were these included, the total would probably be close to 30,000 establishments. Those reporting to the census employed an average of only 11 workers per establishment. This figure must be accepted with the same reservation applicable to any arithmetic average but it is unmistakable evidence that baking is typically a small-scale plant operation.

The most obvious explanation for the predominance of small shops is, of course, the nature of the product. The rapid perishability of bread restricts the size of the market that can be served. With the use of motor delivery some bakers serve markets up to 75 miles distant, but most bakers supply only the immediate neighborhood. Another explanation is to be found in the nature of the process. The optimum size of the proofing unit is about 1,000 lb.; i.e., dough cannot be made satisfactorily in larger batches. A bakery producing in excess of 1,000 loaves a day, as most bakeries do, must therefore have additional fermentation units—it cannot seek lower production costs by making dough in gigantic batches. The size of ovens is likewise limited for reasons of expediency. The technology of baking, therefore, imposes very definite limits upon physical size—stricter limits than are imposed in steel or cement manufacturing by way of contrast.

Consolidations.—Despite the limited advantages of large plant operation, the bread baking industry has had its share of financial consolidations so characteristic of American industry. Consolidations occurred in the baking industry in two periods. The first occurred about 1907 when seven bakeries in St. Louis combined to form the American Bakery Company. Similar combinations were brought about in other cities, and most of these early combinations grew out of local price wars.

A second wave of consolidations culminated in the twenties. Utilizing the holding company device, four large multiplant companies came into existence. These companies, Continental, Ward, Purity, and General, though large concerns, produce only about 14 per cent of the total output of the industry. A comparison of these companies is shown in Table LXVII.

[1] ALSBERG, C. L., Combination in the American Bread Baking Industry, Food Research Institute, Stanford University, California, 1936.

Three of the companies shown in Table LXVII, Continental, Ward, and General, have not always been strictly competitive. They "have at one time or another been affiliated through a community of stock ownership and of organizing personnel and through close association of management."[1] In 1925, the Ward interests, through ownership of voting stock in Continental and General, controlled 151 bakeries representing approximately 20 per cent of the country's commercial bread production and "a much larger per cent of the wholesale production and large-cake production."[2]

TABLE LXVII.—COMPARATIVE SIZE OF THE LEADING BREAD BAKING COMPANIES, 1939

Company	Number of bakeries	Total assets (000,000 omitted)	Net sales (000,000 omitted)
Continental	82	$48	$64
Ward	21	28	32
Purity	55	28	36
General	90	26	39

Source: "Moody's Manual of Investments—Industrials," 1940.

In 1926, Ward sought to organize the Ward Food Products Corporation under a charter which gave the company almost unlimited scope in the production of food products. However, the plan was blocked by the intervention of the Department of Justice on the ground that the proposed corporation would have been a violation of the Sherman Antitrust Act.

Since the ultimate goal of consolidations is to increase profits, a study of the earnings of bakeries may shed some light upon the success of the consolidations.

Profits.—One study of earnings in the baking industry, made by the Federal Trade Commission, reveals an average rate of return upon capital invested of 15.4 per cent for the 6 years 1920–1925, i.e., the period immediately preceding the culmination of the bakery consolidations. Immediately after the consolidation (1926–1930), the leading bakeries earned an average of 13 per cent on their invested capital according to a study made by Poor's Industry Service. These studies are discontinuous and both cover short periods of time. However, the record of earnings is extended by piecing together two additional studies as shown in Fig. 88.

In contrast with the earnings immediately preceding the period portrayed in Fig. 88, it appears that earnings have declined to a lower level. On the basis of these data, financial consolidations have not produced increased profits.

[1] Federal Trade Commission, "Agricultural Income Inquiry," Part I, p. 304, 1937.
[2] *Ibid.*

However, the foregoing data are based primarily upon the earnings of the largest companies. What about the thousands of small bakeries? Very little information of the earnings of small bakeries is available. According to the reports of a certified public accountant who specializes in bakery auditing, small bakeries are earning about the same rate of return on their invested capital as the large bakeries. Again, this statement can be accepted only with certain reservations—the companies are not identified and therefore their size is unknown, the period covered is short, and the sample is small. The most that can be said about the relation between corporate size and earning power in the baking industry is that from the records available it has not been definitely established

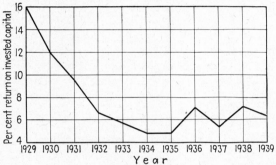

Fig. 88.—Earnings of the "Big Four" bakeries. (*Federal Trade Commission, Agricultural Income Inquiry, Part 1, p. 829, 1937; and Moody's Manual of Investments: Industrials, 1940.*)

that large multiplant companies are more profitable than single-plant enterprises.

It has been alleged that the large multiplant baking company has certain competitive advantages over its small competitors. It is claimed that purchasing large quantities of raw materials makes for lower unit costs; that standardized operating practices produce economies; that national advertising increases returns. These claims are doubtless true but the advantages are not invariably as great as might be supposed. Table LXVIII brings out very clearly the small margin of difference in the principal cost items as between the large and the small bakeries.

The nature of the process and the nature of the product impose limitations upon profits regardless of whether the baking is done by independent bakeries or by many bakeries under a common management. In either case goods in process must go through the plant just as slowly and the bread must be delivered just as rapidly. Excluding the cost of raw materials, it costs about as much to sell and deliver the bread as it does to bake it. Furthermore, as plant size is increased the radius of distribution must be enlarged. Consequently, increased costs of distribution rapidly offset decreased costs of production.

TABLE LXVIII.—COMPARATIVE COSTS OF A LARGE BAKERY AND SEVEN SMALL BAKERIES, 1939

Item	Continental Baking Company,[1] per cent	Average of seven smaller bakeries,[2] per cent
Net sales...................	100.00	100.00
Manufacturing costs..........	61.77	60.81
Delivery and selling exp.......	25.93	24.55
Advertising...............	(2.85)	(3.57)
Management salaries..... ..	......	5.05
Net income.................	6.55	3.72

Sources: [1] "Moody's Manual of Investments," 1940; [2] private communication.

Competition.—Baking is a highly competitive industry. The industry consists of numerous types of enterprises, ranging from the large multiplant companies, engaged in both wholesale and retail baking, to the small neighborhood bakeries. Among these groups there is sharp competition for the existing market. The best evidence of the intensity

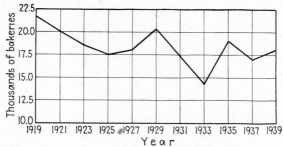

FIG. 89.—Number of baking establishments. (*Census of Manufacturers.*)

of competition is the constant change in the number of enterprises engaged in the industry. This is shown in Fig. 89, which portrays the number of establishments producing, for each of the years indicated, bakery products in excess of $5,000 annually.

The rise and fall of the curve indicates the net changes in the number of bakeries entering and leaving the industry. This does not include the smallest bakeries—those producing less than $5,000 of products annually. Were they included, the fluctuations would doubtless be more pronounced. The constant change in number of enterprises is explained by the fact that it is easy to enter the baking industry. Every master baker is a potential entrepreneur. Not much fixed capital is required, premises can be rented, demand is stable, sales are for cash, and the business has a daily turnover—hence little working capital is required. Baking bread as the staple, the small neighborhood baker often thrives by specializing in the production of pies, cakes, and other dainties that have an especial appeal to his local trade. There is and always will be a market for the products of good craftsmanship.

Competition in bread baking is complicated by the peculiar relationship between costs of raw materials and the retail price of bread. Raw material prices are volatile but bread prices are sluggish. The monthly prices of wheat, flour, and bread are shown in Fig. 90. It is apparent that there is a close relationship between the price of wheat and the price of flour. The price of wheat fluctuates over a wide range for various reasons pointed out in the preceding chapter. The price of flour

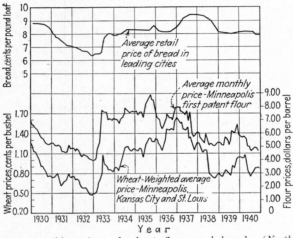

FIG. 90.—Average monthly prices of wheat flour, and bread. (*Northwestern Miller Almanac, Apr. 30, 1941.*)

follows closely upon the heels of the price of wheat, as indeed it must, because, as mentioned in the last chapter, the cost of wheat represents 78 per cent of the total value of the flour produced. The manufacturing operation therefore adds little value.

The price of bread, like the price of flour, wheat, or any other commodity, is of course subject to the fundamental laws of supply and demand, but bread prices are influenced by several conditions peculiar to that commodity. In the first place, it is sold in small units—the pound or half-pound loaf. The smallest increase the baker can make is 1 cent. This represents an increase of 10 per cent on the pound loaf and of 20 per cent on the half-pound loaf, if the base prices were 10 and 5 cents respectively before rising flour costs compelled the bakers to ask for higher bread prices. Any one baker is naturally reluctant to assume the leadership in raising prices until he feels sure most of his competitors will follow. In the second place, bread prices are sluggish because the current price tends to be considered a fair price. For example, if bread has been selling for 10 cents a loaf for a year or more, most buyers will have forgotten the last price change, and an effort on the part of the bakers to raise it to 11 cents will elicit protest against alleged profiteering.

THE BISCUIT AND CRACKER INDUSTRY

This division of the baking industry conforms more closely to the popular concept of American industry—large-scale production, mechanized technology, huge multiplant companies—in short, big business. Seventy-five per cent of the business is in the hands of three companies— National Biscuit, Loose-Wiles, and United Biscuit. Each of these companies has numerous plants located in the principal centers of population.

Cracker Bakeries Are Fewer but Larger.—The outstanding difference between biscuit baking and bread baking is that biscuit and cracker bakeries are fewer but larger. Whereas bread baking is a large-sized, small-scale industry, biscuit and cracker baking is by comparison a small-sized, large-scale industry. This is shown by the census statistics reproduced in Table LXIX.

TABLE LXIX.—CENSUS DATA OF THE BAKING INDUSTRIES, 1939

Item	Biscuit and cracker	Bread
Number of establishments	356	18,049
Number of wage earners	29,173	201,537
Cost of raw materials (millions of dollars)	$ 82	$ 567
Value of products (millions of dollars)	$201	$1,211
Value added by manufacture (millions of dollars)	$119	$ 644

Source: Census of Manufactures, 1939.

The cracker division produces only a sixth as much in dollar volume as the bread division, but its plants are much larger. The average cracker bakery produced about $565,000 worth of products in 1939 in contrast with $67,000 worth for the average bread bakery. The contrast in size of plants is even more pronounced when measured by the average number of workers employed—81 in cracker bakeries as against 11 in bread bakeries.

Individual biscuit and cracker bakeries are larger in physical size primarily because their products are less perishable than bread and related soft-dough products. When properly packaged, biscuits and crackers can be marketed over a much larger territory than bread. Another factor contributing to larger scale operation in cracker baking is the opportunity for greater mechanization. The process is similar to bread baking in sequence of operations but more of the operations are mechanized. This is a natural and inevitable development as a result of the countless numbers of small units of product made in the biscuit and cracker branch. As early as 1813, patents were issued for biscuit-making machinery. The fact that biscuit and cracker baking was done on a commercial basis long before bread baking was taken over by commercial bakeries is another development that explains why the cracker division is larger scale business. The manufacture of ship biscuits goes back to colonial times. Biscuits are specifically mentioned as an American export as early as 1810.

As already indicated, biscuit and cracker baking is also large-scale business from the financial aspect. In this industry, financial consolidations began near the turn of the century at the time when the consolidation movement was rife in all industries. The National Biscuit Company was formed in 1898 by merging three existing companies. Today, this company controls about half of the American biscuit and cracker business. The Loose-Wiles Company, organized in 1902, now controls about 20 per cent of the total. Third in size is the United Biscuit Company of America, created in 1925. It produces about 12 per cent of the total output. The setup of National Biscuit, the leader, is typical of the three companies.

National Biscuit is an integrated company. It owns 47 bakeries located in 23 states. It owns two flour mills which supply flour of the particular kind required to the extent of 80 per cent of its needs. The company has a vast fleet of delivery trucks operating from 250 distributing branches. Its bakeries produce approximately 500 different kinds of crackers, biscuits, cookies, pretzels, etc. Though a large part of its output consists of popular "staples," its "line" is constantly changed to meet or to create new consumer demand. As in the candy business, a clever or well-chosen name is sometimes as effective in building up popular appeal for an individual product as its excellence of taste.

The Profits of Big Business.—The fact that the biscuit and cracker business is dominated by three companies does not automatically mean monopoly profits. In the first place, there is, strictly speaking, no monopoly, and though the business is highly concentrated, there is severe competition among the producers.

Profits have not come up to the expectations of the promoters. In recent years, earnings in this division of the industry have been only slightly above those of the leading bread bakeries, as shown by a comparison of Fig. 88 and Table LXX. In 1936 the editors of a leading business journal expressed the opinion that National Biscuit suffers the penalty of bigness. Table LXX casts some doubt on the accuracy of that opinion—the largest and the smallest of the "big three" show the best profits.

TABLE LXX.—EARNINGS OF THE "BIG THREE" BISCUIT AND CRACKER COMPANIES
(Per cent net income to reported net worth)

Year	National Biscuit	Loose-Wiles	United Biscuit Co. of America
1933	....	6.6	6.6
1934	10.4	5.2	6.7
1935	9.1	5.5	6.5
1936	11.5	5.0	8.4
1937	10.8	2.8	7.1
1938	11.6	3.8	7.4
1939	10.8	4.1	7.7

Source: "Moody's Manual of Investments, Industrials," 1940.

The earning power of biscuit bakers is restricted in a manner somewhat similar to that of bread bakers. Their earnings are reduced by rising raw material prices and enhanced by falling raw material prices. Rising raw material costs cannot be passed on with ease to the consumers, who are sensitive to changes in cracker prices. Biscuits and crackers, unlike bread, are more in the nature of dietary luxuries. Consequently, when raw material prices go up the companies must inevitably absorb some of the increased costs. The leading companies have spent large sums in national advertising to establish brand consciousness on the part of their customers. Consequently they are reluctant to compete with "off brand" cut-price products retailed by some of the large chain stores.

SUMMARY

Baking consists of essentially two industries—the bakers of bread and related soft-dough products and the bakers of biscuits and crackers. The difference in the degree of perishability of their products characterizes the two separate industries. The former was much later to develop commercially but once started, grow more rapidly. It is now a much larger industry, consisting of thousands of small plants located close to their respective markets. Biscuit and cracker baking is characterized by fewer but larger plants. The industry is more highly mechanized, somewhat more profitable, and dominated by fewer companies. Profits in both divisions are sensitive to fluctuating raw material prices and both encounter difficulty in raising the prices of their finished products. Competition is keen in both branches but there is virtually no competition between the two industries.

CHAPTER XXXII

THE SUGAR REFINING INDUSTRY

Refined sugar is so common today and so generally accepted as a necessity of life that it would appear as though it must always have been an important part of man's diet. That, however, is not true. Earlier civilizations obtained their sugar from such foods as bread, cereals, potatoes, and corn, all of which contain starch that is converted into sugar during the process of digestion. Until the nineteenth century sugar was a luxury enjoyed only by the wealthy.

Consumption.—Since sugar was so long a luxury food, and in many countries is still so considered, it is natural that the United States should be the world's largest consumer. Since 1900 per-capita consumption has

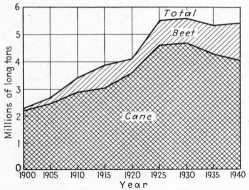

Fig. 91.—United States sugar consumption. (*U. S. Department of Agriculture.*)

grown steadily, having increased from about 73 lb. in that year to almost 110 lb. in 1929. The average annual growth has been slightly less than 5 per cent. The relatively high level of consumption in this country may be explained not only by the higher standard of living, but also by the fact that our huge domestic market makes possible the refining of sugar on a large scale, an indispensable factor for the economical processing of sugar. The growth of consumption is shown in Fig. 91.

The demand for sugar in the United States is not only great but is also relatively stable. About 70 per cent of the total consumption, as shown in Table LXXI, is in the home, and this demand is only moderately affected by changes in business conditions. The remainder is divided

446

among a number of industries, most of them in the luxury class, which means that they are affected by cyclical fluctuations in business. During the depression beginning in 1929 consumption decreased from 5,810,000 tons in that year to 5,200,000 in 1932, a decline of about 10 per cent.

TABLE LXXI.—USES OF SUGAR

	Per cent		Per cent
Household...................	70.0	Other foods..................	1.5
Baking......................	8.2	Dairy products..............	1.1
Confectionery...............	6.1	Chewing gum................	0.5
Canning....................	5.0	Tobacco.....................	0.3
Extracts and flavoring........	2.6	Beverages (alcoholic)........	0.2
Beverages (nonalcoholic).......	2.4	All other....................	0.1
Chocolate...................	2.0	Total....................	100.0

Source: Standard and Poor's Corporation.

The sugar consumed in the United States is produced by two industries—the cane and beet sugar industries. The former, as indicated in Fig. 91, is by far the more important. While there are no important differences between their products discernible by the senses, the economic differences between the two industries warrant separate consideration.

THE CANE REFINING INDUSTRY

This industry has always depended primarily upon foreign sources for its raw materials. While sugar cane is cultivated in many tropical countries, Cuba is our chief source, supplying us with almost 25 per cent of our raw cane requirements. Other sources, in order of importance, are the Philippine Islands, Hawaii, and Puerto Rico.

The cultivation of sugar cane was introduced into Louisiana about 1737, but the development of the industry has been very slow. In 1900 the domestic industry produced about 400,000 tons, an amount that has been increased only slightly. There are large areas in Florida, Louisiana, and Texas that are suitable for sugar-cane cultivation, but the cost of production is so high, primarily because of the short growing season, that the industry can expand only behind a very high tariff wall or with the aid of government subsidies.

Process. *Preparation of Raw Sugar.*—When the sugar cane is mature it is cut and taken immediately to a sugar factory, or centrale, where the raw sugar is prepared. Mature sugar cane contains about 14 per cent sugar, 74 per cent water, 10 per cent cellulose, and 2 per cent impurities. The impurities will cause fermentation of the sugar and a reduction in yield if the sugar is not extracted at once.

The juice is extracted by passing the cane between corrugated steel rollers or mills which press out the juice. The cane juice is raised to a temperature of about 210 to 220°F., and is then run into tanks where lime is added to neutralize the acids and purify the juice. The juice is concentrated into sirup in evaporators which eliminate about 50 to 75 per cent of the water. The sirup then passes through a series of vacuum pans where it is crystallized. The sugar that emerges is still soft and

PLATE 65.—Filtration tanks remove impurities.

damp, and must go through another machine which removes most of the remaining moisture. This machine is known as a centrifugal machine which is a cylindrical-shaped perforated basket surrounded by a solid outside casing. The basket is spun at a speed of from 1,000 to 1,200 r.p.m. until a considerable amount of molasses is thrown off. This sugar, known as "centrifugal sugar," is about 96 degrees sucrose. Almost all raw cane sugar imported into the United States is of this grade.

Refining of Raw Sugar.—Since the raw sugar contains some impurities and is brownish in color, it must be further refined. The raw sugar is poured into centrifugal machines where the crystals are washed with water. The liquid portion is thrown off and the crystals remain in the basket. The washed sugar is removed from the basket, melted in hot water, and then pumped into tanks called "blow ups" where the impurities are precipitated by the addition of milk of lime. Fullers earth is then added and the liquor is run through a series of filters. The liquid sugar, after this operation, still has a yellow color since only a small portion of the impurities has been removed.

The yellow liquid is then pumped to bone-black filters which are huge cylindrical tanks almost completely filled with bone-black, or charred bone-dust, manufactured from animal bones. The liquor passes through the bone-black, which absorbs the impurities, and emerges from the bottom as a colorless fluid. From the filters the liquor goes to evaporators where it is concentrated to almost 68 per cent solids, and is then transferred to vacuum tanks where it is boiled until crystals of the desired size are formed. The crystals are then run into centrifugal machines where, as before, the remaining sirup is eliminated. After the sirup is removed and the sugar washed, it is carried by conveyor to the granulator, a long rotating iron cylinder heated by steam, which dries the sugar. After screening to sort the various sizes, the granulated sugar is packed for shipment. The remaining sirup, from which no more sugar can be extracted, is sold as blackstrap molasses. It is used as cattle food or it may be distilled into alcohol.

Refiner's Margin.—It was stated in Chap. XXIX that the food industries as a class add a comparatively small percentage of value to the raw materials processed. This is especially true of cane sugar refining. The principal item in the cost structure of sugar, excluding tariff and excise tax, is raw material. Labor is a very small proportion of the cost because the process is highly mechanized. The composition of the consumer's sugar price is shown in Table LXXII.

TABLE LXXII.—COMPONENTS OF CONSUMER'S SUGAR PRICE, 1938
(In cents per pound)

World price of raw sugar	1.13
Duty	1.87
Excise tax	0.54
Total	3.54
Refining costs:	
Labor, supplies, maintenance, etc	0.56
Raw sugar shrinkage	0.21
Profit or loss	−0.02*
Total	0.75
Retailing, wholesaling, and transportation costs	1.02
Cost to the consumer	5.31

Source: LYNSKY, M., "Sugar Economics, Statistics and Documents," Supplement, p. 307, U. S. Cane Sugar Refining Association, 1939.

* 1938 was an unprofitable year.

The low value added places the industry in a very speculative position, since it leaves but a small margin between the cost of raw materials and the price of refined sugar, exposing the industry to considerable inventory hazards. The low value added makes it necessary to operate a refinery on a large-scale basis, for only through volume can profits be made sufficiently large to compensate for the necessary capital investment. During the 4-year period 1934–1938, for example, the cane refiners realized a profit of about 4 cents per 100 lb. Capacity operations are very important because a slight decline in volume causes a sharp increase in unit costs.

Organization of the Cane Refining Industry.—The industry comprises 20 companies with 25 plants. The major part of the capacity is located on the Atlantic coast, in Boston, New York, and Philadelphia. Several plants are on the Gulf coast and two are on the Pacific coast.

The American Sugar Refining Company, with five refineries, is the largest company in the industry, and at its organization in 1887 controlled 98 per cent of the capacity. Notwithstanding its dominant position, it was unable to prevent the entrance of new companies and by 1910 its capacity declined to 62 per cent of the total. At the present time, it controls only about 28 per cent. The next largest company is the National Sugar Refining Company with about 14 per cent of the industry's capacity. This company is controlled in part by the American Sugar Refining Company through stock ownership. The third biggest company is the California & Hawaiian Company with about 11 per cent. The three together control slightly over 50 per cent of the industry's capacity.

With the exception of the Gulf refineries, the plants are all large-scale. The majority of them have a daily melting capacity in excess of 2 million lb. and several of the eastern plants have a daily capacity of 4 million lb. There is a considerable amount of excess capacity in this branch of the industry. The annual melting capacity is slightly in excess of 8 million tons, which compares with actual meltings slightly in excess of 4 million tons, or about 50 per cent of capacity.[1]

THE BEET SUGAR INDUSTRY

The beet sugar industry is a much more recent development in the United States than the cane refining industry. As is shown in Fig. 91, it supplied less than 4 per cent of our sugar requirements in 1900, and only after government control was inaugurated in 1934 has it shown a substantial increase.

Unlike the cane refining industry, the beet sugar industry obtains all of its raw materials from domestic sources. The sugar beet can be

[1] DALTON, J. E., "Sugar and National Defense," Twelfth Boston Conference on Distribution, 1940, Boston Chamber of Commerce.

grown over a wide area in the United States, but for economic reasons the principal source, as Table LXXIII shows, is the Rocky Mountain area.

TABLE LXXIII.—SUGAR BEET PRODUCTION, 1940

States	Acres harvested (000 omitted)	Tons of beets (000 omitted)	Tons of sugar (000 omitted)
California	173	2,791	448
Colorado	140	2,034	310
Idaho	72	1,128	142
Montana	85	1,156	166
Nebraska	70	910	111
Utah	48	506	73
Wyoming	47	634	91
Michigan	114	1,004	161
Ohio	41	361	41
Other states	131	1,445	186
Total	921	11,969	1,729

Source: U. S. Department of Agriculture.

Process.—The first step in the processing of beets, after they have been washed and sampled for sugar content, consists of slicing them into long thin pieces called cossettes. The cossettes are placed into a diffusion battery which is made up of a series of tanks connected with each other by pipes. Hot water is introduced into the tanks and percolates through the cossettes, thus extracting the juice which then flows from tank to tank in regular order. As the juice passes from one tank or cell to the next it becomes of greater density, until it attains a density about equal to that of the undiluted beet juice, at which point the action ceases. The remainder of the process is the same in principle as that of cane refining, previously described. The juice is clarified to remove any foreign substances; it is then concentrated into a sirup by means of evaporators; it is next crystallized in vacuum pans; and, finally, the molasses is separated from the sugar by means of centrifugal machines.

Organization of the Beet Sugar Industry.—The sugar beet industry in 1939 comprised about 85 plants, employing 10,000 wage-earners, with a value of products of 134 million dollars. The majority of these plants are controlled by a few companies, the largest of which is the Great Western Company with 21 factories, followed by the Holly Sugar Corporation and the Utah-Idaho Company with 12 plants each.

It is apparent that the scale of operation of this industry is much smaller than that of the cane refining industry. This can be explained by the fact that beets originate over a wide area and costs of transportation are so high that the factories must be near the beet fields. This not only restricts the scale of operations but also the continuity of operations, since the production of beets is seasonal in nature. The average working period for all beet sugar factories is about 3 months; thus for nearly three-fourths of the year the equipment is idle, a condition which makes for heavy overhead costs.

The beet sugar companies have a large measure of control over their raw material supply. Some engage directly in the growing of sugar beets while some have their farms worked by tenants. Others buy their beets from independent farmers on a sliding scale contract based on the refined sugar price.

INSTABILITY OF THE SUGAR INDUSTRY

Although the demand for sugar in the United States has a high degree of stability, the American sugar industry, especially the cane refining branch, has not been able to translate the stable demand into stable operations or earnings. The difficulties of the industry arise from a number of sources: the nature of the product, the existence of excess capacity, competition between beet and cane sugar, and the competition of both of these with "off shore" refined sugar, *i.e.*, sugar from Cuba, Puerto Rico, Hawaii, and the Philippine Islands.

Sugar is characterized by a high degree of uniformity and there is little, if any, consumer preference for any particular brand. Accordingly, to gain a larger share of the total demand, which we have seen is not very elastic, and to utilize their excess capacity to the greatest possible extent, the companies frequently resort to price cutting and demoralizing trade practices.

The competitive position of the cane refiners has been further complicated by competition from the beet sugar industry. The competition between these two branches is not national in scope but prevails only in certain areas. The bulk of the beet sugar is inland and most of it is consumed locally with little competition from cane because the cost of transportation from the seaboard, where all cane refineries are located, is so high that no cane sugar can penetrate into the mountain states. However, there are certain areas where the markets overlap and in those areas the two sugars meet competitively. As is shown in Fig. 91, and for reasons that will be explained later, the sugar beet industry is supplying a larger proportion of the total market, chiefly at the expense of the cane refiners.

Much more important has been the competition from the off-shore refiners. Beginning in 1925 there was a steady increase in the imports of refined sugar from Cuba and our insular possessions. This is shown in Fig. 92. Since the consumption of sugar did not increase, every pound of refined sugar imported from these sources represented a loss to the American refiners. The situation was further complicated by the fact that refining costs in Cuba and the insular possessions were lower than

those of domestic refiners. The tariff on refined sugar did not offer
sufficient protection for the domestic refiners because the spread between
the duty on refined sugar and the duty on raw sugar was not wide enough.

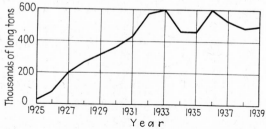

Fig. 92.—United States imports of off-shore refined sugar. (*Sugar Institute, Inc., Statistics
and Agricultural Adjustment Administration.*)

Government Control.—For most of the time since the end of the
First World War the world sugar industry has been in a state bordering
on almost complete collapse. Prior to the war the problem of balancing
supply with demand had been worked out on the basis of experience and
a relatively high measure of stability had been maintained. However,
at the outbreak of the war a very substantial proportion of the world
sugar supply, about 33 per cent, was tied up within the European battle
lines, and European sugar production declined from about 8 million tons
in 1913 to 2.5 million tons in 1919. The resulting high prices encouraged
the expansion of cane production wherever possible, and in the United
States there was an expansion of the beet sugar industry. The end of
hostilities and the elimination of governmental control of prices and
consumption brought about a further increase in both, causing a further
expansion in sugar production.

In 1920 the price of sugar was 22 cents per pound, but in 1921 the
price structure collapsed and sugar declined to 7 cents per pound. Had
the world sugar industry been left to the mercies of an open competitive
market, balance would probably have soon been attained, because the
cost of beet sugar was too high to compete with cane. However, most
countries were determined not only to rebuild their sugar beet industries,
but to expand them either by bounties or high tariff protection. Thus,
the production and processing of sugar is perhaps the most rigidly controlled industry in the world today.

Until 1934 the activity of the government in the domestic sugar
industry was limited to providing tariff protection, chiefly in the interests
of the beet and cane growers. Despite the protective duty, however,
the beet sugar industry was unable to maintain the high levels reached
during the war period. Beginning in 1926, and especially after 1930,
when the duty was again increased, the trend in beet production was

reversed.   The increase in beet acreage was facilitated also by the decline in the prices of alternative agricultural products.   While the tariff reduced imports from Cuba, it did not restrain imports from our insular possessions, whose exports were admitted free.   Since their exports were in increasing amounts in the form of refined sugar,[1] the effect on domestic refiners was severe.

To remedy the unsatisfactory price situation Congress in 1934 enacted the Jones-Costigan Act which directs the Secretary of Agriculture to determine in December of each year the amount of sugar needed to meet requirements for consumers for the following calendar year, and to allocate quotas for the various producing areas, according to fixed percentages set forth in the act.[2]   The quotas for 1941 are shown in Table LXXIV.

TABLE LXXIV.—SUGAR QUOTAS, 1941
(In short tons)

Domestic beet	1,549,898
Continental cane	420,167
Hawaii	938,037
Puerto Rico	797,982
Virgin Islands	8,916
Philippines	1,006,931
Cuba	1,869,060
Foreign countries other than Cuba	25,826
Total	6,616,817

Source: U. S. Department of Agriculture.

To compensate the domestic and insular cane and domestic beet producers for observing production restrictions and minimum wage and maximum hour requirements for farm labor, determined by the Secretary of Labor, benefit payments are paid from an excise tax of .054 cents imposed on all domestic refiners.

The administration of the act has been criticized by the industry chiefly because it has not resulted in prices as high as the manufacturers would like.   This has been due to the fact that the figure of consumers' requirements determined by the secretary has usually been set too high, with the result that the price structure is subjected to the pressure

---

[1] See Fig. 92.

[2] The quotas for the various sugar producing areas are automatically determined from the determination of consumers' requirements in the following manner:

Domestic beet sugar	23.19 %	or 1,549,898	tons, whichever is higher
Continental cane sugar	6.29 %	or 420,167	tons, whichever is higher
Hawaii	14.0 %	or 938,037	tons, whichever is higher
Puerto Rico	11.94 %	or 792,982	tons, whichever is higher
Virgin Islands	0.13 %	or 8,916	tons, whichever is higher
Total domestic areas	55.59 %	or 3,715,000	tons, whichever is higher

The balance of the total is allotted to other producers on the following basis: Philippine Islands 15.4 per cent, Cuba 28.6 per cent, and others 0.41 per cent.

of the excessive supply. Furthermore, there has been considerable criticism of the allotment formula, each of the several interests insisting upon a larger allotment. Since the total demand is relatively fixed, an increase accorded to any one group must be at the expense of all the other interests.

Of the several groups the most favored have been the beet interests, and for a number of reasons. First, the import duty and the quotas give them protection from price competition from the more cheaply produced cane. Second, transportation costs on cane sugar from the seaboard refineries give them additional protection in their own markets. Third, the quotas allotted to the beet producers have usually been in excess of their actual production which meant that, until 1941, when a reduction in acreage was ordered, in effect they operated outside of the quota restrictions. Fourth, the cost of beets to those beet refiners that do not grow their own are governed by sliding-scale contracts, based on the market price of sugar and the sugar content of the beets; those companies that grow beets receive benefit payments from the Treasury for observing acreage restriction and labor standards.

The insular cane producers are also in a favored position. They have low production costs, are not subject to the tariff, and while the marketing control has checked their expansion, their quotas are large enough to give them an assured market at a price higher than the world market. In addition, they too receive benefit payments.

The poorest showing has been made by the domestic refiners of imported cane. Since they receive no allotment under the law, they obtain the remainder of the home market only after the beet industry and the off-shore refining industry have sold their shares.[1] The only protection they receive is a provision in the law that imports of refined sugar from off-shore interests may not exceed 612,863 tons.

Future.—Since the demand for sugar is relatively inelastic, any substantial growth in demand will depend primarily on population growth. Accordingly, the domestic sugar industry cannot look to demand as a solution for its problem. To maintain stability, therefore, the industry must look to the control of supply factors, and since so many varied interests are involved, the control must necessarily be governmental in nature. More than any other industry so far considered in this book, the stability, if not the existence, of this industry depends upon the government. The varied producers, the differences in their costs of production, and the international aspects of the industry make tariffs and quotas necessary. Consequently, the future of the industry as a whole, and the profits of its branches, will be determined by the attitude of the government rather than by economic forces in the market.

[1] DALTON, J. E., Federal Sugar Control, *Harvard Business Review*, Autumn, 1938.

CHAPTER XXXIII

THE MEAT PACKING INDUSTRY

As one of the principal sources of proteins, meat occupies a prominent place in our diet. The average daily consumption of meat is about 6 oz. per person. The total annual meat consumption is approximately 17 billion lb. To supply this huge demand, the meat packing industry slaughters and prepares fifty million to 75 million head of livestock each year. In 1939, the meat packing industry produced about 2.5 billion dollar's worth of meat products. According to the Census of Manufactures, this was about 25 per cent of the value of all food products. The money which the meat packers pay to some 6 million farmers for livestock is their largest single source of cash income. It represents about 25 per cent of the total farm income. The money which meatpackers collect from some 130 million consumers represents a very substantial proportion of the food budgets of American families. Since the packing process adds little value to the product, the packers' profits are precarious. Farmers naturally seek the highest prices for their livestock and consumers can easily shift to other kinds of food when they regard the price of meat as too high. The supply of raw materials is highly irregular and the finished product is highly perishable. The industry is affected by traditional patterns of food consumption, religion, weather, and government control.

The Development of the Industry.—Prior to the heavy industrialization and urbanization of the East and before the agricultural development of the West began, livestock was raised on the Atlantic seaboard close to the market, and the preparation of livestock for consumption was accomplished by local butchers operating small establishments.

As the cities grew and gradually forced livestock raising away from the East, local supplies became inadequate and it was necessary to obtain them from points farther and farther away. The absence of adequate transportation facilities made it necessary to drive the animals across the country to the cities where they were slaughtered and dressed. This was not entirely true of pork which, because it could be cured by salting down or smoking, was shipped already prepared rather than on the hoof. The packing of pork led to the development of several river towns west of the Alleghenies as important packing centers. Prominent in this group was Cincinnati. With the advent of the railroads and the further development of the West as a livestock-raising area, animals were shipped alive in stock cars.

It soon became apparent that the practice of shipping live animals was inefficient since there was considerable loss from shrinkage and deterioration, and freight had to be paid on the entire animal although only about one-half of it, in the case of cattle, could be sold as meat. Notwithstanding these factors, it was impracticable, in fact impossible, to shift the industry to the source of livestock because fresh meat could not be shipped long distances.

It was to be expected that steps would be taken to meet this problem, and in 1870 it was successfully solved by the introduction of the refrigerator car. This development was of supreme importance to the industry, for it not only shifted its location nearer to its raw materials, but changed its entire complexion and gave it characteristics which we today associate with the meat packing industry—large establishments, huge stockyards, refrigerator cars, and a highly developed system of distribution.

The rise of Chicago as a meat packing center began quite early. Although cattle markets had been established there before 1850, it was the Civil War boom that caused Chicago to forge ahead of other centers. In 1865 the Chicago Union Stock Yards were opened and by 1870 Chicago was established as the leading center of the industry. Shortly thereafter Gustavus Swift, a New England butcher, and P. D. Armour, a Milwaukee pork packer, established in Chicago their respective companies which today are the two leading concerns in the industry. The growth of the Western cattle ranges, the rise of the corn belt centering in Iowa, and the linking of these areas with Chicago by numerous railroads gave added impetus to Chicago as a packing center. As early as 1885 over 1 million dollars' worth of livestock was purchased daily by Chicago packers.

The meat packing industry may be represented as a bridge which joins the vast area west of the Mississippi, where two-thirds of the raw materials originate, with the East where most of its products are consumed. In 1939 the industry consisted of 1,478 establishments and it employed 120,000 workers. In that year it converted 2,227 million dollars' worth of raw materials into 2,648 million dollars' worth of meat and allied products. It should be noted that the difference, 421 million dollars, the value added, is only 15 per cent of the value of the product.

Types of Packers.—Meat packing establishments of the United States may be classified into three groups. First are the large interstate or national packers; second, the small interstate packers; and third, the local packers.

The large interstate packers are Swift, Armour, Wilson, and Cudahy. Each of the "big four" sells well over 100 million dollars' worth of products annually and together they control almost half of the total business. Swift and Company is the largest unit in the industry; its sales in 1940 were 772 million dollars. The company operates about 50 plants in various states and Canada and 25 cottonseed-oil mills and refineries. Armour is only slightly smaller than Swift. It operates about 25 meat packing establishments, 300 branch houses, and owns over 5,000 refrigerator cars. Wilson and Cudahy each operate about 12 meat packing plants.

The large national packer came into existence in response to the demand for a mechanism to join the producing areas of the West with the consuming areas of the East.   It will be recalled that over two-thirds of the livestock is raised west of the Mississippi River and two-thirds of the consumers live east of the river.   To assemble animals in sufficient quantity and variety and to distribute the meat in the Eastern market is a large task and requires a huge organization. In addition to the long-distance nature of the industry's operations, the time element of the industry favors the large packer to some extent. Livestock is not sent to the market in a steady stream or in response to demand. The seasonal variation in the receipt of livestock and in meat consumption makes it necessary for some one to hold the meat, especially pork, until the market is prepared to absorb it. This function can best be performed by the large packer.

Another factor which influences the size of establishments is the type of animal slaughtered.   Most cattle are slaughtered by the large packers. Cattle produce a smaller percentage of edible meat than do hogs.   Only 45 to 50 per cent of the live weight of lamb is meat, and 50 to 60 per cent of the weight of a steer is beef, in contrast with 70 to 75 per cent of edible pork products from a hog.   Thus the cattle packers must engage more extensively in by-product processing.

In addition to the advantage of large-scale operations, the large packers have nation-wide marketing and distributing facilities which enable them to sell in all the markets.

The activities of the small interstate packers parallel those of the national packers except that they market their products over a smaller area and confine their business more to pork products which require less by-product processing.   In this class are such companies as Morrell, Hormell, Rath, Dold, and Kingan. Annual sales of these packers are considerably under 100 million dollars each.

The local packers, as the name implies, do a local rather than a national or state-wide business. They buy local supplies of livestock and sell in near-by markets. This makes a heavy investment unnecessary, since they have no need for large-capacity coolers, refrigerator cars, branch storage and distribution houses, etc. Most of the small establishments are in the East, especially in New York and Pennsylvania. Although they use local raw material supplies primarily, they also obtain some livestock from the West. This practice, according to Weld[1] is due to, first, the large kosher demand in New York and other large Eastern cities; second, a preference for locally prepared meats in certain areas such as New England, which is a survival of the early prejudice against Western meats; and third, the fact that meat packing was first established in the Atlantic seaboard states.

PLATE 66.—View of the Union Stockyards of Chicago. (*Courtesy of Swift & Company.*)

Buying Policies of the Packers.—Packers buy most of their livestock either through central markets or through what is known as direct marketing. A central market is a terminal market or public stockyard to which farmers send their cattle for sale to packers or other buyers. The stockyard is purely a service organization; it unloads, weighs, and cares for the cattle until sold. The cattle are kept in pens owned by the stockyard company and these pens are allotted to commission firms that sell the cattle to the packers for cash, deduct rents, commissions, etc., and remit the proceeds to the farmer. There are about 100 central markets but over half of the cattle receipts are handled by the 9 central markets shown in Fig. 93.

[1] WELD, L. D., and A. T. KEARNEY and F. H. SIDNEY, "Economics of the Packing Industry," pp. 122–125, University of Chicago Press, Chicago, 1925.

Direct marketing is the purchase of livestock by the packer directly from the farmer without the service of a commission agent and usually in places other than recognized public stockyard markets. Direct marketing is more important in the case of hogs than in the case of other livestock because of greater concentration of hog raising in the corn belt, but the practice is growing generally as shown in Table LXXV.

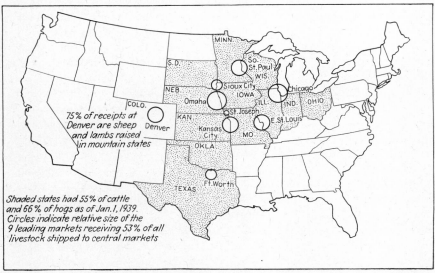

Fig. 93.—Principal cattle raising and meat packing areas. (*Bureau of Agricultural Economics, Livestock Meats, Wool Market Statistics, and Related Data*, 1939, *United States Department of Agriculture*.)

Several factors have helped to bring about more direct buying especially with respect to hogs. The freight on a given amount of pork products from the corn belt eastward is less than the freight of the live hogs required to produce those pork products. This has been a factor leading to the establishment of more packing houses at interior points close to the source of the raw materials. Furthermore, there is less

TABLE LXXV.—DIRECT PURCHASES OF LIVESTOCK IN PERCENTAGE OF TOTAL SLAUGHTERED UNDER FEDERAL INSPECTION*

	Hogs	Calves	Sheep and lambs	Cattle
1923	26.5	14.3	18.1	11.1
1938	51.7	35.8	31.6	25.1

* Balance of Federal Inspected slaughter purchased at public stockyards.

Source: MALOTT, D. W., and B. F. MARTIN, "The Agricultural Industries," p. 95, McGraw-Hill Book Company, Inc., New York, 1939.

concluded that it was the effect of the outside air. Those who followed him also laid great stress upon the effect of the air, and made every effort to secure a high vacuum. When tin cans came into use, they were sometimes vented as many as two or three times in order to secure the desired result. Chemists appointed by the French government to investigate the matter reported substantially the same findings as Appert.

This explanation was accepted until the advent of the new science of bacteriology, which was largely the product of the work of Pasteur. This brought the true explanation. It is now known that all foods, water, air, and the containers are bearers of bacteria and other microorganisms; that the effect of the heat is to destroy them and that the hermetic container merely excludes those from without. Although the application of heat destroys these bacteria, foods immediately become reinfected as soon as the temperature drops low enough to allow microflora to flourish. Hence the importance of an airtight container. The first application of the science of bacteriology to canning in this country was made in 1895, and since that time sufficient work has been done to enable factories to can all kinds of food products with comparative safety. Canning may be defined, therefore, as the preservation of food through sterilization by heat and its maintenance in that condition in an hermetically sealed container.

DEVELOPMENT OF THE CANNING INDUSTRY

The canning industry started in France and England immediately after Appert's discovery. It was brought to the United States soon after, where it has attained its highest development. The first use of the new method in this country was in 1819 in New York where Ezra Daggett and Thomas Kensett commenced packing salmon, lobsters, and oysters. In the next year quinces, cranberries, and currants were first packed in Boston, and, in 1840, oyster canning commenced in Baltimore. In the succeeding years, small canneries sprang up along the coast, packing marine products principally and supplementing those by fruits and vegetables in season. However, very little progress was made in the industry prior to the Civil War, as the advantages of the new process were not generally recognized, and the process was costly and laborious owing to the lack of labor-saving machinery. Furthermore, cities were small and fruits and vegetables of all kinds were grown in their immediate vicinity and delivered fresh by wagon.

It was not until the close of the Civil War decade that the superiority of canned foods over those which were dried, salted, and pickled became common knowledge. Soldiers in camps and hospitals, though meagerly supplied with canned foods, learned of their excellence and value, and later carried the information to every section. About this time, the introduction of calcium chloride enabled a much higher temperature to be obtained in the cooking kettles so that the output of the average cannery was materially increased. It was during these years that the first canneries were established in the Middle West and California, followed in 1878 by the establishment of one in Alaska.

Domestic and commercial canning increased constantly, though somewhat slowly, because of popular prejudice that had to be broken down. In addition, economical methods of manufacture had to be developed. The first step along this line was the invention of the closed

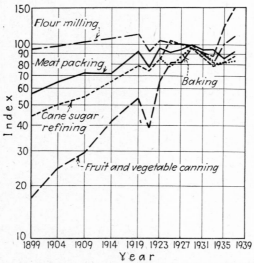

Fig. 95.—Growth of food industries, physical volume (1929 = 100). (*National Bureau of Economic Research, The Output of Manufacturing Industries, 1899–1937, New York, 1941.*)

or pressure kettle which enabled higher temperatures to be obtained. The decade of the nineties brought the automatic capping machine for soldering caps on the cans. This overcame a limitation on production which had been imposed by the cappers' union. During this period, also, the industry witnessed the application of Pasteur's epoch-making discoveries to canning processes, with the result that many fruits and vegetables hitherto unused were canned successfully.

Since 1900, the fruit and vegetable canning industries have grown rapidly, at a faster rate than the other major food industries as shown in Fig. 95. Commercial canning was naturally stimulated by the same basic changes in our habits of living that brought about increasing reliance upon prepared foods. The constantly improved process gradually broke down the prejudice against canned foods and increased the variety of foods successfully packed. Improved technology affected literally every phase of the industry. Selective crops are grown under the direction of canners to insure highest grade raw materials. The solder-top can has been replaced by the modern double-seal sanitary tin. Scientifically determined standards of temperature, pressure, and processing time assure uniformity of quality for each type of food. Costs have been reduced by a widespread adoption of labor-saving machinery. The rapidity of growth has also been due in large part to the rapid expansion in variety of foods processed. For many years the annual pack consisted chiefly of peas, corn, and tomatoes among the vegetables, peaches and pineapples among the fruits, and several sea-foods. Now more than 225 different kinds of foods are successfully packed.

SIZE AND CHARACTER OF THE INDUSTRY

Canning is a large industry. It employs over 100,000 workers and produces in excess of a half billion dollars worth of products annually. The annual output of canned goods and the relative importance of the several classes is shown in Table LXXVI.

TABLE LXXVI.—THE ANNUAL PACK OF CANNED GOODS

	Cases
Vegetables	165,000,000
Fruits	50,000,000
Milk products	40,000,000
Seafoods	17,000,000
Meats and other products	12,000,000
Total	284,000,000

Source: "The Canning Industry," National Canners Association, 1939.

The industry is predominantly small-scale. The typical cannery employs an average of 50 workers; only 9 per cent of the fruit and vegetable canneries employ more than 100 workers each. Because of the seasonal nature of the industry, these figures, based upon yearly averages, somewhat understate the scale of operation. Nevertheless canneries are, for the most part, comparatively small-sized enterprises. Among fruit and vegetable canneries, 15 per cent produce less than $20,000 worth of products annually, and 60 per cent have an output of less than $100,000 annually. Small-scale operation is the rule because the seasonal and perishable nature of most of the raw materials definitely limits the size of economical operation. However, there are several notable exceptions, such as Campbell's, Heinz, and Libby, McNeill and Libby. These companies are far above average size; they operate numerous widely scattered plants and produce a great variety of products.

In spite of the small size of most canneries and their necessarily wide geographical distribution, the quest for the highest grade raw materials has brought about considerable localization.   Each canning crop tends to localize where soil and climatic conditions are most favorable.   Over 50 per cent of our peaches are packed in California.   This state also leads in plum, apricot, asparagus, and spinach canning.   Salmon packing is localized in Alaska, sardines in Maine and California, shrimp in the Gulf states, beets and carrots in New York, pumpkins and squash in Indiana, cherries in Michigan, and pineapples in Hawaii.   The common vegetables—beans, peas, corn, and tomatoes—are grown in many states;

PLATE 68.—Filling and capping cans of peas.   (*Courtesy of American Can Company.*)

consequently vegetable canneries are found in all the major growing areas.

THE CANNING PROCESS

The steps in canning vary with the character of the food, but certain basic operations are common to practically all products.   These operations consist of cleaning and trimming, blanching, filling, preheating, sealing, cooking, cooling, labeling, and packing.

Cleaning and trimming consist of such operations as peeling, coring, and pitting of fruits; shelling, vining, and husking of vegetables.   Many of these operations are done mechanically in all but the smallest canneries. For example, a machine, called the "iron chink," automatically cleans salmon, cuts off the heads, tails, and fins, and removes the entrails—a job formerly done by numerous Chinese laborers.   Pea canners no longer hire laborers by the thousand to pick and hull peas. Automatic machines have been developed which harvest and load the entire stalks like so much hay. The crop is hauled to the cannery where another machine separates the peas from the pods and grades the peas according to size.

Blanching is a preliminary cooking applied to certain vegetables, such as beans and peas, for the purpose of removing natural gummy substances.

PLATE 69.—Cans entering pressure cooker. (*Courtesy of American Can Company.*)

Cans are filled by hand in the case of peaches and salmon, but most products lend themselves to mechanical filling. Some products, such as tomatoes, are put into the cans cold, then put through a steam box for a preheating. This expels the air and prevents the cans from bursting during the cooking operation after the cans are closed.

Sealing is done by the automatic capper. It inserts a gasket and crimps the edge with a double seal, thus assuring airtightness.

The cooking, or sterilizing, process varies with the product. Acid products, such as tomatoes and fruits, do not require temperatures in excess of the boiling point of water. Hence they are cooked in tanks or troughs heated by open steam pipes. However, milk, fish meats, and vegetables require higher temperatures.   For proper sterilization, these products are cooked in steamtight pressure cookers controlled by automatic devices.

After cooking, the cans are removed and placed under cold water sprays to prevent overcooking.   Labeling and sometimes packing are done mechanically, depending upon the size of the cannery.

The importance of harvesting crops at the proper stage of maturity and the necessity of immediate processing calls for the use of speedy

PLATE 70.—Cooling cans in a continuous conveyor-cooling-tank.   (*Courtesy of American Can Company.*)

mechanized operation in almost every stage of the process.   Some evidence of the progress of mechanization is the fact that since 1900 power-driven machinery has increased twenty-five fold whereas the amount of labor employed has only doubled.   Most canneries, except those packing tomatoes and asparagus, require complex and costly machinery.   However, some of the machines can be rented from the machinery or supplies manufacturers.   For example, a $6,000 can capper can be rented from the can manufacturer for $250 a year.

HOW THE CANNERS BUY THEIR RAW MATERIALS

Canners, unlike most other processors of agricultural products, buy their raw materials directly from the farmers.   This direct business relationship between canner and farmer is unique. Cotton and wool manufacturers, by contrast, or meat packers and flour millers, customarily deal through intermediaries—brokers or commission men. The practice of dealing directly with the farmer is advantageous to both the farmer and the canner, as will be seen presently. The relationship between canner and farmer is unique in still another respect. Canners do not buy crops after they are harvested. They buy crops before they are harvested; in fact, before they are planted. Furthermore, they do not buy vegetables; they buy "acres." The method of buying may be explained best by an illustration.

During the winter, or probably as early as November, the individual farmer enters into a contract with the canner wherein the canner agrees to buy the farmer's entire crop of so many acres of, let us say, green peas. The contract specifies the price for peas of first-class quality together with a sliding scale for peas of inferior quality, which serves as an incentive to the farmer to produce only the best. The contract price is determined by the customary bargaining process: it must be high enough to induce the farmer to raise peas rather than some other crop which his land can produce, and at the same time the price cannot be so high as to preclude any prospect of profit for the canner. Since the canner is in reality buying a "future," he must consider, before making a specific price offer, such things as the size of the carryover, the rate at which current canned goods are moving into distributive channels, the acreage devoted to peas in the season just past, prices paid in the past season, probable shifts in consumption, competing supplies of other vegetables, etc. Likewise, the farmer, before signing a contract, must consider the alternative use of his acreage, crop-rotation requirements, investment in specialized agricultural machinery, revenue from the season just closed, etc.

Let us see why this method of buying is beneficial to both canner and grower. By working in close cooperation with the farmer, the canner is able to exert considerable influence over the quality of his raw materials. Having contracted for a definite acreage, the canner can make advance arrangements with respect to machinery and physical facilities required. The principal benefits to the farmer are that he is assured of a market for his product, and furthermore he is guaranteed a definite price. In this respect the farmer growing canning crops is in a much better position than the farmer producing wheat, cotton, or other field crops. The wheat farmer, for example, may plant his crop when the price of wheat is $1.00 a bushel and may receive only 60 cents a bushel when the grain is harvested. Although he may occasionally get a better price than he expected, the point is that he never knows what his crop will bring until it is harvested. His income is, therefore, more speculative

than that of the farmer who sells his crops to canneries. This is shown
in Fig. 96. Throughout the entire period sketched, the price of wheat
fluctuated over a much a wider range than the price of peas, because
wheat is sold in the open market where its price is determined by the
supply and demand forces operative at that particular time. Under
contract marketing the growers of peas and other canning crops achieve a
better adjustment of supply to demand and hence less erratic variations
in income from one season to the next.

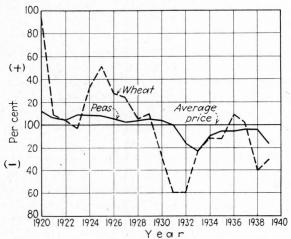

Fig. 96.—Prices paid growers for wheat and peas. (Per cent deviations from average
1920–1939). (*National Canners Association.*)

Cans.—Cans are a very important item in the canner's cost structure;
in fact, the can in some instances costs more than its contents of food.
In tomato canning, for example, cans are 39 per cent of the total cost in
contrast with 25 per cent for raw products and 18 per cent for labor.
In the early days the canner customarily made his own cans, and his
success depended largely upon how good a tinsmith he was—too many
"leakers" spelled financial ruin. Can making gradually became a
separate business and today practically all canners buy their cans.[1]
Heinz is an outstanding exception.

The present-day can supply is virtually controlled by two companies—
American Can, which produces just a shade over half the total, and
Continental Can, which produces half of the remainder. American Can
obtained a working monopoly of the business, 90 per cent of capacity,
when in 1900 its promoters created the company by consolidating about
125 of the 175 then existing can manufacturers. However, its monopoly
was soon undermined by its own price policy. The price of cans was

[1] MAY, E. C., "The Canning Clan," The Macmillan Company, New York, 1937.

raised and this served to attract others into the business, notably Continental Can. Over the years both companies have grown and prospered, but Continental has grown faster, which explains the relative decline of the leader, American Can.

Despite the outward appearance of monopoly, or more correctly "duopoly," competition is very keen between these two companies for the trade of the canners. Though there is sharp rivalry between American and Continental, they do not engage in price wars in the usual sense of the term. The nearest approach to price competition is the practice of protecting their customers against rising can costs. The thin veneer of tin represents two-thirds of the cost of a tin can, and, since the price of tin is notoriously volatile, the can companies revise the price of cans annually, based upon the prevailing price of tin. A novel feature of the contract with the canner is the ceiling clause which protects the canner for one year against rising can prices, and provides for pro-rata rebates in case tin prices decline. Though the two leading can companies do not underbid each other, each tries to build up volume by offering its customers the most attractive contract.

In practice this means that each must meet the other's terms. They cater to the canners' trade by offering cans in a variety of sizes and shapes, by renting and servicing can-closing machinery, by building new plants to serve new canning districts more efficiently, by sending out crews of experts to study and advise canners concerning special problems such as leaks, swells, or food discoloration.

HOW CANNERS MARKET THEIR PRODUCTS

About 65 per cent of all canned goods is sold through brokers. Most canneries are too small and too remote from their markets to undertake the task of marketing. Even chain groceries formerly bought their canned goods through brokers, but since the passage of the Robinson-Patman Act, chain stores have eliminated the broker. Brokers frequently represent more than one canner because in some of the smaller cities the broker must have a variety of canned goods in order to get sufficient volume. As a result of this practice, canners often feel that although they pay the brokerage commissions, the broker works for the buyer. Nevertheless, canners could not assume the expense of doing their own distributing except in the case of the few large canners that have a national market.

Although it is not a general practice, canners sometimes sell futures,[1] *i.e.*, sell for future delivery products that have yet to be processed. If the crop subsequently turns out to be too small, the canner, under the

---

[1] These contracts are not to be confused with futures contracts traded in on organized commodity markets.

terms of the future contract, is relieved from his obligation if he can show: first, that he contracted for enough acreage; second, that he was financially able; and third, that all buyers holding his futures were given equal consideration.

The distributor often insists upon having his own rather than the packer's name appear on the label. This is especially true of the highest quality canned goods. This is in marked contrast with the early days when labeling was frequently deceptive or failed to reveal the name of the responsible canner or distributor. The National Canners Association, formed in 1907, assumed an active leadership in informative labeling. Canners are now so jealous of the quality of their products that they vigorously oppose a recent governmental suggestion that all canned goods be classified according to an A-B-C system of grading. Most canners contend that it would lower the standards of the industry because a grade A, for example, ranging from 90 to 100, would not distinguish the very best goods from those that just managed to make the grade A. They take the position that descriptive labeling is more informative because it enumerates all the essential qualities of the product. In 1940, the Association financed a nation-wide survey, conducted by Elmo Roper, to determine the type of labeling preferred by consumers. The study revealed that "85 per cent of the women of the country have no difficulty in picking out the quality or kind of canned food they want and most people are not aware of the absence of any important information on the labels of canned goods."[1]

PROBLEMS PECULIAR TO THE CANNING INDUSTRY

Seasonality.—Canning is obviously a highly seasonal industry. Active operations usually begin in May and continue to expand each succeeding month until September, after which there is a sharp recession. Between November and April, *i.e.*, during the slack period, the industry employs about 100,000 workers. At the peak of the canning season about 350,000 workers are employed. Despite the acute seasonality of operations, the industry experiences little difficulty in obtaining its peak labor requirements. Most canneries are located in small communities where they can draw upon farm laborers, housewives, students, and others who during the rest of the year engage in other activities.

The greatest burden of seasonality is the need it creates for large working capital. Canners pay cash for their raw materials, which causes a heavy drain upon their resources during the summer months, and since they have to carry the pack until sold, their cash receipts are spread out over the remainder of the year. For this reason, canners, more than any other manufacturers, are always in need of cash.

[1] *Roper Report*, National Canners Association, 1941.

Efforts to lengthen the canning season have been along the lines of product diversification, cooperation with the growers to extend the harvesting season by developing varieties that mature at different times of the season and by staggering planting dates. Despite these efforts, seasonal irregularity remains a major problem. The industry is granted certain specific exemptions under the Wages and Hours Act. Canners are exempt from all overtime provisions of the law for 14 weeks of the year, and for an additional 14 weeks they need not pay overtime rates provided the total hours worked in any one week do not exceed 56.

Can Sizes.—One form of competition between canners of the same product is to offer the consumer greater variety in sizes of cans. Up to a certain point, this kind of competition is advantageous to the consumers for they can buy canned goods to suit their individual needs, ranging from the cafeteria to the kitchenette size. However, in their zeal to win the patronage of customers, canners have introduced so many sizes that the buyer is bewildered. Foods are now being offered in more than 150 different-sized cans; tomato juice alone comes in 52 different sizes of cans.

The National Canners Association has sponsored a movement to reduce and simplify can sizes. One governmental agency proposed a maximum of 7 different sizes, a suggestion which is impractical because it does not make adequate allowance for varieties of size and shape of products, such as peaches, pears, cherries, asparagus spears, corn on the cob, etc., nor does it meet the needs of the consumer, which range from baby-food size to large units required by hotels and restaurants. The association is working along the line of a minimum 20 per cent differential in size, sufficient to be easily recognized by every buyer.

The Size of the Pack.—The central problem of the canning industry which affects profit or loss is the annual change in the size of the pack. The size of the pack of any one fruit or vegetable is a composite of many variables. In the first place, it depends upon the number of acres planted which, in turn, depends upon the aggregate of numerous individual contracts between canners and growers. However, the ultimate size of the crop harvested depends upon the forces of nature which are at best subject to very limited control by man. Variations in climatic conditions from year to year cause marked differences in yield per acre. In 1936, for example, 440,000 acres of sweet corn were planted, which under normal conditions would have produced 23 million cases of canned corn; but as a result of an abnormally low yield per acre, only 15 million cases were realized. In 1939 the actual pack exceeded the expected pack by almost 3 million cases. Since canners contract for acres, they must be prepared to process and sell as much or as little as nature yields.

In determining the acreage to be planted each year, canners and growers are naturally responsive to price. Note in Fig. 97 the relationship between annual variations in green-pea acreage and green-pea prices. Throughout the two decades 1920–1940, rising prices usually stimulated larger acreage and falling prices usually brought about a curtailment.

It is also interesting to note fairly well-defined cycles in acreage planted. Three cycles are apparent—the first runs from a low point in 1921 to a peak in 1924 and ends at a low point in 1927; the second runs to 1932; and the third to 1939. In each of the three cycles there were three successive years of expanding acreage following the low point of the cycle. Furthermore, throughout the entire period, there was a rising secular trend in acreage planted, and a declining secular trend in prices, indicating

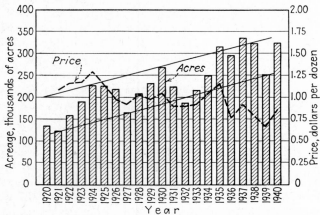

Fig. 97.—Green peas for canning, acreage and price, 1929–1940. (*National Canners Association.*)

that at any price level there was the inevitable cyclical response of acreage expansion to price increase. By connecting the peaks and troughs of the cycles, two parallel lines are obtained which represent a margin of about 90,000 acres. The National Canners Association suggests that this represents the upper and lower limits of expansion and contraction for a given amount of processing machinery installed. That is to say, the capacity of the industry is sufficiently flexible to absorb the increased flow of raw materials for two or three consecutive years, but any further increases can be accommodated only after installing additional equipment. However, the installation of additional capacity is usually followed by a cyclical recession, with the result that the relation between the acreage of the low year and the next peak is the same as it was between the previous peak and its antecedent low point.

The size of the pack of the other principal vegetables—corn, tomatoes, green and wax beans—rises and falls with a cyclical rhythm paralleling that of green peas, indicating that acreage is highly responsive to price changes throughout the vegetable canning industry. However, the supply of fruits is less elastic than that of vegetables because it takes years to mature an orchard while the crop of vegetables can be expanded from one season to the next.

PROFITS IN CANNING

Profits in the canning industry are influenced very largely by the size of the pack. Although the annual consumption of each type of canned goods is fairly constant, the annual pack, as we have seen, fluctuates considerably. On account of the contract system of buying, the canners' raw material unit costs are fixed; volume is unknown until crops are harvested; and sales revenue is unknown until the last case of canned goods leaves the warehouse, which may be 8 or 10 months after financial commitments have been made. Consequently, if the actual crop yield is larger than was anticipated, selling prices must be sacrificed to move the entire pack and profits shrink. Contrariwise, if the total pack is small, selling prices are higher and profits proportionately larger than were expected.

It is difficult to make any generalizations about the adequacy of profits for the canning industry as a whole, because most of the canneries are family-owned concerns that do not publish financial statements. This applies not only to the multitude of small canneries, but also to some of the largest, notably Heinz and Campbell. However, there is substantial evidence that companies in the fruit canning division of the industry have been averaging 10 per cent or better on their net worth in recent years. It may be significant to observe in this connection that fruit canneries are generally larger than vegetable canneries, that the size of the fruit pack is subject to less fluctuation, and that some of the fruit canners control the acreage of fruit grown. For example, the pineapple pack was controlled for many years by the few companies dominating that branch of the industry. Vegetable packers, with few exceptions, are smaller in size, larger in number, and widely dispersed geographically so that there is less opportunity to exert any concerted influence upon the size of the pack.

Stabilization of profits through production control is virtually impossible; there are too many growers—approximately 750,000—and too many canners—about 2,200. The National Canners Association supplies the industry with excellent statistical service embracing for each of the major crops such data as acreage planted, acreage yields, production, prices, stocks on hand, etc. These data are useful to the canners in determining their own individual policies, but the association does not undertake to sponsor production control. Such action, aside from its illegality, would be inimical to the interests of the trade because one group, the corn canners, for example, would naturally oppose lending support to a plan to increase the revenue of the tomato or bean canners.

FROZEN FOODS

A comparatively recent development that may exert considerable influence upon the future course of food preservation is the art of quick-freezing. Quick-freezing differs from the older method of freezing in that the food product is subjected to an extremely low temperature which causes almost instantaneous freezing. Quick-frozen foods retain their natural flavor because the quick-freezing prevents the formation of ice crystals that rupture the cellular structure and cause a loss of natural juices when thawed out preparatory to consumption. Quick-freezing is accomplished by either dipping or spraying the foods in low-temperature brine, or subjecting the food to a blast of frigid air, or by compressing the food between frigid metal plates at a temperature ranging from -5 to $-30°F$.

The frozen-food pack, though small in contrast with the canned-food pack, has grown very rapidly. It has increased from an estimated 10 million lb. in 1934 to approximately 350 million lb. in 1940. There are over 100 companies now in the business, of which the largest is the Frozen Foods Company, a subsidiary of General Foods Corporation, which pioneered with its Birds Eye products. Frozen Foods is a distributing rather than a manufacturing company. It leases its patented freezing equipment to independently operated food packers and distributes its Birds Eye products through thousands of low-temperature cabinets leased to retailers.

Canners have suffered no adverse effects from the advent of frozen foods because the frozen-food pack is very small in contrast with the canned-food pack and many canners, realizing the potentialities of frozen foods, have added quick-freezing to their line. This is a natural development because canners are already equipped with all the facilities except the freezing units which are portable and can easily be rented.

FUTURE

Although the canning industry has grown faster in the present century than the other food industries, it is not likely that its rapidity of growth will be long maintained. In fact, the rate of growth has already slackened. Production of canned goods rose 70 per cent in physical volume in the first decade of the present century. During the second decade it rose 90 per cent, but during the third and fourth decades the rates of growth slackened to 80 and 50 per cent respectively. To a large extent the rapidity of growth reflects a shift from home cooking and preserving to commercial canning and most of this shift has already been consummated.

Nevertheless, the industry is constantly experimenting with new foods for canning and new canning processes. Among the latter are the current efforts to preserve the natural color of green vegetables and "high short" canning, a method based upon the principle of increasing the temperature and reducing the time of sterilization. Foods which are now being processed for 30 minutes at 240°F. are sterilized by "high short" canning for 15 seconds at 300°. The special machinery required has been the principal obstacle to its commercial development thus far.

CHAPTER XXXV

THE LIQUOR INDUSTRY

The term "liquor industry" is used to designate the manufacture of all alcoholic beverages. So defined, the industry produces three principal types of products. Beer and ale, the principal products of breweries, are made from malt, *i.e.*, sprouted barley. Whisky, the principal product of distilleries, is a distillate made from grains, chiefly corn and rye. Wine, the product of wineries, is made principally from fermented grape juice.

One of the outstanding characteristics differentiating these products is their alcoholic content. Beer and ale, commonly called malt liquors, have an alcoholic content ranging from 3 to 6 per cent. Whisky and related products of distilleries, variously referred to as distilled, spirituous, or hard liquor, have an alcoholic content ranging from 40 to 50 per cent. The term "proof" stamped on a bottle of whisky indicates its alcoholic strength. The proof of spirits is twice the percentage of the content, by volume, of ethyl alcohol. Spirits containing 50 per cent ethyl alcohol by volume are accordingly 100 proof. The alcoholic content of wines or vinous liquor falls between the extremes of malt and spirituous liquors. So-called "light wines" have 12 to 14 per cent alcohol, and fortified wines contain 17 to 24 per cent alcohol.

Historical Development.—Rum and whisky were the popular alcoholic beverages from the colonial period to the Civil War. Rum was distilled from molasses, an imported by-product of the sugar cane industry of the West Indies. The manufacture of rum was largely confined to the upper Atlantic seaboard. Whisky was manufactured in the interior and distilleries sprang up almost everywhere that grain was ground. During the early part of this period whisky was cheap—farmers exchanged a bushel of corn for a gallon of whisky. Throughout this period, distilled spirits were generally tax free. Alexander Hamilton's proposed tax of 10 cents a gallon fomented the Whisky Rebellion in western Pennsylvania. The consumption of malt liquor was widely urged to check the excessive consumption of hard liquor.

From the Civil War to the First World War the brewing industry grew much more rapidly than the distilling industry. Annual per capita consumption of spirituous liquors declined from 2 to 1.5 gal., whereas consumption of malt liquor rose from 5 to 20 gal. The year 1914 marks the peak of growth of brewing as measured by total volume of production.   The growing popularity of malt beverages was the result of progressively higher taxes on distilled spirits, and beer was improved in quality as a consequence of the entry of German brew masters following the heavy German immigration after the middle of the century.   As in the previous period brewing continued to be a small-scale local industry. At the turn of the century there were about 2,000 breweries in operation.

Meanwhile distilling took on more of the aspects of big business. The indifferent success of the whisky pools in the seventies and eighties culminated in the consolidation, in 1887, of about 60 distilleries into the Distilling and Cattle Feeding Trust—better known as the Whisky Trust.   Although the trust acquired well over 50 per cent of the total

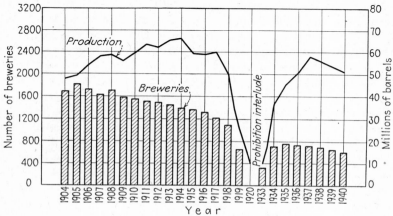

Fig. 98.—United States beer production and number of breweries.   (*W. M. Persons, Beer and Brewing in America, United Brewers Industrial Foundation, New York,* 1940.)

distilling capacity, it never did feast on monopoly gains.   It ran into financial difficulties, it lacked a satisfactory distributing system, and it aroused widespread public antipathy.

The Prohibition Interlude.—Few industries have ever been wiped out by statutory decree, but such was the fate of the liquor industry in 1920, following the passage of the Eighteenth Amendment.   At that time the liquor industry comprised about 300 distilleries and 600 breweries representing a capital investment of approximately 900 million dollars. The spread of state prohibition in the West and the South had caused a marked decline in demand for malt liquor several years before the advent of national prohibition.   Note, in Fig. 98, the decline of both operating breweries and beer production for the period immediately preceding 1920.   During the era of prohibition some breweries continued to operate by producing a cereal beverage with an alcoholic content of not over 0.5 per cent, popularly called "near beer."   Others turned to manufacturing candy, malt sirups, or cheese and other creamery products.

Some of the distilleries also continued to operate, under stringent governmental regulation, to produce alcoholic products for industrial, sacramental, and medical purposes.   The prohibition experiment, however, served to stimulate a nation-wide business in illicit liquor.   This was not a new development.   Ever since liquor has been taxed the moonshine liquor business has flourished.   For example, as early as 1898, Federal officers confiscated over 2,000 illegal stills, and 10 were said to escape for every one seized.   National prohibition, however, caused bootlegging to flourish more than ever before.   Home brewing increased but the bootleg trade was confined chiefly to hard liquor. Because of its greater potency and higher value it could be produced in short runs and distributed in small amounts with less risk of detection. Gin became a popular liquor during this period, because, unlike whisky, its manufacture requires no aging; it is cheaper and was more easily manufactured in the home.   Since the repeal of prohibition in 1933 the liquor industry has returned to a condition in some respects like, but in many respects unlike, its preprohibition status.   We shall return to this after an analysis of the major divisions of the industry.

Divisions of the Liquor Industry.—The literally thousands of alcoholic beverages are produced by three virtually separate branches of the liquor industry based largely upon differences of alcoholic content, as pointed out at the outset.   The three branches are the malt, distilled liquor, and vinous liquor industries.   Their relative importance is shown in Table LXXVII.   Because of the comparatively small size of the vinous division, this branch of the industry may be dismissed with only a few observations.

Wine, made from fermented grape juice, is one of the earliest recorded beverages because of the simplicity of the process and for the same reason a large part of the annual production is homemade.   The industry is small-scale and highly localized in regions adjacent to the vineyards supplying the raw material.   California produces almost 80 per cent

TABLE LXXVII.—SUMMARY DATA OF THE LIQUOR INDUSTRY, 1939

Item	Liquor		
	Malt	Distilled	Vinous
Number of establishments..........................	605	135	301
Wage earners..	36,000	4,100	2,000
*Cost of raw materials (millions of dollars)...........	163	28	19
*Value of products (millions of dollars)..............	526	56	33
*Value added (millions of dollars)..................	363	28	14

* Internal revenue taxes are not included.
Source: Census of Manufactures.

of the commercial output and New York produces half of the remainder. Prohibition greatly stimulated the use of wine. Total annual consumption, which ranged between 40 to 50 million gal. before prohibition, is estimated to have increased to 111 million gal. during prohibition. Since repeal consumption has declined to about 80 million gal. annually.

THE BREWING INDUSTRY

Barley is the principal raw material used in making beer and ale. By weight it constitutes about two-thirds of the total raw materials. It is estimated that the brewing industry utilizes annually about 100 million dollars worth of agricultural raw materials. The cultivation of approximately 3 million acres is required to produce the materials shown in Table LXXVIII.

TABLE LXXVIII.—RAW MATERIALS USED IN BREWING, YEAR ENDING JUNE 30, 1940

	Million Pounds
Malt	1,958
Corn products	441
Rice	189
Sugar and sirups	145
Hops	32
Total	2 765

Source: Annual Report, Bureau of Internal Revenue, 1940.

Process.—The beer making process is comparatively simple. It consists of (1) preparation of the mash, (2) hopping, (3) fermenting, and (4) aging.

The *mash* is prepared by soaking the barley in water until it sprouts. It is then crushed in the malt mill in which some corn and rice is added to obtain the necessary cereal starch. The ground mixture is next mechanically stirred in mashing rakes to which hot water has been added. During this process, which requires about 2 hours, the enzymes of malt convert the starch into sugar (maltose), which is later fermented. A pressure filter next separates the clear liquid, called "wort," from the solid matter. The latter is sold as a by-product for cattle feed.

Hopping is similar to making tea. The wort is concentrated and sterilized for 1 to 3 hours in a brew kettle. During this time hops have been added to counteract the sweetness and give the final product its characteristic flavor. The brew, called "lager," must be cooled to proper temperature before adding yeast.

Fermenting is usually done in two stages. Yeast is added to the lager in a starting vat. After fermentation sets in the lager is pumped to the fermenting vat. This is a huge steel tank lined with glass enamel. Fermenting requires 4 to 8 days. The carbon dioxide liberated during the process is collected and stored for later use. At this stage in the

process, the distinction between beer and ale arises. Traditionally ale
had a stronger flavor, more body, less foam, and slightly more alcohol
than beer. Today the distinction lies in the yeast. Ale yeast works
to the top of the vat. Beer yeast works to the bottom of the vat. Thus
ale yeast produces a drier and lighter taste in the final product.

Aging takes place in underground storage tanks into which the beer is
pumped from the fermenting vat. The beer is kept in these tanks for
2 to 3 months. When ripe it is withdrawn and cooled, some carbon
dioxide gas is reinjected, and the beer is pasteurized and bottled or
barreled.

Location.—The brewing industry consists of slightly over 600 establishments dispersed over a wide area. Practically every state in the
union has one or more breweries, but the distribution is roughly in
proportion to population density; about 60 per cent of the total output
is produced in the six states listed in Table LXXIX.

TABLE LXXIX.—THE LEADING BEER-PRODUCING STATES

	Number of breweries	1940 Production, barrels (000,000 omitted)
New York	64	8.9
Pennsylvania	85	6.2
Wisconsin	73	5.7
Missouri	17	4.3
Illinois	56	3.7
Ohio	51	3.7
All others	259	22.5
Total United States	605	55.0

Source: Census of Manufactures.

At one time brewing was strictly a local industry. In the early
seventies there were over 4,000 breweries in operation. Although
competition has forced many small breweries out of business, as we shall
see in a moment, there are certain factors in favor of the small local
brewery serving its local market. Barley, the principal raw material,
is a dry-climate crop produced in almost every state. Beer, whether
barreled, bottled, or canned, is a bulky product which entails progressively higher distribution costs as more distant markets are sought.
Furthermore, numerous states have set up legal barriers against the
importation of beer made in other states. Most of these laws take the
form of higher licenses exacted from manufacturers and distributors of
"foreign" beer.[1]

[1] U. S. Department of Agriculture, Barriers to Internal Trade in Farm Products,
p. 31, Washington, 1939.

Structure of the Industry.—In 1940, the 600 operating breweries ranged in size from the largest, producing 2.4 million barrels, to very small establishments producing only 5,000 barrels or less; the average was 90,000 barrels. Unlike many of our industries, in the brewing industry, no one company or small group of companies occupies a dominant position. Only 6 companies, shown in Table LXXX, are in the class producing in excess of a million barrels annually and the combined output of these companies is only a sixth of the total production. The 25 leading companies produce only 37 per cent of the total output.

TABLE LXXX.—THE LEADING BREWERS

	Plant location	1940 output, barrels
Anheuser-Busch...................	St. Louis, Mo.	2,468,000
Pabst Brewing Company..........	Milwaukee, Wis. Peoria, Ill.	1,730,000
Jos. Schlitz Brew. Company........	Milwaukee, Wis.	1,570,184
F. & M. Schaefer Brew. Company..	Brooklyn, N. Y.	1,390,000
P. Ballantine & Sons..............	Newark, N. J.	1,322,346
Jacob Ruppert Brewery...........	New York, N. Y.	1,228,400

Source: A National Survey of the Brewing Industry, Research Company of America, 1941 edition.

The brewing industry has an elaborate distributing organization. Shortly after the relegalization of beer, 18,000 wholesalers and 260,000 retailers had entered the business, according to the reports of the Internal Revenue Bureau. Distributors as well as manufacturers had overestimated the anticipated demand. Competition forced numerous distributors to retire; about 11,000 wholesalers and 150,000 retailers remain.

Competition and Profits.—Profits in the brewing industry are exceedingly varied. The medium- and large-sized breweries, according to a sample based upon 25 to 30 companies, have earned an average of 12 to 18 per cent upon their invested capital since repeal. On the other hand, profits earned by the small breweries, with certain exceptions, have been very unsatisfactory. Profits in brewing apparently depend, more than anything else, upon the size of each brewery in relation to its market. For the industry as a whole there is a large amount of idle capacity but it is by no means equally distributed. Most of the idle capacity is found in the smaller establishments. A survey[1] of the brewing industry in 1939 revealed that breweries with an annual capacity of a million barrels or more operated at 80 per cent of capacity; those with a capacity of 500,000 to 1 million barrels operated at 71 per cent of capacity;

[1] Analysis of Brewing Industry, George S. May Business Foundation, Report No. 103, New York, 1940.

those in the 100,000- to 500,000-barrel class operated at 64 per cent of capacity; and breweries with less than 100,000 barrel capacity, which group constitutes over half of the breweries, operated at 50 per cent of capacity.   The entire industry operated at 58 per cent.   Too many enterprisers rushed in immediately after repeal, expecting that the industry would resume where it had left off 13 years earlier.   In fact, many were even more hopeful, basing their optimism upon a potentially larger market as a result of the increased size of the total population. However, a large part of the potential market, estimated at 30 million people, represented a generation that had attained beer-drinking age during prohibition, a time when there was little opportunity to acquire a taste for good beer.   Many of these people were, therefore, poor prospects for the brewing industry.   Whatever the reasons, the fact remains that total consumption after repeal did not attain the preprohibition level as Fig. 98 shows, and most of the burden of excess capacity has fallen upon the smaller brewers.

The brewing industry is peculiarly susceptible to overcapacity because of the seasonal nature of demand.   Beer is a hot weather drink, the consumption of which attains its peak in the summer months.   To supply the peak demand brewers must either provide extra space and storage tanks to hold the beer made in advance of the extra heavy withdrawals or else they must be equipped with adequate brewing capacity to meet the peak.   Most brewers have elected the latter alternative, which means they have seasonally idle productive capacity 7 to 8 months during the year.

Competition has been intensified by the aggressive merchandising of the leading companies, notably Anheuser-Busch, Schlitz, Pabst, and Ballantine.   Unlike most of their smaller competitors, these brewers have attained a national market.   This has been accomplished through national advertising of quality products that command premium prices. The point has been made that brewing is essentially a local industry; nevertheless, by spending large sums for advertising, the large brewers have built up a demand for their products at prices which yield returns far in excess of the added costs of distribution.   For example, it may cost the brewer 6 to 10 cents a barrel more to make a high quality beer, he may spend 85 cents to a dollar more in selling it but by charging an extra $3 per barrel for the product he turns a nice profit.   The growth of nationally advertised beer not only cuts down the market of the local breweries but it leaves them the less profitable part of their markets— the price-conscious end.

Improved transportation facilities likewise make for greater competition.   Local breweries face not only the competition of nationally advertised brands shipped by rail but also the products of competitors who ship by motor truck. Motor-truck delivery greatly enlarges the area of the market and, under pressure of excess capacity, breweries sometimes engage in dumping, *i.e.*, selling in distant markets at prices which cover out-of-pocket costs and some of the overhead.

A postrepeal development which has complicated the competitive situation is the change in relative proportions between sales of draught and packaged beer. Before prohibition, 75 per cent of the consumption was draught beer and 25 per cent bottled beer. After repeal, many companies made large initial investments in cooperage but draught sales declined and packaged beer sales increased; draught sales are now only 42 per cent of the total. Some of the breweries that properly anticipated larger sales of packaged beer erred nevertheless by overinvestments in bottling equipment, because one brewer introduced canned beer and others quickly followed.

Taxation.—One aspect of the brewing industry which is likely to affect its future more than anything else is taxation. At present there is a Federal excise tax on beer of $6 a barrel. State taxes average $1.25 a barrel. Furthermore, there are occupational taxes on brewers plus taxes on distributors, both wholesalers and retailers. Total taxes in some areas amount to as much as $9 a barrel, which represents about 50 per cent of the price paid by the consumer. With rising national defense costs it is almost certain that beer will be taxed more heavily in the future. It is almost equally certain that brewers will pass the tax on to the consumer in the form of higher prices. However, it is by no means certain that the consumers will bear a perpetually increasing tax load. Beer is not a necessity; it is a luxury, primarily the working man's luxury, and if the price goes too high, consumption may shift to soft drinks. While it is recognized that the consumption of beer is habit-forming, like the use of tobacco, it cannot be assumed that the demand is completely inelastic.

THE DISTILLING INDUSTRY

The distilling industry produces a large variety of highly alcoholic beverages, but whisky is the leading item. It accounts for 80 per cent of the total output. Other items are gin, rum, brandy, cordials, liqueurs, etc.

Raw Materials.—Raw materials for whisky depend upon the type of whisky being manufactured. A straight rye whisky, according to the Federal Alcohol Administration regulations, must be made from a mash consisting of at least 51 per cent rye. Usual proportions are 60 per cent rye, 20 per cent corn, and 20 per cent malt. A straight bourbon must have at least 51 per cent corn. The usual formula is two-thirds corn and one-third rye. Corn whisky is made chiefly from corn plus enough barley malt for conversion.

Process.—The manufacturing process is similar to the brewing process except for the semifinal operations—distilling and aging. The grains are ground into a meal. The meal is cooked to a mash. The liquid dripping out of the mash is fermented with yeast. The product of the fermenting vats, called beer, is piped through a continuous still where the "high wine" or raw whisky comes off the top in a steady colorless stream. The raw whiskey is then stored in white oak casks for aging. Aging requires from 2 to 4 years or more depending upon the quality of whisky desired.

Distilling, like brewing, yields valuable by-products, but more of them. The carbon dioxide bubbling out of the mash is converted into dry ice. The fusel oil recovered from the fermenting process is sold to solvent manufacturers to make lacquers. The spent mash is a rich cattle food.

Location.—The distilling industry is more highly localized than the brewing industry. Kentucky is the leading state. Illinois, Indiana, and Pennsylvania rank next in that order. The four states together produce 85 per cent of the total output. Water supply is an important factor influencing location, because distilling requires a large supply of cold limestone water. Tradition also plays an important role.

TABLE LXXXI.—COST ANALYSIS OF A QUART OF FOUR-YEAR-OLD BONDED WHISKEY

Production—labor, material and overhead	$0.10
Barrels, bottles, labels, and handling charges	0.14
Aging, including evaporation, interest, and insurance	0.13
Advertising, selling, and administrative expense	0.13
Federal excise tax	1.00
Distiller's income and excess profits tax	0.04
Distiller's profit	0.13
Distiller's selling price	$1.67
Freight to market	0.02
Wholesaler's margin (15 per cent) covering all expenses and profit	0.15
State tax (average)	0.25
Wholesaler's selling price	$2.09
Retailer's margin (40 per cent) covering all expenses and profit	0.84
Retail price	$2.93

Source: Adapted from Standard and Poor's Corp.

Cost Structure.—Manufacturing is the smallest cost in liquor production. It costs about 67 cents to manufacture a quart of properly aged whisky, but this is only about a fourth of the price the ultimate consumer pays for the product. After adding distribution costs, Federal and state excise taxes, the whisky will cost the consumer about $3 a quart. Only 23 cents of the consumer's dollar for whisky goes to the manufacturer; 35 cents goes for distribution costs, and the tax collectors take 42 cents. A more detailed breakdown of costs is shown in Table LXXXI.

Organization of the Industry.—Distilling is a larger-scale industry than brewing. The principal reason is that distilling has a much longer manufacturing cycle. A large amount of capital is tied up in process inventories because of the necessity for aging whiskey. This is reflected in the ratio of sales to inventories. The ratio in brewing averages 12 to 1, whereas the ratio is only 2 to 1 for distilleries.

The physical size of plants has increased considerably since the pre-prohibition period. The explanation lies in a change in merchandising policy. Formerly, distilleries sold most of their output, about 80 per cent, in bulk to rectifiers. Thus the distiller was relieved of the burden of carrying maturing stocks. Since repeal, bulk sales to rectifiers have averaged only 10 per cent. Distillers, particularly the larger ones, have chosen to strengthen their competitive position by marketing their own branded products instead of allowing rectifiers to put their own labels on the bottles. Many of the small distillers, however, sell both bulk and bottled goods through rectifiers.

Production of spirituous liquors is heavily concentrated among a few companies. Four companies control about 60 per cent of the total output. They are Schenley Distillers Corporation, Distillers Corporation-Seagrams, Ltd., Hiram Walker-Gooderham & Worts, and National Distillers Products Corporation. Each of these companies sells a variety of nationally advertised brands.

The spirituous liquor distributing system presents a highly complex pattern. Within a year after repeal 6,700 wholesalers and 207,000 retailers were struggling for the 45 million gal. trade. Sales volume has since doubled. About 1,000 wholesalers have dropped out but retailers now number a quarter of a million. In addition there are over 200 rectifiers, that is, houses that buy bulk whiskey, blend it, and distribute it.

Profits.—Since repeal, the distilleries, particularly the large companies, have made a good profit showing. The leading producers have averaged about 15 per cent on their investment. The most favorable factor for high initial earnings was the shortage of whisky. At the time of repeal there were only about 5 million gal. of properly aged whisky available. Some of this was blended with freshly made whisky and the rest was sold at fancy prices. The novelty of the regained freedom to consume liquor and consumer purchases for the purpose of laying in a stock also spelled profits during the early years of repeal. However, the inevitable reaction set in, as shown in Fig. 99; note the tendency of the earnings of the "big four" to converge at a lower level. Repeal was greeted with enthusiastic expansion. New plants were erected and

existing plants were enlarged.   Bankers approved capital flotations of
distillers' securities as prime investments.   Whisky production for the
first 6 months after repeal was 76 million gal.   Production for 1935
jumped to 185 million and for 1936 to 245 million gal.   As the mounting
stock in warehouses became more or less properly aged, prices began to
decline.   Since 1934, wholesale liquor prices have dropped 50 per cent.
Furthermore, as the novelty of consumption wore off, the public shifted
to lower priced liquor which yields smaller profits to distillers.   In
1940 the industry had 480 million gal. of maturing whisky in stock, and a
productive capacity of 435 million gal.   Since annual consumption is
about 100 million gal., further price declines and smaller profits seem
inevitable.

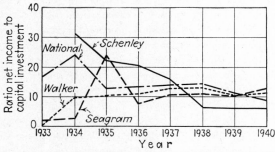

Fig. 99.—Ration of net income to capital investment of "big four" distilleries.   (*Standard
and Poor's Corporation.*)

Competition.—Thus far no definite competitive pattern has emerged.
Since repeal the industry has been in a state of flux.   It shows numerous
evidences of immaturity.

In the first place, it is offering the drinking public a bewildering array
of products.   The consumer may have his choice among whisky, rum,
gin, brandy, or other spirits.   If whisky is preferred, there is rye, Scotch,
bourbon, or corn.   There are "blends" and "straights."   Liquor may
be bought by the quart or the fifth.   There is further choice as to age.
Some is bottled in bond, *i.e.*, kept under government seal for 4 years.
Finally comes the battle of the brands.   Altogether the consumer is
offered 30,000 brands, 3,000 of which are marketed nationally.

Another evidence of immaturity is found in the price policy.   Prices
range from approximately 60 cents a pint to $4 a fifth.   There are no
sharply differentiated price lines, as we find for example in cigars or
clothing.   The same product may appear under various brand names
offered at different prices.   If a certain brand does not sell well, it may
be rebranded and repriced.   There is much overlapping of prices and
brands, resulting in what amounts to a company competing with itself.

The inefficient topheavy marketing system is another characteristic of immaturity. There are too many distributors and they must carry a large stock because of the great variety.

The distilling industry is highly speculative. It is strictly regulated, heavily taxed, and undermined by bootlegging. The Federal Alcohol Administration determines who may legally enter the business and in what capacity. It determines standards, approves labeling, controls unfair competition and unlawful practices. The industry lives in constant fear of statutory extinction. It is striving hard to attain respectability through discreet advertising. Taxes are the largest cost item in manufacturing. The Federal excise tax is $4 per gallon, and state taxes average about $1 a gallon. High taxes therefore make for high cost which serves either to discourage consumption or encourage bootlegging. Illicit liquor production is estimated to be 35 to 40 million gal. a year—equivalent to a third of the legal production.

Another ominous development is the trend toward state economy. Liquor sales are legal in all states except Kansas, Mississippi, and Oklahoma, and certain areas of other states by local option. However, some of the other states, endeavoring to foster local industry, exact discriminatory licenses, fees, or taxes for the privilege of selling within their borders liquor made in another state. This is in effect a state tariff. If this trend continues, distilling, like brewing, may become a local industry. As in the case of the brewing industry, the outlook for the liquor industry depends largely upon future tax policies.

CHAPTER XXXVI

THE TOBACCO MANUFACTURING INDUSTRY

The tobacco industry is peculiarly American. The tobacco plant, of which there are some 70 varieties, is indigenous to this hemisphere. Cured tobacco was an important colonial crop for export—as early as 1618 over 20,000 pounds were exported annually. Present annual production is about 1½ billion lb., of which about a third is exported. America ranks high in the per capita consumption of tobacco and the "blended cigarette" is of American origin. The machinery used in this industry was likewise developed in this country.

Several branches are to be distinguished in the general field of tobacco manufacturing—cigarettes, cigars, pipe tobacco, chewing tobacco, and snuff. Cigarettes account for 75 per cent of the total value of the output of the tobacco industry and the remainder is almost equally divided between cigars and all other forms of tobacco.

CIGARETTE MANUFACTURE

Historical Development.—The cigarette was invented in 1821 by an Egyptian. It came into general vogue in this country shortly after the Civil War, when returning Federal soldiers brought back this form of tobacco consumption from North Carolina. The first cigarettes were hand rolled, but machines appeared as early as 1880. By the end of the eighties, cigarette manufacture had become so standardized and mechanized that the leading manufacturers resorted to ruinous price competition. All this was changed by the consolidation, in 1890, of the five principal producers to form the American Tobacco Company which produced about 90 per cent of the cigarettes. The next significant developments occurred in the period 1912–1916, which marks the appearance of the blended cigarette and the dissolution of the American Tobacco trust.

By 1910 the American Tobacco Company had acquired monopolistic control of every branch of the tobacco industry except cigars, which were still handmade. In 1911 the Supreme Court ordered the dissolution of the company. The partition was effected by the formation of 14 separate companies providing for at least two companies in each of the fields where the trust formerly held a monopoly.

The blended cigarette had its origin in the shortage of imported tobaccos resulting from the Balkan and First World wars. Prior to that time, cigarettes were either the "Piedmont" type, made from domestic or Virginia tobacco or the "Murad" type made from so-called Turkish tobacco. By mixing the two kinds of tobaccos each of the cigarette companies emerging from the trust brought out a product which subsequently attained widespread popularity. Liggett and Myers introduced the Chesterfield in 1912; R. J. Reynolds brought out Camels in 1913; and in 1916 appeared Lucky Strikes, made by the American Tobacco Company. Each of the companies concentrated promotional efforts on its blended product instead of pushing a variety of lines as they had previously done.

These changes, coupled with the introduction of high-speed machinery and heavy advertising expenditures, led to a decrease in the number of

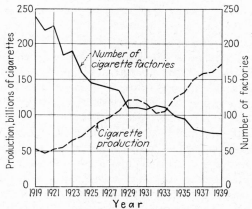

Fig. 100.—United States production of cigarettes and number of cigarette factories. (*Annual Reports of Bureau of Internal Revenue.*)

factories, an increase in the scale of enterprise, and a maintenance of a high rate of expansion in sales. Despite the phenomenal growth in production, shown in Fig. 100, the number of establishments decreased from 381 in 1914 to 34 in 1939.

Technology.—Since the modern cigarette is a blended product, its production calls for a variety of tobaccos. The average blend consists of 53 per cent flue-cured tobacco, 32 per cent Burley, 5 per cent Maryland, and 10 per cent Levantine tobaccos.

Flue-cured tobacco is grown in the Piedmont section of Virginia and North Carolina and in the coastal plain areas of the Carolinas, Georgia, and Florida. The term has its origin in the method of curing the leaves. The leaves are plucked from the stalk as they ripen and strung on sticks which are placed in a curing barn. A firebox is placed outside the barn and in it wood is burned. The smoke passes through an iron flue extending along the ground across the barn and back again. The proper temperature, determined by experience, is maintained for the curing period of 5 days. The leaves, after absorbing enough moisture to permit handling, are bundled and taken to an auction warehouse.

Burley tobacco, formerly used principally in the manufacture of chewing and pipe tobacco, is now an important cigarette tobacco. It is grown in Tennessee, Kentucky, and West Virginia. Burley tobacco is generally air-cured; the leaves are hung in barns for 6 to 8 weeks and exposed to controlled natural ventilation.

Flue-cured and Burley tobaccos, after purchase by tobacco companies at auction, are dried by heat, brought up to 10 to 12 per cent moisture, packed in hogsheads, and aged in warehouses for 2 to 3 years to develop the aroma. After aging, the moisture content is increased to about 20 to 25 per cent to facilitate the removal of stems. The moisture content is then reduced to 12 per cent before the cut tobacco goes to cigarette-making machines. Not much deviation from this optimum figure is permissible. One of the major advances in technology in recent years has been in the exactness of control of moisture content.

Maryland tobacco is used for its exceptional burning quality and Levantine tobacco is added to obtain the proper blend.

The raw materials of cigarette manufacture are leaf tobacco, a hygroscopic agent to enable a cigarette to retain its moisture (glycerine is the principal substance), a small amount of flavoring materials, and cigarette paper. The flavoring materials consist of sugar, honey, essential oils, spices, and various extracts, such as cocoa, chocolate, licorice, ginger, cinnamon, molasses, rum, brandy, maple syrup, oil of anise, juniper, and cloves. The paper is made of a good grade of cellulose derived from linen, hemp, or ramie, with enough filler to give opacity and control the rate of combustion. Prior to the Second World War, cigarette paper was imported from France. It is now being made from linseed-flax straw by a special paper mill recently set up in North Carolina with the aid of 2 million dollars of capital supplied by the large United States cigarette manufacturers.

The cigarette machine has been in a constant state of evolution until today it is capable of turning out 1,200 to 1,600 cigarettes per minute. Other operations are carried on largely by machinery. Only the handling and stemming of the leaf tobacco requires much hand labor. The result is that in the 1939 Census only 27,000 wage earners were employed to handle a volume of product representing 227 million dollars of value added.

Characteristics of Cigarette Manufacture.—Extreme mechanization, heavy inventories, extensive advertising, and heavy taxation characterize this branch of tobacco manufacturing.

The cigarette-making machines are completely automatic. The cigarettes are made, packed, sealed, stamped, and the revenue stamps cancelled in a series of continuous operations. So automatic is the process that labor is one of the smallest items in the cost structure. Wages represent only 2.5 per cent of the value of product, the smallest percentage of any of the major industries, as shown in Table IV, Chap. I.

No industry has so large a proportion of its assets tied up in inventories as the cigarette industry. Inventories account for two-thirds to three-fourths of the total assets. The reason is that the raw tobacco has to be aged for at least 18 months. The companies generally follow the policy of carrying a 2- to 4-year supply of tobacco. This enables a manufacturer to curtail raw material purchases in any one year if he regards prices as too high or if the quality is inferior.

Cigarette manufacturers spend enormous sums for advertising. Lorillard spent 15 million dollars in 1926 to launch Old Golds. In 1929 four companies spent 35 million dollars in advertising. When Camels introduced the Cellophane wrapper they expended 1 million dollars in 7 days. In order to reach the largest potential market the companies use all the principal media—newspapers, magazines, billboards, and radio. It is estimated that expenditures for advertising average between 40 and 50 cents per thousand cigarettes, or roughly 1 cent per pack of 20.

Cigarettes are one of the most heavily taxed commodities. For two decades the Federal tax has been $3 per thousand, which amounts to 6 cents per pack. Consequently the smoker who consumes a pack a day pays the Federal government about $25 a year. Federal taxes represent approximately two and a half times the value added by manufacture. The importance of this source of income to the Federal government is shown by the fact that cigarette manufacturers paid 504 million dollars in 1940, a sum which together with the 76 million dollars borne by other forms of tobacco, represented 10 per cent of the total Federal receipts from all sources.

The Principal Companies.—The major producers of cigarettes are the American Tobacco Company (Lucky Strike), Liggett and Myers (Chesterfield), and R. J. Reynolds (Camels). These three companies together produce two-thirds of the entire output. The relative importance of the leading producers is shown in Table LXXXII.

It is apparent that consumer preferences shift from year to year. Some of the shifts are explained by policies of individual companies. For instance, the strong relative position of the American Tobacco Company at the outset of the period, shown in Table LXXXII, is due in large part to the aggressive advertising campaign begun in 1926. The decline of Camels in 1932–1933 is attributed chiefly to the company's temporary suspension of newspaper advertising. The phenomenal growth of Philip Morris, which rapidly displaced Old Gold from fourth position in the cigarette industry, is the outstanding recent development. The early success of Philip Morris is largely attributed to the use of diethylene glycol instead of glycerine as a hygroscopic agent. The former is alleged to cause less throat irritation, and the company laid much stress upon this feature in its early advertising. Continued sales growth has been maintained by the company's policy of rigid price maintenance which has protected dealers' margins.

TABLE LXXXII.—ESTIMATED CONSUMPTION OF LEADING BRANDS OF CIGARETTES
(In billions)

Year	Luckies	Chester-fields	Camels	Philip Morris	Old Gold	10-cent brands	All others	Total
1930	42.6	25.0	38.0	....	8.0	....	6.0	119.6
1931	44.6	24.6	33.0	....	7.6	*	3.6	113.4
1932	37.0	21.0	24.6	*	5.7	12.0	3.3	103.6
1933	37.5	29.0	26.5	*	5.5	8.5	4.8	111.8
1934	33.5	33.5	32.0	2.8	5.0	13.0	5.8	125.6
1935	32.5	36.0	37.0	3.8	5.3	13.1	6.9	134.6
1936	37.0	38.0	43.0	5.0	6.8	16.0	7.4	153.2
1937	38.5	38.0	45.0	7.5	7.9	19.0	6.7	162.6
1938	38.3	37.4	41.0	9.2	6.3	24.0	7.5	163.7
1939	39.5	36.5	40.0	11.0	5.3	30.0	10.1	172.4
1940	42.0	36.5	42.5	12.5	*	21.8	24.7	180.0

* Included in "All others."
Source: Standard and Poor's Corporation, *Printers' Ink Monthly*, Feb., 1941, p. 5.

Competition.—This branch of the tobacco industry has been unusually profitable. From the dissolution of the trust to 1930 the "big three" earned consistently 10 per cent and over on their invested capital. With Philip Morris taking the place of Lorillard, the earning capacity of the leaders continued substantially unimpaired throughout the depressed years of the thirties as shown in Fig. 101. Even Lorillard, despite the fact that the cigarette branch of its business has been slipping, earned more than 5 per cent on its capital every year except one between 1912 and 1940.

The sustained earning power of the cigarette companies is rooted in the nature of the product. Smoking easily becomes habitual, which assures a steady demand. The First World War was the occasion for the first major spurt in cigarette consumption, because soldiers were freely supplied with this form of tobacco; in fact, it was not until that period that cigarette smoking acquired widespread social respectability. Persistent heavy advertising helped to spread the habit, and in the late twenties the potential market was vastly increased when cigarette companies ventured, first cautiously, then openly, the suggestion of cigarette smoking by women. This industry demonstrates better than any other the power of advertising to create a market and the necessity of advertising to maintain that market. The lavish appropriations for advertising, more than anything else, explains the tenfold increase in consumption within the short space of three decades. Furthermore, the individual companies have discovered through experience that their sales are highly dependent upon advertising. Whenever appropriations are curtailed it is reflected almost immediately in reduced sales. The demand for a specific brand rests upon the conviction of the superiority

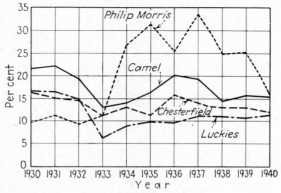

Fig. 101.—Earnings of the leading cigarette companies, (per cent earned on investment). (*Standard and Poor's Corporation.*)

of that brand. This depends not only upon quality but also upon what the advertisers can make the consumers believe.

Competition between the leading companies is based upon brand promotion rather than upon price appeal. This is plainly revealed by the contrast between their advertising policies and their price policies. Despite the heavy advertising, the industry is notably free from price wars. Almost invariably a change in the wholesale price by one of the leaders is quickly followed by the others. Each of the producers has too large a stake in the market to ignore the prices of his competitors and each one realizes that any price policy he can afford to put in effect can be matched by his competitors who are of substantially equal size. Unable to exercise power over one another they follow a uniform price policy and thereby exercise power with one another and all reap the benefits of cultivating a market which is characterized by a comparatively inelastic demand.

Although the demand for cigarettes is generally conceded to be inelastic, the market is not entirely insensitive to price changes. This is demonstrated by the advent of the 10-cent cigarette during the early

thirties.   In the middle of 1931 when leaf tobacco prices were declining
and consumer purchasing power was falling by reason of the widening
business depression, the "big three" cigarette companies raised the
wholesale price of cigarettes from $6.40 to $6.85 a thousand.   The error
of this pricing policy was subsequently appreciated because it opened
the way for the 10-cent package of cigarettes.   In 1932 the 10-cent
brands seized almost 25 per cent of the total business.   Rising tobacco
costs and higher taxes have reduced the margin of profit of these brands,
but they cannot be dismissed as a negligible factor; they continue to
hold about 12 per cent of the market.

Buying and Inventory Policies.—The relations between the 1,602,000
tobacco growers and the cigarette manufacturers are not entirely satisfactory.   Since most of the annual crop domestically consumed is bought
by a handful of companies at prices which yield very meager returns
to the thousands of growers, the farmers naturally feel that the big
companies conspire to keep prices down.   To support their contention
the farmers point to the huge profits made by the manufacturers.   In
1932, for example, the total value of the farm crop was less than the
combined net profits of the 10 leading cigarette manufacturers.

Dissatisfaction on the part of the growers arises largely from the
chaotic system of marketing leaf tobacco.   Most tobacco is sold through
the auction warehouse system.   The farmers sort their tobacco and take
it to a warehouse, where the tobacco is weighed and arranged according to
quality in rows on the warehouse floor.   When the sale starts the
auctioneer proceeds from one basket to another selling to the highest
bidder until the floor is cleared.   The buyers are the manufacturers or
their representatives, exporters, dealers, and speculators.   Sales are
made very rapidly—as many as 360 per hour.   This is disadvantageous
to the farmer because, it is alleged, buyers have to make a hasty appraisal
and to protect themselves they offer less than the tobacco should bring.
The farmer may reject the bid and move his tobacco to another row or to
another warehouse for resale, but he may fare no better and perhaps
worse.   Since tobacco is difficult to grade, each buyer has his own grading
system.   Consequently farmers complain that the same quality tobacco
often brings two different prices in the same auction.   Another unsatisfactory feature is the short marketing period in each tobacco-growing
area.   Starting in the deep South, a small group of expert buyers take
what they want in each local auction and move on northward.   Therefore, if the farmer does not offer his tobacco before the large buyers have
withdrawn their support, he must take what he can get later or incur the
risk and expense of sending his crop to a distant market.

Although the Federal Trade Commission has found no evidence of
collusion among buyers for the purpose of depressing prices, the tobacco-

marketing system has many earmarks of a buyer's market.   Sellers are numerous, small, and impecunious; buyers are few, large, and financially strong.   The market is often glutted because tobacco is an ideal tenant farmer crop—it requires little capital but much labor to raise.   The farmers are ever in urgent need of whatever cash their crop will bring, whereas the manufacturers are seldom in urgent need of tobacco because they have huge stocks in their warehouses to fall back on.

PLATE 71.—Cutting the binder.   (*Courtesy of International Cigar Machinery Company.*)

The "big three" cigarette companies, together with several of the smaller companies, were indicted in 1941 by the Federal Court of the Eastern District of Kentucky for violating the Sherman Antitrust Act. The Department of Justice alleged that the tobacco growers were at the mercy of the manufacturers as a result of their policies of fixing dates and places of auctions, using secret buying grades, avoiding competition by not bidding against each other, and bidding by a method which the farmers cannot understand.   The government also contended that, through control of auctions, the "big three" raised the price of 10-cent tobacco grades and equalized to themselves the average cost of tobacco by simultaneously beating down the prices of top grades of tobacco. It was also alleged that the "big three" almost succeeded in driving the 10-cent brands off the market in 1933 by vigorous concerted price cuts, liberal use of free goods, and prolonged credit terms.   However, the

PLATE 72.—Cigar forming machine and inspection. (*Courtesy of International Cigar Machinery Company.*)

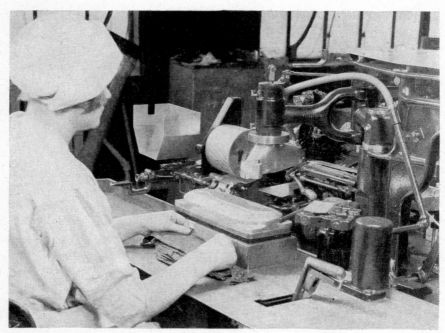

PLATE 73.—Cutting the wrapper. (*Courtesy of International Cigar Machinery Company.*)

case turned largely upon the alleged conspiracy to fix prices of cigarettes at wholesale and retail. According to the testimony offered, any change in the wholesale price made by any one of the "big three" was immediately duplicated by the others. Late in 1941, the court rendered a decision that the companies were guilty of monopolistic practices.[1]

Future Market.—There is a difference of opinion as to the future trend of cigarette consumption. Cigarettes have a number of advantages over other types of consumer goods. Customers are habitual users, renewing their purchase several times a week. The unit of purchase is small—10 to 20 cents. The product is available everywhere; it is estimated that there are 600,000 retail outlets. The future market is not dependent upon population growth. There are still 100 million lb. of chewing tobacco consumed and almost 200 million lb. of smoking tobacco. Furthermore, only a relatively small proportion of women in the country smoke. On the other hand, one student of the industry points out that there is some evidence of a decline in the consumption of cigarettes by women. If women have entered the market for reasons of fashion, they may depart as quickly as they have come in.

CIGAR MANUFACTURE

Cigar manufacture differs from cigarette manufacture at many points. The individual item of consumption is much more expensive; the industry is much older; the market in recent decades has been contracting rather than expanding, the number of companies and factories is much greater.

The Product and Its Manufacture.—Every cigar consists of a filler, a binder, and a wrapper, and a definite type of tobacco has been developed to make each part. The inner part or the filler gives the cigar its principal characteristics. The binder or inner cover holds the filler in shape, giving the cigar style and appearance. The wrapper gives external appearance, such as color and mellowness.

The finest grades of filler are imported from Cuba and Puerto Rico. Pennsylvania is the leading state in the production of domestic filler, with Lancaster and York counties producing all of the state's output. Wisconsin is preeminent in the production of tobacco suitable for cigar binders. Domestic wrapper tobacco is grown in the Connecticut Valley. Imported wrappers come principally from Sumatra, Java, and Cuba.

Cigar manufacturing began in this country at the end of the eighteenth century as a home industry employing hand labor exclusively. It remained an industry of hand labor to almost the end of the First World War. This was not because there were no early efforts to introduce machine processes.

[1] *Time*, Dec. 22, 1941, p. 74.

The American Tobacco Company sought as vigorously as in other branches to dominate the field.   As early as 1898 it gave an assignment to its engineers to devise a cigar-making machine and ultimately expended 7 million dollars over a 20-year period on the problem.   Its early failures to produce a successful machine probably account for the failure of the trust to gain in cigar manufacture the same dominance that it early achieved in cigarettes.

Like most complicated mechanisms, the cigar-making machine is one of gradual development, adaptation, and coordination of separately devised machines.   The machinery-making subsidiary of the American Tobacco Company tested its so-called complete cigar machine in 1915 and by 1919 had so perfected it that installation on an extensive scale began.   By 1922 large cigar manufacturers were installing machines. In 1930, half of the total cigar output was machine-made and it is estimated that these now constitute well over 90 per cent of all cigars. Not only are cigars themselves being made by machines, but tobacco stripping and filling, stem crushing, foiling, banding, boxing, and other operations are mechanically performed.

Scale of Operation.—In 1921, there were 15,000 cigar factories ranging in size from small shops producing annually less than 500,000 cigars each to large factories that produced annually in excess of 40 million cigars each.   The latter class produced about half of the industry's total output.   The mechanization of cigar making had a pronounced effect upon scale of operation.   By 1939, there were only 4,000 cigar manufacturers, and 32 of these were of the large class, producing over 40 million cigars each and accounting for two-thirds of the total industry output.

Along with the growth in mechanization, and largely in consequence of it, came the popularity of the 5-cent cigar.   Between 1926 and 1939, the production of 5-cent cigars rose from 45 to 92 per cent of the total of large cigars.   (See Fig. 102.)   Cigars retailing at 5 cents or less are the only ones that have grown in both relative and absolute amount. Only the 5-cent cigar has been able to hold its own against the fast-growing popularity of the cigarette, and this is largely because mechanization has reduced costs of production to a point where manufacturers can produce the 5-cent cigar at a profit.   Cigar-making machines are so intricate and expensive that only the larger companies can afford to install them, but the machine produces in one hour 50 per cent more cigars than a hand worker can produce in one day.   Taking into consideration the fact that a machine requires four operators, the productivity per worker has been increased about 267 per cent as a result of mechanization.   So great is the differential in cost between machine and handmade cigars that the former have practically driven handmade cigars out of the market except for the higher priced cigars.

Merchandising methods have also undergone a marked change as a result of the larger scale mechanized operation. Formerly, the cigar manufacturers, like the cigarette manu acturers, produced a great variety of branded products. More recently the progressive companies have reduced the number of brands and have concentrated their sales and advertising efforts upon one or a few leading brands, particularly the 5-cent brands. Bayuk Cigars, Inc., in 1933 reduced the price of its "Philly" from 10 to 5 cents, thereby increasing sales fifteen-fold. This company also manufactures other brands, but most of its sales promotion is lavished on the "Philly." For similar reasons the General Cigar Company is best known for its "White Owl," although the company

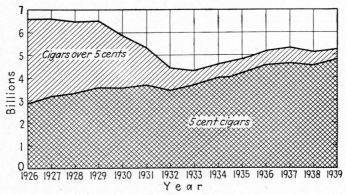

FIG. 102.—Cigar production, 1926–1939. (*Annual Reports, Bureau of Internal Revenue.*)

also makes the "Robert Burns," "Van Dyke," and other well-known brands.

Principal Producers.—General Cigar Company and Bayuk are the leading producers. Each company turns out about 12 per cent of the total output. Their leadership is to be explained chiefly by the popularity of their well-advertised 5-cent brands. Among the outstanding producers in the medium-priced field are the Consolidated Cigar Corporation, known for its "Dutch Masters," and "El Producto," and the Congress Cigar Company. By aggressive advertising tactics, the American Tobacco Company, through one of its subsidiaries, tried to revive one of its popular brands, "Cremo," but sales slumped after advertising support was withdrawn.

Although concentration of production among the leading companies is not so great in the cigar industry as in the cigarette industry, the large companies have a distinct advantage over the small producers. One of the most important qualities affecting the marketability of a cigar is its freshness. Therefore, the faster the cigars get into the hands of consumers the more satisfactory will be the smoke. This redounds to the advantage of the large producers because their well-advertised brands move into consumption more rapidly than the products of the smaller producers.

Manufacturer-grower Relations.—A survey of the important aspects of tobacco manufacturing would be incomplete without some consideration of the relations between the tobacco manufacturers and the growers. These relations, from the farmer's point of view, have been generally unsatisfactory over the years. This is to be accounted for by the following aspects of the situation: the strong position of the manufacturers with respect to both inventories and capital, the lack of serious competition among buyers, the inability of the farmers to withhold tobacco from sale, and the lack of specific tobacco grades which has handicapped the grower in selling his product.

In recent years, governments, Federal and local, have thrown the weight of their influence on the side of the farmers. The result has been the organization of a tobacco-grading service, the rise of cooperative marketing, financial assistance under the Federal Farm Loan Act, the Agricultural Adjustment Act, and more recently, since the AAA has been declared unconstitutional, under the soil conservation policy. The indications seem clear that, in the long run, tobacco manufacturers will not enjoy a buyer's market to the extent they have in the past.

The Future.—The future of the cigar industry is not very promising. The industry appears to have reached its peak in 1920. In fact, its rate of growth between 1899 and 1937 was exactly zero. This stands in marked contrast to the cigarette industry which during the same period grew 4,200 per cent. The shift in demand from cigars to cigarettes will doubtless intensify the competition for the gradually shrinking market. It is not to be inferred that cigar manufacturing is a dying industry, but it is one that has apparently attained maturity.

PART IX
THE CHANGING PATTERN OF AMERICAN INDUSTRY
*

CHAPTER XXXVII

THE CHANGING PATTERN OF HISTORICAL DEVELOPMENT

In the first chapter it was pointed out that manufacturing employs more people and contributes a larger share to our national income than any other branch of economic activity. The analyses of the individual industries have presented the place and importance of each industry. In the present chapter, we shall sketch the development of all manufacturing activity, indicating how it came to occupy so prominent a place in our national economy.

For simplicity of presentation, the long span of American industrial history has been divided into separate periods. They are as follows:

1. Colonial period—to 1783.
2. Period of uncertainty—1783–1823.
3. Period of the American industrial revolution—1823–1860.
4. The emergence of big business—1860–1914.
5. The modern period—1914–1941.

So complex is the field of manufacturing and so closely is it interrelated with agriculture, mining, finance, transportation, and marketing that almost any division into periods or eras must necessarily be arbitrary.

THE COLONIAL PERIOD—TO 1783

During the colonial period, there was a notable scarcity of manufacturing. The colonial economy was built upon agriculture and the extractive industries because these industries supplied the most pressing needs—food, clothing, and shelter. The principal extractive industries were lumbering and fishing.

The reasons for the scarcity of manufacturing were the abundance of land, the scarcity of labor and capital, and the attitude of England, the mother country. Land was plentiful and, therefore, cheap. Labor was scarce and high-priced because most colonists preferred to clear a plot of land and engage in independent farming rather than to work for wages. Manufacturing requires capital, which was as scarce as labor. Furthermore, there were few available markets because of the poor transporta-

507

tion facilities.   In addition to these natural hindrances to manufacturing, England erected some legal barriers.   Operating under the mercantile system, England regarded her colonies as her exclusive markets and as sources of cheap raw materials for her industries.   For example, the Molasses Act of 1733 placed a prohibitive duty on the importation of molasses from the French West Indies.   The colonial rum manufacturers had been getting molasses more cheaply from that source than they could obtain it from the British possessions.   Despite all handicaps, some manufacturing developed during this early period of our history.

Origin and Nature of Colonial Manufactures.—The earliest form of manufacturing was domestic production.   Virtually every household or plantation was a self-contained economic unit.   Wool and linen yarn was spun and woven into cloth for home consumption.   The farmer did his own slaughtering and curing of meat for home use.   Tallow, lard, soap, candles, and leather were by-products of this domestic industry.

There was also some handicraft manufacturing which required more tools and greater skill.   Typical handicraftsmen of the period were the weavers, cobblers, sadlers, and ropemakers.   The shop was frequently the artisan's home and customers often supplied the raw materials.

In addition to domestic and handicraft manufacturing, there were some mill and furnace industries.   Machinery was required for fulling cloth, grinding grain, sawing lumber, felting paper, and forging iron. Some of these establishments were quite large for their time.   For example, the Hasenclever iron works, built in New Jersey before the Revolution, was said to represent a $250,000 investment.   With the passage of time, capital for colonial manufactures was accumulated from a flourishing export trade.   Tobacco, wheat, lumber, and other raw materials were exported to the West Indies and European markets.   The ships to carry the trade were built here, and frequently the ships, together with their cargoes, were sold abroad.   It is estimated that just before the Revolution a third of Britain's sea-borne trade was carried in colonial-built vessels.   As a result of the large colonial foreign trade, shipbuilding was one of the earliest and largest manufacturing industries.

The Revolutionary war had a mixed effect upon colonial manufacturing.   At the outbreak of the war, there were enough iron furnaces and forges to supply military and civilian needs, but some closed down for lack of labor and others discontinued operation because their Loyalist owners fled to England.   Although firearms factories and powder mills were multiplied to supply Washington's army, our producing capacity was inadequate.   Aid sought from France was freely granted because of her traditional rivalry with Great Britain.   The war cut off imports of English woolens, but American patriots gladly put up with the inconvenience of using domestic fabrics.

THE PERIOD OF UNCERTAINTY—1783–1823

From the close of the Revolutionary war to 1823, American manufacturing went through a period of alternating good and bad times. The immediate aftermath of the war was unfavorable. British manufacturers dumped goods on the American market at prices which domestic producers could not meet. American manufacturing methods had undergone very little change, whereas British manufacturing had just gone through a period of revolutionary changes in technology from which the manufacturers emerged with greatly reduced costs. American manufacturers had to contend with higher labor costs, and capital could be put to better use in the rapidly expanding merchant marine.

During this period, economic conditions favored the development of agriculture and trade more than growth of manufacturing. The invention of the cotton gin by Eli Whitney in 1793 gave to the Southern agricultural economy of indigo, rice, and tobacco a new crop which ultimately became its principal source of revenue. The cotton gin increased the daily productivity of separating the fiber from the seed from 1 to 50 lb. per worker. Between 1790 and 1810, cotton production rose from 1 million to 85 million lb. By the end of this period, cotton challenged breadstuffs and tobacco as the chief export. However, shipping rather than exporting was the major industrial activity, primarily because the Napoleonic wars sent ocean freight rates skyward, making shipping an exceedingly profitable business.

American manufacturing was affected indirectly by the European wars of the early nineteenth century because of the immediate effect of these wars on our trade and shipping. Through the issues of decrees and counter-decrees, England and France tried to starve each other into submission. Curiously, these attempted blockades of European and English ports did not discourage American shipping despite the seizure of over 900 ships that ran the blockade. The Embargo Act of 1807, forbidding any vessel to sail from an American to a foreign port, and the Nonintercourse Act of 1809, prohibiting all trade with France and England, caused a sharp decline in our shipping and export trade which, as will be seen later, was never fully recovered. However, the self-imposed isolation from world commerce had the inevitable effect of stimulating American manufacturing. Since imports of British manufactures and foreign markets for our raw materials were cut off, domestic raw materials were processed by American manufacturers for the home market. Furthermore, this diverted the flow of capital and labor from shipping and trading to manufacturing.

The War of 1812 provided only a temporary stimulus to manufacturing. Existing enterprises were expanded and new ones were set up to meet the demand for war materials.   However, the expansion came to an abrupt halt because of the short duration of the war, whereupon manufacturers were confronted with numerous problems of readjustment. Among these was the postwar dumping of British goods upon our markets at prices that were ruinous to American manufacturers.

Toward the close of this period of uncertainty, manufacturing received another setback which grew out of the declining prices of farm crops.   European demand for our agricultural surpluses did not revive as expected.   In 1819, our currency inflation was checked and the ensuing financial crisis had an adverse effect upon our manufacturing industries. This period ended without any permanent gains for manufacturing.   The volume of manufacturing had, of course, grown somewhat, but its basic character had not changed very much from that prevailing at the close of the colonial period.

AMERICAN INDUSTRIAL REVOLUTION—1823–1860

The period from 1823 to the Civil War is characterized by important changes in technology in almost every manufacturing industry.   To a very large extent the technical innovations were not of American origin but were transplanted from England, where the industrial revolution had already been under way.   As pointed out in Chap. XXI, English industry was already on a factory basis by 1825 as a result of the epoch-making inventions in textiles.   In the United States this transition was yet to be made.   It was delayed here because conditions down to the close of the War of 1812, as we have observed, favored a commercial rather than an industrial economy.   Indeed, upon the close of the War of 1812, American industrial interests eagerly awaited a revival of trade and shipping.   These expectations were doomed to disappointment. Other nations had preempted a sizable proportion of our carrying trade and, although American ships and American seamen had no peers, competition was keen.   No longer did foreign commerce alone shape our destiny.   The accumulation of capital, not absorbed in trade and shipping, supplied the resources for our first large manufacturing enterprises.

The Mechanization of Industry.—The American industrial revolution followed the same basic pattern as the English industrial revolution. Here, as abroad, the spinning and weaving of cotton were the earliest processes to undergo extensive mechanization.   Although England attempted to prevent the exportation of machinery, she could not prevent the migration of ideas.   As early as 1790, Samuel Slater erected in Pawtucket, R. I., a cotton mill equipped with Arkwright machinery.

Although English machines for spinning and weaving were reproduced here, there was no dearth of Yankee ingenuity.   In 1828, Charles Danforth invented a device by which the bobbin instead of the spindle rotated. This permitted a speed of 8,000 revolutions per minute in contrast with 4,000 revolutions of the Arkwright spindles. That same year, John Thorp of Providence patented the ring traveler which increased the speed to 12,000 revolutions per minute, and finer yarn was produced. In weaving cloth, Americans displayed a similar propensity for improving upon the ideas and machines imported from England. Before 1824, power weaving had been confined to plain fabrics, but in that year a New England manufacturer perfected a loom for weaving twills, checks, and other pattern fabrics. Extensive improvements were also made in American looms for weaving wool and silk fabrics. The revolutionary character of the new technique is shown by the fact that between 1816 and 1860 the labor cost of making cotton sheeting declined from 18 to 2 cents a yard.

The introduction of machinery requiring mechanical power was an important element in the rise of the factory system. Until about 1830, water power was used almost exclusively because of the abundance of natural falls on New England rivers. The invention of the high-pressure steam engine by Oliver Evans and improvements in steam economy by George Corliss, another American inventor, hastened the shift to steam power during the last decade of this period.

Though the factory system had its origin in the cotton textiles, technological changes were not confined to this industry alone. Factory-made clothing first appeared about 1825, but production was small before 1846 when the sewing machine was invented. Shortly thereafter, the sewing machine was adapted to shoe manufacturing. Other outstanding inventions of the period were the vacuum pan for sugar refining, the vulcanization of rubber, the hot blast for smelting iron, low-cost steel, the slide rest attachment for engine lathes, and numerous improvements on both wood- and metal-working machinery.

A factor which contributed to the acceleration of technical improvements was the reorganization of the patent system. Prior to 1836, patents were issued freely to any inventor without careful examination into the merits of the proffered invention. This resulted in excessive litigation and very little protection to the patent holder. These evils were largely abolished by a revision of the patent system providing, among other things, for the predetermination of the validity of an invention before the grant.

Development of Internal Transportation.—Another important development which aided the growth of manufacturing during this period was the opening of larger markets afforded by improved means of transportation. The cheapness of water transportation focused attention upon canals. The Erie canal, connecting Lake Erie with the Hudson River, completed in 1825, was the first large venture of this character. The anthracite tidewater canals offered low-cost transportation for lumber, grain, and coal to the Philadelphia and Baltimore markets.

During the decade of the thirties, canal building was superseded by a new form of transportation—the steam railroad. Construction of the first railroad began in 1828, and by 1860 over 30,000 miles had been built. This rapid development of railroad transportation aided manufacturing in two ways—it created an immediate demand for construction materials to build the roads and it opened up wider markets for the products of manufacturing industries.

Labor.—The relative scarcity of labor in America, in contrast with abundant labor in Europe, resulted in higher wages which readily attracted immigrants. The potato famine in Ireland, which later spread to the Rhine valley, sent large numbers of Irish and German immigrants to this country. These immigrants were welcomed by manufacturers who were eager for lower cost labor.

Tariff.—The growing importance of manufacturing was also reflected in the changed attitude toward the tariff. Although the first Congress passed a tariff law, the primary purpose of the tariff was to obtain revenue. The fiscal needs of the government continued to shape tariff policies until after the second war with England. Thereafter, the tariff for revenue only began to give way to protective tariffs, and the pressure for tariff protection increased with our growing industrialization. However, there was no unanimity of agreement on this question. The South, predominantly agricultural, vigorously opposed the protectionist sentiment of the Northern manufacturing interests. In fact, the conflict of the interests of the Southern agricultural economy and the Northern industrial economy was an important and, in the opinion of some students, the primary cause of the Civil War.

THE EMERGENCE OF BIG BUSINESS—1860–1914

The Civil War marked a definite turning point in the history of American manufacturing. The industrial revolution which preceded the conflict set the stage for a tremendous industrial expansion. The expansion of the market which followed provided the necessary complementary stimulus. Furthermore, the victory of the North over the South assured the dominance of the industrial over the agricultural interests. During this period, manufacturing lost all vestiges of its colonial characteristics and assumed the characteristics of modern production. New sources of raw materials were discovered, new supplies of cheap labor were tapped, and new markets were opened up. Technology changed from a hand basis to a machine basis, and steam power displaced water power. The form of business organization changed from the single enterprise or the partnership to the corporation and later the trust and the holding company. Aided by none too ethical business practices, monopoly or near monopoly developed in many industries. Such, in general, are the major developments of this period. Let us now turn our attention to the factors that brought them about.

The Attainment of a National Market.—A fundamental cause of the rapid growth in manufacturing after 1865 was the expansion of the market. The discovery of gold in California in 1848 initiated the westward movement of the population, but migration did not assume large proportions prior to the Civil War. After the war, westward migration took on renewed vigor because the settlement of the West was actively fostered by the Federal government. By the Homestead Act of 1862 any citizen who was the head of a family could obtain 160 acres of land for the nominal fee of $10, provided he occupied the land.

The opening of the West was greatly accelerated by the development of a nation-wide system of railroad transportation. The huge expansion in railroad construction came in the decades of the 1870's and the 1880's. From the end of the Civil War to 1873, railroad mileage doubled. Between 1878 and 1893, railroad mileage doubled again, increasing from about 80,000 to 160,000 miles. The promoters were assisted by very generous land grants from the government, and capital was easily obtained through the public offering of securities. Great technical improvements had been made in railway transportation in contrast with the prewar railroads. Steel rails replaced iron rails as a result of the introduction of a low-cost steel, as pointed out in Chap. III. The improved rails accommodated heavier coal-burning locomotives and larger cars. Standard gage tracks were adopted by all roads in 1886, which enabled rolling stock to move freely from one line to another. This period also witnessed the introduction of the sleeping car, the refrigerator car, air brakes, and the completion (in 1869) of the first transcontinental line.

The railroad system was a vast improvement over the inland waterways because most of the rivers run a generally north-to-south course. Railroads offered faster transportation, and they connected the populous East with the land-locked stores of natural wealth in the West. The rich stores of timber, grain, and minerals of the West were afforded better access to the Eastern markets. Iron ore shipments from the Superior district, which began and ended the journey by rail, increased from 1 million tons annually in 1880 to 9 million tons by 1890. Petroleum from western Pennsylvania, copper from Michigan, Montana, and the southwestern mining states, timber from Wisconsin and Michigan, and agricultural products from the Great Plains supplied a swelling volume of railroad traffic.

Technical Changes.—Although the preceding period witnessed the important changes in technology, it was during the second half of the nineteenth century that these new technologies came to fruition. Commercial production of Bessemer steel began in 1867, and by 1880, production passed 1 million tons. Open-hearth production lagged behind for a time, but when its superiority began to be appreciated it surpassed Bessemer steel production.

Machine tools were greatly improved and many new types were developed during this period. Probably the most oustanding improvement was Frederick W. Taylor's high-speed tool steel for cutting metal. Machine tools of heavier construction and greater automaticity appeared in almost endless succession. Standardization and the principle of interchangeability were adopted wherever volume of demand for the products justified the added cost of highly specialized machine tools.

The invention of the internal combustion engine by Seldon gave rise to the automobile industry, which, however, attained its greatest development after the First World War.

In the textile industries, the most revolutionary changes in technology had already taken place. However, some noteworthy progress was made during the period under consideration. Cotton spinning machinery was perfected so as to run at higher speeds. The most important development came in weaving. The Draper-Northrup loom, appearing in 1895, increased the number of looms a weaver could attend from 8 to 24 because of their greater automaticity. The outstanding invention in wool manufacturing was the mechanical comb for separating the tops from the noils which ushered in the worsted industry. Rayon, the first successful man-made fiber, appeared on the market near the close of this period.

In practically every major industry there occurred significant technological changes. The cement industry developed the rotary kiln and adopted a standard specification for its product. The Owens automatic bottle blowing machine reduced the cost of making milk bottles from 75 cents to 10 cents a gross.[1] In the leather industry, mineral tanning was introduced; in the shoe industry, the quality of the product was greatly improved by the invention of the Goodyear-welt process. Numerous technological changes likewise occurred in the food industries. The invention of the refrigerator car transformed meatpacking from a local to a large-scale, centralized industry. Flour millers adopted the European roller system of gradual reduction which improved the quality of flour and opened up new areas of wheat production. Canned goods appeared in ever greater variety and quantity as a result of new sealing devices and pressure cookers.

---

[1] CLARK, VICTOR S., "History of Manufactures in the United States," Vol. III, p. 259, McGraw-Hill Book Company, Inc., New York, 1929.

The Labor Supply.—The unparalleled rapidity of expansion of manufacturing which characterized this period was largely the result of a similarly unparalleled increase in the total population. During the nineteenth century when the world population increased from 600 to 1,600 millions, the population of the United States rose from 5 to 75 millions—a fifteen-fold increase. The phenomenal growth in population constituted an ever-increasing demand for the products of industry and, equally important, an ever-expanding supply of man power to operate industry. A large part of the labor required was supplied by the swelling volume of European immigration. Except for laws restricting orientals, practically no legal restrictions were placed on immigration until 1924. During the century preceding the outbreak of the First World War, approximately 33 million immigrants were admitted, and fully 75 per cent of these entered during the period between the Civil War and the First World War. Manufacturing interests welcomed this influx of cheap labor, and, on the whole, the immigrants enjoyed a higher standard of living here than in their mother countries. After 1890, there was a marked shift in the source of immigrants: fewer of English and German origin and progressively more from southern and eastern Europe.

Protective Tariffs.—In addition to the natural economic forces that favored the growth of manufacturing during this period, there was the benefit of protective tariffs. Although some protectionist sentiment had appeared earlier, the quest for revenue, as previously mentioned, had been the dominant motive behind most of our tariff legislation down to the end of the Civil War. Thereafter, fiscal needs definitely gave way to protection. Except for minor reductions, there was an almost uninterrupted upward trend in tariff rates throughout this entire period. In several instances, when Congress definitely set out to reduce tariffs, the final bills contained more increases than reductions. For example, the Act of 1883 was supposed to revise rates downward, but the duties on cotton, wool, and steel were actually increased. Protected by the progressively higher tariff walls, American industries encountered almost no competition from abroad. The McKinley Act of 1890 gave protection ranging from 50 to 100 per cent. The tariff was especially beneficial to our industries with high labor costs such as cotton, silk, and the clay working industries. It is doubtful whether silk and pottery manufacturing could have been established without tariff protection. The Underwood Tariff of 1913 was the first act since 1860 that provided substantial reductions. Unquestionably the growth of American industry from the Civil War to the First World War was in no small measure due to the generous protection afforded by the tariff.

The Rise of Big Business.—One of the outstanding characteristics of this period was the development of gigantic business enterprises. First through processes of normal growth, and later by means of mergers and consolidations, there emerged such companies as the American Sugar Refining, United Shoe Machinery, American Woolen, Standard Oil, and American Tobacco. In most instances, these companies attained practical control in their respective industries.

The growth of large business combinations was greatly facilitated by changes in the form of business organization. At the outset of this period, the corporate form of organization was little used except in textile manufacturing. However, the widening markets and the greater use of machine processes called for more capital than the individual enterpriser could raise. The corporation supplied the necessary funds to enlarge the scale of operation, and manufacturers were quick to shift to this form of organization. Adoption of the corporate form was accelerated by competition among the states in offering simplified legal procedure for incorporation. Following the leadership of New Jersey, other states eagerly shaped their corporation laws to suit the wishes of promoters.

During the decade of the eighties, another form of organization, the trust, came into popularity. The trust was a device whereby a number of naturally competing corporations could be administered as one company, thus eliminating competition. By exchanging trust certificates for sufficient stock certificates to secure a controlling interest in several companies, the trustees could administer all the concerns in the plan as one company. The Standard Oil Trust, which obtained a complete monopoly of the oil industry, was one of the first and most effective of the trusts.

The growth of big business was not arrested by the passage, in 1890, of the Sherman Antitrust Act which outlawed combinations and conspiracies in restraint of trade. During the nineties there appeared a new form of organization—the holding company—which is a corporation created to control other corporations through the simple expedient of owning a major part of their voting stock. Utilizing this form of organization, a rising wave of consolidation began just before the turn of the century. After the panic of 1893 had run its course, prosperity returned and the hope of monopoly gains revived. Abundant funds for investment had accumulated before the expiration of the century, and promoters took the opportunity to inflate their consolidations with large amounts of watered stock. The consolidation movement attained its climax with the creation of the United States Steel Corporation which was the first billion-dollar corporation.

In addition to the improved business conditions and the quest for monopoly gains, there were other reasons for the rising trend in consolidations. The movement received the aid and support of the bankers who saw in it fertile sources of underwriting profits. Most of the new companies formed were of such huge size that banker assistance was required to float and distribute the securities. Another factor was the desire on the part of some of the captains of industry to retire from active business—notably Rockefeller and Carnegie. Since there were few, if any, individuals with sufficient wealth to buy their business empires, the only way to retire was to offer their businesses for public subscription.

In several industries, the concentration of control grew to such an extent that virtually complete monopoly resulted. This growth of power aroused widespread public resentment which found its most vigorous expression in Theodore Roosevelt's "trust busting" threats. However, it was during the administration of Taft that the first really effective enforcement of the Sherman Antitrust Act was carried out in manufacturing industries, resulting in the dissolution of the American Tobacco and Standard Oil trusts. The effect of these decisions rendered in 1911 was to curb some of the activities of big business, but it did not stop the apparently irresistible trend toward big business. In almost every industry there arose a "big three" or a "big four" that dominated or had the power to dominate the industry. The real or fancied power wielded by the big companies give widespread currency to the belief that huge size is a curse. However, the Supreme Court did not subscribe to that belief. In the so-called "rule of reason" promulgated in 1911 the Court held that mere size or the power to exercise monopolistic control is in itself no cause for condemnation. The test is whether that power is abused or used wisely. Toward the close of this period characterized by the dominance of big business the government began to play an increasingly important role in the control of big business to prevent the abuse of power in the hands of private interests.

THE MODERN PERIOD—1914–1941

The period from the First World War to the Second World War was one during which competition in manufacturing industries took on an essentially different character. In almost every industry there had appeared a few leading companies of sufficient size to wield their influence throughout the entire industry. The leading companies respected each other and were respected by their smaller competitors. Competition did not disappear; on the contrary, it was intensified, but it took on a new form. More emphasis was placed upon internal administration and less upon price competition because rising overhead costs made price cutting a perilous road to profits.

Influence of the First World War.—The general character of this period was largely determined by the First World War. Manufacturing facilities were greatly expanded in response to the receipt of war orders shortly after the outbreak of hostilities.   From 1914 to 1917, our exports to Europe rose from 1.5 to 4 billion dollars.   After the entrance of the United States into the war, in 1917, demand for the products of industry increased as never before.   Expansion was not confined to the metal, chemical, and machine industries that produced the implements of war; it involved such industries as flour milling, canning, and wool manufacturing because modern warfare requires materials of all kinds.   According to the Census, between 1914 and 1919 the value added by manufacture expanded from 10 to 25 billions.   Allowing for changes in the purchasing power of the dollar, the increased output was attained by a vast expansion of productive capacity.   When the war ended, industry was equipped to produce far in excess of the peacetime demand.   This intensified the struggle for survival which impelled manufacturers to seek new ways to escape the rigors of competition.

Industry Turns to Internal Administration.—After the war, there was a widespread renewal of interest in the adoption of that body of management principles and practices known as "scientific management." The movement antedated this period, for its founder, F. W. Taylor, had done his pioneer work before the war, but its adoption was delayed because many believed scientific management was useful only in the metal industries where Taylor had carried on his experimentation. However, under stress of greater competition, manufacturers in other fields eagerly sought whatever scientific management had to offer.   They discovered many sources of economies in production through professional advice in such things as: factory layout for continuous flow of production, advanced production planning, the establishment of output and operating standards, and inventory control.   The short but severe depression of 1920–1921 taught a lasting lesson on the value of careful buying.   Having suffered heavy losses from depreciation on excessive inventories, many companies adopted hand-to-mouth buying as a definite purchasing policy. The application of rational technique to plant administration was given additional impetus by the formation of professional societies for the advancement of management, the addition of management courses in college curricula, and the rise of reputable management consultants.

Another phase of internal administration which had its origin before the war, but its greatest development after the war, was personnel administration.   Whereas scientific management stressed the technical and physical aspects of production, personnel administration focused greater attention upon the human factor.   Manufacturers realized that efficiency of production required more than scientific control of equipment, machines, and materials.   Just as important, if not more important, was a capable, stable, and cooperative work force.   Out of this realization grew the various efforts to secure the most efficient utilization of industrial man power. This involved job analysis to determine the kinds of skill required, scientific selection of workers, careful training, incentive wages, promotion programs, employee representation, profit sharing, sick benefits, pension plans, and other devices to promote harmonious employer-employee relationships.

Manufacturers likewise turned their attention to marketing techniques. The outstanding change in this realm of administration was the popularization of installment selling. Though not a new practice, installment selling was used to a greater extent in this period than ever before. Without it the automobile industry could not have grown so rapidly. This form of selling was also widely used by clothing manufacturers and by the manufacturers of household appliances such as washing machines, sewing machines, and vacuum cleaners. Product design was given more careful attention. Products were redesigned more frequently with more emphasis upon style so as to enhance their salability. Furthermore, products were designed to sell at a certain price so as to appeal to the largest possible market. Market analysis and market research were entirely new tools of merchandising developed during this period. By studying the characteristics of markets in different areas and analyzing the results of various marketing practices, manufacturers accomplished more effective results than were obtained by the familiar high-pressure methods of former periods.

The improved cultivation of internal administration was not confined to plant management, personnel, and marketing. It was likewise applied to finance and research. Realizing the necessity for more careful planning and more rigid control over costs, the practice of budgeting gained widespread usage. As opportunities in the capital markets were presented, numerous companies converted their bonded indebtedness into stocks, thereby securing greater flexibility in their financial structure. Organized research was another avenue through which many companies forged ahead of their competitors during this period. In 1940 there were 3,480 industrial research laboratories employing 70,000 people. These laboratories spend 300 million dollars annually seeking to develop new products and new processes.

Technological Developments.—The institutionalization of scientific research very naturally brought a rich harvest of technological improvements. It was during this period that the steel industry introduced continuous rolling. The cement and copper industries developed the flotation process. Newsprint manufacturers shifted to southern pine. Petroleum refining was revolutionized by the new cracking and polymerizing processes. Almost endless improvements were made in the automobile so that its manufacture became one of our leading industries. Automobile tire mileage increased almost tenfold because of better chemical processing of rubber. In shipbuilding, welding supplanted riveting. The airplane, once a machine flown only by daredevils, became an accepted mode of travel. In the textile field, there were such advances as long draft spinning, the introduction of rayon, Nylon, and other synthetic fibers. Food processing witnessed new techniques of preservation such as quick freezing and mechanical refrigeration. Throughout all industry, there was a continuous stream of new products such as Neoprene, Lucite, Cellophane, plastics, radios, and sound movies. One index of technological change is the increase in patents issued by the United States patent office. The annual issue of patents during this period was in the neighborhood of 40,000, contrasted with an average of about 20,000 for the preceding period.

The changes in industrial processes were accompanied by the installation of machines on a vaster scale than ever before. The mechanization of American industry is familiar to everyone. Regardless of its capital cost, machinery is installed whenever it reduces the cost of production. The great increase in mechanization during this period was in large part due to the comparative scarcity of labor. In 1924, immigration was sharply restricted by the imposition of the quota system. Consequently, manufacturers no longer had an endless supply of cheap foreign labor as in earlier periods.

Industrial Consolidations.—During the decade preceding the depression of 1929, there was a second wave of industrial consolidations. It is interesting to note, however, that the combinations effected during the twenties were, on the whole, of a different character from those which occurred at the turn of the century. The earlier merger movement was characterized by the formation of gigantic consolidations in which promoters were none too discriminating in their choice of companies to be united. Sheer size was expected to bring increased profits. However, increased size in business units does not necessarily produce increased earning power, as the operating results of many of these early consolidations reveal.

The consolidations during the twenties were less spectacular; they did not embrace large numbers of manufacturing units collected indiscriminately. Instead, the process was usually a piecemeal absorption of companies. When one company absorbed a competitor, it was to gain some particular advantage that that competitor had to offer, such as a strategic location or highly specialized equipment or a well-established market.

Commercial and distributive factors rather than technical considerations were the dominant motives behind most of the mergers of this period. The art of production was well advanced; the problem confronting industry was how to sell the goods so easily produced. By consolidation, wasteful duplication of selling forces and distributive facilities could be reduced. Nation-wide distribution and advertising could be more effective, trade-marks and trade names could be more fully utilized. These factors rather than the internal economies of large-scale production were behind such consolidations as General Mills, General Foods, International Paper, and Texas Corporation. Admitting some obvious exceptions, the mergers and consolidations of this period were, on the whole, a more rational attempt to meet the rigors of increasing competition.

The Trade Association.—The intensified competition of this period brought about pronounced industry-wide efforts to curb the worst effects of competition. The rapid growth of some of the newer industries such as automobile manufacturing had an adverse effect upon the older industries. Manufacturers in the older industries became more and more impressed with the need for organized self-defense. The trade association or trade institute was the best instrumentality to achieve this form of industry-wide cooperation.

The trade association had made its appearance in the preceding period, but during the postwar years there occurred a great increase in both the number of such institutes and in the activities they performed. More than two-thirds of the 1,500 national or regional associations in existence in 1938 were formed during this period. Over 250 were created in the depression years 1933 to 1935 as a result of the stimulus of the National Industrial Recovery Act. At that time, trade associations had government sanction to promote cooperative efforts for the elimination of excessive competition.

The nature of trade associations is best revealed by their activities. These include: (1) The promotion of efficiency in production and distribution through product simplification and standardization; marketing and merchandising research; collection and circulation of cost data. (2) Development of new products and publicizing of qualities and new uses for existing products; quality standardization and labeling; cooperative advertising; promotion of technical and commercial exhibits. (3) Elimination of coercive practices, misrepresentation of products and services by cooperation with the Federal Trade Commission. (4) Cooperation in dealing with government bodies, trade, labor, and consumer groups. (5) Serving as a means of exchange of ideas and experience of mutual interest.[1]

The Expanding Role of the Government in Industry.—Until recently the government has played a comparatively unimportant role in industry. Such control as the government did exercise was usually in the form of tariff legislation and laws to prevent the sale of harmful foods and drugs.

[1] Lyon, L. S., and Victor Abramson, "Government and Economic Life," The Brookings Institution, Washington, D. C., 1940.

Matters like price fixing, hours of work, rates of pay, and the acquisition of capital by public offering of securities were left to the marketplace.

The depression that began in 1929 changed all this. Within the short span of 3 years our economy toppled from what was widely heralded as permanent prosperity into the worst business depression ever experienced. National income dropped from 81 to 40 billion dollars. Industrial production declined from an index of 319 to 170, salary and wage payments dropped from 49 to 30 billion dollars, unemployment rose to an estimated 14 million workers. The collapse was so devastating that demands arose from all sides for governmental action to stabilize and stimulate industry. The demands came from businessmen who suffered severe losses, from workers who had no jobs, and from farmers who faced foreclosure.

The government responded with a comprehensive legislative program aimed at immediate recovery and ultimate reform. The first law regulating manufacturing industries was passed in 1933—the National Industrial Recovery Act. Under the sponsorship of their respective trade associations, codes of fair competition were drawn up by the major industries. Following approval by the Recovery Administration and the President, the codes became binding upon all members of the industry. All codes contained provisions for minimum wages and maximum hours and many codes also provided for control of prices and production. Although the NRA was declared unconstitutional in 1935, it served as the opening wedge for subsequent government regulation of industry.

The extension of governmental power over industry is clearly revealed in our recent labor legislation, and this is in the nature of permanent reform. The same year that the NRA was outlawed, Congress passed the National Labor Relations Act which reasserted the right of employees to organize for purposes of collective bargaining and defined a series of unfair labor practices which employers were forbidden to exercise. Underlying this law was the recognition that labor did not have equality of bargaining power and the philosophy that collective bargaining is socially desirable. Labor immediately seized the opportunity to organize the low-wage mass-production industries. Though the law was bitterly assailed from numerous quarters, the government has shown no indication of withdrawing from the position of throwing its weight on the side of labor.

With the passage of the Fair Labor Standards Act of 1938, the Federal government reasserted and strengthened its determination to control the process of free bargaining in industry. This act put a floor under wages and a ceiling over hours. Its purpose was to increase purchasing power and reduce unemployment by spreading work and also to buttress health and living standards of workers. Behind all of this labor legislation was the belief that one of the principal causes of the acute depression of the thirties was the collapse of mass purchasing power.

The expanding role of the government is illustrated in a variety of ways. By the Connally Act of 1935, Federal assistance was given to the oil-producing states in their efforts to curb overproduction of petroleum. The Bituminous Coal Act of 1937 brought the coal industry under closer government control. The Wheeler-Lea Act of 1938 strengthened the powers of the Federal Trade Commission. The Robinson-Patman Act restricts price discrimination, and the Miller-Tydings Act curbs price competition by legalizing resale price maintenance. In 1938, the problem of the impact of monopoly upon our economy was reexamined in an exhaustive survey undertaken by the Temporary National Economic Committee. However, before any major governmental action was taken as a result of this study, we were forced by the trend of world events to turn our attention to the more pressing problem of national defense.

The period closes with active government participation with industry in a gigantic task of fighting a Second World War. Soon after the outbreak of the war American industry received large orders for war materials from France, England, and the other European democracies. As the European countries collapsed, one by one, under the vastly underestimated military strength of Germany, our industries were called upon for desperately needed war supplies. Foreseeing the danger ahead, we at last began to arm ourselves, but the program of national defense manufacturing had scarcely begun when we were attacked by Japan. For obvious reasons the government must perform the leading role in the control of industry for successful prosecution of the war. Upon the termination of the war there will be enormous problems of readjustment in which government control will be just as indispensable.

CHAPTER XXXVIII

TECHNOLOGY: THE COURSE IT HAS TAKEN AND THE PROBLEMS IT RAISES

In the first chapter manufacturing was defined as the creation of utility, *i.e.*, the conversion of raw materials into forms that will better satisfy human wants. The manufacturing method employed to achieve the conversion and the extent to which utility is enhanced, as measured by value added, varies considerably from one group of industries to another. In some industries, as has been shown in the preceding chapters, the processes are very elaborate and complex, involving the use of large amounts of mechanical equipment and labor, and the value added is substantial; in others, the methods are simple, requiring neither much equipment nor much labor, and the finished products issue from the factories worth only a fraction more than the raw materials that entered the receiving departments. In either case, however, the technology has an all-pervasive influence on the industry's structure and its performance in our economy. It is, as we have seen, an important, if not the most important, factor in determining the degree of concentration in an industry, the nature of its cost structure, its competitive pattern, its responsiveness to price changes, and its labor problems, to mention only a few aspects of industry.

TECHNOLOGY IS DYNAMIC

All technologies in manufacturing involve the use of men, machines, materials, and money. These factors of production can usually be combined in various proportions, depending upon the method of manufacturing employed, to achieve the desired result—a finished and useful product. However, while there are usually alternative methods of producing a product, at any given time in the development of an industry there is always one most efficient method—one that invokes the lowest combination of costs—and this method becomes the prevailing process or technology. It is significant to note, however, that the prevalent method does not long prevail. Since the prices at which the factors of production are made available to businessmen constantly change and since our scientific knowledge is always expanding, a new combination of men, machines, materials, and money becomes more economical and, therefore, displaces the former method. The new combination may not only be a new method of making a product, but may also result in a new product to fill some hitherto unsatisfied human want. This process of change, which we have encountered in practically every industry described in this book, is known as technological progress, and in all instances the objective was the same—to obtain more and more goods from less and less of the limited supply of the factors of production. In short, the purpose of technological progress is to economize in the use of the factors of production.

The need for economy has always been a compelling force in human history, regardless of the nature of the prevailing social organization. Mankind, today no less than formerly, has always been confronted with the economic problem that results from the existence of unlimited human wants and only limited means to satisfy them. A constantly improving technology is the only solution to this age-old problem.

FORMS OF TECHNOLOGICAL PROGRESS

Technological progress, as we have seen in the preceding chapters, has assumed a variety of forms. The changes that have occurred in the technology of American industry are too numerous to detail here but most of them fall into one of the following principal types:
1. Increased use of machinery.
2. Economy of raw materials.
3. Changes in products.
4. More rational organization of plants.

Increased Use of Machinery.—The most spectacular manifestation of technological progress is the increased use of machinery and mechanical processes. The primary purpose of mechanization has been to reduce directly both the amount and kind of labor required to produce a good. As long as goods were produced entirely or in large part by hand, output depended upon the endurance, skill, and willingness of labor. With the application of a mechanical process, the output of labor per hour was greatly increased, and since, in many industries, the necessary skill was built into the machine, a lower grade of labor, and therefore less costly labor, could be employed. Thus a double economy was realized.

Not all mechanical improvements are made with the direct object of reducing the amount of labor required. In the petroleum industry, for example, the chief cause of mechanical improvements has been the desire to obtain a greater yield of gasoline from each barrel of petroleum processed. In other instances, mechanical changes were made because the new process produced products that had wider uses. Thus, for example, the open-hearth process replaced the Bessemer process, in part, because the product of the former could be more generally used.

Economy in Raw Material Consumption.—Many processes have been introduced to make possible the manufacture of existing products with cheaper raw materials or waste materials. Thus, there was introduced into the copper industry the flotation process, which permitted the utilization of low-grade copper ores, theretofore too costly for such use. The rubber industry learned to use reclaimed rubber, thereby decreasing our dependence upon the costlier virgin rubber, imported from great distances. Similarly, the steel industry developed methods to use scrap iron and steel, and the textile industry perfected processes to respin reclaimed fibers. Other processes were installed to conserve existing raw materials. The cement industry, for example, increased the size of the rotary kiln to save coal, and the by-product coke oven was adopted to save the valuable gases which were formerly permitted to go unutilized. Again, other processes were introduced to use existing raw materials to make new products to replace higher cost products. Thus, rayon and Nylon, made of common raw materials available in large amounts, came to the market to replace silk, a luxury product that depended upon the slow processes of nature.

Changes in Products.—Some technological developments do not involve important changes in machinery or raw materials but arise from changes in the product itself. In many of our industries, products have been standardized in design to permit continuous manufacture in large volume, thus decreasing the idle time in plants while shifting from one design to another. Productive capacity is therefore increased with little or no change in equipment or in the labor force. In other industries technological progress involves changes in design to increase the life of the product and to reduce the replacement demand for it. A good example of this type of technological development occurred in the rubber tire industry which reduced tire prices through mechanization and increased tire mileage by improvements in design and structure.

More Rational Organization of Plants.—Many technological changes affected only the organization of the plant and its internal operation and management. For example, the integration of a blast furnace plant with an open-hearth plant permitted the use of pig iron in a molten state, eliminating the time necessary for cooling and reducing the cost of handling and reheating. The integration of pulp and paper mills similarly reduced the cost of manufacturing paper. Better plant layout, permitting the direct flow of work from one machine to another, reduced the amount of labor required in handling the work; better scheduling prevented the work from piling up at one machine while another machine, further along in the process, stands idle. Closer supervision of labor and frequent inspection of goods in process reduced the amount of spoilage; detailed instructions to labor on methods and order of work eliminated useless motions and idle time. Similarly, minute subdivision of work and specialization have increased the output of labor and, at the same time, decreased the need for skilled workers. Careful control of inventories to avoid either shortages which might cause a shutdown or the building up of excess supplies which would increase working capital requirements, is a technological change which economizes the use of capital. Some of the best examples of technological improvements of this character are found in the automobile industry. Regional assembly plants are supplied with parts and subassemblies, made in the central manufacturing plants at Detroit, on schedules as accurate and precise as if they were coordinated departments in a single factory.

DIRECT REASONS FOR TECHNOLOGICAL CHANGES

All these technological changes, and many others that might be mentioned, have been the results of efforts to economize in the use of the factors of production and to maximize our human satisfactions with our limited resources. While this has been the basic factor underlying technological progress, it has seldom, if ever, been the direct cause of such changes, in our type of social organization. Technological innovations usually spring from other causes.

Without a doubt the most important single cause is the quest for profits. Businessmen make a profit by buying the factors of production at their respective prices and reselling them, in the form of finished goods, at a higher price. The spread between the cost prices and the selling prices is the profit margin. Businessmen in their quest for profits constantly try to increase this spread. If they are unable to achieve this objective by increasing selling prices, they attempt to achieve it by decreasing costs through the economies described above. If one or more succeed in doing so, their competitors, in order to maintain their position in the market, must do the same. Consequently, the quest for profits and the forces of competition compel the adoption of new and more efficient methods of production.

In other instances, innovations are brought about not by the urge for profits, but by the exercise of curiosity—the inclination to seek a new and better way of making a good or the desire to find a substitute for an existing product, for no other reason than to satisfy one's curiosity that it can be done. In still other cases, the search for profit is combined with the instinct of curiosity. Our patent system rests upon this dual basis. It holds out the hope of financial reward to those who have an urge to apply their curiosity in the industrial arts and sciences. Whatever the direct cause may be for technological innovations the result is the same— the increase of human satisfactions from our limited resources.

THE BENEFITS OF TECHNOLOGICAL CHANGE

The technological changes cited above, and many others not mentioned, are the basis of our present high level of material well-being.

Without them economic society as we now know it could not exist, and our standard of living, measured by the amount, quality, and variety of goods and services consumed, would differ little, if at all, from that which prevailed in early colonial America. The benefits flowing from these changes have not been restricted to any one group, but have been shared by all members of economic society—the manufacturer, the workers, and society as a whole.

Benefits to the Manufacturer.—Since technological changes are usually inaugurated by the manufacturer it is logical, in a discussion of the benefits of technological change, to begin with the advantages that accrue to him. The manufacturer's interest in such changes, as has been shown, arise from the hope of a greater profit. If any of the changes mentioned above enable him to reduce his costs, his profits per unit of production will increase—provided, of course, that competition will permit him to maintain his former price—and his total profits will likewise increase. Maintenance of prices with a larger profit per unit is not, however, the only objective. A reduction in price made possible by a reduction in costs may cause expansion in the manufacturer's market, and although profit per unit will be smaller, his total profits and the rate of profit per dollar of investment will be considerably greater. Such results may be expected in the case of products with a highly elastic demand. In some instances, as has been indicated, technological changes are instituted not to reduce costs but, through a change in the product, to give it a new and wider use. The expansion in the market makes possible an increase in production, a greater utilization of productive capacity with lower per unit costs and greater total profits. Other changes, such for example as the improvement in the quality of rubber tires, are inaugurated for a competitive advantage that may prove to be only temporary. Thus, each of the tire companies, engaged in a fierce competitive struggle, tried to obtain for itself a larger share of the market by producing a better tire than its competitor.

In a competitive economy, no manufacturer or industry can hope to retain for long all the economies that arise from technological change. If profits, as measured by the rate of return on invested capital, are larger than in industry generally, additional capital, in the form of new companies, will flow into the industry, and the added output will force a decline in prices and a reduction in the rate of profits.

Benefits to the Workers.—To workers, as a group, the benefits flowing from technological changes have taken the form of shorter hours of labor, better working conditions, and higher real wages.

In the latter part of the nineteenth century, a work week of six 12-hour days was not unusual, and as late as 1890 the average work week in manufacturing industries was 60 hours, usually six 10-hour days. During the first two decades of the present century the work week in manufacturing declined to an average of 51 hours, and by 1937 the average was 42 hours per week. Since then, in the majority of industries, the maximum number of hours of work, without payment of an extra rate for overtime, has become fixed at 40 hours per week.

The great reduction in the hours of work, without a comparable decline in weekly earnings, would not have been possible without technological changes. The great increase in the productivity of labor, through the application of one or more of the changes mentioned above, has enabled workers to produce a larger amount of goods in a shorter period of time, permitting a reduction in the work week without a comparable decline in production or the employment of more workers to produce the same volume of output.

More leisure is not, however, the only benefit that has come to labor from technological change. Better working conditions and less back-breaking toil have also followed in its wake. With greater reliance on machinery, with more mechanical lifting and internal transportation appliances, the worker's function often consists of no more than tending a machine or supervising its operation.

In addition to these benefits, technological changes in the long run have increased the worker's wages, both real and money wages. Without such changes, in most instances, wage increases would have increased the costs and prices of goods, and the higher prices, in turn, would have caused a decline in the demand for the goods and, therefore, a decrease in the demand for labor. As a result of technological changes, wages could be increased without a comparable increase in prices, and, in many industries, prices have decreased without a decrease in wages.

Benefits to Society.—Important as the benefits of technological change have been to manufacturers and to labor, the greatest beneficiary has been society as a whole. It should be noted here that both of the former groups, as members of society, have also shared in these general gains; indeed, their indirect gains as members of a society undergoing rapid technological change are probably greater than the benefits that come to them as a result of the specific advances in their respective industries.

To society as a whole our advancing technology has meant the production of more goods, of new goods, and of better goods, at lower and lower prices. Without the technological changes described in the preceding chapters, our present standard of living could not have been attained. There would not be enough resources, of labor, raw materials, capital, and management, to produce the huge stream of goods that flow annually from our factories, if we depended upon the technology that prevailed before the American industrial revolution got under way.

THE COSTS OF TECHNOLOGICAL CHANGE

Great as the benefits of technological changes have been, they have not been achieved without certain costs. The costs, like the benefits, have been and are being paid by the manufacturer, the worker, and society.

Costs to the Manufacturer.—The changes in technology have greatly increased the risks that confront the manufacturer. As manufacturing processes became more mechanized and, therefore, depended less upon labor, the manufacturer's cost structure changed—a larger proportion of his total costs became fixed costs and a smaller proportion remained variable costs. In periods of business prosperity, when his plant is operated at or very near to capacity, his profits are substantial because there are more units of output over which his fixed costs can be spread. However, in periods of declining business activity, the opposite condition obtains. Small decreases in production result in sharp increases in unit costs and a corresponding shrinkage in the profit margin. If the contraction in capacity utilization is great, substantial losses are incurred. Since a large proportion of his total costs are fixed, the manufacturer has less ability than formerly to adjust his costs to market conditions. In some industries, as we have seen, the relentless pressure of overhead costs causes the manufacturer to attempt to obtain a larger share of the available market by reducing prices. To prevent him from accomplishing his objective of greater volume, his competitors are obliged to meet his prices. If the demand for his product is inelastic, the entire price structure is imperiled and heavy losses are sustained by the entire industry. This result, as was shown in the preceding chapters, obtains from time to time in such industries as the cement and newsprint manufacturing industries. Thus, large investments in plant and equipment, with their attendant heavy fixed costs, create pressures which if left uncontrolled cause severe competition and violent fluctuations in earnings.

Wide fluctuations in earnings are not the only risks that accompany the use of mechanical equipment. Of equal importance is the risk that changes in technology may render the equipment obsolete much earlier than was anticipated at the time of purchase and before its costs are fully recovered. The obsolescence may be caused by the development of more efficient machines, and failure to keep abreast with such changes may force a company out of the industry. This, for example, was the experience of some of the rayon manufacturers, many of whom fell by the wayside during the industry's period of most vigorous expansion. In other instances, plants have been rendered obsolete by changes in the design of the product or by the development of cheaper or more efficient substitutes.

The increasing rate of technological change and the consequent acceleration of technological obsolescence have increased the difficulties of managing manufacturing enterprises. The absence of cost accounting methods that give adequate recognition to the problem of obsolescence, the payment of large dividends, and the failure to establish sufficient reserves have forced many companies into bankruptcy.

The Costs to the Worker.—It has been indicated that technological change affects the type of workers employed, the number of workers required, and the conditions of their employment. Usually the first effect upon the workers is a reduction in the need for their skill—the skill they acquired during a lifetime of work. A series of changes may completely eliminate their skills and reduce them to the level of unskilled, or at best semiskilled, labor, with corresponding reductions in their rates of pay.

Inability to sell their acquired skill is not their only loss. If their productivity is greatly increased and the market for their products fails to respond sufficiently, they are completely and permanently detached from the industry in which they had worked their entire adult lives, and must look for employment in other occupations that may require complete retraining of their talents.

Those who are fortunate enough to retain their jobs often find their way of work completely changed. Once skilled workers, they are now machine tenders. No longer can they regard the finished article as a product of their own handicraft; instead they perform monotonously one small task which is merged with those of their fellow workers, and the product of their effort can no longer be identified. Instead of determining, as they once did, the sequence of operations and the speed of performing them, the machine determines what they must do and the pace they must follow. If they are unable to keep up with the pace they are discharged and replaced by younger men, with the result that in many industries men who are over 40 years of age can not obtain a job.

Costs to Society.—Technological changes have not been, and are not now, confined to one industry but proceed along the entire front of all industry. The consequences of these changes to both the employer and the worker are sometimes of such magnitude that they are no longer the problems of these two groups alone but assume the proportions of a social problem. When thousands of coal miners are economically stranded as a result of mechanization or the competition of fuel oil, their unemployment becomes a problem for the entire community. When the textile industry shifted to the South, a migration that was hastened by technological changes, the burden of the shift was felt not only by the employer whose plant was abandoned and by the workers who were left jobless but by the community at large. The social problem that is created by such a change is vividly portrayed by the following account of the experiences of Manchester, N. H.[1]

Catastrophe was the only word to describe the effect of Amoskeag's collapse on Manchester's 76,000 inhabitants.   Manchester grew up around the Amoskeag mills.   Over half of the very land it stands on was sold or deeded to the city by Amoskeag owners.   Since 1805 Amoskeag has provided the city's business life-blood.   At the peak of its prosperity in 1921, Amoskeag's red-brick plants, stretching for almost a mile along the Merrimack River, employed 18,000 workers, paid nearly one-half the city's industrial payroll.   Last week Amoskeag's workers, jobless for ten months, had at least the certainty that they would never work for Amoskeag Manufacturing Co. again.

Early last summer Amoskeag began closing down, mill by mill.   By last September every gate was locked, every worker on the street.   As dust gathered on Amoskeag's 20,000 cotton looms, the citizens of Manchester endured a bad winter, a cheerless spring.   Amoskeag workers who had been getting $13 a week from the mills were thrown on relief of $2 per week with $1 more for each family.

The experiences of Manchester have been duplicated in many other towns and cities, in Paterson, N. J., for example, where the silk mills and silk workers were left idle because of the rise of rayon as a substitute, and in many steel towns that were left stranded by the introduction of the continuous rolling mill that displaced the hand rolling mills.

Similarly, the displacement of "over age" employees ceases to be an individual problem when it assumes large proportions; it becomes a social problem of first magnitude with which only society is competent to deal.

RESISTANCE TO TECHNOLOGICAL CHANGE

Despite the admitted long-run benefits of technological changes, all groups affected try to resist them or to minimize their effects.   Employers attempt to protect their earnings by maintaining prices, either by administrative policy or by collusion with their competitors.   They try to protect their investments by a reluctant acceptance of new processes and sometimes by a deliberate suppression of new patents.

The workers, especially if organized into strong unions, attempt to minimize the impact of technology on their jobs and earnings by imposing rules and restrictions on the use of new machines.   Thus, when the automatic loom was introduced into the textile industry, the textile unions limited the number of looms per weaver in order to spread work.   When the spray gun was introduced the painter's union vigorously opposed its adoption, and in some cities its use by union members is still prohibited. In other instances, unions have attempted to reduce the displacement of workers by insisting upon shorter hours and by requiring the payment of time and one-half or double time for overtime.   Still other unions have

[1] *Time*, Aug. 3, 1936.

placed severe limits upon the number of units a worker may produce in one day. These are only a few of the many types of restrictions by which labor tries to ease the burden of technological change.

Society, acting through the government, has also tried to mitigate the adverse effects of rapid technological change. In the belief that machines are the principal cause of our recent mass unemployment, the government has imposed limits on the length of the work day and work week in our manufacturing industries. Proceeding on the theory that labor is unable to purchase the goods it produces because it receives too small a share of the value of the product, the government has also fixed limits below which minimum wages cannot fall. So great have been the effects of technological change and so persistent is the belief that they are the root of most of our economic troubles that the demand has grown in many quarters to call a halt to further mechanization. Indeed, a few years ago a prominent member of the House of Representatives introduced a bill to suspend the issue of patents on new inventions.

THE FUTURE OF TECHNOLOGICAL CHANGE

Whatever the costs of technological change, it is likely that in the future the rate will increase rather than decrease. Industry today is more conscious than ever of the importance of research work and is making greater expenditures than ever on research. It is estimated that in 1920 private industry supported 300 laboratories with a personnel of 9,300; in 1930 the number of laboratories expanded to 1,625 with a personnel of 34,200; and by 1940 the industrial laboratories numbered 3,480 with a personnel of over 70,000 research workers. In addition to the research efforts of industry, research is carried on by the government, trade associations, and the colleges and universities of the country. Since research workers today begin their efforts with a greater knowledge and understanding of both the pure and applied sciences than was true in the past, it is a fair assumption that progress in the future will be made at a faster rate. Thus we can look forward to the development of new products, new processes, and new fields of application for existing products and materials.

On these developments rests the realization of our hopes for a more abundant life for all. The great question that remains to be solved is whether the benefits of technology can be obtained without paying the heavy social and economic costs that were paid for our earlier achievements. The answer to this depends upon the wisdom and skill with which we adapt our social and economic institutions to the inevitable technological changes.

CHAPTER XXXIX

COMPETITION

In the preceding chapter the point was made that our society, like all other societies, is confronted with an economic problem because we have unlimited wants and only limited means to satisfy them. In order to maximize our satisfactions, it is necessary to economize in our use of resources, so that our most important needs will be satisfied first.

In earlier societies, when man produced primarily for his own use, the task of resolving this problem was less difficult than it is today. He knew what goods he wanted, and he could allocate his time and effort in accordance with his wants. Today no man or family is self-sufficient. Indeed, the vast majority of men do not make any of the things they need. Instead, as we have seen, we have highly specialized producers who produce for the needs of others, and who use the income they receive from the sale of their products to purchase from other specialized producers the goods and services they need.

If the activities of the specialists are to be properly coordinated and our limited resources used efficiently, some guidance of our economic system is necessary, otherwise it will get out of balance. It might produce too much flour and not enough meat; too many shoes and not enough clothes; too much cotton and not enough rayon; too much of all these goods and not enough blast furnaces, steel, looms, and other machines necessary to process them. Guidance of the system today, then, as before, resolves itself into the problem of:

1. Determining what goods and how much of each shall be produced; and

2. Directing the flow of labor, capital, and land so that the "right" goods will be produced and in the "right amounts"; and

3. Producing the goods as efficiently as possible.

PRICES AS A BAROMETER AND A GUIDE

Men engage in business to make a profit. Therefore, they will produce those goods which will yield them the greatest profit; and profit depends upon the prices they pay for the factors of production and the price they receive for the goods they sell. Businessmen compare the price of each good and its cost of production with the prices and costs of all other goods, and on the basis of this comparison decide which to produce.

Every time a person spends a dollar for rayon hosiery rather than cotton hosiery, he increases the demand for the former and decreases the demand for the latter. If many other people do the same, the price of cotton hosiery will decline and that of rayon hosiery will increase, and hosiery manufacturers will lower the production of the former and increase the production of the latter.

TABLE LXXXIII.—COTTON PRINT CLOTH: TOTAL COSTS OF GRAY GOODS, IRRESPEC-
TIVE OF CONSTRUCTION, IN 21 MILLS (EXCLUDING SELLING AND INTEREST PAID)
IN MARCH AND OCTOBER, 1931–1934, INCLUSIVE, AND IN MARCH, 1935,
ARRANGED IN ASCENDING ORDER OF COSTS IN MARCH, 1935

(In cents per pound)

Mill number	1931		1932		1933		1934		1935
	March	October	March	October	March	October	March	October	March
1	29.92	21.01	19.99	18.89	17.39	30.76	33.62	33.48	31.03
8	28.87	21.47	20.36	18.01	16.40	30.26	34.03	35.44	31.70
18	24.97	20.30	18.00	17.15	16.55	29.33	30.87	32.30	31.74
15	24.73	18.67	17.91	19.24	15.02	30.28	29.66	31.75	32.14
2	29.28	25.95	18.47	17.39	16.40	29.93	30.17	32.49	32.65
6	24.32	19.36	19.87	17.88	17.07	29.61	31.73	32.72	32.75
19	26.40	20.38	19.01	17.77	16.92	31.12	31.90	34.03	32.76
20	25.29	22.48	19.91	19.76	18.48	31.38	33.56	37.87	33.13
4	27.41	19.39	20.12	18.45	16.92	31.06	33.49	34.08	33.15
10	33.73	23.07	20.29	22.13	18.18	36.40	36.55	39.14	33.21
3	24.23	18.57	19.88	16.16	16.08	30.23	31.67	33.67	33.47
11	24.93	19.10	17.23	17.05	16.79	31.14	29.46	34.07	33.53
17	29.76	24.65	23.20	23.16	18.67	31.90	33.87	40.70	33.55
21	29.23	23.44	20.03	23.92	19.54	31.40	31.49	34.61	33.89
13	29.31	20.76	20.88	17.85	17.33	34.73	35.02	35.72	33.94
7	26.68	21.39	20.67	19.71	18.20	32.71	35.10	36.54	35.12
16	31.76	21.00	20.12	19.29	18.82	33.91	33.25	36.47	35.35
12	28.02	21.62	20.78	18.71	18.97	34.00	34.04	34.68	35.82
9	23.86	22.17	20.76	19.54	16.39	33.22	32.87	34.52	36.27
14	32.29	25.52	23.25	19.56	18.09	32.99	30.39	36.19	36.31
5	28.34	19.30	19.67	18.60	18.34	33.71	35.23	35.72	37.11
Average	27.78	21.41	20.02	19.06	17.45	31.91	32.76	35.06	33.74

Source: "Report to the President on Cotton Cloth," U. S. Tariff Commission, April, 1936.

The flow of labor, capital, and land necessary for production is directed by the same process that guides the manufacturer of hosiery. Capital and land are privately owned, and each worker controls his own labor power. They can be obtained only upon the payment of a price, and will go to that industry which can pay the highest price. And these industries, of course, are the ones for whose products there exists the greatest demand and from which the greatest profits can be realized. Until the needs of these industries for the productive factors have been satisfied, other industries, whose products have a smaller demand, cannot obtain them.

It is important not only that the "right" goods be produced in the right amounts, but that they be produced as efficiently as possible. It is unusual, as we have seen in the earlier chapters, for a product to be produced entirely by one establishment or one company. An industry usually comprises several companies, and often, as in textiles and clothing, the number of companies is in the hundreds and thousands. It would be most unusual if each company showed the same costs. Some are better located than others and can obtain their raw materials or reach their customers at a lower cost; some have more efficient labor or more modern equipment; others are managed more efficiently. The wide range in costs of manufacture in an industry is well illustrated in Table LXXXIII. It will be noted that in March, 1935, between the highest cost mill and the lowest cost mill there was a difference of 6.08 cents per pound of cloth. Of equal importance is the fact that few mills maintained their position of March, 1931, throughout the period. Some became more efficient, and others less so. It is to the best interests of society, insofar as is possible, that production be concentrated in the more efficient plants.

Thus, prices determine what goods shall be produced, in what amounts they shall be produced, and also what companies shall produce them.

COMPETITION

Since we rely so much upon prices to guide the economic system, it is necessary that prices be free to move so that they will accurately reflect the supply of and demands for goods and also the supply of and demand for the factors of production that are necessary for the manufacture of goods. This freedom of movement can be assured only when there is competition between the sellers for the available factors of production and for the market and competition between the buyers for the available supply of a product.

Economists, for purposes of economic analysis, distinguish several types of competition. Competition is said to be perfect when (1) sellers exist in such number that no one of them controls enough of the supply so that a change in his output will materially affect the total supply, and conversely buyers must be equally numerous, (2) the product offered by the sellers is identical in quality, (3) sellers and buyers have complete knowledge of the market and of market conditions, (4) there is no restraint or collusion on the part of either sellers or buyers, and (5) there are no obstacles to the entrance to or elimination from the market. *Pure* competition exists when only the first two conditions exist, *i.e.*, many sellers and buyers exist and an identical product is offered and sought for.

Monopoly is the antithesis of perfect or pure competition. Strictly speaking, monopoly means the control of the supply of a product by one producer, such control giving him the ability to increase his profits by fixing the price at which he sells or by fixing the number of units he offers for sale. It also implies that the product is indispensable and that no substitute for it exists.

Not a single industry described in this book meets one of these three descriptions. Many of them have large numbers of sellers and buyers, as, for example, the textile, clothing, and shoe industries, but complete standardization of product is certainly a characteristic of neither of them. The companies in the copper and cement industries, on the other hand, produce identical products, but production is concentrated in relatively few hands. The Aluminum Company of America was until recently the sole producer of virgin aluminum in this country, but its power over price was not complete because substitutes, in the form of other metals, were available. Similarly, some of the industries are relatively easy to enter, but in all but a few cases, especially in those industries where considerable specialized equipment is necessary, the elimination of units is very difficult. Accordingly, however useful the terms *perfect* competition, *pure* competition and *monopoly* are to the economist for purposes of theoretical economic analysis, they are much less useful for analyzing and understanding the operation of specific industries. Actual conditions in the industries described in this book lie between the extremes of perfect competition, on the one hand, and pure monopoly on the other. Some industries are more competitive than others, though none of them meets the requirements of perfect competition; others with a high degree of concentration are able to augment their profits, by virtue of such concentration, much more easily than other industries with a comparable degree of concentration. A more realistic approach would be to determine not whether the conditions that prevail in a specific industry are those of perfect competition, pure competition, or pure monopoly, but, rather, whether the conditions that do obtain and the interplay of those conditions yield the results that we expect from competition. In short, we can agree that nowhere in this book can we find industries in which perfect competition or even pure competition exists—but there are many in which *effective* competition exists, *i.e.*, sufficient competition to achieve the results society expects.

FACTORS THAT INFLUENCE THE NATURE OF COMPETITION

As we have seen in the course of this book, competition in an industry is determined by a number of factors, among the more important of which the following may be listed:

1. The number of companies in the industry.
2. The capital requirements of the industry.
3. The character of the product.
4. The nature and source of the raw material.
5. The maturity of the industry.

The Number of Companies.—As we have seen in the preceding chapters, the number of companies in an industry varies considerably from one industry to another, from (until recently) one company in the aluminum industry to 18,000 in the baking industry. Usually, though by no means always, the intensity of the competition varies directly with the number of companies in the industry—the larger the number of companies, the greater the competition—and usually it is resolved into price competition. The existence of a large number of companies may be said to make an industry inherently competitive and makes it most difficult to obtain and maintain agreements to restrain competition. In the aluminum industry, when only one company produced the entire virgin aluminum supply, the price[1] was relatively stable over long periods of time, notwithstanding large fluctuations in the sales of the product. In other industries with few companies, such as the automobile and cigarette industries, such competition as does exist between the companies does not manifest itself primarily in price competition, but, respectively, in quality and advertising. On the other hand, the rubber tire industry, which is substantially under the control of only four companies, has in recent years been engaged in vigorous price competition and has not been able to augment its profits by virtue of the high degree of control.

Capital Requirements.—Closely associated with the number of companies are the capital requirements necessary to enter the industry. Small capital requirements facilitate the ease of entrance, and in profitable periods new units do enter the industry and do increase competition. Conversely, in periods of low or nonexistent profits, companies leave the industry, their exit facilitated by the fact that they have little capital tied up in specialized equipment and that which they do have can be liquidated at a small loss. These conditions obtain in such industries as clothing, baking, and silk weaving.

On the other hand, industries with large capital requirements cannot adjust themselves as quickly to changing conditions. The automobile industry, as we have seen, has been one of our most profitable industries, but the high profits have not attracted new companies. Automobile manufacturing can be conducted profitably only on a large-scale basis, and the difficulties of securing a substantial share of the market in the presence of the existing "big three" are almost insurmountable. The same situation existed for many years in the steel industry.

[1] See p. 102.

Large capital requirements, in periods of declining business, should tend to increase price competition because of the pressure to cover at least part of the company's overhead costs. In the newsprint industry[1] this did occur, and in the cement industry[2] it happens from time to time. On the other hand, in other industries, knowledge of what such pressure might do to the price structure has tended to restrain companies from initiating price cuts in periods of declining activity. This was true for many years in the steel industry[3] and the rayon yarn industry,[4] in both of which short-run changes were seldom reflected by price changes.

Large capital requirements also tend to place obstacles to the elimination of companies from an industry. With large investments in specialized equipment which cannot be shifted to the manufacture of a different product, the company continues to produce at a loss in the hope of recovering at least part of the capital. To remain in business the company attempts to increase its share of the market by reducing prices, with the hope that a greater volume will reduce its unit costs. It may fail to make adequate provision for depreciation and obsolescence, and increase the number of shifts. Other companies cannot ignore the prices of the hard-pressed competitor, and are obliged to meet his price, cut by cut. This process may continue for a long time before liquidation of productive capacity occurs; and during this process many companies may finally be liquidated. This condition prevailed for many years in the cotton textile industry, and also in the newsprint industry.

Character of the Product.—The character of the product manufactured has a definite influence upon the nature of competition. In an industry where the product turned out by one manufacturer is practically identical in its physical characteristics with the products of every other manufacturer, competition centers upon price. Deprived of the ability to claim superiority of quality, a producer can compete with his rivals only by offering his product at a lower price if he seeks to obtain a larger share of the market. The best illustration is furnished by the copper industry. Electrolytic copper is perfectly homogeneous, and for that reason competition turns entirely upon price despite the small number of producers. Homogeneity of the product is likewise a factor causing occasional breaks in the price of cement.

The durability of manufactured products affects the character of competition. Durable goods, such as automobiles or floor coverings, are serviceable for a number of years; consequently the demand for them is

[1] See p. 262.
[2] See p. 184.
[3] See p. 69.
[4] See p. 348.

irregular. Since a general decline in purchasing power undermines the demand for durable goods more than that for nondurable goods, competition among the producers of the former is intensified.

If the product is one that is in joint demand with another product, violent price competition often occurs. The demand for tires, the principal product of the rubber industry, is inseparable from the demand for automobiles. If the production and use of automobiles is insufficient to absorb the productive capacity of the tire industry, producers cut prices drastically in order to build up their volume. However, because the demand is relatively inelastic, the entire price structure may be imperiled without any substantial increase in total sales.

The effectiveness of price as a competitive weapon depends to a large extent upon whether the product is a producer's or a consumer's good. When a paper box manufacturer buys his raw material, paper board, he makes certain specifications with respect to tensile strength, thickness, ease of folding, etc., and he will tend to buy from that board manufacturer who can meet the specifications at the lowest price. Sales or advertising pressure by competing vendors of paper board will be of no avail unless they meet or quote a lower price. Among producers of consumer's goods, on the other hand, price competition frequently gives way to the methods of persuasion. We have observed in Chap. XXXVI that the producers of cigars and cigarettes adhere fairly well to established price lines and that competition takes the form of intensive cultivation of the market through advertising.

Nature of the Raw Material.—The nature of the raw material is another important factor that influences competition. For example, in the petroleum industry we have observed how the law of capture affects the entire industry. High gasoline prices stimulate production of crude oil, but low gasoline prices do not immediately retard production of crude oil.

The industries that process agricultural raw materials are faced by the constant problem of fluctuating raw material costs. The size of the cotton crop, for example, varies greatly from one year to another because it is the product of thousands of farmers who act independently in determining what acreage to plant and also because very little control can be exercised over the yield per acre owing to the forces of nature. As a result of these factors, the annual crop is subject to considerable fluctuation in volume and therefore in price. Confronted with highly irregular raw material prices, the cotton manufacturer who, through foresight or good fortune, gets his raw material cheaper than his competitors can undersell them in the cloth market. It is apparent how such conditions make for greater instability in the cost structure, thus adding to the intensity of competition.

Competition is especially keen in those industries where the raw materials constitute a large proportion of the total manufacturing costs. We have noted that such is the case in most of the food industries. The high ratio of raw material costs to total costs leaves these manufacturers only a small margin from which all other costs and profits must be obtained. Since most of these industries utilize agricultural raw materials characterized by great price irregularity, competition is particularly acute, and this is reflected in the customarily narrow and irregular profit margins.

Maturity of the Industry.—The nature of competition in an industry is also determined by its maturity. A mature industry is one that has attained the last stage in secular growth, characterized by stability or decline, as described in Chap. I. As long as an industry has an expanding market to exploit, competition is none too rigorous and all but the grossly inefficient manage to survive. However, sooner or later a point is reached when the market becomes saturated and will expand no further unless prices are reduced. Although industries frequently find ways to avoid price competition, such steps are usually taken only after the disastrous effects of price wars have been experienced.

When an industry attains maturity it is subject to another form of competition that might be termed "external competition," *i.e.*, the tendency for purchasing power to be siphoned away in favor of new industries that are enjoying rapid growth. The substitution of paper containers for cotton bags is a case in point. The effect is the same even though the product of the new industry is not a direct substitute for the product of the mature industry. There can be little doubt that new industries like automobile and radio manufacturing have had adverse effects upon older industries such as textiles and leather.

Another factor which makes the competitive going more difficult for mature industries is the inevitable decline in the vigor of older companies. Competitive strength, built up in earlier years, wastes away as patents run out and become public property, as customers are lost to rivals, and as products are imported from foreign producers.

Excess producing capacity is an almost inevitable characteristic of mature industries which adds to the severity of competition. Theoretically, the economic system is supposed to purge itself of excess capacity by way of overproduction bringing about, in turn, lower prices, disappearing profits, and bankruptcies. However, we have noted that in the mature industries such as textiles, bankruptcies do not eliminate productive equipment as rapidly as is commonly supposed. Another producer may step in, buy the equipment at bargain prices, and intensify the competition by his ability to manufacture at greatly reduced overhead costs. The removal of excess capacity is at best a slow and painful process in industries where technological changes are minor and infrequent.

THE COSTS OF COMPETITION

The unbalance in industry that results from the factors listed above may, and frequently does, create heavy burdens that are shared in varying degree by all groups in our economy—by the manufacturers, the workers, and society as a whole.

The manufacturer pays his share of the costs in the form of low profits or heavy losses. If, for any of the reasons stated above, the restoration of balance is long delayed, he pays for it by a deterioration of his plant, by the dissipation of his assets, and eventually the liquidation of his plant. If the process of liquidation extends over a long period, the impact is felt by all companies in the industry. Indeed, it is not unusual to find in some of the industries described in this book that often the first victims of competition have been technically the most efficient companies, which despite their technical efficiency could not meet on a price basis the competition from less efficient companies that were reorganized, after bankruptcy, at a fraction of the original investment.

Most companies, especially those with large capital investments, do not shut down when sales cannot be made at a profit. The very existence of these investments, with their concomitant overhead costs, makes it impossible for them to do so. They make every effort to continue operation and resort to every economy that will, in their judgment, permit them to do so. Often the only sizable economy is a reduction in labor costs, which is achieved by lowering wage rates or increasing work loads, or both. Similar action by competing firms may result in a complete breakdown of existing labor standards. If competition is between regions with wide differences in both costs and standards of living, as was the case in the cotton textile industry,[1] it may result in not only the breakdown of labor standards but abandonment of plants in the high-cost area and the permanent detachment of a large number of workers from the industry. The same displacement occurs in competition between different industries. It has been estimated that approximately 74,540 coal miners have been permanently displaced by the rise of substitute fuels. A comparable displacement occurred in the silk weaving industry of Paterson, N. J., owing to the rise of rayon.

When many industries, companies, and workers are affected by severe competition, the costs cease to be the concern of only the manufacturers and labor—it likewise becomes an important social problem. Reference was made in the preceding chapter to the effect of the closing down of the Amoskeag Mills in Manchester, N. H. This experience can be dupli-

[1] See p. 312.

BIBLIOGRAPHY

The Iron and Steel Industry

(Chapters 2, 3, 4, and 5)

American Iron and Steel Institute: *Directory of the Iron and Steel Works of the United States and Canada*, various years, New York.

————: *Steel Facts*, monthly, New York.

American Metal Market, *Metal Statistics*, Annual, New York.

BRIDGE, J. H.: "The Inside Story of the Carnegie Steel Company," Aldine Publishing Company, New York, 1903.

BROOKS, R. R.: "As Steel Goes, Unionism in a Basic Industry," Yale University Press, New Haven, 1940.

CAMP, J. M., and C. B. FRANCIS: "Making, Shaping and Treating of Steel," The Carnegie Steel Company, Pittsburgh, 1925.

DAUGHERTY, C. M., C. DE CHAZEAU, and S. S. STRATTON: "The Economics of the Iron and Steel Industry," McGraw-Hill Book Company, Inc., New York, 1937.

DAVIS, H. B.: "Labor and Steel," International Publishers Co., Inc., New York, 1933.

Federal Trade Commission: Pittsburgh Plus, *Docket* 760, Washington, D. C., 1924.

————: Practices of the Steel Industry under the Code, *Senate Document* 159, Washington, D. C., 1934.

————: *Report to the President with Respect to the Basing-point System in the Iron and Steel Industry*, Washington, D. C., 1934.

FETTER, F. A.: "The Masquerade of Monopoly," Harcourt, Brace and Company, New York, 1931.

GULICK, C. A.: "Labor Policy of the United States Steel Corporation," Columbia University Press, New York, 1924.

Institute of Scrap Iron and Steel: *Yearbook*, New York, 1939.

Iron Age, various issues.

Iron Trade Review (now *Steel*), various issues.

MACCALLUM, E. C.: "The Iron and Steel Industry in the United States," P. S. King & Son, Ltd., London, 1931.

O'CONNOR, H.: "Steel-dictator," The John Day Company, New York, 1935.

Report of N.R.A. on Operation of Basing-point System in the Iron and Steel Industry, Nov. 30, 1934.

Statistical Report of American Iron and Steel Institute, annual.

Steel, various issues.

TARBELL, I. M.: "The Life of Elbert H. Gary," D. Appleton-Century Company, Inc., New York, 1925.

Temporary National Economic Committee: *The Basing-point Problem, Monograph* 42, Senate Committee Print, 76th Congress, 3d Session, Washington, D. C., 1941.

————: Final Report and Recommendation, *Senate Document* 35, 77th Congress, 1st Session.

————: *Price Discrimination in Steel, Monograph* 41.

U. S. Steel Corporation, *United States Steel Corporation T.N.E.C. Papers*, New York, 1940.

U. S. Tariff Commission: Iron and Steel, *Report* 128, Second Series, Washington, D. C., 1938.

VANDERBLUE, H. B., and W. L. CRUM: "The Iron Industry in Prosperity and Depression," McGraw-Hill Book Company, Inc., New York, 1927.

WENKLER, J. K.: "Incredible Carnegie," The Vanguard Press, New York, 1931.

WORTHING, MARION: Comparative Assembly Costs in the Manufacture of Pig Iron. *Pittsburgh Business Review*, Vol. VIII, No. 1, Jan. 31, 1938.

The Copper Industry

(Chapter 6)

American Bureau of Metal Statistics: *Yearbook*, various years.

DAVIS, WATSON: "The Story of Copper," Century Company, New York and London, 1924.

ELLIOTT, W. Y., E. S. MAY, J. W. F. ROWE, A. SKELTON, and D. H. WALLACE: "International Control in Non-ferrous Metals," The Macmillan Company, New York, 1937.

INGALLS, W. R.: Economics Rule Use of Old Metals, *Waste Trade Journal*, November, 1935.

KNIGHT, C. L.: "Secular and Cyclical Movements in the Production and Price of Copper," University of Pennsylvania Press, Philadelphia, 1935.

Metal Statistics, New York, various years.

Minerals Yearbook, Bureau of Mines, various years.

National Association of Purchasing Agents: Copper, *Report* A-4 (Mimeograph), New York, 1933.

U. S. Tariff Commission: Copper, *Report* 29, Second Series, Washington, D. C., 1932.

VOSKUIL, W. H.: "Minerals in Modern Industry," John Wiley & Sons, Inc., New York, 1930.

Aluminum Industry

(Chapter 7)

Aluminum Company of America: "An Outline of Aluminum," Pittsburgh, Pa., 1940.

Federal Trade Commission: *Report on the House Furnishing Industry*, Vol. III, 1925.

Fortune, May, 1941.

HOBBS, D. B.: "Aluminum," The Bruce Publishing Company, Milwaukee, 1938.

National Recovery Administration, Division of Research and Planning: *Report on the Aluminum Industry*, April, 1935.

NOURSE, E. G., and H. B. DRURY: "Industrial Price Policies and Economic Progress," The Brookings Institution, Washington, D. C., 1938.

U. S. Department of Justice: *Report of Special Assistant to Attorney General Concerning Alleged Violation by Aluminum Corporation of America of Decree against It*, Washington, D. C., 1926.

United States of America v. Aluminum Company of America et al., Petition of U. S. Department of Justice, April, 1937. Answer of Aluminum Company of America, June, 1937. Opinion of U. S. District Court, Southern District of New York, 1941.

WARSHOW, H. T.: "Representative Industries of the United States," Henry Holt and Company, Inc., New York, 1928.

Making Assembled Metal Products: The Development of Mass Production

(Chapter 8)

DONALD, W. J., Editor: "Handbook of Business Administration," McGraw-Hill Book Company, Inc., New York, 1931.

National Machine Tool Builders Association: *Machine Tools*, various issues.
————: "Machine Tools and You," Cleveland, 1941.
PERAZICK, G. SCHIMMEL, H. ROSENBERG, and BENJAMIN ROSENBERG: Industrial
    Instruments and Changing Technology, Works Progress Administration, *National
    Research Project Report* M-1, Philadelphia, Pa., 1938.
ROE, J. W.: "English and American Tool Builders," Yale University Press, New
    Haven, 1916.
USHER, A. P.: "History of Mechanical Invention," McGraw-Hill Book Company,
    Inc., New York, 1929.

The Shipbuilding Industry
(Chapter 9)

CARMICHAEL, A. W.: "Shipbuilding for Beginners," The Industrial Service Depart-
    ment, Emergency Fleet Corporation, Washington, D. C., 1918.
Fortune, July, 1941.
HURLEY, E. N.: "The New Merchant Marine," Century Company, New York, 1920.
JAMES, F. C.: "Cyclical Fluctuations in the Shipping and Shipbuilding Industries,"
    The Westbrook Publishing Company, Philadelphia, Pa., 1927.
National City Bank of New York: Shipping Losses and Our Shipping Program,
    Bulletin, January, 1941.
National Council of American Shipbuilders: various reports.
New York Trust Company: "The American Merchant Marine," Index, autumn, 1938.
SMITH, H. GERRISH: "Shipbuilding and Its Relation to the Iron and Steel Industry,"
    American Iron and Steel Institute, New York, 1931.
Society of Naval Architects and Marine Engineers: New York, various reports.
U. S. Maritime Commission: "New Ships for the Merchant Marine," Washington,
    D. C., 1940.

The Automobile Industry
(Chapters 10 and 11)

Automobile Facts and Figures, Automobile Manufacturers Association, various years.
Automotive Industries, various issues.
"A Chronicle of the Automotive Industry in America," Eaton Manufacturing Com-
    pany, Cleveland, Ohio, 1936.
"The Dynamics of Automobile Demand," Based upon papers presented at joint meet-
    ing of the American Statistical Association and the Econometric Society, Detroit,
    Mich., Dec. 27, 1938.
EPSTEIN, R. C.: "The Automobile Industry," McGraw-Hill Book Company, Inc.,
    New York, 1928.
Federal Trade Commission: Report on Motor Vehicle Industry, *House Document* 468,
    Washington, D. C., 1939.
KENNEDY, E. D.: "The Automobile Industry," Reynal & Hitchcock, Inc., New York,
    1941.
McPHERSON, W. H.: "Labor Relations in the Automobile Industry," The Brookings
    Institution, Washington, D. C., 1940.
PARLIN, C. C., and FRED BREMIER: "The Passenger Car Industry," Curtis Publishing
    Company, Philadelphia, 1932.
Poor's Publishing Company: "The Automobile Industry," pamphlet, Wellesley,
    Mass., 1933.
POUND, ARTHUR: "The Turning Wheel," Doubleday, Doran & Company, Inc., New
    York, 1934.

Proceedings of the 1938 *Ohio Conference of Statisticians,* Ohio State University Publications, College of Commerce Conference, Series 5, Columbus, Ohio, 1938.

SCOVILLE, J.: "Reasons for the Fluctuations in Automobile Production," an address before the Ohio Conference of Statisticians on Business Research, Columbus, Ohio, Nov. 12, 1938.

SELTZER, L. H.: "Financial History of the Automobile Industry," Houghton Mifflin Company, Boston, 1928.

SMITH, T. H.: "The Marketing of Used Automobiles," Bureau of Business Research, Ohio State University, Columbus, Ohio, 1941.

The Aircraft Industry
(Chapter 12)

Aeronautical Chamber of Commerce: *Aircraft Yearbook,* various issues.

DODD, P. A.: "Financial Policies in the Aviation Industry," Philadelphia, Pa., 1933.

Fortune, April, 1932; May, 1935; July, 1938; September, 1938; December, 1939; March, 1940; June, 1940; July, 1940; August, 1940.

"Handbook of the Air Transport Industry," J. S. Bache and Company, New York, 1940.

KENNEDY, T. H.: "An Introduction to the Economics of Air Transportation," The Macmillan Company, New York, 1924.

MINGOS, HOWARD: "The Birth of an Industry," The W. B. Conkey Company, New York, 1930.

ROSS, DONALD: "Aviation—Manufacturing, Transportation," White, Weld and Company, New York, 1940.

Vultair, various issues, Vultee Aircraft, Inc., Vultee Field, Calif.

Cement
(Chapter 13)

Federal Trade Commission: "Cement Industry," Washington, D. C., 1933.

————: *Report of the Federal Trade Commission on Price Bases Inquiry,* Washington, D. C., 1932.

GLOVER, J. G., and W. B. CORNELL: "The Development of American Industries," Prentice-Hall, Inc., New York, 1932.

LESLEY, R. W.: "History of the Portland Cement Industry in the United States," International Trade Press, New York, 1924.

Portland Cement Association: *Cement and Concrete Reference Book,* various issues.

U. S. Tariff Commission: Cement, Report to the President, *Report* 38, Washington, D. C., 1932.

WILCOX, J. G.: "Portland Cement Industry," Robert Morris Associates, Lansdowne, Pa., 1928.

WILLIS, H. P., and J. R. B. BYERS, "Portland Cement Prices," The Ronald Press Company, New York, 1924.

YAWORSKI, N., *et al.:* Fuel Efficiency in Cement Manufacture, 1909–1935, Works Progress Administration, National Research Project, *Report* E-5, Philadelphia, 1938.

The Clayworking Industries
(Chapter 14)

CHUTE, A. H.: *Marketing Burned Clay Products,* Ohio State University Press, Columbus, Ohio, 1939.

————: Labor Productivity in the Leather Industry, Studies in Changing Labor Productivity, *Report* B-1, National Research Project, October, 1937.

National Association of Purchasing Agents: Leather, *Report* A-2, New York, 1932.

U. S. Department of Labor, Bureau of Labor Statistics: Labor Productivity and Displacement in the Leather Industry, *Monthly Labor Review*, September, 1932.

WARSHOW, H. T.: "Representative Industries of the United States," Henry Holt and Company, New York, 1928.

The Shoe Industry
(Chapter 28)

DAVIS, H. B.: "Shoes: The Workers and the Industry," International Publishers Co., Inc., New York, 1940.

HOOVER, E. M., JR.: "Location Theory and the Shoe and Leather Industry," Harvard University Press, Cambridge, Mass., 1937.

KEIR, M.: "Manufacturing Industries in America," The Ronald Press Company, New York, 1928.

NORTON, T. S.: "Trade Union Policies in the Massachusetts Shoe Industry, 1919–1929," Columbia University Press, New York, 1932.

PERLMAN, J.: Earnings and Hours in Shoe and Allied Industries, U. S. Department of Labor, Bureau of Labor Statistics, *Bulletin* 670, Washington, D. C., 1939.

SCHNITZER, J. G.: "Leather Footwear: World Production and International Trade," U. S. Department of Commerce, Bureau of Foreign and Domestic Commerce, Washington, D. C., 1937.

United Shoe Machinery Corporation: "How Modern Shoes Are Made," Boston, Mass., 1936.

U. S. Department of Labor, Bureau of Labor Statistics: Labor Productivity in the Boot and Shoe Industry, *Monthly Labor Review*, February, 1939.

Foods
(Chapter 29)

Facts in Food and Grocery Distribution, *The Progressive Grocer*, January, 1940.

National Resources Committee: "Consumers' Expenditures in the United States," Washington, D. C., 1939.

————: "The Structure of the American Economy," Washington, D. C., 1939.

"Report of the Committee on Recent Economic Changes in the United States," Vol. I, McGraw-Hill Book Company, Inc., New York, 1929.

Temporary National Economic Committee: *Large-scale Organization in the Food Industries, Monograph* 35, Senate Committee Print, 76th Congress, 3d Session, Washington, D. C., 1940.

U. S. Department of Agriculture: "Economic Analysis of the Food Stamp Plan," Washington, D. C., 1940.

————: "Food and Life," Washington, D. C., 1939.

U. S. Department of Labor: "Changes in Family Expenditures in the Post-war Period," 1938.

The Flour Milling Industry
(Chapter 30)

BAGNELL, D. B.: "Analysis of Open Commitments in Wheat and Corn Futures on the Chicago Board of Trade, Sept. 29, 1934," U. S. Department of Agriculture, Washington, D. C., May, 1936.

DAVIS, J. S.: "Wheat and the A.A.A.," The Brookings Institution, Washington, D. C., 1935.

KUHLMANN, C. B., "The Development of the Flour-milling Industry of the United States," Houghton Mifflin Company, Boston, 1929.

The Northwestern Miller, various issues.

The Northwestern Miller Almanac, Apr. 30, 1941.

PICKETT, V. G., and R. S. VAILE: "The Decline of Northwestern Flour Milling," University of Minnesota Press, Minneapolis, 1933.

"Wheat and Flour Primer," Washburn-Crosby Company, Minneapolis, Minn.

"Wheat Studies of Food Research Institute," Stanford University Press, Stanford University, Calif., various issues.

The Baking Industry

(Chapter 31)

ALSBERG, C. L.: "Combination in the American Bread Baking Industry," Food Research Institute, Stanford University Press, Stanford University, Calif., 1926.

Federal Trade Commission: "Agricultural Income Inquiry," Part I, Washington, D. C., 1937.

————: "Bakery Combines and Profits," Washington, D. C., 1927.

KYRK, HAZEL: "The American Baking Industry, 1849–1923," Stanford University Press, Stanford University, Calif., 1925.

The Northwestern Miller Almanac, Apr. 30, 1941.

PERLMAN, J.: Wages, Hours and Working Conditions in the Bread-baking Industry, 1934, U. S. Department of Labor, Bureau of Labor Statistics, *Bulletin* 623, Washington, D. C., 1937.

The Sugar Refining Industry

(Chapter 32)

ADAMSON, R. K., and M. E. WEST: Beet Sugar, Works Progress Administration, National Research Project, *Report* N-1, Philadelphia, 1938.

DALTON, J. E.: "Sugar, A Case Study of Government Control," The Macmillan Company, New York, 1937.

GLOVER, J. G., and W. B. CORNELL: "Development of American Industries," Prentice-Hall, Inc., New York, 1932.

LYNSKY, MYER: "Sugar Economics, Statistics and Documents," United States Cane Sugar Refiners' Association, New York, 1938.

————: "Supplement, Sugar Economics, Statistics, and Documents," United States Cane Sugar Refiners' Association, New York, 1939.

MALOTT, D. W., and B. F. MARTIN: "The Agricultural Industries," McGraw-Hill Book Company, Inc., New York, 1939.

U. S. Tariff Commission: Report to the President on Sugar, *Report* 73, Washington, D. C., 1934.

WRIGHT, P. G.: "Sugar in Relation to the Tariff," McGraw-Hill Book Company, Inc., New York, 1924.

The Meat Packing Industry

(Chapter 33)

DALE, E. E.: "The Range Cattle Industry," University of Oklahoma Press, Norman, 1930.

DUDDY, E. A., and D. A. REVZAN: "The Changing Relative Importance of the Central Livestock Market," University of Chicago Press, Chicago, 1938.

FITZGERALD, D. A.: "Livestock under the A.A.A.," The Brookings Institution, Washington, D. C., 1935.

JORDAN, E. M.: "Livestock, Meats and Wool Market Statistics and Related Data," U. S. Department of Agriculture, Washington, D. C., 1940.

MALOTT, D. W., and B. F. MARTIN: "The Agricultural Industries," McGraw-Hill Book Company, Inc., New York, 1939.

MAYER, O. G.: "America's Meat Packing Industry," pamphlet, The Newcomen Society, American Branch, Princeton University Press, Princeton, N. J., 1939.

"Meat—Reference Book of the Industry," a pamphlet of the American Meat Institute, Chicago, Ill., 1941.

WELD, L. D., A. T. KEARNEY, and F. H. SIDNEY: "Economics of the Packing Industry," University of Chicago Press, Chicago, 1925.

The Canning Industry

(Chapter 34)

BENNING, LOTYS: "The Vegetable Canning Industry," National Youth Administration of Indiana, Indianapolis, 1938.

CAMPBELL, CARLOS: "Factors Affecting Production and Distribution of Canned Peas, Corn, Tomatoes and Soup Beans," National Canners Association, Washington, D. C., 1936.

CAROTHERS, NEIL, "Some Phases of the Canning Industry," National Canners Association, Washington, D. C., 1942.

LYON, L. S.: "Some Trends in the Marketing of Canned Foods," The Brookings Institution, Washington, D. C., 1929.

MAY, E. C.: "The Canning Clan," The Macmillan Company, New York, 1937.

MONTGOMERY, E. G., and C. H. KARDELL: "Apparent Per Capita Consumption of Principal Foodstuffs in the United States," U. S. Department of Commerce, Bureau of Foreign and Domestic Commerce, Washington, D. C., 1930.

National Canners Association: "Canned Peas, A Product of Cooperation between Grocer and Canner," Washington, D. C., 1935.

————: "Production Planning Statistics," Washington, D. C., 1940.

————: "Roper Report," 1941.

————: "The Canning Industry," Washington, D. C., 1938.

"Nutritive Aspects of Canned Foods," The American Can Company, 1937.

The Liquor Industry

(Chapter 35)

ABRAHAMSON, A.: "The Incidence of Public Tolerance in Price Policy," in "Price and Price Policies," Walton Hamilton, Editor, McGraw-Hill Book Company, Inc., New York, 1938.

Annual Report of Bureau of Internal Revenue, various years.

George S. May Business Foundation: Analysis of Brewing Industry, *Report* 103, New York, 1940.

PERSONS, W. M.: "Beer and Brewing in America," United Brewers Industrial Foundation, New York, 1940.

Research Company of America: "A National Survey of the Brewing Industry," New York, 1941.

Temporary National Economic Committee: Hearings, "The Liquor Industry," Part 6, Washington, D. C., 1939.

U. S. Department of Agriculture: "Barriers to Internal Trade, Farm Products," Washington, D. C., 1939.

The Tobacco Manufacturing Industry

(Chapter 36)

Annual Report of Bureau of Internal Revenue, various years.

BAER, W. N.: "The Economic Development of the Cigar Industry in the United States," The Art Publishing Company, Lancaster, Pa., 1933.

COX, REAVIS: "Competition in the American Tobacco Industry," Columbia University Press, New York, 1933.

CREAMER, D., and G. W. SWACKHAMER: Cigar Makers—After the Lay-off, *Report* L-1, Works Progress Administration, National Research Project, Philadelphia, 1937.

GOTTSEGEN, J. J.: "Tobacco: A Study of Its Consumption in the United States," Pitman Publishing Corporation, New York, 1940.

LEMERT, B. F.: "Tobacco Manufacturing Industry in North Carolina," National Youth Administration of North Carolina, Raleigh, 1939.

MACK, R. H.: "The Cigar Manufacturing Industry," University of Pennsylvania Press, Philadelphia, 1933.

ROWE, H. B.: "Tobacco under the A.A.A.," The Brookings Institution, Washington, D. C., 1935.

U. S. Department of Agriculture: Tobacco Statistics, *Annual Report,* various years.

U. S. Department of Labor: Mechanization and Productivity of Labor in the Cigar Manufacturing Industry, *Bulletin* 660, Washington, D. C., 1939.

U. S. Department of Labor, Wage and Hour Division: "The Cigar Industry," Washington, D. C., 1941.

General

ARNOLD, T. H.: "The Bottleneck of Business," Reynal & Hitchcock, Inc., 1940.

BEARD, C., and MARY BEARD: "The Rise of American Civilization," The Macmillan Company, New York, 1927.

BLISS, C. A.: "The Structure of Manufacturing Production," National Bureau of Economic Research, New York, 1939.

BOGART, E. L., and C. E. LANDON: "Modern Industry," Longmans, Green and Company, New York, 1927.

BURNS, A. R.: "The Decline of Competition," McGraw-Hill Book Company, Inc., New York, 1936.

BURNS, ARTHUR F.: "Production Trends in the United States since 1870," National Bureau of Economic Research, New York, 1934.

CHASE, S.: "Government in Business," The Macmillan Company, New York, 1935.

CLARK, J. M.: "Economics of Overhead Costs," University of Chicago Press, Chicago, 1923.

————: "Social Control of Business," University of Chicago Press, Chicago, 1926.

CLARK, V. S.: "History of Manufactures in the United States," M Graw-Hill Book Company, Inc., New York, 1929.

FABRICANT, SOLOMON: "The Output of Manufacturing Industries 1899–1937," National Bureau of Economic Research, New York, 1940.

FRASER, C. E., and G. F. DORIOT: "Analyzing Our Industries," McGraw-Hill Book Company, Inc., New York, 1932.